Priced per Lot.

EXECUTORS' SALE.

J. SABIN, Auctioneer.

CATALOGUE

OF THE

THEATRICAL & MISCELLANEOUS LIBRARY

OF THE LATE

WILLIAM E. BURTON.

Also, a small but select collection of Curiosities, Antiquities, Washington and Napoleon's Repeaters, Shakspearian Medals and Relics, Library Furniture, Bookcases, Tables, Antique Side Board, Fire Proof, and some **CHOICE OIL PAINTINGS**, &c.

Which will be sold at Auction by

J. SABIN & CO.,

AT THEIR AUCTION ROOM,

Cor. of Broadway, Fourth Street, and Lafayette Place,

NEW YORK.

On Monday, October 8, 1860, and following days.

COMMENCING EACH DAY AT 2 O'CLOCK.

The undersigned respectfully inform the public, that they have leased the very eligible premises situated at the corner of

"Fourth Street and Lafayette Place,"

(One door east of Broadway,)

NEW YORK,

AS AN

AUCTION ROOM

FOR THE SALE OF

MERCHANDISE IN GENERAL,

BUT ESPECIALLY OF

Books, Paintings, Water-color Drawings, Engravings, Autographs, Coins, Medals, Bronzes, Antiquities, &c., and all other articles connected with Literature and the Fine Arts.

The room is 130 feet in depth by 40 feet in width, and is by far the most spacious and best lighted Auction Room in the city of New York. Its proximity to Broadway, the principal hotels, the Astor and Mercantile Libraries, &c., and its comparative quiet, render it specially available for the purposes for which it has been leased.

The respective partners have each had an experience of over twenty years in the Auction business, and bring to the conduct of this enterprise all the advantages of large capital, an extensive knowledge of books and their value, and a determination to use every exertion in their power to secure the entire value of goods consigned to their care.

That the cataloguing department will have a proper attention will be evident on an inspection of the present as well as many anterior specimens.

Booksellers desirous of reducing their stock, Librarians having duplicates and Executors having estates to close up, are invited to avail themselves of our services.

JOSEPH SABIN & CO.,

Liberal cash advances on Consignments.

Orders to purchase at this sale will be attended to by the Auctioneers, or any of the following Booksellers of New York: D. Davidson, R. H. Johnson, J. Miller, C. B. Norton, and C. B. Richardson; *or,* H. Rodd, *Philadelphia.*

Eng'd by W. G. Jackman, New York, from a Daguerreotype by Brady

W E Burton

N.Y. D. Appleton & Co.

BIBLIOTHECA DRAMATICA.

CATALOGUE

OF THE

THEATRICAL AND MISCELLANEOUS LIBRARY

OF THE LATE

WILLIAM E. BURTON,

THE DISTINGUISHED COMEDIAN,

COMPRISING AN IMMENSE ASSEMBLAGE OF BOOKS RELATING TO THE STAGE,

And including interesting specimens of the Early English Drama, exceeding in extent any collection that has ever been submitted to the public competition, commencing with the earliest dawn of Histrionic Art, and brought down to the present time. Among these will be found the first four folio Shakspeares', and seventy other editions; also about 1,500 vols. of Shakspeariana. An unrivalled collection of Books of Wit and Humor; a complete series of the History of the Stage, containing Music, Pageants, &c. Old English Poetry of the Elizabethan era, including all of the contemporaries of Shakspeare. Indeed the collection is at once magnificent and unique, and offers to buyers a rare opportunity of collecting books not to be obtained except in the dispersion of Private Collections.

Also, a small but select collection of Curiosities, Antiquities, Shakspearian Models, &c. Library Furniture, Bookcases, Tables, Antique Side Board, Fire Proof, some CHOICE OIL PAINTINGS, &c.

TO BE SOLD AT AUCTION BY

J. SABIN & CO.,

AT THEIR AUCTION ROOM,

Corner of Broadway, Fourth Street, and Lafayette Place, New York,

On Monday, October 8, 1860, and following days.

COMMENCING EACH DAY AT 2 O'CLOCK.

The Books will be on view one week before the Sale, and Catalogues may be had of the Auctioneers at the above address, also of Booksellers generally.

NOTICE.

The Catalogue of Books, now offered to the public, comprises the entire library of the late Mr. Wm. E. Burton, the eminent Comedian, who devoted many years to its collection, and it is believed to be by far the largest Library of Dramatic Literature ever offered at public auction in this or any other country.

It contains a most surprising mass of rare old English Plays; Works on the Drama, History of the Stage, Theatres, Theatrical Characters and Biography, Pageants, Royal Progresses, and Processions, Mimes, Pantomimes, Masquerades, Mummeries, Mysteries, and Morris Dancers, Fantoccini, Olympian Games, Feats of the Circus, Carnivals, Cavalcades, and every other description of Exhibition which were all objects of Mr. B.'s research; indeed, such was Mr. Burton's enthusiasm that nothing was too trivial that tended in any way to illustrate the profession which he was so eminently qualified to fill.

Old English Poetry, will be found not only voluminous, but abounding in rare and choice copies, including many English translations of the classics of very early dates; while the Dramatic collection is replete with the first editions of most of the Plays of importance. Shakspeariana is especially rich, not only in rare books, but in some presque *unique copies* of books printed for presentation only.

Amidst such a variety of really choice and rare books it would be almost invidious to make a special reference to any particular work or works; but the fact of there being the First Four Folio Editions of Shakspeare's Works is too important to overlook. Also, all the collected editions from that of Rowe to Halliwell's folio. For a further account of this department, the reader is referred to page 335.

Topographical Works, however rare or expensive, were not forgotten, nor Antiquities of Greece and Rome. Among the former is a fine copy of the first edition of Dugdale's Warwickshire, containing the earliest engraving of the Monument of Shakspeare, by the elaborate, accurate, and most industrious Hollar, which differs materially from all the more recent representations of it, either from the burin of the engraver, or the numerous plaster casts. Dugdale's St. Paul's, Weever's Funeral Monuments, Wren's Parentalia, and Nichols' Royal Progresses will also be found.

Mr. Burton's speciality as an author of Comic Pieces naturally led him to the collection of Books of Wit and Humor; of this fact there will be sufficient evidence on referring to the departments of Facetiæ and Jest Books, among which will be found many works of rarity—books of this class being cheaply got up, are especially liable to mutilation.

Polonius's description of the players whom Rosencrantz and Gilderstern "coted on the way" from the Academy at Wittenburg to the Court of Elsinore, as "being the best actors in the world, either for Tragedy, Comedy, History, Pastoral, Pastoral-comical, Historical-pastoral, Tragical-historical, Tragical-comical, Historical-pastoral, Scene indivisible, or Poem unlimited," conveys some idea of the thorough completeness of this dramatic collection. "Seneca was not too heavy, nor Plautus too light."

The Curiosities and Antiquities comprise some desirable rarities, including Statues, Busts, Models, Casts of Shakspeare's Monument and Bust at Stratford, including Clara Fisher's Museum, and the celebrated Mulberry Tree Tea Caddy, one of the choicest Souvenirs of the Tree in existence, and perfectly unique. Also, many Bronze Medals, a Watch formerly belonging to Washington, and Talma's Repeater, presented by Napoleon.

The Library Furniture comprises a series of Book Cases of Gothic Pattern, made for a room thirty feet square. An Oak Book Case and four Mahogany Book Cases, Library Table, Chairs, two Fire-proofs, &c. Also, a magnificent Antique Buffet, or Sideboard, Gas Fixtures, Billiard Table, &c.

There are also a few of the best of the Oil Paintings which were not sold with the Gallery.

Of the Catalogue, let it suffice to observe that the books are all faithfully represented, and distant buyers may rely upon the condition of the books being truly expressed. Its arrangement has been attended with much labor, but the convenience to the buyer will be self-evident.

J. SABIN & CO.

CONTENTS.

CONDITIONS OF SALE.

1. THE highest Bidder to be the Buyer; and if any Dispute arise between two or more Bidders, the Lot so disputed shall be immediately put up again.
2. The Purchasers to give in their Names and Places of Abode, and to pay down 25 per cent., if required, in part of payment of the Purchase-money; in default of which, the Lot or Lots purchased to be immediately put up again and re-sold.
3. The Lots to be taken away, with all faults, at the Buyer's Expense, immediately after the conclusion of the Sale; in default of which the Auctioneers will not hold themselves responsible if lost, stolen, damaged, or otherwise destroyed, but they will be left at the sole risk of the Purchaser. If at the expiration of ONE WEEK after the conclusion of the Sale, the Lots are not cleared or paid for, they will then be Catalogued for immediate sale, and the expense, the same as if re-sold, will be added to the amount at which they were bought. The Auctioneers will have the option of re-selling the Lots uncleared either by public or private sale, without any notice being given to the defaulter.
4. To prevent inaccuracy in delivery, and inconvenience in the settlement of the purchases, no Lot can on any account be removed during the time of sale, except for cash; and the money must absolutely be paid on the delivery.
5. Upon failure of complying with the above conditions, the money required or deposited in part of payment shall be forfeited; *and if any loss is sustained in the reselling of such Lots as are not cleared or paid for, all charges on such resale shall be made good by the defaulter at this sale.*

Gentlemen who cannot attend the Sale, may have their Commissions faithfully executed by the Auctioneers.

CATALOGUE.

AFRICA—HISTORY OF, AND VOYAGES TO.

1 ALEXANDER (*J. E.*) Expedition to Africa, 2 vols. 12mo. Phil. 1833

2 AYALA (*J. L. de*), History of Gibraltar, translated by Bell, *cloth*, 12mo. Lond., *Pickering*, 1845

3 GARDNER (*Capt. A.*) Visit to the Zoolu Country, *colored plates*, *cloth*, 8vo. Lond. 1836

4 MARCO-POLO, Travels of, edited by Murray, *cloth*, 12mo. 1844

5 OGILBY (T.) Africa, being an exact Description of Egypt, Barbary, Lybia, Guinea, Ethiopia, and Abyssinia, folio, *numerous fine plates by* HOLLAR, *half calf.* Lond. 1670

Ogilby may be considered the English De Bry. His works are similar in their object, compilation, and mode of illustration.

6 PONCET (*Dr.*) Voyage to Ethiopia, *calf*, 18mo. Lond. 1709

7 RUSSELL (*M.*) History of the Barbary States, *cloth*, 18mo. N. Y. 1855

8 SALAMÉ (*A.*) Expedition to Algiers, *boards*, 8vo. Lond. 1819

AMERICA—WORKS RELATING TO.

9 ALBERT (*Lieut.*) Notes on the Wisconsin Territory, particularly with reference to the Iowa District, or Black Hawk Purchase, *with maps*, 18mo., pp. 53. Phil. 1836

10 ALEXANDER (*Capt. J. E.*) Transatlantic Sketches of North and South America, West Indies, &c., with notes on Negro Slavery, and Canadian Emigration, 8vo. Phil. 1833

11 ALLEN (*Col. Ethan*), A Narrative of the Life of, written by himself, *half cloth*, 12mo. Burlington, 1838

12 AMERICAN Almanack, 1830–9, 10 vols., *sewed.* Bost. v. d.

13 AMERICAN Institute, Annual Reports from 1847 to 1854, 8 vols. 8vo. *cloth.* . Albany.

14 ANDERSON (*Mr.*) History of the Life and Adventures of, containing his Strange Varieties of Fortune in Europe and America, compiled from his own papers, *half calf*, pp. 243, 12mo. Berwick, 1782

"The author was kidnapped to the colonies and sold for a slave at Sennepuxon Inlet, Maryland, and afterwards joined in the Indian and French campaign."

15 ANDRE: A Tragedy in Five Acts, as performed by the Old American Company, New York, 1798. With authentic documents respecting André. The Cow Chace, Court Martial, &c., 8vo. *with full length portrait of André, very rare, half bound.* N. Y. 1798

16 ASHE (*Thomas*), Travels in America, performed in 1806, 12mo. *sheep.* Newburyport, 1808

17 AUTOBIOGRAPHY of an English Soldier in the U. S. Army, 12mo. *cloth.* N. Y. 1853

18 BANCROFT (*George*), A History of the United States, vols. I. II. & III. *cloth.* Boston, 1834

——— BEHN (*Mrs.*) Widow Ranter. *Vide* Drama.

19 BIRKBECK (*M.*) Letters from Illinois, *with a map* showing Mr. Birkbeck's journey from Virginia to Illinois, 12mo. Phil. 1818

20 BLUE Laws of Connecticut, The Code of, 1650, *half cloth*, 18mo. Hartford, 1830

21 BONNYCASTLE (*Sir R. H.*) Canada and the Canadians in 1841, *cloth*, 2 vols. post 8vo. 1841

22 BOSTON, Horrid Massacre in, A short Narrative of the, 8vo. *cloth.* N. Y. Repub. 1849

23 BOSWORTH (*N.*) Hochelaga Depicta; the Early History and Present State of the City and Island of Montreal, *with numerous illustrative engravings, cloth*, 12mo. Montreal, 1839

24 BOTTA (*Carlo*), Storia della Guerra Americana, 3 vols. 8vo. *half morocco.* Livorno, 1825

25 BRADFORD (*Alden*), History of Massachusetts, from July, 1775 to 1789, 8vo. *boards.* Boston, 1825

26 BROWN (*H.*) Illinois, The History of, 8vo. *cloth.* N. Y. 1844

27 BRYAN (*Hugh and Mary Hutson, of South Carolina*), Diaries and Letters of, with Preface by Conder and Gibbons, 12mo. *sheep.* Lond. 1760

28 Bucaniers of America, The History of, 24mo. *calf.* Lond. 1800

29 Buenos Ayres: A Five Years' Residence during the years 1820 to 1823; containing remarks on the Country and Inhabitants; and a Visit to Colonia del Sacramenta, by an Englishman; with an Appendix, containing Rules and Police of the Port of Buenos Ayres, Navigation of the River Plate, &c. &c. Pp. 176, 8vo. *calf.* Lond. 1825

30 Californie, Histoire Naturelle et Civile de la, 3 vols. *sewed,* 12mo. Paris, 1767

31 Campbell (*William W.*) Annals of Tryon County, or the Border Warfare of New York during the Revolution, 12mo. *boards.* N. Y. 1831

32 Candler (*J.*) Brief Notices of Hayti, with its Condition, Resources, and Prospects, 12mo. *cloth,* pp. 175. Lond. 1842

33 Carlton (*Robert*), The New Purchase, or Early Years in the Far West, 12mo. *cloth, illustrated.* New Albany, 1855

34 Carver (*Jon.*) Travels through the Interior parts of North America in 1766-8, *with plates,* 8vo. *half calf.* 1778

"This valuable work lately attracted much attention from its description of parts near to the supposed Northwest Passage."—*Lowndes.*

35 Carver (*John*), Sketches in New England, or Memories of the Country, *cloth,* post 8vo. N. Y. 1842

35* Catlin's Illustrations of the Manners, Customs, and Condition of the North American Indians: in a series of Letters and Notes, during Eight Years of Travel and Adventure among the wildest and most remarkable Tribes now existing, 2 vols. impl. 8vo., containing *engravings* from the author's original paintings, *cloth.* 1844

"Catlin,—one of the most admirable observers of manners who ever lived among the aborigines of America."—*Humboldt's Cosmos,* vol. ii. p. 609 (Bohn's ed.).

"A faithful and well-authenticated declaration, not only of a most interesting portion of the globe, as it at present exists, in a state of nature, but of a race of innocent, unoffending men so rapidly perishing, that too truly may it be said of them,

"'Apparent rari nantes in gurgite vasto!"

Quarterly Review.

36 Chandler (*P. W.*) American Criminal Trials, 2 vols. *cloth, scarce,* 12mo. Bost. 1844

37 CHAPMAN (*Isaac*), Wyoming, A Sketch of the History of, 12mo. *half cloth.* Wilkesbarre, Penn. 1830

38 CHASTELLUX (*Marquis de*), Travels in North America in 1780–'82, 2 vols. 8vo. *maps, calf.* Dublin, 1787

"Nothing escapes the eager eye and minute attention of this lively traveller, and we owe to him the most graphic account of the private life of the Revolutionary era."

39 CHEEVER (*Dr. G. B.*) Journal of the Pilgrims at Plymouth in New England in 1620, *cloth, gilt.* N. Y. 1848

40 COBBETT (*William*), The Emigrant's Guide in Ten Letters, addressed to the Tax Payers of England, with letters from English residents in America. 12mo. *boards.* Lond. 1830

41 ——— Bloody Buoy, thrown out as a Warning to the Political Pilots of America, 4 *plates*, 18mo. *calf.* Phil. 1796

"It appears, then, that these bloody revolutionists, who styled themselves the friends of freedom and of mankind, destroyed in one city of France a population equal to that of the United States."

42 ——— Life and Adventures of Peter Porcupine, with a full and fair account of all his authoring transactions, &c., by himself, 12mo. *half bound, curious and scarce.* Phil. 1797

——— Life of General Jackson, *vide* Biography.

43 COE (*Joseph*), The True American, with lives and political characters of Washington, Adams, and Jefferson, inaugural addresses, 12mo. *cloth.* Concord, N. H. 1840

44 COLUMBUS, Memorials of: or, a Collection of Authentic Documents of that celebrated Navigator, from the original MSS., by order of the Decurians of Genoa, *with portrait and plates*, 8vo. *calf.* Lond. 1823

This valuable work is a translation of the Codice Diplomatico Columbo-Americano, published at Geneva, in 1823.

45 CONNECTICUT, Blue Laws of, by an Antiquary, 12mo. *cloth.* Hartford, 1838

46 COOPER (*J. F.*) History of the Navy of the United States of America, from the Earliest Period to the Peace of 1815, 2 vols. 8vo. *cloth.* Phil. 1839

These volumes are filled with the graphic records of daring adventure, and contain, in their narration of facts, a treasure to the lovers of Sea-Romance.

47 CORTES (*Hernando*), Despatches of, translated, with introduction and notes, by George Folsom, 8vo. *boards.* N. Y. 1843

48 Coxe (*Daniel*), Description of the English Province of Carolana, called by the Spaniards Florida, and by the French Louisiana, the Great River Meschacebe, &c., *large and curious map, old calf, gilt.* Lond. 1741

The whole of this tract was claimed by the author under a grant from the crown. The name Carolana is probably of his own invention.

49 Crockett (*David*), Narrative of the Life of, 12mo. *boards uncut.* Phil. 1834

50 Cuba, Album Pintoresco de la Isla de Cuba, by May & Co., *beautifully colored plates, oblong 4to. cloth.* Berlin

51 Dana (*Rich. Henry*), To Cuba and Back, a Vacation Voyage, 12mo. *cloth.* Bost. 1859

52 Darley (*F. O. C.*) Scenes in Indian Life, a series of original designs portraying events in the Life of an Indian Chief, drawn and etched on stone by F. O. C. Darley, to which is added an illustration of the Death of the War Eagle, a pseudo-biographical sketch, with copious notes, 5 parts, *oblong* 4to. 14 *plates.* Phil. 1843

53 Davis (*A.*) Antiquities of Central America and the Discovery of New England by the Northmen 500 years before Columbus, a lecture, 8vo. pp. 24. Rochester, 1843

54 ——— (*M. L.*) Memoirs of Aaron Burr, with miscellaneous correspondence, *portraits,* 2 vols. 8vo. *sheep.* N. Y. 1837

"The extraordinary history of Aaron Burr is here displayed by Mr. Davis with great integrity and ability. The work is full of instruction to public men. Perhaps no one has illustrated in a more striking manner the fate of unprincipled ambition, the prostitution of great talents, the wreck of a splendid career. To the common reader the memoirs have much of the interest of tragedy."—*Griswold.*

55 Day-Breaking if not the Sun-Rising of the Gospel with the Indians in New England, *wanting last leaf, rare,* 4to. Lond. 1647

In a curious lot of old sermons mostly imperfect.
This appears to be the *second* of the relations of the progress of the Gospel among the Indians of New England. The former is known as New England's First Fruits.

56 Dennett (*J. F.*) Voyages and Travels of Captains Parry, Franklin, Ross, and Mr. Belzen, forming an Interesting History of the Manners, Customs, and Characters of various Nations, visited by enterprising travellers, 8vo. *half calf.* Lond. 1826

57 Denton (*Daniel*), A Brief Description of New York, formerly called New Netherlands, with the places thereto adjoining; likewise, a brief relation of the Customs of the Indians there. A new edition, with an introduction and copious historical notes by Judge Furman, 8vo. *cloth.* N. Y. 1845

58 Description of the New World, wants a title page (? by R. Burton), *old and torn*, 18mo. Lond. 1650

60 De Tocqueville (*Alexis*), Democracy in America, 2 vols. in 1, 8vo. *cloth.* N. Y. 1848

"Let me earnestly advise your perusal of M. De Tocqueville's work. His testimony, as well from actual personal experience as on account of freedom from prejudice, is above exception."—*Sir R. Peel.*

61 Duboccage (*Mme.*) La Colombiade ou la foi porté au Nouveau Monde, Poëme en dix chants, 8vo. *calf.* Paris, 1756

62 Dunn (*John*), A Collection of Curious Observations on the Manners, Customs, Usages, Languages, Ceremonies, Religion, Medicine, Physics, Natural History, Commerce, &c., of Asia, Africa, and America, translated from the French, 2 vols. 8vo. *old sheep.* Printed for the translator. Lond. 1750

A very scarce and interesting privately printed book, chiefly relating to the primitive inhabitants of America.

63 Duyckinck (*E. A. & Geo. L.*) Cyclopædia of American Literature, embracing Personal and Critical Notices of Authors, and Selections from their Writings, from the earliest period to the present day. With 225 portraits, 425 autographs, and 75 views of colleges, libraries, and residences of authors, 2 vols. royal 8vo. *cloth.* N. Y. 1856

64 Dwight (*Theodore*), History of the Hartford Convention, with a Review of the Policy of the United States Government which led to the war of 1812, 8vo. *cloth.* N. Y. 1833

65 Eastern Penitentiary of Pennsylvania, History of, by a Member of the Legislature, 8vo. *cloth.* Phil. 1835

66 Edwards (*Jonathan*), Account of the Life of Mr. David Brainard, 8vo. *old calf.* Boston, 1749

67 ——— (*F. S.*) Campaign in New Mexico with Colonel Doniphan, 12mo. Phil. 1848

68 Emmons (*Richard*), The Fredoniad: or, Independence Preserved, an Epic Poem of the Late War of 1812. 4 vols. 12mo. *calf, neat, with portrait.* Phil. 1832

69 Exposition of the Weakness and Inefficiency of the United States Government, 12mo. *half roan.* 1845

70 Falls of Niagara, with Sketches of the Way, 8vo. *half morocco.* N. Y. 1829

71 Far West: or, a Tour beyond the Mountains, 2 vols. 12mo. N. Y. 1838

72 Faux (*W.*) An English Farmer, Memorable Days in America, being a Journal of a Tour to the United States to ascertain the Condition and Probable Prospects of British Emigrants, including accounts of Mr. Birkbeck's Settlement on the Illinois, 8vo. *boards.* Lond. 1823

73 Ferris (*Mrs. B. G.*) Mormons at Home, 12mo. *cloth.* N. Y. 1856

74 Fidler (*Rev. Isaac*), Observations on Professions, Literature, Manners, and Education in the United States and Canada in 1832, 12mo. *cloth.* N. Y. 1833

75 Findlay (*W.*) History of the Insurrection in the Four Western Counties of Pennsylvania, 8vo. *half sheep, wants title.* Phil. 1796

This is known as the "Whiskey Insurrection." It is the only history of that rebellion, and is now scarce.

76 Flint (*Timothy*), Recollections of the Last Ten Years in the Valley of the Mississippi, 8vo. *boards, loose.* Boston, 1826.

77 Franklin (*Benj.*), The Private Life of, originally written by himself and now translated from the French, to which are added some account of his public life, a variety of anecdotes concerning him, by MM. Brissot, Condorcet, Rochefoucault, Le Roy, &c., and the eulogium of M. Fauchet, 8vo. *boards, uncut.* Lond. 1793

This work is but little known in the United States.

78 Gage (*Thos.*) Travels: New Survey of the West Indies, a Journal of 3,300 miles within the main land of America, the only Protestant that ever was known to have traversed those parts. First edition, folio, *calf, gilt.* Lond. 1648

Contains many curious accounts of the Devil in sorceries and witchcraft. His travels are principally in Mexico, Guaxaca Chiapa, Guatemala, Vera Pax, Nicaragua, Costa Rica, Panama, &c. In the third edition, a chapter which was said to reflect on Archbishop Laud is omitted.

79 Gayerre (*C.*) Romance of the History of Louisiana, 12mo. N. Y. 1848

80 Georgia Scenes—Characteristics, Incidents, &c., in the First Half Century of the Republic, 12mo. *boards.* August, 1835

81 Georgia Scenes, by a Native of Georgia, 12mo. N. Y. 1855

82 Gessner (*M.*) Death of Abel, in two books; attempted from the German of Mr. Gessner, by Mary Collyer, *sixth edition*, pp. 117. London, *printed;* New York, *reprinted by H. Gaine, at the Bible and Crown, in Hanover Square.* 1765

One of the first books printed by Hugh Gaine, in the city of New York.

83 Godwin (*Caleb*), Men and Manners in America, 2 vols. 12mo. *cloth.* Phil. 1833

84 Gordon (*Th. F.*) Gazetteer of the State of New York, 8vo. *sheep.* 1836

85 ——————— Gazetteer of the State of Pennsylvania, comprehending the Colonial History, &c. 8vo. *sheep.* Phil. 1832

It contains a large amount of historical information, not to be found elsewhere.

86 ——————— History of America, containing the History of the Spanish Discoveries prior to 1520, 2 vols. *cloth*, 12mo. Phil. 1832

87 Grayson: Memoirs of a Life chiefly passed in Pennsylvania, within the last 60 years, 8vo. *boards.* Edin. 1822

88 Gregg (*Josiah*), Commerce of the Prairies, 2 vols. 12mo. *cloth.* N. Y. 1844

89 Hacke (*Capt. W.*) Collection of Original Voyages, *illustrated with maps and draughts*, 8vo. *calf.* Lond. 1699

This Collection contains part of the original material for the History of the Buccaniers, Capt. Cowley's Voyage round the Globe, Capt. Sharp's Journey over the Isthmus of Darien and Expedition to the South Seas, Capt. Wood's Voyage to the Straits of Magellan, &c.

90 Hale (*Capt. Nathan*), Memoir of, 8vo. pp. 16. New Haven, 1844

91 Haliburton (*Thos. C.*) An Historical and Statistical Account of Nova Scotia, *with maps of the province and several engravings*, 2 vols. 8vo. *half cloth.* Halifax, 1829

92 Hall (*A. Oakey*), Manhattaner in New Orleans, or Phases of "Crescent City" Life, 12mo. *cloth.* N. Y. 1851

Presentation copy, with the author's autograph.

93 Hall (*James*), Legends of the West, 12mo. *boards.* Phil. 1832

94 HARRIS (*J. M.*) Discourse on the Life and Character of Sir W. Raleigh, 8vo. pp. 71. Balt. 1846

95 ——— (*Thos.*) Life and Services of Commodore William Bainbridge, U. S. Navy, 8vo. *cloth.* Phil. 1837

96 HAYES (*John L.*) Vindication of the Rights and Titles of Alexander, Earl of Stirling and Dovan, 8vo. *cloth.* Wash. 1853

97 HEAD (*George*), Forest Scenes and Incidents in the Wilds of North America, being a Tour through the Canadas, post 8vo. Lond. 1829

98 HENRY (*John Joseph*), An accurate and interesting Account of the Hardships and Sufferings of that band of Heroes who traversed the Wilderness by the route of Kennebec and Chaudiere River to Quebec, in 1775, 12mo. *sheep.* Lancaster, 1812

99 HERBERT (*Thomas*), Some Years' Travels into Africa and Asia the Great, especially describing the famous Empires of Persia and Industant, as also *divers other Kingdoms in the Oriental Indies and Isles adjacent*, folio, *half calf.* Lond. 1677

This work has 50 curious plates, among them the city of Babylon, with a key. It contains many ingenious quotations from the ancient Greek and Latin authors, to show that they had some idea of the continent of North America. It also gives a somewhat detailed account (page 355) of the discovery of this country by Madoc, a Welshman, who planted a small colony here 322 years before Columbus.

100 HEROES of the Lake: A Poem, in two books, written in the Autumn of 1813, *with plate*, 18mo. *boards*, pp. 108. N. Y. 1814

101 HINTON (*J. H.*) History and Topography of the United States, *illustrated by about* 80 *very fine steel plates*, 2 vols. 4to. *sheep.* Bost. 1834

102 HOPKINSON & Nicholson: Pennsylvania State Trials, 8vo. *sheep.* Phil. 1794

103 HOSKINS (*Nathan*), A History of Vermont, from its Discovery and Settlement to the close of 1830, *half cloth*, 12mo. Vergennes, 1831

104 HOUSTON (*Mrs.*) Texas and the Gulf of Mexico. Port. of Santa Anna, 16mo. *cloth.* Phil. 1845

105 HULL (*Brig. Gen. W.*) Defence of, written by himself, 12mo. *bds.* Bost. 1814

106 HUMBOLDT (*Alex.*) The Island of Cuba, from the Spanish, 12mo. *cloth.* N. Y. 1856

107 HYDE (*John, Jr.*) Mormonism, its Leaders and Designs, 12mo. *cloth.* N. Y. 1857

108 INDIAN Fairy Book, *with illustrations by McLenan*, 12mo. *cloth.* N. Y. 1856

109 IRVING (*Washington*), Life of George Washington, *illustrated edition*, 4 vols. royal 8vo. *cloth.* N. Y. 1855

110 ——— Astoria, or Anecdotes of an Enterprise beyond the Rocky Mountains, 2 vols. 8vo. Phil. 1836

111 ——— The Rocky Mountains, or Scenes, &c., in the Far West, 2 vols. 12mo. *cloth.* Phil. 1837

112 ——— Voyages and Discoveries of Columbus, 2 vols. *sheep*, 1839. Do. of the Companions of Columbus, forming vol. 3, uniform, 1835. 3 vols. 8vo. Phil. v. y.

113 JOHNSTON (*Dr. John*), A History of the Haunted Caverns of Magdelanna, an Indian Queen of South America, 12mo. *bds.* Phil. 1821

114 JONES (*George*), Tecumseh and the Prophet of the West, an original historical Israel-Indian Tragedy, 8vo. *cloth.* Lond. 1844

115 JUAN AND ULLOA'S Voyage to South America, describing at large the Spanish Cities, Towns, and Provinces of that extensive Continent, with Notes on the Brazils, *translated by J. Adams*, 2 vols. 8vo. Lond. 1806

"Juan and Ulloa's travels may be selected as the most entertaining and satisfactory work of its kind; they are the acknowledged source of much that has been published in other forms."—*Retrospective Rev.*

116 KENDALL (*G. W.*) The War between the United States and Mexico, illustrated, *embracing Pictorial Drawings of all the Principal Conflicts, by Carl Nebel*, with a Description of each Battle, large folio size, elegantly colored, in a Portfolio. N. Y. n. d.

This magnificent work has long been scarce, and commands more than its original price.

117 KENNEDY (*J. P.*) Discourse on the Life and Character of George Calvert, Lord Baltimore, 8vo. Balt. 1845

118 KOSTER (*Henry*), Travels in Brazil, from Pernambuco to Serara, *with map, and plates of costume*, 2 vols. 8vo. *bds.* Lond. 1817

119 LA HONTAN (*Baron de*), Nouveau Voyage du, dans l'Amerique Septentrionale, et Relation des differents Peuples qui y habitant, &c., 2 vols. 18mo. *maps and curious plates, old calf.* La Haye, 1703

"An ardent and enterprising man, whose accounts bear every mark of authenticity, and are quite confirmed by contemporary and subsequent writers."—*N. A. Rev.*

At the end of the second volume is a "Dictionary of the *Algonkin* Language."

120 LEE (*Henry*), Memoirs of the War in the Southern Department of the United States, 8vo. *half cloth.* Wash. 1827

"Lee's memoirs are very interesting, and as fascinating as a romance, though they undoubtedly contain true history."—*Chancellor Kent.*

121 LEWIS AND CLARK, Travels to the Source of the Missouri River, and across the American Continent to the Pacific Ocean, in 1804–6, *with large map of the route, &c.*, 2 vols. 8vo. *sheep.* Phil. 1814

"This is an interesting work, and exhibits not only some valuable geographical notices, but very copious and amusing details respecting the manners, habits, and diversions of the Indian North American tribes."—*Critical Review.*

122 LEWES (*J. C.*) Aboriginal Portfolio, Part 1, 4to. N. Y. 1853

123 LIEBER (*Francis*), The Stranger in America, or Letters to a Gentleman in Germany, 8vo. *half cloth.* Phil. 1835

124 LIFE on the Lakes, by the Author of "Legends of a Log Cabin," 2 vols. 12mo. N. Y. 1836

125 LLOYD'S Steamboat Directory, &c., 4 vols. *cloth.*

126 LONG (*J.*) Voyages and Travels of an Indian Interpreter and Trader, describing the Manners and Customs of the North American Indians, *map, uncut, clean copy,* a very interesting work, containing a valuable Vocabulary of the Chippewa and other Indian Languages, 4to. *half calf.* Lond. 1791

"A most faithful picture of the life and manners of the Indian and Canadian traders."—*Volney.*

127 MAINE Historical Society, Collections of, Vol. 1, 8vo. *cl.* Portland, 1831

128 MAP of Cuba and Plan of Havana, 12mo.

129 MARION (*Gen. Francis*), The Life of, 12mo, *sheep.* Phil. 1841

130 MARQUETTE (*Le P.*) ET ST. JOLIET, Voyage et Découverte de Quelques Pays et Nations de l'Amérique Septentrionale, *map*, sm. 8vo. *morocco.* Paris, 1681, rep. 1845

Only 125 copies reprinted.

131 MARRYAT (*Capt.*) Diary in America, 3 vols., 1st and 2d series, 12mo. *cloth.* Phil. 1839

132 MARTIN'S (*Montgomery*) History of the British Colonies, complete, *numerous maps and engravings,* 10 vols. fcap. 8vo. *cloth.* 1837, &c.

This popular and excellent work comprises the Canadas, New South Wales, Cape of Good Hope, East and West Indies, Nova Scotia, Newfoundland, Gibraltar, possessions in the Indian and Atlantic Oceans.

133 Maturin (*Ed.*), Montezuma, the Last of the Aztecs, a Historical Romance, 2 vols. 12mo. *paper.* N. Y. 1845

134 Mathews (*C.*) A Pen and Ink Panorama of New York City, 18mo. *cloth.* N. Y. 1853

135 McConnel (*J. L.*) Western Characters, or Types of Border Life, 12mo. *cloth, illustrated.* N. Y. 1853

136 Mead (*Ch.*) Mississippian Scenery, a Poem, Descriptive of the Interior of North America, 18mo. *sheep.* Phil. 1819

137 Melville (*H.*) Typee and a Voyage Thither, 12mo. *cloth.* N. Y. 1852

138 Memoirs of a Life Passed Chiefly in Pennsylvania, 12mo. *sheep.* Harrisburg, 1811

139 Mexico, Life in, being a Residence in that Country, 2 vols. 12mo. *cloth.* Boston, 1843

140 Mexico Versus Texas, a Descriptive Novel of Living Persons, 12mo. *cloth.* Phil. 1838

141 Miranda (*Don Francisco*), The History of his Attempt to effect a Revolution in South America, 12mo. *cloth.* Bost. 1810

142 Molino (*Don J. Ignatius*), The Geographical, Natural, and Civil History of Chili, from the Italian, with notes and appendices by the Translator, 2 vols. 8vo. *sheep.* Lond. 1808

Contains a valuable essay and vocabularies in the Chilian or Araucanian language.

143 Neal (*John*), The Battle of Niagara, with other Poems, 16mo. *bds.* Balt. 1819

144 National Portrait Gallery of Distinguished Americans, conducted by James Herring, of New York, and Jas. B. Longacre, Philadelphia, under the Superintendence of the American Academy of Fine Arts, containing one hundred and forty-nine engraved Portraits of the most eminent Persons who have occupied a Place in the History or Contemporary Annals of the United States, all of which are executed on steel, by the best artists, and from the most esteemed likenesses known or extant, and each portrait accompanied by a concise, authentic, and characteristic Biographical Sketch of the individual, in the preparation of which the work has been aided by the ablest writers in the country, and recourse has been had, invariably, to the most competent and unequivocal authorities in the statement of facts, 3 vols. 4to., *fine early impressions of the plates.* Phil. 1837

"These are deeds which should not pass away,
And names that must not wither, though the earth
Forgets her empires with a just decay,
The enslavers and the enslaved, their death and birth."

Nothing has yet come from the hands of American engravers to equal, in delicacy of handling and beauty of finish, these fine portraits of American statesmen, scholars, and heroes. There is the true texture of the flesh, the indications of color, which is the highest achievement of the artist who is confined to light, shade, and truthfulness of expression, the faultlessness of drawing. Each portrait is accompanied by a biographical sketch from the hands of our first writers, among whom are the names of John Quincy Adams, Prof. Ticknor, Robert Y. Hayne, Dr. Francis, and others equally renowned.

144*National History of the United States, comprising the Colonial, Revolutionary, and Constitutional Records of the Country, based upon and including the State Documents of the Federal Constitution, by Benson J. Lossing and Edwin Williams, in 2 vols. royal 8vo. *half calf.* Lond. n. d.

145 Negro (*The*), Equalled by few Europeans, to which are added Pœms by Phillis Wheatly, 2 vols. 12mo. Phil. 1801

146 Norman (*B. M.*) Rambles by Land and Water: or, Notes of Travel in Cuba and Mexico, including a Canoe Voyage up the River Panuco, and Researches among the Ruins of Tamaulipas, 12mo. *cloth.* N. Y. 1845

147 Northmore (*Thos.*) Washington: or, Liberty Restored, a Poem, 18mo. *sheep.* Balt. 1809

148 Novus Orbis (*Grynæus' New World*) Regionum ac Insularum Veteribus Incognitarum, una cum Tabula, Cosmographia, &c., *folio, in old calf, tall copy, rare.* Basil, 1637

This valuable work (the first collection of the wonderful relations of the maritime discoveries of the age) contains the voyages of Columbus, Vespucius, Marco Polo, Magellan, Haython, Peter Martyr's Decades, &c. &c.

149 Ocaropucerio, a Peruvian Journal, 4 vols. 4to. *half morocco.* Peru, 1837—42

150 Origin and Progress of Despotism in the Oriental and other Empires of Africa, Europe, and America, 8vo. *half calf.*
Amst. (*i. e. the private press of John Wilkes*) 1764

151 Payne (*A. R. M.*) The Geral Milco; or, the Narrative of a Residence in a Brazilian Valley, or the Sierra Paricis, 12mo. *boards.* N. Y. 1852

152 PHELPS (*Capt. Mathew*), Memoirs and Adventures of Capt. Mathew Phelps, formerly of Harwington, in Conn., now resident in New Haven, Vermont, particularly in Two Voyages from Connecticut to the River Mississippi, from Dec., 1773, to Oct., 1780, compiled by Anthony Haswell, 12mo. *sheep.* Bennington, 1801

153 PISONIS (*Guil.*) De Indiæ utrusque Re Naturali et Medica, with woodcuts. Georgii Margravii de Regionibus et Indigenis Brasiliæ et Chili ejusdem Continentis.—Jac. Brontii Historiæ Naturalis Medicæ Indiæ Orientalis, *with fine plates and cuts, folio, half calf.* Amst., *Elzevir*, 1658

Contains Georgius Maregravius on the Country and Aborigines of Chili and Brazil, Brontius's Natural History of the East Indies, &c.

"The climate, &c., of Brazil have been described by two eminent naturalists, Piso and Margrave, who observed it with a philosophical accuracy, unusual in accounts of American provinces."—*Robertson.*

154 PHILADELPHIA Souvenir, by J. E. Hall, 12mo. Phila. 1826

155 PIZARRO in Peru: or, the Death of Rolla, a Play in Five Acts, from the German of A. Von Kotzebue, 8vo. pp. 92. N. Y. 1800

156 POLICE Regulations of City of New York.

POWERS (*T.*) Impressions, *vide* Dramatic Biography.

157 PRIEST (*Josiah*), American Antiquities and Discoveries in the West, 8vo. *sheep.* Albany, 1834

158 PRIOR (*Aug. S.*) All the Voyages Round the World, from the first by Magellan, in 1520, to that of Trajanet, in 1820, 18mo. *sheep.* N. Y. 1841

159 PRESIDENTS' Messages and Documents, 6 vols. 8vo. *cloth.* 1849—58

160 PURCHAS, His Pilgrimage, or Relations of the World and the Religions observed in all ages and places discovered, from the Creation until this present, &c., by Samuel Purchas, *folio, fine copy in old calf, gilt.* Lond. 1614

The synopsis and complement of the collection of voyages edited by the venerable author, of which it forms the fifth volume.

161 PYM, Narrative of Arthur Gordon Pym, of Nantucket, 12mo. *half calf.* N. Y. 1838

RALEIGH (*Sir W.*) Guiana, *vide* Shakspeariana.

162 RALEIGH, History of the World, by Oldys, *fine portrait by Vertue, folio, calf.* 1666

"The design of this great work was equal to the greatness of the author's mind, and its execution to the strength of his parts and the variety of his learning. His style is pure, nervous, and majestic, and much better suited to the dignity of history than that of Lord Bacon."—*Dr. Drake.*

163 REPORT of the Commissioners appointed for the Common Schools, *thick* 8vo. *sewed.* Albany, 1858

164 ——— Of the Common Council of New York on the Reception of Kossuth, 8vo. *cloth.* N. Y. 1852

165 RIGHTS of Great Britain asserted, being an Answer to the American Declaration of Independence, 12mo. *half roan.* Lond. 1786

166 ROBERTSON'S (*J. P. & W. P.*) Paraguay, and Francia's Reign of Terror, comprising an Account of Four Years' Residence in that Republic under the Government of the Dictator Francia, *plates*, 4 vols. 12mo. *boards.* Phil. 1838—39

"These are very pleasant volumes; more agreeable travelling companions we have not lately met with. We recommend our readers to get the work as soon as possible."—*Athenæum.*

167 ROBERTSON (*William*), History of America, with a General History of North and South America, and a Complete History of the United States, *thick*, *royal* 8vo. pp. 1146. Lond. 1834

168 ROBINSON (*Fayette*), An Account of Organization of the Army of the United States, *with thirty-six portraits*, 2 vols. 12mo. Phil. 1848

169 ——— Mexico and her Military Chieftains, *plates*, 12mo. *sheep.* Phil. 1847

170 ROGERS (*Rev. Ammi*) Memoirs of a Clergyman of the Episcopal Church in Connecticut, 12mo. *half sheep.* Schen. 1826

171 ——— (*T. J.*) American Biographical Dictionary, 12mo. *sheep.* Phil. 1829

172 ROSENBERG (*C. G.*) Jenny Lind's Tour through America and Cuba, pp. 226, 12mo. *cloth.* N. Y. 1851

173 RULES for the Government of the Board of Guardians of the Almshouse Hospital, 8vo. *sheep.* Phil. 1835

174 RUSCHENBERGER (*W. S. W.*) A Voyage Round the World, including an Embassy to Muscat and Siam in 1835, 1836, and 1837, 8vo. *sheep.* Phil. 1838

175 SAFFORD (*Wm. H.*) The Life of Harman Blennerhassett, 12mo. *cloth.* Chilicothe, O. 1850

176 SAVAGE (*Ex-Mid. Timothy*), The Amazonian Republic, recently discovered in the interior of Peru, 12mo. *boards.* N. Y. 1842

177 SCHOOLCRAFT (*Henry Rowe*), Algic Researches, or Inquiries respecting the Mental Characters of the North American Indians, 2 vols. *cloth*, 12mo., *scarce.* N. Y. 1839

178 SCHUYLKILL Fishing Company, Authentic Historical Memoir of the, from 1732 to 1830, *cloth*, 8vo. Phil. 1830

179 SEATSFIELD: Life in the New World, or Sketches of American Society, 8vo. *cloth, covers loose.* N. Y.

180 SEWARD'S Monody on Major André, *embellished with engravings*, pp. 22, 12mo.; and other tracts, as follows: Galatea, a Pastoral Romance; imitated from Cervantes, by M. de Florian, translated into English; to which is added, Amelia, or the Faithless Briton; and Amelia, or Malevolence Defeated. Bost. 1796

181 SHARP (*Granville*), The Law of Retribution against Tyrants, Slaveholders, &c.; or, A Serious Warning to Great Britain and her Colonies, 12mo. *boards.* Lond. 1776

182 SHERIDAN and Kotzebue: The Surprising Adventures of Pizarro, preceded by a brief sketch of the Voyages and Discoveries of Columbus and Cortez; to which are subjoined the Histories of Alonzo and Cora, &c. 8vo. *proof plate*, pp. 144. Lond. 1793

183 SHIRREFF (*Patrick*), Tour through North America, with a View of the Canadas and United States, as adapted for Agricultural Emigration, 8vo. Edin. 1835

184 SIMMONDS (*P. L.*) Franklin and the Arctic Regions, 12mo. *cloth.* 1852

185 SIMMS (*W. Gilmore*), The Life of Francis Marion, 12mo. *cloth.* N. Y. 1844

186 SIMON (*Mrs.*) Ten Tribes of Israel Historically Identified with the Aborigines of the Western Hemisphere, *boards*, 8vo. Lond. 1836

This work consists principally of extracts from the sixth volume of Lord Kingsborough's Antiquities of Mexico, with Mrs. Simon's remarks.

187 SMITH (*J. T.*) The Discovery of America by the Northmen in 10th century, Translation of all the Icelandic Sagas, Narratives, &c., *maps and plates, cloth*, 12mo. Bost. 1839

A very interesting volume, principally translated from the Icelandic, Danish, and Latin "Antiquitates Americanæ," published by the Northern Antiquaries of Copenhagen.

188 ——— (*Jerome, V. C., M. D.*) Natural History of Fishes of Massachusetts, with an Essay on Angling, 12mo. *cloth.* Bost. 1833

189 SMYTH (*Capt.*) Sketches in the Canadas, 26 *large and beautiful plates, equal to drawings*, by HULLMANDEL. impl. folio, *half morocco.* Lond. n. d.

190 SNOWDEN (*Richard*), The American Revolution, written in Scriptural or ancient Historical style, to which is added the Columbiad, 12mo. *sheep, rare.* Balt. n. d.

191 SONGS and Ballads of the American Revolution, with Notes and Illustrations by FRANK MOORE, 12mo. *cloth.* N. Y. 1856

192 SOUTHWEST (*The*), By a Yankee, 2 vols. 12mo. *cloth.* N. Y. 1835

193 SPARKS (*Jared*), The Life of Benjamin Franklin, containing his Autobiography, with Notes and a Continuation, 8vo. *cloth.* Bost. 1844

194 SPENCER (*J. A.*) History of the United States, from the Earliest Period to the Present Time, *illustrated with original portraits and historical scenes*, in 52 parts, 4to., wants parts 6 and 26. N. Y. 1856

195 STEWART (*Com. Chas.*) Biographical Sketch and Services of, royal 8vo., pp. 50. Phil. 1838

196 SWAN (*John*), Speculum Mundi, or a Glass representing the face of the World, small 4to. *calf.* Camb. 1644

Contains a "Curious Conjecture how America came to be at the first unknown."—pp. 226–7.

197 ST. DOMINGO, Secret History of the Horrors of, in a Series of Letters to Col. Burr, by a Lady, 12mo. *sheep., very scarce.* 1808

198 TAYLOR and his Generals, including an Account of the Mexican War, 12mo. Phil. 1847

199 THOMAS (*L. F.*) Cortez, the Conqueror, a Tragedy (founded on the conquest of Mexico), 8vo. Wash. 1857

200 THOMPSON (*Benj. F.*) History of Long Island, containing an Account of the Discovery and Settlement, to the Present Time, 8vo. *half cloth.* N. Y. 1839

201 TOWNSEND (*John K.*) Narrative of a Journey across the Rocky Mountains, 8vo. *cloth.* Phil. 1839

202 TRACTS, A volume of interesting, on the subject of taxing America: I. Conduct of the Administration; II. Proceedings of Congress at New York; III. Examination of Dr. Franklin; IV. Two curious papers written in 1739, by Mr. Joshua Gee and others; *scarce*, 8vo., wants covers. Lond. 1767

203 TRAITS of the Tea Party, being a Memoir of George R. T. Hewes, a scion of the little band of patriots who drowned the Tea in Boston Harbor in 1773, by a Citizen of New York, 16mo. *cloth.* N. Y. 1835

204 TRANSACTIONS of the New York State Agricultural Society for 1851, 1853, 2 vols. 8vo. *cloth.* Albany, 1854

205 ——— of the American Institute for 1851, 8vo. *cloth.* Albany, 1852

206 TROLLOPE (*Mrs.*) Domestic Manners of the Americans, 8vo. *half calf.* Lond. 1832

207 ——— Domestic Manners of the Americans, *plates*, 8vo. *cloth.* N. Y. 1832

208 TROLLOPE (*Frances*), The Life and Adventures of Jonathan Jeff. Whitlaw, or Scenes on the Mississippi, 8vo. *sheep.* Paris, 1836

209 TRUMBULL (*John*), Autobiography, Reminiscences, and Letters of, from 1776 to 1841, 8vo. *cloth, numerous etchings and fine port.* N. Y. and Lond. 1841

210 ——— (*Henry*), History and Discovery of America, *half roan*, 8vo. Bost. 1832

211 UNITED STATES, an Accompaniment to Mitchell's Reference and Distance Map of the, *half roan*, 8vo. Phil. 1834

212 VALENTINE (*D. T.*) History of the City of New York. Illustrated by *numerous plates*, 8vo. *cloth.* N. Y. 1853

213 VAN HEUVEL (*J.*) El Dorado; a History of the Reports in the 16th Century, of a Rich and Splendid City in S. America, with a Defence of Sir Walter Raleigh, &c. *map*, 8vo. N. Y. 1844

214 VISION of Rubeta, an Epic Story of the Island of Manhattan, *with illustrations*, 8vo. *boards.* Bost. 1830

215 VOICE to America; or the Model Republic, its Glory or its Fall; with a Review of the Causes of the Decline and Failure of the Republics of South America, Mexico, and the Old World, applied to the Present Crisis in the United States, *cloth extra*, 18mo. N. Y. 1855

216 VOYAGES and Discoveries in South America. I. Voyage up the river of Amazons to Quito in Peru, by Chris. D. Acugna. II. Up the river of Plata, and thence by land to the Mines of Potosi, by M. Acarete. III. From Cayenne to Guiana, in search of the Lake of Parima, "reputed the richest place in the World," by M. Grillet and Bechamel, done into English from the originals, 8vo. *curious maps, old calf.* Lond. 1698

Acugna's Voyage appeared in Spanish in 1641. Acarete's Relation is in Thevenot's Collection. The Original of Grillet and Bechamel's Voyage has not yet been discovered.

217 WAKEFIELD (*John A.*) History of the War between the United States and the Sac and Fox Nations of Indians, *half sheep*, 12mo. Jacksonville, Ill. 1834

218 WARD (*H. G.*) Travels in Mexico, during the years 1825, '26, and '27, with an Account of the Mining Companies, and of the Political Events in that Republic to the present day, 15 *maps and plates*, 2 thick vols. 8vo. *cloth.* Lond. 1829

"A sterling work upon a subject of great and growing interest, the very merits and elaborate nature of which prevent us from doing it justice: we can only say we have seen enough of it to be satisfied with its features of particular attraction and general importance."—*Literary Gazette.*

219 WARDEN (*Thos. J. M. D.*) America Vindicated, 12mo. *cloth.* N. Y. 1855

220 WASHINGTON (*Geo.*) Letters from, to Sir John Sinclair, on Agriculture and other interesting topics, *engraved from the original letters, so as to be an exact fac simile of his handwriting*, 4to. Phil. 1839

221 WATSON (*John F.*), Annals of Philadelphia and Pennsylvania, from the Earliest Settlement down to the year 1844, 2 vols. 8vo. *cloth.* Phil. 1844

In speaking of this work, Washington Irving says, "Its author has done an important service to his country." It deals with the interesting facts of olden time; traces the origin of much that is new about us; and shows the changes which have passed over customs and localities; calls up and places before the view, the scenes, the buildings, and the persons who were memorable in the days of our forefathers.

222 WEBBER (*C. W.*) Old Hicks, the Guide, or Adventures in the Camanche Country, 2 vols. 12mo. N. Y. 1848

223 WEBSTER (*Noah*), A Collection of Essays and Fugitive Writings on Moral, Historical, and Literary Subjects, *with fine Autograph Letter*, 8vo. *sheep, gilt.* Bost. 1790

Printed in the author's peculiar style of orthography; *scarce.*

224 ——— —— Letters to a Young Gentleman Commencing his Education, 8vo. *bds.* New Haven, 1823

225 WESTERN PILOT; containing Charts of the Ohio and Mississippi Rivers, 8vo. *half calf.* Cincinnati, 1847

226 WESTERN BORDER LIFE, or what Fanny Hunter saw and heard in Kansas and Missouri, 12mo. *cl.* N. Y. 1856

227 WHITE (*G. S.*) Memoir of Samuel Slater, the Father of American Manufactures, with a History of the Rise and Progress of Cotton Manufacture in England and America, 8vo. *sheep.* Phil. 1836

228 WHITE Sulphur Papers in Western Virginia, by Mark Pencil, *cloth*, 12mo. N. Y. 1839

229 WILKES (*Geo.*) History of Oregon, Monsieur Violet, &c. 4 vols. 8vo. N. Y.

230 WILKINSON (*Eliza*), Letters of, during the Invasion of Charlestown by the British in the Revolutionary War; from the original MS., by Caroline Gilman, 8vo. *cloth.* N. Y. 1839

231 ——— (*Gen. James*), Memoirs of My Own Times, 3 vols. 8vo. *half mor. neat, scarce.* Phil. 1816

232 WILKINSON (*Jemima*), History of a Preacheress of the XVIII. Century, containing an Authentic Narrative of her Life and Character, and of the Rise, Progress, and Conclusion of her Ministry, by Dav. Hudson, 12mo. *bds.* pp. x. 208, with Appendix, pp. xx. Geneva, 1821

233 WOOD (*John*), The Suppressed History of John Adams, with Notes by John H. Sherburne, *fine port.*, 12mo. *cl.* Phil. 1846

234 WYTHE (*John*), Portraits to the Life and Manners of the Inhabitants of that Province in America called Virginia, afterwards engraved by Theodore de Bry, 1590, 24 *plates*, 8vo. *half calf.* N. Y. 1841

AMERICAN POETRY.

235 ADAMS (*J. Q.*) Dermot Mac Morragh. Bost. 1832

236 ADAMS (*J. T.*) Poems, 12mo. *bds.* New Haven, 1825

237 AHASUERUS, a Poem, by a Virginian, 12mo. *cloth.* N. Y. 1842

238 ALLEN (*Miss E.*) The Silent Harp, or Fugitive Poems, 12mo. *half cloth.* Burl. 1832

239 ALLEN (*Mr.*) Pastorals, Elegies, Odes, Epistles, &c., 12mo. *sheep.* Abingdon, Md., 1806

240 ALLSTON (*W.*) Sylphs of the Seasons, 8vo. *half calf.* Bost. 1813

241 AMERICAN Manners, or the Atlantic Voyage, a Moral Poem, 12mo. *cloth.* Lond.

242 BARRY (*G.*) Poems, 12mo., *scarce.* Balt. 1807

243 BARTLETT (*J.*) Physiognomy, a Poem, 12mo. Portsmouth, 1810

244 BATES (*David*), The Æolian, 12mo. *cloth.* Phil. 1849

245 BATTLE of Lepanto, The Fall of Delhi, and other Poems, by W., 12mo. *bds.* Phil. 1829

246 BRIDAL of Vaumond, a Metrical Romance, 12mo. *bds.* N. Y. 1817

247 BUTLER, Nothing to Wear, 12mo. *cloth.* N. Y. 1857

248 Cairns (*J.*) Miscellaneous Poems, 12mo. *bds.* Jedburgh, 1832

249 Cannon (*Chas. J.*) Poems, Dramatic and Miscellaneous, 12mo. *cloth.* N. Y. 1851

250 Caprices, 12mo. *bds.* N. Y. 1849

251 Chivers (*T. H.*) Nacoochee, 12mo. *cloth.* N. Y. 1837

252 Clarke (*Macdonald*), Poems by, sq. 16mo. *paper.* N. Y. 1844

253 Cliffton (*Wm., of Philad'a*), Poems, chiefly occasional, some account of a manuscript found among the papers of a French emigrant, entitled Talleyrand's Descent into Hell, with his Life and Portrait, *scarce*, 18mo. *sheep.* N. Y. 1800

254 Curse of Liberty, with other Poems, 18mo. *half roan.* N. Y. 1817

255 Dabney (*R.*) Poems, 12mo. Phil. 1815

256 Dabney (*Richard*), Poems, original and translated, 18mo. *bds.* Phil. 1815

257 Darwin (*E.*) Temple of Nature, 8vo. *sheep.* Balt. 1804

258 Davidson (*Lucre. M.*) Amir Khan, and other Poems, the Remains of, 12mo. *bds.* N. Y. 1829

259 Davis (*R. B.*) Poems, with Life, 12mo. *sheep.* N. Y. 1807

260 Dawes (*Rufus*), Geraldine, Athenia of Damascus, and Miscel. Poems, 12mo. *cloth.* N. Y. 1839

261 Democratiad, a Poem, 8vo. *half mor.* Phil. 1796

262 Earle (*Pliny, M.D.*) Marathon, and other Poems, 12mo. *cloth.* Phil. 1841

263 Echo (*The*), Printed at the Porcupine Press, by Pasquin Petronius, *plates*, 8vo. *sheep.* N. Y. 1807

264 Fairfield (*Sum. L.*) Lays of Melpomene, 12mo. *cloth, port.* 1824

265 ——— Last Night of Pompeii, and Lays and Legends, 8vo. *cloth.* N. Y. 1832

266 ——— Abaddon, 8vo. *bds.* N. Y. 1830

267 Flint (*M. P.*) Hunter, and other Poems, 12mo. *bds.* Bost. 1826

268 ——— Hunter and other Poems, 12mo. Bost. 1826

269 Foster (*Wm. C.*) Poetry on different subjects, written under the signature of Timothy Spectacle, 12mo. *shp.* Salem, 1805

270 Glance at the Nations, and other Poems, 12mo. *cloth.* Bost. 1835

271 Goodrich (*S. G.*) Poems by, 8vo. *cloth gilt, illustrated.* N. Y. 1851

272 Guido, a Tale, Sketches from Memory, and other Poems, by Ianthe, 12mo. *half cloth.* N. Y. 1828

273 Halm (*Fried.*) The Son of the Wilderness, a Dramatic Poem, 12mo. *pl.* N. Y. 1848

274 Hill (*G.*) Ruins of Athens, 8vo. *cloth.* Bost. 1839

275 Hitchcock (*D.*) Social Monitor, a Series of Poems, 12mo. *half calf.* Stockbridge, 1812

276 Horace in New York, and other American Poems, 8vo. v. d.

277 Jerusalem, The Destruction of, 12mo. *shp.* Phil. 1809

278 Jones (*J. B.*) Rural Sports, 12mo. Phil. 1849

279 Judgment, a Vision, and Percy's Masque, 12mo. *bds.* N. Y. 1821

280 Judgment, a Vision, 8vo. *bds.* N. Y. 1821

281 Journals of the Ocean, and other Miscellaneous Poems, by a Seaman, 12mo. N. Y. 1826

282 Kettel (*S.*) Specimens of American Poetry, with Critical and Biographical Notices, *uncut*, 3 vols. 8vo. *bds.* Bost. 1829

283 Lexington, with other Fugitive Poems, 8vo. *bds.* (privately printed?) N. Y. 1830

284 Linn (*J. B.*) Powers of Genius, a Poem, 18mo. *bds.* Phil. 1802

285 Lone, or the Heart's Ordeal, a Dramatic Sketch.

286 Low (*Samuel*), Poems, 2 vols. 12mo. *sheep.* N. Y. 1800

287 Lowell (*J. Russell*), Conversations on some of the Old Poets, 8vo. *half morocco.* Lond. 1845

288 Lunt (*Geo.*) Poems by, 12mo. *cloth.* N. Y. 1839

289 Marsh (*Wm.*) England, and other Poems, 12mo. *cloth.* N. Y. 1839

290 McDonald (*Mrs. M.*) Poems, 8vo. *cloth.* N. Y. 1844

291 McHenry (*James*), The Blessings of Friendship, and other Poems and Harmoniæ Cœlestes, by Geo. Bettner, M. D., 2 vols. 12mo. N. Y. and Lond.

292 Misanthrope of the Mountain, 12mo. N. Haven, 1833

293 Miriam, a Dramatic Poem, 12mo. *pr.* Bost. 1838

294 Miscellaneous Poems, by Osander, 12mo. *bds.* Hudson, 1811

295 Month of Freedom, 12mo. *cloth.* N. Y. 1837

296 Morris (*G. P.*) Deserted Bride, and other Poems, 8vo. *cloth.* N. Y. 1838

297 Muzzy (*Mrs. Harriet*), Poems, Moral and Sentimental, 12mo. *bds.* N. Y. 1821

298 NACK (*James*), Earl Rupert, and other Tales and Poems, with a Memoir by P. M. Wetmore, 12mo. *cloth.* N. Y. 1839

299 ——— An Ode on the Proclamation of General Jackson, with a Memoir of the Author, 8vo. *sewed.* N. Y. 1833

300 NOAH, a Poem, by Paul Allen, 18mo. *bds.* Balt. 1821

301 O TEMPORA! O Mores! 12mo. N. Y. 1844

302 OCEAN Harp, a Poem written in Two Cantos, and a Monody on the Death of John Syng Dorsey, M. D., by the author of Lord Byron's Farewell to England, 12mo. Phil. 1819

303 ORIGINAL Poems, by a Citizen of Baltimore, 12mo. *shp.* Balt. 1809

304 OSANDER, Poems, 12mo. *bds.* Hudson, 1811

305 OSGOOD (*F. S.*) A Wreath of Wild Flowers from New England, 8vo. *cloth.* 1838

306 PIERCE (*W. L.*) The Year, a Poem, 18mo. *bds.* N. Y. 1813

307 PIERPONT (*John*), The Portrait, a Poem, 8vo. *half mor.* Bost. 1812

308 PINDARIC Shop Opened, 12mo. *bds.* Bost. 1801

309 POEMS on Different Subjects, 18mo. *bds.* Bost. 1813

310 POEMS, Original and Select, by a Stranger, 12mo. *cloth.* Alb. 1827

311 POEMS, Miscellaneous, selected from U. S. Literary Gazette, 18mo. Bost. 1826

Contains the early effusions of Bryant, Longfellow, &c.

312 POETICAL Wanderer (The), 12mo.

313 PRAY (*Isaac C.*) Poems of, sd. 8vo. Bost. 1837

314 Progress of Society, a Poem, 12mo. N. Y. 1817

315 POET (*The*), A Metrical Romance of the 17th Century, 12mo. *cloth.* Phil. 1840

316 RUINS of Athens, and other Poems, 8vo. *cloth.* Wash. 1831

317 RUINS of Athens, &c., 8vo. *boards.* Wash. 1831

318 SANDS (*R. C.*) Writings of, in Prose and Verse, with Memoir of the Author, 2 vols. 8vo. *half cloth.* N. Y. 1835

319 SAUNDERS (*Jas. M.*) Pieces in Prose and Verse, 18mo. *cloth.* Phil. 1834

320 SAUNDERS (*J. M.*) Poems, 18mo. *cloth.* Phil. 1834

321 SAXE (*J. G.*) Poems, 12mo. *cloth.* Bost. 1856

322 SEARSON (*John*), Mount Vernon, a Poem, *portrait of Washington*, 8vo. *sheep*, *soiled.* Phil.

323 SEARSON (*John*) Poems, 8vo. *sheep.* Phil. 1797

324 SELIM'S New Haven, a Poem, satirical and sentimental, with explanatory notes, 8vo. *half mor.* N. Y. 1809

325 SIMMONS (*J. W.*) The Maniac's Confession, a Fragment of a Tale, 12mo. *boards.* Phil. 1821

326 SPRAGUE (*C.*) Writings of, 8vo. *cloth.* N. Y. 1841

327 STORY (*Joseph*), The Power of Solitude, a Poem in 2 parts, 12mo. *sheep.* Salem, 1804

328 STUART (*J.*) Poems on Various Subjects, 12mo. *boards.* Balt. 1812

329 SUKEY, a Poem, Barnyard Rhymes, and other vols. of American Poetry, 8vo. v. d.

330 SWANWICK (*J.*) Poems, 18mo. *sheep.* Phil. 1797

331 TAGGART (*Cynthia*), Poems, 12mo. *cloth.* Provid. 1834

332 TRIUMPH of Peace, and other Poems, 12mo. *cloth.* N. Y. 1840

333 UNTAUGHT Bard (The), 12mo. *sheep.* N. Y. 1804

334 WAKONDAH, The Moth of Life, 8vo. *boards.* N. Y. 1841

335 WARREN (*Mrs. M.*) Poems, Dramatic and Miscellaneous, 12mo. *sheep.* Bost. 1790

336 WEEKES (*R.*) Poems, 12mo. N. Y. 1823

337 WHITTIER (*J. G.*) Poems by, 12mo. *roan*, *damaged.* Phil. 1838

338 ZELIA, a Poem, 12mo. N. Y. 1830

ANECDOTES.—*See also* BIOGRAPHY AND FACETIÆ.

339 ADDISONIANA, or Anecdotes of Addison, 2 vols. 12mo. *half calf.* Lond.

340 AMERICAN Anecdotes, Original and Select, by an American, 2 vols. 8vo. *cloth*, *one title-page gone.* Bost. 1830

341 ANDREWS (*James Petit*), Anecdotes, Ancient and Modern, *calf*, 8vo. Lond. 1789

342 ANECDOTES of the most Distinguished Persons, &c. 2 vols. 8vo. *sheep.* *Sine loco et anno.*

343 ANECDOTIANA, being Select Gems of Anecdote and Wit, *sewed*, 32mo. Lond. 1826

344 ANONYMIANA, or Ten Centuries of Observations on various Authors and Subjects, 8vo. *half sheep.* Lond. 1818

345 ATTERBURYANA, being Miscellanies by the late Bishop of Rochester, 16mo. *sheep.* Lond. 1727

346 ARVINE (*K.*) Cyclopædia of Anecdotes of Literature and the Fine Arts, containing a copious and choice selection of Anecdotes of the various forms of literature, of the arts, architecture, engraving, music, poetry, painting, and sculpture, and of the most celebrated literary characters and artists of different countries and ages, &c., *with numerous illustrations*, royal 8vo. *half calf.* Bost. 1855

This is unquestionably the choicest collection of anecdotes ever published.

347 BEAUMARCHAISIANA, ou recueil d'anecdotes, bons mots, sarcasmes, repartees &c. de Beaumarchais, *half mor.* 18mo. Par. 1832

Beaumarchais is known as a dramatist, a speculator, a diplomatist, and political intriguer.

348 BENTHAMIANA, or Select Extracts from the Works of Jeremy Bentham, 8vo. *cloth.* Phila. 1844

349 BIOGRAPHIANA, by the Compiler of Anecdotes of Distinguished Persons (Miss SEWARD). 2 vols. 8vo. *calf.* Lond. 1799

350 BLOSSOMS of Anecdote and Wit, or Mirth for the Parlor, 12mo. *boards.* Lond. 1823

351 CHARACTERISTIC Anecdotes, from the History of Russia, 8vo. *boards.* Lond. 1805

*** Cobleriana *vide* Shakespeariana.

352 COLMAN (*George*), Circle of Anecdote and Wit; to which is added a Choice Selection of Toasts and Sentiments, *boards*, 18mo. N. Y. 1825

353 CRISPIN Anecdotes, comprising interesting notices of Shoemakers, who have been distinguished for genius, enterprise, eccentricity, &c. *half cloth*, 18mo. Sheffield, 1827

354 DEMOCRAT (The), Interspersed with Anecdotes of well-known Characters, 2 vols in 1, *calf*, 16mo. Lond. 1795

355 DOUGLAS (*James*), Travelling Anecdotes through various parts of Europe, 8vo. *sheep.* Lond. 1786

355* FRENCH Anas, or Literary Table-Talk Translated, viz. Perroniana, Poggiana, Huetiana, Scaligeriana, Menagiana, St. Evremondiana, &c., 3 vols. 12mo. *half bound.* Lond. 1805

France was very fruitful of that miscellaneous literature which, desultory and amusing, has the advantage of remaining better in the memory than more systematic books.—*Hallam.*

356 FUNGUSIANA, or the Opinions and Table-Talk of the late Barnaby Fungus, Esq., 12mo. *boards.* Lond. 1809

357 GALANTERIANA, ou Choix de Propos et d'Anecdotes Galantes, Anciennes et Modernes, 2 vols. 12mo. *paper.* Paris, 1814

358 GASCONIANA, ou Recueil des Bons Mots, 18mo. *old calf.* Amst. 1708

HOGARTH, Anecdotes of, *vide* Fine Arts.

359 JOHNSONIANA, or Collection of Anecdotes, &c., illustrative of the Life and Character and Writings of Dr. Johnson, 4to. 50 *beautiful plates, portraits, views, fac-similes, &c., half calf.* Lond. 1836

This amusing work, collected by Piozzi and others, is a supplement to Boswell's Johnson.

360 JOINERIANA, or the Book of Scraps, 2 vols. 18mo. *calf.* Lond. 1772

361 JOLYANA, ou Choix de Bons Mots, 18mo. *paper.* Paris, 1816

362 LIBER Facetiarum, being a Collection of Curious and Interesting Anecdotes, 12mo. Newcastle-upon-Tyne, 1800

363 MANGIN (*E.*) The Parlor Window, or Anecdotes, Original Remarks on Books, etc., 12mo. *cloth.* Lond. 1841

364 MALCOLM (*James Feller*), Miscellaneous Anecdotes of the Manners and History of Europe in the Reigns of Charles II., James II., William III., and Queen Anne, 8vo. *calf.* Lond. 1811

365 MENAGIANA, ou Bons Mots, Pensees Judicieuses et Observations Curieuses, De M. Menage, 18mo. *calf.* Paris, 1694

366 PEGGE (*Sam'l*) Curialia Miscellanea, or Anecdotes of Old Times, Regal, Noble, &c., including Anecdotes of the Royal Household, &c., *with portrait,* 8vo. *half calf.* Lond. 1818

367 PIOZZIANA, or Recollection of the late Mrs. Piozzi, 12mo. *boards.* Lond. 1833

368 PRANZERIANA, A Select Collection of Fugitive Pieces, published since the Appointment of the Present Provost of the University of Dublin, 12mo. *sheep.* Dublin, 1775

369 RAILWAY Anecdote Book, a Collection of the newest Anecdotes and Tales to the present day, 8vo. *sewed.* Lond. n. d.

370 ROGERS (*Samuel*), Recollections of the Table-Talk of, to which is added Porsoniana, 12mo. *cloth.* N. Y. 1856

371 SELDENIANA, or the Table-Talk of John Selden, Esq., 18mo. *calf.* Lond.

372 TAVERN Anecdotes, including the Origin of Signs and Reminiscences connected with Taverns, Coffee-Houses, Clubs, &c., MS. notes by G. Furman, of Brooklyn, *portrait*, 12mo. *half calf.* Lond. 1825

373 WALPOLIANA, being a Collection of Anecdotes of Horace Walpole, 18mo. *boards.* Lond. 1820

374 WARRENIANA, with Notes, Critical and Explanatory, 12mo. *boards.* Bost. 1824

ANTIQUITIES.

375 ANTICHITA DI ERCOLANO, Pitture, &c., 9 vols. royal folio, *with many hundred fine large engravings, calf.* Napoli, 1757—92

"Ouvrage très curieux et magnifiquement executé; vendu 820 francs, Trudaine, 760 fr. Clos."—*Brunet.*

This great work was begun under the auspices of King Charles of Naples, in 1757, and completed in 1792, and is the most learned, elegant, and valuable work ever published on the discoveries made in the buried City of Herculaneum. It is richly embellished with many thousands of beautiful engravings.

376 ANTIQUARIAN (*The*) and Architectural Year Book, large 8vo. *cloth, engravings.* Lond. 1845

*** Contents—Primeval Antiquities of the Channel Islands, Roman London, Confessionals, Medieval Antiquities, Ancient Frescoes, Stained Glass, Tombs, Ancient Irish Amulets, Bibliography, &c.

377 ANTIQUARIAN Repertory, by Grose, Astle, and other Eminent Antiquaries, *with upwards of* 200 *fine and scarce portraits and engravings, best edition,* 4 vols. royal 4to. Lond. 1775—84

A most interesting assemblage of Topography, History, Biography, Customs, and Manners, intended to illustrate and preserve several valuable Remains of Old Times.

This valuable work throws abundant light on ancient manners and customs, and embraces with minuteness the value of money, houses, land, &c., the provision usually made for the younger branches of great families, accounts of ancient furniture, religious ceremonies, tournaments, theatrical exhibitions, &c.

378 BARKER's Lares and Penates, or Cilicia and its Governors, from the Earliest Times to the Present Day, *map and numerous engravings,* 8vo. *cloth.* Lond. 1853

This interesting volume includes a description of some household gods of the Ancient Cilicians broken up by them on their conversion to Christianity.

379 Battely (*John*), Opera Posthuma; viz., Antiquitates Rutupinæ et Antiquitates S. Edmundi Burgi ad annum 1272 perductæ, 4to. *boards, maps, and* 16 *plates, besides tail pieces.* Oxon. 1745

*** "Written in pure Latin, it is an undeniable proof of the author's excellent judgment and learning, and will be a lasting monument of his profound skill in our most early antiquities."—*Hearn's Life of John Leland.*

"An elegant posthumous discourse."—*Bp. Nicholson.*

380 Bayardi (*O. A.*) Catalogo Degli Antichi Monumenti, 2 vols. folio, *calf.* Napoli, 1755

This important work contains numerous pamphlets of the Antiquities of Herculaneum, and is a part of Lot 375.

381 Boze (*Gros de*), Dissertation sur la Culte que les Anciens ont rendu a la Deese de la Santé; Dissertation sur Janus des Anciens; Dissertation d'une Inscription Antique trouvée a Lyon, est de Sacrifices Tauroboles, *curious plates of medals, &c., relating to each subject,* 8vo. *old binding.* Paris, 1705

382 Brayley's Graphic and Historical Illustrator, an Original Miscellany of Literary, Antiquarian, and Topographical Information, 150 *wood-cuts*, 8vo. Lond. 1834

383 Champollion-Figeac (*M.*) Egypte Ancien, 8vo. *hf. cf.* Par. 1839

384 Champollion le Jeune, Monuments de l'Egypte et de la Nubie, 4 vols. elephant folio, *containing* 537 *splendid engravings, many of which are beautifully colored to represent the originals, half mor.* 1835

In consequence of the irregularity of the manner in which this magnificent work was published, it is impossible to ascertain the perfection of copies from the prefatory list of plates; some there mentioned not appearing in the body of the work, and, on the other hand, no less than 26 being published beyond the number (511) specified in the list.

385 Cottoni Posthuma—Divers Choice Pieces by that renowned antiquary, Sir R. Cotton, 12mo. *old calf.* Lond. 1672

A valuable book, showing how the Kings of Scotland consult with their Peers. It includes Questions of Precedency, 24 Arguments against Popery, Sir P. Sydney's "Valour Anatomized in a Fancy," Walsingham's "Anatomy of Ambition," &c.

386 Cumberland (*Bp.*) Originis Gentium Antiquiminæ, or Attempts for Discovering the Times and First Planting of Nations, 8vo. *calf.* Lond. 1724

"A valuable and important work."—*Lowndes.*

387 DAWSON (*Thos.*) Memoirs of St. George, the English Patron, and of the Most Noble Order of the Garter, 8vo. *calf.* Lond. 1714

388 DESCRIPTION of the Townley Gallery in the British Museum, 2 vols. 12mo. *cloth, gilt.* Lond. 1836

389 DROGONTEO (*S.*) Storia di Alesa antica citta di Sicilia, col rapportes de 'suoi più insigni Monumenti, Statue, Madaglia, Iscrizioni, &c., 4to. *vellum, fine plates of antiquities, &c.* Palermo, 1753

390 DUGDALE (*Sir W.*) Monasticon Anglicanum, a History of the Abbeys and other Monasteries, Hospitals, Friaries, and Cathedral and Collegiate Churches in England and Wales, and all such Scotch, Irish, and French Monasteries as were in any manner connected with the Religious Houses in England, translated with Additions and a Continuation by Capt. Stevens, *with brilliant impressions of the numerous fine engravings of cathedrals, costume, &c., by Hollar,* 3 vols. folio, *very fine copy.* Lond. 1718–22

"What Dugdale has done is prodigious. His memory ought to be venerated and held in everlasting reverence."—*Anthony Wood.*

The clergy, the lawyer, the antiquary, the historian, the architect, and the topographer, as well as the possessor of real property, will find the Monasticon Anglicanum one of the most interesting and indispensable works that has ever issued from the press.

391 DUGDALE (*Wm.*) Antiquities of Warwickshire, illustrated, from Records, Leiger Books, &c., *portrait, maps, and plates, including the monument to Shakspeare at Stratford upon Avon,* folio, *calf.* Lond. 1656

This celebrated county history, the result of twenty years' indefatigable research, is not only considered the *chef d'œuvre* of Sir William, but, in the words of Mr. Gough, "it must stand at the head of all our county histories." There are works which scrupulous accuracy united with stubborn integrity have elevated to the rank of legal evidence; such is this first edition of Dugdale's Warwickshire, it being the only one admitted as evidence in a court of law.

392 ——— History of St. Paul's Cathedral in London, from its foundation until this time, *fine plates by Hollar,* folio, *half calf.* Lond. 1658

393 ELGIN and Phigaleian Marbles of the Classic Ages, in the British Museum, described by Sir Henry Ellis, 200 *cuts,* 2 vols. 12mo. *cloth.* Lond. 1833

394 FORSYTH (*J. S.*) Antiquary's Portfolio, or Cabinet Selection of Historical and Literary Curiosities, 2 vols. 8vo. *boards.* Lond. 1825

"A selection of historical and literary curiosities on subjects principally connected with the manners, customs, &c., of Great Britain during the middle and later ages."—*Lowndes.*

395 GODWIN (*Bp.*) An English Exposition of the Roman Antiquities, wherein many Roman and English Offices are parallel'd, and divers obscure Phrases explained, with his Moses and Aaron, in 1 vol. 4to. *calf.* 1680

"Godwin's memory cannot but be precious in succeeding ages."—*Anthony Wood.*

396 GROSE'S Antiquities of England and Wales, the original edition, large paper, *with very fine impressions of the numerous engravings of castles, abbeys, &c.*, 4 vols. royal 4to. *calf.* Lond. 1772–6

First and best edition; this is evidently a superior and very early copy, being printed on very thick paper.

397 HAMMER (*Joseph*), Ancient Alphabets and Hieroglyphic Characters explained, in the Arabic by Ahmad Bin Abubeke Bin Wahshih, and in English by Joseph Hammer, 4to. *cloth.* Lond. 1806

A very curious and rare work.

398 HEATH (*Chas.*) Historical and Descriptive Account of the Ancient and Present State of Tintern Abbey, 8vo. *uncut.* Monmouth [1823]

399 HEWLETT (*Rev. J.*) Vindication of the Authenticity of the Parian Chronicle, in answer to a dissertation on that subject lately published, 8vo. *calf.* Lond. 1789

400 HULME (*Dr.*) Account of a Brick brought from the Site of Ancient Babylon, &c. Lond. 1801

401 LIPSII (*J.*) Admiranda, sive de Magnitudine Romana 1617, de Militia Romana 1614, Poliorceticon, et Dissertativncvla in Plinii, 4 vols. in 1, folio, *vellum.* Antverp, Plantin, 1605–17

402 MASCHENS (*A. G.*) Die Gottesdienlichen Altethümer der Obortriten aus dem Temple zur Rhetra am Tollenzer-See, *numerous singular plates of ancient wooden idols, &c.*

An extract of a letter from the Rev. M. Masch, of Strelitz, read at the Antiquarian Society, giving an account of this extraordinary collection, and of the intended publication of this rare volume, is inserted. The idols were dug up at Prilwitz, in the neighborhood of Strelitz, where formerly stood the Temple of Rethra, burned in 1150.

403 LANDSEER (*J.*) Engraved Gems brought from Babylon, considered with reference to Early Scriptural History, 4to. Lond. 1817

404 LAURENT (*P. E.*) Manual of Ancient Geography, *cloth*, 8vo. Oxford, 1840

405 LUMSDEN (*A.*) Remarks on the Antiquities of Rome and its Environs, being a Classical and Topographical Survey of the Ruins of that celebrated City, 50 *plates*, 4to., *cloth.* Lond. 1812

406 MALLET'S Northern Antiquities, or a Description of the Manners, Customs, Religion, and Laws of the Ancient Danes, including those of our own Saxon Ancestors, with a Translation of the Edda, or System of Runic Mythology, and other Pieces from the Ancient Icelandic Tongue, translated, with Additional Notes, by Bp. Percy, *cloth*, post 8vo. 1847

"Highly valuable."—*Lowndes.*

407 MISCELLANEA Pictica; containing the History of the Picts, (supposed to be written) by Mr. H. MAULE. Sir R. SIBBALD'S Account of the Picts, from his History of Fife and Kinross, and a Description of Pictish Antiquities remaining in Scotland and the Northern Islands, 8vo. *half morocco, gilt top.* Edin. 1818

408 MONTFAUCON, L'Antiquité Expliquée et Representée en Figures, avec le Supplement, 15 vols. Monumens de la Monarchie Françoise, 5 vols.; together 20 vols. folio, *original editions, upwards of* 1600 *plates, fine impressions, very neat and uniform, in French marbled calf, gilt backs, marbled edges.* Paris, 1719, '33

A work still unsurpassed in utility; of great importance to classical scholars and artists.

A very fine original library copy. This is the great storehouse from which all succeeding writers on the subject have borrowed; no historical library should be without Montfaucon.

409 NENNIUS' "Historia Brittonum," from a Manuscript lately discovered in the Vatican, edited in the 10th century by Mark the Hermit, with an English Version, Notes and Illustrations by the Rev. W. GUNN, *facsimile of the MS.*, royal 8vo. *boards, uncut.* 1819

410 O'CONWAY (*M. J.*) The Knights Templars; a Historical Tragedy, with Notes, 8vo. *boards, uncut, portrait of Jaques de Molay.* 1809

Prefixed is an interesting history of the origin, character, and persecution of that illustrious order, the mode of receiving members, &c.

411 ORDONNANTIE des Coninghs op het Reglement van Signe Munte, 4to. *numerous plates of coins.* Antwerp, 1744

412 PEARSALL (*R. L.*) The Kiss of the Virgin; a Narrative of Researches made in Germany, for the purpose of ascertaining the mode of inflicting that ancient punishment, 4to. 1857

413 PIGNORIA (*Lorenzo*), Origin di Padova, *curious woodcuts, old binding*, 4to. Padova, 1625

414 PINELLI (*B.*) Principali Fatti della Storia Greca Antica e compendiosamente descritta nelle tre lingua; Italiana, Greca e Francese, oblong 4to. *boards.* Venezia, n. d.

This volume contains 100 engravings of the principal incidents of Grecian history, engraved by Pinelli.

415 ———— Gran Quadro della Storia di Roma Anticha; é descritto nelle tre lingue Italiana, Tedesca e Francese, oblong 4to, *boards.* Venezia, n. d.

416 PUTZ (*W.*) Handbook of Mediæval Geography and History, 12mo. *half bound.* N. Y. 1850

417 RELIQUES of Antiquity, or Remains of Ancient Structures, with other Vestiges of Early Times in Great Britain, accompanied with Descriptive Sketches, 4to. *half mor. uncut.* Lond. 1811

India proof impressions of the numerous plates.

418 REMARKS on Some Passages in Mr. Bryant's Publications respecting the War of Troy, by the Editor of the Voyage of Hanno, 8vo. pp. 62. Lond. 1799

419 RICHARD of Cirencester; The Description of Britain, with the Original Treatise, De Situ Britanniæ, *illustrated with maps*, 8vo. *calf.* Lond. 1809

420 SIBILLINÆ; Sibyllina Oracula ex vett. codd. emendata ac restituta et commentarius diversorum illustrata; op. et stud. Servetii Gallæi, accedunt etiam oracula magica Zoroastris, Jovis Appollinis, etc. Astrumpsychi oneirocriticum, etc. Gr. et Lat. cum notis varior, 1689, et S. Gallæi, Dissertationes de Sibillis earumque Oraculis, 1688, *beautiful plates*, by ROMAN DE HOOGE, 2 vols. 4to. *vellum.* Amst. 1688-9

This is a new recension from a MS. in the possession of the Oxford Professor, Ed. Bernard, and a careful collection of the exegetical apparatus that has hitherto appeared.

421 SIX Old English Chronicles, viz., Asser's Life of Alfred, and the Chronicles of Ethelwerd, Nennius, Geoffrey of Monmouth, and Richard of Cirencester, *cloth*, post 8vo. Bohn. 1848

422 THOMSON (*Richd.*) An Historical Essay on the Magna Charta of King John, and the Charter in Latin and English; also, the Charters of Henry III. and Edward I., with Notes thereon, &c., with the *arms of* 600 *of the nobility and gentry of the period, beautifully printed, and illustrated with vignettes and ornamental borders, uncut, boards*, royal 8vo. Lond. 1829

423 THURY (*Hericart de*), Descriptions des Catacombs de Paris, *plates, half morocco*, 8vo. Paris, 1815

424 TRYPHIODORUS: The Destruction of Troy, being the Sequel of the Illiad; Translated from the Greek by J. MERRICK, 8vo. *calf.* Oxford, 1739

425 WARNER'S (*Rev. R.*) Antiquitates Culinariæ, or Curious Tracts relating to the Culinary Affairs of the Old English, with a Preliminary Discourse, Notes and Illustrations, royal 4to. *large paper, with the* 2 *scarce colored plates of a Saxon Entertainment and a Peacock Feast, boards, uncut.* 1791

A most curious and entertaining book. Copies in large paper are very scarce, and have been sold for £5 5s. and upwards, each.

426 WEEVER (*John*), Ancient Fvnerall Monvments within the Vnited Monarchie of Great Britaine, Ireland, and the Islands adiacent. *Printed by Tho. Harper, and are to be sold in Little Britayne by Laurence Sadler, at the signe of the Golden Lion; fine portrait, and engraved frontispiece by Cecill, and curious woodcuts, fine, clean copy, rare, half russia*, folio. Lond. 1631

This miscellany of epitaphs and inscriptions, collected in various parts of the kingdom, is of great utility to antiquaries and historians. Sold in Brockett's sale for £4 10s.

427 WESTON (*S.*) Opinions of Various Writers on the Identical Place where the Ark of Noah Rested, Gog and Magog, &c. 4to. 1815

428 WILKINS (*W.*) Account of the Prince's Chapel, Cambridgeshire (Soc'y of Antiquaries). 1801

429 WILLIAM of Malmesbury's Chronicle of Kings of England, post 8vo. Bohn. 1847

ARTS AND SCIENCES IN GENERAL.

See also FINE ARTS.

429* ACCUM (*Fred.*) Culinary Chemistry, exhibiting the scientific principles of Cookery, 12mo. *cloth.* Lond. 1821

430 ADLUM (*John*), Cultivation of the Vine in America, 12mo. *boards.* Wash. 1828

431 ALEXIS, The Secrets of, containing many excellent Remedies against Divers Diseases, small 4to. *old calf.* Lond. 1615

This work, which has been translated and published in every European language, is by Haller attributed to Hieronymi Roselle.

432 ALLEN (*J. Fisk*), on the Culture and Treatment of the Grape Vine, 12mo. *cloth.* N. Y. 1858

433 American Repertory of Arts and Sciences, from 1840 to 1842, 8vo. *half calf.* N. Y. v. y.

434 Antrim (*B. J.*) Pantography and Pasiography, 12mo. *sheep.* 1843

435 Bacon (*Francis* Lord Verulam), Silva Silvarum, or a Natural History in Ten Centuries: also the New Atlantis, published by W. Rawley, D. D., folio, *old calf.* Lond. 1678

436 Bank Notes: Report of the Society of Arts on Preventing the Forgery of, *with six small notes*, 8vo. *boards.* Lond. 1819

437 Beckmann (*J.*) History of Inventions, Discoveries, and Origins, revised and enlarged by Francis & Griffith, *portrait*, 2 vols. post 8vo. *cloth.* Lond. 1846

438 Bennett's Toxicological Chart; or, a Synoptical Table of Poisons and their Effects, 12mo. *cloth.* Edin. 1825

439 Bewick (*Thos.*) A General History of Quadrupeds, *excellent impressions of the wood-cuts*, 8vo. *half calf.* Newcastle, 1807

440 Blake (*J. L.*) Conversations on Vegetable Physiology, 12mo. *sheep*, Phil. 1837

441 Blith (*W.*) The English Improver Improved, or The Survey of Husbandry Surveyed, small 4to, *sheep.* Lond. 1653

"A well known and very ingenious work."—*Quarterly Review.*

442 Breakfast, Dinner, and Tea, viewed Classically, Poetically, and Practically, and containing numerous Dishes and Feasts of all Times and Countries, small 4to. *cloth.* N. Y. 1859

443 Brillat Savarin: Physiologie du Gout, ou Meditations de Gastronomie Transcendante, suivis de la Gastronomie, Poeme en quatre Chants par Berchoux, 12mo. *half morocco.* Paris, 1842

444 Buist (*R.*) The Rose Manual, 12mo. *cloth.* Phil. 1844

445 Burton (*F. B.*) Elective Polarity the Universal Agent, 8vo. *cloth.* Lond. 1845

446 Cass (*M. P. A.*) Le Museum D'Histoire Naturelle, 8vo. *cloth, colored plates.* Paris, 1859

447 Castle (*Thos.*) Essay on Poisons, *colored plates*, 24mo. *cloth.* Lond. 1837

448 Cavallo (*Tiberius*), The History and Practice of Aerostation, 8vo. *half sheep, portrait and plates.* Lond. 1785

449 Chorlton (*W.*) The Cold Grapery, 12mo. N. Y. 1853

450 Chemical Amusements, &c., 10 vols. children's books.

451 CLAXTON (*Tim.*) Hints to Mechanics on Self-Education, 12mo. *cloth.* Lond. 1839

452 COINS and Medals, Catalogue of W. Bentham's Collection of, 8vo. pp. 33. 1838

453 COINS. A Report Containing an Essay for the Amendment of the Silver Coins, by W. Lowndes, 8vo. *calf.* Lond. 1695

454 COMBE (*A.*) On the Management of Infancy, 12mo. *cloth.* Phil. 1840

455 COOPER (*D. and Geo. Busk*), The Microscopic Journal and Structural Record for 1841 and 1842, 2 vols. 8vo. Lond. 1842

457 ——— (*Thomas*), The Introductory Lectures of, 8vo. *boards.* Carlisle, 1812

458 DARBY (*Wm.*) Mnemonika, or the Tablet of Memory, being a Register of Events from the earliest period to the year 1829, etc., 12mo. *cloth.* Balt. 1829

459 DEAN (*Wm.*) Historical and Descriptive Account of Croome d'Abilot, with a Hortus Croomensis and Observations on the Propagation of Exotics, 12mo. *boards.* Worcester, 1826

460 DICK (*Thos.*) The Practical Astronomer, illustrated, 12mo. *cloth.* N. Y. 1846

461 DIGGES (*Leonard*), Prognostications, containing Plain, Briefe, Pleasant, and Choice Rules to judge the weather, &c., by the Sunne, Moone, and Starres, 4to. *half bound, rare.* Lond. 1556

462 DOWNING (*A. J.*) Theory and Practice of Landscape Gardening, illustrated, 8vo. *cloth.* N. Y. and Lond. 1844

463 ——— Landscape Gardening adapted to North America, 8vo. *cloth.* N. Y. 1853

464 DOYLE (*Martin*), The Flower Garden, 12mo. *cloth.* N. Y. 1835

465 DUNCAN (*Rev. Henry*), Sacred Philosophy of the Seasons, adapted to American Readers, by F. W. P. Greenwood, 4 vols. 12mo. *cloth.* Bost. 1839

466 DUNLAP (*John*), Drinking Usage in Great Britain and Ireland, 12mo. *cloth.* Lond. 1839

467 ELLIS (*Mrs.*) Family Monitor, or Domestic Guide, 8vo. *cloth.* N. Y.

468 FAMILY Oracle, or the Science of Good Living, *wants title-page, curious plate,* 8vo. *half cloth.* Lond.

469 FISHER (*Jon.*) Scripture Animals, or Natural History, *cuts,* 12mo. *cloth.* Portland, 1834

470 FITCH (*Sam. S.*) On Diseases of the Heart, Apoplexy, Dyspepsia, &c., 8vo. *cloth.* N. Y. 1859

471 FRASCATORII (*Hieronymi*) Syphilis, sive Morbus Gallicus, *fine portrait*, 4to. *calf.* Lond. 1720

472 FULKE (*William*), A goodly Gallery with a most Pleasant Prospect into the Garden of Natural Contemplation, to behold the Naturall Causes of all kind of Meteors, *imprinted by William Griffith*, 16mo. *calf extra*, **Black Letter.** Lond. 1571

"An excellent performance."—*Lowndes.*

473 GALEN'S Bookes of Elementes, as they be in the epitome (which may very aptly, in my judgement, be entituled for the better understanding of the readers, the originall of all things naturall in the whole worlde; confuting as well the errours of all them that went before time as that hath, or shal folowe hereafter of the Paracelcians; maruelious pleasaunt and most acceptable for all sharpe wittes, desirous of wisdome). Published foorth of Latine into English by John Jones, Phisition. *Imprinted by William Jones, dwelling in Paule's Church-Yarde, at the Southwest doore of Paule's, and are there to be solde, very rare, fine, clean copy, paper.* **Black Letter,** 4to. Lond. 1574

474 GARDENS and Menagerie of the Zoological Society delineated, 2 vols. 8vo. *cloth.* Lond. 1825

This work is illustrated with some of the most beautiful specimens of modern wood engraving from drawings by Harvey.

475 GERANIUM (*The*), Its Propagation, 12mo. *colored plates.* Lond. 1843

476 GILES (*G. A.*) Class Book of General Information, 12mo. *edition.* Lond. 1836

477 GIRAUD, Jr. (*J. P.*) Natural History of the Birds of Long Island, 8vo. *cloth.* N. Y. 1844

478 GRAETER (*Francis*), Hydriatics, or Manual of the Water Cure, 12mo. *cloth.* N. Y. 1844

479 GRAHAM (*Jas. M. D.*) Medical and Chirurgical Practice Exhibited, 12mo. *paper.* Lond. 1779

480 GREY (*Dr. R.*) Memoria Technica, or Method of Artificial Memory, 12mo. *half cloth.* Ox. 1841

481 GROSMAN (*J.*) A Treatise for the Service of Chemistry in General, 4to. *boards.* 1766

482 HALLIWELL (*Jas. O.*) A Collection of Letters illustrative of Science in England, 8vo. *paper.* Lond. 1841

483 HARRIS (*John, D.D.*) The Pre-Adamite Earth, 12mo. *cl.* Bost. 1850

484 HARVEI (*Guilielmis*), Exercitationes de Generatione Animalium, 18mo. *old calf, rare.* Amst., *Elzevir*, 1651

485 HERVIG (*H. M.*) Art of Curing Sympathetically or Magnetically proved to be most true, both in its Theory and Practice, *wants 4 leaves*, 12mo. Lond.

486 HERMAN (*Johan*), Tabula Directionum, Profectionum, &c., 4to. Venetiis, MCCCCXC.

487 HILL (*Benson E.*) The Epicure's Almanac, or Diary of Good Living, 12mo. *cloth.* Lond. 1841

488 HINTS for the Table, or the Economy of Good Living, 16mo. *cloth.* Lond. 1838

489 HIPPOCRATIS de Morbis Popularibus comment. I Friend, 8vo. *vellum.* Lond. 1717

490 HISTORY of Wonderful Inventions, *illustrated*, 2 vols. 12mo. *paper.* N. Y. 1849

491 HORTICULTURIST (*The*), Vols. 2, 3, 4, 6, royal 8vo. *cloth.* Albany, 1848, &c.

492 HOUGHTON (*R. S.*) Bulwer and Forbes on Water Treatment, revised edition, 12mo. *cloth.* N. Y. 1851

494 LANGHAM (*W., Practitioner in Physicke*), The Garden of Health, containing the sundry Rare and Hidden Vertues and Properties of all Kindes of Simples and Plants, etc., original edition, small 4to. *cf.*, **black letter.** Lond. 1579

495 LIFE beneath the Waters, *plates*, 12mo. *cl.* N. Y. 1858

496 LYELL (*Sir Chas.*) A Manual of Elementary Geology, *illustrated*, 8vo. *cloth.* Lond. 1851

497 MACHIAVEL (*Nicholas*), Arte of Warre set foorth in English, with an Addicion of other like Marcialle Feats and Experimentes, by Peter Withorne, student at Graie's Inne, 4to., **black letter**, *partly mildewed.* 1573

Sold in Horne Tooke's sale for 1*l.* 16*s.* 0.

498 MARKHAM (*Gervase*), Masterpiece, containing all Knowledge belonging to Smiths and Diseases of Horses, *cur. vig.*, 4to. *old calf.* Lond. 1723

"Gervase is the first English writer who deserves to be called a hackney writer. All subjects seem to have been alike to him; yet, as his thefts were innumerable, he has now and then stolen some very good things."—*Harte.*

499 MAPES (*J. J.*) American Repertory of Arts, Sciences, and Manufactures, 4 vols. royal 8vo. *half calf.* N. Y. 1840

500 MARTINEAU (*Harriet*), How to Observe, 12mo. *cloth.* Phil. 1838

501 MASON (*Monk*), Aeronautica, or Sketches of the Theory and Practice of Aerostation, *with plates*, 8vo. *cloth.* Lond. 1838

502 MEAD (*Rich.*, *M. D.*) Medical Account of Poisons, 12mo. *sheep.* Lond. 1702

503 MILLINGEN (*J. G.*, *M. D.*) Curiosities of Medical Experience, 2 vols. 8vo. *boards.* Lond. 1837

504 MNEMONIKA, or Artificial Memory, 18mo. *sheep.* Balt. 1812

NATURAL HISTORY, *vide* Sports and Games.

505 NATURAL HISTORY—Third Annual Report of the Regents of the University on, 8vo. *cloth.* Albany, 1850

506 NEWMAN (*J. C.*) Harmonies of Creation, 18mo. *calf.* Balt. 1836

507 OINOS KRITHINOS, or a Dissertation concerning the Origin and Antiquity of Barley Wine, 4to. *half calf.* Lond. 1750

508 PARK (*R.*) Pantology, or a System of Human Knowledge, 8vo. *cloth.* Phil. 1842

509 PATENT Office Report, 1854. Wash. 1855

510 PEREIRA (*J.*) on Food and Diet, 8vo. N. Y. 1843

511 PEYTON (*G.*) How to Detect Counterfeit Bank Notes, 8vo. *cloth.* N. Y. 1856

512 PHILOSOPHICAL Theories and Philosophical Experience, by a Pariah, 12mo. Lond., *Pickering*, 1845

513 PHYSIC and Physicians, a Medical Sketch-Book, 2 vols. 18mo. Phila. 1845

514 PLAT (*Sir Hugh*), The Jewel House of Nature and Art, containing rare and profitable Inventions, together with sundry new Experiments in the Art of Husbandry, Distillation, and Moulding. G. Furman's Autograph, square 8vo. *half calf.* Lond. 1653

515 PLAYFAIR (*John*), Outlines of Natural History, 2 vols. 8vo. *boards.* Edin. 1812

516 POLEHAMPTON (*Rev. E.* and J. M. Good, F. R. S.), The Gallery of Nature, or a Tour through Creation, Science, and Art, *numerous plates*, 6 vols. 8vo. *calf.* Lond. 1821

An interesting work, compiled with considerable judgment.

517 RALPH'S Agricultural Catalogue, and other tracts, 80 Nos. 8vo. N. Y. v.d.

518 ROADS AND RAILROADS; Vehicles and Modes of Travelling of Ancient and Modern Countries, 18mo. *cloth.* Lond. 1839

519 ROSE (*J. S., M. D.*) The Reformed Practice of Medicine, 12mo. *half cloth.* Phila. 1845

520 ROUSSEAU (*J. J.*) Emilius and Sophia, or a New System of Education, 4 vols. 12mo. *calf.* Lond. 1783

521 SAYERS (*E.*) *American Flower Garden Companion,* 12mo. *cloth.* Bost. 1839

522 SCHENCHZERO (*Jo. Jac.*) Helvetius sive Itinera per Helvetiæ Alpinas Regionis, plates and maps, curious, 2 vols. 4to. *uncut boards.* Lug. Bat. 1723

523 SCIENTIFIC and Literary Journal for Diffusion of Useful Knowledge, 8vo. *half sheep.* Bost. 1837

524 SCIENTIFIC TRACTS and Family Lyceum, conducted by J. V. C. Smith, M. D. New series, 4 vols. 12mo, *half cloth.* Bost. 1834

525 SCIENTIFIC TRACTS. Sunderland (*La Roy*) Pathetism; Whewell on the Creation; Von Leonhard on Geology; Discussion on Marriage and Mutual Instruction, 5 vols. N. Y. and Lond.

526 SHEW (*Joel*), Hydropathy, or the Water Cure, 8vo. *cloth.* N. Y. 1849

527 SPOON, with 100 illustrations, 8vo. *sheep, scarce.* (See 538, p. 40.) N. Y. 1844

528 STOCKHARDT'S Principles of Chemistry, 8vo. *cloth.* Cambridge, 1852

529 SULPITII VERULANI (*Jo.*) de Nersuum Scancione, de Syllabarum quantitate, de Heroici Carminis decoro, &c.; and Nigri (*Francisco*), Opusculum Scribendi Epistolis, 2 vols. in 1, 4to. *vellum.* Romæ, MCCCCXCIV

530 SYSTEMATISCHE, Bilder-Gallerie (Natural History), 4to. 1839

531 TATHAM (*W.*) Historical and Practical Essay on the Culture and Commerce of Tobacco, 8vo. *boards.* Lond. 1806

532 TIMBS (*John*), Popular Errors Explained and Illustrated, 12mo. *cloth, plates.* Lond. 1851

533 TREASURIE of Hidden Secrets, commonly called the good Housewife's Closet of Provisions, for the Health of her Household, **Black Letter**, 4to. *sewed.* R. Johnes, Lond. 1596

534 VESTIGES of the Natural History of Creation, with sequel, 2 vols. 12mo. *cloth.* N. Y. 1845

535 WARD (*N. B.*) Growth of Plants in closely glazed Cases, post 8vo. *cloth.* Lond. 1852

536 WATER-CURE JOURNAL, edited by Joel Shew, M. D., 6 vols. in 3, 8vo. *cloth.* N. Y. 1845

537 WEISS (*Dr. J.*) Handbook of Hydropathy, 12mo. *cloth.* Phil. 1849

538 WESTMAN (*Hab'k O.*) The Spoon, *with upwards of* 100 *illustrations, primitive, Egyptian, Roman, &c.*, 8vo. *half mor.* N. Y. 1844

539 WHEWELL (W.) Astronomy and General Physics, 12mo. *cloth.* 1836

540 WHITE (*Rev. Gil.*) The Natural History of Selborne, 16mo. *half cloth.* Phil. 1832

541 WILSON (*J. M.*) The Potato, an Essay on its Diseases, &c., 2 *colored plates.* Edinb. 1850

542 WISE (*John*), A System of Aeronautics, 8vo. *cloth.* Phil. 1850

543 WONDERS of the Heavens displayed in 20 Lectures, *with numerous engravings*, 12mo. *cf., neat.* Lond. 1821

544 WORCESTER (*Marquis of*), Century of Inventions, edited by John Buddle, 8vo. *calf.* Newcastle, 1813

First discoverer of the power of steam.

545 Year Book of Facts in Science and Art, 1839 to 1844, 6 vols. 12mo. *cloth, illustrated.* Lond. 1839 to '40

546 YOUTH'S Handbook of Entertaining Knowledge, 12mo. *cloth.* Lond. 1844

547 YOUNG (*Geo., M. D.*) A Treatise on Opium, 8vo. *calf.* Lond. 1753

BIBLIOGRAPHY AND TYPOGRAPHY.

See also LITERATURE.

548 ALLIBONE (*S. Austin*), Dictionary of Authors, a Critical Dictionary of English Literature and British American Authors, living and deceased, from the earliest accounts to the middle of the Nineteenth Century, containing upwards of thirty thousand Biographies and Literary Notices, vol. I., super royal 8vo. *half morocco.* Phil. 1859

I have never referred to this book without finding the information for which I sought; and judging from the numerous written testimonials to the same effect, from such persons as Lords Macaulay, Campbell, Cardinal Wiseman, and others, it is fair to presume it will, when complete, be the best bibliographical work ever produced in this or any other country.

549 APPLETON, Library Manual, containing a catalogue raisonné of upwards of twelve thousand of the most important works in every department of knowledge, &c., 8vo. *half mor.* N. Y. 1847

550 BIBLIOGRAPHICAL and Retrospective Miscellany, 12mo. *boards.* Lond. 1830

551 BIBLIOTHECA DRAMATICA, Priced Catalogue of the Dramatic Libraries of W. B. Rhodes and John Fields, 2 vols. in 1, 8vo. *half calf.* 1825

552 BIBLIOTHECA PARISIANA, a Catalogue of a collection of Books formed by a gentleman in France, *fine clean copy, with the prices in manuscript,* 636 lots, total amount of sale £7,076 17*s.* 6*d.*, 8vo. *boards, uncut.* Lond. 1791

The most extraordinary collection ever disposed of by auction. The average was upwards of £11 per lot.

"Then you might have seen the most notorious Bibliomaniacs, with blood inflamed and fancies intoxicated, rushing towards the examination of the truly matchless volumes contained within this collection."—*The Bibliomania.*

553 BIOGRAPHIA DRAMATICA, or a Companion to the Playhouse, containing Historical and Critical Memoirs and Original Anecdotes of British and Irish Dramatic Writers, &c., Lists of their Works, the Dates when printed, &c., with an Introductory View of the Rise and Progress of the British Stage, &c., by Baker, Reed, and Jones, *best edition, uncut,* 4 vols. 8vo. *hf. cf.* Lond. 1812

"I cannot resist the opportunity of strongly recommending the last and best edition of Baker's Biographia Dramatica. * * * It is the best production on the subject extant, and is a stock book in a dramatic library."—*Dibdin, Lib. Comp.*

554 BOHN (*H. G.*) Catalogue of Books, vol. 1, 8vo. *hf. mor.* 1848

555 BRUNET, Manuèl du Libraire et de l'Amateur des Livres, quatrième édition, entierement revue et augmentée par l'auteur, 5 vols. roy. 8vo. *half mor., scarce.* Par. 1842–4

Last and best edition, containing an immense number of articles not in the previous one.

556 BRYDGES (*Sir Egerton*), Censura Literaria, containing Titles, Abstracts, and Opinions of old English Books, with original Disquisitions, Articles of Biography, and other Literary Antiquities, 10 vols. 8vo. *cf., neat.* 1805–9

Is the same in contents as the second edition, only in that edition the books are arranged chronologically.

"A work justly held in high estimation by all antiquaries in literature." —*Lowndes.*

557 Brydges (*Sir Egerton*), Censura Literaria, *first series*, 3 vols. 8vo. *half calf*. Lond. 1805

558 ——— Restituta, or Titles, Extracts, and Characters of old Books in English Literature Revived, 4 vols. 8vo. *calf, gilt*. Lond. 1814

"My aim shall be to revive those forgotten works which the most enlightened will admit to be among the due apparatus of a curious library, and not detain the reader too long by the technical minutiæ of Bibliography."—*Editor*.

This valuable work contains extracts from a vast number of rare books, interspersed with much curious information on a variety of literary subjects.

559 Catalogues of Books, in all over 1250.

560 ——— of the Basherfield, Bowman, Malmaison, and Queen's Libraries, and Museum Duplicates, 8vo. *hf. cf.* 1817-19

561 ——— of Ibbot, priced, Hollis, Disney, Utterson, and Kemble's Library, 8vo. *half calf*. 1817-21

562 Catalogue of the Printed Books in the Library of the Society of Antiquaries of London, 4to. Lond. 1816

563 ——— of the Library of Stowe House, *prices and names*, 4to. 1849

Several of the books from this collection are in this catalogue.

Catalogue of Five Hundred Celebrated Authors, *vide* Faulder, Lot 579.

565 Coggswell (*Dr.*) Alphabetical Index (of Short Titles) to the Astor Library, 8vo., *scarce*. N. Y. 1851

566 Corwin (*E. B.*) Catalogue of the Rare, Curious, and Valuable Library of, by J. Sabin, 8vo. N. Y. 1856

Replete with scarce books published in America, and other curious and rare books.

567 Davis (*Wm.*) Journey round the Library of a Bibliomaniac, small 8vo. *boards, uncut*. Lond. 1821

A cento of notes and reminiscences concerning rare, curious, and valuable books.

567* De Bure (*G. F.*) Bibliographie Instructive, ou Traité de la Connaisance, des livres rares et singuliers, 7 vols. 8vo. *half morocco*. Paris, 1763

The author was a bookseller of eminence in Paris, and has furnished a large amount of reliable information.

568 De Foe, Catalogue of the Writings of, 8vo. 1835

569 Dibdin (*Dr. T. F.*) Bibliomania, or Book Madness, containing some account of the History, Symptoms, and Cure of this Fatal Disease, in an epistle addressed to Richard Heber, Esq., *first edition, uncut*, 8vo. Lond. 1809

570 DIBDIN (*Dr. T. F.*) Bibliomania, or Book Madness, a Bibliographical Romance, illustrated with cuts, a New and Improved Edition, to which are now added preliminary observations, and a supplement including a key to the assumed characters in the drama, *engravings*, *uncut*, royal 8vo. Lond. 1842

"The Bibliomania is written in dialogues or conversations; the characters introduced are well known book collectors of the author's acquaintance. This work has in a great degree given a stimulus to the collecting of our early literature and bibliography in this country, on which subjects it will always be consulted as a first authority."—*Lowndes.*

"It would now be useless to pass an encomium on this work, as its merits are so fully established as to have more than doubled the original price of a volume now with difficulty to be obtained."—*Gent's Mag.*

571 ——— Bibliographical, Antiquarian, and Picturesque Tour in France and Germany, containing numerous beautiful Portraits, Plates, Vignettes, and Wood-cuts, 3 vols. 8vo. *cloth.* Lond. 1829

572 ——— Introduction to the Greek and Latin Classics, Polyglott, Hebrew, and Greek Bibles, Greek Testaments, Greek and Latin Fathers, best edition, 2 vols. 8vo. *cloth.* Lond. 1827

573 ——— A Descriptive Catalogue of the Books printed in the Fifteenth Century, lately forming part of the Library of the Duke di Cassano Serra, and now the property of George John, Earl Spencer, K. G., *large paper*, *uncut*, impl. 8vo. Lond. 1823

574 ——— Portraits to Illustrated Dibdin's Tour through Germany, &c., 17 *plates, proofs on India paper.*

575 ——— Bibliophobia; Remarks on the Present Depressed State of Literature and the Book Trade, in a letter addressed to the author of the Bibliomania, by Mercurius Rusticus, with notes by Cato Parvus, *uncut*, 8vo. Lond. 1832

576 DULAU'S Catalogue of Foreign Books, 8vo.

577 EGERTON, Theatrical Remembrancer, containing a complete list of all the Dramatic Performances in the English Language, their several editions, dates, and sizes, &c., from the earliest production of the English Drama to the end of the year 1787, &c., 8vo. Lond. 1788

578 FAULDER (*R.*) A Catalogue of Five Hundred Celebrated Authors of Great Britain now living; the whole arranged in alphabetical order, and including a complete list of their publications, with occasional strictures and anecdotes of their lives, 8vo. *calf.* Lond. 1788

579 EDWARDS (*Edward, formerly of the British Museum, and late Librarian of the Manchester Free Library*), Memoirs of Libraries, including a Handbook of Library Economy, containing the following illustrations: *Eight Copper-plates of the Manuscripts of Herculaneum; Thirty-four Wood-cuts of Interiors and Exteriors of celebrated Libraries; Eight Plates of Fac-similes of the Types employed by Early Printers; Seven Chromo-Lithographic Plates of Bookbinding, St. Augustine's Monastery, Canterbury, and several Plans of Ancient Libraries*, 2 vols. royal 8vo. *cloth.* 1859

This important work was in preparation during upwards of thirteen years. Neither France nor Germany can boast of a work treating the subjects with a similar comprehensiveness; and in England the work has certainly had no predecessor. Of this valuable work, a very limited number was printed.

580 FERRIAR (*J.*) Illustrations of Sterne, giving a Bibliographical and Critical Account of the Books from which Sterne pillaged in composing his "Tristram Shandy," 2 vols. in 1, small 8vo. 1812

"The ingenious Dr. Ferriar, with most singular patience, has traced Sterne through the hidden sources whence he borrowed most of his learning and many of his most striking and peculiar expressions." —*Sir W. Scott.*

581 FOURNIER (*W. I.*) Nouveau Dictionnaire Portatif de Bibliographie, 8vo. *vellum.* Paris, 1809

A very useful volume for reference; with lists of the Aldine and other celebrated editions of books, Continental and English.

582 FRY, Bibliographical Memoranda in Illustration of Early English Literature, small 4to. *calf, extra, fine copy.* Bristol, 1816

Presentation copy, *one hundred only* printed, contains extracts from rare old English poetical authors.

583 GOODHUGH (*W.*) English Gentleman's Library Manual, or a Guide to the Formation of a Library of Select Literature, 8vo. *boards.* 1827

Contains some unpublished letters of Thomson the poet.

584 HALLIWELL (*J. O.*) Manuscript Rarities of the University of Cambridge, 8vo. *half calf.* Lond. 1841

A companion to Hartshorne's "Book Rarities."

585 HALLIWELL (*J. O.*) Catalogue of the Early Edition of Shakspeare's Plays, and of the Commentaries and other Publications illustrative of his works, *with MS. additions and corrections by Mr. Burke, boards*, 8vo. Lond. 1841

586 HEBER (*R.*) Catalogue of Heber's Collection of Early English Poetry, with prices and names, the Drama, Ancient Ballads, and Broadsides, rare and curious books on English, Scottish, and Irish History, and French Romances, with notice by Collins, *half morocco*, 8vo. Lond. 1840

If collectors find any specimen of early English poetry not described in this catalogue, they may be certain that their value will be much increased by the rare distinction of having been wanting in the Heber collection.

587 JARVIS (*Dr. S. F.*), Catalogue of the Library of, sold in Nov., 1851, 8vo. N. Y. 1851

588 JOHNSON (*J.*) Typographia, or the Printer's Instructor, including an Account of the Origin of Printing, with Biographical Notices of the Printers of England, from Caxton to the close of the Sixteenth Century, &c. *engraved titles and portraits*, *uncut*, 2 vols. 24mo. Lond. 1824

589 LELANNE (*L.*) Curiosités Bibliographiques, 18mo. *half russia.* Paris, 1845

590 LONDON Catalogue of all Books published from 1814 to 1834, 8vo. *cloth.* Lond. 1835

591 LONGMAN'S Catalogue of Rare Books, pp. 602, 8vo. *boards.* Lond. 1816

592 LOWNDES (*W. T.*) The Bibliographer's Manual of English Literature, containing an Account of Rare, Curious, and Useful Books, published in or relating to Great Britain and Ireland, from the invention of printing, with Bibliographical and Critical Notices, Collations of the Rarer Articles, and the prices at which they have been sold in the Present Century, 4 vols. 8vo. *half calf.* Lond. 1834

As indispensable in a library as a Dictionary in a school.

593 LUMLEY'S Catalogue of Books. 1836

594 MAITTAIRE (*M.*) Annales Typographici ab Artes Inventæ Origine ad Annum M. D., 5 vols. in 1, *old calf.* Hagæ., Com., 1719

"Mattaire's valuable annals are indispensable in every bibliographical library."—*Henry.*

595 PETTIGREW (*Thos. J.*) Bibliotheca Sussexiana, a Descriptive Catalogue, accompanied by Historical and Biographical Notices of the Manuscripts and Printed Books contained in the Library of the Duke of Sussex, 2 vols., *uncut boards*, royal 8vo. Lond. 1827

596 PHILADELPHIA Library, Catalogue of the, 3 vols. 8vo., *with supplement.* Phil. 1835–44

597 REED (*John Watson*) A Catalogue of the Genuine Library of 1790. Lond. 1790

598 RENOUARD, Annales de l'Imprimerie des Alde, *portraits*, 3 vols. *calf*, 8vo. Paris, 1803

"Renouard, in his description of the Aldine Poets, is without a rival." —*Beloe's Anecdotes.*

599 REED (*I.*) Bibliotheca Reediana, a Catalogue of the Curious and Extensive Library, *portrait, half morocco, gilt top*, 8vo. Lond. 1807

"Few collections attracted greater attention before, and during the sale of it, than did the library of the late Mr. Isaac Reed."—*Dibdin.*

600 RHODES (*W. B.*) Bibliotheca Dramatica, a Catalogue of the entire curious and extensive Dramatic Library, *prices, uncut, paper*, 8vo. Lond. 1825

601 RIMBAULT (*Dr.*) Bibliotheca Madrigaliana, a Bibliographical Account of the Musical and Poetical Works of the XV. and XVI. centuries, under the titles of Madrigals, Ballets, Ayres, &c., *boards*, 8vo. Lond. 1847

It records a class of books left undescribed by Ames, Herbert, and Dibdin, and furnishes a most valuable Catalogue of Lyrical Poetry of the age to which it refers.

602 RITSON (*J.*) Bibliographica Poetica, a Catalogue of English Poets, of the twelfth, thirteenth, fourteenth, fifteenth and sixteenth centuries, with a short account of their works, *calf*, 8vo. Lond. 1802

603 RODD (*T.*) Catalogue of Books, 8vo. 1836

604 SABIN (*J.*) Catalogue of the Library of Dr. S. F. Jarvis, sold Nov. 1851, 8vo. N. Y. 1851

This valuable collection sold for over $11,000; it was the largest theological collection in this country.

605 ——— Catalogue of the Library of E. B. Corwin, sold 1856, royal 8vo. N. Y. 1856

The most extraordinary *omnium gatherum* ever made in this country, sold for 9,245 dollars; very rich in early American books.

606 ——— Catalogue of the Library of A. E. Douglas, G. R. Hazewell and others, 3 vols. v. y.

607 ——— Catalogue, "Bibliotheca Americana," *largely annotated*, 8vo. N. Y. 1856

The above catalogues are all annotated, digested and alphabetically arranged for immediate reference.

608 SPENCE (*Jos.*) Anecdotes, Observations and Characters of Books and Men, collected from the Conversation of Mr. Pope and other Eminent Persons of his Time, published from Original Papers, with Notes and Life of the Author, by Samuel Weller Singer, 8vo. *cloth.* Lond. 1820

SMITH'S Bibliography of Dialects, *vide* Dialects.

609 SOTHEBY (*S.*) Typography of the Fifteenth Century; being specimens of the productions of the Early Continental Printers, exemplified in a collection of Fac Similes from 100 Works, together with their Water Marks, *half morocco*, folio. Lond. 1845

610 STEEVENS (*G.*) Bibliotheca Steevensiana, a Catalogue of the curious and valuable Library, *rare, large paper, prices and names*, royal 8vo. *half calf.* Lond. 1800

"The wit, taste and classical acquirements of George Steevens are everywhere recorded and acknowledged.—Wit, elegance, gaiety and satire, combined with almost perfect erudition in English dramatic antiquities."—*The Bibliomania.*

611 STRAKER'S Catalogue of Theological Books. 1834–35

612 STRONG (*W.*) Catalogue of Books, 8vo. v. d.

613 THORPE (*Thos.*) Catalogue of Curious and Rare Books, 8vo. *half morocco.* 1842

614 ——— Idem, *various parts*, 8vo. v. d.

615 THEOBRANE, Bibliographique Description, et Analyse d'un Livre Unique par Theobrane, 8vo. por. Mescha, 1849

616 TROW (*J. F.*) Specimen of Types, &c., 8vo. N. Y. 1856

617 TRUE, Perfect, and Exact Catalogue of all the Comedies, Tragedies, Tragi-Comedies, Pastorals, Masques, and Interludes, that were ever yet printed and published till this present year, 1671, interleaved, 4to. *half calf.* Kirkman, 1671

618 WILLET (*R.*) Merly Library; a description of that well known and celebrated library, *fine plates, privately printed*, folio, *half calf.* Lond. 1813

"With that winter of the same year there was fought such a fight, as, take it for all in all, the like again hath not been witnessed since the memorable day of the Roxburghe battle. I would be understood here emphatically to allude to the Willet contest, or to the sale of the Merly Library."—*Bibliographical Decameron.*

BIOGRAPHY.—*See also* Dramatic Biography and Portraits.

619 Appleton's Cyclopedia of Biography, edited by Dr. Hawks, 8vo. *cloth.* 1856

Agathocles, vide *Spence*, under England.

620 Andryane (*Alex.*) Memoirs of a Prisoner of State with Count Confalonieri and Silvio Pellico, translated by Randi, 2 vols. 12mo. *cloth.* Lond. 1848

621 Angelo (*H., Fencing Master*), Reminiscences, with Memoirs of his Father and Friends, *portrait*, 2 vols. 8vo. *boards.* 1828-30

Contains original anecdotes and curious traits of the most celebrated characters that have flourished during the last eighty years, (Fox, Sheridan, Gainsborough, Dr. Dodd, Byron, &c.)

622 Barnum (*P. T.*) Life of, 12mo. *cloth.* N. Y. 1855

623 Bell (*R.*) Life of Rt. Hon. George Canning, 12mo. *cloth.* Lond. 1846

624 Bennett (*James G.*) Life and Writings of, 8vo. pp. 64. N. Y. 1844

625 Biographical Magazine, each page illustrated by a Portrait and Biography, 8vo. *calf.* Lond. 1794

Biographical Mirror, *vide* Portraits.

626 Biographical Sketches of Eminent Persons whose Portraits form part of the Duke of Dorset's Collection at Knole, 8vo. *calf.* Lond. 1795

627 Boos (*Martin*) Life and Persecution of, edited by Gossner, 12mo. *cloth.* Lond. 1836

628 Boys (*Capt. E.*) Narrative of a Captivity and Adventure in France and Flanders, 12mo. *cloth.* Lond. 1831

629 Brewer (*Thos.*) Memoir of John Carpenter, Town Clerk of London, in the Reigns of Henry V. and VI., 8vo. Lond. 1836

630 Brougham (*Lord*), Sketches of Statesmen who flourished in the Time of George III., with Remarks on Party, and on the French Revolution, 4 vols. 12mo. *cloth.* Phil. 1839

This well known and interesting work comprises upwards of sixty biographies.

631 Brougham (*Lord*), Lives of Men of Letters and Science who flourished in the time of George III., 12mo. Phil. 1845

Containing Lives of Voltaire, Rousseau, Hume, Robertson, Joseph Black, James Watt, Dr. Priestley, Sir Humphry Davy, and Simson.

632 BROUGHAM (*Lord*), Sketches of Public Characters, 2 vols. 12mo. *cloth.* Phil. 1839

633 BROUGHAM (*Henry Lord*), Letters and Speeches on various Subjects, 2 vols. 12mo. *cloth.* Phil. 1840

634 BRIDGES (*Sir E.*) Autobiography, Times, Opinions, and Contemporaries of, 2 vols. 8vo. *cloth.* Lond. 1834

"A man to all the book tribe dear."

635 BUCKINGHAM (*Villiers, Duke of*), Historical and Biographical Memoirs of, *portraits*, 4to. Lond. 1819

636 BURNEY (*Dr.*) Memoir of Metastasio, with Translation of his principal Letters, 3 vols. 8vo. *half calf.* Lond. 1796

637 BURTON (*J. H.*) Lives of Simon Lord Lovat, and Duncan Forbes, of Culloden, post 8vo. *cloth.* Lond. 1847

638 CAGLIOSTRO (*Count*), or Joseph Balsamo, Life of, his singular and uncommon Adventures, Trial before the Inquisition, Confessions concerning the Egyptian Masonry, &c., 8vo. *calf, very scarce.* Lond. 1787

639 CAMPBELL (*T., the Poet*), Life of Petrarch, with Notices of Boccacio and his illustrious Contemporaries, second edition, *with fine portraits and plates*, 2 vols. 8vo. *cloth.* 1843

"The standard Life of Petrarch, and one of the most interesting and important historical works of our time."—*Athenæum.*

640 CARSON (*Mrs. Ann*), History of, written by herself, 12mo. *sheep.* Phila. 1822

641 CASPER Hauser, Tracts relating to, by Earl Stanhope, 12mo. *cloth, scarce.* Lond. 1830

Account of an individual kept in a dungeon, separated from all communication with the world from early childhood.

642 CARY (*H.*) Memoirs of the Rev. H. F. Cary, translator of Dante, 2 vols. 12mo. Mexico, 1847

643 CELLINI (*Benvenuto*), Memoirs of his own Life, with the Notes of Carparn, translated by Thomas Roscoe, royal 8vo. 1839

"Cellini was one of the most extraordinary men of an extraordinary age. His Life, written by himself, is more amusing than any novel I know."—*Horace Walpole.*

644 CHATTERTON Dix (*Jno.*), Life of, 12mo. *cloth.* Lond. 1851

645 CHILD (*Mrs.*) Biographies of Mme. de Stael and Roland, 12mo. Bost. 1832

647 CICERO, MIDDLETON (*Dr. Conyers*), History of the Life of Marcus Tullius Cicero, 8vo. *calf.* Lond. 1837

"An elaborate, learned, and admirably written performance. The style of Middleton is considered a model of pure English."—*Didbui.*

4

648 Cicero—Hollings (*J. F.*) Life of, 12mo. *cloth.* Lond. 1839

649 Collingwood (*Admiral*), Selections from the Public and Private Correspondence of, 8vo. *half calf.* N. Y. 1829

650 Cook (*Capt. J.*) Life of, 18mo. Lond. 1822

651 Costello (*Miss*), Memoirs of Jacques Cœur, the French Argonaut, and his Times, *portrait and woodcuts*, 8vo. *cloth.* 1847

Jacques Cœur, chief adviser and governor of the Finances of Charles VII. of France, was "one of the most remarkable personages of his time."

652 Costello (*L. S.*) Memoirs of Eminent Englishwomen, *numerous highly finished portraits*, 4 vols. 8vo. *cloth.* Lond. 1844

652*Dallas (*R. C.*) Recollections of the Life of Lord Byron from 1808 to 1814, 8vo. *boards.* Phil. 1825

653 Dana's Two Years before the Mast, 18mo. 1855

654 D'Aubigne (*Theodore Agrippa*), Life of, containing a Succinct Account of the most Remarkable Occurrences during the Civil Wars of France, 8vo. *calf.* Lond. 1772

655 Davenport (*R. A.*) Narrative of his Perils and Sufferings, 2 vols. 16mo. *cloth.* Lond. 1840

656 Davenport (*Dr. K. A.*) Dictionary of Biography, comprising the most eminent Characters of all Ages and Professions, *embellished with more than* 300 *portraits inserted in the text*, 8vo. *cloth.* Lond., *Tegg*, 1831

A most useful and interesting book for autograph collectors, for the correctness of portraits and dates.

657 De La Sarre (*Mme.*) Life and Adventures of, containing a great many incidents presumed to be new, by Thos. Crowley, 12mo. *half calf.* Rotterdam, 1751

658 Demerville (*J. C.*) Vies des Enfants Célèbres, roy. 8vo. *cloth. gilt.* Paris, 1842

659 D'Ewes's (*Sir Simonds*) Autobiography and Correspondence, during the Reigns of James I. and Charles I., edited by J. O. Halliwell, *portraits*, 2 vols. 8vo. *cloth.* 1845

660 De Tott (*Baron*), Memoirs of, and the State of the Turkish Empire, 2 vols. 8vo. *hf. cf. gilt.* Lond. 1786

"The best memoirs I know of are those of Baron de Tott. I hardly know of a book so necessary for a young man to read and remember."—*Lord Chesterfield.*

661 DICTIONAIRE des Girouettes, ou nos contemporains peints d'après eux-mèmes. 8vo. *calf, gilt.* Paris, 1815

A scarce and suppressed work. Each person's biography is preceded by as many weathercocks as he has changed his opinion.

662 DUMAS (*Comt.*) Memoirs of his own Time, 2 vols. 12mo. *boards.* Phil. 1839

663 FAIRFIELD (*S. L.*) Life of, by Jane Fairfield, 12mo. *cloth.* N. Y. 1847

664 DAN MARBLE, a Biographical Sketch, by Falconbridge, 12mo. N. Y. n. y.

664* DUNLAP (*William*), Memoirs of Charles Brocden Brown, the American Novelist, 8vo. *cloth.* Lond. 1822

665 FENN'S Paston Letters, 2 vols. 12mo. *sewed.* 1840

The original edition of this very curious and interesting series of historical letters is a rare book, and sells for upwards of ten guineas. The present is not an abridgment.

666 GOETHE, Memoirs of, written by himself, 2 vols. 8vo. *boards.* Lond. 1824

667 GOOCH (*Mrs.*) The Life of, written by herself, dedicated to the Public, 2 vols. in 1, *calf.* Lond. 1792

668 GOODRICH (*S. G.*) Recollections of a Lifetime, or Men and Things I have seen, &c., 2 vols. 8vo. *cloth.* N. Y. 1856

669 GORDON (*Peter*), Narrative of the Imprisonment and Escape of, from the French, 8vo. *half calf.* 1816

670 GRAY (*Thomas*), Letters of, 2 vols. in 1, sq. 18mo. *hf. cf.* Bost. 1820

671 HAMILTON (*Count A.*) Memoirs of Count Grammont, a new translation, *with 76 portraits, fine impressions,* 2 vols. 12mo. *calf.* Lond. 1818

"The beginning of the eighteenth century witnessed the publication of perhaps the most popular volume of memoirs ever put forth in France, under the title of Mémoires de Grammont, of which Anthony Hamilton was the author. All the better French critics unite in extolling the style, wit, and sentimentality of this book up to the skies."—*Dibdin.*

672 HAMILTON (*Elizabeth*), Memoirs of the Life of Agrippina, the Wife of Germanicus, 2 vols. 8vo. *shp.* Lond. 1811

673 HAMILTON (*Lady*), Memoirs of, with Illustrative Anecdotes, 18mo. *half calf.* N. Y. 1815

674 HEBER (*Bp.*) Life of, by his Widow, 2 vols. 4to. *cloth.* Lond. 1830

675 HEMANS (*Mrs.*) Memoir of the Life and Writings of, 12mo. Phil. 1839

HERBERT of Cherbury, *vide* Shakspeariana.

676 HUTTON (*Wm., Stationer, of Birmingham*), Life of. Lond. 1841

677 JACKSON (*Andrew*), Life of, by Wm. Cobbett, 12mo., *scarce.* N. Y. 1836

678 JAMES (*G. P. R.*) Lives of Cardinal de Retz, Colbert, De Witt, and the Marquis de Louvois, 2 vols. 12mo. Phil. 1837

678*JAMESON'S (*Mrs.*) Beauties of the Court of Charles the Second, with their Portraits after Sir Peter Lely and other eminent Painters; illustrating the Diaries of Pepys, Evelyn, Clarendon, &c., third edition, considerably enlarged, with an Introductory Essay, and additional Anecdotes, illustrated by 21 beautiful Portraits, comprising the whole of the celebrated suite of Paintings by Lely, preserved in the Windsor Gallery, and several from the Devonshire, Grosvenor, and Althorp Galleries, *original edition*, 2 vols. imp. 8vo. *cloth.* Lond. 1838

"This truly beautiful and splendid production is equally a gem among the fine arts and in literature. Mrs. Jameson's diligence of research—her charms of style—the acuteness, force, and justice of her remarks—her characteristic touches—the racy and piquant manner with which she relates an anecdote, are too well known to require eulogy from us."—*Court Journal.*

JOHNSON, Life, *vide* Dramatic Biography.

——— Lives of the Poets, *vide* Dramatic Biography.

679 KNIGHTON (*Sir Wm.*) Memoirs of, during the Reign of George IV., including his Correspondence, 8vo. *cloth.* Phil. 1838

680 KORNER (*C. T.*) Life of, written by his Father, with selections from his Poems, Tales, and Dramas, by Richardson, *portrait*, 2 vols. post 8vo. *half morocco.* Lond. 1827

A most interesting biography of the "Hero Poet of Germany."

681 LAFARGE (*Mme, the Poisoner*), Memoirs of, written by herself, 12vo. *cloth.* Phil. 1841

682 LAFAYETTE (*Genl.*) Recollections of the Private Life of, by Dr. Jules Cloquet, *embellished with numerous engravings*, 8vo. *cloth.* Lond. 1835

683 LAUD, *Abp.* (*Prynne, Wm.*) Breviate of the Life of, Extracted for the most part out of his own Diary, and other writing under his own hand, *curious plate of the trial*, folio. *calf.* Lond. 1644

684 LEIGH HUNT, Autobiography of, with Reminiscences of Friends and Contemporaries, 2 vols. 12mo. *cloth.* N. Y. 1850

685 Life and Writings of James Gordon Bennett, Editor of the New York Herald, 12mo. pp. 64. N. Y. 1844

686 Lilly (*W., the astrologer*), History of his own Life and Times, from 1602 to 1681, *fine portraits by Cooper*, 8vo. *boards.* Lond. 1822

687 Lives of Distinguished Shoemakers, 12mo. *cloth.* Portland, 1849

688 Lives of Eminent Characters in Essex, Suffolk and Norfolk, *with* 68 *portraits, unbound,* 8vo. Lond.

689 Lives (*The*), of those Eminent Antiquaries John Leland, Thomas Hearne, and Anthony à Wood; also, *several engravings of Antiquity, never before published,* 2 vols. 8vo. *boards, scarce.* Oxford, 1762

690 Louvet (*J. B.*) Narrative of the Dangers to which I have been Exposed since 1793, with Historical Memoranda, 8vo. *half calf.* 1795

Louvet is well known as the author of the celebrated Adventures of the Chevalier de Faublas.

691 MS. Obituary and Nativity of Eminent Men in every day of the year, from July 1st to December 31st, and Remarkable Events, *vellum,* folio.

692 Markoull (*John*), Abuses of Justice, illustrated in my own case, 8vo. *boards.* Lond. 1812

693 Massinger (*Philip*), Some account of the Life and Writings of, *sewed,* 8vo. Lond. 1789

694 Memoir of the Life of Artemi of Wagarschapat Armenia, 8vo. *half bound.* Lond. 1822

695 Meredith (*W. G.*) Memorials of Bernadotte, King of Sweden and Norway, illustrative of his Character, of his relations with the Emperor Napoleon, and of the History of his Kingdoms, with a Discourse on the Political Character of Sweden, 8vo. *cloth,* Lond. 1829

"A work that exhibits much of the rise and fall of nations, and we may say contains the seeds of history."—*Literary Gazette.*

696 Milton (*John*), His Life and Times, Religious and Political Opinions, by J. Journey, 12mo. *boards.* N. Y. 1833

697 Mirabeau, Letters of, during his residence in England, with Anecdotes, Maxims, &c., *fine full length portraits,* 2 vols. 8vo. *half cloth.* Lond. 1832

698 Moore (*Th.*) Memoirs, Journals and Correspondence of, edited by Lord J. Russell, 2 vols. royal 8vo. *cloth.* N. Y. 1857

699 Moreau (*Genl.*) Some Details Concerning, by Paul Svinine, 12mo. *half calf.* Boston, 1814

700 NAUNTON (*Sir Robert*), Memoirs of, Author of "The Fragmentaa Regalia," *portraits, large paper*, folio. Lond. 1814

701 NICOLAS (*Sir Harris*), Life and Times of Sir Christopher Hatton, Chancellor to Queen Elizabeth, *portrait*, 8vo. *cloth.* 1847

Includes secret letters of the Queen, and correspondence of the most distinguished statesmen.

702 NOBLE (*M.*) Memoirs of the Protectoral House of Cromwell, as also the Lives of such persons as were distinguished by the Cromwells, *plates*, 2 vols. 8vo. *calf.* Lond. 1787

703 PEPYS (*Samuel*), The Life, Journal, and Correspondence of, 2 vols. 8vo. *cloth.* Lond. 1841

"The ablest picture of the age in which the writer lived, and a work of standard importance in English literature."—*Sir W. Scott.*

704 PRINCE EUGENE, of Savoy, Memoirs of, containing all those passages which have been suppressed by order of the French Government, with Notes, Historical and Biographical, of the Amours with Females of the Highest Rank in France, 12mo. *half calf.* N. Y. 1811

705 PUBLIC Characters of 1799–1800, 8vo. *calf.* Lond. 1799

706 RAMBLE (*Jas.*), Life and Adventures of, 2 vols. 12mo. *calf.* Lond. 1770

Autograph of John Theobald.

707 RIENZI (*Nicholas Gabrini de*), Memoirs of, who Raised Himself from a Low and Despicable Situation to the Sovereign Authority in Rome, 12mo. *calf, scarce.* Lond. 1730

708 RITSON (*Joseph*), The Letters of, with a Memoir of the Author, by Sir Harris Nicolas, 2 vols. 8vo. *cloth.* Lond., *Pickering*, 1833

709 ——— Life of King Arthur, 12mo. *cloth.* Lond. 1825

No library can be called complete in Old English lore which has not the whole of the productions of this laborious and successful antiquary.

710 ROCHESTER (*Earl of*), Some Passages in the Life and Death of, by Bp. Burnet, 12mo. *calf.* Lond. 1787

711 ROGERS (*T. J.*), American Biographical Dictionary, &c. 8vo. *sheep.* Easton, 1824

712 ROSCOE'S (*W.*) Illustrations, Historical and Critical, of the Life of Lorenzo de Medici, with an Appendix of Original Documents, 8vo. *portrait of Lorenzo and plates, boards.* Lond. 1822

713 ROSCOE'S (*H.*) Life of Wm. Roscoe, 2 vols. 12mo. Bost. 1833

714 ROSE'S Biographical Dictionary, A Specimen of Amateur Criticism on, 8vo. Lond. 1839

715 RUSSELL (*Lord J.*), Memoirs, Journals, and Correspondences of the late Thomas Moore, in 8 parts, 8vo. *sewed.* N. Y. 1843

716 SEWARD (*Anna*), Memoirs of the Life of Dr. Darwin, with Anecdotes of his Friends, 8vo. *sheep.* Phil. 1804

717 SHIPP (*John*), Memoirs of the Extraordinary Military Career of, 2 vols. 12mo. *boards.* N. Y. 1829

718 SIAMESE Twins, A Few Particulars of, 8vo. pp. 16. N. Y. 1836

719 SMITH (*Horace*), Memoirs, Letters, &c., in Prose and Verse, of the late J. Smith, in 2 vols. 8vo. *cloth.* Phil. 1841

720 SOCRATES, Life of, by Dr. G. Wiggers, translated from the German, 12mo. *cloth.* Lond. 1840

721 STOTHARD (*C. A.*) Memoirs of, including Original Journals, Letters, Papers, and Antiquarian Tracts, by Mrs. Stothard, 8vo. *half calf, gilt.* Lond. 1823

722 SULLY (*Duke of*), Memoirs of, by A. Jamieson, 2 vols. 18mo. *boards.* Lond. 1823

"The example of Sully, that master of written portraits, shows that the study of history is practically useful to a statesman."—*Horace Walpole.*

723 SWIFT (*Dr. Jon.*) Remarks on the Life and Writings of, in a series of Letters from John, Earl of Orrery, to his Son, *old calf,* 12mo. Lond. 1752

724 THOMPSON (*J. P.*) Memoir of David Hale, with selections from his Miscellaneous Writings. Hartford, 1850

725 THORBURN (*Grant*), Life and Writings of, 12mo. *cloth.* N. Y. 1852

726 UNIQUE (*The*), by George Smeetar, 2 vols. 18mo. *half calf, five portraits.*

727 WARBURTON (*Bp.*) Letters from a late eminent Prelate to one of his Friends, 8vo. *half calf.* N. Y. 1809

728 WELLINGTON (*Duke of*), Military Memoir of, by Capt. Sherer, 2 vols. 12mo. *cloth.* Phil. 1833

729 WESTMINSTER Abbey, Smyth (*G. L.*) Biographical Illustrations of Celebrated Authors interred in Westminster Abbey, including Chaucer, Spenser, Milton, Shakspeare, Ben Jonson, Congreve, Rowe, Sheridan, Addison, Foote, Gay, &c. &c., complete in one vol. 8vo. *cloth.* Lond. 1843

730 WHITE (*S. and his Son*), Miscellanea Nova, containing remarks on Boswell's Johnson, &c., 8vo. *calf.* Dub. 1801

731 WOOLRYCH'S (*H.*) Memoirs of Judge Jeffreys, 8vo. *cloth.* Phil. 1852

An excellent and strictly impartial piece of historical biography, embracing details of Monmouth's rebellion and the "Bloody Assizes."

732 WOTTON (*Sir Henry*), Reliquiæ Wottonianæ; or, a Collection of Lives, Letters, Poems, with characters of sundry personages, edited by Izaak Walton, *fine portraits* of Lord Essex and the Duke of Buckingham, *old calf*, 8vo. Lond. 1672

733 WREN (*Stephen*), Parentalia; or, Memoirs of the Family of the Wrens, but chiefly of Sir Christopher Wren, *with portraits*, folio, *calf.* Lond. 1750

734 WOOD (*A. a*), Athaenæ Oxoniensis, an exact history of all the writers and bishops who have had their education in the most ancient and famous University of Oxford, from the fifteenth year of Henry the Seventh Dom. 1500 to the end of the year 1690, representing the birth, fortune, preferment, and death of all those authors and prelates, the great accidents of their lives, and the fate and character of their writings, &c., 2 vols. in one, folio. Lond. 1691–92

"All hail to thee, old Anthony a Wood! May the remembrance of thy researches, amidst thy paper and parchment documents, stored up in chests, pews, and desks, and upon which, alas! the moth was 'feeding sweetly'—may the remembrance of these, thy laborious researches, always excite sensations of gratitude towards the spirit by which they were directed!"

CHINA.

735 ANTIQUITY of China, an Historical Essay, &c., 12mo. *half calf.* Lond. 1678.

736 CHINESE, a small volume printed in Chinese characters, *sewed*, 12mo.

737 CUNYNGHAME (*A.*), Recollection of China, 18mo. Phil. 1845.

738 LE COMPTE (*Louis*), Memoirs of China, 8vo. *calf* Lond. 1737.

"The best account of China previous to Du Halde's work, though in many particulars extremely partial to the Chinese."—*Lowndes.*

739 PALAFOX (*Sieur.*), History of the Conquest of China by the Tartars, 12mo. *calf.* Lond. 1671

740 STAUNTON'S (*Sir G.*) Account of the Embassy of the Earl of Macartney to China, the second edition, corrected, 8vo. *half calf.* Lond. 1797

A most valuable, and at the present time a peculiarly interesting work upon the Celestial Empire, the manners, customs, &c. of its inhabitants, &c.

741 WOOD (*W. W.*) Sketches of China, 12mo. *boards.* Phil. 1830

CHIVALRY.

742 DIGBY (*Kenelm*), Broad Stone of Honor, or the true Sense and Practice of Chivalry, 12mo. *cloth gilt.* Lond. 1844

743 MILLS, The History of Chivalry, 2 vols, 8vo. *cloth.* Lond. 1826

"This was an appropriate undertaking for the able author of the Crusades, and he has executed it with equal learning, fidelity and elegance."—*Monthly Review.*

744 VERTOT (*Abbe*), History of the Knights of Malta, *illustrated with the heads of the Grand Masters, and with maps and plans of Malta, and a complete index to the whole*, 2 vols. folio, *calf* Lond. 1728

December, 1737. J. W. N.

This history was ye last performance (it seems) of ye justly celebrated Abbot Vertot. * * * Besides ye importance of ye subject (viz., ye rise, progress and manners of ye famous Knights of *Malta*), our author easily appears to have recomended this performance, by ye beauty of ye stile, by ye elegance and perspicuity of the narration, and by ye various and artful episodes interwoven thro'out, which to me seem to comprehend a general idea of ye affairs of Europe, and are a kind of a history in miniature of ye establishment of Mahometism, of the Crusades, of several of the Popes, of ye Emperors of ye East, of the Turkish Sultans, of the K'gs of Jerusalem, Tripoli and Cyprus, together with other remarkable personages and events.

Our author says, "The first rise of ye Order of ye Knights, &c., was owing to "*Devotion*"—I wd. rather say to "*Superstition.*" For to what else can be justly ascribed ye frequent pilgrimages to the Holy Land, &c.?"—*From a MS. note in the first volume. Dated* 1737.

COSTUME.—*Vide* HISTORY OF THE STAGE.

DIALECTS.

"Vether it's worth while goin' through so much to learn so little, as the Charity-boy said ven he got to the end of the alphabet, is a matter of taste."—*Pickwick Papers.*

745 CARR, Dialect of Craven, West Riding of York, "*chaste and nervous language of its unlettered natives*," with Copious Glossary, illustrated by Authorities, from Ancient English and Scottish Writers, and Exemplified by Familiar Dialogues, *best edition, much enlarged*, 2 vols. *pub.* Lond. 1828

This learned Glossary shows the relationship of the Yorkshire Dialect to the Anglo-Saxon, Danish, Gothic, German, Moeso-Gothic, Suio-Gothic, Scottish, etc. Ample quotations from Popular Songs, Gower, Shakspeare, Chaucer, illustrate the work.

The Deanery of Craven is situated in the Northern part of the West Riding of the County of York; it embraces a small portion of the Wapentakes of Skyrack, Claro, and Ewcross, and the whole of the Wapentake of Staincliffe. Pent up by their native mountains, the inhabitants had no opportunity of corrupting the purity of their Language.

746 CLARK (*C.*) John Noakes and Mary Styles: a Poem, exhibiting some of the most striking Lingual Localisms, peculiar to Essex, with a Glossary, by C. Clark, *portrait*, 8vo. *cloth.* Lond. 1839

Full of quaint wit and humor.—*Gent's Mag.*

747 CORNWALL, Specimens of Cornish Provincial Dialect, collected and arranged by Uncle Jan Treenoodle, with some Introductory Remarks and a Glossary by an Antiquarian Friend, also a selection of Songs and other Pieces connected with Cornwall, post 8vo. *with curious portrait of Dolly Pentreath, cloth.* 1846

748 ——— Another copy. 1846

749 EXMOOR Scolding in the Propriety and Decency of Exmoor Language between two Sisters, as they were Spinning, also an Exmoor Courtship, with Notes and a Glossary, 12mo. *half morocco, uncut, scarce.* Lond. 1771

750 ——— Another Edition, with Notes and a Glossary, *boards.* Lond. 1839

Two very amusing Farces in the Devonshire Dialects; the Forest of Exmoor, however, is for the most part in the County of Somerset.

"A very rich bit of West of Englandism."

751 Dorset, Poems of Rural Life, in the Dorset Dialect, with a Dissertation and Glossary, by the Rev. William Barnes, B. D., *second edition, enlarged and corrected*, royal 12mo. *cloth.* 1848

A fine poetic feeling is displayed through the various pieces in this volume; according to some critics nothing has appeared equal to it since the time of Burns; the "Gentleman's Magazine" for December, 1844, gave a Review of the First Edition some pages in length.

752 Forby (*Rev. R.*) Vocabulary of East Anglia, an attempt to record the vulgar tongue of the twin sister Counties, Norfolk and Suffolk, as it existed in the last twenty years of the Eighteenth Century, and still exists; with proof of its Antiquity from Etymology and Authority, 2 vols. post 8vo. *cloth.* Lond. 1831

753 Glossary of Provincial and Local Words used in England, by F. Grose, F. S. A. with which is now incorporated the Supplement, by Samuel Pegge, F. S. A., post 8vo. *cloth.* 1839

The utility of a Provincial Glossary to all persons desirous of understanding our ancient poets, is so universally acknowledged, that to enter into a proof of it would be entirely a work of supererogation. Grose and Pegge are constantly referred to in Todd's "Johnson's Dictionary."

754 Halliwell, Dictionary of Archaic and Provincial Words, Obsolete Phrases, Proverbs, and Ancient Customs, from the time of Edward I., 2 vols. 8vo. closely printed in columns, in parts. 1844

This useful work begins with a History of the English Provincial Dialects; to every word in the whole Dictionary an illustration from an Ancient or Provincial Poet or other source is given, and when purely Provincial, the name of the County is added, where the word or phrase is used.

An indispensable book to the reader of the old Poets, Dramatists, Theologians, amd other writers, whose works abound with allusions of which explanations are not to be found in ordinary Dictionaries and books of reference.

755 Hunter (*I.*) Hallamshire Glossary, 8vo. *cloth.* 1829

An Appendix contains Thoreby's Catalogue of Words used in the West Riding of Yorkshire; a second Appendix contains Watson's Halifax Glossary. The district called Hallamshire is on the southern border of Yorkshire.

756 Kent, Dick and Sal, or Jack and Joan's Fair: a Doggerel Poem, in the Kentish Dialect, third edition, 12mo.

757 Smith (*J. R.*) A Bibliographical List of the Works that have been published towards illustrating the Provincial Dialects of England, 12mo. Lond. 1839

758 MOORE (*Ed.*) Suffolk Words and Phrases, 12mo. Woodbridge, 1823

759 SPECIMENS of the Yorkshire Dialect, exemplified in various Dialogues, Tales, and Songs, applicable to the County, with a Glossary, 12mo. Knaresborough, 1833

760 TOM CLADPOLE'S Journey to Lunnun, told by himself, and written in pure Sussex Doggerel, by his Uncle Tim, 18mo. n. d.

761 WESTMORELAND and Cumberland Dialects: Dialogues, Poems, Songs, and Ballads, by various Writers, in the Westmoreland and Cumberland Dialects, now first collected, to which is added a Copious Glossary of Words peculiar to those Counties, 12mo. *cloth.* Lond. 1839

This collection comprises, in the Westmoreland Dialect, Mrs. Ann Wheeler's Four Familiar Dialogues, with Poems, &c.; and in the Cumberland Dialect, I. Poems and Pastorals by the Rev. Josiah Relph; II. Pastorals, &c. by Ewan Clark; III. Letter from Dublin by a young Borrowdale Shepherd, by Isaac Ritson; IV. Poems by John Stagg; V. Poems by Mark Lonsdale; VI. Ballads and Songs by Robert Anderson, the Cumbrian Bard (including some now first printed); VII. Songs by Miss Blamire and Miss Gilpin; VIII. Songs by John Rayson; IX. An extensive Glossary of Westmoreland and Cumberland Words.

DICTIONARIES AND BOOKS OF REFERENCES.

762 AINSWORTH'S Latin Dictionary, reprinted from the best folio edition, with numerous Additions, Emendations, and Improvements, by the Rev. B. W. Beatson, A. M., revised and corrected by W. Ellis, Esq., A. M., impl. 8vo. *boards.* 1834

763 ALPHABETICAL Index to Subjects treated in the Reviews, 8vo. N. Y. 1848

This is the first edition of Poole's Index.

764 APPLETON'S New American Cyclopædia, XIX Numbers, 8vo. *sewed.* N. Y. 1858

765 ASH (*Dr.*) Complete English Dictionary, with a Supplement, 2 vols. 8vo. Lond. 1775

Replete with a multitude of obsolete, provincial, vulgar, and cant words and phrases, besides technical terms, &c.

766 BAILEY'S (*N.*) Universal Etymological English Dictionary, comprising explanations of Proverbs, Cant and Slang Words, Technical Terms, &c., 8vo. *calf.* Lond. 1724

"A favorite book of Lord Chatham's, which he was accustomed to read regularly through."—*Thos. Moore's Journal.*

767 BAYLE (*Peter*), Historical and Critical Dictionary, 4 vols. folio, *old calf.* Lond. 1710

"Such were the materials, and such the genius of the man, whose folios, which seemed destined for the retired few, lie open on parlour tables. The men of genius of his age studied them for instruction, the men of the world for their amusement. Amidst that mass of facts he has collected, and those enlarged views of human nature his philosophical spirit has combined with his researches, Bayle may be called the Shakspeare of dictionary makers.—*D'Israeli, Curiosities of Literature, 2d series, 1st vol.*

"If Bayle wrote his Dictionary to empty all the collections he had made, without any particular design, he could not have chosen a better plan. By the double freedom of a Dictionary and of Notes, he could pitch on what articles he pleased, and say what he pleased on those articles."

768 BOHUN (*Edmund*), a Geographical Dictionary, representing the Present and Ancient Names of all the Countries, Provinces, &c., &c., of the whole world, 8vo. *calf, front. curious issue.* Lond. 1688

769 BOYER'S French Dictionary, 8vo. *sheep.* Boston, 1844

770 ——— French Master, &c., 3 vols. 1794

771 CAREY (*J.*) Latin Prosody, 8vo. *boards.* L. n. d.

772 COBBETT (*W.*) English Grammar, 12mo., *sheep.* N. Y. 1812

773 COLES (*C.*) English Dictionary, 12mo., *old calf.* Lond. 1696

774 ENCYCLOPEDIA Americana, edited by Prof. Lieber, 13 vols. 8vo., *sheep.* Phil. 1836

775 FALCONER (*Wm.*) New Universal Dictionary of the Marine, 4to. *calf.* Lond. 1784

FLORIO'S Dictionary, *vide* Shakspeariana.

776 GRADUS ad Parnassum, 12mo. *vellum.* Coloniæ, n. d.

777 HAYDN (*Joseph*), Dictionary of Dates, relating to all Ages and Nations, for universal reference, 8vo. *cloth,* Lond. 1841

"A volume containing upwards of 10,000 articles, and, perhaps, more than 10 times 10,000 facts. What the Directory is to the merchant, this Dictionary of Dates will be found to be to those who are searching after information, whether classical, political, domestic, or general."—*Times.*

778 HURD (*S. T.*) Grammatical Corrector and others, 4 vols. 1847

779 KER (*J. B.*) An Essay on the Archæology of our Popular Phrases and Nursery Rhymes, 2 vols. 12mo. Lond. 1837

780 KNOWLES (*James*), Pronouncing and Explanatory Dictionary of the English Language, founded on a correct development of the Nature, the Number, and the Various Properties of all its Simple and Compound Sounds, as combined into Syllables and Words. *A new edition*, in medium 8vo. *cloth.* 1845

781 LEMPRIERE'S Classical Dictionary, by Anthon, Barker and Giles, 8vo. *cloth.* Lond. n. d.

782 LESLIE (*Jas.*) Dictionary of the Synonymous Words and Technical Terms in the English Language, 8vo. *sheep.* Edin. 1806

783 MANESCA'S French Course, vol. 1, 8vo. N. Y. 1834

784 MIEGE (*Guy*), The Great French Dictionary, 2 *parts, Fr. and Eng. and Eng. and Fr.*, thick folio, *calf.* 1688

Illustrated with opposite Phrases and Proverbs, the hard words explained, the Proprieties adjusted with two Grammars, English and French; also the Ancient and Modern Orthography, and contains several hundred words not to be found in any other Dictionary.

785 MONBODDO (*Lord*), Of the Origin and Progress of Language; 6 vols. 8vo. *half calf, uncut.* 1774

Contains the appendix with the author's last corrections.

"Those who were partial to modern literature, on account of their ignorance of that of antiquity, or who, not unacquainted with the more popular of the ancient authors, were strangers to the deeper mysteries of Greek erudition, condemned this work of Lord Monboddo, with bitter and contemptuous censure. In the late Mr. Harris, however (the philosopher of Malmsbury), he found an admirer and a literary friend, who was exceedingly delighted to meet with one that had cultivated those studies with equal ardour, and worshipped the excellence of the ancient Greeks, as far above all other excellencies."—*Chalmers' Biog. Dict.*

786 OSWALD (*J.*) Etymological Dictionary of the English Language, 12mo. Phil. 1836

787 PHILLIPS (*E.*) The New World of Words, or a general English Dictionary, etc., *frontispiece of portraits of Chaucer, Spenser, Sidney, Bacon, Selden, etc.*, folio, *calf, neat.* Lond. 1671

*** Among the names of Learned Persons contributory to this Work, are, Ashmole, Evelyn, Dugdale, Boyle, Hollar, Faithorne, Isaac Walton, Col. Venables, &c., &c.

788 RICHARDSON'S Large Dictionary of the English Language, combining Explanations with Etymology, with quotations from the best authorities, 2 thick vols. 4to. *half calf.* Lond., *Pickering*, 1838

This celebrated dictionary is the most important achievement in English Lexicography since the days of Johnson.

789 READ (*A.*) A Dictionary of the English Language, containing the Pronunciation, etc., 12mo. *sheep.* N. Y. 1845

790 ROWBOTHAM (*J.*) New Derivative and Etymological Dictionary of such English Words as have their Origin in the Greek and Latin Languages, &c., 12mo. Lond. 1838

791 SCHADE (*C. B.*) German Grammar, 12mo. *sheep.* Phil. 1838

792 SCHREVELII Lexicon Greco-Latinum, *sheep*, 8vo. Lond. 1814

793 TOOKE (*J. H.*) Epea Pteroenta, or the Diversions of Purley, with the author's additions, 2 vols. 8vo. *calf.* 1829

"What an epoch in many a student's life has been his first acquaintance with 'The Diversions of Purley.'"—*Trench on the Study of Words.*

794 WALKER (*J.*) Rhyming Dictionary, 12mo. *cloth.* Lond. 1836

795 WARD (*John*), Four Essays upon the English Language, 8vo. *calf.* Lond. 1768

796 WEBSTER (*N.*) Dictionary Abridged, square 8vo. *cloth.* 1856

797 WILSON (*J.*) French-English and English-French Dictionary, containing full Explanations, Definitions, Synonyms, Idioms, Proverbs, Terms of Art and Science and Rules of Pronunciation in each Language, imperial 8vo. *sheep.* 1833

OLD ENGLISH AND FOREIGN DRAMAS, MYSTERIES, INTERLUDES, MASQUES, ETC.

See also PAGEANTS.

Most of the collected works in this department are uniformly bound in *half blue calf; contents lettered.* The thin volumes have generally several leaves of thick writing paper before and after the text.

798 ABDICATED Prince, or Adventures of Four Years, a Tragi-Comedy, interleaved, *half calf.* Lond. 1690

Relating to James the Second, who is charged with the murder of Charles 2d; the Duke of Marlborough is the hero."—*See MS. Note.*

799 ADDISON (*Joseph*), Drummer, or the Haunted House, a comedy, prefaced by Sir R. Steele, 4to. Lond. 1722

800 ALARBAS: A Dramatic Opera, written by a gentleman of quality, 4to. *half calf.* Lond., 1709

801 ALFIERI (*Vittorio*), The Tragedies of, translated from the Italian by Charles Lloyd, 3 vols. 12mo. *cloth.* Lond. 1815

The Tragedies of Alfieri are noble poems. He displays consummate skill in unfolding and conducting his plots; he is always eloquent, always able to keep the imagination alive; and the uniform dignity of his manner is in the highest degree imposing.—*Quarterly Review.*

802 ANCIENT Mysteries, from the Digby MSS. in the Bodleian Library at Oxford: Mind, Will, and Understanding, a Morality inserted, both printed for the Abbotsford Club, 4to. Edinb. 1837

803 ANDRE: A Tragedy in five acts by W. Dunlap, as now performing at the theatre in New York; to which is added The Cow Chase: a Satirical Poem by Major André; with the Proceedings of the Court Martial, and authentic Documents concerning him, *large print,* 4to. *half roan.* Lond. 1799

804 APPARITION (*The*), or The Sham Wedding, a comedy, 4to. *half calf.* Lond. 1714

805 ARCHERS or Mountaineers of Switzerland, by W. Dunlap, *sewed,* 8vo. N. Y. 1796

806 ARIOSTO (*L.*) Scolastica Comedia, *vellum,* 12mo. Venez, 1553

807 ARISTOPHANES, Comedies, translated by Wheelwright, 2 vols. *cloth,* 8vo. 1837

808 ARMIN (*Robert*), The Valiant Welshman, or the True Chronicle History of the Life and Valiant Deeds of Caradoc the Great, King of Cambria, now called Wales, *woodcut of a Knight on horseback,* 4to. Lond. 1663

809 ——— Italian Taylor and his Boy, *woodcut, reprint,* 4to. Lond. 1609

810 ARROWSMITH, Reformation, a Comedy, acted at the Duke's Theatre. 4to. *half calf.* Lond. 1673

This is ascribed to Arrowsmith by Langbaine; it is the only play by its author.

811 B. (*G.*) Love the Leveller, or the Pretty Purchase. small 4to. *half calf.* Lond. 1704

812 B. (*T.*) [Anthony Brewer] The Countrie Girl, a Comedie. *sewed,* 4to. Lond. 1647

813 BAILLIE'S (*Joanna*) Series of Plays, delineating the stronger passions of the mind, each passion being the subject of a Tragedy and Comedy. 2 vols. 8vo. *half calf.* 1800

Unquestionably the greatest dramatist who has appeared here since the Reformation.—*Neale's Lectures on English Poetry.*

814 BAILLIE (*Jo.*), Bride, and others. 12 vols. v. y.

815 BAKER (*Thomas*), Tunbridge Walks, or the Yeoman of Kent, a Comedy. 4to. Lond. 1703

816 ——— Act at Oxford, a Comedy. 4to. Lond. 1704

817 ——— Fine Lady's Airs, or an Equipage of Lovers, a Comedy. 4to. Lond. 1709

"Wit, pure and genuine; satire, just and poignant."—*Baker.*

——— (*Dd.*), Biographia Dramatica, vide Bibliography.

818 BALE (*John, Bishop of Ossory*), Kynge Johan, a Play in Two Parts, edited from the recently discovered MS., by J. Payne Collier, small 4to. *half calf.* Lond. 1838

"Occupies an intermediate space between moralities and historical plays."

819 ——— Promises. 4to. *half calf.* Lond. 1780

820 BANCROFT (*John*), Tragedy of Sertorius, 1679; King Edward the Third, 1691; Henry II. King of England, with the death of Rosamond, in 1 vol. 4to. Lond. v. y.

821 BANISHED DUKE, or the Tragedy of Infortunatus. "The scene lies in Belgium—the character of 'Banished Duke' is intended for the Duke of Monmouth, and those of Romanus and Papessa for James II. and his queen." 4to. *half calf.* 1690

822 BANISHED VIRGIN (*The*), from the Italian, *folio calf.* Lond. 1635

823 BANKES (*John*), The Rival Kings. 4to. Lond. 1677

824 ——— Cyrus the Great. 4to. Lond. 1696

825 ——— Virtue Betrayed, or Anna Bullen. 4to. Lond. 1683

826 ——— Unhappy Favorite, or the Earl of Essex, a Tragedy. 4to. Lond. 1702

827 BARNES (*Barnaby*), The Divil's Charter with the Life and Death of Pope Alexander the Sixth, title written by John Kemble. 4to. *calf.* Lond. 1607

828 BARREY (*Lo.*), Ram-alley, or Merry Trickes, a Comedy. 4to. *half morocco.* Lond. 1636

Charles Mathews' copy, with his book-plate.

829 BATTELL OF ALCAZAR, fought in Barbarie, betweene Sebastian, King of Portugall, and Abdelmelee, King of Morocco, with the Death of Capt. Stukeley. 4to. *half morocco, very scarce.* Lond. 1594

Shakspeare has pointed his ridicule at this play in a parody on the words, Feed, and be fat, &c.

830 BEAUMARCHAIS' Œuvres, *half calf*, 3 vols. 24mo. Paris, 1825

831 BEAUMONT and Fletcher's Comedies and Tragedies, never printed before, *very fine impression of the portrait of Fletcher by Marshall*, title laid down, folio, *very neat old calf, fine clean copy*, sold in Roscoe's sale, £4 5*s.*; Drury's, £6 6*s.* 1647

First collected edition, with numerous commendatory pieces by Cokaine, Lovelace, Habington, Stanley, Buck, Earle, Cartwright, Ben Jonson, Herrick, &c. &c.

832 BEAUMONT and Fletcher's Comedies and Tragedies, Edited by George Colman, 4 vols. 8vo. *half calf.* Lond. 1811

833 BEAUMONT and Fletcher, Works, with an Introduction by George Darley, 2 vols. royal 8vo. *half calf.* *Maxon*, Lond. 1839

834 BEAUMONT and Fletcher, The Works of; the Text formed from a New Collation of the Early Editions, with Notes and a Biographical Memoir, by the Rev. Alexander Dyce, 12 vols. 8vo. *half calf*, lettered contents. Lond. 1843

"Elaborate, without being overloaded. It has done for the text of the united Dramatists, perhaps, nearly all that it was possible to do." —*Quarterly Review.*

"Two men once united by friendship and forever by fame, the Dioscuri of our Zodiac, rose upon the horizon as the star of Shakespeare, though still in its fullest brightness, was declining in the sky. In Comedy they founded a new school, at least in England, the vestiges of which are still to be traced in our theatre. Their language brilliant with wit, their measure, though they do not make great use of prose, very lax and rapid, running frequently to lines of thirteen and fourteen syllables. Few of their comedies are without a mixture of grave sentiments or elevated characters; and though there is much to condemn in their indecency and even licentiousness of principle, they never descend to the coarse buffoonery not unfrequent in their age. Never were dramatic poets more thoroughly gentlemen according to the standard of their times."—*Hallam.*

835 BEAUMONT and Fletcher, Woman Hater, acted with great applause, 4to. *half calf.* Lond. 1648

836 ——— The same, first edition, *sewed*, 4to. Lond. 1607

837 ——— The Knight of the Burning Pestle, 4to. *half morocco.* Lond. 1635

838 ——— The same, 4to. *half vellum.* Lond. 1635

839 ——— Cupid's Revenge, 4to. *half morocco.* Lond. 1635

840 ——— Another edition, 4to. *sewed.* Lond. 1630

841 ——— Scornefull Lady, a Comedy, 4to. *half vellum.* Lond. 1639

842 BEAUMONT and Fletcher, King and no King, 4to. *half vellum.* Lond. 1631

843 ——— Philaster, or Love lies a Bleeding, 4to. *half vellum.* Lond. 1639

844 ——— Another copy, 4to. *sewed.* 1652

845 ——— The Tragedy of Thierry, King of France, and his Brother Theodoret, 4to. *rare.* Lond. 1621

846 ——— Another edition, 4to. *sewed.* Lond. 1631

847 ——— Faithful Shepherdesse, by John Fletcher, 4to. *sewed.* Lond. 1629

848 ——— Elder Brother, a Comedy, by John Fletcher, 4to. *half calf.* Lond. 1637

849 ——— Monsieur Thomas, a Comedy, 4to. *sewed.* Lond. 1639

850 ——— Wit without Money, a Comedie, 4to. *half morocco.* Lond. 1639

851 ——— Tragedy of Rollo, Duke of Normandy, 4to. *half morocco.* Lond. 1640

852 ——— The Night-Walker, or the Little Thiefe, a Comedy, 4to. *half vellum.* Lond. 1640

853 ——— Spanish Curate, 4to. *half vellum.* Lond. 1718

854 ——— Beggar's Bush, 4to. *half vellum.* Lond. 1717

855 ——— Another edition, 4to. *half morocco.* Lond. 1661

856 ——— The Coxcombe, a Comedy, 4to. *half vellum.* Lond. 1718

857 ——— The Loyal Subject, a Tragic Comedy, *half vellum.* Lond. 1717

858 ——— Humorous Lieutenant, 4to. *sewed.* Lond. 1697

859 ——— Another edition, 4to. *half vellum.* Lond. 1717

860 ——— Maid in the Mill, a Comedy, 4to. *half calf.* Lond. 1718

861 ——— Prophetess, 4to. *half vellum.* Lond. 1717

862 ——— Scornful Lady, a Comedy, 4to. *half vellum.* Lond. 1691

863 ——— Royal Merchant, or Beggar's Bush, a Comedy (same as Beggar's Bush), 4to. *half vellum.* Lond. v. d.

864 ——— Bloody Brother, or Rollo, a Tragedy, 4to. *half vellum.* Lond. 1718

865 ——— Maid's Tragedy, 4to. *sewed.* Lond. 1686

866 ——— Rule a Wife and Have a Wife, a Comedy, 4to. *sewed.* Lond. 1697

867 ——— A King and no King, 4to. *sewed.* Lond. 1686

868 ——— Demetrius and Enanthe, being the Humorous Lieutenant, a Pleasant Comedie, edited by Alex. Dyce, 8vo. *sewed.* Lond. 1830

869 BEAUMONT and Fletcher, Wilde Goose Chase, a Comedie, Retrieved, by and for the benefit of, John Lowin and Joseph Taylor, *fine copy*, folio. Lond. 1652

"Beaumont and Fletcher are lyrical and descriptive poets of the first order; every page of their writings is a *florilegium*; there is hardly a passion, character, or situation, which they have not touched in their devious range, and whatever they touched, they adorned with some new grace or striking feature; they are masters of style and versification in almost every variety of melting modulation or sounding pomp, of which they are capable: in comic wit and spirit, they are scarcely surpassed by any writers of any age."—*Hazlitt.*

"In the romantic Drama, Beaumont and Fletcher are almost supreme. Their plays are, in general, most truly delightful. I could read the Beggar's Bush from morning to night. How sylvan and sunshiny it is! The Little French Lawyer is excellent. Lawrit is conceived and executed from first to last in comic humor. Monsieur Thomas is also capital. I have no doubt whatever that the first act and the first scene of the second act of The Two Noble Kinsmen, are Shakespeare's."—*Coleridge.*

870 BEAUTIES and Spirit of English Tragedy, a Companion to the Beauties of Shakspeare, *half calf*, 12mo. Lond. 1833

871 BECKET (*Gilbert Abbot*), Dramatic and Prose Miscellanies, 2 vols. 8vo. *cloth.* Lond. 1838

The author was one of the wittiest writers of the day.

873 BECKINGHAM (*Chas.*) Henry IV. of France, a Tragedy, 8vo. *curious portrait, rare, half bound.* Lond. 1720

874 BEHN (*Mrs.*) The Dramatic Works of, 2 vols. 8vo. *very rare, half calf, stained.* Lond. 1702

Mrs. Behn's Comedy, "The Widow Ranter," is founded on the story of Col. Bacon's Insurrection in Virginia, on which obscure part of history it throws much light, exhibiting strongly the mismanagement of the Colony, the incompetence of the authorities, &c., and the state of affairs which led to the outbreak.

875 ——— City Heiress, or Sir Timothy Treat All, 4to. Lond. 1682

876 ——— False Count, or a New Way to Play an Old Game, 4to. Lond. 1697

877 BELL'S British Theatre, consisting of the most esteemed English Plays, *with upwards of* 300 *fine scene and character Prints, after designs by Smirke, Fuseli, and others* (*including portraits of the most celebrated performers*), 34 vols. 12mo. *half calf.* 1791-95

"But of the modern stage down to the writings of Morton and Reynolds, get possession of a choice copy, considered with reference to the plates, of Bell's edition. The portraits of the actors, in the principal parts of the respective dramas, are admirably executed, and exhibit the dresses in which the scenes were first performed."—*Dibdin.*

878 BELL (*A.*) Count Clerment and Cain's Poranius, 12mo. *cloth.* Lond. 1841

879 BETTERTON (*Thos.*) The Prophetess, wants title, 4to. Lond. 1690

880 BLACKET (*Joseph*), Remains, Poems, Dramatic Sketches, &c., and Memoirs of his Life, by Pratt, 2 vols. 12mo. *boards, uncut.* Lond. 1811

881 BLADEN (*Morton*), Solon; or Philosophy no Defence against Love, a Tragi-comedy, 4to. *half calf.* Lond. 1705

882 BOILEAU (*Nicolas*), Œuvres de, *fine plates*, 2 vols. 4to. *old calf.* Amsterdam, 1718

"Boileau may be compared to the dog, whose sagacity is remarkable, as well as its fawning on its master, and its snarling on those he dislikes. If Boileau was too stern to admit the pliancy of grace, he compensates by good sense and propriety. He is like (for I will drop animals) an upright magistrate, whom you may respect, but whose public justice and severity leave an awe that discourages familiarity."—*Works of Hor. Walpole*, vol. V, p. 660.

883 ——, The Works of, made English from the last Paris edition by several hands, to which is prefixed his Life, by Des Maiseaux, *plates*, 2 vols. 8vo. Lond. 1712

"Boileau is the analogue of Pope in French Literature."—*Hallam.*

884 BOOTH (*H.*) Sebastian, a Tragedy, 8vo. pp. 96. Lond. 1823

885 BOUNDEN (*James*), Fortress of Rotzberg, or the Swiss Patriots, a Play, 8vo. *half morocco.* Lond.

886 BOYLE (*C. Earl of Orrery*), As You Find It, a Comedy, *half calf*, 4to. 1703

887 —— (*Roger, Earl of Orrery*), Dramatic Works of, *with portrait*, 2 vols. 8vo. *half calf.* Lond. 1739

888 BRATHWAIT (*Richard*), Mercurius Britanicus, or the English Intelligencer, a Tragi-comedy, at Paris, small 4to. 1641

Political subjects, Ship money, Judges Hutton and Cooke, are attacked in it; Prynne is introduced as Prinner, &c.

889 BREWER (*Anthony*), The Love-sick King, an English Tragical History, with the Life and Death of Cartesmunda, the fair nun of Winchester, *sewed*, 4to. Lond. 1655

890 —— Another copy, 4to. *half morocco.* Lond. 1655

—— *vide* Lots 812 and 1099.

891 BRIDE of Fort Edward, founded on an incident of the Revolution, 12mo. *cloth*, pp. 174. N. Y. 1839

892 British Enchanters, or no Magick like Love: A Tragedy, *sewed*, 4to. Lond. 1706

This is by Lord Lansdowne. "Its success was great."—*Baker.*

893 British Farces, a collection of, 6 vols. 12mo. Edin. 1786

893*Do. vols. 2, 3, 4, and 5, 12mo. Edin. 1786

894 British Theatre, Collection of the best Tragedies and Comedies, *numerous fine plates, costumes, portraits*, &c., 19 vols. 12mo. *calf.* Lond. 1776

894*British Theatre, *plates, calf*, 19 vols. 8vo. (vol. 3 missing.) Lond. 1776

895 British Theatre, Inchbald's excellent edition, with biographical and critical notes, and numerous engravings, containing portraits of eminent actors in their favorite characters, 20 vols. 12mo. *cloth.* 1808–9

896 Brome (*Richard*), The Northern Lasse: A Comedie, sm. 4to. Lond. 1632

897 ——— Queene's Exchange: A Comedy, sm. 4to. Lond. 1657

898 ——— Sparagus Garden, acted 1635, sm. 4to. Lond. 1640

899 ——— Joviall Crew, or The Merry Beggars: A Comedie, sm. 4to. Lond. 1652

900 ——— Another Edition, la. 4to. Lond. 1708

901 ——— Five new Plays—Madd Couple Well Macht; Novella; Court Begger; City Witt; Damoiselle. 1653

902 ——— Five new Plays—English Moor, or the Mock Marriage; Love-Sick Court; Covent Garden Weeded; New Academy; Queen and Concubine, 1659, 2 vols. *uniform, half calf*, 8vo. Lond.

Brome was a servant to Ben. Jonson, but wrote himself into notice.

903 Brooke (*Fulke Greville, Lord*), Learned and Elegant Works, containing Alaham and Mustapha, Tragedies, &c., autograph of T. Warton, *half calf*, folio. Lond. 1633

"Passion, Character, and Interest of the highest order, all frozen and made rigid with intellect."—*Charles Lamb.*

904 Brown (*D. P.*) Sertorius and Prophet of St. Pauls, 2 vols. in 1, 8vo. *calf, extra gilt.* Phil. 1830–36

905 Brown (*Tom*), Physick Lies a Bleeding, or the Apothecary Turned Doctor: A Comedy, acted every day in most of ye Apothecaries' Shops in London, 4to. Lond. 1697

906 BUCKINGHAM (*Duke of*), the Chances, altered from Beaumont and Fletcher, *half morocco*, 4to. Lond. 1692

907 BUCKINGHAM (*George Villiers, Duke of*), genuine Works, *half calf*, 12mo. Edin.

908 BULLOCK'S Octavius, a Tragic Drama in Five Acts, *sewed*, 8vo. Lond. 1834

909 BURGOYNE (*Lieut. Gen. T.*) Dramatic and Poetical Works, to which is prefixed a memoir of the author, *embellished with copper-plates*, 2 vols. 8vo. Lond. 1808

910 BURKE (*J.*) Female Patriotism, or the Death of Joan D'Arc, 12mo. N. Y. 1798

911 BURN (*D.*) Plays and Fugitive Pieces, 8vo. *boards*. Hobart Town, 1842

912 BURNABY (*Chas.*) Reformed Wife, a Comedy, *l.* 4to. Lond. 1700

913 ——— the same, 2d Edition, La. 4to. Lond. 1700

914 ——— Ladies' Visiting-Day, La. 4to. Lond. 1701

915 ——— Modish Husband, La. 4to. Lond. 1702

916 CÆSAR AND POMPEY (*The Tragedy of*), or Cæsar's Revenge ("*a later edition of this play was published in* 1607, *stating it was acted by the students of Trinity Coll., Oxford*"), 4to. *G. E. for John Wright.* Lond. n. d.

917 CALDERON DE LA BARCA, Comedie, 2 vols. 8vo. Paris, 1823

"His boundless and inexhaustible fertility of invention, the loftiness and purity of his sentiments, and the rich facility of his verse, entitle him to a high rank as to the Imaginative and Creative faculty of a poet."—*Quar. Review.*

918 CAMILLO (*Giulio*) Opere; Discorso in Materiá del suo Theatro, &c. 2 vols. 18mo. *vellum.* Venez. 1584

919 CAMPEZZI (*R.*) Il Tancredi Tragedia, 4to. *vellum, from Jolly's Library.* S. n. Y. a.

920 CARLELL (*Lodowicke*), Deserving Favorite, acted at Blacke-Friers, 1st Edit., 4to., *interleaved.* Lond. 1629

921 ——— another Copy, *sewed*, 4to. 1629

922 ——— another Edition, *frontispiece*, 4to. Lond. 1659

923 ——— Heraclius, Emperour of the East, a Tragedy from Corneille, 4to. *half calf.* Lond. 1664

924 ——— Arviragus and Philicia, in two parts, 12mo. *interleaved in* 4to. Lond. 1639

925 ——— The Passionate Lovers, 8vo. *interleaved in* 4to. Lond. 1655

926 CARLILE (*James*), The Fortune Hunters, 4to. *half calf.* 1689

CARLISLE, Earl of, *see* Howard.

927 CARPENTER (*Richard*), New Play called The Pragmatical Jesuit, *interleaved*, 4to. Lond., *circa* 1657

928 CARTWRIGHT (*Wm.*) Comedies, Tragi-comedies, with other Poems, by Mr. William Cartwright, late student of Christ Church in Oxford, and Proctor of the University. The Ayres and Songs set by Mr. Henry Lawes, servant to his late Majesty in his publick and private musick, *rare*, *Portrait*, 8vo. Lond. 1651

Cartwright died at the early age of thirty-two, but he lived long enough to earn the distinguished praise of Ben Jonson, who used to say of him "My son, Cartwright, writes all like a man."

Judging from the commendatory poems, which are more than fifty in number, attached to this volume, it would appear that Cartwright was much beloved and admired by all the great writers of the time. The last of the commendatory poems is by Isaac Walton. "On the Death of my dear Friend, Mr. William Cartwright," one of the few specimens of the muse of the good old Isaac.

929 ——— Another copy, *no title or portrait.*

930 CARTWRIGHT (*W.*) The Royal Slave, a Tragi-comedy, presented to the King and Queen by the Students of Christ Church, Oxford, 1st edition, small 4to. MS. Note by John Mitford. Oxford, 1639

931 CARYL (*John*), An English Princess, or Death of Richard the Third, a Tragedy written in 1666–1667; Sir Salomon, or The Cautious Coxcomb, a Comedy, 1691, in 1 vol. 4to. Lond. 1691

932 CENTLIVRE (*Susannah*), Original editions of her Plays, The Man's Bewitched, Love at a Venture, 1706; The Gamester, 1708; A Bickerstaff's Burying, or Work for the Upholders, a Farce, in 1 vol. La. 4to. Lond.

933 ——— The Beau's Duel, or a Soldier for the Ladies, a Comedy, La. 4to. Lond. 1702

These plays are justly admired for their lively incidents, genteel language, and humorous descriptions of real life.

934 CHAMBERLAINE (*Robert*), Swaggering Damsell, a Comedy, *half morocco*, 4to. Lond. 1640

935 ——— (*William*), Love's Victory, a Tragi-comedy, *half morocco*, 4to. Lond. 1658

This play was afterwards acted under the name of Wits led by the Nose.

936 CHAPMAN (*George*), Al Fooles, a Comedy, *sewed*, 4to. Lond. 1605

937 ——— All Fools, and Wisdom's Tears, 4to. *half calf*, *large paper copy.* Lond. 1780

938 CHAPMAN (*George*), Jonson, and Marston, Eastward Hoe, as it was playd in the Black-friers, *stained*, 4to. 1605

*** The first edition, containing the passage reflecting on the Scots, which gave such offence to James I. that the authors were imprisoned for writing it, and were compelled to cancel it in the subsequent edition.

939 ——— Gentleman Usher, *half morocco.* Lond. 1606

940 ——— Monsieur D'Olive, a Comedie, *half calf.* 4to. Lond. 1606

941 ——— Bussy D'Ambois, a Tragedie, *sewed*, 4to. Lond. 1641

942 ——— Cæsar and Pompey, a Roman Tragedy, first and only edition, *small* 4to. *sewed.* Lond. 1631

943 ——— The Conspiracie and Tragedie of Charles, Duke of Byron, Marshal of France, *sewed*, 4to. Lond. 1608

944 ——— Another edition, *half calf*, 4to. Lond. 1625

945 ——— Another copy, *half calf*, 4to. Lond. 1625

946 ——— Second Part, *sewed*, 4to. Lond. 1625

947 ——— May-day, a witty Comedie, *half calf*, 4to. Lond. 1611

948 ——— The Revenge of Bussy D'Ambois, a Tragedy, as it hath been often presented at the private playhouse in the White Fryers, first edition, *small* 4to. *sewed.* Lond. 1613

949 ———Another edition, 4to. Lond. 1623

950 ——— Widdowe's Teares, a Comedie, 4to. *half calf.* 1612.

951 ——— Old English Drama, Two Wise Men and all the rest Fooles, or a Comicall Morall, censuring the follies of this age, *half morocco*, 4to. Lond. 1619

952 ——— The Tragedy of Alphonsus, Emperor of Germany, *first and only edition*, small 4to. *sewed.* Lond. 1654

953 ——— Second Maiden's Tragedy, *sewed*, 8vo. Lond. 1824

954 ——— The Tragedie of Chabot, Admirall of France, as it was presented by her Majesty's Servants at the Private House in Drury Lane, written by George Chapman and James Shirley, small 4to. *half calf*, *scarce.* 1639

Shirley, the principal author of this play, was once of Gray's Inn, and a poet much esteemed in the days of Charles I.; he wrote 37 pieces and died shortly after. Chapman was well received among the poetic writers of that age for his translations as well as his original writings. He joined with Ben Jonson in composing the play called Eastward Hoe. He also translated Homer, Hesiod and Musæus, which works were esteemed well done in that infancy of translation. His theatrical pieces are 13 in number.

955 CHENIER (*M. J. de*), Théatre de, 3 vols. 18mo. Paris, 1821

956 CHERRY (*A.*) The Travellers, Soldier's Daughter, and Peter the Great, 8vo. *half calf.* 1806

957 CHESTER Plays, a collection of Mysteries, edited by Wright, (Sh. Soc.) 2 vols. 8vo. *half calf.* 1843

958 CHETTLE (*Henry*), Tragedy of Hoffman, or a Revenge for a Father, 1631. Kind-Heart's Dream, edited by E. F. Rimbault, in 2 vols. *half calf*, 4to. Lond. 1841

959 ——— Kind-Heart's Dream, 8vo. *sewed.* Lond. 1841

960 CIBBER (*Colley*), Plays, 2 vols. large 4to. Lond. 1721

961 ——— Plays, 5 vols. *half calf*, 12mo. Lond. 1777

962 ——— Clue to the Comedy of the Non Juror, by N. Rowe, 1718; 3 Letters on Cibber, &c., 4 Tracts, 12mo. Lond.

Cibber's name is frequently introduced in Boswell's Life of Johnson. Boswell—"Cibber was a man of observation?" Johnson—"I think not."

963 CICERO, A Drama, 4to. *cloth.* Lond. 1847

964 CLIVE (*Mrs.*) The Rehearsal, or the Boys in Petticoats, a Comedy, 8vo. *half calf.* Lond. 1753

965 COKAIN (*Sir Aston*), Choice Poems of several sorts: with 3 new Plays, viz.: The Obstinate Lady, a Comedy, Trappolin supposed a Prince, a Tragi-Comedy, The Tragedie of Ovid, 12mo. *calf.* Lond. 1669

According to Ellis, Cokain may be consulted with advantage by those who search after anecdotes of contemporary characters or pictures of their manners. Many of the poems, epigrams, &c., are addressed to various Gentry in Derbyshire and Staffordshire.

966 COLLECTION of Dramatic Pieces, vol. 1, *boards.* Lond. 1795

967 COLMAN (*Geo. the Younger*), The Iron Chest, a Play, with a preface and postscript, 2d edition, 8vo. *half calf, port inserted.* Lond. 1796

The title is as follows:—

"The Principal Characters"
"By Mr. Kemble, &c."

Drury Lane Play-bill.

"I had as lieve the town-crier had spoke my lines."

Shakspeare.

968 COMIC Theatre; a Free Translation of all the best French Comedies, by Samuel Foote, Esq., and others, 5 vols. 12mo. *calf.* Lond. 1762

969 COOKE (*John*), Green's Tuquoque Comedy, *interleaved, no title*, 4to. Lond. 1599

970 CONGREVE (*William*), Mourning Bride, a Tragedy, La. 4to. Lond. 1697

"If I were required to select from the whole mass of English poetry the most poetical paragraph, I know not what I could prefer to an exclamation in the Mourning Bride."—*Dr. Johnson.*

971 ——— Love for Love, a Comedy, La. 4to. Lond. 1704
972 ——— another copy, La. 4to. Lond. 1695
972* ——— Double Dealer, a Comedy, La. 4to. Lond. 1694

"We have had in Congreve a humorous observer in another school to whom the world seems to have had no moral at all, and whose ghastly doctrine seems to be that we should eat and drink and be merry when we can, and go to the deuce (if there be a deuce) when the time comes."—*Thackeray.*

COREY, *See* CORYE.

973 CORNEILLE (*P.*) Les chef d'Œuvres de, 12mo. *calf.* Oxford, 1746

Horace Walpole's copy, with his autograph and book-plate.

974 CORNEILLE, Theatre de, *calf*, 8vo. 1764

975 CORNEILLE (*P.*) Othon Tragedie, *sewed*, 12mo. Paris, 1666

"The greatest of the French dramatic poets. He was born at Rouen, in 1606, and for some time practiced in that city as an advocate. His first dramatic performance was 'Mélite,' a comedy, which met with such distinguished success, that he was encouraged to devote his rare powers to the drama. The tragedies of 'Medea,' 'The Cid,' 'The Horatii,' and 'Cinna,' followed, and established for their author a pre-eminent station among French dramatists. Besides the foregoing, he wrote many other tragedies, and translated Thomas à Kempis, 'On the Imitation of Jesus Christ.' It is melancholy to reflect that Corneille, who had achieved fame equally for himself and his country's literature, ended his days in poverty and distress. Died 1684."

976 CORNISH Plays, two Ancient Cornish Plays, Mount Calvary and the Creation of the World, written in the Cornish language with the translation, by J. Keigwin, edited by Davies Gilbert, 2 vols. in 1, *half calf*, 8vo. (See also Dialects.) Lond. 1826–7

977 CORNWALL (*Barry*), *i.e.* Proctor's Dramatic Scenes, with other Poems, 12mo. *cloth.* Bost. 1857

978 CORYE (*J.*) Generous Enemies, or the Ridiculous Lovers, a Comedy, *half calf*, *l.* 4to. Lond. 1672

A compilement or rather plagiarism from other authors.—*Lowndes.*

979 ——— Cure for Jealousie, a Comedy, 1701, Metamorphosis, translated from Moliére, in 1 vol, *half calf*, *large* 4to. Lond. v. y.

980 COSTLIE Whore, a Comicall Historie acted by the companie of the Revels, *interleaved*, 4to. Lond. 1633

COWLEY (*A.*) The Works of, *vide* Poetry.

983 COWLEY (*A.*) The Guardian: A Comedie acted 1641, *half calf.* Lond. 1650

"This title was changed, and the play much altered; it was called the Cutter of Colman Street."—*See MS. Note.*

984 ——— Love's Riddle, a Pastoral Comedy; Naufragium Joculare, *unbound*, folio. Lond. 1681

985 COWLEY (*Mrs.*) The Runaway, 8vo. 1776

986 COXE (*C. C.*) Saul, a Mystery, 12mo. *boards.* N. Y. 1845

987 CROESIUS, King of Lydia, a Tragedy, 4to. *cloth.* *Pickering*, 1845

988 CRAUFURD (*David*), Love at First Sight, a Comedy, 4to. Lond. 1704

989 CREBILLON (*P. J. de*), Œuvres Completes, 3 vols. 8vo. *calf, gilt edge.* Paris, 1785

990 CRICKET on the Hearth, a MS. prompt copy and sundry others.

991 CRISP, Virginia, a Tragedy, 8vo. Lond. 1754

992 CRITICAL Remarks on the Four Taking Plays of this Season, *sewed*, 12mo. Lond. 1719

993 CROSS (*J. C.*) Dramatic Works, 8vo. *boards.* Lond. 1812

994 CROKER (*Thomas Crofton*), Recollections of Old Christmas, a Masque, *wood-cuts, sewed, privately printed*, 4to. 1850

995 CROWNE (*John*), Juliana, Charles 8th of France, The Country Wit, The Chaste Nimph, &c., &c., from 1671 to 1693, all first editions, 4 vols. 4to. *half calf, fine.* Lond.

996 CROWNE (*John*), The Dramatic Works of, containing 13 plays, the original editions, collected and bound in 4 vols. 4to. *half calf, very rare.* Lond. v. y.

"Crowne was the son of an Independent Minister in New England, who sought his fortune in England, and became a dramatic writer of considerable eminence, being patronized by the Earl of Rochester, and put forward by him in opposition to Dryden; no collected edition of his works has appeared; they are, consequently, very rare."

999 CUMBERLAND (*Geo.*) Mysterious Husband, a Tragedy, *interleaved*, 8vo. *half calf.* Lond. 1785

1000 DABORN (*Robert*), Christian Turned Turke; or, The Tragical Lives and Deaths of the two famous Pyrates, Ward and Dansiker, 1612. The Poore Man's Comfort, a Tragi-comedy, *half calf*, 4to. Lond. 1655

1001 DANIEL (*Saml.*) The Queene's Arcadia, a Pastoral Tragi-comedy, *sewed*, 4to. Lond. 1623

"Both in prose and poetry he is, as to language, among the best writers of his time."—*Hallam.*

1002 DANCER (*John*), Agrippa, King of Alba, from Mons. Quinault, La. 4to. Lond. 1675

——— Nicomede, a Tragi-comedy, translated from Corneille, La. 4to. Lond. 1671

1003 D'ANCOURT, Œuvres, augmentées de plusieurs Comedies qui n'avoient point été imprimées, *plates*, 9 vols. *calf*, 12mo. Paris, 1729

1004 D'AVENANT (*Charles*), Circe, a Tragedy, as acted at the Duke of York's Theatre, 4to. *half calf*. Lond. 1685

1005 ——— (*Sir Wm.*) The Works of Sir William d'Avenant, Kt., consisting of those which were formerly printed, and those which he designed for the press, now published out of the author's original copies, *portrait by Faithorne*, bound in 2 vols., folio. Lond. 1673

1006 ——— The Rivals, a Comedy (not in his works), 4to. Lond. 1668

1007 ——— Another copy.

1008 ——— The Cruell Brother, a Tragedy, sm. 4to. Lond. 1630

1010 ——— Salmacida Spolia, a Masque, presented by the King and Queene's Majesties, at Whitehall, Jan'y 21, 1839, *invention, ornament, scenes, &c., by Inigo Jones, musick by Lewis Richard; masques, Charles I., Henrietta Maria, Duke and Bp. of Lenox, Earl of Carlisle, Ctss. of Carnarvon, Earl and Ctss. Newport, &c.* (not in his works), sm. 4to. 1639

1011 ——— Siege of Rhodes, 2 parts, La. 4to. Lond. 1663

1012 ——— Siege of Rhodes, part I., imperfect, 4to. Lond. 1659

1013 DAVENPORT (*Robert*), a Pleasant and Witty Comedy, called a New Tricke to Cheat the Divel, *sewed*, 4to. Lond. 1639

1014 ——— The City Night Cap, or Crede quod habes, et habes, a Tragi-comedy, *half russia*, 4to. Lond. 1661

1015 ——— New Tricke to Cheat the Divel, 1639; Bloodie Banquet, 1639, by T. D. (see MS. note of Fullerton); King John and Matilda, 1655; The City Night-Cap, 1661, in 1 vol., *morocco extra, calf back*, 4to. Lond. v. y.

1016 DAY (*John*), The Isle of Gulls, 1633; Humor out of Breath, a Comedy, 1608; The Parliament of Bees, with their proper characters, or a Bee-hive furnisht with twelve Honey-combes, as pleasant as profitable, *woodcuts, interleaved, unbound*, 4to. 1641

1017 DAY (*John*), The Travaills of the Three English Brothers, Sir Thomas, Sir Anthony, and Mr. Robert Shirley, historical play, *fine copy*, 4to. 1607

The author was assisted in this by Wm. Rowley and Geo. Wilkins.

1018 DEKKER (*Thomas*), Pleasant Comedie of Old Fortunatus, *black letter*, *unbound*, 4to. Lond. 1600

1019 ——— Satiro-mastix, or the Untrussing of the Humorous Poet, *fine copy*, *interleaved*, 4to. Lond. 1602

——— Satiro-mastix, or the Untrussing the Humorous Poet, a Play, privately acted by the children of Paules, 4to. *calf*. 1602

A very rare and curious satire, in which Dekker ridiculed Ben Jonson under the name of Horace.

1020 ——— Second Part of the Honest Whore, with the Humors of the Patient Man, *sewed*, 4to. Lond. 1630

1021 ——— Honest Whore, Dodsley's edition, 8vo. *interleaved* in 4to. Lond. 1780

1022 ——— and Webster, Westward Hoe, *half morocco*, 4to. Lond. 1607

1023 ——— and Webster, Northward Hoe, *sewed*, 4to. Lond. 1607

1024 ——— Whore of Babylon, *sewed*, 4to. Lond. 1609

1025 ——— The Roaring Girle, or Moll Cut-purse, a Play, 1611, Dodsley's reprint, 8vo. *interleaved* in 4to. Lond. 1780

1026 ——— If it be not good the Divel is in it, a new Play, *half morocco*, 4to. Lond. 1612

1027 ——— A Tragi-comedy, called Match Me in London. *sewed*, 4to. Lond. 1632

1028 ——— Another copy (title wanting), 4to. Lond.

1029 ——— The Wonder of a Kingdome. 1636

1030 ——— Another, *half calf*, 4to. Lond. 1636

1031 ——— Shoemakers' Holiday, or Gentle Craft, with the Humorous Life of Simon Eyre, shoemaker, and Lord Mayor of London, *half morocco*, 4to. Lond. 1618

1032 ——— Sun's Darling, a Moral Masque, by John Foard and , *half morocco*, 4to. Lond. 1657

1033 ——— Reprint, 8vo. Lond. n. d.

1034 ——— Virgin Martyr, a Tragedy, *half morocco*, 4to. Lond. 1651

1035 ——— Another edition, *half vellum*, 4to. Lond. 1661

1036 ——— Another copy, *half calf*.

1037 ——— Patient Grissel, a Comedy, by Dekker, Chettle, and Haughton. (Shakesp. Soc.) 8vo. Lond. 1841

1038 DEKKER (*Thomas*), History of Patient Grissell, two early Tracts, *sewed*, 8vo. (Percy Soc.) Lond. 1842

1039 ——— A Knight's Conjuring, Done in Earnest, Discovered in Jest, edited by Rimbault, *sewed*, 8vo. (Percy Soc.) Lond. 1842

1040 ——— Witch of Edmonton, by Rowley, Dekker, and Ford, *sewed*, 8vo. Lond. n. d.

1041 ——— The Gull's Hornbook, reprint, *half calf*, 4to. Bristol, 1812

"The pamphlets and plays of Dekker alone would furnish a more complete view of the habits and customs of his contemporaries in vulgar and middle life, than could easily be collected from all the grave annals of the times."—*Quarterly Review*.

1042 DELAVIGNE (*C.*) Theatre de. 2 vols. 8vo. Par. 1826

1043 ——— Œuvres Complètes de. Royal 8vo. *half calf.* Paris, 1836

1044 DENHAM (*Sir John*), Poems and Translations, with the Sophy, a Tragedy. 8vo. *half calf.* Lond. 1709

1045 DENNIS (*John*), Select Works. 2 vols. 8vo. *half calf.* Lond. 1718

1046 ——— A Plot and no Plot, a Comedy. 4to. *sewed.* Lond. 1697

1047 ——— Rinaldo and Armida, a Tragedy. 4to. *sewed.* Lond. 1699

1048 ——— Iphigena, a Tragedy. 4to. *sewed.* Lond. 1700

1049 ——— Comical Gallant, or the Amours of Sir John Falstaff (altered from Shakspeare's Merry Wives of Windsor), 4to. *sewed.* Lond. 1702

1050 ——— Liberty Asserted, a Tragedy (autograph of the Duke of Lauderdale), 4to. *sewed* Lond. 1704

1051 ——— Gibraltar, or the Spanish Adventure, a Comedy, 4to. *sewed.* Lond. 1705

1052 ——— Invader of his Country, a Tragedy, 8vo. *sewed.* Lond. 1720

1052* ——— Rinaldo and Armida, 10 vols. 4to. Lond. v. d.

1053 DE VADÉ, Œuvres Complettes, 2 vols. 18mo. Troyes, 1798

1054 D'HARLEVILLE (*C.*) Œuvres Choises, 18mo. Paris, 1822

1055 DIGBY (*Lord*) Eloisa, or the Worst not always True, a Comedy, small 4to. *calf.* Lond. 1667

1056 Dilke (*Thomas*), Lover's Luck, a Comedy, 4to. *sewed.* Lond. 1696

1057 ——— Pretenders, or the Town Unmaskt, a Comedy, 4to. *sewed.* Lond. 1698

1058 Dilke's (*T. W.*) Old English Drama. Old Plays, edited by C. W. Dilke, 6 vols. 8vo., *calf gilt, scarce.* Lond. 1844

Contains plays by Chapman, Marston, Rowley, Tourneur, Lily, &c., not reprinted in Dodsley, or any of the modern collections.

1059 Dodsley's Select Collection of Old Plays, 12 vols. 12mo. *half calf.* Lond. 1744

1060 ——— Old Plays, best edition. Select Collection of Old English Plays (comprising the Works of the Elizabethan Dramatists), new edition, with Notes, Corrections, and Additions, by Isaac Reed, Oetavius Gilchrist, and the Editor (J. Payne Collier, Esq.), 13 vols. small 8vo. *half calf, contents of each volume lettered on the back, scarce.* Lond. 1825

We may here perceive how this noble generation of poets, some of whose names are not familiar to us, have moulded our language with the images of their fancy, and strengthened it by the stability of their thoughts."—*D'Israeli.*

1061 Drue (*Thos.*) The Life of the Duches of Suffolke, as it hath been divers times acted (ascribed by Langbaine to Heywood), 4to. 1631

1062 Druræi (*Guilielmo, Nobili Anglo*), Dramatica Poemata. Alvredus, Tragico Comœdia, Mors, Comœdia, Reparatus, Tragico Comœdia, *half calf,* 24mo. Duaci, 1628

1063 Dryden (*John*), Works, with Notes, Historical, Critical, and Explanatory, and a Life of the Author, by Sir Walter Scott, 18 vols. 8vo. *half calf, lettered.* Lond. 1808

Pope's admiration of Dryden is well known; he declared, "he could select from his works better specimens of every mode of poetry, than any other English writer could supply. Speaking of his writings, he says, 'as to his writings, I may venture to say, in general terms, that no man hath written in our language, so much, and so various matter, and in so various manners, so well.' . . . His prose had all the clearness imaginable, together with all the nobleness of expression, all the graces and ornaments proper and peculiar to it, without deviating into the language of poetry."—*Congreve.*

1064 ——— Dramatic Works of, being a Collection of the Original Quartos, Collected and Collated by W. E. Burton, 3 vols. *fine half calf,* 4to. Lond. 1669 to 1680

∴ 17 plays in all, a rare collection of the original editions.

1065 DRYDEN (*John*), Albion and Albanius, 4to. *sewed.* Lond. 1691

1066 —— King Arthur, or The British Worthy, 8vo. *boards.* Lond. 1691

1067 —— Cleomenes, the Spartan Hero, a Tragedy, 8vo. *boards.* Lond. 1692

1068 —— Don Sebastian, King of Portugal, a Tragedy, 4to. *sewed.* Lond. 1692

1069 —— All for Love, or World Well Lost, 4to. *sewed.* Lond. 1703

1070 —— Aurengzebe, a Tragedy, 4to. *sewed.* Lond. 1694

1071 —— Amboyna, a Tragedy, 4to. *sewed.* Lond. 1691

1072 —— Conquest of Granada, 4to. *sewed.* Lond. 1695

1073 —— Tyrannick Love, or The Royal Martyr, a Tragedy, 4to. *sewed.* Lond. 1693

1074 —— Sir Martin Marall, or Feigned Innocence, a Comedy, 4to. *sewed.* Lond. 1691

1075 —— Rival Ladies, a Tragic Comedy, 4to. *sewed.* Lond. 1664

1076 —— Another edition, 4to. *sewed.* Lond. 1693

1077 —— Wild Gallant, a Comedy, 4to. *sewed.* Lond. 1694

1078 —— Spanish Fryar, or the Double Discovery, 4to. *half bound.* Lond. 1717

1079 —— Love Triumphant, or Nature will Prevail, 8vo. *boards.* Lond. 1694

1080 —— The Revolter, a Trage-Comedy, acted between the Hind and Panther, and Religio Laici, &c. 4to. *half morocco.* Lond. 1687

1081 DUCIS (*J. F.*) Œuvres, 24mo. *half morocco.* Paris, 1824

"M. Lemercier ranks this writer, and very justly, above Crebillon, who with the terrible has no mixture of tenderness. M. Ducis unites them both."—*Ventouillac.*

1081* DUNLAP'S Collection of Plays, 8vo. *Autograph of J. H. Hackett.* N. Y. 1800

1082 D'URFEY (*Thos.*) Madam Fickle, or The Witty False One, a Comedy, 4to. *sewed.* Lond. 1642

1083 —— Love for Money, or The Boarding-School, a Comedy, 4to. *sewed.* Lond. 1691

1084 —— Wonders in the Sun, or the Kingdom of the Birds, a Comick Opera, 4to. *sewed.* Lond. 1706

1084* EFFINGHAM (*C.*) Virginia Comedians, 2 vols. 12mo. *cloth.* (vol. 1.) N. Y. 1856

1085 ENGLISH and American Stage, &c. 15 vols. odd, 12mo.

1086 ENGLISH Theatre, 8 vols. 12mo. *calf*, odd. Lond. 1776

1087 ETHEREGE (*Sir George*), Works, containing his Poems and Plays, 8vo. *half calf.* Lond. 1704

1088 ——— Works, containing his Poems and Plays, 12mo. *half calf.* Lond. 1735

1089 ——— Comical Revenge, or Love in a Tub, 4to. *half vellum.* Lond. 1669

1090 ——— Another edition, 4to. *sewed.* Lond. 1697

1091 ——— Another edition, 4to. *sewed.* Lond. 1689

1092 ——— Man of Mode, or Sir Fopling Flutter, a Comedy, 4to. *sewed.* Lond. 1684

1093 EURIPIDES' Tragedies, translated by Woodhull, 3 vols. 8vo. *half calf.* Lond. 1809

1094 FAIR Captive, a Tragedy, by E. Haywood, 8vo. *half calf.* 1721

1095 FALKLAND (*Henry Lucius Cary*), The Marriage Night, a Play, *half calf*, 4to. Lond. 1664

1095*——— Another copy.

1096 FAMOUS Tragedie of King Charles I., basely Butchered, &c., *fine copy, surreptitiously printed*, 4to. 1649

"This play seems to have been written by some very strong party man, who thought at so critical a juncture the declaration of his name would have been attended with hazard, perhaps, even his life." —*Biographia Dramatica.*

1097 FANE (*Sir Francis*), Love in the Dark, or the Man of Business, 4to. *half calf.* Lond. 1675

1098 FARQUHAR (*Geo.*) Love and Business, in a collection of occasionary verse, on the death of General Schomberg, killed at the Boyne, &c., *half calf*, 8vo. Lond. 1702

1099 ——— Twin Rivals, a Comedy, *half vellum*, 4to. Lond. 1703

1100 ——— Constant Couple, or a trip to the Jubilee, a Comedy, *sewed*, 4to. Lond. 1701

1101 ——— Inconstant, or the Way to win Him, a Comedy.

1102 FATAL Legacy, a Tragedy, 8vo. *half calf.* Lond. 1723

1103 FAUGERES (*M. V.*) Belisarius, a Tragedy, 8vo. N. Y. 1795

1104 FENTON (*Elijah*), Mariamne, a Tragedy, 8vo. *half calf.* Lond. 1723

1105 FIELD (*Nathaniel*), A Woman is a Weathercock—Amends for Ladies, a Comedy, edited by T. P. Collier, *sewed*, 8vo. Lond. 1821

1106 FISHER (*Jasper*), Fuimus Troes, Æneid 2, The True Trojanes, *half calf*, 4to. Lond. 1633

1107 Fletcher (*John*), Tragedy of Rollo, Duke of Normandy, 4to. *half calf.* Oxford, 1640

1108 Foote (*Samuel*), Dramatic Works, *calf*, 2 vols. 12mo. Lond. 1797

1109 ——— Comic Theatre, vols. 2 and 5, 12mo. 1762

1110 ——— Roman and English Comedy, considered and compared, with remarks on the Suspicious Husband, *sewed*, 8vo. Lond. 1747

1111 ——— Mayor of Garratt, a Comedy, in two acts, illustrated by Seymour, *sewed*, 12mo. Lond. 1831

1112 Ford (*John*), The Dramatic Works of, with Notes, by Henry Weber, Esq., 2 vols. 8vo. *calf*, *fine*. Edin. 1811

1113 ——— Vol. 1, of the same.

1114 ——— The Dramatic Works of, by Hartley Coleridge, 8vo. *half calf.* Lond., *E. Moxon*, 1843

1115 ——— The same, Harper's Ed., 8vo. *calf.* N. Y. 1831

"Ford was of the first order of poets; he sought for sublimity, not by parcels in metaphor or invisible images, but directly where she has her full residence, in the heart of man, in the actions and sufferings of the greatest minds."—*Charles Lamb.*

1116 Ford (*John*), Chronicle Historie of Perkin Warbeck, *interleaved*, *half morocco*, 4to. Lond. 1634

1117 ——— Love's Sacrifice, a Tragedie, Roxburgh copy, *autograph of A. Dyce*, 4to. Lond. 1633

1118 ——— Fame's Memoriall, or the Earle of Devonshire, deceased, *half morocco*, 4to. Lond. 1606

1119 ——— Ladies' Triall, acted in Drury Lane, *half vellum*, *fine copy*, 4to. Lond. 1639

1120 ——— Tis Pitty Shee's a Whoore, corner of the title torn off, otherwise fine copy, *half calf*, 4to. Lond. 1633

1121 ——— Tis Pitty Shee's a Whoore, acted at the Phœnix, *half russia*, 4to. Lond. 1633

1122 ——— Tis Pity Shee's a Whore, *interleaved*, 4to. *half calf.* Lond. 1633

1123 ——— Tracts by, edited by Jos. Haselwood Kent. 1819

1124 Forde (*Thomas*), Love's Labyrinth, or the Royal Sheperdess, a Tragi-Comedie, 8vo. Lond. 1660

1125 Four Old Plays. Three interludes, Thyrsites, Jack Jugler, Heywood's Pardoner, and Frere and Jocasta, a Tragedy, by Gascoigne and Kinwelmash, with an introduction and notes, 12mo. *half calf.* Cambridge, U. S. 1848

1126 FREEMAN (*Sir Ralph*), Imperiale, a Tragedy, *fine copy, half vellum*, 4to. Lond. 1655

1127 ——— Another copy, *half morocco*. Lond. 1655

Highly praised by Langbaine.

1128 Female Fop, or the False One Jilted (by Mr. Sanford), 8vo. *half calf*. 1724

1129 FRENCH Plays, various, royal 8vo. *half calf*. Paris, n. d.

1130 FRENCH Tragedies, a collection of, in two thick vols., 8vo. *half calf*. 1820

1131 GAMBOLD (*J.*) Martyrdom of Ignatius, a Tragedy, 8vo. *half calf*. Lond. 1773

1132 GARRICK (*David*), The Dramatic Works of, with the Life of the Author, 3 vols. 12mo. *calf*. Lond. 1798

"Whose death eclipsed the gaiety of nations."—*Dr. Johnson.*

1134 GAY (*John*), Plays, *with portrait*, 18mo. *calf*. Lond. 1760

1135 GAYTON (*E.*) Will Bagnal's Ghost, or the Merry Devil of Gadmunton, *half calf*, 4to. Lond. 1655

Not mentioned in the Biographia Dramatica.

1136 GAZUL (*Clara, a Spanish Comedian*), Plays of, with Memoir, 12mo. *boards*. Lond. 1825

1137 GERBIER (*George D' Ouvilly*), False Favourite Disgrac'd, and the Reward of Loyalty, a Comedy, 12mo. *half calf*. Lond. 1657

1138 GERMAN Plays, 5 vols. 12mo. v. d.

1139 GHOST (*The*), or The Woman Wears the Breeches, 4to. 1640.

1140 GIRAUD (*Geo.*) Comedie Scelte, 12mo. *half bound*. Paigi, 1829

1141 GLAPTHORNE (*Henry*), The Hollander, a Comedy, *sewed*, 4to. Lond. 1640

1142 ——— Another copy.

1143 ——— Argalus and Parthenia, *sewed*, 4to. Lond. 1639

1144 ——— The Ladies' Priviledge, acted at the Cock-pit, Drury-lane, *sewed*, 4to. Lond. 1640

1145 ——— Wit in a Constable, a Comedie, *sewed*, 4to. Lond. 1640

1146 ——— Tragedy of Wallenstein, Ladies' Priviledge, *half calf*, 12mo. Lond. 1640

"One of the chiefest dramatic poets of that age (Charles I.)"—*Winstanley.*

1148 GOFFE (*Thos.*) The Raging Turke, or Bajazet the Second, *1st edition, rare*, 4to. Lond. 1631

1149 GOFFE (*Thos.*) Couragious Turk, or Amurath the First, 1*st edition rare, vellum,* 4to. Lond. 1632

1150 ——— Three Excellent Tragedies, viz., The Raging Turk, or Bajazet the Second; The Courageous Turk, or Amurath the First; and the Tragedie of Orestes, *half calf,* 8vo. Lond. 1656

1151 ——— Raging Turk, 8vo., 1656; Courageous Turk, 8vo., 1656; Orestes, 8vo., 1656; Careless Shepherdes, a tragic comedy, (without the alphabetical catalogue of all such plays that ever were printed), 1656, *interleaved,* in 2 vols. *half calf,* 4to. Lond. 1656

1152 GOLDONI (*Carlo*), Commedie, 3 vols. 12mo. *half calf.* Milan, 1825

1153 ——— Commedie, 31 *plates to illustrate.*

"Les Italiens considèrent Goldoni comme ayant porté l'art dramatic à son plus haut degrè de perfection. Goldoni est aujourd'hui, le seul roi de la scêne comique."—*Sismondi.*

1154 GOMERSALL (*Robert*), Poems. Tragedie of Lodovick Sforza, Duke of Milan, &c., *half calf,* sm. 8vo. Lond. 1633

1155 GORING (*Charles*), Irene, or the Fair Greek, a Tragedy, *half calf,* la. 4to. Lond. 1708

1156 GOUGH (*J.*) Strange Discovery, a Tragic Comedy, *interleaved, half calf,* 4to. Lond. 1640

1157 GOULD (*E. S.*) "The Very Age," a Comedy, 12mo. N. Y. 1850

1158 GOULD (*Robert*), Rival Sisters, or the Violence of Love, a Tragedie, *sewed,* 4to. Lond. 1696

1159 GRANVILLE (*George, Lord Lansdowne*), The Sea-gallants, a Comedy, 4to. *sewed.* Lond. 1696

1160 ——— Heroick Love, a Tragedy, *sewed,* 4to. Lond. 1698

1161 GRATIÆ Theatrales, or a choice Ternary of English Plays; Thorney-abbey, or the London-maid, a Tragedy, by T. W.; The Marriage Broker, or the Pandar, by M. W.; Grim, the Collier of Croydon, or the Devil and his Dame, with the Devil and St. Dunstan, a Comedy, by J. T., *half calf,* 12mo. Lond. 1662

1162 GREENE (*Robert*), Quip for an Upstart Courtier, or a Quaint Dispute Between Velvet Breeches and Cloth Breeches, *black letter, woodcut rare, sewed,* 4to. Lond. 1635

Priced £7 7s. in Bib. Ang. Poetica.

1163 GREENE (*Thomas*) and Thomas Lodge, a Looking-Glasse for London, England, *half morocco*, 4to. Lond. 1617

Sold at Nassau's sale for £7 7*s*.

1164 ——— Honorable Historie of Frier Bacon and Frier Bongay, *sewed cut close*, 4to. Lond. 1630

1165 ——— Dramatic Works and Poems, with Life of the Author, and Notes by the Rev. Alex. Dyce, 2 vols. 8vo. *half calf*, *Pickering*. 1831

Greene was one of the most popular poets of the Elizabethan period. His dramas contain much real poetry, and are especially valuable as pictures of the wild roystering life of the age.

1166 HABINGTON (*William*), The Queene of Aragon, a Tragi-comedie, folio, 1635, with Castara, 12mo. 1635, inter-leaved, in folio, *half calf*. Lond. v. d.

1167 HALM (*Frederich*), Son of the Wilderness, a Dramatic Poem in five acts, translated by Anthon, *sewed*, 8vo. N. Y. 1848

1168 HARDING (*Samuel*), Sicily and Naples, or The Fatal Union, a Tragedy, *sewed*, 4to. *rare*. Oxford, 1640

1169 HARDY (*Alex.*) Le Theatre de, 7 pieces, 12mo. *vellum*. Paris, 1621

1170 HARRIS (*Jos.*) Mistakes, or the False Report, a Tragi-comedy, *sewed*, 4to. Lond. 1691

1171 HARTSON (*H.*) The Countess of Salisbury, a Tragedy, 8vo. Lond. 1767

1172 HAUSTED (*P.*) Rivall Friends, a Comedie, 1632; Senile Odium, 8vo. 1633, Ad Populum, or a Lecture to the People, with a Satyre against Separatists, in 1 vol. 4to. Lond. 1675

1173 HAWKINS (*Thomas*), Origin of the Old English Drama, illustrated in its various species, viz: Mystery, Morality, Tragedy, and Comedy, by specimens from our earliest writers, 3 vols. *half calf*, 12mo. Oxford, 1773

Contains Hycke Scorner, A Morality, Lusty Juventus, do., King Cambises, The Spanish Tragedy, Ferrex and Porrex, Satiro Mastix, Return from Parnassus, etc.

1174 HAYWARD (*John*), The Four P's, The Pardoner, &c., 2 vols. 8vo. *half calf*. Lond. 1780

1175 HEYWOOD (*Thomas*), Love's Mistresse, or the Queene's Masque, publickly acted by the Queene's Comedians, *sewed*, 4to. Lond. 1640

Inglis' copy of original sold for £3 3*s*.

1176 ——— Challenge for Beautie, as it hath beene sundry times acted, *sewed*, 4to. Lond. 1636

1177 HEYWOOD (*Thomas*), Silver Age, including the Love of Jupiter and Alcmena, the Birth of Hercules, and Rape of Proserpine, concluding with the arraignement of the Moone, first edition, *calf extra, very scarce*, 4to. Lond. 1612

1178 —— and William Rowley, Fortune by Land and Sea, a Tragi-comedy, *half calf*, 4to. Lond. 1655

1179 —— Another copy, *half morocco*, 4to. Lond. 1655

1180 —— Pleasant Comedy, called a Mayden-Head well lost, as it was acted at the Cocke-pit, *curious woodcut, half russia*, 4to. Lond. 1634

1181 —— A Woman Kilde with Kindnesse, *half calf*, 4to. Lond. 1617

1181* —— Brazen Age; Death of the Centaure Nessus; Tragedy of Meleager; Jason and Medea; Vulcan's Nest, &c., *calf, cut close*, 4to. Lond. 1613

1182 —— Wise woman of Hogsdon, a Comedy, *sewed, cut close*, 4to. Lond. 1638

1183 —— Rape of Lucrece, a true Roman Tragedy, indifferent copy, *sewed*, 4to. Lond. 1608

Nassau's copy sold for £18 7*s*. 6*d*.; Inglis's, £6 12*s*. 6*d*.

1184 —— Rape of Lucrece, 4th edition, *half russia*, 4to. Lond. 1630

1185 —— The Rape of Lucrece, 5th edition, with sundry Songs before omitted now inserted in their right places, *sewed*, 4to. Lond. 1638

1186 —— Fayre Maide of the Exchange, together with the Merry, Humorous, and Pleasant Passages of the Cripple of Fanchurche, furnished with a varietie of delectable mirth, *half russia*, 4to. Lond. 1625

1187 ——The English Traveller, as it hath beene publikely acted at the Cock-pit in Drury Lane (dedicated to Sir Henry Appleton, Knight Baronet, &c.), *sewed*, 4to. Lond. 1633

1188 —— Pleasant Dialogues and Dramas, selected out of Lucien, Erasmus, Textor, Ovid, &c., with sundry emblems extracted from the most elegant Jacobus Catsius, as also certaine Elegies, Epitaphs, and Epithalamions, or Nuptiall Songs, Anagrams and Acrosticks, with divers speeches (upon severall occasions) spoken to their most excellent majesties, King Charles and Queen Mary, with other fancies, translated from Beza, Buchanan, and sundry Italian poets, *rare*, 8vo. Lond. 1637

Bindley's sale, £1 9*s*.; Bib. Ang. Poet., £2 12*s*. 6*d*.

1189 HEYWOOD (*Thomas*), Iron Age, first and second parts, *woodcut*, *sewed*, first part wants title, *sewed*, 4to. Lond. 1632

1190 ——— and W. Rowley, two Plays, 8vo. Lond. 1845

1191 ——— King Edward the Fourth, *unbound*. Lond. 1626

1192 ——— Golden and Silver Ages, &c. 4 vols. 8vo. *cloth*. Lond. 1851

1193 ——— Royall King and the Loyall Subject, acted with great applause, first edition, *one leaf MS.* (F. 1), *half morocco*, 4to. Lond. 1637

1194 ——— Funerall Elegy on Prince Henry, in conjunction with Tourneur and John Webster, beautiful clean large copy, *half calf*, 4to. Lond. 1613

1195 ——— Exemplary Lives and Memorable Acts of Nine the most worthy Women in the World; three Jewes, three Gentiles, three Christians, *rare portraits of Queen Margaret, Queen Elizabeth, and Henrietta Maria, &c.*, *calf*, 4to. Lond. 1640

1196 ——— Apology for Actors, containing three brief Treatises; I. Their Antiquity; II. Their Ancient Dignity; III. The True Use of their Quality, *half russia*, 4to. Lond. 1612

1197 ——— The same, reprint. Lond. 1841

Heywood, whom Lamb styled the prose Shakespeare, was the most voluminous dramatic writer that England produced. See Langbaine and Biographia Dramatica.

1198 HIGGINS (*Bevil*), The Generous Conqueror and Timoleon, or the Revolution, anon., 4to. *half calf*. Lond. 1702

1199 ——— Generous Conqueror, or The Timely Discovery, a Tragedy, 4to. *sewed*. Lond. 1702

1201 HILL (*A.*) Works of, consisting of, Letters on various Subjects, and Original Poems, moral and facetious, with an Essay on the Art of Acting, 4 vols. 8vo. *calf*. Lond. 1754

1202 ——— Do. do. vol. 2, 8vo. *calf*. 1760

1203 HISTORICAL Tragedies, by Beaumont and Fletcher, Nat. Lee, Southerne, and Dryden, 4 Plays in 1 vol. Lond. v. d.

1204 HISTRIO-MASTIX, or The Player Whipt, 4to. *half morocco extra, by Rivicre*, printed for Th. Thorp. 1610

This curious play was written towards the close of Elizabeth's reign, though not printed till 1610. It contains a ridicule or burlesque on the passage of Shakespeare's Troilus and Cressida, where Troilus, at parting, presents his sleeve to Cressida, and she gives him her glove. *Sold at Sotheby's sale in* 1823 *for* £4 16*s*.

1205 HITCHCOCK (*M.*) The Macaroni, a Comedy, 12mo. pp. 82. Phil. 1774

1206 HOLIDAY (*Barten*), Texnogamia, or The Marriage of the Arts, a Comedie, 4to. *half russia.* Lond. 1618

1207 HOME (*John*) Dramatic Pieces, 12mo. *portrait inserted, half calf.* Lond. 1760

David Hume, in dedicating his Four Dissertations to the author of Douglas, bestows the highest possible praise on him; observing that he possessed the true theatric genius of Shakespeare and Otway.

1208 HOPKINS (*Charles*), Pyrrhus, King of Epirus, a Tragedy, 1695; Boadicea, Queen of Britain, 1697; Friendship Improved, or the Female Warriour, 1700; all first editions, in 1 vol. 4to. *half calf.* Lond. v. y.

1209 HORATII, a Tragedy, 8vo. *sewed.* Lond. 1846

1210 HORDEN (*Hild.*) Neglected Virtue, a Play, 4to. *half calf.* Lond. 1696

1213 How a Man may Choose a Good Wife from a Bad, Second Maiden's Tragedy, 12mo. *half calf.* Lond. 1824

1214 HOWARD (*Ed.*) The Usurper, a Tragedy, 4to. *sewed, rare.* Lond. 1668

"The character of Damocles is intended to point at that of Oliver Cromwell."

1215 ——— Another copy, 4to. *half calf, sewed.* Lond. 1668

1216 HOWARD (*H.*) Dramas adapted for the Representation of Juvenile Persons, 18mo. *half calf.* Lond. 1819

1217 HOWARD (*James*), All Mistaken, or The Mad Couple and the English Monsieur, 4to. *half calf.* Lond. 1672

1218 HOWARD (*Sir Robt.*) Poems, including the Blind Lady, a Comedy, 8vo. *inlaid in folio, half calf.* Lond. 1660

1219 HUGHES (*Thomas*), Misfortunes of Arthur, edited by J. Payne Collier, 12mo. *half calf extra.* Lond. 1828

1220 HUNT (*Leigh*), The Dramatic Works of Wycherly, Congreve, Vanbrugh, and Farquhar; with Biographical and Critical Notices, portrait of Wycherly, 4 vols. royal 8vo. *portraits, half calf.* Lond. 1851

"In some respects Mr. Leigh Hunt is excellently qualified for the task which he has now undertaken. His style is well suited for light, garrulous, desultory ana; half critical, half biographical, we do not always agree with his literary judgments; but we find in him what is rare in our time—the power of greatly appreciating and heartily enjoying good things of very different kinds. He has paid particular attention to the history of the English drama from the age of Elizabeth down to our own time; and has every right to be heard with respect on that subject."—*Edinburgh Review.*

1221 HOWARD (*Sir R.*), Five New Plays, viz. the Surprisal, Committee, Indian Queen, Vestal Virgins, and Duke of Lerma, folio, *uniformly bound in 2 vols. with portrait, half calf.* Lond. 1692 v. d.

The Author was known in his own time as "Sir Positive At All," because of his conceit. He is highly praised by Langbaine, Jacob, and Gildon.

1221* INTERLUDES—Interlude of Youth, from the rare black letter edition, printed by Waley, about 1554, Bande, Ruffe, and Cuffe, a Costume Show; News out of Islington; and a Derbyshire Mummer's Play, all edited by J. O. Halliwell, and privately printed at *Brixton Hill, half calf,* 4to. 1840

1222 ISLAND Princess, or the Generous Portugal (by Beaumont and Fletcher), *half vellum,* 4to. Lond. 1669

IT Cannot Rain but it Pours. *Vide* London.

1224 JACKE Drum's Entertainment, or the Comedie of Pasquill and Katherine, as it hath bene sundry times plaide by the Children of Fowles, 1st edition, *rare, interleaved,* 4to., for Richard Olive. Lond. 1601

"Bindley's copy sold for £5 15*s.* 6*d.*"
The incident of Mammon's poisoning Katharine's face, seems borrowed from Demagora's treatment of Parthenia, in Argalus and Parthenia.

IRELAND'S Vortigern, *vide* Shakspeariana.

1225 JACOB (*H.*) Fatal Constancy, a Tragedy, 8vo. *half calf.* Lond. 1723

1226 JAY (*Steph.*) Tragedies of Sin Contemplated, in Ruine of the Angels, Fall of Man, Destruction of the World, Confusion of Babel, Conflagration of Sodom, &c., 12mo. *sheep, very scarce.* Lond. 1689

1227 JONES (*John*), Adrasta, or Woman's Spleene, and Love's Conquest, a Tragi-Comedie, *interleaved, half calf,* 4to. Lond. 1635

1228 JOHNSON (*Charles*), The Cobler of Preston, acted at Drury Lane, 8vo. Lond. 1716

A similar character, and founded upon Christopher Sly, in the Taming of the Shrew.

1229 JONSON (*Ben*), The Works of Benjamin Jonson, *printed by Richard Bishop, and are to be sold by Andrew Crooke, in St. Paule's churchyarde, portrait by Vaughan, frontispiece by Hole, rare,* 2 vols. folio. Lond. 1640

Sold in Roscoe's sale, £3 15*s.*
At the end of Every Man in his Humour, occurs the name of WILL. SHAKESPEARE among those of THE PRINCIPAL COMEDIANS.
A very rare edition; the second collected one of his Works—supposed, by Gifford, to have been printed surreptitiously.

1230 JONSON (*Ben*). The Works of Ben Jonson, *portrait by Vertue and plates by Guernier*, 6 vols. 8vo. *half calf.* Lond. 1716

*** The first edition containing Plates, much esteemed by the curious, as displaying the costume of the time in the dressing of the characters.

1231 ——— Ben Jonson's Works, with Notes, Critical and Explanatory, and a Biographical Memoir, edited by Gifford, 9 vols. 8vo. *half calf.* 1816

"Best edition by the ablest of modern commentators, through whose learning and generous labors Old Ben's forgotten works and injured character are restored to the merited approbation and esteem of the world."—*J. P. Kemble.*

1232 ——— Beaumont & Fletcher, vol. 4, *boards*, 8vo. Lond.

1233 ——— 19 Comedies by, with Notes, by George Coleman, Esq., royal, 8vo. *half calf.* Lond. 1811

1234 ——— Comicall Satyre of Every Man out of his Humour, *wanting the first leaf, half morocco*, 4to. printed for *Nicholas Linge.* Lond. 1600

1235 ——— Volpone, or the Fox, 1st edition, sm. 4to. *calf, fine copy, with Bindley's bookplate.* 1607

"Murphy, and afterwards Cumberland, in speaking to me of this Comedy, described it as the most perfect of any existing."—*MS. note by Mr. Rogers.*

1236 ——— Mask of the Queens, and the Twelfth Night's Revels, from a MS. in the British Museum, *sewed*, 8 vo. n. p.

1237 ——— Catiline, his Conspiracy, a Tragœdie, *sewed*, 4to. Lond. 1674

1238 ——— G. Chapman, and John Marston, Eastward Hoe, as it was played in Black Friers, *half calf*, 4to. Lond. 1605

"The authors were accused of reflecting on the Scots, for which they were committed to prison, and were in danger of losing their ears and noses."—*Loundes.*

1238½ JORDAN (*T.*) Money is an Asse, a Comedy, 4to. 1663

1239 JULIETTA GORDONI, a Play, *not published*, 8vo. N. Y. 1839.

1240 KETELLAS (*Caroline M.*) Last of the Plantagenets, 8vo. *sewed.* N. Y. 1844

1241 KILLEGREW (*Henry*), The Conspiracy, a Tragedy, as it was intended for the Nuptials of the Lord Charles Herbert and the Lady Villiers, *sewed*, 4to. Lond. 1638

1242 KILLEGREW (*Thomas*), Comedies and Tragedies, *fine and rare portrait, by Faithorne, with picture of Charles I. and his favorite dog, half calf*, folio. Lond. 1664

1243 —— The Prisoners and Claracilla, two Tragi-Comedies, 12mo. Lond. 1840–41, inlaid on 4to. paper, with the Dramatis Personæ, written by a hand of the time, several congratulatory Poems, by William Cartwright and others, *half calf.* Lond.

" Henrietta Maria, Queen of Charles I, appears to have been the Patroness of this Theatre. Killegrew was the favorite page of Charles I., and companion of his familiar hours."

" Perhaps there is no writer of plays who throws so much light upon, and illuminates the customs, habits, and ways of living among the higher classes of his time as Killegrew."

1244 —— (*Sir William*), Three Plays, Selindra, Pandora, Ormasdes, *half calf*, 8vo. Lond. 1665

1245 —— Four New Plays, Siege of Urbin, Selindra, Love and Friendship, Pandora, *calf*, folio. Oxford, 1668

1246 KIRKE (*J.*) The Seven Champions of Chistendome, acted at the Cock-pit and the Red Bull, and never printed till this year, 4to. 1638

1247 KIRKMAN (*Francis*), The Wits, or Sport upon Sport, in selected pieces of Drollery, both parts, *original frontispiece*, with the scene in the Old Red Bull Playhouse of Sir John Falstaffe, &c., 2 parts, *half calf.* 8vo. Lond. 1671

1248 KNAVE in Graine, new Vampt, a witty Comedy, acted at the Fortune many days together with great applause, 1640; The Blind Beggar of Bednal-Green, with the Merry Humor of Tom Strowd the Norfolk-Yeoman, 1659, *both interleaved, in all* 3 vols. *half calf*, 4to. Lond.

1249 KNEVET (*Ralph*), Rhodon and Iris, a Pastorale, as it was presented at the Florist's Feast in Norwich, 4to. Lond. 1631

1250 KNOWLES (*J. S.*) The Hunchback, *with portrait of Miss. Kemble inserted*, 8vo. *half calf.* Lond. 1832

" Judge Furman's copy, with a long account of Miss Kemble's acting, the Influence of the Stage, &c.

1251 KOTZEBUE (*Augustus Von*), Plays, translated from the German, by Smith, 8vo. *calf.* N. Y. 1800

1252 —— Happy Family, Pizarro and 3 others, 8vo. *half calf.* N. Y. 1800

1253 —— Abbé de l'Epee, or the Orphan, 8vo. N. Y. 1801

1254 —— The Writing Desk, 8vo. N. Y. 1801

1255 KYD (*T.*) The Spanish Tragedy, or Hieronimo is Mad Againe, containing the lamentable end of Horatio and Belinperia, *woodcut half russia*, 4to. Lond. 1633

1256 ——— Cornelia, Hieronimo is Mad Againe, Solyman and Perseda, *half calf*, 12mo. Lond. 1780

1257 LACY (*John*), Sawney the Scott; Sir Hercules the Buffoon; The Old Troope, 3 plays. Lond. 1672–98

1258 LADY'S Visiting Day, a Comedy, by Charles Burnaby, *half morocco*, 4to. Lond. 1701

1259 LAMB (*C.*) John Woodvil, a Tragedy, to which are added Fragments of Burton, the author of the Anatomy of Melancholy, 12mo. *bds. very scarce.* 1802

A warm admiration of the Elizabethan Dramatists led him to imitate their style and manner, in a tragedy named John Woodville, which was published in 1802. There is much that is exquisite, both in sentiment and expression in Lamb's Play, and the following description of the Sports in the Forest, has a truly antique air, like a passage in Heywood or Shirley—
"To see the sun to bed, and to rise."—*Hazlit.*

1260 ——— Specimens of English Dramatic Poets who lived about the time of Shakespeare, with Notes, 2 vols. *half calf.* 1844

"A selection in which is displayed the utmost judgment and taste. The critical notices are extremely valuable, and above any praise of mine."—*Singer's Preface to Chapman's Hymns of Homer.*

1261 LANCI (*C. C.*) Il Vespa Commedia, 24mo. *in vellum.* Firenze, 1586

1262 LANSDOWNE (*G. Granville, Lord*), Dramatic Works, 12mo. Lond. 1752

1263 LATOUCHE (*M. H. de*) Le Reine d'Espagne, 8vo. Paris, 1831

1264 LEE (*Nat.*) Twelve Tragedies by, Original Editions, as acted at the Royal Theatre, *small* 4to. *calf.* Lond. 1675–1690

1265 ——— Four Plays: Theodosius, Cæsar Borgia, The Rival Queens, The Princess of Clene, 4 vols. 4to. Lond. 1684 to 1697

1266 ——— Mithridates, King of Pontus, a Tragedy, *sewed.* 4to. Lond. 1685

1267 ——— The Rival Queens, or the Death of Alexander, 4to. *calf.* Lond. 1694

"The Rival Queens, about which play much nonsense has been talked. It is true there is bombast in it, and one or two speeches that smack of Bedlam; but there is not more bombast than in other plays of the epoch, and there is ten times as much fire."—*Charles Reade.*

"Lee was a true poet in all the excesses of poetical feeling."—*D'Israeli.*

1268 Le Sage (*M.*) Recueil des pieces mises au Théatre François, 2 vols. 12mo. *half morocco.* Maestrecht, 1774

1269 Lillo (*George*), Dramatic Works, with Memoirs by Davies, 2 vols. 12mo. *boards.* Lond. 1810

1270 Lilly (*John*), Sixe Court Comedies, often presented and acted before Queen Elizabeth by the Children of her Majestie's Chappel, and the Children of Paules, 12mo. *half calf.* Lond. 1632

The author is called by the editor, E. Blount, "the only rare poet of that time, the wittie, comical, facetiously quicke, and unparallel'd John Lilly," and in his curious address ("to the Readers)" he says, "These his playes crown'd him with applause, and the spectators with pleasure. Thou canst not repent the reading of them over, when old John Lilly is merry with thee in thy chamber, thou shalt say few (or none) of our poets now are such witty companions, and thanke mee that brings him to thy acquaintance."

1271 Lingua, or the Combat of the Tongue and the Five Senses for Superiority, a pleasant Comoedie, *very small* 4to. *half morocco rare.* Lond. 1617

Act IV. Scene 4, is a curious Allegory, in which "Tobacco, apparelled in a Taffata Mantle," is introduced and speaks an "unknown" tongue. Attributed to the witty Antony Brewer. It is said that Oliver Cromwell once acted the part of Tactus in this curious old Droll or Merriment, from which he first imbibed his sentiments or ambition.

1272 Longfellow (*H. W.*) Spanish Student, a Play, 12mo. *boards.* Camb. 1844

1273 Longinus, A Tragedy, &c., 8 Plays.

1274 Lottery (*The*), A Comedy, 8vo. *half calf.* Lond. 1728

1275 Love in the Dark, by Sir F. Ford, and 4 plays, 5 vols. 4to. Lond. v. d.

1276 Lawyer's Fortune or Love in a Hollow Tree, by Lord Grimstone, 8vo. *sewed.* Lond. 1736

1277 Lower (*Sir William*), Horatius, a Roman Tragedie, *half calf,* 4to. Lond. 1656

1278 Lucan, Translations from, occasion'd by the Tragedy of Cato, *unbound,* 8vo. Lond. 1713

1279 Lyndsay (*D.*) Dramas of the Ancient World, 8vo. *bds.* Edinb. 1822

1280 McDonald (*Andrew*), Miscellaneous Works, including the Tragedy of Vimonda, and those productions which have appeared under the signature of Matthew Bramble, Esq., &c., 8vo. *calf.* Lond. 1791

1281 Machin (*Lewis*), The Dumbe Knight, an Historical Comedy, 4to. *sewed.* Lond. 1633

1282 Macklin (*Charles*), Man of the World, a Comedy, 4to. *with fine portrait.* Lond. 1793

1283 MANLEY (*Mrs.*) Lucius; Almyna, or The Arabian Vow; The Lost Lover; 3 vols. 4to. *pr.* Lond. 1696

1284 MAGASIN Theatral, vol. 3, 8vo. Paris, 1835

1285 MS. DRAMAS, 4to. *vellum.* v. d.

CONTENTS.—I., The Generous Courtezan, from the Macklin Collection, as well as the other two, were purchased at Jolly's sale; II. Green-Room Chitchat, formerly from the library of Isaac Reed; III. Cambas and Thewingia, 1736, from the Rhodes Collection.

1286 MARKHAM (*Gervase and William Sampson*), True Tragedy of Herod and Antipater, with the Death of Marriam, interleaved, 4to. *morocco.* Lond. 1622

1287 MARLOWE (*Kit*), Works, 3 vols. cr. 8vo. *half calf.* *Pickering*, 1826

"Marlowe, renowned for his rare art and wit,
Could ne'er attain beyond the name of Kit."—*Heywood.*

1288 MARLOWE (*Christopher*), Dramatic Works, with Prefatory Remarks, Notes, &c., 12mo. *half calf.* Lond. 1827

"There is an awful melancholy about Marlowe's Mephistophiles, perhaps more impressive than the malignant mirth of that fiend, in the renowned work of Goethe.—*Hallam.*

"What mortall soule with Marlo might contend,
That could 'gainst reason force him stoope or bend?
Whose silver-charming toung mou'd such delight,
That men would shun their sleepe in still darke night
To meditate upon his goulden lynes,
His rare conceyts, and sweete-according rimes."
Henry Petowe.

1289 MARLOW (*Christopher*), Famous Tragedy of the Rich Jew of Malta, 4to. *half calf.* Lond. 1633

1290 ——— Tambarlaine the Greate, with his Impassionate Furie for the Death of his Lady and Love, faire Zenocrate, &c., part 2, **Black Letter**, *stained*, 4to. *half calf.* Lond. 1606

1291 ——— Troublesome Raigne and Lamentable Death of Edward the Second, King of England, 4to. *half calf.* Lond. 1622

1291* MARLOW and Nash, Tragedie of Dido, Queen of Carthage. 1594

"The original edition is one of the rarest of Plays, only two known to exist." Steevens's copy sold for £17.

1292 MARMION (*Shakerly*), Holland's Leaguer, an excellent Comedy, 1632; Fine Companion, acted before the King and Queene at White Hall, 1633; The Antiquary, a Comedy, 1641; in 3 vols. interleaved, 4to. *half calf.* Lond. v. y.

1293 MARSHALL (*Thomas, of King's Norton*), Histrio-Mastix, A Whip for Webster (as 'tis conceived), the Quondam Player, or an Examination of one John Webster's Delusive Examen of Academies, &c., 12mo. *sewed.* Lond. 1654

1294 MARSTON (*John*), The Dramatic and Poetical Works of, now first collected, and edited by J. O. Halliwell, 3 vols. 18mo. *cloth.* Lond. 1856

"This edition deserves well of the public; it is carefully printed, and the annotations, although neither numerous nor extensive, supply ample explanations upon a variety of interesting points. If Mr. Halliwell had done no more than collect these plays, he would have conferred a boon upon all lovers of our old dramatic poetry."
Literary Gazette.

1295 ——— Plays of, interleaved and unbound, printed 1598, reprinted Lond. 1764

1296 ——— Parasitaster; or, The Fawne, as it hath bene divers times presented at the Blacke Friars, by the Children of the Queene's Maiestie's Reuels, 4to. *half calf, large print, rare.* Lond. 1606

1297 ——— Another copy, 4to. *half morocco.* Lond. 1606

1298 ——— Insatiate Countesse, a Tragedie, 4to. Lond. 1631

1299 ——— The Malcontent, 1604; Eastward Hoe, by Chapman, Jonson, and Marston, 4to. Lond. 1605

1299* ——— Insatiate Countesse, 4to. Lond. 1616

1300 ——— Insatiate Countesse, 8vo. Lond. 1820

1301 ——— Second Maiden's Tragedy, 12mo. Lond. 1824

"A poet of distinguished celebrity in his own day, no less admired for the versatility of his genius in tragedy and comedy, than dreaded for the poignancy of his satire; in the former department the colleague of Jonson, in the latter the antagonist of Hall."
Rev. P. Hall.

1302 MASON (*John*), An excellent Tragedy of Muleasses the Turke, and Borgias, Governor of Florence, *interleaved, half calf,* 4to. 1632

1303 MASSINGER (*Phil.*) Dramatic Works, edited by Hartley Coleridge, royal 8vo. *half calf, neat, portrait.* Lond., *Moxon,* 1840

"On a level with, if not one degree above the writings of Fletcher, follow the purer and more chastened productions of Philip Massinger, a poet of unwearied vigour and consummate elegance."—*Drake's Shakspeare and his Times.*

1304 ——— Plays, with Notes, Critical and Explanatory, by W. Gifford, 4 vols. 8vo. *hf. cf. extra, marbled edges.* 1805

"This is the best edition of an English Dramatist that we have ever seen; the editor has done everything which was necessary and nothing more."—*Annual Review.*

1305 MASSINGER (*Phillip* and T. Dekker), Virgin Martyr, *sewed*, 4to. Lond. 1631

1306 ——— Another edition, *sewed*, 4to. Lond. 1661

1307 ——— Injured Virtue, or the Virgin Martyr, an alteration, by Benj. Griffin, *sewed*, 12mo. Lond. 1715

1308 ——— The Duke of Millaine, *sewed*, 4to. Lond. 1638

1309 ——— The Bondman, an ancient storie, as it has beene often acted, *sewed*, 4to. Lond, 1638

1310 ——— Another edition, *sewed*, 4to. Lond. 1624

1311 ——— The Renegado, a Tragie-Comedie, *first edition*, dedicated to George Harding, Baron of Barkley, with commendatory verses by James Shirley and D. Lakin, *half morocco*, 4to. Lond. 1630

1312 ——— The Picture, a Tragæ-Comedie, *sewed*, 4to. Lond. 1630

1313 ——— Emperour of the East, a Tragæ-Comedie, *sewed*, 4to. Lond. 1632

1314 ——— Maid of Honour, *sewed*, 4to. Lond. 1632

1315 ——— Fatal Dowry, a Tragedy, *sewed*, 4to. Lond. 1632

1316 ——— New Way to Pay Old Debts, *sewed*, 4to. Lond. 1633

1317 ——— Great Duke of Florence, a Comicall History, *half calf*, 4to. Lond. 1636

1318 ——— Unnaturall Combat, a Tragedie, *first edition*, *clean, large copy, half morocco*, 4to. Lond. 1639

1319 ——— Another copy, *sewed*, 4to. Lond. 1639

1320 ——— The Virgin Martyr, *with six designs*, by Pickersgill, *half calf*, square 8vo. Lond. 1844

1321 ——— Another copy, *cloth.* Lond. 1844

1322 ——— Beauties of, *half calf*, 12mo. Lond. 1847

"Pure and chastened Massinger, a Poet of unwearied vigour and consummate elegance, exhibits a perfectibility, both of diction and versification, of which we have, in dramatic poesy at least, no corresponding example. A transparency, perspicuity, sweetness, harmony, ductility, blended strength and ease, in structure of his Metre, which delight and never satiate."—*Dr. Draper.*

"The tragedies of Massinger have a calm and dignified seriousness, a lofty pride, that impresses the imagination very strongly. His genius was more eloquent and descriptive than impassioned or inventive; yet his pictures of suffering virtue, its struggles and its trials, are calculated to touch the heart, as well as gratify the taste. His versification is sweetly smooth and mellifluous."—*Chambers.*

1323 MAY (*Thomas*), The Tragedie of Cleopatra, Queen of Egypt, *calf*, 12mo. Lond. 1639

1324 ——— (*Thomas*), The Old Couple, a Comedy, *sewed*, 4to. Lond. 1658

1325 MAY (*Thomas*), The Heire, an excellent Comedie, *half calf*, 4to. Lond. 1622

1326 MAYNE (*Jasper*), Amorous Warre, a Tragi-Comedy, *interleaved*, 4to. Lond. 1648

1327 ——— The City Match, a Comœdy, and the Amorous Warre, a Tragi-Comœdy, *red morocco, calf back*, 1 vol. small 4to. Oxford, 1658–9

1328 MEAD (*Robert*), Combat of Love and Friendship, a Comedy, *sewed*, 4to. Lond. 1654

1329 ——— Another Copy, 4to. Lond. 1654

1330 MEDBURNE (*Mathew*), St. Cecily, or the Converted Twins, a Christian Tragedy, 1660, Tartuffe from Moliere, 1670, 1 vol. *half calf*, 4to. Lond.

1331 MEDEA in Corinth, a Tragic Opera, in 2 acts, *sewed*. 12mo. Lond.

1332 MEILAN (*M. A.*) Dramatic Works, 8vo. *calf.* Lond. n. d.

1333 MERCIER, Theatre, complete, 4 vols. *calf.* 12mo. Amst. 1778

1334 MERITON (*Thomas*), Love and War, a Tragedy, n. d., Wandering Lover, a Tragi-Comedy, 2 vols. in 1, *old calf, fine copies*, 4to. Lond. 1658

1335 ——— Love and War, a Tragedy, *curious*, 4to. *half bound.* Lond. 1658

"Certainly the meanest dramatic writer that England ever produced."—*Langbaine.*

1336 MERRIE Devill of Edmonton, reprint of an Elizabethan Drama, by an unknown author, 12mo. Lond.

"I wish it could be ascertained that Drayton was the author, it would add a worthy appendage to his renown."—*C. Lamb.*

1337 METASTATIO (*Pietro*). Opere, 4 vols. *half calf*, 12mo. Milan, 1822

1338 MICKLE (*W. J.*) Poems and a Tragedy, 4to. *calf.* Lond. 1704

1339 MIDDLETON (*Thomas*), The Dramatic Works of, now first collected, with some account of the Author, and Notes by the Rev. Alexander Dyce, 5 vols. 8vo. *half calf.* Lond. 1840

Most of his plays are pre-eminently beautiful, many portions only inferior to Shakspeare. They have hitherto been almost inaccessible from their rarity ; the value averaging from £20 to £30 a play.

"Mr. Dyce's unpretending and excellent edition."—*Edinburgh Review.*

"We take the opportunity of expressing our very high opinion of the diligence, skill, and judgment of Mr. Dyce, whose editions leave little to desire, and less to improve."—*Quarterly Review.*

1340 MIDDLETON (*Thomas*) The Phœnix, as it hath beene sundrie times acted by the Children of Paules, 4to. *half morocco.* Lond. 1630

1341 ——— Another copy, *calf, extra, large margin*, 4to. Lond. 1630

1342 ——— Michelmas Terme, *title soiled, half calf*, 4to. Lond. 1630

1343 ——— Mad World My Masters, a Comedy, *half calf*, 4to. Lond. 1640

1344 ——— A Game at Chess, as it was acted nine days together at the Globe on the Bankside, *no title, sewed*, 4to. Lond. 1624

This very curious and rare old play was suppressed, and the authors and actors imprisoned, as they had presumed to introduce on the stage the persons of the King of Spain, Count Gondomar, and the Bishop of Spalatro, whose portraits are on the frontispiece. Sir M. Sykes' copy sold for 6*l.* 2*s.* 6*d.*; Rhodes' for 4*l.* 14*s.* 6*d.*; and Towneley's for 4*l.* 15*s.*

1345 ——— Fletcher and Jonson, Widdow, a Comedie, *sewed*, 4to. Lond. 1652

1346 ——— and (W. Rowley). The Changeling, 4to. 1652

1347 ——— The Spanish Gipsie, a Comedy, 4to. 1661

1348 ——— Mayor of Quinborough, a Comedy, *half morocco*, 4to. Lond. 1661

1349 ——— Another copy, *half vellum*, 4to. Lond. 1778

1350 ——— Tragi-Comedie, called the Witch, 8vo. *boards, uncut.* 1778

Only 100 copies printed by Mr. Reed for presents. To this curious old play Shakspeare was greatly indebted for his Witches in Macbeth, &c. "Humor, wit, and elegance are to be found in the comedies of Middleton, and occasionally a pleasing interchange of elegant imagery and tender sentiment."—*Drake's Shakspeare and his times.*

1351 MINSHULL (*J.*) Rural Felicity, Sprightly Widow, She Stoops to Conquer, and Merry Dames, 8vo. N. Y. 1801–5

1352 MR. TURBULENT, or the Melanchollicks, a Comedy, as it was acted at the Duke's Theatre, 4to. interleaved, *half calf.* Lond. 1682

1353 MODERN Drama, vol. III., &c., 4 vols.

1354 MOLIERE, Les Œuvres de, avec des Remarques, &c., splendid old quarto edition, *with plates to each play, by Boucher*, &c., *elegant copy in French, cf. gt.*, 6 vols. 4to. Paris, 1734

1355 MOLIERE (*J. B.*) Œuvres, 4 vols. 18mo. *calf.* Utrecht, 1713

1356 MOLIERE, the Works of, the French Text with an English Translation on the opposite page, 10 vols. 12mo., with *plates* to each Play by Hogarth, &c., *old calf, neat, scarce, the only English translation.* Lond. 1755

1357 MOLIERE, French and English, vol. 8, 12mo. 1739

1358 MOLIERE, The Metamorphosis, or the Old Lover Outwitted, a Farce, 4to. *sewed.* Lond. 1704

1359 MONCRIEFF (*W. T.*), Selections from the Dramatic Works of, *cloth*, 3 vols. 8vo. Lond. 1851

1360 MONTI (*Vincenzo*), Tragedie, editio revista e corretta dall' autor, port. *Firenze* 1822; Lamento del Tasso di Lord Byron, recato in Italiano de Michele Leoni, Pisa 1818, in 1 vol. *large paper, uncut, half morocco*, 8vo. v. y.

1361 ——— Tragedie, 8vo. *vellum.* Firenzi, 1825

1362 MOORE (*Sir Thos.*) Mangora, King of the Timbusians, or the Faithful Couple,. 4to. *half calf.* Lond. 1718

The scene of this curious play is laid in Spanish America. The characters are Spaniards and Indians.

1363 MODERN British Drama (Tragedies, Comedies, Operas, and Farces), 5 vols. royal 8vo. *boards, Vignettes.* Lond. 1811

This very capital selection made by Sir Walter Scott, is ILLUSTRATED WITH NUMEROUS SCENIC PLATES. See also Lot 1572.

1364 MORAL Plays—Keep Your Temper; Fate of Ivan; Miss Betsy Bull, 8vo. *boards.* Lond. 1832

1365 MORE Ways than One, and other Plays, 8 vols.

1366 MOTTEUX, Loves a Jest, a Comedy, 1696; The Novelty, Every Act a Play, 1697; Beauty in Distress, 1698; Island Princess, 1699; Four Seasons, or Love in Every Age, 1699; Arsinœ, 1705; Thomyris, 1707; Love's Triumph, 1708; 8 vols. 4to. *sewed.* Lond.

1367 ———Loves a Jest, a Comedy, 4to. *sewed.* Lond. 1696

1367* ——— Island Princess, 4to. 1669

1368 MOTTLEY, The Imperial Captives, a Tragedy, 8vo. Lond. 1720

1369 MONTAGUE (*W.*) The Shepheard's Paradise, a Comedy, privately acted before the late King Charls, by the Queen's Majesty and ladies of honour, *scarce*, 8vo. Lond. 1659

1369* MOUNTFORT (*W.*) Successful Strangers, a Tragi-Comedy, 4to. 1690

1370 MOWATT (*A. C.*) Armand, presentation copy, with Author's Autograph, pp. 60, 12mo. Lond. 1849

1371 Munday (*Anthony*), John a Kent and John a Cumber, a Comedy, edited by J. P. Collier (Shakspeare Society), 8vo. *cloth.* Lond. 1851

1372 ——— Downfall of Robert, Earl of Huntington; Munday and Chettle's Death of Robert, Earl of Huntington, both edited by J. P. Collier. Lond. 1852

1373 Mysteries: Early Mysteries, and other Latin Poems of the XII. and XIII. Centuries, from original MS., &c., edited by T. Wright, *half calf.* Lond. 1845

1374 Nabbes (*Thomas*), Playes, Maskes, Epigrams, Elegies, and Epithalamiums, collected into one volume, 1639; Totenham-Court, a pleasant Comedy, 1639; Microcosmus, a Morall Maske, 1637; Hannibal and Scipio, an Historical Tragedy, 1637; The Spring, a Maske, 1639; Unfortune Mother, a Tragedie, 1640; Pride, a Comedie, 1640, in 2 vols. 4to. *half calf.* Lond. v. y.

1375 Nabbes' Microcosmus, 4to. 1772, and the Bride, 4to. 1640, 2 vols. in 1, *half calf.* Lond. v. d.

1376 Nash (*Th.*), Dido, Queen of Carthage, 1594; The Tragedy of Pierce Penniless; An Almond for a Parrot, reprint, 3 vols. Lond. v. d.

1377 Neville (*Henry*), Shuffling, Cutting, Dealing, in a Game at Pickquet, being acted from the year 1653 to 1658, as it was acted by Oliver Protector and others with great applause, 4to. *uncut.* Lond. 1659

1378 New British Theatre, a collection of Original Dramas, *Valpy*, 4 vols. 8vo. *half calf.* Lond. 1814

1379 New-Market Fayre, a Tragi-Comedy, called, or a Parliament Out-Cry of State Commodities; (Actors' names, Fairfax, Crum, their wives, Ireton, Mildmay, Skippon, Pride, &c.,) 4to. *half vellum, privately printed.* 1649

Written by some loyalist to satirize the Parliamentarians.

1380 New Theatrical Dictionary and Alphabetical Catalogue of Dramatic Writers, 12mo. *half calf.* Lond. 1792

1381 Nota (*Alb.*) Commedie, 4 vols. *cf.* 12mo. Milan, 1821

1381* Œdipus, a Tragedy, by Dryden and Lee, 4to. 1679

1382 O'Keefe (*John*), Dramatic Works, Author's own edition, 4 vols. 8vo. *calf, extra.* Lond. 1798

1383 Old English Plays, a selection from Early Dramatic Writers (by Dilke), 6 vols. 8vo. *large paper, half calf, fine copy.* 1814

A desirable accompaniment to Dodsley's collection. Contains Plays by Chapman, Marston, Rowley, Tourneur, Lily, &c., not reprinted in Dodsley, or any of the modern collections.

1384 OLDMIXON (*John*), Amintas, Grove, and Governor of Cypress, 4to. *half calf.* 1698–1703

1385 ——— Governour of Cypress, a Tragedy, 4to. *half morocco.* Lond. 1703

1386 OLD Plays, a Select Collection, 12 vols. imperfect, 12mo. Lond. 1780

1387 ORRERY (*Boyle, Earl of*), Six Plays, folio, *half calf.* Lond. 1694

1388 ORRERY (*Earl of*), Herod the Great, and Killigrew (*T*), The Prisoners, 1664, 2 vols. folio. Lond. v. d.

1389 OTWAY (*Thomas*), Works of, consisting of Plays, Poems, and Letters, 2 vols. 8vo. *half calf.* Lond. 1812

1390 ——— Alcibiades, a Tragedy, 1675; Don Carlos, Prince of Spain, a Tragedy, 1679; Titus and Berenice, a Tragedy, 1677; Friendship in Fashion, a Comedy, 1678; History and Fall of Caius Marius, 1692; The Orphan, 1696; Souldier's Fortune, 1683; Atheist, 1684; Venice Preserved, 1704; Heroick Friendship, 1719; all original editions, collected by W. E. Burton, 2 vols. 4to. *half bound, calf.* Lond.

1391 ——— Venice Preserved, and The Soldier's Fortune, 2 vols. 4to. Lond. 1681–2

1392 ——— The Atheist, or the Second Part of the Soldier's Fortune, 4to. *sewed.* Lond. 1684

"Next to Shakspeare, the greatest genius that England ever produced in Tragedy."—*Goldsmith.*

1393 OWEN (*Robert*), Hypermuestra, or Love in Tears, a Tragedy, 4to. *half calf.* Lond. 1703

1393* P. (*L.*), LANGUISHING Lady, a Pastoral, 12mo. *unbound,* Lond. 1718

1394 PADLOCK (*The*), A Comic Opera, 8vo. *half calf.* Lond. 1768

1394* PARNELL, A very Good Wife, 4to. *half calf* 1693

1395 PALAPRAT, Œuvres de, 18mo. La Haye, 1797

1396 PATHOMACHIA, or the Battell of Affections, shadowed by a faigned Siedge of the Citie of Pathopolis, a Comedy, 4to. 1690

1397 PATRIOT (*The*), or the Italian Conspiracy, a Tragedy, 4to. *sewed.* Lond. 1703

1398 PAULDING (*J. K. & W. I.*) American Comedies, 12mo. *boards.* Phil. 1847

1399 ——— Another copy, 12mo. *bds.* Phil. 1847

1399* PAYNE (*Nevil*), The Morning Rambles and The Just General, 2 vols. 4to. *half vellum* 1673

1400 PEAPS (*Wm.*) Love in its extasie, or the large Prerogative, a kind of Royall Pastorall, *cut close, half morocco*, 4to. Lond. 1649

1401 PEELE (*Geo.*) Dramatic Works, edited, with Life and Notes, by Dyce, 3 vols. 8vo. *half calf.* Lond. *Pickering*, 1829

"Peele and Marlowe were the contemporaries of Shakspeare; both had exquiste feelings for Poetry, and excelled in description, to which the former lent beauty, the latter sublimity."—*Gifford.*

1402 PEPOLI (*Aless.*) Tragedie, 8vo. Parma, 1783

1403 PERCY (*Wm.*) Cuck-Queanes and Cuckolds Errants, or the Bearing Down the Irene, a Comedye—and the Faery Pastorall, or Forest of Elves, 4to. *half calf.* 1824

Two most curious early English Dramas, printed from the original MS. found in the Roxburghe collection. Dent's copy sold for £3 11*s.*

1404 PELITOT, Repertoire Generale du Theatre Francais ou Collection des Chefs d'Œuvres Dramatique, &c., *beautiful edition, with fine engravings, &c.*, to each play, 23 vols. 8vo. *fine copy, full calf gt. contents lettered on each vol.* Paris, 1803

1405 PLEASANT conceited Comedy, How a Man May Choose a Good Wife from a Bad, *interleaved, half calf*, 4to. Lond. 1621

1406 ——— Another copy, 4to. *half calf.* Lond. 1634

1407 PHILIPS (*Katharine*), Poems, to which is added Corneille's Pompey and Horace, Tragedies, port. *half calf*, folio. Lond. 1678

1408 PICCOLOMINI (*Aless.*) Comedia, 24mo. *velum.* Venezia, 1612

PLAYS BOUND IN VOLUMES, AND IN PARCELS, SOME CURIOUS AND SCARCE.

1409 PLAYS, Tragedies, Comedies, &c., a very large collection of all the most popular Dramatic pieces which have been collected together at various times, altogether about 300, with list of contents in each volume, by Arch-deacon Wrangham, 59 vols. 8vo. v. y.

1410 ——— A large collection of popular plays in the time of George III., almost all corrected for the stage, many by the late W. E. B. *half morocco*, 10 vols. 8vo. Lond. v. y.

1411 ——— Alexander the Great, 5 vols. Manuscript Plays.

1412 ——— Alfred the Great, 22 Plays, *unbound.*

1413 PLAYS, Alfred, Donna Charitea, and Blue Beard, *three privately printed and acted plays*, in 1 vol. 12mo. *morocco extra, from Lord Ellesmere's collection.* 1841–3

1414 ——— Art of Poetry and Plays, 8 vols. odd. 12mo.

1415 ——— Barnett (*Moses*), The Tempest as a Lyrical Drama, 1850; Marriage Trump, by T. Heywood; Love's Mistress, by do.; Plays and Poems, by Marston; The Shade of Alex. Pope; Harlequin, Dr. Faustus; the Bard of Love, 7 poems, 8vo. v. p.

1416 ——— Belles' Stratagem, Blind Boy, Cælia, Gazette Extraordinary, and the Rivals, 8vo. *half calf.* v. d.

1417 ——— Bohemian (*The*), &c., 11 plays.

1418 ——— Brothers, Ways and Means, Don John, School for Friends, and Zoriuski, 8vo. *half morocco.* 1777, &c.

1419 ——— The Carib Chief, &c., 17 vol. plays, 12mo.

1420 ——— Child of Passion, &c., 12 plays.

1421 ——— Clandestine Marriage, 1766; Magic Picture, altered from Massinger by Bate; Ahab; Fall of the Mogul; Elfrida; Edwy; and Trip to Scarborough, 8vo. *half calf.* v. d.

1422 ——— Comedies, by Dryden, Beaumont, and Fletcher, Crown, &c., 8 plays, small 4to. Lond. v. d.

1423 ——— Conscious Lovers, &c., 10 vols.

1424 ——— Counterfeit, a Farce, &c., in all 20 vols.

1425 ——— Deserter, Three Weeks after Marriage, &c., 12mo.

1426 ——— Drummer, &c., 9 vols.

1427 ——— The Triumphs of Virtue and Fruitless Revenge, by Scott, 4 vols. 4to. *paper.* Lond. 1697

1428 ——— Esop, a Comedy, and three others, small 4to. Lond. 1697

1429 ——— First Love; Count of Narbonne; Vimonda; Word to the Wise; Siege of Sinope; Sultan; Law of Lombardy; Douglas and Percy, in 1 vol. 8vo. *half calf.* v. d.

1430 ——— False Delicacy and others.

1431 ——— Independent Patriot, 1737; The Knights, 1754; Livery Rake, 1733, 3 vols. in 1, *half calf.* v. d.

1432 ——— King Lear, Lord Cromwell, Venice Preserved, Morning Bride, Lady Jane Gray, Jane Shore, and Don Sebastian, 18mo. *calf.* 1733, &c.

1433 ——— The Orphan, Governour of Cyprus, by Oldmixon; The Cornish Comedy, 3 vols. 4to. *half calf.* Lond. v. d.

1434 PLAYS, Lease and Release, 7 plays.

1435 ——— Love's Mistress, &c., 10 plays.

1436 to 1485 ——— Comedies, Tragedies, Tragi-Comedies, Farces, and Operas, a large collection (over 3,000) arranged in parcels of from 25 to 100 in each lot, further particulars at the time of sale.

Many of these plays are prompt-books, and have the autograph alterations of W. B. Wood and W. E. Burton.

1486 ——— Malvina, Three Strangers, Benyowsky, Death of Ugolino, Saracens and Cantostarlos, Narrative of the Material Facts in relation to the Building of the Two Great Frigates, 8vo. v. d.

1487 ——— The Man's Bewitched, Beau's Duel, Abra-Mule and Xerxes, 12mo. *calf.* 1737, &c.

1488 ——— Odd vols. of, 8 vols. 16mo. *bound.*

1489 ——— Paris and London, 9 plays, *various.*

1490 ——— The Distrest Mother, a Tragedy, by Mr. Philips, 1712, La Creole, 2 vols. 4to. *half vellum.* Lond. and Paris

1491 ——— (*Pix, Mrs. Mary*), The Innocent Mistress, 1697; The Deceiver Deceived, 1698; The False Friend, 1699. 3 vols. in 1, 4to. *half vellum.* Lond.

1492 ——— *various*, 12mo. *bound*, 7 vols. v. d.

1493 ——— *various*, 16mo. 8 vols. v. d.

1494 ——— and Farces, a collection bound in 21 vols. 12mo. nearly all printed at Dublin, including many curious and rare local and provincial pieces not otherwise to be found, *half calf.* v. y.

1495 ——— Polly, Wedding Day, Robin Hood, Songs in Jack the Giant Killer, and Chrononhotonthologas 8vo. *half calf.* v. d.

1496 ——— Prince (*The*) is Come, a Farce; £20,000, or London Love, 2 vols. in MS.

1497 ——— Remorse, by S. F. Coleridge, editor of the Black Prince, The Drummer, Haunted House, Maid of the Mill, Tarrataria, Dido, 6 vols. 12mo. Lond. v. d.

1498 ——— Reparation, Step-Mother, Cabin Chief, The Sultan, Siege of Cuzco, Feudal Times, Self-Immolation, Prince of Tunis, 1 vol. 8vo. *half calf.* 1773, 1823

1499 ——— Riches, The Exile, Emelia Galotti, Bondman, Maid of Honour, Fatal Dowry, Foundling of the Forest, Man and Wife, Venani, New Way to Pay Old Debts, Alfonso, and Free Knight, 8vo. *calf.* Phil. v. d.

1500 PLAYS, Rinaldo and Armida, by Dennis, &c. 4 plays, 4to. Lond. v. d.

1501 ——— Select Plays, 8 vols. 12mo. Lond. v. d.

1502 ——— Talfourd's Athenian Captive, Knowles' Maid of Mariendorpt (autograph of Knowles), St. Leon, Jones' Spartacus and Bird's Cosmo, 1 vol. 8vo. *half calf.* Lond. 1835–38

1503 ——— Tempest, How to Grow Wise, and The Devil to Pay, 3 vols. in 1, *calf.* 1785

1504 ——— Tracy's Penander, Cibber's Papal Tyranny, Mitchell's Fatal Extravagance, Hospital for Fools, T. Cibber's Lover, Timon in Love, Universal Passion.

1505 ——— Twelfth Night, The Confederacy, Douglas, and Who's the Dupe, 18mo. *cloth.* Boston, 1823

1506 ——— Veteran, The Beggar's Opera, Guy Mannering, Duenna, Waterman, Purses, Broken Sword, Musical Lady, and The Woodman's Hut, 8vo. *half calf.* v. d.

1507 ——— Venice Preserved and others, 9 vols.

1508 ——— Collected by W. E. Burton, &c., 16 vols. 12mo.

1509 ——— Whims and Oddities, 10 vols.

1510 ——— Young's Revenge, Revised by J. P. Kemble; the Poetical, by Dr. Johnson; the Cabinet, by Thomas Dibdin; the Grecian Daughter; All in the Wrong, a Comedy; Isabella, or the Fatal Marriage; Man of the World, 7 vols. 12mo. Lond. v. d.

1511 POCAHONTAS, a Historical Drama, *sewed*, 8vo. N. Y. 1837

1512 PORTER (*Henry*), The Two Angry Women of Abington, edited by Alexander Dyce, *half calf.* 8vo. Lond. 1841

1513 ——— (*Thos.*) The Villain, The French Conjuror, a Comedy, and two others, 2 vols. 4to. *half calf.* Lond. 1678

1514 POWELL (*George*), Alphonse King of Naples, a Tragedy, 1691; Very Good Wife, a Comedy, 1691; Treacherous Brothers, a Tragedy, 1696; Imposture Defeated, or a Trick to Cheat the Devil, 1698; Cornish Comedy, 1696; Bonduca, altered by Powell, 1696; Brutus of Alba, 1697; Collected in 1 vol. *half calf.* 4to. Lond.

1515 ——— (*G.*) A new Opera called Brutus of Alba, *sewed*, 1697; Cornish Comedy, *sewed*, 1696; Alphonse King of Naples, *sewed*, 1691; A Very Good Wife, *half calf.* 1693, 4to. Lond.

1516 POWELL (*Th.*) The Blind Wife, or the Student of Bonn, 8vo. Lond. 1843

1517 PRESTON (*Thomas*), A Lamentable Tragedie, mixed full of pleasant mirth, containing the Life of Cambises King of Percia, from the Beginning of his Kingdome unto his Death, &c. **Black Letter**, *sewed, imprinted by Edward Allde.* Lond. v. d.

Bindley's copy sold for £12 15*s*. At Sotheby's, 1821, it sold for £15. Written about 1561. Langbaine imagines Shakspeare meant to ridicule this performance, when, in his play of Henry IV., Part I., Act II., he makes Falstaff talk of speaking *in King Cambyses' vein.*

1518 PROLOGUES and Epilogues, Collection of more than 800 (including all those written by Garrick), with Notes, &c., by Griffith, 4 vols. 12mo., *fine character portraits, calf, gilt.* Lond. 1779

1519 PROVERBES Dramatiques, Manuel de, 12mo. *boards.* 1830

1520 QUARLES (*Francis*), The Virgin Widow, a Comedie, 4to. Lond. 1656

1521 QUEENE of Arragon, by W. Habington and others. 6 Plays, in 2 vols. small 4to. Lond. 1640–1702

1522 RALPH Roister Doister, a Comedy, Udal, and the Tragedy of Gorbodne, by Norton and Sackville, edited by W. D. Cooper, 8vo. *Shakspeare Society*, Lond., 1847

1523 RAMSAY (*Allen*), Gentle Shepherd, a Scots Pastoral Comedy, 12mo. Edin. 1776

1524 RANDOLPH (*Thomas*), Poems with the Muses, Looking-Glass, and Amyntas, &c., *wants front.*, 12mo. Lond. 1668

1525 ——— Aristippus, or the Joviall Philosopher, Demonstratively proving that Quartes, Pintes, and Pottles, are sometimes necessary authors in a Scholar's Library, to which is added the Conceited Pedlar, *sewed, uncut*, 4to. Lond. 1630

1526 ——— The Jealous Lovers, by Reviére, *half red morocco, extra*, 4to. Camb. 1632

1527 ——— Pleasant Comedie, entitled Hey for Honesty Down with Knavery, *half calf*, 4to. Lond. 1651

1528 RAVENSCROFT (*Edward*), The Dramatic Works of, being a collection of the Original Quartos collected and collated by W. E. Burton, 2 vols. 4to. *half calf, neat.* v. y.

1529 ——— The Anatomist: or, the Sham Doctor, a Farce, 8vo. *sewed, uncut.* Lond. 1807

1530 RAWLINS (*Thomas*), Rebellion, a Tragedy, *sewed*, 4to. Lond. 1646

1531 —— Tom Essence: or, the Modish Wife, a Comedy, *sewed*, 4to. Lond. 1677

1532 REPERTOIRE Général du Theatre Français, 66 vols. 12mo. *half morocco.* Paris, 1818

1533 —— Dramatique de la Scene Française, 176 numbers, *sewed*, 18mo. Bruxelles, 1829

1534 —— Dramatique, 8 vols. 18mo. Bruxelles, 1830

1535 —— de Theatre de Moderne, 8 vols. 18mo. Paris, 1827

1536 REVENGE (*The*), or Match in Newgate, a Comedy, small 4to. *boards.* Lond. 1680

1537 RIDER (*W.*) The Twins, a Tragi-Comedy, acted at the Private House, Salisbury Court, *sewed*, 4to. Lond. 1655

1538 ROCHESTER (*Earl of*), Valentinian, a Tragedy, as acted at the Royal Theatre, with a long and very curious preface concerning the author and his writings, 4to. *half calf.* Lond. 1685

1539 ROUX (*A. A.*) Louise Necker, a Comedy, 12mo. N. Y. 1850

1540 ROWE (*Nicholas*), Ambitious Step-Mother, 1701; Tamerlan e, a Tragedy, 1703; Fair Penitant, a Tragedy, 1703; The Biter, a Comedy, 1705; Ulysses, 1706; Royal Convert, a Tragedy, 1708; Tragedy of Jane Shore, n. d.; Tragedy of Lady Jane Gray, 1715; *original editions*, 2 vols. *half calf*, 4to. Lond. v. y.

1541 ROWLEY (*Samuel*), When you see Me you know Me, or the Famous Chronicle History of King Henry the Eighth, &c., *woodcut of Henry VIII*, 1632; The Noble Souldier, or a Contract Broken Justly Revenged, a Tragedy, 1634, *both interleaved*, 2 vols. 4to. Lond.

1542 ROWLEY (*William*), A New Wonder, A Woman Never Vext, a Comedy, 4to. Lond. 1622

1543 —— All's Lost by Lust, a Tragedy, 4to. Lond. 1633

1544 —— A Match at Midnight, a Comedie, 4to. Lond. 1633

1545 —— A Shoo-maker a Gentleman, a Comedy, 4to. Lond. 1638

1546 —— Birth of Merlin, by William Shakespear and W. Rowley, *half russia*, 4to. Lond. 1662

The following plays were written in conjunction with others.

1547 ROWLEY, Day and Wilkins, The Travailes of the Three English Brothers: Sir Thomas, Sir Anthony, and Mr. Robert Shirley, as it is now played by her Majesties Servants, *interleaved*, *sewed*, 4to. Lond. 1607

1548 ——— and Middleton, A Farie Quarrell, with new additions of Mr. Chaugh's and Trimtram's Roaring and the Baud's Song, 4to. Lond. 1622

1549 ——— and Middleton, A Courtly Masque, The Device called The World Tost at Tennis, *curious old woodcut*, 4to. Lond. 1640

1550 ——— and Middleton, Changeling, as it was acted (with great applause) *half morocco*, 4to. Lond. 1653

1551 ——— Massinger and Middleton, Excellent Comedy, called the Old Law, 4to. *half calf*. Lond. 1656

1552 ——— and Webster, Cure for a Cuckhold, a pleasant Comedy, *half morocco*, 4to. Lond. 1661

1553 ——— and Webster, Thracian Wonder, a comical History, by T. Webster and W. Rowley, *sewed*, 4to. Lond. 1661

1554 ——— and Middleton, Spanish Gipsie, 4to. Lond. 1653

1555 ——— and Heywood, Fortunes by Land and Sea, a Tragi-Comedy, by Heywood and Rowley, 4to. Lond. 1655

1556 ——— Search for Money, 12mo. Percy Society, 1840

1557 RUGGLE (*George*), Ignoramus, Comedia, *large paper*, 12mo. *half calf*. Westminster, 1731

1558 ——— Ignoramus, a Comedy, Latin and English, with Notes, Glossary and Life, by J. S. Hawkins, *frontispiece after Stothard*, *old calf*, 8vo. Lond. 1787

"This comedy was played by the Students at Cambridge, before King James I. It was composed with a view to ridicule the common Law and Lawyers of England, a subject extremely agreeable to James, who detested all laws the people had any hand in framing."

"The English Notes and Glossary contain a fund of information on historical, philological, and legal points."

1559 RUTTER (*Joseph*), Shepheard's Holy Day, 1635; The Cid, Tragi-Comedy, 1650; The Cid, 1650, with the original, by Corneille, 1666, 3 vols. *uniform*, *half calf*, 12mo. Lond. v. y.

1560 RYLEY (*S. W.*) Roderic Random, a comic Opera, and the Civilian, a Musical Farce, and several comic Songs, 12mo. *half calf*. Huddersfield, n. d.

1561 RYMER (*Thomas*), Edgar, or the English Monarch, *sewed*, 4to. Lond. 1678

1562 ——— Another copy, 4to. *half calf*. Lond. 1678

1563 S. (*S.*) The Honest Lawyer, acted by the Queene's Majestie Servants, interleaved, *half calf*, 4to. Lond. 1616

1564 SAGGIONE (*J.*) The Temple of Love, &c., 5 Plays in 1 vol. Lond. 1706

1565 SAMPSON (*William*), The Vow Breaker, or the Faire Maide of Clifton, Nottinghamshire, 4to. Lond. 1636

1566 SAVAGE (*Richard*), Tragedy of Sir Thomas Overbury, 8vo. *half calf.* Lond. 1724

1567 SAUNDERS (*C.*) Tamerlane the Great, a Tragedy, interleaved, 4to. *half calf.* Lond. 1681

1568 SAVIÑON (*Don Antonio*), Roma Libre, Tragedia, 18mo. *red morocco.* Cadiz, 1812

1569 SCHILLER (*F.*) Don Carlos, translated, 8vo. Balt. 1834

1570 SCHILLER'S William Tell and other Poems, by W. Peter, 18mo. Phila. 1840

1571 SCOTT (*Thomas*), Unhappy Kindness, or a Fruitless Revenge, *half calf*, 4to. Lond. 1697

1572 SCOTT (*Sir W.*) Ancient British Drama, 3 vols. royal 8vo. *half calf.* (See Lot 1363.) Lond. 1810

This collection is chiefly founded on the old plays of Dodsley, to which are added a large number not included in that collection, but which have kept possession of the stage, and are still popular.

1573 SECOND Maiden's Tragedy, from the MS. in the Lansdown collection, *sewed*, 12mo. Lond. 1804

1574 SEDLEY (*Sir Chas.*) Bellamira, 4to. 1687

1575 ——— Anthony and Cleopatra, a Tragedy, *half calf*, 4to. Lond. 1677

1576 ——— The Mulberry Garden, a Comedy, *half calf*, 4to. Lond. 1673

1577 SELECT Dramatic Pieces, viz: Boarding School Miss, One and All, Disguise, Musico, Who's Afraid, and the Bulse, 8vo. *calf.* Lond. 1787

1578 SELECT London Stage, a collection of the most reputed Tragedies, Comedies, Operas, Melo-Dramas, Farces, and Interludes, 8vo. *cloth.* Lond. n. d.

1579 SETTLE (*Elkanah*), Cambyses, King of Persia, a Tragedy, *half calf*, 4to. Lond. 1691

1580 ——— Conquest of China by the Tartars, a Tragedy, *sewed*, 4to. Lond. 1676

1581 ——— Female Prelate, being the History of the Life and Death of Pope Joan, a Tragedy, *half calf*, 4to. Lond. 1680

1582 SETTLE (*Elkanah*), The New Athenian Comedy, *half vellum*, 4to. Lond. 1693

1583 ——— The World in the Moon, an Opera, *half calf*, 4to. Lond. 1697

1584 ——— The City Ramble, or Play-house Wedding, a Comedy, *half calf*, 4to. Lond. 1711

For an account of this author (who was the last of the City Poets) vide D'Israeli's Curiosities.

1585 SHADWELL (*Charles*), Five Plays—The Hasty Wedding, The Sham Prince, Rotherick O'Conner, King of Connaught, The Plotting Lovers, Irish Hospitality, *half calf*, 12mo. 1720

1586 SHADWELL (*Thomas*), Royal Shepherdess, 1669; Sullen Lovers, 1668; Humourists, 1671; Epsom Wells, 1673; Psyche, 1675; The Libertine, 1676; The Virtuoso, 1691; Timon of Athens (altered from Shakspeare), 1678, in 1 vol. *half calf*; The Miser, 1691; True Widow, 1679; Squire of Alsatia, 1688; Busy Fair, 1689; Scowrers, 1691, all *unbound*, forming vol. 2, 4to. London, v. y.

1587 ——— Timon of Athens, 4to. *half calf.* Lond.

1588 ——— Lancashire Witches, Amorous Bigot, Woman Captain, and Libertine, 4to. *half calf.* Lond. 1691 to 1705

1589 ——— Epsom Wells, a Comedy, 4to. *boards.* Lond. 1676

1590 ——— Squire of Alsatia, a Comedy, *many alterations and corrections in an old hand*, *calf*, 4to. Lond. 1688

This play is full of the slang of the day.
"The plays of Shadwell have in them fine strokes of humour; the characters are often originals, strongly marked, and well sustained."

SHAKSPEARE and Shakspeariana. *See* separate headings: SHAKSPEARIAN GALLERY, Statues, Busts. *See* Curiosities, &c.

1591 SHARPE'S British Theatre, *beautifully printed*, 18 vols. 24mo. *calf.* Lond. *Whittingham*, 1805

1592 SHARPE (*Lewis*), The Noble Stranger, as it was acted at the Private in Salisbury Court, interleaved, 4to. *half calf.* Lond. 1640

1593 SHARPHAM (*Edward*), The Fleire, a Comedy, no title, 4to. *half vellum.* Lond.

1594 ——— Another edition, fine copy, interleaved. 1615

1595 ——— Cupid's Whirligig, 4to. *half calf.* Lond. 1616

(This play has been attributed to Shakspeare.)

1596 SHEPPEARD (*S.*) Committee Man Curried, a Comedy, 4to. Lond. 1647

This is a satire, and surreptitiously printed.

1597 SHERBURNE (*Edward*), Troades, or the Royal Captives, a Tragedy, translated from Seneca, 8vo. interleaved in 4to. Lond. 1679

1598 SHERIDAN (*R. B.*) Dramatic Works, edited by Leigh Hunt, royal 8vo. Lond. *Moxon*, 1846

1599 ——— School for Scandal, interleaved, 18mo. *sheep.* 1786

This edition was privately printed; the present copy wants the last leaf, but the matter is supplied in MS. by the Author, Hon. R. B. Sheridan.

"Whatever Sheridan has done has been *par excellence*, always the best of its kind. He has written the best comedy (School for Scandal); the best drama (The Duenna); the best farce (The Critic); and the best address (Monologue on Garrick); and to crown all, delivered the very best oration (the famous Begum Speech) ever conceived or heard in this country."—*Byron.*

1600 SHERLEY (*Sir Anthony, Sir Robert, and Sir Thomas*), The Three Brothers' Travels in Persia, Russia, Turkey, Spain, &c., *portraits, calf,* 8vo. Lond. 1828

1600*a* SHIRLEY (*Henry*), The Martyr'd Souldier, as it was sundry times acted with generall applause, at the Private House in Drury Lane, and at other Publicke Theatres, interleaved, 4to. *half calf.* Lond. 1638

1600*b* ——— Another copy, *half calf, ib. ib.*

1600*c* ——— Another.

1600*d* SHIRLEY (*James*), Dramatic Works and Poems of, with his Life, &c., edited by Wm. Gifford and Rev. A. Dyce, *large paper,* 6 vols. royal 8vo. *portrait, half calf, lettered contents.* Lond. 1833

"Shirley claims a place among the worthies of this period, as the last of a great race, all of whom spoke nearly the same language, and had a set of moral feelings and notions in common."—*Charles Lamb.*

1600*e* ——— The Wedding, acted at the Phenix, 1st edition, 4to. *half morocco.* Lond. 1629

1600*f* ——— Another edition, 4to. *sewed.* Lond. 1633

1600*g* ——— Another edition, 4to. *sewed.* Lond. 1660

1600*h* ——— Grateful Servant, 4to. interleaved.

1600*i* ——— Changes, or Love in a Maze, a Comedie, 4to. *half morocco.* Lond. 1632

1600*j* ——— Another copy, 4to. *sewed.* Lond. 1632

1600*k* ——— Contention for Honour and Riches, a Masque, 4to. *sewed.* Lond. 1633

1601 SHIRLEY (*James*), The Witty Fair One, 4to. *half morocco.* Lond. 1633

1602 ——— Triumph of Peace, a Masque, 4to. *half morocco.* Lond. 1633

1603 ——— Bird in a Cage, a Comedie, 4to. *sewed.* Lond. 1633

1604 ——— Traytor, a Tragedy, 4to. *sewed.* Lond. 1635

1605 ——— Lady of Pleasure, a Comedie, 4to. *sewed.* Lond. 1637

1606 ——— Another copy, 4to. *sewed.* Lond. 1637

1607 ——— Young Admirall, 4to. *sewed.* Lond. 1637

1608 ——— The Example, a Tragi-Comedy, 4to. Lond. 1637

1609 ——— Gamester, 4to. *sewed.* Lond. 1637

1609* ——— Royal Master, 4to. interleaved.

1610 ——— Duke's Mistress, a Comedie; Autograph of, and Notes by O. Gilchrist, interleaved, 4to. *sewed.* Lond. 1637

1611 ——— Another edition, 4to. *half morocco.* Lond. 1638

1612 ——— Maide's Revenge, a Tragedy, 4to. *sewed.* Lond. 1639

1613 ——— Tragedie of Chabot, Admirall of France, by Chapman and Shirley, 4to. *sewed.* Lond. 1635

1614 ——— The Ball, a Comedie, 4to. *sewed.* Lond. 1639

1615 ——— A Pastorale, called the Arcadia, 4to. *sewed.* Lond. 1640

1616 ——— Humorous Courtier, a Comedy, 4to. *half calf.* Lond. 1640

1617 ——— Opportunitie (no title), 4to. *sewed.* Lond. 1640

1618 ——— St. Patrick for Ireland, *sewed,* 4to. Lond. 1640

1619 ——— Love's Crueltie, a Tragedy, *sewed,* 4to. Lond. 1640

1620 ——— Constant Maid, a Comedy, *half morocco,* 4to. Lond. 1640

1621 ——— Coronation, written by John Fletcher, *interleaved, sewed,* 4to. Lond. 1640

1622 ——— Brothers, a Comedie, *sewed,* 8vo. Lond. 1652

1623 ——— Sisters, a Comedie, *sewed,* 8vo. Lond. 1652

1624 ——— Doubtful Heire, a Tragi-Comedie, *sewed,* 8vo. Lond. 1652

1625 ——— Cardinal, a Tragedie, *sewed,* 8vo. Lond. 1652

1625* ——— The Imposture, 4to. *interleaved.*

1625† ——— Court Secret, 4to. *interleaved.*

1625‡ ——— Gentleman of Venice, 4to. *interleaved.*

1626 ——— Politician, a Tragedy, *half morocco,* 4to. Lond. 1655

1627 SHIRLEY (*James*), Cupid and Death, a Masque, 4to. *half calf.* 1659

1628 ——— Honoria and Mammon, 8vo. Lond. 1659

1629 ——— Royal Master, and Maid's Revenge, and Love's Mistress, by Heywood, in 1 vol. *half calf*, 8vo. *reprints.* Lond. 1792–3

1630 ——— Plays of, The Duke's Mistris, Love Tricks, The Example, 3 vols. 4to. *interleaved.* Lond. 1637

Shirley and his wife both died from fright, within twenty-four hours, at the great fire in London, 1666, after having removed from his house in Fleet Street to St. Giles in the Fields.

1631 SIEGE and Surrender of Mons, a Tragedy-Comedy, exposing the Villany of the Priests, and the Intrigues of the French, *half calf*, La. 4to. Lond. 1691

1832 SIR GYLES' Goose-Cappe, a Comedy lately acted with great applause at the private house in Salisbury Court, *half calf*, *interleaved*, 4to. Lond. 1635

1633 SIX Old Plays, on which Shakspeare founded his Measure for Measure, Comedy of Errors, Taming of the Shrew, King John, Kings Henry IV. and V., and King Lear.
See also under Shakspeariana.

1634 SMITH (*Edmund*), Phædrus and Hippolitus, a Tragedy, *half calf*, La. 4to. Lond. 1707

1635 ——— (*W.*) Hector of Germany, or the Palsgrave, Prime Elector, a new play, an Honorable History, *sewed*, 4to. Lond. 1615

1636 SMOLLETT (*T.*) The Reprisal, or the Tars of England, a Comedy, 8vo. *half calf.* Lond. 1757

1637 SOPHOCLES' Electra and Œdipus, translated by Theobald, 2 vols. 12mo. 1714–15

1638 SOUTHERNE (*Thomas*), Plays, *first collected edition by Evans*, 3 vols. *half calf*, 12mo. Lond. 1774

1639 ——— Disappointment, or the Mother in Fashion, a Play, *sewed*, 4to. Lond. 1684

1640 ——— Oroonoko, a Tragedy, *sewed*, 4to. Lond. 1696

1641 ——— Fate of Capua, a Tragedy, *sewed*, 4to. Lond. 1700

1642 ——— Money the Mistress, a Play, *half calf*, 8vo. Lond. 1726

1643 SPANIARDS in Peru, expressed by Instrumentall and Vocall Music, and by Art of Perspective in Scenery, represented daily at the Cock-pit, in Drury Lane, at three afternoons punctually, 4to. *half calf.* Lond. 1648

1644 SPANISH Exile, a Play, 12mo. pp. 38. Charleston, 1844

1645 STAPYLTON (*Sir Robert*), The Slighted Maid, 1663; Step-Mother, a Tragi-Comedy, 1664; Tragedie of Hero and Leander, 1669, in 1 vol. *half calf.* 4to. Lond. v. y.

1646 STEELE (*Sir Richard*), Dramatick Works, Conscious Lovers, Funeral, Tender Husband, Lying Lover, *half calf*, 12mo. Lond. 1736

1647 ——— The Funeral, or Grief a-la-mode, *sewed*, 4to. Lond. 1704

1648 ——— Lying Lover, or the Ladies' Friendship, *sewed*, 4to. Lond. 1704

1649 ——— Another copy, 4to. *half vellum.* Lond. 1704

1650 ——— Ladies' Friendship, *sewed*, 4to. Lond. 1704

1651 STEPHENS (*G.*) Dramas for the Stage, comprising Nero and Sensibility, Tragedies; Self-Glorification, a Chinese Play; Rebecca and her Daughters, a Comedy; Philip Basil, or a Poet's Fate, etc., 2 vols. 8vo., *only 150 copies privately printed.* 1846

"Genius there is in George Stephens."—*Times.*

1652 ——— (*John*), Cinthia's Revenge, or Menander's Extasie, *interleaved, half calf.* 4to. Lond. 1613

1653 STEPMOTHER, by the Earl of Carlisle, 8vo. *half calf.* 1800

1654 STERLINE (*William Alexander, Earl of*) Recreation of the Muses, Four Monarchicke Tragedies, Doomesday, &c., folio, *half calf.* Lond. 1635

1655 STOCK Plays, Oxberry's edition, 6 vols. 16mo. Bost. 1832

1656 STRUTT (*Joseph*), Test of Guilt, a Dramatic Tale, *boards*, 4to. Lond. 1808

1657 SUCKLING (*Sir John*), Fragmenta Aurea, a collection of all the Incomparable Pieces of, The Tragedy of Brenneralt, The Goblins, a Comedie, Aglaura, Poems, Letters, etc., 8vo. *calf, gilt, first edition scarce.* Lond. 1658

1658 ——— Poems, Plays, Letters, &c., 8vo. *half calf.* Dub. 1766

As a writer, Sir John Suckling will command admiration, so long as a taste for whatever is delicate and natural in poetry shall remain. In description of feminine grace and beauty he is peculiarly happy; and his ballads and songs, the grace and elegance of which, says Mr. Ellis, are inimitable, will render his fame imperishable.

1659 ——— Aglaura, 1st edition, *interleaved, half calf.* Lond. 1638

1660 SUCKLING (*Sir John*), The Discontented Colonell, *sewed*, 4to. Lond. n. d.

1661 ——— Selections from the Works of, with a Life of the Author, with Critical Remarks on his Genius, by Rev. Alfred Suckling, royal 8vo. *port. half calf.* Lond. 1836

This darling of the muses was worthy to be crowned with a wreath of stars.—*Winstanley*.

1662 SWETNAM (*Joseph*), The Arraignment of Lewd, Idle, Froward, and Unconstant Women, or the Vanity of Them, Chuse You Whether, *wood cut*, 1667; Swetnam, the Woman-hater, Arraigned by the Women, a new Comedie, *wood cut*, 1620, *in 1 vol. both very scarce, half calf.* 4to. Lond. v. y.

1663 SWINY (*Owen Mac*), Camilla, an Opera, *boards*, 4to. Lond. 1706

1664 ——— Pyrrhus and Demetrius, an Opera, *sewed*, 4to. Lond. 1709

1665 TAYLOR (*Robert*), The Hogge hath lost his Pearle, a Comedy, divers times publikely acted by several London Prentices, 4to. *half russia.* Lond. 1614

This scarce and very curious old play is enumerated by Beloe as not among Garrick's rare plays in the British Museum.

1666 TATE (*Nahum*), Ingratitude of a Commonwealth, or the Fall of Caius Martius Coriolanus (altered from Shakspeare), with Songs set to Music, *sewed*, 4to. Lond. 1688

1667 ——— Island Princess, or the Generous Portugal, a Comedy (altered from Beaumont and Fletcher), *sewed*, 4to. Lond. 1669

1668 ———Cuckold's Haven, or an Alderman no Conjuror, *sewed*, 4to. Lond. 1685

1669 ———Injured Lover, or the Cruel Husband, a Tragedy, *sewed*, 4to. Lond. 1707

1670 ——— Another copy, *half calf.* Lond.

1671 ——— Brutus of Alba; Loyall General, 1680; History of Richard the Second, 1681; History of King Lear, 1681, *all fine copies from Lutterel's Collection, the two last altered from Shakspeare, sewed*, 4to. Lond. v. y.

1672 TATHAM (*John*), Distracted State, a Tragedy, written 1641, *sewed*, 4to. Lond. 1651

1673 ——— Scots Figgaries, or a Knot of Knaves, a Comedy, *sewed*, 4to. Lond. 1652

1674 ——— The Rump, or Mirror of the Late Times, a Comedy, *sewed*, 4to. Lond. 1661

1675 TAYLOR (*H.*) Henry the Fair, 4to. N. Y. 1843

1676 TEATRO Comico di Augusto Bon, *calf*, 12mo. Milan, 1823

1677 TEATRO Italiano, *vellum*, 12mo. Verona, 1723

1678 ——— Italiano Antico, 10 vols. *half bound*, *fine portraits.* Milano, 1808

*** A very excellent collection, containing the whole of the comedies of Pietro Aretino, and the principal dramatic pieces of Allemanni, Ariosto, Berni, Chiabrera, Dolce, Giraldi Cinthio, Tasso, and other equally esteemed authors.

"Recueil recherche, et peu commun."—*Brunet.*

1679 TERENCE's Comedies, translated by Cooke, 2 vols. 12mo. Lond. 1749

1680 ——— Comedies, translated by G. Colman into familiar blank verse, *illustrated with portraits*, 2 vols. *half calf*, 8vo. Lond. 1768

"A better translation can scarcely be expected; it is such as Terence deserved, and done by a man of almost equal comic powers with himself.—*Clarke.*

1681 THEATRE Burlesque, 2 vols. 18mo. Paris, 1840

1682 ——— Complet des Latins, par J. B. Levee, et le Monnier, *half calf*, 15 vols. 8vo. Paris, 1820

Composed of the following authors in Latin and French : Plautus, 8 vols. by Levee ; Terence, 3 vols. by Monnier ; Seneca, 3 vols. by Levee ; Fragments of Ennius, &c., 1 vol. by the same.

1683 ——— De la Foire, ou l'Opéra Comique, les meilleures pièces qui ont été représentées aux Foires de St. Germain et de St. Laurent, 9 vols. 12mo. *numerous engravings with the music of the songs*, *fine impressions*, *old calf gt. curious.* Amsterdam, 1723

1684 ——— Espagnol, Lope de Vegá, traduit en Francais, *half morocco extra*, 2 vols. 8vo. Paris, 1827

1685 ——— Français Repertoire, par Lepeintre, 1 to 4; 8 to 30, 34 to 36; 38 to 40; 42 to 47; 62 to 67; 72 to 76; 78 and 80; Fin de Repertoire 2 to 10; 13, 15, 27 and 41; Fin 2nde ordre, 6 odd vols. *sewed*, 18mo.

1686 THEOBALD (*L.*) The Fatal Secret, a Tragedy, 8vo. *half calf.* Lond. 1735

1687 THOMPSON (*B.*) German Theatre, translated by B. Thompson, *cl.* 6 vols. 12mo. Lond. 1811

1688 ——— Another copy, *bds.* 6 vols. 12mo. Lond. 1811

1689 THURMOND (*George*), Harlequin Doctor Faustus, with the Mask of the Deities, *half calf*, 8vo. Lond. 1724

1690 THYESTES, a Tragedy, translated out of Seneca, to which is added Mock Thyestes in Burlesque, *half calf*, 12mo.. Lond. 1674

1691 TIMON of Athens, &c., 6 old plays.

1693 TOMKIS, Albumazar, a Comedy, *half morocco*, 4to. Lond. 1634

1694 TOURNEUR (*Cyril*), The Revenger's Tragedy, Atheist's Tragedy, 4to. *half calf.* Lond. 1780–92

1695 TRAGEDIES, by Dennis, N. Tate, J. Shirley, and Hopkins, 4 vols. 4to. *paper.* Lond. 1637 to 1700

1696 ——— A Collection of, in three thick vols. 8vo. *half morocco.* 1798, &c.

1697 TRAPP (*Joseph*), Tragedy of Saul, 1703; Abra-Mule, 1704, first edition in 1 vol. *half calf*, 4to. Lond. v. y.

1698 TRIAL for Murder: or, the Siege of Calais Besieged, 4to. Lond. 1765

1699 TRIUMPHS of Virtue, a Tragi-Comedy, 4to. *half calf.* 1697

1700 TRUE and Exact Catalogue of all the Plays and other Dramatick Pieces that were ever yet printed in the English Tongue in Alphabetical order, continued down to April, 1732, 12mo. *half calf.* Lond. 1732

1701 TUKE (*S.*) Adventures of Five Hours, a Tragi-Comedy, *interleaved, half calf*, folio. Lond. 1663

Pepys' favorite play.—*See his Diary.*

1701* VALIANT Welshman, a Tragi-Comedy, 4to. 1615

1702 VANBRUGH (*Sir John*), Plays, 2 vols. *half calf*, 12mo. Lond. 1719

1703 VERBRUGGEN (*John*), New Opera called Brutus of Alba, *half calf*, 4to. Lond. 1697

1704 VOLTAIRE, Theatre Choisi, *half morocco, top edges gilt, uncut*, 7 vols. 8vo. Paris, 1831

1705 ——— (*M. de*), The Dramatic Works of, translated by Downman and Williams, 2 vols. 8vo. *half calf, very neat.* Lond. 1781

Contains Œdipus, Brutus, Mariamne, Death of Cæsar, the Tattler, Nanine, the Prodigal, the Coffee House, Lord of the Manor, &c.

1706 W. (*J.*) The Valiant Scot, a Play, *fine copy, scarce*, 4to. Lond. 1637

From the History of Sir W. Wallace, dedicated to the Marquis of Hamilton by Wm. Bowyer.

1707 WALKER (*William*), Victorious Love, a Tragedy, *sewed*, 4to. Lond. 1698

1708 WALLER (*Edmond*), Pompey the Great, a Tragedy, *sewed*, 4to. Lond. 1664

1709 WARD (*Henry*), Works of, consisting of Dramatic Pieces, Poems, Prologues, Epilogues, Epigrams, Epitaphs, Songs, Tales, &c., 8vo. *half calf.* Lond. 1746

1710 WEBSTER (*John*), Dramatic Works Complete, edited by Dyce, *best edition, scarce*, 5 vols. 12mo. *half calf.* Lond., Pickering, 1830

A very elegant edition of the works of Webster, who is allowed to be one of the finest of the Elizabethan dramatists, and scarcely inferior to Shakspeare.

1712 ——— (*John and T. Dekker*), Westward Hoe, acted at St. Paule's, *sewed*, 4to. Lond. 1607

1713 ——— Northward Hoe, *sewed*, 4to. Lond. 1607

1714 ——— (*John*), Devil's Law-Case, or when Women goe to Law the Devil is full of Business, a Tragi-Comedy, 4to. *sewed.* Lond. 1623

First edition, and very scarce. Field's copy sold for £1 10*s*., and Inglis' for £1 5*s*.

1715 ——— (*and W. Rowley*), Thracian Wonder, a Comical History, *sewed*, 4to. Lond. 1661

1716 ——— White Devil, or the Tragedy of Paulo Giordano Ursin, Duke of Brachiano, &c., *half calf*, 4to. Lond. 1631

1717 ——— The Dutchesse of Malfi, a Tragedy, *sewed*, 4to. Lond. 1640

1718 ——— Duchess of Malfi, reconstructed by R. H. Horne, folio, *half calf.* Lond. 1850

1719 WEST (*Richd. Lord Chan. of Ireland*), Hecuba, a Tragedy, as played at Drury Lane, 4to. *half calf.* Lond. 1726

1721 WESTON (*Jo.*) Amazon Queen, or the Amours of Thalestrius, a Tragi-Comedy, 4to. *sewed.* Lond. 1667

1722 ——— Another copy, *half calf.* Lond. 1667

1723 WHEELWRIGHT'S Comedies of Aristophanes, translated into blank verse, 2 vols. 8vo. *cloth.* Oxford, 1837

1724 WHITE (*T.*) Old English Drama, reprints of, *rare old plays*, 4 vols. *half calf.* Lond. 1830

1725 WILD'S Dramas, 18mo. *half morocco.* Lond. 1805

1726 WILKINS (*G.*) Miseries of Inforst Marriage, *sewed*, 4to. Lond. 1637

1727 ——— Another copy, 4to. *half morocco.* Lond. 1637

1728 WILSON (*Arthur*), The Inconstant Ladie; with long Appendix, 4to. *half calf.* Oxford, 1811

1729 WILSON (*John*), The Cheats, a Comedy, *half morocco*, 4to. Lond. 1664

1730 ——— Another edition, 4to. Lond. 1693

1731 ——— Andronicus Comnenius, a Tragedy, 4to. Lond. 1664

1732 WILY Beguil'd, a wittie Comedie, *half calf, no title*, 4to. Lond. 1606

1733 WINDSOR Castle, and others, 2 vols. of Plays.

1734 WISEMAN (*Jane*), Antiochus the Great, or the Fatal Relapse, sm. 4to. *half calf.* Lond. 1702

1735 Wit and Science, a Moral Play, edited by Halliwell, *half calf*, 8vo. Lond. 1848

1736 WOLSELY's Valentinian, a Tragedy, 4to. *title cut, sewed.* Lond.

1737 WRIGHT (*Thomas*), The Female Vertuosos, a Comedy, 4to. *half calf.* Lond. 1693

1738 ——— Another copy, *unbound.* Lond. 1693

1739 WYCHERLY (*William*), Plays, 2 vols. *half calf*, 12mo. Lond. 1720

1740 ——— The Plain-dealer, a Comedy, *half vellum*, 4to. Lond. 1694

1741 ——— Another edition, *sewed*, 4to. Lond. 1686

1742 ——— Love in a Wood, or St. James' Park, a Comedy, *half vellum*, 4to. Lond. 1694

"As long as Men are false and Women vain,
Whilst gold continues to be Virtue's Bane,
In pointed satire Wycherly shall reign."—*Evelyn.*

1743 ZOUCH (*Richard*), The Sophister, a Comedy, *half calf*, 4to. Lond. 1639

DRAMATIC BIOGRAPHY.—*See also* HISTORY OF THE STAGE, BIOGRAPHY, &c.

1743* ACTORS by Daylight, or Pencillings in the Pit, 2 vols. in 1. 8vo. *half calf.* Lond.

1744 ADDISON (*Joseph*), Life of, by Miss Aiken, illustrated by many of his Letters and Private papers never before published, 8vo. *half calf.* Phil. 1846

"Her book contains the first complete life of Addison ever put forth. As a literary biography it is a model; and its pages are besides enriched by many hitherto unpublished letters of Addison."
Athenæum.

1745 ALFIERI (*Vittorio*), Autobiography, translated by Lester, 12mo. N. Y. 1841

1746 ALLEYN (*Edward, founder of Dulwich College*), Memoirs of, by Collier, 8vo. *half calf.* Lond. 1841

1747 BADDELEY (*Sophia, actress*), Memoirs of, by Elizabeth Steele, 6 vols. bound in 3, 12mo. *half calf.* Lond. 1787

1748 BAKER (*David Erskine*), Companion to the Play-house, 2 vols. 12mo. *half calf.* Lond. 1764

BAKER Biographia Dramatica, *vide* Bibliography, Lot 553.

1749 Bannister (*John, comedian*), Memoirs of, by Adolphus, 2 vols. 8vo. *half calf.* Lond. 1839

1750 Barnum (*P. T.*) Life of, written by himself, *cloth,* 12mo. Redfield, 1855

1751 Barrymore (*Earl of*), Life of, by Anthony Pasquin (John Williams), 8vo. *half calf, portrait.* Lond. 1793

1752 Bell's Lives of the most Eminent and Scientific Men of Great Britain, 2 vols. 8vo. *half calf.* Lond. 1839

1753 Brummell (*Geo.*) Life of, commonly called Beau Brummell, by Jesse, 8vo. Phil. 1844

1754 Bellamy (*George Anne*), Apology for the Life of, written by herself, 6 vols. in 3, 12mo. *half calf* Lond. 1785

"Apology! this lewd female should have termed it a sort of defence of her long course of licentious infamy."

1755 Bernard (*John*), Retrospections of the Stage, 2 vols. 8vo. *half calf.* Lond. 1830

1756 Betterton (*Thomas, tragedian*), Life of, written by himself, *portrait,* 12mo. *half calf.* Lond. 1710

1757 Betty (*Henry West, the Young Roscius*), Memoirs of the Life of, 12mo. *half calf.* Liverpool, 1704

1758 Billington (*Mrs.*) Memoirs of, by herself, 8vo. *half calf.* Lond. 1792

1759 Booth (*Barton, comedian*), Life of, 8vo. *half calf.* Lond. 1733

1760 ——— Another copy, *unbound.* 1733

1761 Boyle Family (*Earls of Orrery*), Memoirs of the, by E. Budgell, 8vo. *calf.* Lond. 1737

1762 British Theatre, containing the Lives of the English Dramatic Poets, 12mo. *half calf.* Lond. 1752

1763 Bunn (*Alfred*), Old England and New England, in a series of views taken on the spot, 2 vols. in 1, 12mo. *cloth.* Lond. 1853

1764 ——— The Stage, both before and behind the Curtain, 3 vols. 12mo. *half calf.* Lond. 1840

1765 Burney (*Dr.*), Life of Metastasio, with translations of his principal Letters, *portraits,* 3 vols. 8vo. *boards.*

1766 Butler (*Frances Anne Kemble, now Mrs.*) Journal, 2 vols. 8vo. *half calf.* Phil. 1835

1767 Byron (*Lord*), Letters and Journals of, edited by Thos. Moore, 2 vols. 8vo. *half calf.* N. Y. 1830

1768 Catley (*Ann,* Actress), Life and Memoirs of, by Miss Ambross, 12mo. *half calf.* Lond.

1769 CHARKE (*Charlotte*, Actress, Daughter of Colly Cibber), Narrative of the Life of, by herself, 12mo. *half calf.* Lond. 1755

1770 ——— Another edition, 12mo. *half bound.* Lond. 1827

A singular piece of autobiography, full of the vicissitudes of life arising from a wild and dissipated disposition, and so unsuitable to her sex.

1771 CIBBER (*C.*) An Apology for the Life of Mr. Colley Cibber, written by himself, and interspersed with Characters and Anecdotes of his Theatrical Contemporaries, the whole forming a complete history of the stage for the space of forty years, &c., *portrait, uncut,* with a MS. Index, 4to. *half calf.* Lond. 1740

1772 ——— Another copy, *unbound,* 4to. Lond. 1740

1773 ——— Another edition, 8vo. *half calf.* Lond. 1822

"One of the most amusing specimens of biography in the language, and the best history of the English stage during the time."

1774 ——— (*Theophilus*), The Lives of the Poets of Great Britain and Ireland to the Time of Dean Swift, compiled from ample materials scattered in a variety of books, and especially from the MS. notes of the late ingenious Mr. Coxeter and others, collected for this design, 5 vols. 12mo. Lond. 1753

Contains the lives and curious particulars relative to obscure poets, nowhere else to be found.

1775 ——— Letter to David Garrick, Life of Barton Booth, and other tracts, *plates,* 8vo. Lond. v. d.

1776 CLAIRON (*Hyppolite*, the famous Actress), Memoirs of, by herself, translated from the French, 2 vols. 12mo. *half calf.* Lond. 1800

1777 COLMAN Family, Memoirs of the, by R. B. Peake, including their Correspondence with the most Distinguished Personages of their Times, *ports.* 2 vols. 8vo. *half calf.* Lond. 1841

1778 COOKE (*George Frederick*), Memoirs of, by W. Dunlap, with Anecdotes of his Theatrical Contemporaries, 8vo. *half calf.* 1813

1779 CONGREVE (*William*), Memoirs of the Life, Writings, and Amours of, by Charles Wilson, 8vo. *half calf.* Lond. 1730

1780 CONSTANTINI, Vie de Scaramonche, 12mo. *half calf.* Brusselles, 1699

1781 COWELL (*Joe*, Comedian), Thirty Years Passed Among the Players of England and America, 8vo. *half calf.* Lond. 1824

1782 CROUCH (*Mrs.*, Actress), Memoirs of, including a Retrospect of the Stage during the Years she Performed, by M. J. Young, 2 vols. 12mo. *half calf, neat, fine ports.* 1806

1783 CRUSIUS (*L.*) Lives of the Roman Poets, containing a critical account of them and their writings, with large quotations of their most celebrated passages, &c., in 2 vols. 12mo. *calf.* Lond. 1733

1784 CUMBERLAND (*Richard*, Dramatic Author), Life of, by William Mudford, 8vo. *half calf.* Lond. 1812

1785 DIBDIN (*Charles*, Actor), The Professional Life of, written by himself, with 600 of his songs, 4 vols. 8vo. *half calf, portrait and sixty plates by his daughter.* Lond. 1803

1786 ——— (*Thomas*), Reminiscences, comprising his Correspondence with Sheridan, G. Colman, Whitbread, Douglas Kinnaird, P. Moore, &c., *portrait*, 2 vols. 8vo. *half calf.* 1827

This work abounds in lively Theatrical Anecdotes, curious secrets of the Green Room, accounts of the destruction by fire of Covent Garden and Drury Lane Theatres, &c.

1787 DRYDEN (*John*), Life of, 12mo. *half calf.* Lond. n. d.

1788 DYER (*Robert*), Nine Years of an Actor's Life, *cloth*, 12mo. Lond. 1833

1789 EBERS (*John*), Seven Years of the King's Theatre, 8vo. *half calf.* Lond. 1828

1790 ECCENTRICITIES of J. Edwin, the Comedian, with several hundred original Anecdotes, &c., by Ant. Pasquin [J. Williams], 2 vols. 12mo. *half calf.* Dublin, 1791

1791 EGAN (*Pierce*), Life of an Actor, *with numerous fine spirited engravings, highly colored*, royal 8vo. *half calf.* Lond. 1825

1792 ELLISTON (*R. W.*, the celebrated Comedian and Manager of Drury Lane Theatre), Memoirs of, by G. Raymond, 2 vols. 8vo. *fine portrait and humorous illustrations, by Geo. Cruikshank, half calf, gilt.* Lond. 1846

"Great wert thou in thy life, Robert William Elliston. Joyousest of once embodied spirits! whither at length hast thou flown? Magnificent were thy caprices on this Globe of Earth."—*Charles Lamb.*

1793 EVERARD (*Edward Coke*, Comedian), Memoirs of an Unfortunate Son of Thespis, being a Sketch of his Life, by himself, *half calf*, 12mo. Edin. 1818

1794 FENNELL (*James*), Apology for the Life of, 8vo. *half calf.* Phil. 1814

1795 FOOTE (*Samuel*), Memoirs, with a collection of his Bon Mots, Anecdotes, Opinions, &c., and Three Dramatic Pieces not in his Works, by W. Cooke, *portrait*, 2 vols. 12mo. *half calf.* N. Y. 1806

1796 GALT (*John*), Lives of the Players, and Biography of the most Distinguished Actors and Actresses of the English Stage, 2 vols. post 8vo. *half calf, gilt.* Lond. 1831

1797 GARRICK (*David*), Private Correspondence with the most Celebrated Persons of his Time, illustrated with Notes and Biographical Memoir by Boaden, *portrait*, 2 very large thick vols. royal 4to. *half calf.* 1831

A most amusing and interesting collection of upwards of 2,000 letters by the most eminent men and women of the time in which Garrick lived.

1798——— Life of, by Arthur Murphy, 8vo. *half calf.* Dub. 1801

1799 ——— Memoirs of the Life of, by Thos. Davies, interspersed with Characters and Anecdotes of his Theatrical Contemporaries, including a History of the Stage for Thirty-Six Years, 12mo. *half calf.* Bost. 1813

1800 GOLDONI (*Carl*), Memorie di, 3 vols. 8vo. *half boards.* Prato, 1822

1801 GOLDONI'S Memoirs, forming a complete History of his Life and Writings, Translated by Black, 2 vols. 8vo. *half calf.* 1814

"The Memoirs of Goldoni are more truly dramatic than his Italian Comedies."—*Gibbon.*
An admirable specimen of Autobiography.

1802 GOLDSMITH (*Oliver*), Life of, by Prior, 2 vols. 8vo. *half calf.* Lond. 1837

These volumes will ever constitute one of the most precious "wells of English undefiled."—*Quarterly Review.*

1803 GOETHE, Characteristics of, from the German of Talh Von Muller, with Notes, original and translated, illustrative of German Literature, by Sarah Austin, 3 vols. 8vo. *half calf.* Lond. 1833

1804 ——— Autobiography of, by Park Godwin, 2 vols. 12mo. *half calf.* N. Y. 1846

1805 GRIMALDI (*Joseph*, Clown), Memoirs of, by Dickens, *illustrated by Cruikshank*, 2 vols. 8vo. *half calf.* Lond. 1838

1806 GUIZOT'S Corneille and his Times, *elegantly printed in large type*, thick 8vo. *cloth.* 1852

1807 HARLEY (*George, Davies*), Biographical Sketch of the Life, Education, and Personal Character of William Henry West Betty, the young Roscius, 8vo. *half calf.* Lond. 1804

1808 HENDERSON (*John*), A Genuine Narrative of the Life and Theatrical Transactions of, 8vo. *sewed.* Lond. 1778

1809 ——— Letters and Poems of, by Ireland, 12mo. *half calf.* Dublin, 1786

1810 HILL (*B. E.*) Playing About, or Theatrical Anecdotes and Adventures, with Scenes of a general nature from the Life, in England, Ireland, and Scotland, 2 vols. 8vo. *half calf.* Lond. 1811

1811 HILL (*G. H., called Yankee Hill*), Life and Recollections of, by W. K. Northall, 12mo. *cloth.* N. Y. 1850

1812 HOLBERG (*Lewis*), Memoirs of, by himself, 12mo. *half calf.* Lond. 1827

1813 HOLCROFT (*Thomas*), Memoirs of, written by himself, in 3 vols. 12mo. *half calf.* Lond. 1816

1814 ——— Narrative of Facts relating to a Persecution for High Treason, with an Address to the Jury and the Defence, 8vo. *half calf.* Lond. 1795

1815 INCHBALD (*Mrs.*) Memoirs of, by Boaden, 2 vols. 8vo. *half calf.* Lond. 1803

1816 JOHNSON (*Dr.*) Account of the Life of, by Miss Hill Boothby, 12mo. *boards.* Lond. 1805

1817 ——— Russell's Life of, 12mo. *cloth.* Lond. 1847

1818 ——— Lives of the Poets, with Annotations, by Mrs. Thrale (Piozzi). The Lives of the most eminent English Poets, with Critical Observations on their works, by Samuel Johnson, in 4 vols. 8vo. (*portrait after Reynolds*). *First edition, in the original old calf binding.* Lond. 1781

In the whole range of English literature it would, perhaps, be impossible to select a more intrinsically valuable and gratifying literary gem than the present. It is the copy of Dr. Johnson's Lives of the Poets, presented to his friend, Mrs. Thrale, and enriched throughout with *copious notes and annotations by her*, which are entirely unpublished. The late editions of "Boswell's Life" have shown the eagerness with which every scrap relating to Dr. Johnson has been collected and cherished, though often of trivial value; while these volumes present an *untouched mine* of entirely new material, from one, of whose house he was so long an inmate, and who soothed with feminine attention and the luxuries of wealth the declining years of the "Colossus of Literature." It may be doubted whether an equally valuable addition to our knowledge of Dr. Johnson is in existence. On the fly-leaf of vol. 1 is the signature "*H. L. Thrale,*

1781," and the notes with which the margins abound appear to have been written on various perusals between that time and 1817, (which is the last date noticed), four years previous to Mrs. Piozzi's death, in 1821, in her 82d year. In a note to Boswell, Mr. Croker says of Mrs. Piozzi's hand, "Her writing is an almost perfect specimen of calligraphy, and this power remained unimpaired to the last years of her long life;" a fact to which these volumes testify—indeed some of the later notes are almost microscopic, though perfectly clear and legible. The notes, which are many hundreds in number, and of various extent, from a few words to a long paragraph, may be roughly classed as unpublished anecdotes of Dr. Johnson, anecdotes of English literary men and their works, derived from a constant intercourse with the highest sources of information, and original critical remarks, &c., by Mrs. Piozzi herself, frequently displaying great vivacity and talent. A specimen or two, chiefly of the first class, is given merely to show their character and importance:—

"When I expressed my grief and anger at seeing Young's character so mangled, (*by Herbert Crofts, who supplied the Life in Johnson's Collection*), 'Why, pry'thee, my dear, (says Dr. Johnson), why didst not do it thyself?' 'I did not possess any materials for such a work,' was my reply. 'Nor I, (answered Johnson), and I was glad of good help. So now, let's hear no more on 't.'"—*Life of Young*, vol. iv., p. 359.

"When Johnson had finished his preface to Shakspear, Mr. Thrale said, 'Oh, sir, you have driven Pope quite into shade.' 'I fear *not*, sir,' was our doctor's reply, 'the little fellow has done wonders.'"—*Pope*, vol. iv., p. 73.

"Dr. Johnson requested Lord Westcote, in my hearing, to write this life (*Lord Lyttleton*) for him, (though I am sure he neither loved nor esteemed the man.) Lord Westcote declined the work, with many complimentary expressions; said his dear brother was in the best possible hands, &c.; and after it was written flew in a rage, and ran to Mrs. Montagu, complaining of Dr. Johnson, who sat still and laughed at my Lord Parenthesis, as he called Billy Lyttleton."—*Lyttleton*, vol. iv., p. 489.

"'The beauty who is totally free from disproportion of parts and features, cannot be ridiculed by an overcharged resemblance,' &c., *Johnson*," finely said, and accurately illustrated; and it was Johnson's conversation opinion, too. He liked Mr. Thrale, he said, because he had no *trick* about his manner, no emphasis in his talk; he could no more be taken off (as the phrase is) than Beauclerc. 'And what, sir, (said I,) do you think, then, of your favorite, Burney?' 'Oh, (said he,) Burney could not be taken off, certainly, because he is *all trick*.'"—*Dryden*, vol. ii., p. 121.

"Dr. Johnson was very angry that he was not called upon by Garrick to write the Ode, (in the Shakespeare Jubilee,) which for that reason he always ridiculed."—*Dryden*, vol. ii., p. 110.

"I have heard Dr. Johnson say, what 'tis plain he would not *write*, how Parnell could not get through a sermon, without turning his head, even in the pulpit, to drink a dram."—H. L. P., 1802.—*Parnell*, vol. ii. p. 306.

"Richardson quotes as Otway's lines, verses now well known to be Shakespeare's; but to Garrick, that *mine of mercury striated with gold*, we owe the revivification of Shakespeare, though none of us had influence enough with Dr. Johnson to make him confess it in his Preface or Notes. Mr. Thrale would not try—Garrick had refused him a favor. He would not patronize Poll Hart, who afterward married Reddish."—*Otway*, vol. i., p. 340.

For a very curious anecdote of Rochester, see vol. i., p. 301; and of Thomson, vol. iv., p. 271; which would take too much space to extract. It is hoped that the above specimens, out of *some hundred* notes, will be sufficient to give an idea of the value of this Unique Contribution to the Literary History of England, and Memorial of one of her Greatest Writers.

1819 JOHNSON (*Samuel*), The Life of, by James Boswell, edited by J. W. Croker, *Variorum Edition*, including the Tour to the Hebrides, Johnson's Diary of his Tour in Wales, Unpublished Letters, and two Supplementary Volumes of Johnsoniana, from various sources, edited and arranged by T. Wright, 10 vols. 12mo. *with* 50 *beautiful Plates*, *Portraits*, *Views*, *Facsimiles*, *&c. half calf.* Lond. 1848

"Boswell's Life of Johnson is one of the best books in the world. It is assuredly a great, a very great book. Homer is not more decidedly the first of Heroic poets—Shakspeare is not more decidedly the first of dramatists—Demosthenes is not more decidedly the first of orators, than Boswell is the first of biographers. He has distanced all his competitors so decidedly, that it is not worth while to place them; Eclipse is first, and all the rest, nowhere. We are not sure that there is in the whole history of the human intellect so singular a phenomenon as this book. Many of the greatest men that have ever lived have written biography—Boswell has beaten them all." *Macaulay, in Edinburgh Review.*

1820 JOHNSONIANA: a Collection of Miscellaneous Anecdotes and Sayings, gathered from nearly a hundred different publications, and not contained in Boswell's Life of Johnson, edited by J. W. Croker, M. P., fcap. 8vo. *half calf.* 1845

This entertaining collection comprises the whole of the two supplementary volumes of Croker's edition of Boswell's Life of Johnson.

1821 JONSON (*Ben*) Memoirs of the Life and Writings of, with an abstract of the lives of Somerset and Buckingham; collected from the writings of the most eminent historians, and interspersed with the pasquils of those times; to which are added two Comedies (wrote by Ben Jonson, &c., and not printed in his works), called the Widow and Eastward Hoe, 12mo. *scarce, calf.* Dublin, 1756

1822 JORDAN (*Mrs.*) Boaden's Life of, including original Private Correspondence and Anecdotes of her Contemporaries (Duke of Clarence, &c.) *portrait*, 2 vols. 8vo. *half calf.* Lond. 1831

1823 KEAN (*Edmund*), Life of, 2 vols. 8vo. *half calf.* Lond. 1835

1824 KELLY (*Michael*), Reminiscences of, and Anecdotes of Distinguished Personages, Political, Literary, and Musical, 2 vols. post 8vo. *half calf.* Lond. 1826

"The best addition to our Theatrical History since Colley Cibber;" it was, in reality, written by Theodore Hook.

1825 KEMBLE (*John Philip*), Memoirs of, by Williams, 12mo. *sewed.* Lond. 1817

1826 ——— Life, including a History of the Stage from the time of Garrick, by J. Boaden, 2 vols. royal 8vo. *half calf.* 1821

1827 KOTZEBUE (*Augustus Von*), Sketch of the Life and Literary Career of, written by himself, 2 vols. 12mo. *half calf.* Lond. 1827

1828 LEMAZURIER (*P. D.*) Galerie Historique des Acteurs Théatre Français depuis 1600, Jusqu'a nos jours, 2 vols. 12mo. *half calf.* Paris, 1810

1829 LEWIS (*Monk*), Life and Correspondence, with many pieces in prose and verse never before published, 2 vols. 8vo. *portrait and fac-simile, half calf.* 1839

"I'd give a world of sugar cane,
Mat Lewis were alive again."—*Byron.*

The "wonder-working Lewis," as he was styled by Byron, was the friend and associate of nearly all the most celebrated men of his day.

"Crammed full of anecdotes as these volumes are—theatrical, political, and literary—there is not a dull page throughout."—*Court Journal.*

1830 LIVES of the English Dramatick Poets, begun by Langbaine, continued by Gildon, 12mo. *calf.* Lond. 1698

"Of all the early catalogues of the English Stage, Langbaine's is the only one to be relied on implicitly for it's fidelity.—*Lowndes.*

1831 LIVES of British Dramatists, by miscellaneous authors, in 2 vols. 8vo. *half calf.* Phil. 1846

1832 MACKLIN (*Charles*), Memoirs of the Life of, by Kirkman, 8vo. *half calf.* Lond. 1799

1833 MACREADY (*Mrs.*) Memoirs of, 8vo. Chicago, 1857

1834 MALIBRAN (*Madame*), Memoirs of, by the Countess de Merlin, 2 vols. 12mo. *cloth.* 1840

"These Memoirs of this extraordinary woman are full of interesting details, much of which is entirely new to the public: the Letters and Anecdotes are characteristic and amusing."

1835 MASSINGER (*Philip*), Account of the Life and Writings of, 8vo. *half calf.* Lond. 1789

1836 MILTON (*John*), Life of, by C. Simmons, 8vo. *half calf.* Lond. 1822

1837 MATHEWS (*Mrs.*) Anecdotes of Actors, with other Desultory Recollections, &c. 8vo. *cloth.* Lond. 1844

1838 MATHEWS (*Charles, the Comedian*), Memoirs, including his Autobiography and Diary, Anecdotes of his Contemporaries, American Tours, &c., edited by Mrs. Mathews, *portrait and plates*, 4 vols. 8vo. *cloth.* 1838

A rare book, a book of jest and anecdote. The eccentricities of old Johnny Winter—the natty neatnesses of Colman—the practical jesting of Hook—these, and the passing glances at Curran, Kemble, the Prince Regent, Q. Charlotte, &c., are given in excellent style. "Indeed it is 'heaped up and running over' with anecdotes of the most singular and diverting nature."—*Athenæum.*

1839 MILLER (*D. P.*) Life of a Showman, 12mo. *sewed.* Lond. 1849

1840 MOLÉ, Mémoires de, précédés d'une notice sur cet acteur par M'Tienne, 8vo. *half calf.* Paris, 1825

1841 MOORE (*T.*) Memoirs, Journal, and Correspondence, edited by Lord John Russell, complete, with copious Index, *portraits and vignettes*, 8vols. post 8vo. *cloth.*

An exceedingly interesting work, abounding in anecdotes and sketches of the principal literary and political persons of the present century.

1842 MORE (*Hannah*), Life of, by Thompson, 8vo. *half calf*, 2 vols. in one. Phila. 1838

1843 MOWATT (*Anne Cora, Actress*), Autobiography of, or eight years on the stage, *port.*, *cloth*, 12mo. Bost. 1854

1844 MOZART, Life of, by Holmes, 12mo. *half calf.* N. Y. 1845

1845 MUNDEN (*Joseph, Comedian*), Memoirs of, by his Son, 8vo. *fine portrait, half calf.* Lond. 1844

"He is not one, but Legion, not so much a comedian as a company," &c.—*C. Lamb.*

1846 MURRAY (*Arthur*), Life of, by Jesse Foot, 4to. *half calf.* Lond. 1811

1847 NASH (*Rd. Master of the Ceremonies at Bath*), Life of, 8vo. *calf.* Lond. 1762

1848 O'NEILL (*Miss*), Memoirs of, containing her public character, private life, and dramatic progress, by J. C. Jones, *portrait*, royal 8vo. *half calf.* Lond. 1816

1849 O'KEEFE (*John, the celebrated Dramatist*), Recollections of the Life of, including Anecdotes of Royal, Noble, and Distinguished Persons, *fine portrait*, 2 vols. 8vo. *half calf.* 1826

The above work is full of entertainment; introducing nearly all the gay celebrities of the last and present age.

1850 OLDFIELD (*Anne, Actress*), Faithful Memoirs of the Life of, 8vo. *half calf.* Lond. 1751

1851 OXBERRY'S New Series of Dramatic Biography and Green Room Spy, 6 vols. 12mo. *half calf.* Lond. 1825

1852 PALMER (*John, Actor*), A Monody on. Ed. Forrest's Oration, &c., &c., 8vo. v. p.

1853 PARKER (*George*), Life's Painter of Variegated Characters in Public and Private Life (Cant Dictionary, Freemasonry, &c.), 8vo. *half morocco.* Lond. 1789

1854 PARSONS (*William, Comedian*), Life of, by Bellamy, 8vo. *half calf.* Lond. 1795

1855 PAYNE (*J. H., The American Roscius*), Memoirs of, with Criticisms on his Acting in the various Theatres of America, England, and Ireland, also the Plays of Belisarius, &c., 8vo. *boards.* Lond. 1815

1856 PETITE, Biographie des Acteurs et Actrices des Theatre Française, *half calf,* 32mo. Paris, 1826

1857 POPE (*Alexander*), Life of, by Owen Ruffhead, 8vo. *half calf.* Lond. 1769

1857*POWERS (*Tyrone*), Impression of America during the years 1833–5, 2 vols. 8vo. *boards.* Lond. 1836

Poor Powers, who was lost in the steamship President.

1858 QUINN (*James, Actor*), Life of, no title, *half calf,* 12mo. Lond.

1859 REEVE (*John*), Life of, by Douglas Banister, *portrait by Wageman, sewed,* 8vo. Lond. n. d.

1860 REYNOLDS' (*F., Dramatist*), Life and Times, with Anecdotes of his Contemporaries, *portrait,* 2 vols. 8vo, *half calf.* Lond. 1827

1861 ROBINSON (*Mrs.*) Memoirs of, by herself, *half bound,* 12mo. Lond. 1826

Better or worse known as the Mistress of George IV.

1862 ROCHESTER (*Earl of*), Familiar Letters by, with letters by Thos. Otway and Mrs. K. Philips, 2 vols. 12mo. *cloth.* Lond. 1697

1863 ROSSINI (*G.*) Vie de, par un Dilettante, 12mo. *half calf.* Anvers, 1859

1864 RYLEY (*S. W.*) The Itinerant, or Memoirs of an Actor, 5 vols. *half calf,* 12mo. Phil. 1810

1865 SAVAGE (*Richard, Poet*), Account of the Life of, 8vo. *half calf.* Lond. 1744

1866 SCHILLER (*Frederich*), Life of, 8vo. *half calf.* N. Y. 1837

1867 SCOTT (*Sir Walter*), Life of, by Lockhart, 12mo. *half calf.* Lond. 1839

1868 SHERIDAN (*Mrs. Frances, mother of R. B. Sheridan*), Memoirs of the Life and Writings of, by her granddaughter, 8vo. *half calf.* Lond. 1824

1869 SHERIDAN (*Richard Brinsley*), Life of, by Thomas Moore, *original* 4to. *edition, with fine portrait of Sheridan, Fac Similes, etc., half calf.* Lond. 1825

"This is as magnificent a piece of biography as we have in our language."—*Monthly Rev.*

1870 SHARP (*J.*) Les Petites Aventures de, professeur de physique Amusante, 8vo. *calf.* Bruxelles, 1789

1871 SIDDONS (*Mrs.*) Life of, by Campbell, 2 vols. 8vo. *half calf.* Lond. 1834

"The life of Mrs. Siddons, the imperial Queen of Tragedy, is brief and beautiful, full of spirited details, amusing anecdotes and interesting incidents, which are most agreeably and eloquently told. There is nothing heavy or cumbersome in the biography to mar the interest, or to fatigue the mind of the reader; for the style is marked by a sprightly simplicity that now and then, unknown to the author, borrows the modest grace of unaffected eloquence."

1872 ——— Memoirs of, by James Boaden, with Anecdotes of Authors and Actors, *fine portrait after Lawrence,* 8vo. *half calf.* Phil. 1827

1873 SMITH (*Sol., Comedian*), Theatrical Apprenticeship and Anecdotal Recollections, 12mo. *half calf.* Phil. 1846

1874 ST. ALBANS (*Miss Mellon, afterwards Duchess of*), Memoirs, by Mrs. C. Baron Wilson, *portraits,* 2 vols. post 8vo. *half calf, scarce* 1839

"A most interesting life of this very extraordinary woman, whose career was so plethoric of good fortune, and whose singular destiny placed her in so many and such varied situations."

1875 STOCKDALE (*Percival*), Life and Memoirs of, written by himself, 2 vols. 8vo. *half calf.* Lond. 1809

1876 SUMBELL (*Mrs., late Wells*), Memoirs of, by herself, 3 vols. 8vo. *half calf.* Lond. 1811

1876*——— Another copy. 1811

1877 TAYLOR (*J.*) Records of my Life, 2 vols. 8vo. *half calf.* 1832

1878 THEATRICAL Biography of the Principal Performers of the Three Theatres Royal, 2 vols. *half calf,* 12mo. Lond. 1772

1879 THESPIAN Dictionary, or Lives, Productions, &c., of all the Principal Managers, Dramatists, Composers, Commentators, Actors and Actresses, thick 12mo. *neatly bound,* 22 *portraits, including Kemble and Mrs. Siddons.* 1805

"A very satisfactory and authentic work."

1880 THEATRICAL Times, a Weekly Magazine of Thespian Biography, 2 vols. royal 8vo. *half calf.* Lond. 1847

1881 TOBIN (*John*), Memoirs of, by Miss Benger, 8vo. *half calf.* Lond. 1820

1882 VEGA (*Lope de*), The Life of, and account of his Writings, by Lord Holland, 8vo. *half calf.* Lond. 1806

1883 VESTRIS (*Madam*), Memoirs of the Public and Private Life of, *portrait*, 8vo. *sewed.* N. Y. n. d

1884 WEMYSS (*F. C.*) Twenty-six years of the Life of an Actor and Manager, 2 vols. 8vo. *half calf.* N. Y. 1847

1885 WESTON (*Thomas, Comedian*), Memoirs of, 8vo. *half calf.* Lond. 1776

1886 WILKS (*Robert, Comedian*), Life of, 8vo. *half calf.* Lond. 1733

1887 WILKINSON (*Tate*, Patentee of the Theatres Royal, York and Hull), Memoirs of his own Life, 2 vols. 12mo. *half calf, scarce.* York, 1793

"If I had held *my Pen* but half as well as I have held *my Bottle*, what a charming hand I should have wrote by this time."—*Motto of title page.*

1888 YANKEE Hill, Life and Recollections of, 12mo. *cloth.* N. Y. 1850

1889 ZCHOKKE (*Heinrich*), Autobiography of, 8vo. *half calf.* Lond. 1845

DUELS AND DUELLING.

1890 C. (*T.*) A Discourse of Duels, small 4to. *boards.* Lond. 1687

1891 CHALMERS (*Rev. Peter*), Two Discourses on the Sin, Danger, and Remedy of Duelling, 16mo. Edin. 1822

1892 MASSALI (*Antonii*), Contra usum Duelli, small 4to. *sheep.* Romæ, 1554

1893 MILLINGEN (*J. G.*) History of Duelling, 2 vols. 8vo. *cloth.* Lond. 1841

1894 SABINE (*Lorenzo*), Notes on Duels and Duelling, 12mo. *cloth.* Bost. 1855

SAVIOLE, *vide* Shaksperiana.

EGYPT AND THE HOLY LAND.—*See also* ANTIQUITIES.

1896 ADDISON (*G. G.*) Damascus and Palmyra, 2 vols. 12mo. *cloth.* Phil. 1858

1897 ANNALS of the Jewish Nation during the Period of the Second Temple, 12mo. *cloth.* N. Y. 1832

1898 Cooley (*J. Ewing*), American in Egypt, with Rambles through Arabia Petræa and the Holy Land in 1839–40, 8vo. *cloth.* N. Y. 1841

1899 Edrehi (*Rabbi Moses*), Account of the Lost Ten Tribes of Israel, settled beyond the River Sambatyon, in the East, 8vo. *map, &c., half calf, gilt.* Lond. 1830

1900 Expedition to Egypt, 12mo. *sheep.* 1803

1901 Eothen, or Traces of Travel brought Home from the East, 12mo. *cloth.* N. Y. 1850

1902 Geramb (*Baron*), Pilgrimage to Jerusalem and Mount Sinai, 2 vols. 12mo. Phil. 1840

1903 History of Egypt, Treating of the Pyramids, the Inundation of the Nile, according to the Opinions and Traditions of the Arabians, 12mo. *half calf.* Lond. 1672

1904 Maundevile's (*Sir J.*) Voiage and Travaile (MCCCXXII. &c.) which Treateth of the Way to Hierusalem and the Marvayles of Inde, &c., edited by Halliwell, 8vo. *cloth.* Lond. 1839

Our earliest prose author of any consideration, and our very first narrator of travels.

1905 Prime (*W. C.*) Boat Life in Egypt and Nubia, 8vo. *cloth.* N. Y. 1857

1906 Rennel (*Major*), Dissertation on the Topography of the Ancient Babylon, 4to. Lond. 1813

1907 Rich (*C. J.*) Babylon and Persepolis, 8vo. *cloth.* Lond. 1839

1908 Seymer (*John Gunning*), The Romance of Ancient Egypt, 2 vols. 12mo. *boards.* Lond. 1835

1909 Sharpe (*S.*) History of Egypt under the Ptolemies, 4to. *cloth.* Lond. 1838

1910 Travels of Alladin, Sultan of Egypt, 2 vols.

EMBLEMS.

1911 Alciati (*Andriæ*), Emblemata denuo ab ipso Auctore recognita, 8vo. *vellum, neat, with* 215 *wood-cut emblems.* Lugd., *Rovilium*, 1550

1912 Boudin (*J.*) Iconologie, ou explication nouvelle de Plusieurs Images, Emblemes, &c., *figures by C. Ripa*, folio. Par. 1644

Brunet puts this under Boudard.

1913 Burgundia (*Antonius a.*) Mundi Lapis Lydices, sive vanitatas per vanitatem falsa accusata et convicta, *beautiful plates, one torn, and title wanting*, 4to. Antv. 1639

1914 CAMERARII (*J.*) Symbolarum ac Emblematum Ethico-Politicorum, 12mo. *calf.* Mogunt, 1702

1915 CATS (*J.*) Zinne, en Minne Beelden, Selfstryd, a work on emblems and other works, *many curious plates*, 12mo. *vellum.* Amst. 1717

1916 DARET, Le Doctrine de Moralité, 100 *fine plates by Otho Vœniis*, folio. Paris, 1646

This large paper copy includes ten books in the finest condition.

1917 DARET'S Doctrine of Morality, with descriptions, English and French, and verses by De Gomberville, *portrait and* 103 *fine engravings*, folio, *calf gilt.* Lond. 1726

These engravings exhibit a very curious picture of human life, according to the Stoic philosophy.

1918 GOMBERVILLE (*Talasius Basilides a*). Doctrine of Morality, translated by T. M. Gibbs, 103 *fine plates, calf*, folio. Lond. 1721

1919 JUNII (*Hadriani*), Emblemata; Antv. *Plantin*, 1565 Ovidii Matamorphoses, illustratæ, I. Sprengiani, Francof, 1563, in 1 vol. *both works illustrated by beautiful wood cuts, old calf*, 8vo. v. y.

1920 QUARLES (*Francis*), Emblems Divine and Moral, 12mo. *half morocco.* N. Y. 1816

The best proof of Quarles' merit is the rarity of copies not worn to rags. He possesses much genuine fire, happy similes, admirable epithets, compound words, smooth versification, and keeps one in perpetual alarm.

1921 RICHARDSON (*George, Architect*), Iconology, a collection of emblematical figures, containing four hundred and twenty-four remarkable subjects, moral and instructive, &c. engraved by Malpas, Bartolozzi, W. Sharpe Hall, &c. 4 books in 3 vols. 4to. Lond. 1779

With particular explanations of the figures, their attributes and symbols, from classical authors, &c.

This work will be found extremely useful to artists, as it gives the received or established figures of all the virtues, vices, qualities, muses, seasons, senses, arts, sciences, and other matters of which the personifications are ideal.

1922 SCHOONHOVII (*Florentii Goudani*), Emblemata, partim Moralia partim etiam Civilia, 4to. *vellum, wants one leaf.* Amsterdam, *Elzevir*, 1626

1923 SMIDS (*Lud.*) Emblemati Heroica, fig. de Schronebeck, 8vo. *calf.* Amsterdam, 1712

1924 SYMBOLA Divina et Humanas Pontificum Imperatorium Regun, *numerous beautiful engravings by Egedum Sadeler*, 3 vols. in 1, folio *old calf.* Francof. 1601

1925 VAENI (*Othonis*), Emblemata Horatiana, in Latin, German, French, and Dutch, 103 *curious plates*, 12mo. Amsterdam, 1784

1925* VIEW of the Human Heart, in a series of allegorical designs, illustrative of the Evil Passions, 8vo. *boards*. Lond. 1832

ENGLAND, CHRONOLOGY AND GENERAL HISTORY, PARTICULAR LIVES, GOVERNMENT, BIOGRAPHY, TOPOGRAPHY, &c.

1926 ANDREWS (*J. P.*) History of Gt. Britain connected with the Chronology of Europe, with Anecdotes of the Times, Lives of the Learned and Specimens of their Works, 2 vols. 4to. in 1, *russia*. Lond. 1794–5

1927 BAKER (*R.*) Chronicle of the Kings of England, from the Time of the Roman Government unto the Death of King James, folio, *no title*. Lond. 1641

1929 ——— Another edition, to which is added the Reigns of King Charles the First and of Charles the Second, folio, *plates*. Lond. 1696

A book rendered familiar to most readers, from Addison in his Roger de Coverley, it has been the delight of the English peasant from its first appearance to the present day.

Formerly one of the most popular of our Chronicles, no less than twelve editions having been printed, the author has modestly informed us that if all other Chronicles were lost, posterity would be sufficiently informed by reading his own. Anthony Wood, Daines Barrington, and Alex. Chalmers speak favorably of his labors.

1930 BURTON (*Richard*) The Wars in England, Scotland, and Ireland, or an Impartial Account of all the Battels, Sieges, and other remarkable Transactions, from 1625 to 1660, *with curious cuts, first edition*, 12mo. *calf*. 1681

1931 BRIEF Account of the Morall and Political Acts of the Kings and Queens of England, 8vo. *calf*. Lond. 1793

1932 CABINET History of England, *copper plate* edition, 8vo. *calf*. Lond. n. d.

1933 COTTON (*Sir Robert*), Abridgement of the Records in the Tower of London from King Edward the Second unto Richard the Third, by Prynne, small folio, *calf*. Lond. 1657

"This Abridgement records the substance of Acts of Parliament, and other particulars that are not extant in print among the Statutes or the Parliament Rolls."—*MS. note on title.*

1934 DANIEL (*Samuel*), Collection of the Historie of England, engraved title, folio, *half calf*. 1618

"Written with a freedom from all stiffness and a purity of style which hardly any other work of so early date exhibits."—*Hallam.*

1935 FROISSART'S (*Sir John*), Chronicles of England, France, and Spain, and adjoining Countries, translated by Mr. Johnes of Hafod, 2 vols. impl. 8vo. *cloth.* 1839

The period embraced in this amusing work is from the latter part of the reign of Edward II. to the Coronation of Henry IV. Mr. Johnes has prefixed a Life of the Author, an Essay on his Works, a Criticism on his History, and a Dissertation on his Poetry.

Sir Walter Scott, in his "Tales of My Landlord," thus speaks of the above—"Did you ever read Froissart?" "No," said Morton. "I have half a mind," said Claverhouse, "to contrive you should have six months' imprisonment in order to procure you that pleasure. His chapters inspire me with more enthusiasm than even poetry itself. And the noble Canon; with what true chivalrous feeling he confines his beautiful expressions of sorrow to the death of the gallant and high-bred Knight, of whom it was a pity to see the fall, such was his loyalty to his King, pure faith to his religion, hardihood towards his enemy, and fidelity to his lady-love."

1936 ——— Chronicles of, 74 illuminated plates to illustrate Froissart, printed in gold and colours, being fac similes from the drawings in the illuminated copy at the British Museum, and Bibliotheque Nationale de Paris, in impl. 8vo. *half red morocco, gilt edges.* 1846

The illuminations are admirably executed, and highly characteristic representations of authentic costume, &c.

1937 GRANGER (*Rev. J.*) A Biographical History of England from Egbert the Great to the Revolution; consisting of Characters disposed in different classes, and adapted to a methodical Catalogue of engraved British Heads, interspersed with Anecdotes and Memoirs of a great number of Persons not to be found in any other Biographical work; with upwards of 400 additional Lives, fifth edition, 6 vols. 8vo. *calf, fine copy.* Lond. 1824

"I have no hesitation in designating Granger's a delightful and instructive book; and considering that he may be said to have first walked the field alone, it is surprising what he has done. His Catalogue of engraved British Heads is immense, his style is always clear, pointed, and lively."—*Dibdin.*

1938 GRAFTON'S Chronicle History of England, to which is added his Table of the Bailiffs, Sheriffs, and Mayors of the City of London, 2 vols. 4to. *half calf.* Lond. 1809

1939 HALL (*Edward*), Chronicle, containing the History of England during the reign of Henry the IV. and the succeeding Monarchs, to the end of the reign of Henry the VIII., carefully collated with the editions of 1548 and 1550, edited by Sir H. Ellis, 4to. *half calf.* Lond. 1809

Shakspeare was much indebted to this Chronicle.

HOLINGSHED'S Chronicles, *vide* Shakspeariana.

1940 HIGDEN (*Ranulph*), Polychronicon, containing the Berynges and Dedes of many Tymes, fol. **Black Letter**, *calf, in fine clean state, wants two last leaves.* Wynken de Worde, MDCCCCXCV.

A most desirable specimen of Wynken de Worde's press, and of English typography in the XV. century.

1941 ——— Polychronicon, conteyning the Berynges and Dedes of many Tymes, *with curious old wood cuts*, thick folio, *newly bound in antique calf extra, gilt leaves, fine copy.* Southwerke, P. Treveris, MDXXVII.

"A splendid and rather uncommon impression. Indeed the volume is in every respect a curiosity; and enables us, perhaps, with some degree of certainty, to date the origin of *Vignettes* in this country in which the Human Figure is introduced. On the reverse of fol. 182 is a representation of a Battle; the first which I have met with in this country on an enlarged scale, having the arms designated by the respective standards and pennons which they bore."—*Dibdin.*

1942 KENNETT (*Dr.*) Complete History of England, with the Lives of all the Kings and Queens, from the earliest accounts to the time of the death of William III.; containing also a faithful account of the Affairs of State, Ecclesiastical and Civil. *The whole illustrated by a series of very fine portraits*, 3 vols. folio, *calf, fine copy.* Lond. 1706

This History forms a collection of various authors, arranged and continued from Charles I. to William III. by Bishop Kennett; amongst them are Milton's History of England up to the Conquest, Daniel's Lives of the Norman Kings, Huntingdon's Edward IV., Sir Thomas Moore's Lives of Richard III. and Edward V., Lord Bacon's Henry VII., Lord Herbert's Henry VIII., Camden's Annals of Elizabeth.

Of the "Complete History of England usually attributed to Bp. Kennett, I have little hesitation in affirming, that considering the interesting materials of which it is composed, it must be entitled to a conspicuous place in the library of the careful collector."—*Dibdin's Lib. Comp.*

1943 KIMBER (*Edward*), History of England, as well Civil as Ecclesiastical, from the earliest period to the Twelfth Parliament, together with the History of Scotland and Ireland, &c., also of the Settlement, Progress, &c., of the British Empire in America, *plates*, 10 vols. 8vo. *calf.* Lond. 1766

1944 LARREY (*M. de*), Histoire d'Angleterre, d'Ecosse, et d'Irlande. With many portraits, 4 vols. folio, *calf.* Rotterd. 1707

This work has a dissertation on the origin of Parliaments, combating the opinions of Spelman, Prynne, and Brady.

1945 MACAULAY (*Catherine*), History of England, from the Accession of James the First to the elevation of the House of Hanover, 5 vols. 4to *half calf.* 1763

Written with great spirit and ability, and full of the freest, noblest sentiments of liberty.

1946 MOLEVILLE (*Bertrand de*), Chronological arrangement of the History of Great Britain, from the Romans to George III., 4 vols. royal 8vo. *splendid large paper copy, calf extra.* Lond. 1811

1947 MONSTRELET'S Chronicles, from the year 1400 to 1467, and continued by others to 1516; translated by Col. Johnes, 2 vols. impl. 8vo. *cloth.* 1840

These Chronicles commence at the exact period where Froissart finishes. They relate not only to the affairs of France, but also to those of England, Scotland, Ireland, Spain, and some other parts of Europe. Monstrelet's Chronicles are real history, wherein are found all the characteristics of historical writing. He traces events to their source, developes the causes, and follows them with the minutest details; and what renders these Chronicles infinitely precious is, his never-failing attention to report all Edicts, Letters, Treaties, etc. as proofs of the truth of the facts he relates.

1947*NAVAL Chronicle, complete from its commencement in 1799 to 1816 inclusive, illustrated with many fine portraits and engravings of Sea Fights, &c., 36 large vols. royal 8vo. *half bound.* 1799–1816

This very interesting work gives the fullest and most graphic accounts of the brilliant exploits of the British Navy during 16 years, with Memoirs of the Commanders, Officers, &c., including many no where else published; also Naval Tales, Anecdotes, Obituaries, &c.

Amongst the biographies will be found:

Admiral Earl Howe,	Sir J. Moore,	Willet Payne,
" Sir C. Knowles,	Lord Duncan,	Capt. Brodie,
" Lord Bridport,	Sir Sidney Smith,	" Harvey,
" *Lord Rodney*,	*Sir Hyde Parker*,	" *Ellison*,
" Lord Nelson,	Lord Keppel,	" Jervis,
" Earl of St. Vincent,	Lord Mulgrave,	Sir E. Gough,
" Lord Graves,	Sir G. Pocock,	Sir E. Hamilton,
" Cornwallis,	Lord Radstock,	Sir R. Curtis,
" Lord Anson,	Sir R. Onslow,	Sir P. Parker,
" Lord Keith,	Earl of Northesk,	Sir N. Dance,
" Lord Hood,	Sir E. Pellew,	Hon. Rich. Walpole,
" Collingwood,	Capt. M. Seymour,	Sir H. R. Popham,
" Lord Gambier,	Lord Gardner,	Sir T. Duckworth,
" Sir C. Hardy,	Sir R. Dacres,	Lord Cochrane,
" Sir C. M. Pole,	Sir R. Calder,	Hon. J. Forbes,
" Earl of Nottingham,	Capt. Flinders,	Sir Cloudesly Shovel,
Lord Seymour,	Lord Hawke,	and many others.

1948 NETHERCLIFT'S Collection of One Hundred Characteristic and Interesting Autograph Letters, written by Royal and Distinguished Persons of Great Britain, from the 15th to the latter part of the 18th Century, copied in perfect fac-simile from the originals, with explanatory Letterpress and Translations, large 4to. Lond. 1835

Indispensable to the autograph collector.

1949 PICTORIAL History of England, being a History of the People as well as a History of the Kingdom, illustrated with 2000 wood-cuts and plates of Monumental Records; Coins; Civil and Military Costume; Domestic Buildings, Furniture, and Ornaments; Cathedrals and other works of Architecture; Sports and other illustrations of Manners; Mechanical Inventions; Portraits of Eminent Persons; and Remarkable Historic Scenes, by George L. Craik and Charles Macfarlane, assisted by other Contributors, 8 vols. super-royal 8vo. *cloth.* 1849

"The 'Pictorial History of England' now before us seems to be the very thing now required by the popular taste of the present day; adding to the advantage of a clear, historical narrative, all the varied illustrations of which the subject is capable. Almost every page in the earlier volumes is enriched with appropriate wood-cuts, generally of able execution—dresses, arms, industrious employments, sports, copied from illuminated manuscripts of the periods to which they belong."—*Edin. Review.*

1950 POLYDORI Virgilii, Historia Anglicæ, folio, *limp vellum.* Basil, 1548

Polydore Virgil, who came to England in the retinue of Cardinal Corneto, to collect the Papal tribute called Peter-Pence, and whose fine and elegant style as a Latinist is preferred to almost any of his contemporaries, recommended himself so much to Henry VIII. that the King promoted him to several church preferments, and among others to the rich Archdeaconry of Wells.

In this work will be found the origin of various religious rites and ceremonies.

1951 RAPIN and Tindal's England: The History of England, by M. Rapin de Thoyras; translated and continued to the Reign of George II. by N. Tindal, 4 vols. folio, illustrations by Virtue and Houbraken—Heads and Monuments of the Kings, Portraits of Illustrious Persons, Maps, Military Plans, Medallic History, &c., *half calf.* Lond. 1743

"Let me assure the well educated and tasteful collector of books, that he can have no brighter or more desirable ornament in the historical department of his library than the folio edition of Rapin and Tindal, adorned by the heads of Virtue and Houbraken."—*Dibdin.*

1952 RANDALL (*M. D.*) History of England, 12mo. *boards.* Lond. 1829

1953 RAPIN'S Acta Regia, or an Account of Treaties, Letters and Instruments, between the Monarchs of England and Foreign Powers, published in Rymer's Fœdera, which are the basis of English History, 4 vols. 8vo. *calf.* Lond. 1726

1954 REPORTS of the Commissioners upon the Public Records of Great Britain, 4 vols. folio. Lond. 1801–37

"A treasure of Historical Information. Vol. 3 is a collection of all the plates from the various works published by the Commission, and contains 86 of the finest fac similes ever made.

"These Reports are particularly interesting to those who have occasion to search after the Records of the Kingdom, and contain much important and truly valuable information. The plates of fac similes will prove highly useful to those engaged in deciphering old Records, Deeds, &c.

1955 TURNER (*Sharon*), History of the Anglo-Saxons from the Earliest Period to the Norman Conquest, 3 vols. 8vo. Paris, 1840

"There is good information to be found in the book of the laws, languages, and manners of the Anglo-Saxons, their religion and their superstitions; the constitution of their government, their kings, their poetry, literature and arts. These are all subjects very interesting, and can only be exhibited by an antiquarian who, Mr. Turner, offers them so completely and agreeably."—*Prof. Smyth.*

1956 SLATYER (*W.*) Palæ Albion, or the History of Great Britaine from the first peopling of this Island to this present Raigne of our happy and peaceful Monarke K. James, printed by W. Stansby, for Ric. Meighen and are to be sold at his shop at St. Clement's Church, *fine engraved frontispiece, fine clean copy in the original binding, rare,* folio, *calf.* Lond. 1621

*** Sold in Sir M. M. Sykes' sale for £4 4*s.*, and priced in Bib.-Ang-Poet, £3 3*s.*

1956*SPEED'S Chronicle, or the History of Great Britaine under the Conquests of ye Romans, Saxons, Danes and Normans; the Originals, Manners, Habits, Warres, Coines, Seales, &c. &c., folio, *calf, Gibbons' copy, large paper, very rare.* Lond. 1627

"Speed was a person of extraordinary industry and attainments in the study of antiquity."—*Nicholson.*

1957 SIEGE of Calais, by Edward of England, 12mo. *calf,* Lond. 1740

1958 RICHARD II., Life and Reign of, by a person of quality, 12mo. *vellum.* Lond. 1681

1959 IDOL of the Clownes, or Insurrection of Wat the Tyler, with his fellow kings of the commons, against the English Church, the king, the lawes, nobility and gentry, in the fourth yeare of King Richard the 2d, Anno. 1381, with Lidgate's leaf of Black Letter Poetry, *rare, fine copy.* Lond. 1654

"This volume contains a vast deal of curious information, and was much read at the time."

1960 HALSTEAD (*C. A.*) Life and Times of Richard the Third, as Duke of Gloucester and King of England: in which all the Charges against him are carefully investigated and compared with the Statements of the Contemporary Authorities, portraits and other illustrations, 2 vols. 8vo. Lond. 1844

"Many new lights are thrown on the career of Richard, many new facts elicited, and the injustice of four centuries vindicated by this intrepid and indefatigable champion of historical truth."

Metropolitan Magazine.

1960*—— Idem, 8vo. *cloth.* Phil. 1844

1961 WALPOLE (*Horace*), Historic Doubts on the Life and Reign of King Richard 3rd, 4to. *plates, calf, wants all after page* 50. Lond. 1768

"A masterpiece of historical criticism."

1962 GOODWIN (*Thos.*) History of the Reign of Henry V. of England, *portrait,* folio, *calf.* Lond. 1704

"Compiled from good authorities."—*Nicholson.*

1963 BLUNT (*Rev. P. J.*) The Reformation in England, 12mo. *cloth.* Phil. 1837

1964 FENN'S (*Sir John*), Original Letters of the Paston Family, written during the reigns of Henry VI., Edward IV. and V., Richard III., and Henry VII., by various persons of Rank and Consequence, 2 vols. 4to. *half calf.* Lond. 1787

A most singular and valuable work, containing many curious anecdotes relative to this turbulent and bloody, but hitherto dark, period of history, and elucidating not only public matters of state, but likewise the private manners of the age, &c. &c.

1965 HARINGTON (*Sir John*), Nugæ Antiquæ; a Collection of Papers in Prose and Verse, written in the reigns of Henry VIII. to James I., 3 vols. 12mo. *calf.* Lond. 1792

The first volume comprises a brief view of the state of the Church of England as it stood in the reigns of Elizabeth and James, being a Character and History of the Bishops, written for the use of Prince Henry upon occasion of that proverb—

"Henry the Eighth pulled down monks and the cells,
Henry the Ninth should pull down bishops and their bells."

1966 HAYWARD'S (*Sir J.*) Life and Raigne of King Edward VI., *fine portraits by Vaughan and Pass*, small 4to. *vellum*. Lond. 1630

1967 ——— Annals of the First Four Years of the Reign of Queen Elizabeth, 4to. *cloth*. (*Camden Society*), Lond. 1840

1968 HEYWOOD (*Thos.*) England's Elizabeth, her Life and Troubles, *rare and curious*. Lond. 1634

1969 NAUNTON (*Sir Robt.*) Fragmenta Regalia, or Observations on the late Queen Elizabeth, her Times and Favorites, *with autograph of* "*G. Furman*," small 4to. *half morocco, rare*. Lond. 1642

1970 A TRUE RELATION of the Facts and Circumstances of the Intended Riot and Tumult on Queen Elizabeth's Birth-Day, 12mo. *half roan*. Lond. 1711

1971 MEMOIRS of the Peers of England during the Reign of King James I., *numerous fine portraits inserted*, 2 vols. 4to. *half morocco*. n. d.

1972 SANDERSON (*W.*) Charles I., Complete History of the Life and Reign of his Majesty, from his Cradle to his Grave, *with fine portrait by Faithorne*, thick folio, *half calf*. Lond. 1658

1973 CHARLES I., Trial of, for High Treason before the High Court of Justice, with additions, by J. Nalson, LL.D., 12mo. *sheep*. Lond. 1740

1974 ——— Eikon Basilike, the Pourtraiture of his Sacred Majesty in his Solitude and Sufferings, 8vo. *old binding*. Lond. 1648

1975 ——— Eikon Basilike, the Portraiture of his Sacred Majesty in his Solitudes and Sufferings, post 8vo. *plates, calf*. 1648, *Reprinted*, Lond. 1824

"Had it appeared a week sooner, it might have preserved the king's life, so extraordinary was the effect it produced. Fifty editions appeared in one year."—*Laing.*

1976 ——— Hollingworth (*Rich.*) Death of Charles I. proved to be downright Murder, 1693; Walker, True Account of the Author of a Booke entituled Eikon Basilike, &c., 1693; Ludlow (*Gen.*) Truth Brought to Light, or the Gross Forgeries of Dr. Hollingworth Detected, &c., 1693, *see MS. notes by Furman*, in 1 vol. 4to. Lond. v. y.

1977 CLARENDON'S History of the Rebellion and Civil Wars in England, *illustrated with* 88 *portraits of the personages referred to therein*, folio, *calf*. *Bp. Jarvis' copy*, Oxford, 1732

"One of the noblest historical works of the English nation."—*Lord Jeffrey.*

1978 WORDSWORTH (*Christ.*) D.D., "Who Wrote Eikon Basilike?" Considered and Answered, in Two Letters to the Archbishop of Canterbury, 8vo. *half calf.* Lond. 1824

*** Who wrote 'Eikon Basilike'" is a question that has not yet received a *satisfactory* answer. "This work has, however, been attributed to Dr. Gauden, who was incapable of writing the book, though not of disowning it."—*Disraeli.*

1979 BURTON (*John*), Genuineness of Lord Clarendon's History of the Rebellion Vindicated, 8vo. *sewed.* Oxford, 1744

1980 CAULFIELD (*J.*) High Court of Justice, comprising Memoirs of the Principal Persons who sat in Judgment on King Charles the First and Signed his Death Warrant, *illustrated with their portraits, autographs, and seals collected from authentic materials*, 4to. *boards.* Lond. 1820

1981 MEMOIR of King Charles I. and the Loyalists who suffered in his Cause, *illustrated with their portraits from Vandyke*, 4to. *boards, uncut, large paper.* Lond. 1798

1982 CATTERMOLE (*Rev. R.*) Illustrated History of the Great Civil War of the Times of Charles I. and Cromwell, with 30 highly finished engravings on steel, after Cattermole, by Rolls, Wellmore, Holl, Heath, Varral, and other first-rate artists, imperial 8vo. *cloth.* 1845

*** This is unquestionably the most perfect illustrated volume of an historical character which has ever been published.

1984 ——— Another copy, 4to. *cloth, gilt.* n.d.

1985 MAY (*Thomas*), History of the Long Parliament, edited by F. Maseres, with Life of May, 4to. *portrait and plate, half calf.* Lond. 1812

"This history is written with much temper, moderation, and judgment, and with great vigor of style and sentiment."—*Lowndes.*

The great Lord Chatham considers this "a much honester and more instructive book of the period than that of Lord Clarendon."

1986 CABAL: sive Scrinia Sacra, Mysteries of State and Government, in Letters and Negotiations of Illustrious Persons and Great Ministers, Foreign and Domestic, from Henry VIII. to Charles I., small 4to.

"An important and valuable collection, constantly referred to by writers on the Reigns of Elizabeth, James I., &c.

1987 BATE (*Geo.*) Elenchus motuum nuperorum in Anglia simul ac juris Regii et Parliamentario brevis Narratio, *portrait of Charles I.*, 12mo. Lond. 1663

Bp. Warburton says this is a book worth reading.

1988 Bolton's Nero Cæsar, or Monarchie Depraved, an Historical Work, dedicated to the Duke of Buckingham, *engraved title by Delaram*, folio, *calf.* 1627

Contains interesting description of Roman Britain.

Cromwell and the Commonwealth.

1989 Noble (*Mark*), Memoirs of the Protectoral House of Cromwell, as also the Lives of such persons as were distinguished by the Cromwells, *plates*, 2 vols. 8vo. *calf.* Lond. 1787

1990 Burton (*T.*) Cromwellian Diary, with an Historical Introduction and Notes, by J. T. Rutt, *plates*, 4 vols. 8vo. *cloth.* Lond. 1828

The very curious and important manuscripts from which these volumes were printed, were discovered among the papers of Henry Hyde, Earl of Clarendon, and owe their publication to the same assiduous bibliographer who brought to light the Memoirs of Evelyn and Pepys.

1991 Cromwell (*Oliver*), A Short Critical Review of the Political Life of, &c., by a gentleman of the Middle Temple, 12mo. *old calf.* Lond. 1747

1992 Cromwelliana, a Chronological Detail of Events in which Oliver Cromwell was engaged, from 1642 to his Death, 1658, with a Continuation to the Restoration, *plates*, folio, large paper, *boards.* 1810

One of the most interesting works relating to this very celebrated man, taken from the tracts, newspapers, &c. &c., of the period, by Stace, and containing many curious and authentic anecdotes, &c. &c., not generally known.

1993 Allen (*William, i. e. Col. Silas Titus*), Killing noe Murder, briefly discoursed in three Questions, &c. *half morocco*, 4to. 1689

The real author of this famous pamphlet, which is said to have struck such a terror into the mind of Cromwell as to render the concluding part of his life miserable, was the celebrated Col. Titus Loundes.

1994 Agathocles, the Syracusan Tyrant, or the Life of Agathocles (*e. i. O. Cromwell*), with some reflections on the practices of our Modern Usurpers, *curious plate, containing a portrait of Cromwell, inscribed "Tyrannus"* 12mo. *half calf.* Lond. 1661

This book, intended as a parallel to Cromwell, was written by R. Perrinchief; the portrait is an adaption of the copperplate of Edward Waterhouse, a furred cap being the alteration.

1995 Peters (*Hugh*), Historical and Critical account of, after the manner of Mr. Bayle, by Wm. Harris, 8vo. *half calf.* Lond. 1751

1996 PETERS (*Hugh*), History of, with an Appendix, by the Rev. Samuel Peters, 2 vols. in 1, 8vo. *half calf.* N. Y. 1807

CHARLES II., RESTORATION, &c.

1997 MONARCHY Revived, being the Personal Memoirs of Charles the Second, from his Earlier Years to the Restoration, *with* 14 *portraits*, 8vo. *boards, uncut.* 1822

1998 REGICIDES and Murderers, an exact and most impartial accompt of Twenty-Nine, and of his late Sacred Majesty (Charles I.), small 4to. *calf.* Lond. 1660

1999 SPEECHES and Prayers of Harrison, Cooke, Hugh Peters, Scott Scroop, Axtell, Clement, Jones, and Hacker, at their Execution 1660; also the Speeches, Discourses, and Prayers of Col. John Berkstead, Col. John Okey, and Mr. Miles Corbet, upon the 19th of April, being the day of their suffering at Tyburn, together with the Occasion and Manner of their taking in Holland, etc. 2 vols. in 1, small 4to. *old calf.* 1660–62

An universal feeling of sadness appeared among the spectators of their several deaths. They were all quartered and their several quarters taken back to Newgate to be boyled.

*** Sold in Bindley's sale for £1 7*s*., and in Towneley's for £1 9*s*.

2000 BURNET (*Bp.*) History of his Own Time, 2 vols. folio, *calf*, first edition. Lond. 1724

Bishop Atterbury *said* on the appearance of this edition, "Damn him, he has told a good deal of truth, but where the devil *did he find it?*"
"Burnet's History of His Own Times is a truly valuable book."—*Coleridge.*

2001 KING James II., True Account and Declaration of the Horrid Conspiracy against, folio, *calf.* Lond. 1685

2002 ABDICATED Prince, or the Adventures of Four Years, a Tragi-Comedy, surreptitiously printed, 4to. Lond. 1696

Relating to James the 2d, and the Duke of Monmouth, Father Peters, &c.

2003 NOBLE (*Mark*), House of Stuart, *half calf*, 4to. Lond. 1795

2004 JESSE'S Memoirs of the Court of England during the Reign of the Stuarts, including the Protectorate, *fine engravings*, 4 vols. 8vo. *cloth.* 1840

"Without it no library can be complete."—*Times.*

JAMEISON'S Beauties, vide Lot 678*.

2005 THOMSON'S (*Mrs.*) Memoirs of the Jacobites of 1715 and 1745, *portraits*, 3 vols. 8vo. *cloth.* Lond. 1845

"This useful and interesting work may assert its place in the standard literature of the country."—*Lit. Gaz.*

2007 ESSEX'S Innocency and Honour Vindicated, or Murther, Subornation, Perjury, and Oppression justly charged on the Murtherers of that Noble Lord and true patriot, Arthur, (late) Earl of Essex, *rare and curious*, 4to. *boards.* Lond. 1690

2008 D'ORLEANS (*P. J.*) History of the Revolution in England, 8vo. *calf.* Lond. 1722

2009 SAMSON (*P. A.*) Histoire de Guillaume III., 3 vols. 12mo., *vellum, numerous portraits and plates.* La Hay, 1703

2010 ENGLAND'S Remembrancer, 18mo. *old calf.* Lond. 1713

2011 WALPOLE'S (*Horace*) Memoirs of the Last Ten Years of the Reign of George II. *eleven fine portraits*, 2 vols. royal 4to. *half calf, uncut.* 1822

"The most valuable addition made to English Memoirs since the publication of Burnet and Clarendon, and we know of no works in our language that contain such minute and circumstantial details from an eye-witness of so many persons remarkable in our history."—*Edinburgh Review.*

2012 COURT and Times of George IV., Diary illustrative of, by Lady Charlotte Bury, *Maid of Honour to Queen Caroline*, with Original Letters by Q. Caroline, Princess Charlotte, &c., 4 vols. *boards.* Phil. 1838

A most remarkable work, comprehending the *Secret* History of the Courts; full of curious and authentic anecdotes, related by a person conversant with the scenes she describes.

2013 GRANT—British Senate, 2d Series of Random Recollections, 2 vols. 12mo. *cloth.* Phil. 1838

2014 JOURNAL of the Movements of the British Legion, 8vo. *boards.* Lond. 1836

2015 STAR Chamber, Outline of its History and account of its Jurisdiction, and other pieces, 4to. 1833

2016 BURTON'S Historical Works—History of the Kingdom of Scotland, by Richard Burton, 4to.; Historical Remarks on the Ancient and Present State of London and Westminster; History of the House of Orange, and of King William and Queen Mary; History of the Kingdom of Ireland, 4 vols. in 1, 4to. *reprinted from the original editions, numerous curious cuts, half morocco.* Lond. 1810

2017 BRADY, Clavis Calendaria, or a Compendious Analysis of the Calendar, with Ecclesiastical, Historical, and Classical Anecdotes, 2 vols. 8vo. *calf.* Lond. 1815

2018 REGNAULT (*E.*) Annual History of the English Government, 12mo. *cloth.* N. Y. 1843

2019 JONES (*C. C.*) Recollections of Royalty, 2 vols. 8vo. *half morocco.* 1828

2019*a* RITSON (*J.*) Letters, with a Memoir, by Sir H. Nicolas, 2 vols. 12mo. *cloth.* Long., *Pickering*, 1833

2019*b* GORDON (*D.*) General History of the Lives, Trials, and Executions of all the Royal and Noble Personages that have suffered in Great Britain and Ireland for High Treason or other Crimes from Henry VIII. to the present time, 3 vols. 8vo. *calf, numerous portraits, fine copy.* Lond. 1760

2019*c* WOOLRYCH (*H. W.*) Life of Judge Jeffreys, 12mo. *cloth.* Phil. 1852

2020 CUNNINGHAM (*G. G.*) Lives of Illustrious Englishmen, from Alfred the Great to the Latest Times, *with fine series of portraits*, 8 vols. in 4, *half calf.* Glasgow, 1836

"Embodying the history of England in the lives of Englishmen and the nearest approach compatible with truth, to the historical plays of Shakspeare, and the historical novels of Scott. We warmly recommend the work as a mine of valuable information presented in the most attractive form."—*Tait's Edin. Mag.*

2021 ENGLAND'S Worthies, under whom all the Civil and Bloody Warres, since Anno 1642 to Anno 1647, are related, by John Vicars, *with copies of the* 18 *rare portraits after Hollar, &c.*, 12mo. *half morocco.* 1819

Copies of the original edition sold at from £16 to £20.

2022 RICRAFT'S Survey of England's Champions, with 20 fine portraits of the most celebrated Personages connected with the Civil War, whose Lives are given, 8vo. *half morocco, uncut* 1810

Reprinted from the rare edition of 1647, which has sold for £33.

2023 GEORGEAN Era: Memoirs of the most Eminent Persons who have flourished in Great Britain, 4 vols. 8vo. *boards.* Lond. 1832

2024 GILPIN (*Wm.*) Lives of John Wicliff and of the most Eminent of his Disciples, 8vo. *calf.* 1765

ENGLAND, SCOTLAND, WALES AND IRELAND.—Topography and Antiquities, London and Westminster, Channel Isles, Foreigners' Travels in.

2025 Barbers's Isle of Wight, illustrated by 45 fine steel plates (including a portrait of Her Majesty) with a Map of the Island, and Dr. Mantell's Geological Map, 8vo. *cloth, gilt.* 1850

2026 Beattie (*Dr. W.*) Castles and Abbeys of England, royal 8vo. *cloth*, 250 *plates, imperfect.* Lond. n. d.

2027 Beauties of England, or a Description of the Public Edifices, Palaces, Noblemen's and Gentlemen's Seats, &c., *numerous plates*, 2 vols. 8vo. *old calf.* Lond. 1773

2028 Brayley and Britton, Durham, Topography and History of, 8vo. *boards.* Lond. n. d.

2029 ——— Cambridge, Topography and History of, 8vo. *boards.* Lond. n. d.

2030 Burton (*William*), Commentary on Antoninus, his Itinerary, or Journies of the Romane Empire, so far as it concerneth Britain, with the scarce portrait and map by Hollar, *beautiful copy*, folio, *original binding.* Lond. 1658

This writer is highly commended, by Ant. à Wood.

2031 Canterbury, a Collection of Tracts relating to the City of; including the Book of Chronicles, by an Old Woman, Life of Betty Bolaine, Essay on Courtenay, &c., 8vo. *boards.* Lond. 1836

2032 Compton (*Th.*) North Cambrian Mountains, oblong 4to. *half calf.* 1816

2033 Crosby, Gazetteer of England and Wales, 12mo. Lond. 1818

2034 Darell (*Rev. W.*) History of Dover Castle, 4to. *half morocco.* Lond. 1797

2035 Dover and Dover Castle, 12mo. *boards, imperfect.* 1828

2036 Dugdale's England Delineated, vols. 1, 2, and 5, 3 vols. 8vo. *cloth.* v. d.

2037 Englefield (*Sir H.*) Walk Through Southampton, 8vo. *morocco, fine plates of its antiquities.* Southampton, 1805

2038 Fittler (*J.*) Views of the Public Buildings, &c., of Newcastle upon Tyne, oblong 4to. n. d.

2039 Fosbroke (*T. D.*) British Monachism, or Manners and Customs of the Monks and Nuns of England, *plates, half calf*, royal 8vo. Lond. 1843

2040 Harraden (*R. B.*) Cantabrigia Depicta, containing an Historical and Descriptive Account of the most Picturesque and Interesting Edifices in the University of Cambridge, with Views of each, 35 *fine line engravings by Byrne, calf*, 4to. Lond. 1811

2041 Hone's Every Day Book and Table Book; Everlasting Calendar of Amusements, Times and Seasons, and complete History of the Year, 3 vols. 8vo. *engravings by Cruikshank, &c. boards.* Lond. 1850

> "I like you and your book, ingenuous Hone,
> In whose capacious, all-embracing leaves,
> The very marrow of tradition's shown,
> And all that History—much that Fiction—weaves."
> *Charles Lamb.*

2042 Howitt (*Wm.*) Visits to Remarkable Places, Old Halls, Battle Fields, &c. 2d series, 8vo. *cloth.* Phil. 1842

2043 Old England, a Pictorial Museum of National Antiquities, Regal, Ecclesiastical, Baronial, Municipal, and Popular, *with* 3000 *wood cuts, and* 24 *coloured engravings*, 2 vols. folio, *cloth.* 1845

The engravings embrace Druidical Remains, Cathedrals, Churches, Castles, Mansions, Sepulchral Monuments, Portraits, Famous Localities, the Great Seals and Arms of the Monasteries, &c.

2044 Liverpool Riots, Report of the Proceedings of the Trial before Sir Robert Graham, 8vo. Liverp. 1810

2045 Martin's Civil Costume of England, from the Conquest to the present period, a series of sixty-one plates, (mostly portraits of royal and noble persons, drawn from Ancient Manuscripts, Tapestries, &c.,) beautifully illuminated in gold and colors, royal 4to. *cloth.* Lond. 1842

This elegant work, executed by two sons of the celebrated painter, John Martin, Esq., is the only one which presents the authentic costumes of various ranks of society, from the Norman Conquest to the present day. It is especially valuable to artists.

Martin and Strutt's Works are the principal authorities for English Costume, and have, of late, been largely consulted for Her Majesty's splendid Bal Masque.

2046 REPRINTS of Rare Tracts, and Imprints of Ancient Manuscripts, &c., chiefly illustrative of the History and Biography of the Northern Counties, *beautifully printed on fine thick paper, with fac simile titles, initial letters in colours, &c., forming* 7 vols. post 8vo., *complete, with general titles and contents, boards, uncut,* (pub. at £7 7*s.*) Newcastle, 1844–49

This Collection comprises no less than 62 Tracts of the most interesting kind, edited by Mr. M. A. Richardson, assisted by several antiquaries in the northern counties. Only 100 copies of the Collection were printed, which were all sold by the printer before he sailed for Australia.

2047 SPRAT'S (*Bp.*) History of the Royal Society of London, *plates,* 4to. *calf, neat.* 1722

"One of the few books, which selection of sentiment and elegance of diction have been able to preserve."—*Chalmer's Biog. Dic.*

2048 STRUTT (*Joseph*), Dresses and Habits of the People of England, from the Establishment of the Saxons in Britain to the present time; with an Historical and Critical Inquiry into every branch of Costume: new and greatly improved edition, with Critical and Explanatory Notes, by J. R. Planche, Esq., F. S. A., 2 vols. royal 4to., 153 *colored plates, half morocco.* 1842

2049 ——— Regal and Ecclesiastical Antiquities of England, containing Authentic Portraits of all the Monarchs from Edward the Confessor to Henry VIII., and many Eminent Persons, and Contemporary Paintings of Important Events, 72 *beautifully colored plates,* royal 4to. *half morocco, gilt top.* Lond. 1842

Uniform with Strutt's dresses.

2050 SPORTS and Pastimes of the People of England, edited with Index, &c., by W. Hone, 140 *curious cuts from ancient illuminations, large paper, the cuts colored,* impl. 4to. *sheep.* 1801

LONDON.

"I pray you let us satisfy our eyes
With the memorial and things of fame
That do renown this city."

2051 AINSWORTH (*Wm. Harrison*), The Tower of London, a Historical Romance, *ill. by Geo. Cruckshank,* 8vo. *cloth.* Lond. 1845

2052 BEE (*John*), Living Picture of London, from 1828, 18mo. *cloth.* Lond.

2053 BAYLEY (*J*). Tower of London, History and Antiquities of, with Memoirs of Royal and Distinguished Personages, *highly finished engravings*, 2 vols. 4to. *half morocco.* 1821

2054 BRAYLEY, Brewer, and Nightingale, Beauties of London and Middlesex, 125 *plates*, 5 vols. 8vo. *half calf.* Lond. 1810

2055 BRIEF History of Christ's Hospital, 12mo. *boards.* Lond. 1820

2056 CHRONICLES of London Bridge, by an Antiquary, *numerous wood cuts, half morocco.* Lond. 1827

One of the most curious and interesting antiquarian books upon London ever published.

2057 DUGDALE (*William*), History of St. Paul's Cathedral, in London, from its Foundation to these Times, &c., edited by Ellis, 6 *parts*, folio, *unbound.* Lond. 1814

2058 GRANT'S Every-day Life in London, 12mo. Phil. 1839

2059 GRANT, Great Metropolis, 2 vols. 12mo. *cloth.* Phil. 1838

2060 GRANT'S Sketches of London, 2 vols. 12mo. Phil. 1839

2061 HUGHSON (*D.*) Walks through Islington, 2 vols. 12mo. *boards.* Lond. 1817

2062 IRELAND (*S.*) Picturesque Views in the Inns of Court, royal 8vo. *boards, uncut.* 1800

2063 JESSE (*J. H.*) Literary and Historical Memorials of London, *maps and plates*, 2 vols. 8vo. *cloth.* 1847

A very entertaining work, containing anecdotes of every remarkable locality, and also of the eminent inhabitants of the metropolis.

2064 JONES, Views of London in the 19th Century, 4to. Lond. 1827

2065 KNIGHT'S Pictorial History of London, Ancient and Modern, *extensively embellished with fine woodcut illustrations of the buildings, objects of art and interest, processions and customs, antiquities, &c.*, 6 vols. roy. 8vo. 1841

One of the most delightful works on London ever published, comprising a vast amount of topographical and antiquarian information, detailed in a lively and pleasant manner.

2066 LAMBERT'S History and Survey of London and its Environs from the earliest period, *numerous engravings and portraits*, 4 vols. 8vo. *sheep.* Lond. 1806

2066*London Strew'd with Rarities, or It cannot Rain but it Pours, (an account of the arrival of a White Bear in Bishopgate Street, the Copper Farthing Dean, the Singing Woman, the Wild Man, &c.,) 8vo. 1726

2067 London and its Environs Described, containing an Account of whatever is Remarkable in the City and 20 Miles Round, *many plates, several of which are additional*, 6 vols. 8vo. *calf, neat.* Dodsley, 1761

This work contains much curious information not to be found elsewhere, especially lists of celebrated collections of pictures, viz: Devonshire House, Foot's Cray Place, Blackheath, Sir G. P. Turner, &c.

2068 Select Views of London, *cold. plates*, royal 8vo. Lond. 1816

2069 Defoe's History of the Great Plague of London, in 1665, *front.* 8vo. *calf.* 1819

A fictitious narrative—so well drawn, however, that Dr. Mead supposed it genuine.

2070 Mahew's (*Henry*) London Labor and London Poor; a Cyclopedia of the condition and earnings of those that *will* work, those who *cannot* work, those that *will not* work, *woodcuts of the streets-folk of London*, 2 vols. in numbers.

The further publication of this work was interdicted by the authorities.

2071 Malcom (*J. P.*) Anecdotes of the Manners and Customs of London during the XVIII Century, including the Charities, Depravities, Dresses, and Amusements of the Citizens during that Period, 45 *plates, some colored*, 2 vols. 8vo. *calf.* 1810

This work is full of biographical notices, curious anecdotes, local peculiarities, charters, presentments, &c.

2072 Malcolm (*J. P.*) Miscellaneous Anecdotes of the Manners and History of Europe, with Reigns of Charles II., James II., William III., and Queen Ann, 8vo. *half calf.* Lond. 1811

2073 Noorthouck (*John*), History of London, including Westminster and Southwark; to which is added a Survey of the whole, describing the Public Buildings, late Improvements, &c., thick 4to. *numerous plates.* Lond. 1773

2074 Pennant (*Thos.*) Antiquarian and Picturesque Account of London, with numerous portraits and engravings of famous Buildings, &c., 3d edition, 4to. *half morocco.* Lond. 1793

"Pennant's account of London is one of the most pleasing topographical performances that ever appeared in any language."
Boswell's Life of Johnson.

2075 Pennant (*Thos.*) Antiquities of London, and Anecdotes of Eminent Persons, 8vo. *half calf*, 55 *plates.* Lond. 1814

2076 Percy (*S. and R.*) London, or Interesting Memorials of its Rise, Progress, and Present State, *portrait and engravings*, 3 vols. 18mo. *calf.* 1824

2077 Roscoe (*T.*) Account of the London and Birmingham Railway, *illustrated*, 8vo. *cloth.* Lond. n. d.

2078 Smith (*Albert*), Gavarni in London: Sketches of Life and Character, with Illustrative Essays by Popular Writers, 4to. *half calf, extra.* Lond. 1849

2079 Smith (*J. T.*) Antiquities of London and its Environs, 96 fine engravings of Old Houses, Monuments, Statues, &c., many of which no longer exist, impl. 4to. *half morocco.* Lond. 1791

2080 ——— Streets of London, 12mo. *cloth.* Lond. 1849

WESTMINSTER.

2081 Westminster: Antiquities in Westminster Abbey, Ancient Oil Paintings, and Sepulchral Brasses, from drawings by Harding, and Descriptions by Thomas Moule, folio. Lond. 1825

2082 Westminster: Brief Account of Ancient and Modern Westminster, 8vo. pp. Lond. 1839

"If you ask a well-educated American, when he visits England, what objects in the mother country have impressed him most, he will answer, "Its Cathedrals." Place him in York-minster, or Westminster Abbey, and he no longer thinks of comparing England to America: the *religio loci* makes itself felt; it awakens in him an ancestral feeling of which he was before unconscious, and he then begins to understand that, in the thoughts and emotions which carry us back to past ages, and connect us with the generations which are gone, there is something more soothing, more salutary for the heart, and more elevating also, than in all the anticipations with which a young and emulous nation looks onward to the future."—(*Southey? in*) *Quarterly Review.*

2083 History of the Famous Election for Westminster, between Fox, Admiral Hood, and Sir Cecil Wray, including all the Electioneering Squibs, Satires, &c., and 16 large caricature plates by Gilray of the beautiful Dutchess of Devonshire (who was so active a canvasser for Fox. *See* Wraxall's Memoirs, &c.) 4to. *boards, scarce.* Lond. 1784

2084 LYSON'S Environs of London, with the Additional Middlesex Parishes, with fine impressions of the numerous engravings of Buildings and Antiquities, 5 vols. royal 4to. *boards.* 1800–11

Few topographical works possess so much merit as this, and no pains or expense were spared to obtain authentic information.

2085 LYSONS' Britannia Depicta, a Series of Views of the most Interesting and Picturesque Objects in Great Britain, from Drawings by Hearne, Farrington, &c., engraved by Scott, Middiman, Pye, &c., with Descriptions, 6 parts, in 1 vol. oblong folio, containing 129 *fine copper-plate engravings, half morocco.* 1806–18

This series of views was published to illustrate Lysons' Magna Britannia, and contains the Counties of Bedfordshire, Berks, Bucks, Cambridgeshire, Cheshire, Cornwall, Cumberland, and Derbyshire, being all published.

2087 MACKENZIE (*A. Slidell*), The American in England, 2 vols. 12mo. *roan, gilt.* N. Y. 1835

2088 MUDIE (*R.*) Channel Islands, *plates*, royal 8vo. Winchester, n. d.

2089 PICTURESQUE Tour of the River Thames, illustrated by upwards of 100 highly finished wood engravings, steel plate engravings by Cooke and others, royal 8vo. *calf, gilt.* Lond. 1845

Full of entertaining anecdotes and descriptions ; a delightful Guide-book to Richmond, Windsor, and Hampton Court.

2090 ROBY (*J.*) Traditions of Lancashire, Historical, Legendary, and Romantic, 3 vols. small 8vo. *cloth.* Lond. 1841

"Tales that are as true as History, and yet possess the animation of Romance."

2091 TINDAL (*Wm.*) History and Antiquities of the Abby and Borough of Evesham, 4to. *half calf.* Evesham, 1794

2092 WALKS and Talks of an American Farmer in England, 8vo. N. Y. 1852

2093 WESTALL (*W. and Samuel Owen*), Picturesque Views on the River Thames, *cloth,* 24 *plates, colored,* imperial 4to. Lond.

2094 BORDERER'S Table Book, or etching of the local history and romance of the English and Scottish borders, *with* 900 *wood-cuts,* 4 vols. 8vo. *cloth.* Newcastle, 1846

EUROPE.—*See also* ENGLAND, FRANCE, GERMANY, ITALY, GREECE, &c.

2095 BREVAL (*J.*) History of the House of Nassau, 8vo. *half bound.* Lond. 1734

2096 BURTON (*Richard*), History of the House of Orange, *reprint*, 4to. 1814

2097 SOUTHEY'S (*R.*) Chronicle of the Cid, from the Spanish, 8vo. *cloth.* Lowell, 1840

"This is certainly one of the most interesting productions of the Spanish mind; it gives a full length picture of Spain in those dark ages in which the costume of other countries is so indistinct and confused."

2098 GLEANINGS in Europe, England, by an American, 2 vols. 12mo. *cloth.* Phil. 1837

2099 GLEANINGS in Europe, Italy, by an American, 2 vols. 12mo. *cloth.* Phil. 1838

2100 Noah (*M. M.*) Travels in England, France, Spain, and the Barbary States, 8vo. N. Y. 1819

FABLES.

2101 ÆSOP: Mythologia Æsopica, in qua Æsopi et aliorum Fabulæ, Gr. et Lat. cura J. Niveleti; 12mo. *numerous plates, half calf.* Francof. 1610

2102 ——— Fables, paraphrased in verse and adorned with sculptures by John Ogilby, *many fine plates*, 2 vols. *half calf*, folio. Lond. 1665

2103 ——— Fables of, and other eminent Mythologists, with morals and reflexions by Sir Roger L'Estrange, *binding broken*, folio. Lond. 1704

2104 ——— Fabulæ cura Desbillons; accesserunt plus CLXX., novæ, numerous beautiful etchings by Egidius Verhelst, 2 vols. in 1, 8vo. Mannh. 1768

"Verhelst was an artist of celebrity, and is noticed by Bryan (Stanly's edition); these plates are singular, as many of those having figures are in the full costume of George II., and Æsop is represented with an eyeglass looking at some others wearing spectacles, in court dresses, with cocked hats, bag-wigs, and pig-tails."

2105 ——— Fabulæ; 41 beautiful etchings by G. Kartsch, *vellum, clasps*, 18mo. no title.

2106 ——— in Rhyme and others, 4 vols. 8vo.

2107 ——— Junior in America, being a series of fables written for the people of the U. S., in America, *half calf*, 12mo. N. Y. 1834

2108 AYRES (*Philip*), Mythologia Ethica, or Three Centuries of Æsopian Fables in English Prose, done from Æsop, Phædrius, Camerarius, and others, *curious cuts*, 8vo. Lond. 1689

Rare, not in Lowndes.

2109 DRYDEN (*J.*) Fables, Ancient and Modern, translated into verse from Homer, Ovid, Boccace, and Chaucer, with original poems, folio, *old calf.* Lond. 1700

2110 FÆRNI, Fabulæ Centum ex antiquis Auctoribus Delectæ et a Gab. Færne carminibus explicatæ, 100 *plates after Titian*, *calf*, *extra*, 4to. Romæ, 1565

Editione originale, recherchée et peu commune.

2111 FÆRNI (*G.*) Fabulæ Centum; Cent Fables Choisies des Anciens Auteurs, mises en Vers Latins, et traduites en Français par Perrault, royal 4to. 100 *plates*, *calf.* Lond. 1743

2112 FONTAINE (*J. de la*), Fables avec figures de Simon et Coiny, 6 vols. *sewed*, 12mo. Paris, 1796

"Edition ornée de jolies gravures."—*Brunet.*

2113 ——— Excerpta en Fables Choisies, avec des notes nouvelles, &c., par de la Harpe, 8vo. N. Y. 1810

2114 NORTHCOTE'S Artist's "Book of Fables," comprising a Series of Original Fables, *illustrated by* 280 *exquisitely beautiful engravings on wood by Harvey and other eminent artists*, post 8vo. *cloth.* 1845

*** The late Mr. Northcote bequeathed upwards of three thousand pounds to his executors for the purpose of bringing out this volume, and the whole sum was expended on it.

2115 PHÆDRI, Fabulæ, edit. J. Lawrentio, 8vo. *vellum.* Amst. 1672

2116 WALLBRIDGE (*A.*) Bizarre Fables, a Series of Eccentric Historiettes, 40 *wood-cuts*, *cloth*, 12mo. Lond. 1843

FACETIÆ.

Let those laugh now who never laugh'd before,
And those who always laugh'd now laugh the more.

i. e. Let those bid now who never bid before,
And those who always bid give one bid more.

2117 ABEILLARD and Heloisa, a Nineteenth and Familiar History of the Lives and Loves of, by Rabelais, Jr., in Verse, *plates*, *boards*, 8vo. Lond. 1819

2118 A'BECKETT (*Gilbert A.*) Comic Blackstone, *sewed*, 12mo. Phil. 1846

2119 ADOLPHUS, Histoire des Diables Modernes, 12mo. *pr.* Cleves. 1771

2120 ADVENTURES of a Batchelor, or Stolen Vigils, *half calf*, 12mo. Phil. 1837

2121 ——— Black Coat, containing a Series of Remarkable Occurrences and Entertaining Incidents, *scarce*, 12mo. Edin. v. d.

2122 ——— Lazarillo De Tormes, *plates*, *half calf*, 12mo. Lond. 1821

For wit, spirit, and fun, there is nothing like it. Lazarille presents the very pattern of a good knave, the perfection of trickery.

2123 ——— Signor Gaudentia di Lucca, *half calf*, 12mo. Lond. 1821

2124 ——— To the Moon and Other Worlds, 8vo. Lond. 1836

2125 ALMANACK du Diable, contenant des predictions tres curieux et absolument infaillables, pour l'annee, 1738. Aux. Enfers, n. d.

2126 ——— of the Month, a Review of Everything and Everybody, edited by Gilbert Abbot à Beckett, *woodcuts*, 2 vols. 18mo. *cloth.* Lond. 1846

2127 ALEMAN (*Matheo*), The Rogue, or Life of Guzman de Alfarache, translated by James Mabbe, 1634; The Spanish Bawd, represented in Celestina, or the Tragicke-Comedy of Calisto and Melibea, in 1 vol. *half calf*, folio. Lond. 1631–4

"The Spanish Proteus, which, though writ,
But in one tongue was formed with the world's wit;
And hath the noblest mark of a good booke,
That an ill man doth not securely looke
Upon it; but will loathe or let it passe
As a deformed face doth a true glasse."—*Ben Jonson.*

The most ample portraiture of the Catariberas or the gayer one of Picaros, that is to be found in Spanish Literature. It was very successful falling in with the vices and humors of the times of the loose Court of Philip III. after the hypocrisy and constraints of the last dark years of Philip II.

2128 AMERICAN Bards, a Satire, 8vo. Phil. 1820

2129 ——— Comic Annual, *plates*, 12mo. Bost. 1831

2130 ——— Miscellany, or Popular Tales, Essays, Sketches, Poetry, and Jeux d'Esprit, by Transatlantic Authors, royal 8vo. *half calf.* Lond. 1840

2131 ——— Museums, or Repository of Ancient and Modern Fugitives, Pieces in Prose and Verse, 7 vols. *boards*, 8vo. Phil. 1781

2132 Anstey (*C.*) New Bath Guide, 12mo. Lond. 1773

Dodsley declared the Bath Guide was the most successful work he had ever published.

2133 Apecian Morsels, or Tales of the Table, Kitchen, and Larder, by Dick Humbbergius Secundus, *illustrated*, 8vo. *half cl.* N. Y. 1829

2134 Apuleius' Metamorphoses, or the Golden Ass, a free translation reprinted from the scarce edition of 1709, 2 vols. 8vo. *new half calf, gilt.* 1822

This is *modern* Apuleius—the actors monks and nuns—a scandalous book.

2135 Arthur O'Leary, His Wanderings and Ponderings in Many Lands, *illustrated by George Cruikshank*, 8vo. Lond. 1845

2136 Ass on Parnassus, and from Scotland Ge-ho!! Comes Roderigh Vichneddy Dhu, ho! Jerve!!! or a Poem entitled, What are Scot's Collops? a Prophetical Tale in imitation of the Lady of the Lake, 18mo. Phil. 1815

2137 Astonishing History and Adventures of Miss Betsy Warwick, the Female Rambler: The Life of Fanny Nugent, 8vo. *half morocco.* Manchester.

2138 Athenian Oracle, with the Supplement and History of the Athenian Society (by J. Dunton); also, Athenian Sports (very free), together, 6 vols. 8vo. *calf, gilt.* 1707–28

These volumes comprise an entire collection of all the valuable Questions and Answers in the Old Athenian Mercuries, also Two Thousand Paradoxes merily Argued to Amuse and Divert the Age—Apparitions, Adultery, Beauty, Polygamy, Mary-land, a Strange Account, are Quaker Marriages Lawful, &c. &c. No man sees but he that is stark blind; the Restored Maidenhead, or a Marryed Woman may be Twice a Virgin; the Virgin Paradox, or a Young Lady may Love and Hate the same Person at the same time; the Living Shrew, or the Kindest Women are the most Cruel, &c.

2139 Attachè, or Sam Slick in England, 8vo. Phil. 1843

2140 Authentic Memoirs, Memorandums, and Confessions of the King of the Swindlers, 8vo. *boards.* Lond. n. d.

2141 Bachelor Butterfly, &c., other comicalities. N. Y. n. d.

2142 Bacon (*Dr.*) Humorous Ethics, an Attempt to Cure the Vices and Follies of the Age, by a Method Entirely New, in Five Plays, &c., 8vo. *calf.* Lond. 1775

2143 Barber (*John*), Impartial History of the Life, Character, Amours, Travels, and Transactions of, *portrait inserted*, 8vo. *half calf.* Lond. 1741

2144 Barlow, Hasty-Pudding, a Poem, in three cantos, *written in the Savoy*, 1795, 12mo. *half morocco.* N. Y. 1796

2145 Battersby (*John*), Tell-tale Sophas, an eclectic Fable, 3 vols. (vols. 2 and 3) 12mo. Lond. 1814

2146 Bayley (*P. Haynes*), David Dumps; or the Budget of Blunders, a Tale, 12mo. *half calf.* Phil. 1838

2147 ——— (*F. W. N.*) New Tale of a Tub, an Adventure in Verse, *with illustrations designed by Lieut. J. S. Cotton*, 4to. *cloth, gilt.* Lond. 1845

2148 ——— (*P. Haynes*), Weeds of Witchery (in verse), *ludicrous plates*, 4to. Lond. 1837

2149 Behn (*Mrs. Aphra*), Seventeen Histories and Novels by, 2 vols. 8vo. *sheep.* Lond. 1718

"A very curious collection, illustrative of the license of the times," scarce.

2150 Ben Saddi (*Nathan*), The Chronicle of the Kings of England, *written in the manner of the ancient Jewish historians*, 8vo. Newport, R. Island, 1744

2151 Beresford (*James*), Miseries of Human Life, or the Groans of Sam Sensitive and Tim Testy, with a few Supplementary Sighs from Mrs. Testy, in 12 Dialogues, 2 vols. 12mo. *calf, extra.* 1806

To peruse these amusing Dialogues is certainly not one of the Miseries of Human Life.

2152 ——— Antidote to the Miseries of Human Life, 12mo. *boards.* Lond. 1810

2153 ——— Sequel to the Antidote, &c. 12mo. *boards.* 1811

2154 ——— Miseries of Human Life, vol. 2, 12mo. *boards.* 1826

2155 Bergerac Satyrical Characters and Handsome Descriptions in Letters, translated from the French, 8vo. Lond. 1658

An account of this singular and amusing work will be found in the *Retrospective Review*, I. 279–87.

2156 Bertin (*Le. Chev. de*) Œuvres, 2 vols. 18mo. *old French calf, gilt.* Paris, 1791

2157 Biographical Sketches of Eccentric Characters, 18mo. *half calf.* Bost. 1832

2158 BIOGRAPHIE des Préfets, Biographié des Cardinaux, Archeveques, &c., Biographié des Souveraines du XIX Siècle, in 1[illegible] vols. 32mo. 1826

2159 BLANCHARD (*Laman*), Sketches from Life, with a Memoir by Sir Edward Bulwer Lytton, 3 vols. 12mo. *engravings by G. Cruikshank, cloth.* 1849

A charming work, full of wit and wisdom, humour and pathos—an admirable companion for a wet day or long journey, for there is something to suit every temper and season. There are upwards of 100 Essays, Tales, and Sketches.

2160 BOCCACIO Decameron, translated, *with* 21 *plates*, 12mo. *cloth.* Lond. 1850

——— Idem, *vide* Shakspeariana.

2161 BOCCALINI (*Trajan*), Advertizement from Parnassus, with the Politick Touchstone, translated by H. Carey, Earl of Monmouth, folio, with autograph of H. Drake, Commentator on Shakspeare. Lond. 1674

2162 BOSTON Book, being specimens of Metropolitan Literature, *cloth*, post 8vo. Bost. 1850

2163 BOWER of Bliss, and other Amatory Poems, including the Loves of Abelard and Heloise, 8vo. *bds. uncut.* Lond. 1814

2164 BOWL of Punch, or Selections from the London Charivari, illustrations by Leech, &c. 12mo. *sewed.* Phil. 1844

2165 BOYLE (*Robt.*) Voyages and Adventures of, interspersed with the Story of Mrs. Villars, 12mo. *old calf.* Lond. 1771

2166 BRACKENRIDGE (*H. H.*) Adventures of Captain Farrago, 12mo. *sewed.* Phil. n. d.

2167 ——— Adventures of Major O'Regan, 8vo. *sewed.* Phil. 1856

2168 BRANDT (*Sebastian*), Ship of Fooles, wherein is shewed the Follie of all States, imperfect at beginning and end, translated by Barkely, *bad copy*, folio, *half calf.* Lond. n. d.

The design of this most curious and amusing work was to ridicule the prevailing follies and vices of every rank and profession, under the allegory of a ship freighted with fools: and in this metrical translation Barclay has given a variety of characters drawn expressly from his own countrymen, and added his advice to the various fools, which possesses at least the merit of good sense and morality.

2169 ——— Narren Speel-Schuyt, *one hundred wood-cuts*, and same designs as in Barclay's translation, *half russia*, 4to. Leyden, 1610

2170 BRAITHWAIT (*Richard, the Facetious Poet*), Drunken Barnaby's Journal, Travels to the North, &c., with Bessy Bell, and Chevy Chase, in Monkish Latin Rhyming Verse and English, 12mo. *rare.* Lond. 1723

"An exquisite piece of humorous drollery."

2171 BREMOND (*M. S.*) The Pilgrim, a Pleasant Piece of Gallantry, 18mo. *calf.* Lond. 1684

2172 BRITISH Apollo, containing about 2000 Answers to Curious Questions in most Arts and Sciences, Serious, Comical, and Humorous, 8vo. *calf.* Lond. 1708

The "Notes and Queries" of the last century.

2173 BROUGHAM (*John*), Basket of Chips, *plates*, post 8vo. *cloth.* N. Y. 1855

2174 BROWN (*Tom*), Works, Serious and Comical, with a Key to all his Writings, to which is prefixed a Character of Mr. Brown, by Drake, 4 vols. 12mo. *fronts., calf, nt.* Dub. 1778

"An Author, who disgraced great natural talents, humour and erudition, by an unhappy taste for ribaldry and libertinism." His works are valuable historically for their vivid pictures of English life, in all its coarseness, &c., during the "Augustan Age" of Queen Anne.

2175 BUCKINGHAM (*John Sheffield, Duke of*), Works, 2 vols. 8vo. *calf.* Lond. 1729

2176 BURKE (*Edmund*), The Wisdom and Genius of, with a Summary of his Life, 8vo. *sheep.* Lond. 1844

2177 BURNHAM (*George P.*) The History of the Hen Fever, a Humorous Record, *illustrated, cloth,* 8vo. Boston.

2178 BURNETT (*Thomas*), A Second Tale of a Tub; or, the History of Robert Powell, the Puppet-Showman, post 8vo. *old calf, front.* Lond. 1715

A Satire on Sir Robert Walpole.

2179 BURROUGHS (*Stephen*), Memoirs of the Notorious, 2 vols. in 1, 18mo. *boards.* Bost. 1832

2180 BUSSI-RABUTIN, Lettres, et Lettres Nouvelles, avec les Responses, 6 vols. 12mo. *calf.* Amst. 1768

For the liberties this witty author and courtier took with the characters of the French ladies, and his allusions to the partiality of Louis XIV. for Mad. de la Vallière, he was committed to the Bastile.

2181 BUSTLE, a Philosophical and Moral Poem, *paper*, 12mo. Boston, 1845

2182 BURLESQUE Translation of Homer, in Verse, 4to. Lond. 1774

"This clever and amusing, but rather too broad performance was written by Thos. Brydges, Esq."—*Lowndes.*

——— Another copy. *Vide* lot 2344.

2183 Burton (*W. E.*) Cyclopedia of Wit and Humor of America, Ireland, Scotland, and England, 600 *engravings*, 2 vols. *cloth*, royal 8vo. N. Y. 1857

2184 ——— Cyclopedia of Wit and Humor, *many plates*, &c., 2 vols. royal 8vo. *cloth.* N. Y. 1858

2185 Burton's Cyclopedia of Wit and Humor, Nos. 1 to 24, wants 2, 4, 5, 8, 11—19 Nos.

2186 ——— do. 12 to 24—13 Nos.

2187 ——— do. 12 to 24—13 Nos.

2188 ——— do. 12 to 24—13 Nos.

2189 ——— do. 3 Nos. sunds., 1 Lot.

2190 Burton (*W. E.*) Waggeries and Vagaries, *sewed*, 12mo. Phila. 1848

2191 Butler (*Samuel*), Hudibras, *original plates by Hogarth*, *stained*, 12mo. *calf.* Lond. 1726

2192 Butler (*W. A.*) Barnum's Parnassus, 12mo. N. Y. 1850

2193 Butler (*W. A.*) Nothing to Wear, an Episode of City Life, *cuts*, 12mo. *cloth.* N. Y. 1857

2194 Byroniana, Bozzies and Piozzies, *half calf*, 8vo. Lond. 1825

2195 Cabinet of Momus, a choice selection of Humorous Poems, from Peter Pindar, Swift, &c., *half sheep*, 12mo. Phila. 1827

2196 Cabinet Satyrique ou recueil des vers piquans et gaillards de ce temps, 2 vols. 12mo. *morocco*, *extra gilt leaves*, *beautiful copy*, *scarce.* Imprimé au Mont Parnasse, 1697

2197 Callot (*Jaques*), Miseries of War, a *series of plates*, *good impressions*, *mounted and bound*, an oblong 8vo.

2198 Cambridge Tart, Epigrammatic and Satiric Effusions, &c., Dainty Morsels served up by Cantabs on various occasions, fcap. 8vo. *half calf.* 1823

2199 Caricatures by Heath and others, French and English, *colored and plain*, a large lot.

2200 Caricature Magazine, by Woodward, 2 odd vols.

2201 Journal de Caricatures, 2 vols. fol. *hf. cf.* Paris, 1830–2

Complete copy of this famous series till stopped by the Government, apparently it has belonged to the Artist himself (Mr. Philipon), as it contains *the original sketches made by him in the Court of Justice when defending himself against the charge of caricaturing Louis Philippe under the form of a Pear.*

2202 Caricatures and Colored Engravings, a collection of, 25 in 1 vol. oblong 4to.

2203 CATULLUS, Adventures of, and History of his Amours with Lesbia, *intermixed with choice Poems*, thick 12mo. *old calf, frontispiece, scarce.* 1707

2204 CAUDLE (*Mrs.*) Curtain Lectures (Douglas Jerrold), &c., 12mo.

CERVANTES, vide *Novels*.

2205 CHAPELLE (*De la*), Le Ventriloque ou l'engastrimythe, *old French calf*, 12mo. Lond. 1772

2206 CHRONICLES of Pineville, *illustrated, sewed*, 12mo. Phila.

2207 CHARACTER of a Towne Misse, Printed by W. L. 1675; The Towne Misses Declaration, an Apology, or an Answer to the Character of a Towne Misse, printed for J. T. 1675, very rare, not in Lowndes, two tracts in one vol., fine copies, from the Library of Thos. Jolley, *sewed*, 4to. Lond. 1675

2208 CHEAP JOHN, the Chapman, the History of, containing above a hundred merry exploits done by him, 12mo. *half calf.* Glasgow, 1808

COBBLERIANA, *vide* Shakspeariana.

COLLET, Relics of Literature, *vide* Shakspeariana.

2210 COLMAN (*George the Younger*), The Lady of the Wreck, or Castle Blarneygig, 12mo. *half calf.* Bost. 1812

2211 ——— Poetical Works of, edited by E. D. Ingraham, 12mo. *cloth.* Phila. 1834

2212 COMIC Almanack, edited by Horace Mayhew, B. Brough, &c., with most humorous coloured and other engravings by G. Cruikshank, 10 vols. 12mo. v. d.

This is without exception the most humorous and witty series of books ever published. Every page is redolent of fun, heightened by the inimitable illustrations of George Cruikshank.

2213 COMIC Latin Grammar, a new and facetious introduction to the Latin tongue, with numerous illustrations, *cloth.* Lond. 1840

2214 COMIC Miseries of Human Life, 12mo. *cloth.* N. Y. n. d.

2215 COMIC Wandering Jew, 8vo. pp. 104. N. Y. 1847

2216 COOMBE (*Wm.*) English Dance of Death, from the designs of Thomas Rowlandson, with Metrical Illustrations by the Author of "Doctor Syntax," seventy-two colored plates of the Dance of Death by Rowlandson, 2 vols. royal 8vo. *scarce* Lond. 1815

This is the chef d'œuvre of Coombe and Rowlandson. Rhyme and Art go hand in glove together. The very bones of grisly death dance in apt unison to the poet's measure. Author and Artist are both excellent—most excellent.

2217 COOMBE (*Wm.*), The Dance of Life, by the same author and artist, uniform with the above, *complete*, royal 8vo., 26 *colored plates, extra gilt.* Lond. 1817

2218 ——— History of Johnny Quæ Genus, the little Foundling of the late Doctor Syntax, a Poem, 8vo., with numerous coloured laughable plates by Rowlandson, *scarce.* Lond., *Ackermann*, 1822

"Coombe, as is well known, lived a lively frolicsome life, full of ups and downs. In this work he is supposed to have included a portion of his own biography."

2219 ——— Tours of Dr. Syntax, Search of the Picturesque, &c. (in Hudibrastic Verse), illustrated with humourous coloured engravings by Rowlandson, 2 vols. royal 8vo. *half calf, imperial edition.* 1813

2220 CORNU-COPIE, Pasquil's Night-cap, or Antidote for the Head-ache, 1612, *half morocco, reprint*, 12mo. Chiswich, 1819

2221 COTTON (*Charles*) The Genuine Works of, containing Scarronides, or Virgil Travestie, Lucian Burlesqued, Wonders of the Peake, The Planter's Manual, *with many curious cuts, engraved by the best artists*, 8vo. *calf, neat.* 1771

2222 COYNE (*S. J.*) Pippins and Pies, or Sketches out of School, *illustrated, sewed*, 12mo. Lond. 1855

2223 COZZENS (*F. S.*) The Sparrowgrass Papers.

2224 CROCKETT'S (*Col.*) Exploits and Adventures in Texas, written by himself, *cloth*, 12mo. Phil. 1827

CROWQUILL *vide* Seymour.

2225 CRUIKSHANKIANA, a most singular and extensive collection of his comic sketches, folio, 81 *plates.* Lond. n. d.

CONTENTS.—Travelling in England, Ditto in France, Dancing Dolls, Dancing Lessons, Chess, to Calais; from the West Indies, November Fog, Gout, Stale Mate, Check Mate, Money Hunting, English Manners and French Politeness, Radical Parliament, Breaking up, Black Monday, Party of Pleasure, Raining Cats, Dogs, &c.; Return from Paris, London Dandies, Sailor's Progress, and numerous others; also, Deighton's London Nuisances; each design inimitable in character and execution, affording a stern Moral, in the most effective manner, a neverfailing source of Amusement.

2226 CRUIKSHANK (*Geo.*) Three Courses and a Dessert with Decorations, by, 8vo. *half roan.* Lond. 1830

2227 ——— Comic Album, 12mo. *cloth.* Lond. 1832

2228 ——— Table Books, edited by Gilbert Abbott a'Becket, royal 8vo. Lond. 1845

2229 CRUIKSHANK (*Geo.*) Illustrations of Humphrey Clinker, Roderick Random, Peregrine Pickle, &c., 41 *plates*, 12mo. *cloth.* Lond. 1836

2230 CUPID and Psyche, Loves of, translated from Apuleius and Fontaine by Lockman, 8vo. Lond. 1744

2231 CUNNINGHAM (*J. W.*) Sancho, or the Proverbialist, 12mo. *cloth.* Phil. 1833

2232 ——— (*Peter*), Story of Nell Gwyn and the Sayings of Charles the Second, 8vo. *cloth.* Lond. 1852

2233 CURIOSITIES for the Ingenious Selected from the most Authentic Treasures of Nature and Art, *illustrated*, *boards*, 12mo. Lond. 1822

2234 DAN MARBLE, a Biographical Sketch, 12mo. *sewed.* Phila. n. d.

2235 DANCE of Death, La Socialisme Nouvelle, Danse des Morts confreur et Dessinée, par A. Rethel, lithographiée par A. Collette, 6 *plates.* Paris, n. d.

——— *vide* Coombe and Holbein.

2236 DASHES of American Humor, 12mo. N. Y. 1853

2237 D'ARNAY (*M.*) Private Life of the Romans, *boards*, 12mo. Edin. 1808

2238 DAVENPORT (*R. A.*) Common-Place Book of Epigrams, 18mo. Edin. 1825

2239 DAVENPORT'S Exquisite Effusions of Wit and Humor, Nos. 2, 5, 7, 12mo. Lond. v. y.

2240 DE VADE, Œuvres Choises de, 8vo. Paris, 1834

2241 DEATH'S Doings, consisting of Numerous and Original Compositions, *thirty plates after R. Dagley*, 2 vols. 8vo. *half calf.* Bost. 1828

DECKER'S Gulls Handbook, *vide* Shakspeariana.

2242 DEFOE (*D'l*), The Consolidator: or, Memoirs of Sundry Transactions from the World in the Moon, translated from the Lunar Language by the author of the True-Born Englishman, 8vo. *calf.* Lond. 1705

This prose satire contains the first hints of many of the ideas which Swift afterwards embodied in Gulliver, and also a great many sly hits at all the authors of the time, from Dryden to Tom D'Urfey.

2243 ——— Ancient and Modern History of the Devil, 12mo. *sheep*, 2 vols. in 1. Phil. 1837

2243* DE LA MOTTE ROULLANT, Les Facetieux Deviz des Cent et Six nouvelles Nouvelles, tres recreatives pour reveiller les bons et joyeux esprits Françoys, *calf*, *fine copy*, *very rare*, 18mo. Lyon, 1576

This edition was not known to Brunet.

2244 DEMOCRITUS Redivivus, sive Campus Recreationum Honestarum cum Exorcismo Melancholiæ, 18mo. *with the sphere.* Amst. 1649

2245 DIABLE (*Le*), à Paris, Paris et les Parisiens, Texte par George Sand, Léon Gozlan, F. Soulié, etc., *illustrations par Gavarni*, 2 vols. royal 8vo. *half morocco.* Paris, 1845

This fine work is illustrated most profusely and beautifully.

2246 DICKENS (*Charles*), Picnic Papers, by various hands, *illustrated by Cruikshank, cloth*, 8vo. Lond. 1841

2247 ——— Public Life of Mr. Tulrumble, once Mayor of Mudfog, *boards*, 12mo. Phil. 1837

2248 DIOGENES, About 120 Numbers of, a Parcel. v. d.

2249 DISCOURSE (*A*), of Drinking Healths, by Peter, Lord Bishop of Cork and Rosse, 12mo. *old calf.* Lond. 1716

2250 D'ISRAELI (*John*), Flim-Flams, or the Life and Errors of my Uncle, 3 vols. no vol. 3, *half calf*, 12mo. Lond. 1806

2251 DIX HUIT, Scenes d'Amourettes, 4to. *colored plates.* Paris, n. d.

2252 DOESTICKS, History and Records of the Elephant Club, compiled from authentic documents now in the possession of the Zoological Society, 8vo. N. Y. 1857

2253 DODSLEY (*R.*) Trifles, viz: The Toy Shop, The King and the Miller of Mansfield, The Blind Beggar, &c., 8vo. *calf.* Lond. 1745

2254 ——— Fugitive Pieces on several subjects, by several authors, 2 vols. 8vo. *calf.* Lond. 1761

*** A curious collection, containing "A modest defence of gaming," "A project for raising an Hospital for decayed authors," Vindication of Natural Society, by Bolingbroke, Fragments of Ancient Poetry collected in the Highlands, Hentzner's Journey into England in the year 1598, Spence's Parallel, Lucina sine Concubitu, proving that Women may conceive without Commerce with Man, &c. &c.

2255 DOMESTIC Miseries, oblong 4to. 6 *plates.* Lond. n. d.

2256 DORAN (*Dr.*) Table Traits with something on them, 12mo. *cloth.* N. Y. 1855

2257 DOWNING (*Major Jack*), Letters of, to his old friend Mr. Dwight, of New York, *illustrated, cloth*, 12mo. N. Y. 1836

2258 DROZ (*F. X. J.*) Art of being Happy, translated by T. Flint, 12mo. *sewed.* Lond. 1834

2259 DRUDGE, (*The*), or the Jealous Extravagant, a Piece of Gallantry, 12mo. *old calf.* Lond. 1673

2260 DUNLAP (*W.*) Thirty Years Ago, or the Memoirs of a Water Drinker, 2 vols. *cloth*, 12mo. N. Y. 1856

2261 D'URFEY (*Thomas*), Wit and Mirth, or Pills to Purge Melancholy, being a collection of the best Merry Ballads and Songs, fitted to all Humours, having each their proper tune, together with his several Orations, spoken by himself on the stage, 5 vols. 12mo. *half calf.* Lond. 1712

This facetious writer, who possessed a double genius for Poetry and Music, was well adapted for these "pleasant and divertive" mementos of his time. In his dedication he says, I have added 100 new pieces, hoping they will happily be received by you when read, or performed in your merry and vacant hours.

2262 ——— Comical History of Don Quixote, as it was acted at the Queen's Theatre, *autograph of G. Vertue, both parts calf.* 4to. Lond. 1694

Tom Durfey was censured for the looseness of this piece.

2263 ——— (*T.*) Tales, tragical and comical, 8vo. *calf, fine copy, scarce.* Lond. 1704

2264 ——— (*Tom*), New Operas, with Comical Stories and Poems, 8vo. *calf, fine copy.* 1721

Containing the Two Queens of Brentford, Grecian Heroine or Fate of Tyranny, Athenian Jilt, or the Intriguing Cullies, Plague of Impertinence, Love the Best Philosopher, etc.

2265 DUMPLINGS, a Learned Dessertation on, with a Word upon Pudding, and many other useful Discoveries, of great benefit to the public, 12mo. *calf.* Lond. 1726

2266 EBRIETATIS Encomium, or the Praise of Drunkenness, wherein is proved the Necessity of frequently getting Drunk, and that the Practice is most Ancient, Primitive, and Catholic, 12mo. original edition, *calf gilt, scarce.* Pinted for E. Curll, 1723

2267 EGAN (*Pierce*), Anecdotes of the Chase, the Turf, the Road, and the Stage, *thirteen colored plates*, 8vo. *calf extra.* Lond. 1827

2268 ——— Life in London, Day and Night Scenes, Rambles and Sprees through the Metropolis of Jerry Hawthorn and Corinthian Tom, accompanied by Bob Logic, *colored plates by Cruikshank*, royal 8vo. 1821

2269 ——— Finish to the Adventures of Tom and Jerry, and Logic, *illustrated by R. Cruikshank, plates colored, boards*, royal 8vo. Lond.

2270 ELECTRIC Telegraph of Fun, illustrated by Alfred Crowquill, 12mo. Lond. 1852

2271 Eloge de l'Enfer, Ouvrage Critique, Historique, et Moral, 2 vols. 12mo. *half calf.* La Haye, 1759

2272 Encyclopædia of Wit, thick 18mo. imperfect. n. d.

2273 English Spy, original work, Characteristic, Satirical, and Humorous, comprising Scenes and Sketches in every rank of Society, &c. *colored plates, &c. by R. Cruikshank,* 2 vols. royal 8vo. Lond. 1825

2274 ——— Entertaining Medley, a Collection of Genuine Anecdotes, Stories, Frolick of Wit and Humour, &c. 12mo. *calf.* Lond. 1767

2275 Errata, or the Works of Will. Adams, 2 vols. 12mo. *boards.* N. Y. 1823

2276 Erasmi (*Disid.*) Morias Encomium, Stultitiæ laus, figures Holbenianes adornate Holbein Delin, C. M. Sculp. *portraits of Erasmus and Holbein, old calf, fine copy,* 8vo. Basil, 1676

Archdeacon Wrangham's copy, with his autograph and MS. notes.

2277 Erasmus, L'Eloge de la Folie, trad. du Latin par Guendeville, *plates,* 12mo. 1761

2278 Epigrams, Collection of, with a Critical Dissertation on this species of Poetry, 2 vols. 12mo. *calf, rare.* 1735

"How does the little Epigram delight,
And charm us with its miniature of wit."

*** A collection of nearly 1000 singular and curious epigrams.

2279 ——— Collection of, *calf.* 12mo. Lond. 1727

2280 Epigrammatist's Annual or Humourist's Almanac, *half morocco,* 32mo. Lond. 1833

2281 Essays, Moral, Philosophical and Stomachical, on the important subject of Good Living, 12mo. Lond. 1823

2282 Etiquette for Ladies, 24mo. *cloth.* Phil. 1836

2283 Eunuchism Display'd, Describing all the different sorts of Eunuchs, by a Person of Honour, 12mo. *calf.* Lond. 1718

2284 Fabliaux, or Tales abridged from French Manuscripts of the XII and XIII Centuries, by Le Grand, translated into English verse by G. L. Way, 3 vols. *half morocco,* 8vo. Lond. 1815

2286 Facetious Tracts—1. On Heads; 2. Battle of the Authors; 3. Artificer's Looking Glass, and six others, 8vo. *half calf.* Lond. 1785

2287 Faces in the Fire, by Redgap, *illustrated,* 12mo. *cloth.* Lond. n. d.

2288 Facetiæ Cantabrigienses, consisting of Anecdotes, Smart Sayings, Satires, Retorts, &c., by Celebrated Cantabs, 12mo. 1836

2289 FANCIES of a Whimsical Man (by John S. Taylor), post 8vo. *cloth.* N. Y. 1852

2290 FASHION, or the Art of Making Breeches, 8vo. pp. 19. Phil. 1800

2291 FEAST of the Poets, with Notes, and other Pieces in Verse, 12mo. *boards.* N. Y. 1814

2292 FEMALE Favorites, A History of Marie de Padilla, Livia, Julia Farnesa, Agnes Sorel and Matilda, 8vo. *calf.* Lond. 1772

2293 FESSENDEN (*T. G.*) Terrible Tractoration, 12mo. *boards.* N. Y. 1804

2294 FEMALE Jockey Club, or a Sketch of the Manners of the Age, the Three Parts Complete, thick 8vo. 1794

This famous satirical work in which are brought forward all the most distinguished personages of the day, has been attributed to G. Canning.

2295 Fifteen Comforts of a Good Parliament, and the Fifteen Plagues of a Bad One, 12mo. *sewed.* Lond. 1711

2296 FOOLS and Jesters, and Tarleton's Jests (Shak. Socy.), 8vo. *half calf.* 1844

2297 FOREIGN Tour of Messrs. Brown, Jones, and Robinson, being the History of what they saw, and did, in Belgium, Germany, Switzerland, and Italy, by Richard Doyle, 4to. *cloth.* Lond. 1855

2298 Fosdick (*W. W.*) Arill and other Poems, *illustrated with designs by Dallas*, 8vo. N. Y. n. d.

2299 FOUNDLING Hospital for Wit, intended for the reception and preservation of such Brats of Wit and Humour whose Parents chuse to drop them; containing Satires, Odes, Ballads, Epigrams, &c., 6 vols., together with the New Foundling Hospital, 4 vols.—in all 10 vols. 12mo. *calf.* Lond. 1785

A collection of Fugitive Pieces, Humorous and Satirical Poetry, Lampoons, &c., during the times of Wilkes, Lord North, and the American War.

2300 FRANCAISES (*les*) ou XXXIV. examples choises dans les Mœurs actuelles propre à diriger les filles, les femmes, les epouses et les mères, *beautiful plates,* 4 vols. 12mo. *calf.* Neufchatel, 1786

2301 FRENCH BITE (*The*), or Adventures of the Marquess Dul Bruce, his several memoirs and warme intrigues, *curious frontispiece,* 8vo. *half calf.* Lond. 1753

2302 Friar Gerund (The History of the Famous Preacher); otherwise called Gerund Zotes, translated from the Spanish, 2 vols. 8vo. Lond. 1772

This celebrated Satire on the Fathers of the Dominican and Mendicant orders, written by Father Isla, a Jesuit, caused probably a greater sensation than any work of the kind which ever issued from the press. Denounced in unmeasured terms by the Bishops and the greater part of the Clergy, while upheld stoutly by the Inquisition it came before the general council of Castile, by whose orders it was rigorously suppressed. Copies are now rare.

2303 Fun and Earnest, by the author of Musings of an Invalid, &c. 12mo. *cloth.* N. Y. 1853

2304 G. (*I.*) Parson's Horn-Book. Contents—Churchman's Alphabet, Chapter on the Church, "Simony Hall," &c. *plates,* 8vo. Dub. 1831

2305 Gascoigne (*George*), A Delicate Diet for Daintie Mouthde Droonkardes, 8vo. pp. 24. Lond. 1789

2306 Gavarni in London, Sketches of Life and Character, edited by Albert Smith, *plates by Vizetelly,* royal 8vo. *cloth.* Lond. 1849

2307 Gelli (*Sig. Giovanni Battista*), The Circe of, from the Italian, by Mr. Thos. Brown, 8vo. *old calf.* Lond. 1702

2308 Gifford's Baviad and Mæviad; Pasquin *versus* Faulder, Epistle to Peter Pindar, Byron's English Bards and Scotch Reviewers, 18mo. Lond. 1827

2309 Gomberville (*Mar. le Roy de*), La Cytherée, 4 vols. 8vo. *calf.* Paris, 1642

2310 Goodfellow's Calendar and Almanack of Perpetual Jocularity, &c. 12mo. *boards.* Lond. 1826

2311 Goodrich (*S. G.*) Sketches from a Student's Window, post 8vo. *cloth.* Bost. 1841

2312 Gordon (*Thomas, Esq.*) Cordial for Low Spirits, being a Collection of Curious Tracts, 2 vols. 12mo. *calf.* Lond. 1763

2313 Grand Historical Pictures, *a series of comical plates,* 4to. *cloth.* Lond. n. d.

2314 Grand Master, or Adventures of Qui Hi in Hindostan, a Hudibrastic Poem, in eight cantos, 8vo. *half calf.* Lond. 1816

2315 Gratian (*Baltasar*), The Compleat Gentleman, by T. Saldkeld, from the Spanish, 8vo. *calf.* Lond. 1730

2316 Graves (*Richard*), Spiritual Quixote; or summer's ramble of Mr. Geoffrey Wildgoose, a comic romance, 3 vols. 12mo. *calf.* Dodsley, 1754

2317 Greaves (*John*), Miscellaneous Works, a description of the Pyramids in Egypt, Discourse of the Roman Foot of Denarius, Description of the Grand Seignor's Seraglio, &c., edited by T. Birch, *plates*, 2 vols. *calf*, 8vo. Lond. 1737

2318 Green Room Gossip: or, Gravity Gallinipt, a Gallimaufry consisting of Theatrical Anecdotes, Bon Mots, Chit-Chat, Drollery Entertainment, Fun, Gibes, Humor, Jokes, Kickshaws, Lampoons, Mirth, Nonsense, Oratory, Puns, Quizzery, Repartee, Stories, Tattle, Vocality, Wit, Yawning, Zest, got up to guile Gymnastical and Griniocratic Governments, 12mo. *half calf*. Lond. 1809

2319 Griggs (*William N.*) Celebrated Moon Story, with its Origin and other Incidents, *cloth*, 12mo. N. Y. 1852

2320 Grose (*Captain*), Dictionary of Buckish Slang, Universely Wit and Pickpocket Eloquence, 8vo. *boards*. Lond. 1811

"Ken ye aught of Captain Grose?"—*Burns*.

2321 Guzman (*Aleman*, of Alfarache), Pleasant Adventures of, 3 vols. *half calf*, 12mo. Lond. 1816

Contains a fund of acute and comprehensive observations on almost every rank in society.

2323 H. (*P.*) Essay on Laughter, *half calf*, 12mo. Lond. 1769

2324 Haliburton (*Judge*), Bubbles of Canada, 12mo. Phil. 1830

2325 ——— The Clockmaker, or Sayings and Doings of Sam'l Slick, 12mo. Phil. 1840

2326 ——— Another copy.

2327 ——— Traits of American Humor, 3 vols. 8vo. *half calf*. Lond. 1852

2328 Handbook of Humbug, *sewed*, 18mo. Lond. 1848

2329 ——— of Swindling, by the late Barnabas Whitefeather, edited by Jackdaw, *illustrations by Phiz*, *sewed*, 12mo. Lond. 1839

2330 Harrison (*W. H.*) The Humourist, a Companion for the Christmas Fireside, *fifty engravings after Rowlandson*, 12mo. Lond. 1831

2331 Harvey's (*G.*) Pierce's Supererogation, or the New Praise of the Old Ass (Book III.), also a new letter of noble contents, &c., *half morocco*, 1593; *reprinted*, 1815.

Only 250 copies of this reprint were published.

2332 HANGER'S (*Celebrated Colonel George, afterwards Lord Coleraine*) Life, Adventures and Opinions, to which is added Advice to the Prelates, Advice to the lovely Cyprians, History of the lovely Ægyptia, Paragon of the Egyptian Race, the Author's Marriage with her and her Cruel Infidelity and Elopement with a Travelling Tinker, and a History of the King's Bench written during the Author's Custody, 2 vols. 8vo. *calf, scarce.* 1801

"A very curious book; the author served with distinction in the American war, and on the death of his brother succeeded to the title of Lord Coleraine."

2333 HEADS of the People, or Portraits of the English, with a Biographical History of the most Noted Characters, by Douglas Jerrold, Lemon Rede, Leigh Hunt, etc., 83 *characteristic engravings by Kenny Meadows*, 2 vols. 8vo. Lond. 1840

A very curious work relative to the people of London.

2334 HISTOIRE d'une Epingle, *colored plates*, 4to. Paris, n. d.

2335 HISTORY of the Grand Viziers, Mohamet and Achmet, 12mo. *old calf.* Lond. 1677

2337 ——— Royal Malady, with Stricture on Horne Tooke, respecting Mrs. Fitzherbert, 4to. *half calf.* Lond. 1789

2338 HOFFMAN (*E. T. A.*) Devil's Elixir, from the German, 2 vols. 12mo. Edin. 1824

2339 HOGARTH, The Rake's Progress, or the Humours of Drury Lane, a poem in eight cantos, *illustrated with eight plates which are stolen from Hogarth's designs, but altered*, 8vo. *cloth.* Lond. 1735

The book is a description of a Young Man About Town, in 1735, and *very rare.*

2340 HOOD'S (*Thos.*) Comic Annual, *full of humorous engravings*, 12mo. 1834

Who has not laughed with laughter-loving Hood?

2341 ——— Endless Fun, or a Comic Annual, 12mo. Phil. 1838

2342 ——— Tylney Hall, *cloth*, 12mo. N. Y. 1835

2343 ——— Humorous Poems, 12mo. *cloth.* Bost. 1856

2344 HOMER Travestie, a Burlesque Translation of Homer's Iliad, in Verse, *numerous curious etchings*, 2 vols. 8vo. *cloth, best edition.* 1797

Said to be written by T. Bridges; full of wit and humor, but which often transgresses the bounds of decency.

——— Another copy, *vide* Lot 2182.

2345 HORACE in London, 12mo. *boards.* 1813

A series of clever parodies and imitations of the Odes of Horace by the Messrs. Smiths, the talented authors of "Rejected Addresses."

2346 ——— in New York, Part I. all published, by James M. Campbell, *sewed,* 12mo. N. Y. 1826

2347 HUARTE (*J.*) The Examination of Men's Wits, in which by discovering the varietie of natures is shewed for what proffession each one is apt, and how far he shall profit therein, by John Huarte, translated out of the Spanish tongue by M. Cammillo Camilli, Englished out of his Italian by R. Carew, Esq., 4to. Lond. 1616

2348 HUARTES, Tryal of the Wits, translated by Bellamy, 8vo. Lond. 1698

2349 HUMOURIST, being Essays upon several Subjects, viz. News Writers, Enthusiasm, the Spleen, Love, History of Miss Manage, Ghosts and Apparitions, &c., Punishment of Staying Home on Sunday, 2 vols. 12mo. *calf.* Lond. 1724

2350 HUMORIST, edited by Theodore Hook, 12mo. *half cloth.* Phil. 1837

2351 HUMPHREY (*Ravelin*), The Lucubrations of, 8vo. *half calf.* Lond. 1823

2352 HUNT (*Leigh*), Bucchus in Tuscany, from the Italian, 12mo. *boards.* Lond. 1825

2353 ——— Poetry of, Wit and Humor, 12mo. N. Y. 1846

2354 ——— A Jar of Honey from Mount Hybla, illustrated by Doyle, 8vo. *ill. boards, gilt.* Lond. 1848

2355 ——— Selections from the English Poets, Wit and Humor, 8vo. *cloth.* Phil. 1854

2356 IMITATIONS of Celebrated Authors, or Imaginary rejected Articles, in Prose (by Lamb, James and Horace Smith, Professor Wilson, Hazlitt, Leigh Hunt, &c.), post 8vo. *cloth.* 1844

2357 INGOLDSBY Legends; or, Mirth and Marvels, new edition, with all the humorous plates by George Cruikshank and John Leech, 2 vols. post 8vo. *cloth.* 1856

"We cannot open a page of the book that is not sparkling with its wit and humor, that is not ringing with its strokes of pleasantry, satire, &c."—*Examiner.*

2358 INVESTIGATOR (*The*), An Essay on Ridicule, 8vo. *calf.* Lond. 1753

2359 JACK RANDALL'S Diary of Proceedings at the House of Call for Genius, edited by Mr. Breakwindow, 12mo. *boards.* Lond. 1820

2360 JERROLD (*Douglas*), Collected Works, 22 Nos. 8vo. wants parts 17, 22, and after 24. Lond. 1851

2361 ——— Wit, arranged by his Son, 12mo. Bost. 1858

JEST BOOKS.—*Vide* LOTS 3377 TO 3397.

2362 JOCKEY Club, or a Sketch of the Manners of the Age, some curious Amorous Gallantries of the D—ke of C—r—ce, D—ke of Y—k, P—— of W—l—s, and other Aristocratics, 8vo. *scarce.* 1794

2363 ——— Another copy. Lond. 1794

2364 JOKEBY, a Burlesque on Rokeby, 12mo. Bost. 1813

2365 JONES (*J. B.*) Adventures of Colonel Gracchus Vanderbomb, also the Exploits of Mr. Numerius Plutarch Kippe, post 8vo. Phil. 1852

2366 JORROCK'S Jaunts and Jollities; or, The Hunting, Shooting, Racing, Driving, Eating, and other Exploits of that Renowned Sporting Citizen, John Jorrocks of St. Botolph's Lane, &c. 2 vols. 12mo. *half cloth.* Phil. 1838

2367 KELLEY (*J. F.*) Humors of Falconbridge, a Collection of Humorous and Every-day Scenes, 8vo. *cloth.* Phil. n. d.

2368 KETT (*Rev. H.*) Flowers of Wit, or a Collection of Bon Mots, &c. 2 vols. in 1, 12mo. *half morocco.* Lond. 1814

KISSES, *vide* Secundus.

2369 KOCK (*C. Paul de*), The Modern Cymon, from the "Jean," 2 vols. 12mo. *calf.* Phil. 1833

2370 ——— Barber of Paris, 2 vols. 12mo. Phil. 1839

2371 ——— Translations of Rose-Marie, &c. 8vo. *half morocco.* N. Y. 1846

The most lively, piquant, and witty of the modern French novelists.

2372 LA SILHOUETTE, revue Satirique Encyclopedie de l'apropos, 4to. *half calf.* Paris, 1845

2373 LACONICS, 2 odd vols. 12mo. *cloth.*

2374 LADY and the Saints, in three Cantos, ten vignettes by R. Cruikshank, 12mo. *cloth.* Lond. 1839

2375 LAIRD of Logan, or Anecdotes and Tales, illustrative of the wit and humour of Scotland, *cloth,* 12mo. Glasgow, 1845

2376 L'ISLE des Hermaphrodites, Nouvellement Descouverte, 24mo. *calf, wants title.* Paris.

2377 L'ANE Promeneur, ou Critès promenez, par son ane, par Gorsas membre de la Convention, decapité, 1793, *sewed,* 12mo. Pampelune chez Democrite, &c. 1788

2378 LAUGH and be Fat, or the Merry Companion, containing great variety of comical and diverting stories, &c., 12mo. Lond. n. d.

2379 LAUGHTER, Essay on, 12mo. *calf.* Lond. 1769

2380 LAY of the Scottish Fiddle, attributed to Sir W. Scott, 12mo. N. Y. 1813

2381 LAZARILLO de Tormes, Vida del, 12mo. Mad. 1811

2382 ——— the Adventures of, translated by D. Rowland, *portrait and plates*, 12mo. *half calf, reprint.* 1821

> "The man whose picture here you see,
> A thousand pranks has played,
> A rogue he was, and none could be
> More dextrous at his Trade."

2383 LANCERS (*The*), or the Memoirs of Lady Sarah B., and the Countess P., 8vo. *calf.* Lond. 1769

2384 LE GRAND: Fabliaux or Tales, by the Anglo-Norman Trouveurs of the 14th Century, from the collection of M. Le Grand, translated with notes, by G. L. Way and George Ellis, 2 vols. royal 8vo. *half calf, gilt, cuts by Bewick.* Lond. 1800

2385 ——— Tales of the Minstrels, translated from the French, *calf*, 12mo. Lond. n. d.

2386 LE MELANGES: Chateau des Demons, Nouveau petit catéchisme poissard pour le Carnaval, Diable Fourré pratout recueil de bons tours de Moines et Nonains, 1 vol. *half morocco*, 18mo. Par. v. y.

2387 LE SAGE: Les Aventures de M. Rob. Chevalier dit de Beauchêne, 2 vols. 12mo. Maestrecht, 1780

2388 LE ROUX: Dictionnaire Françaisе, Comique, Satyrique, Critique, Burlesque, Libre et Proverbiale, *best edition*, 2 vols. *half gr. morocco, uncut, gilt tops*, 8vo. Pampelune, 1786

> "The most complete edition."—*Brunet.*

2389 L'ESTRANGE (*R.*) Five Love Letters, from a Nun to a Cavilier, with the Cavilier's answers, 18mo. *cloth.* Lond. 1693

2390 LETTER Bag of the Great Western, or Life in a Steamer, 12mo. Phil. 1840

LIFE in London *vide* Egan, Lot 2268.

2391 LITERARY Lounger, *half cloth*, 8vo. Lond. 1826

2392 LOWELL (*J. R.*) The Biglow Papers, edited with Notes, Glossary, and Index, by H. Wilbur, 12mo. Boston, 1854

2393 ——— Fable for Critics, 12mo. *boards.* N. Y. 1848

2394 Lloyd: The Legend of Captain Jones, relating his strange adventure at sea; his first landing, and strange combat with a mighty bear; his furious battel with his six and thirty men against the army of eleven Kings, with their overthrow and deaths; his relieving of Kemper Castle; his strange and admirable sea fight, with six huge gallies of Spain, and nine thousand soldiers, &c. &c., 8vo. Lond. 1766

2395 Love in Captivity, or future felicity anticipated, in a series of eccentrical epistles between several celebrated Heroes and amorous British Beauties bound to Botany Bay, 8vo. *unbound.* 1787

2396 Love and Madness, a story too true, in a series of letters, 8vo. *half sheep.* Lond. 1780

Relating to the murder of Miss Martha Reay, who was the mistress of the Earl of Sandwich, and shot by the Rev. John Hackman.

2397 Lunn (*J.*) Horæ Jocosæ, or the Doggerel Decameron, 12mo. *half morocco.* Lond. 1823

2398 M. (*R.*) Scarronides, or Virgile Travestie, a Mock-Poem, being a continuation of the former story, *pristine state,* 12mo. Lond. 1665

2399 Mack (*Doctor Ebenezer*), Cat Fight, a mock heroic Poem, *plates, half calf,* 12mo. N. Y. 1824

2400 Mackenzie (*R. Shelton*), Bits of Blarney, *cloth,* 8vo. N. Y. 1854

2401 Malcolm (*J. P.*) Historical Sketch of the Art of Caricaturing, with Graphic Illustrations, 4to. *half calf.* Lond. 1813

2402 Maginn (*W.*) Fraserian Papers, 12mo. *cloth.* N. Y. 1857

2403 ——— O'Doherty Papers, 2 vols. 12mo. *cloth.* N. Y. 1853

2404 Major Jones' Travels, and other Humorous Books, 16 vols. 12mo. v. d.

2404*Mandeville (*R.*) Fable of the Bees, or Private Weaknesses Public Benefits, with Essay on Charity, and Charity Schools, &c., 2 vols. *calf.* Edin. 1772

"Had Shakspeare written a book on the motives of human actions, it is extremely improbable that it would have contained half so much able reasoning on the subject as is to be found in the Fable of the Bees."—*Macaulay.*

2405 Manley (*Madame*), L'Atlantis contenant les Intrigues politiques et Amoureuses de la Noblesse D'Angleterre, &c., 3 vols. 12mo. *sh.* à Londres, 1714

2406 Martineau (*Harriet*), Sketches from Life, *plates, cloth*, 12mo. Lond. 1856

2407 Masques Arraches (les) ou vies privées de L. E. Henri Vander-Noot et van Eupen, &c., par Jacques le Sueur, 2 vols. in 1, 18mo. Lond. 1790

2408 Masse (*E. N.*) Amours et Intrigues des Prêtres Français, 18mo. Paris, 1837

2409 Mathews (*Cornelius*), Moneypenny, or the Heart of the World, *boards*, 12mo. Lond. n. d.

2410 Mathews' Comic Pieces, Songs, &c., 20 Tracts. v. d.

2411 Maxims of Kit Larcosse, the Lord Mayor's Fool, 12mo. *boards.* Lond. 1840

2412 Mayhew (*Horace*), Model Men Moulded by, sculptured by H. G. Hine, *sewed*, 12mo. N. Y.

2413 ——— Letters at the Pastry-Cook's, *illustrated*, po. 8vo. Lond. 1854

2414 Mayer (*Joh. Godofr.*), Historia Diaboli, seu commentatio de Diaboli, 8vo. *half calf.* Tubing. 1780

2415 Merry Tales of the Three Wise Men of Gotham, edited by the author of John Bull in America, *boards*, 12mo. N. Y. 1826

2416 Memoirs of an Old Wig, *boards, uncut, p.* 8vo. Lond. 1815

2417 Midnight Merriment, or a Nocturnal Ramble through St. Giles', containing a funny but faithful picture of that quarter, 12mo. *frontispiece, rare tract.* n. d.

2418 Miscellanea Aurea, or the Golden Medley, consisting of a Voyage to the Mountains of the Moon, Account of Bad and Good Women, &c., 8vo. *scarce.* Lond. 1720

Some of the letters are curious, "On Players, Love is a Warfare, That our sleeping hours are as valuable as our waking," &c.

2419 Mirror of Merit and Beauty, 18mo. N. Y. 1808

2420 Moulinet (*N. de*), Vraye Histoire Comique de Francion, 2 vols. *cf. gilt*, 12mo. Leyde, 1721

2420 Miscellanies, History of the Tea Plant, Tributary Lines to the Memory of the Princess Charlotte, Man in the Moon, Non mi ricordo, and several political squibs on George the 4th, by Hone, and other tracts, *in all* 16, *with MS. list of contents*, 8vo. Lond. v. y.

2421 Modus Salium, a Collection of such Pieces of Humor as Prevailed at Oxford in the Time of Anthony à Wood, *sewed*, 12mo. Oxford, 1751

2422 Momus at Home, or a Feast of Good Things for the Merry and the Melancholy, by a bon-vivant, *cloth*, 12mo. Ithaca, 1842

2423 Monastic Life, Meliton, l'Apocalypse de Meliton, ou Revelations des Mysteres Cenobitiques, *scarce*, 12mo. 1665

2424 Moncrief (*W. T.*) Old Booty, a Serio-Comic Sailor's Tale; Sunday under Three Heads, as it is, as Sabbath bills would make it, as it might be made; Matthews' Comic Annual, by Pierce Egan; Margate, a humorous poem, in 1 vol. *wood-cuts*, 12mo. *cloth*. Lond. v. y.

2425 Moore (*A.*) Annals of Gallantry, or the Conjugal Monitor, being a collection of Curious and Important Trials for Divorces, 2 vols. *half morocco*. Lond. 1814

2426 ——— (*Thomas*), Fables for the Holy Alliance, Rhymes on the Road, &c., *boards*, 12mo. Lond. 1823

2427 Moore's New Miscellany, 8vo. *half calf*. Lond. 1750

2428 Mouse-Trap, To the Majesty of the People, The Christian Political Mouse-Trap, or the World Reformed, by Order, Truth, and Good Humour, *curious*, 8vo. *paper*. Lond. 1790

2429 Mrs. Peck's Pudding, by Tom Hood, a Humorous Paper by Charles Dickens, and a Dramatic Sketch by Sir E. L. Bulwer, *sewed*, 12mo. N. Y. 1845

2430 Mulock (*Miss*), Olive, the Ogilvies, 1854; Agatha's Husband, 1853; Head of the Family; Avillion, 1854, &c., in 1 vol. 8vo. N. Y. v. y.

2431 My Own Home and Fireside, being illustrative of the speculations of Martin Chuzzlewit & Co., 12mo. Phil. 1846

2432 Neal (*Joseph C.*) Peter Ploddy and Peter Faber, 2 vols. 12mo. Phil. n. d.

New Foundling Hospital, *vide* Lot 2299.

2433 New Journey to the World in the Moon, *sd.* 8vo. Lond. 1741

2434 No Jest like a True Jest, 2 vols.

2435 No-Slur Else-Slur, a Dancing Poem, by Nobody; Life of Tom Thumb, &c., 6 *tracts*, 12mo. v. p.

2436 Noel (*Nath.*) Conversations on Love and Gallantry, originally in French, 18mo. *calf*. Lond. 1676

2437 Nonpareil, or the Quintessence of Wit and Humor, being a choice selection of those pieces that were most admired in the ever-to-be-remembered Midwife, or Old Woman's Magazine (by Smart), 12mo. Lond. 1757

2438 NOUVEAUX Contes a rire, et aventures plaisantes de ce Tems, 12mo. *half morocco.* Breux. 1723

2439 NUITS de Paris, ou Spectateur Nocturne, 16 vols. 12mo. *sewed.* (Par.) 1788

2440 NUTS and Nut Crackers, *illustrated by Phiz*, 12mo. *cl., gilt leaves.* Lond. 1845

2441 ODDITIES of London Life, 2 vols. 12mo. Phil. 1838

2442 ŒUVRES choisies de Vadé et de ses imitateurs, contenant different sujets pour les Halles, Ports, Marches, &c., Le Bavard universel ou le Farceur sans pareil, Des Calembourgs comme s'il en pleuvait déluge de traits d'esprit, &c., in 1 vol. 12mo. Paris, v. y.

2443 OLIO (*The*), Collected by a Literary Traveller. (Contents—Joe Haynes, Strong Lines, Macklin's Shylock, Journey to Dublin, &c.) 12mo. *cloth* Bost. 1833

2444 ORIENTAL Chronicle of the Times, by Confucius, the Sage, curious Political Work, *with caricature plate*, 12mo. *half calf, gilt.* Lond. n. d.

2445 OSTEWALD (*Rev. J. F.*) The Nature of Uncleanness Considered, and a Discourse on the Nature of Chastity, 8vo. *sheep.* Lond. 1708

2446 OUFLE (*Mons.*) A History of the Ridiculous Extravagances of, from the French, 8vo. *old calf.* Lond. 1711

2447 OXFORD and Cambridge Nuts to Crack, or Quips, Quirks, &c. of Oxford and Cambridge Scholars, *illustrated*, 12mo. *cloth.* Lond. 1835

2448 ——— The Oxford Sausage, or Select Poetical Pieces, written by the most celebrated Wits of the University, *numerous curious cuts.* 1764

This celebrated jeu-d'esprit is generally considered to have been the work of Warton.

2449 PADLOCK Open'd, or Mungo's Medley, a collection of miscellaneous pieces, in prose and verse, serious and comic, &c. 1771; Letters addressed to Clarinda by Robert Burns, Dublin, 1816; Midnight Assassin, and other pieces, in 1 vol. 12mo. *half calf.*

2450 PAMPHLETS, Le Dragon, Fine Etchings, Paris, 1839; Fantasies Artistiques, sqr., Widow Rugby's Husband, Race in Kentucky, 4 vols.

2451 ——— (*Curious*), Three Jacks of Rosemary Lane; Adventures of John Daniel, Bamfylde Moore Carew; The Dancing Master, 12mo. *half cl.* Lond.

2452 Pamphlets, Odes, and Epistles; A Letter to the Club at White's, by Mumford; Papers Pro and Con; The Amours of Zeokinizul, &c. 8vo. *old calf.* Lond. 1739 &c.

2453 ——— Torpedo (*The*) (by Jas. Perry, Esq.); Electric Eel, by do.; The Inamorata, to the author of the Electrical Eel, by a Lady; Adam's Tail, or the First Metamorphosis, said to be by Perry, 4 vols., *rare tracts,* 4to. Lond. 1774

2454 ——— Bozzy and Piozzy, by Peter Pindar, 1786; Epistle to James Boswell, Esq., by Pindar, 1786.

2455 Parnassus in Pillory, a Satire by Motley Manners, 12mo. *cloth.* N. Y. 1851

2456 Parterre du Parnasse François par M. Bonafons, 12mo. Amst. 1709

2457 Passe-Temps-Royal de Versailles, les Amours secretes de Madame de Maintenon, suivi de nouveaux Mémoires tres-curieux, 18mo. Col. 1712

2458 Patin (*Guy*) L'Esprit de; tiré de ses conversations, &c., *portrait,* 12mo. Amst. 1700

2459 Pedrille del Campo, la vie de, Roman comique, par M. T., G. D. T., *plates,* &c., 12mo. Amst. 1720

2460 Percy Anecdotes, to which is added American Anecdotes, 2 vols. *half calf,* 8vo. N. Y. 1832

2461 Perrault (*Ch.*) Contes du Temps Passé, royal 8vo. *half mor.* Paris, 1843

2462 Personal Adventures of "Our Own Correspondent" in Italy, 8vo. N. Y. 1852

2463 Petronii Arbitre, Satiricon, cum Petronium Fragmentis, 12mo. Helenope, 1610

2464 Phantasmagoria of Fun, edited and illustrated by A. Crowquill, 2 vols. po. 8vo. Lond. 1843

2465 Phenix (*The*), or a Revival of scarce and valuable Pieces from the remotest antiquity down to the present times, being a collection of Manuscripts and printed Tracts, nowhere to be found but in the closets of the curious, 2 vols. 8vo. *calf* 1707

2466 Phenix, vol. 1, 8vo. *calf.* 1707

2467 Philadelphia Book, or Specimens of Metropolitan Literature, *cloth,* 8vo. Phil. 1836

2468 Philipan (*Ch.*) Les Compensations, a collection of amusing caricatures, &c., 4to. Paris, n. d.

2469 Philosophy of Kissing Anatomically and Physiologically Explained, with *illustrations, cloth,* 18mo. N. Y.

2470 PHILOSOPHY, Mock and Absurd, or a Word to the Reasonable, by one who salutes all, 12mo. *boards.* Bost. 1811

2471 PHYSIOLOGIE du Ridicule, ou suite d'observations, par une société de gens Ridicules, *half morocco*, 12mo. Brux. 1833

2472 PIECE of Family Biography, 3 vols. 12mo. Lond. 1799

2473 PILLS, Poetical, Political, and Philosophical, prescribed for the purpose of purging the publick of piddling philosophers, or puny poetasters, of paltry politicians, and petty partizans, by Peter Pepperbox, Poet and Physician, *boards*, 12mo. Phil. 1809

2474 PINDAR (*Peter*, i. e. *Dr. Walcott*), The original editions of several of his Satyrs with caricatures, Bozzy and Piozzi, *plate, in* 1 *thick volume*, 4to. Lond. v. y.

2475 PINDARIANA, or Peter's Portfolio, *unbd.* Dublin, 1795

2476 PINDAR (*Peter*), The Works of, *with a portrait*, 8vo. *sh.* Phil. 1835

2477 PLAISIRS de l'Amour ou recueil de contes, histoires et poemes galans, 2 vols. *plates*, 12mo. *calf.* 1782

2478 PLURIBUSTAH, a Song that's by no Author, "a deed without a name," illustrated by Q. R. Philander Doestick, P. B., (in verse), *cloth*, 12mo. N. Y. 1856

2479 POCKET Miscellany in Prose and Verse, 12mo. *sheep.* Phil. 1798

2480 POETICAL Farrago, being a miscellaneous assemblage of Epigrams and other jeux d'esprit, 2 vols. *calf, extra*, 12mo. Lond. 1794

2481 POETICAL Tit Bits, or Leaves from Momus's Day-Book, by Moncrief, Pierce Egan, Dibdin, &c., 40 *humorous engravings, cloth*, 12mo. Lond. 1840

2482 POETICAL Vagaries of a Knight of the Folding Stick, of Paste-Castle, to which is annexed the History of the Garret, &c., 18mo. Gotham, 1816

2483 POINTS of Misery, Humour, &c., illustrated by George Cruikshank, royal 8vo. *half calf, gilt*, "*most spirited etchings*," *scarce.* Lond. 1823

2484 POLITICAL History of the Devil, interspersed with many of the devil's adventures, a description of the devil's dwelling, vulgarly called hell, by D. Defoe, *calf*, 12mo. Lond. 1754

2485 POOLE (*John*), Sketches and Recollections by, 8vo. Phil. 1835

2486 Polyanthea (*The*), or a collection of interesting Fragments in Prose and Verse, 2 vols. *calf.* Lond. 1804

2487 Polyanthos (*The*), a Periodical Publication, Oct. 1812 to Sept. 1813, 2 vols. *half calf,* 8vo. Boston, 1814

2488 Pompadour (*Marchioness de, Mistress to the French King*), History of, 2 parts in 1 vol. 12mo. Lond. 1760

2489 Portraits of Famous London Courtezans, by Holbein, with their terms, small 4to. *half morocco.* Lond. n. d.

2490 Potiphar Papers, reprinted from Putnam's Monthly, 8vo. N. Y. 1853

2491 Powell (*The*), Count de Foix, a Tale, 8vo. Lond. 1842

2492 Priapeia, sive diversorum poetarum ad Priapum lusus, cum comment Gasp. Scioppii, etc., accedunt Jose Scaliger in Priapeia comment, *original binding, rare,* 8vo. Patav, 1664

2493 Primaudaye (*Peter de la*), The French Academie, wherein is discoursed the institution of Maners, &c., dedicated to the most Christian King, Henry III., 8vo *old sheep.* Lond. 1601

2494 Puckle (*James*), The Club, or a Gray Cap for a Green Head, a Dialogue between a Father and Son, *illustrated,* 8vo. *cloth.* Lond. 1710

2495 ——— Another edition, 12mo. Lond. 1834

2496 Punch, or the London Charivari, 128 Nos. 4to. v. d.

2497 ——— Another lot, 4to. n. d.

2498 Punch and Diogenes, 2 vols. 4to. *folded.*

2499 Punchiana and other Pieces, from Punch, 9 vols. 12mo. v. d.

2500 Punch's Snapdragons for Christmas, *sewed,* 12mo. Lond. 1844

2501 ——— Guide to the Chinese collection, *wood-cuts,* 12mo. Lond. 1844

2502 ——— Medical Student and other Pieces, 9 vols. 12mo. v. d.

2503 ——— Almanacks, 1842 to 1851, 4to. Lond. 1852

2504 Quevedo (*Francisco de*), Six Visions of Hell, being satires of the corruptions and vices of all degrees of mankind, *plates, calf,* 12mo. Lond. 1756

2505 ——— Visions, translated by W. Elliot, 12mo. Phil. 1832

"Quevedo was one of the best writers of the age, his Humorous Pieces have a certain ease and pleasantry peculiar to themselves."

2506 QUILLET (*Claudius*), Callipœdia, a Poem, with his Life, by Bayle, translated by Rowe, 8vo. *old calf, gilt, scarce, and curious.* Lond. 1712

2507 QUINZE Joyes de Mariage, *Gothic letter,* imprime à Paris par Jehan Preperel, demeurant sur le pont Nôtre Dame a lymage Sainct Laurente, reprint by Techener, square 8vo. *red morocco, extra, uncut.* Paris.

2508 ——— Joies de Mariage, *only* 106 *copies printed, yellow morocco,* square 8vo. Paris.

2509 QUODLIBET: Containing some Annals thereof, and an authentic account of the origin and growth of the Borough, *cloth,* 8vo. Phil. 1840

2510 ——— Another Copy, *cloth,* 8vo. Phil. 1840

2511 RABELAIS (*Francis*), Works, or the Lives, Heroic Deeds and Sayings of Gargantua and Pantagruel, translated by Sir T. Urchard and Matteux, 5 vols. in 4, 12mo. Lond. 1694

"I could write a treatise in praise of the moral elevation of Rabelais's Works which would make the Church stare and the conventicle groan, and yet it would be the truth. I class Rabelais with the creative minds of the world—Shakspeare, Dante, Cervantes, &c." —*Coleridge.*

2512 RABELAIS the younger, 18mo., no title.

2513 RABUTIN (*Bussy*), Histoire Amoreuse des Gaules, 3 vols. 8vo. *half calf.* Paris, 1829

2514 RADCLIFFE (*A.*) The Ramble, an anti-heroick Poem, together with some Terrestrial Hymns and Carnal Ejaculations, printed for the author, and are to be sold by Walter Davis in Amen Corner, 1682; Ovid Travestie, a burlesque on Ovid's Epistles, by Alexander Radcliffe, of Gray's Inn, printed for Jacob Tonson, at the Judge's Head in Chancery Lane, near Fleet Street, 1681, *scarce, in the original binding,* 8vo. Lond. 1681–82

2515 RAYMOND (*G.*) Drafts for Acceptance, 18mo. N. Y. 1856

2516 REACH (*Angus B.*) Claret and Olives, from the Garonne to the Rhone.

2517 ——— Man in the Moon, *with illustrations,* vols. 3, 4 and 5, *cloth,* 12mo. Lond.

2518 REAL Life in London, or the Life and Adventures of Bob Tallyho, Esq., and his Cousin Tom Dashall, through the Metropolis, *numerous colored plates,* 2 vols. *cloth,* 8vo. Lond. 1831

2519 REMARKABLE Satires, Causicade, Triumvirade, Porcupinade, Processionade, 'Piscopade, Scandalizade, and the Pasquinade, with notes variorum, *calf*, 8vo. Lond. 1760

2520 REPOSITORY of Anecdote and Wit, containing Smart Sayings, Singular Adventures, Eccentric Biography, Curious Incidents, &c. 2 vols. 12mo. *boards, uncut.* Lond. 1784

2521 REVERIES of an Old Maid, embracing Important Hints to Young Men, 43 *engravings*, 12mo. N. Y. 1856

2522 REVERIE, or a Flight to the Paradise of Fools, 2 vols. *calf*, 12mo. Dub. 1762

2523 REYNOLDS (*George W. M.*) Alfred de Rosan, or Adventures of a French Gentleman, *half calf*, 12mo. Phil. 1839

2524 REPTON (*Humphrey*) Odd Whims and Miscellanies, by the author of the Works on Landscape Gardening, 2 vols. 8vo. *large paper copy, colored plates, calf.* Lond. 1801

An amusing and well written book, in which first occurs the story of the Bashful Man.

2525 RICHELIEU (*Mademoiselle de*), Travels and Adventures, who made the Tour of Europe, dressed in Men's Clothes attended by her Maid Lucy, as her Valet-de-Chambre, 3 vols. 12mo. *calf.* Lond. 1744

*** These are, indeed, the marvellous adventures of a most remarkable Woman.

2526 RIDLEY (*James*), The Schemer, or Universal Satirist, by Helter Van Skelter, 12mo. *calf.* Lond. 1763

2527 RILEY (*H. H.*) Puddleford Papers, or Humors of the West, *illustrations*, 8vo. N. Y. 1857

2528 ROBERT Macaire et Son Ami Bertrand, 18mo. *half morocco.* Paris, 1841

2530 ROBINSON, Intriguing Milliner and Attorneys' Clerks, a mock Tragedy, 12mo. *half calf.* Lond. 1738

2531 ROLLIAD (*The*), Probationary Odes for the Laureateship, and Political Miscellanies, with Criticisms and Illustrations, 8vo. *calf.* Dublin, 1797

An extraordinary collection of *jeu d'esprits* of the age just preceding the Poetry of the Anti-Jacobin.

2532 RUSSEL (*G.*) Works of, including a translation of the Lettres Galantes of Fontenelle, 2 vols. 8vo. *calf.* Cork, 1769

2533 SALONS Célèbres, par Mrs. Sophie Gay, *half morocco*, 12mo. Brux. 1857

2534 SAM Slick, Tammany Hall, &c. 3 vols.

2535 SANDERSON (*T.*) Royal Hero, 4to. Lond. 1733

2536 SANSOVINO (*F.*) The Quintessence of Wit, being a Corrant of Conceites, Maximies, and Poleticke Deuises, selected and gathered together by Francisco Sansovino, wherein is set forth sundrye excellent and wise sentences, worthie to be regarded and followed, translated by Captaine Hitchcock, *with a woodcut of his coat of arms, a fine copy of a very rare book,* **Black Letter,** 4to. *Edward Allde,* Lond. 1590

Lowndes says 1596, and that it sold for £4 7*s.* in Townley's sale.

2537 SAILLIES d'Esprit ou choix curieux de traits utiles et Agreables pour le Conversation, entrelassés d'Histoires Singuliers, d'Anecdotes Intereportés, &c. pour Gayot de Pitaval, 2 parts in 1, 8vo. Paris, 1727

2538 SCARRON, Novels Translated by John Davies, of Kidwelly, *portrait, calf,* 8vo. Lond. 1683

2539 ——— Roman Comique, 4 vols. in 2, 12mo. *calf.* Paris, 1820

2540 ——— Sixteen Engravings after Marillier to illustrate any edition of the Roman Comique, 8vo. Paris, 1832

"That pleasantly extravagant book, the Comic Romance, has more of the English cast of humor than any other work of the same country."—*Retrospective Review.*

2541 SCRIBE (*Eugene*), Proverbes et Nouvelles, 12mo. Paris, 1840

2542 SECUNDUS (*J.*) The Basia, or Kisses of, with his Epithalamium, &c., the Latin Text and English Translation in Verse, with his Life, 12mo. *plate.* Dub. 1787

2543 SECRET Memoirs of the Court of Petersburg, and particularly during the end of the Reign of Catharine II., 8vo. *sheep.* Phil. 1802

2544 ——— History of the Loose and Incestuous Loves of Pope Gregory VII. and Richelieu, 12mo. *sheep.* Lond. 1722

2545 SEYMOUR'S Humorous Sketches, comprising 86 caricature etchings, *illustrated in prose and verse,* 8vo. *half russia, neat.* Lond. 1841

2546 ——— Comic Album, 18mo. *cloth.* Lond. n. d.

2547 SHILLABER (*B. P.*) Life and Sayings of Mrs. Partington and other Members of the Family, *cloth,* 8vo. N. Y. 1854

2548 Six Hints to Bachelors, or the Secret of Happiness, 8vo. Bost.

2549 Sketches from St. George's Fields, by Georgione Di Castel Chiuso, in verse, *boards*, *uncut*, 12mo. Lond. 1820

2550 Smith (*Albert*), The Wassail-Bowl, *cuts*, 2 vols. *cloth*, post 8vo. Lond. 1843

2551 ——— (*Ben.*) The Motley Book, a Series of Tales and Sketches, *plates*, *cloth*, 8vo. N. Y. 1838

2552 ——— Gaieties and Gravities, a Series of Essays, Comic Tales, &c., 2 vols. *half calf*, 12mo. Phil. 1825

2552* ——— (*Sydney*), Wit and Wisdom, *calf*, 12mo. N. Y. 1856

2553 Southey, The Common-Place Book, edited by his son-in-law, 8vo. *cloth*. Lond. 1849

2554 Specimens of Marcaronic Poetry, 8vo. *cloth*. Lond. 1831

2555 Spence, Pig's Meat, or Lessons for the Swinish Multitude, 2 vols. 12mo. *half bd.* Lond. n. d.

2556 Spette (*Ant. Mar.*), La Sage-Folie, Fontaine d'Allegresse, mère de plaisir, et reyne de belles humeurs, trad. par Marcel, *rare*, 2 vols. *crimson morocco*, *extra fine copy*, 12mo. Lyon, 1628

2557 Spirit of the Public Journals, a Selection of Jeux d'Esprits from the Journals printed in 1824, *with explanatory notes and plates*, 8vo. Lond. 1825

2558 Spouter's Companion, or Theatrical Remembrancer, together with the Spouting Club in an Uproar, &c. &c., *half calf*, 12mo. Lond. 1786

2559 Squatter Life and Backwoods, 2 vols. 1847

2560 ——— and other Humorous Works, 7 vols. 12mo. v. d.

2561 Stamford Toasts, or Panegyrical Characters of the Fair Ones Inhabiting the Good Town of Stamford, in Lincolnshire, etc., by Mr. Pope, *not the undertaker*, 12mo. Lond. 1726

2562 State Triumvirate, a Political Tale, and the Epistles of Brevet Major Pindar Puff, 12mo. N. Y. 1819

2563 Stephens (*H.*) Comic Natural History of the Human Race, *colored caricature plates*, royal 8vo. *cloth*. Phil. n. d.

2564 Sterne, Funeral Discourse Occasioned by the Much Lamented Death of Mr. Yorick, *sewed*, *scarce*. *Printed at Aretopolis, Capital of Eutopia*, 1761

2565 STEVENS (*Geo. Alex.*) Lecture on Heads, with additions by Mr. Pilon, *large paper*, *half russia*, 8vo. Lond. 1799

2566 ——— Choice Spirit Chaplet, or a Poesy from Parnassus, *calf*, 12mo. Whitehaven, 1771

2567 ——— The Adventures of a Speculist: or, a Journey through London, with a Life of the Author by the Editor, 2 vols. *half calf*. Lond. 1788

These amusing and scarce volumes contain a picture of the manners, fashions, and amusements of the Metropolis about a century ago. The chapters are entitled a Visit to the Fleet—Visit to Bedlam—Authentic Life of a Woman of the Town—Description of what Covent Garden Was, and what it Is. The whole singularly curious and interesting.

2568 ——— Distress upon Distress, or Tragedy in True Taste, a Heroi-Comi-Parodi-Tragedi-Farcical Burlesque, 8vo. Lond. 1752

2569 ——— Court of Alexander, an Opera, 8vo. Lond.

2570 STRAY Subjects arrested and bound over, being the Fugitive Offspring of the Old 'Un and the Young 'Un, illustrated by Darley, 8vo. *sewed*. Phil. 1848

2571 STUDENT'S Common Place Book, or Selections on Life, Manners, and Literature, 12mo. *boards*. Edin. 1820

2572 STULTIFERA Navis, or the Modern Ship of Fools, 12mo. Phil. 1807

A smart original Poem, with notes, in which the author (the late ingenious W. H. Ireland, the framer of the celebrated Shakspeare papers). Among the 36 sections satirized by his pen are—"Foolish and Unprofitable Books," "Of Fools who collect Old Books and Prints," "Of Foolish Antiquaries," &c. &c.

2573 SURE Guide to Hell, in seven sections—to Parents, to Youth, &c., by Beelzebub, 8vo. *calf*. Lond. n. d.

2574 SWIFT and Pope—Supplement to their Works, now first collected into one volume, 12mo. *calf*. Dub. 1732

2575 SYLVIUS (*Æneas*), The History of the Amours of Count Schlick, Chancellor to the Emp. Sigismund, 8vo. Lond. 1708

SYNTAX'S Tours, *vide* Coombe, lots 2500 to 2506.

2576 TAKINGS, or Scenes in the Life of a Collegian, a Poem, 36 *engravings by Dagley*, *half calf*. Lond. 1821

2577 TALES of a Parrot, from the Persian of Pooti Nameeh, 8vo. *boards*, *uncut*. Lond. 1792

2578 TALES of Humour, Gallantry, and Romance, selected and translated from the Italian, post 8vo. *wood-cuts*, *boards*, *uncut*. Lond. 1824

Contains a story of the Merchant of Venice, &c.

2579 TALE of the Basyn and the Frere and the Boy, edited by Wright, square 12mo. *half morocco.* Lond. 1836

2580 TALE (*A*), and no Tale: That is to say, A Tale, and no Tale of a Tub, thin 8vo. *half calf.* Lond. 1715

2581 TARANTULA (*The*), or Dance of Fools, 2 vols. in 1, 12mo. Lond. 1809

2582 THACKERAY (*W. M.*) Rose and the Ring, *cuts*, square 8vo. N. Y. 1855

2583 ——— English Humorists of the Eighteenth Century, 12mo. *cloth.* N. Y. 1854

2584 ——— Yellowish Papers, 12mo. *cloth.* N. Y. 1853

2585 ——— Kickleburys on the Rhine, 12mo. *sewed.* N. Y. 1851

2586 THEOPHRASTUS, Characters of, illustrated by Physiognomical Sketches, &c., *woodcuts, cloth,* 12mo. Lond. 1831

2587 THOMAS of Reading, or the Sixe Worthie Yeomen of the West (by Thos. Deloney), from the edition of 1632, edited by W. J. Thoms, 12mo. Lond. *Pickering,* 1827

2588 THORPE (*T. B.*) The Hive, or the Bee-Hunter, 12mo. *plates, cloth.* N. Y. 1854

2589 THREE Courses and a Dessert, the decorations by Geo. Cruikshank, 8vo. Lond. 1830
See also under Cruikshank.

2590 Tickler (*The*), a Newspaper from January 23, 1811, to April 21, 1813, with a few numbers of Folwell's Spirit of the Press, folio. Phil.

2591 TIM BOBBIN'S Human Passions Delineated, 44 *colored plates, containing upwards of* 120 *droll, satirical, and humorous figures, illustrative of the passions, with verses,* royal 8vo. *half morocco.* 1773, rep. n. d. [1846]

A very clever and humorous work in the style of Hogarth.

2592 TIN Trumpet, or Heads and Tails for the Wise and Waggish, by the late Paul Chatfield, M. D., *portrait,* 12mo. Phil. 1836

This clever work is attributed by some to Sir F. Head, and by others to James Smith, one of the authors of the Rejected Addresses.

2593 'TIS Merry when Gossips meet, *curious woodcut,* 8vo. *half calf.* Reprinted for J. Deane, 1843

This *scarce* little dialogue has been attributed to Samuel Rowlands, and it is valuable as a lively satiric picture of female manners in the middle class of society at that period. Very few copies reprinted.

2594 TORPEDO, a Poem, by James Perry, Editor of the Morning Chronicle. 1777

2595 ELECTRICAL Eel, a Poem. 1777

2596 ELEGY on the Death of the Electrical Eel, a Poem, 4to. Lond. 1779

2597 TOUR of Doctor Prosody in Search of the Antique and Picturesque, through Scotland, the Hebrides, the Orkney, and Shetland Isles, *twenty humorous plates, colored, half calf*, 8vo. Lond. 1821

2598 TRACTS, a volume containing, among others, Grubb Street Miscellany, 1731, several literary prospectusses, and Life of John Hales, of Eton, *half calf*, 8vo. Lond. 1719

2599 TRACTS, containing Pope's Literary Correspondence, Vol. 2, 1735; Life and Heroick Actions of the Eighth Champion of Christendom, *wood-cut*, 1739: No Fool like the Old Fool, 1731; Virgil's Husbandry, 1724, in 1 vol. 8vo. v. y.

2600 TOUR of Doctor Syntax in search of the Picturesque, designs by Crowquill, *cuts, damaged*, 12mo. *cloth*. 1844
See also Lots 2216 to 2219.

2601 TRAVELS in America, by George Fribbleton, ex-barber to her Majesty (dedicated to Mrs. Trollope), 12mo. N. Y. 1853

2602 TRUE Politeness, or Etiquette, *sewed*, 12mo. Boston, 1846

2603 TOURNAMENT of Totenham and the Feest, edited by Wright, *reprint in* black letter, 12mo. *half morocco*. Lond. 1836

2604 UNCLE Sam's Recommendations of Phrenology to his Millions of Friends, *cloth*, 12mo. N. Y. 1842

2605 VOLTAIRE, La Pucelle d'Orleans augmentée de cinq chants nouveaux et de Notes, 8vo. *hf. cf.* Lond. 1766

2606 W. (*W.*) New help to Discourse, or wit, mirth, and jollity intermixed with more serious matter, 12mo. *binding loose*. Lond. 1672

2607 WAGSTAFF'S (*W.*) Works, with Life, *portrait and two curious plates,* to Tom Thumb and Crispin the Cobler, 8vo. *neat*. Lond. 1726

"Valued in his profession—admired for his wit and facetiousness."

2608 WARD (*Ned*), Helter-Skelter, or the Devil upon two Sticks, a Comedy, as it hath been acted between High-Church and Low-Church in most Taverns about London (satirical), *half calf*, *Roxburgh copy*, 4to. Lond. 1704

2609 WARD (*Thomas*), England's Reformation, from the time of Henry VIII. to the end of Oates's Plot, a Poem in four cantos, *calf*, 12mo. Lond. 1715

"Full of impious abuse put in a strain apt enough to take with those who are disposed to divert themselves with a show of wit and humour, dressed up to make the Reformation appear both odious and ridiculous."—*Bp. Burnet.*

2610 WARWICK (*Eden*), Nosology, or Hints on Noses, 12mo. *cloth.* Lond. 1848

2611 WATMOUGH (*Edward C.*) Scribblings and Sketches diplomatic, piscatory, and oceanic, *cloth*, 12mo. Phil. 1844

2612 WEWITZER (*R.*) School for Wits, containing a choice collection of Bons-Mots, Anecdotes, Epigrams, &c., *half morocco*, 12mo. Lond. 1815

2613 WHITEHEAD (*W.*) The Nymph of Bristol. 1751

2614 WHORE'S (*The*) Rhetorick, calculated to the meridian of London, and conformed to the Rules of Art, *with portraits of noted Courtezans and Procuresses*, 4to. *half morocco, uncut*, (*very few copies printed.*) Lond. 1683; Reprinted at Edinb. 1836.

"A very singular and amusing performance, written with infinite ability, and valuable from the exposure it affords of Cyprianic diplomacy."

2615 WIELAND, Socrates out of his Senses, or Dialogues of Diogenes of Sinope, 2 vols. in 1, 12mo. Newburg, 1797

2616 WHIMSICAL History of some parts of the Iron Age, set forth in a predictical manner. Lond. 1707

2617 WITS of Men, a Discourse concerning the different, 12mo. *sheep.* Lond. 1669

*** Locke is said to have taken several of his ideas from this Tract.—*Translated from Huarte.*

2618 WITTY Apophthegms delivered by King James, King Charles, the Marquess of Worcester, Lord Bacon, and Sir T. Moor, 12mo. Lond. 1669

2619 WILSON (*John*), Noctes Ambrosiana, 4 vols. 8vo. *half morocco.* Phil. 1843

2621 YANKEE Doodle, 2 vols. 4to. 1st vol. *cloth*, 2d vol. *sewed.* N. Y. 1843

2622 YANKEE Notions, a Medley, by Timo. Titterwell, 12mo. *cloth.* Bost. 1838

—— —— Another copy.

2623 YANKEE Story Teller's Own Book, 18mo. Phil. n. y.

2624 YANKEE Stories, &c., 5 vols. 12mo. v. d.

2625 Yates (*E. H. and R. R. Brough*), Our Miscellany, 12mo. *boards.* Lond. 1856

2626 York-shire-Ale, The Praise of, with the Humours of most sort of Drinkers, 16mo. *half calf.* Dublin, 1719

FINE ARTS.—Architecture, Painting, Books of Prints, Emblems, Fables, &c. For Music, *vide* History of the Stage.

2627 Album of Drawings, oblong 8vo. Phil. n. d.

2628 American Art Union Journal, 18 *parts.*

2629 Annales du Salon de Gand et de L'Ecole Moderne des Pays-Bas, 8vo. *half calf.* Gand. 1823

2630 Art Union Journal, *fine plates*, 4to. *cloth.* Lond. 1848

2631 ——— Journal for 1850–51, 48 *parts*, 4to.

2632 ——— Journal for 1854, 12 *parts*, 4to.

2633 ——— Journal, 25 Nos., *various dates.*

2634 Baglione (*Geo.*) Le Vite de' Pittori Scultavi et Architetti, Roma, 1643; Bellori (*G.*) Vita di Carlo Maratti Pittore, 2 vols. in 1, 4to. *calf.* Roma, 1732

2636 Barry (*J.*) Cartoons: A Series of Etchings, from his original and justly celebrated Paintings in the Great Room of the Society of Arts, Adelphi, atlas folio, containing fifteen very large and highly finished etchings, with a fine etching of Barry's picture of Pandora by Schiavonetti, *neatly half bd.* 1808–10

This series of Paintings by Barry is one of the glories of the English School. Introduced are the portraits of a vast number of eminent individuals: the above desirable copy has the usually deficient plate of "Pandora," by Schiavonetti, on India Paper.

2637 Book of Art, Cartoons, Frescoes, Sculpture and Decorative Art, as applied to the New Houses of Parliament, 111 *plates*, 4to. *cloth, gilt.* Lond. 1846

2638 ——— of Beauty for 1837, by the Countess of Blessington, *plates*, post. 8vo. Lond. 1837

5639 Boydell (*J. & J.*) Catalogue of the Pictures of, 4to. Lond. 1803

2640 Bryan's (*R.*) Dictionary of Painters and Engravers, new edition, corrected, greatly enlarged, and continued to the present time, with the addition of more than 1300 articles, by George Stanley, Esq., complete in one large volume, impl. 8vo. *numerous plates of monograms, cloth.* Lond. 1849

2641 BUCHANAN (*W.*) Memoirs of Painting, with a Chronological History of the Importation of Pictures by the Great Masters into England since the French Revolution, 2 vols. 8vo. *boards.* 1824

2642 CABINET of Modern Art, edited by A. A. Watts, 3d series, 8vo. *boards, uncut.* 1837

2643 CASTLES, A Scrap Book, with a large collection of prints of Ancient Castles in England, Ireland, and Scotland, &c. pasted in it, 4to. *boards.*

2644 CATALOGUES of Sales of Oil Paintings, &c., about 50.

2645 CAULFIELD (*J.*) Calcographiana: The Printseller's Chronicle, and Collectors' Guide to the knowledge and value of British Portraits, 8vo. *boards.* Lond. 1814

CHALCOGRAPHIMANIA, *vide* Ireland.

2646 CHINESE Drawings on Rice Paper of Landscapes, Shells, Insects and Flowers, 3 vols. oblong 4to.

2647 CHOICE Examples of Art Workmanship. Lond. 1849

2648 COPPER-Plate Magazine, or Elegant Cabinet of Picturesqe Prints, consisting of sublime and interesting views in Great Britain and Ireland, *beautifully engraved,* 5 vols. oblong 4to. *morocco, extra.* Lond. n. d.

Fine old Plates by Grignon, Watts, Cooke, &c., after Lebrun, Moreau, Kneller, Eisen, Sandby, and others.

2649 COTTINGHAM (*L. N.*) Catalogue of his Museum of Mediæval Art, 4to. Lond. 1850

2650 CRUIKSHANK (*G.*) Essay on the Genius of, with numerous illustrations of his works (from the Westminster Review) with additional etchings, 8vo. *cloth.* Lond. 1840

2651 CUMBERLAND (*G.*) Essay on the utility of collecting the best works of the Italian School; accompanied by a Critical Catalogue, with interesting anecdotes of the engravers, 4to. *boards.* Lond. 1827

2652 CUNNINGHAM (*A.*) Gallery of Pictures, 12 parts, royal 8vo. *fine impression of the plates.*

2653 DU FRESNOY (*C. A.*) Art of Painting, translated by Dryden, 8vo. *calf.* Lond. 1716

The preface contains a parallel betwixt poetry and painting.

2654 DUNLAP (*W.*) History of the Rise and Progress of the Arts and Designers of the United States, 2 vols. 8vo. *boards, uncut, very scarce.* N. Y. 1834

2655 EDWARDS (*E.*) Anecdotes of Painters who have resided or been born in England, 4to. *half calf.* Lond. 1808

Intended as a continuation of Walpole's Anecdotes of Painting.

2656 EVANS (*E.*) Catalogue of Engraved Portraits, 8vo. *boards.* Lond. n. d.

2657 FABLES: Gabrielis Færni, Cremonensis, Fabulæ Centum, 4to. *calf.* Lond. 1743

2658 FERGUSON (*Jac.*) Historical Inquiry into the true principles of Beauty in Art, more especially with reference to Architecture, 8vo. *cloth.* Lond. 1849

2659 ENGRAVINGS from a collection of pictures by the Italian, Flemish, and Dutch Masters, exhibiting at the Saloon of Arts, with Biog. and Critical Notices, &c., by Gillow, 4to. 90 fine etchings by Vendramini and Aglio, with descriptions, *half morocco, top edge gilt, scarce.* Lond. 1818

2660 FIELDING (*T. H.*) Art of Engraving, with the various modes of Operation, 8vo. *cloth.* Lond. 1844

2661 ——— on the Knowledge and Restoration of Old Paintings, and the means of judging between copies and originals, 12mo. *cloth.* Lond. 1841

2662 FINDEN'S Views of Ports, Harbors, Watering Places, and Fishing Villages on the English Coast, containing highly-finished engravings after Harding, Creswick, Cooke, Bartlett, &c., vol. 1, 4to. 1838

2663 FLATTER'S Compositions from Milton: The Paradise Lost of Milton, Illustrated in a Series of Fifty-Four Plates of the Human Figure, for the Use of Sculptors, Artists, &c., by J. J. Flatters, Sculptor, with 54 beauful outline engravings, with Quotations in English and French, folio, *half morocco, uncut.* 1851

2664 FLAXMAN (*G.*) Atlante Dantesco, 120 *fine etchings,* 4to. Milan, 1822

2665 ——— Compositions from Dante; 111 *plates in outline,* oblong folio. Carlsruhe, n. d

"Flaxman has translated Dante best, for he has translated it into the universal language of nature."—*Lord Byron.*

2666 FLAXMAN et SCHULES, Sujets de l'Illiade et l'Odyssee d'Homere, royal 8vo. Carlsruhe, n. d.

"Flaxman's unequalled Compositions from Homer, Æschylus, and Hesiod, have long been the admiration of Europe; of their simplicity and beauty the pen is quite incapable of conveying an adequate impression."—*Sir Thomas Lawrence.*

2667 GODEY'S Gallery of Splendid Engravings, royal 8vo. *sewed.* Phil. n. d.

2667*FLEURY (*Claude*) Traité du Choix et de la methode des etudes, 12mo. Paris, 1740

2668 Frommel (*C.*) Dreissig Ansichten Griechenlands zu den Werken Griechischer Autoren, 3 *parts*, royal 8vo. Carlsruhe, 1830

2669 Flindall (*J. M.*) Amateur's Pocket Companion, 18mo. *boards.* Lond. 1813

2670 ——— Amateurs Pocket Companion, *interleaved*, 1813

2671 Gavards (*Ch.*) Galerie Historiques de Versailles, fine etchings, 8vo. *boards.* Paris, 1838

2672 Glances at the Metropolis, a hundred illustrated Gems, 4to. *morocco.* N. Y. n. d.

This volume contains one hundred fine English Engravings, with one hundred business puffs; cost one hundred dollars.

2673 Hamilton (*G.*) English School of Painting and Sculpture, 4 vols. 12mo. Lond. 1833

2674 Harding's Landscape Illustrations of the Tourist in Italy, 74 plates in 2 portfolios. 1833

Hayley (*Wm.*) Life of George Romney, *vide* Romney.

2675 Heath (*Chas.*) Book of Beauty, 1837–45, 10 vols. 8vo *in silk and morocco.* Lond. v. d.

2676 ——— Book of Beauty for 1849, 8vo. *silk.* Lond. 1849

5677 Hogarth (*W.*) Works, 79 Plates published by Sayer, folio, *half calf.* Lond. 1768

2678 ——— Works, from the Original Plates, restored by James Heath, Esq. R. A., with the Addition of many subjects not before collected, to which is prefixed a Biographical Essay on the Genius and Productions of Hogarth, and Explanations of the Subjects of the Plates, by John Nichols, 119 *large Plates*, atlas fol. *half russia.* 1812

Published at £31 10*s.*; and the impressions are very much superior to the usual copies now offered for sale, which have been worked off more recently.

Hogarth is indispensable in the library, and is still unrivalled as a drawing-room table-book.

2679 ——— Graphic Illustrations of, from Pictures, Drawings, and Scarce Prints in the Possession of Samuel Ireland, *upwards of* 100 *Plates*, imperial 4to. *large paper, cloth.* 1794

An indispensable companion to every edition of Hogarth, containing matter nowhere else to be found. The subjects of the plates and letterpress are particularly interesting.

"I was pleased with the reply of a gentleman, who being asked which book he esteemed most in his library, answered 'Shakspeare;' being asked which he esteemed next best, replied, 'Hogarth.'"—*Charles Lamb.*

"To the student of history, these admirable works must be invaluable, as they give us the most complete and truthful picture of the manners, and even the thoughts, of the past century."—*Thackeray.*

2680 HOGARTH (*W.*) Illustrations of, *i. e.* Hogarth Illustrated from Passages in Authors he never read, and could not understand, *portrait inserted*, 8vo. Lond. 1816

2681 ——— Moralized, by Mr. Trusler, *upwards of* 78 *plates, brilliant impressions*, 8vo. *calf, extra gilt.* Lond. 1831

*** While I moralize I study to explain, and while I explain I study to moralize. The prints in this exceedingly pretty edition combine much spirit and delicacy.

2682 ——— Biographical Anecdotes of, with Catalogue of his Works, by J. Nichols, *third edition, enlarged, portrait*, thick 8vo. *calf.* Lond. 1782

"Necessary to the completion of the Literary Anecdotes to which it was originally intended as a Note."

2683 HOLBEIN (*Hans*) Alphabet of Death, illustrated with old borders engraved on wood, with Latin sentences and English Quatrains, selected by Anatole de Montaiglon, 12mo. Paris, Didot, 1856

2684 ——— Dance of Death, with an Historical and Literary Introduction by an Antiquary, small 8vo. *with* 54 *engravings, being the most accurate copies ever executed of these gems of Art, morocco extra, gilt leaves*, 8vo. Lond. 1849

"The designs are executed with a spirit and fidelity quite extraordinary. They are indeed most truthful."—*Athenæum.*

"Ces 53 Planches de Schlotthauer sont d'une exquise perfection."—*Langlois, Essai sur les Dances des Morts*, 1852.

HURET (*Gregoire*), *vide* Lot. 2737.

2685 ILLUSTRATIONS to the Book of Exodus, oblong 4to. Lond. 1830

2686 ILLUMINATED Calendar for 1846, *on card board, coloured, splendidly bound in kid, inlaid with blue and gold*, 4to. Lond. 1846

This choice book is copied from the Hours of the Duke of Anjou, and is a fine example of art, at a period when such works were rare.

2687 IRELAND (*W. H.*) Chalcographimania, or the Portrait Collector and Printseller's Chronicle, with infatuations of every description, a humorous Poem in four books, with copious Notes explanatory by Satiricus Sculptor, Esq., *portrait of Will Somers, half morocco*, 8vo. Lond. 1814

This was written by W. H. Ireland, the Shakspearean forger. It is a clever satire on the extravagant prices given for single prints, and upon the eccentricities of all the printsellers and auctioneers of the day.

2688 JACOB ET SERE, Histoire des Corporations Ouvrieres, le Livre d'Or des Métiers, Nos. 1 to 133, *numerous illuminated illustrations.* Paris, v. d.

A most beautiful work, now in course of publication. It is a perfect cyclopædia on the subject of which it treats, and the engravings are published in a style commensurate to the importance of the work.

2689 JAMESON (*Mrs.*) Sacred Legendary Art, 2d edition, 8vo. *cloth.* Lond. 1850

2690 ——— Legends of the Monastic Orders, 2d edit., 8vo. *cloth.* Lond. 1852

2691 ——— Legends of the Madonna, 8vo. *cloth.* Lond. 1852

"Few subjects are of greater interest than the history of Sacred and Legendary Art. It is the symbolism of the Christian faith, a record of the hate which persecuted, of the constancy which overcame, of a gloomy fanaticism, and the subjugation of the old mythology 'that had peopled space with life and mystical predominance,' by another of a purer nature, through the medium of similar agencies. . . . . Mrs. Jameson has shown great qualifications in its composition. Her reading is extensive, and confirmed by a personal knowledge of the best works of Art in the most valuable public and private galleries."

2692 ——— Memoirs and Essays, Illustrative of Art, Literature, and Social Morals, 12mo. *cloth.* Lond. 1846

2693 ——— Companion to the Private Picture Galleries in London, containing accurate Catalogues arranged Alphabetically, preceded by a Historical and Critical Introduction, and an Essay on Art, Artists, Collectors, and Connoisseurs, post 8vo. *cloth.* 1844

"Mrs. Jameson knows her subject thoroughly, and is so skilful a mistress of language, that few who care about painting will lay down the volume when once taken up."—*Athenæum.*

2694 ——— Handbook to the Public Galleries of Art in and near London, 12mo. *cloth.* Lond. 1845

"Pleasant to read, useful to consult, and valuable as a vade mecum to the visitor."—*Spectator.*

2694*LACROIX (*M. Paul*), Le Moyen Age, et Le Renaissance, Histoire et Description des Mœurs et Usages du Commerce, et de l'Industrie, des Sciences, des Arts, des Litteratures et des Beaux Arts en Europe, 4to. *half morocco.* Paris, 1848

This superb work contains many hundred illustrations, large illuminations in gold and colors, wood engravings, &c. It is the most richly embellished work ever published relating to the Middle Ages. Each subject—as Costume, Architecture, Poetry, Illuminated Manuscripts, Arms and Armor, Sculpture, Enamels, Romances of Chivalry, Painting, Stained Glass, &c.—has a separate dissertation devoted to it, by the most competent literary men best acquainted with it; forming a perfect encyclopædia of the Middle Ages. The richness and quantity of the plates must be seen to be appreciated. In no other country than France could such a work be produced.

2695 JOURNAL of Design, 9 Parts, 8vo. 50 *plates.* Lond. 1849

2696 LA FAGE (*Ramon*), Recueil de 123 pièces d'apres ses dessins, grav. par Andran Simoneau, etc., folio, *calf.* Paris, 1689

2697 ETRURIA Pittrice ovvero Storia della Pittura Toscana; de dotta dai suoi monumenti che si esibiscono in Stampa del Secolo X. sino al presente (en Italien et en Français, la description par Lastri), 2 vols. folio, *half morocco.* Firenze, 1791–5

This work is now exceedingly scarce; it comprises 120 large engravings, and an equal number of vignettes, all engraved in the best Italian style.

2698 LE BLANC, Histoire des Peintres de toutes les Ecoles depuis la renaissance jusqu'a nos jours, avec notes, recherches, &c., in 279 numbers, *portraits of the artists, and specimens of their works,* folio. Paris, n. d.

This most beautifully illustrated work is a history of the painters of all nations with examples of each artist, and contains lives and specimens of the most famous works of Murillo, Teniers, Ruysdael, Valentin, Boucher, Vernet, Rubens, and others; it is not yet completed.

2699 LE BRUN Travestied, or Caricatures of the Passions, by Woodward and Rowlandson, 20 *spirited plates,* 4to. *half morocco.* Lond. 1800

2700 LESTER (*C. E.*) Artists of America, a Series of Biographical Essays of American Artists, *with portraits and steel plates,* 8vo. N. Y. 1846

2701 LONDON Art Union Prize Annual, vol. 3, folio, *cloth, gilt.*

2702 MAGAZINES of the Fine Arts and Journal of Literature and Science, 4 vols. 8vo. *cloth.* Lond. 1833

2703 MALCOLM (*J. P.*) Historical Sketch of the Art of Caricaturing, with graphic illustrations, 4to. *half calf.* Lond. 1813

2704 MARCENAY De Ghuy, Œuvres de, contenant différens Morceaux d'Histoires, Portraits, Paysages, Batailles, etc., imperial 4to., with above 50 remarkably fine engravings by this elegant artist, after paintings by Poussin, Vandyck, Rembrandt, and others, including portraits of Charles I., the Maid of Orleans, Sully, &c., *fine impressions, half morocco,* folio. Paris, 1755

2705 MIFFLIN (*J. H.*) On the Fine Arts in America, an Address, pp. 19, 8vo. Phil. 1833

2706 MOSES (*H.*) Engravings of Benjamin West's Pictures, 4to. Lond. 1811

2707 MODERN Gallery of British Artists, consisting of a Series of Engravings of their most admired Works, with illustrative descriptions, 4to. *cloth, gilt.* Lond. 1836

2708 MUSEUM of Painting and Sculpture, or Collection of the Principal Pictures, Statues, and Bas-Reliefs in the Public and Private Galleries of Europe, 17 vols. crown 8vo. *containing* 1150 *outline plates by Reveil, with descriptions in French and English by Duchesne, uncut.* Paris, 1820–33

This valuable work contains 1200 outline engravings, executed in a masterly style of art, and will be found extremely useful as a book of reference to the amateur and collector of pictures.

2709 NASH'S Characteristics of British Palaces of the Olden Times, with Descriptions by Mrs. S. C. Hall, in verse and prose, 13 *large and fine colored plates, illustrative of interesting events in history,* royal 4to. *cloth, gilt leaves.* 1849

2710 NOLLEKINS and his Times, comprising his Life and Memoirs of Contemporary Artists, from Roubiliac, Hogarth, and Reynolds, to Fuseli, Flaxman, and Blake, by J. T. Smith, *portrait,* 2 vols. 8vo. *boards.* 1829

A delightful book; in it will be found some curious anecdotes of George III., Princess of Wales, Lords Mansfield and Londonderry, Sir P. Lely, Pitt, Fox, Garrick, Mrs. Siddons, Mr. Coutts, Barry, Bannister, Dr. Johnson, Goldsmith, Burney, Wolcott, Gainsborough, and a host of other celebrities.

2711 PAYNE'S Universum, or Pictorial World, edited by G. C. Edwards, 4to. *cloth, gilt.* Lond. n. d.

2712 PERELLE, Les Œuvres de, Vues Nouvelles des plus beaux Lieux de France et d'Italie, oblong 4to. Paris, 1685

A collection of one hundred and sixty views of landscapes, gardens, ruins, &c., by this celebrated French engraver, in a folio volume. Perelle is the Hollar of France, both in his style of engraving, and the esteem with which his views are held.

2713 PICART (*B.*) Impostures Innocentes, ou recueil d'estampes gravées dans le gout de differens maitres celebres, des trois ecoles, par B. Picart, folio, 80 *fine plates engraved in exact facsimile of the original drawings* (*hence the name*), *fine impressions, half calf, rare.* Amst. 1734

2714 PLANS of Temples, &c. 4to. no title. Lond. 1795

2715 RAPHAEL'S Cupid and Psyche, les Amours de Cupidon et Psyche; Gravées d'apres les dessins de Raphael, avec le Poeme de La Fontaine, royal folio, 32 *beautiful plates by Fragonard, &c. half morocco gilt.* Paris, 1820

"See the beautiful Allegoric Tale of Cupid and Psyche in Apuleius, the tasks imposed on her by the jealousy of her Mother in Law and the agency by which they are at length self-performed, are noble instances of that hidden wisdom, 'where more is meant than meets the ear.'"—*Coleridge.*

2716 RAPHAEL, Cattermole (Revd. R.) Book of the Cartoons of, 8vo. *cloth.* Lond. 1846

Richardson, speaking of the Cartoons, piously exclaims, "God be praised that we have so near us such an invaluable blessing."

"Ille hic est Raphael, timuit quo sospite vinci
Rerum magna parens, et moriente mori."
Epitaph at Rome.

2717 REYNOLDS (*Sir Joshua*), Works, including his Discourses, Commentary on Fresnoy, Art of Painting, &c., with Explanatory Notes, and Life by Edward Malone, Esq., 3 vols. 8vo. *portrait, half calf* 1798

This copy belonged to the celebrated artist who is so well known as the illustrator of Blair's Grave, and other works. It is illustrated with very numerous MS. notes, written with all the spirit of a good hater and excessively vituperative; the following note is written on the title page:—

"This man was hired to Deprave Art."

This is the opinion of William Blake, my proofs are *given in* the [following] notes. The reader is referred to the work, it is full and running over with marginal notes, all written in the spirit already indicated.

"Blake is a real name I assure you, and a most extraordinary man he is, if he be still living. He is the Blake whose wild designs accompany a splendid edition of Blair's Grave. He paints in water colours marvellous strange pictures—visions of his brain, which he asserts that he has seen. They have great merit. I have heard of his Poems, but have never seen them. There is one to a tiger, which I have heard recited, beginning:—

'Tiger! Tiger! burning bright,
Through the deserts of the night,' &c.

which is glorious. But, alas, I have not the book, and the man is flown, whither I know not—to Hades, or a madhouse—but I must look on him as one of the most extraordinary persons of the age."—*C. Lamb.*

"The most original, and in truth the only new and original version of the Scripture idea of *Angels* which I have met with, is that of William Blake, a poet painter, somewhat mad as we are told, if indeed his madness was not rather the 'telescope of truth,' a sort of poetical *clairvoyance*, bringing the unearthly nearer to him than to others."—*Mrs. Jameson's Sacred and Legendary Art.*

Of Reynolds, however, it may not be amiss to say with Sotheby:—

"Hail! guide and glory of the British School,
Whose magic line gave life to every rule."

2718 Rheinesches Jahrbuch, *fine lithographic illustrations.* Koln, 1846

2719 Richardson's Catalogue of Portraits, India Drawings, &c., with the Prices and Buyers at Auction. 1799

2720 Robinson's Designs for Lodges and Park Entrances, 48 *plates*, 4to. *half morocco.* Lond. 1837

2721 Romney (*George*), Life of, by William Hayley, *illustrated by numerous fine examples of his Works*, 4to. *fine copy, calf.* Chichester, 1809

He was famous in his profession, and it was his great right to be so.

2722 Rubens (*P. P.*) His Life and Genius, translated from the German of Dr. Waagen, by Noel, edited by Mrs. Jameson, 8vo. *cloth.* Lond. 1840

2723 Sandrart (*J. de*) Sculpture Veteris Admiranda sive delineatio vera perfectissimarum Statuarum, folio, *calf.* Norimb. 1680

2724 ——L'Academia Todesca della Architettura, Scultura et Pittura, folio, *vellum.* 1675

All the works of Sandrart are held in great esteem.

2725 Scrap Book, 4to. containing a great variety of miscellaneous prints, some very old and scarce, Theatrical, &c.

2726 Scott (*Sir W.*) Book of Waverley Gems, in a series of engraved illustrations of Incidents and Scenery in Sir Walter Scott's Novels, *fine impressions, thick paper, cloth.* 8vo. Lond. 1848

2727 Serie Degli Momini I Piu Illustri nella Pittura, Scultura Architettura con i Loro Eloge, i Ritratti incisi in Rome, Cominciando dall suo prima Restaurazione Sino ai Tempo Presenti, 12 vols. 4to. *vellum, containing over* 300 *fine portraits.* Firenzi, 1769

Sold for £5 5*s.* at the Penelli sale.

2728 Shee (*Martin Ar.*) Rhymes on Art, or a Remonstrance of a Painter, 12mo. *cloth.* Phil. 1815

2729 Smith (*John*), Catalogue Raisonné of the Works of the most eminent Dutch, Flemish, and French Painters, with Biographical Notices of their principal Pictures, a Statement of the Prices at which they have been sold, and the Galleries or Collections in which they are at present; Names of the Artists by whom they have been engraved; and Notices of the Scholars and Imitators, *complete with Supplement,* in 9 large vols. royal 8vo. 7 vols. in *half morocco,* 1 vol. 8vo. and Supplement in *cloth.* Lond. 1829–42

This elaborate work, by Mr. Smith, the eminent picture dealer, is indispensable to the collector of pictures.

2730 STATUES: Delle Antiche Statue Greche e Romane, che nell' Antisala della Libreria di San Marco, e in altri luoghi pubblice di Vinezia si trovano, 100 *plates*, 2 vols. in 1, folio. Venezia, 1740

2731 ——— A large collection of Ancient Statues, Busts, Illustrative of Ancient Sculpture, from Examples in the British Museum, &c., *all proofs before letters, including many private plates*, folio. n. d.

2732 STOTHARD (*Thos.*) Life of, with Personal Reminiscences, by Mrs. Bray, 4to. *cloth.* Lond. 1851

2733 STOWE Catalogue, priced and annotated by H. R. Fowler, 4to. *half morocco.* Lond. 1848

2734 STRAWBERRY Hill: Catalogue of the Contents as sold by George Robins, 1842, with the printed prices, also a Catalogue of the Engraved Portraits, copiously and beautifully illustrated, *half red morocco gilt leaves*, 4to. Lond. 1842

2735 TAYLOR: History of the Fine Arts in Great Britain and Ireland, 2 vols. 8vo. *cloth.* Lond. 1841

"The best View of Modern art."—*United Service Gazette.*

2736 TEMPLE of The Muses, or the Principal Histories of Fabulous Antiquity, represented in 60 Sculptures, by the famous engraver, Bernard Picart, folio, *fine early impressions, rare, calf.* Amst. 1733

2737 THEATRUM Dolorum Iesv Christe Dei-Hominis pro Hominibus Patientis, a series of 26 very fine engravings, by Huret, neatly mounted and bound in royal large folio vol. *half morocco,* from La Forest's collection. Paris, 1664

2738 TIBALDI (*Pellegrino,* e Nicolò Abbati), Le pitture esistenti nell' Instituto di Bologna, descritte ed illustr. da Giam. Pietro Zanetti, *fine plates,* folio, *half morocco.* Venezia, 1756

Vendu, 75 fr. La Valliere, 60 fr. St. Ceran.

2739 TOPHAM (*J.*) Description of an Ancient Picture in Windsor Castle, representing the Embarkation of Henry VIII. Lond. 1787

2740 TURNBULL (*Dr. Geo.*) Treatise on Ancient Painting: its Progress and Decline among the Greeks and Romans, and connection with Poetry and Philosophy, folio, 50 fine plates of ancient frescoes, etc., including the Aldobrandini Marriage, and other celebrated works, *half calf.* Lond. 1744

2741 Van Roy (*J. J.*) Vie de Pierre Paul Rubens, 8vo. Bruxelles, 1840

2742 Versailiarum Consecrata Memoria, Monicart et Le Tertie, 2 vols. 4to. 100 *fine plates.* 1720

2743 Walpole's (*H.*) Anecdotes of Painting in England, with some account of the principal artists, and incidental notes on other arts, collected by the late Mr. George Virtue, digested and published from his original MSS., with considerable additions by Rev. James Dallaway, 3 vols. 8vo. *cloth.* Lond. 1849

"In the good old times of Bibliomania, this work would have walked, of its own accord, into the mahogany book cases of half the collectors of London."—*Dibdin's Bibliomania.*

2744 Wanderings of a Pen and Pencil, by Palmer and Crowquill, royal 8vo. *cloth.* 1846

2745 Ware (*William*), Lectures on the Works and Genius of Washington Allston, 12mo. *cloth.* Boston, 1852

2746 West (*Benj.*) A Gallery of Pictures painted by; Engraved in outline, by H. Moses, *large paper*, folio, *half calf.* Lond. 1811

2747 White (*R. G.*) Companion to the Bryan Gallery of Christian Art, presentation copy with autograph, 8vo. *cloth.* N. Y. 1853

2748 Winkles's English Cathedrals, Architectural and Picturesque illustrations of the Cathedral Churches of England and Wales, 186 plates beautifully engraved, with historical and descriptive accounts, 30 parts. 1851

This beautiful and interesting work contains twenty-eight Cathedrals, whilst that of Britton illustrates but fourteen.

2749 Wood (*J.*) Origin of Building, or the Plagiarism of the Heathens detected, in 5 books, folio, *half calf.* Bath, 1741

2750 Young (*John*), Catalogue of the Pictures at Grosvenor House, *etchings, half calf,* 4to. Lond. 1821

2751 Young (*J.*) Catalogue of Pictures (Leicester Gall.), with *etchings* of the whole collection, 4to. *cloth.* Lond. 1825

2752 Ziegler's Views of the Lodges, &c., in Windsor Park, folio, *half morocco.* Lond. 1839

FRANCE.

2753 Arnould et Prejol, Histoire de Bastile, *numerous fine plates*, 2 vols. in 1, *half calf*, 8vo. Paris, 1844

2754 Blanchard (*P.*) Beautés de l'Histoire de France, 12mo. Paris, 1810

2755 Carr (*Sir J.*) Stranger in France, 8vo. *half calf.* Lond. 1807

2756 Carrel, History of the Counter Revolution, 12mo. *cloth.* Lond. 1846

2757 Another Copy. 1846

2758 Caricatures, a Collection of 24, illustrative of the French Revolution, 12mo. *sewed.* Lond. 1831

2759 Caussidiere (*Citizen*, ex-Prefect of Police, and Representative of the People), Memoirs of, 2 vols. 12mo. Lond. 1848

Contains a full account of the Revolution of 1848.

2760 Chambray (*M. de*) Histoire de la Expedition de Russie, 3 vols. 8vo. *half calf.* Paris, 1825

2761 Daniel (*Gabriel*), Histoire de la Milice Françoise, *plates*, 2 vols. 4to. *old calf.* Amst. 1724

2762 Chateaubriand (*M. de*) The Congress of Vienna, comprising a portion of Memoirs of his own times, 2 vols. 8vo. *boards.* Lond. 1838

2763 Cobbett (*J. P.*) Ride in France, 12mo. *boards.* Lond. 1844

2764 La Chaize (*Pere Confesseur du Roi Louis XIV.*) Histoire du, 18mo. *calf.* Cologne, 1693

2765 Comines (*Messire Philippe de*), Memoires conténant l'histoire des Rois Louis XI. et Charles VIII. 1464–1498, folio, *half calf.*

"Comines was long in the service of Charles le Terrible, last Duke of Burgundy, and of Louis XI., King of France." "Le Sire de Comines ecrivit des beaux recits, et il porta des jugemens sur les princes de son temps avec tant de reflexion et de sagesse que la posterité les adopta presque entièrement."—*Barante.*

2766 Crowe (*E. E.*) History of France, 3 vols. 12mo. Phil. 1836

2767 Dewint (*P.*) Vicinity of the River Rhone displayed, *plates engraved by Cooke*, oblong 4to. Lond. 1823

2768 Dumourier (*Genl.*) Memoirs of, written by himself, translated by *John Fenwick*, 2 parts in 1 vol. 8vo. *sheep*, pp. 260. Phil. 1794

2769 Duncan (*Jon.*) The Religious Wars of France, 12mo. *cloth.* Lond. 1840

2770 Foster and English's French Revolution of 1848, 8vo. *cloth.* Phil. 1848

2771 FRANCE and Napoleon's Second Reign, collection of Works on, Visit to Paris, and Paris Re-visited, by John Scott; Paul's Letters to his Kinsfolk; Eustace's Letters from Paris; Shoberl's Account of Waterloo, &c., in 4 vols. 8vo. *half calf.* Lond. 1815

2772 FRANCE Illustrated from Drawings by Allom, with descriptions by G. N. Wright, *beautiful engravings of Landscape Scenery, Antiquities, Architecture, &c., fine early impressions,* 3 vols. 4to. *gilt leaves.* 1850

2773 FRENCH Revolution, Journées Illustrées de la Revolution de; 1848.

2774 FROISSART'S Chronicles of England, France, and Spain, translated by Johnes, 2 vols. *cloth.* Lond. 1849

"Froissart is a historian consulted and cited by every writer whose subject leads him to the period in which he wrote; he is the chief, if not the only authentic source of information we are possessed of with regard to one of the proudest and most striking portions of our national annals. Even the readers of novels and romances, if ever they have in the course of their lives read anything of real history, must be gratified and even charmed with Froissart, for there is as much gallantry, love, and adventure, in the Chronicles of Froissart, as in any romance, Don Quixote scarcely excepted."

Quarterly Review.

2775 GLEIG (*G. R.*) Story of the Battle of Waterloo, 2 vols. 12mo. N. Y. 1847

2776 HEAD (*Sir F.*) A Faggot of French Sticks, 12mo. N. Y. 1852

2777 HISTORICAL Collection of the most Memorable Accidents and Tragicall Massacres of France, under the Reigns of Henry II., Francis II., Charles IX., Henry III., and Henry IV. (by Thos. Tymme), folio. Lond. 1598

2778 JANIN (*Jules*), L'Hiver et L'Etè à Paris illustrées par M. Eugene Lami, 2 vols. 4to. *cloth, gilt.* Lond. n. d.

2779 JOBSON (*D. W.*) History of the French Revolution, 8vo. *cloth.* Lond. 1853

2780 LA VALLIERE (*Mme. de*), Vie Penitente de, par Mme. de Genlis, 12mo. *calf.* Paris, 1807

2781 LABAUME (*E.*) Napoleon's Campaign in Russia, 8vo. *sheep.* 1817

2782 LAMARTINE (*A. de*), History of the French Revolution of 1848, 2 vols. 12mo. Bost. 1849

2783 LANGON (*Baron*), Evenings with Cambaceres, Arch-Chancellor of the Empire, second Consul of the French Republic, *Reminiscences of the Imperial Court, &c.,* 2 vols. *half calf, gilt.* Lond. 1837

2784 Long (*George*), Pictorial History of France and its Revolutions (comprising the period 1789 to 1848), impl. 8vo. *with fine portraits, and numerous large wood-cuts, after designs by Harvey, cloth.* Lond. 1850

2785 L'Urne, Des Stuarts et des Bourbons, ou Le Fond de mer Consciencé, 8vo. Paris, 1815

2786 Mathieu, The Heroyk Life and Deplorable Death of the Most Christian King Henry the Fourth; addressed to his immortal memory by P. Mathieu, Councellor and Historiographer of France, translated by Ed. Grimeston, Esq., *portrait, printed by Geo. Eld, scarce,* 4to. *half calf.* Lond. 1612

*** At the end is a poem of 27 pages, "The Tropheis of the Life and Tragædiæ of the Death of that Vertuous and Victorious Prince Henry the Great, late of France and Navarre," by Iosvah Sylvester.

2787 Memoirs of Madame de la Rochejacquelin, and History of the Insurrection in La Vendée, by herself, with Introduction, &c., by Sir Walter Scott, 8vo. *map of the seat of war, half calf, gilt.* Edin. 1817

2789 Miscellaneous Remains of Cardinal Perron, President Thuanus, &c., 2 vols. 12mo. *calf.* Lond. 1707

2790 Memoirs of Philip de Comines, Lord of Argenton, with his Life, etc., *calf*, 8vo. Lond. 1674

"The memoirs of Comines make an epoch in historical literature; if Froissart be reckoned the Livy of France, she had her Tacitus in P. de Comines."—*Hallam.*

2791 Merimee (*Prosper*), Chronicle of the Times of Charles the 9th, Translated from the French of, 8vo. N. Y. 1830

2792 Museum Parisien Histoire Physiologique, Pittoresque, Philosophique et Grotesque, de toutes les bétes curieuses de Paris, &c., par M. Louis Huart, 350 *vignettes,* royal 8vo. *half calf.* Paris, 1841

2793 Moore (*H. N.*) The Reign of Terror to the Fall of Robespierre, 16mo. *cloth.* Phil. 1846

2794 Napoleon, The Court of: or, Society under the First Empire, by Frank B. Goodrich (Dick Tinto), *with colored portraits on steel of its Beauties, Wits, and Heroines,* royal 4to. *morocco.* N. Y. 1857

2795 ——— Gallery, Parts 2—4, 6—15, 12mo. Lond. v. d.

2796 ——— and his Times, by Caulincourt, Duke of Vincenza, 2 vols. 12mo. *boards.* Phil. 1838

2797 ——— in the Other World, written by himself and found near his Tomb at St. Helena, by Xongo, Tee, Foh, Tchi, Mandarin, 8vo. *half calf, gilt, curious.* Lond. 1827

2798 ——— Another copy, *half morocco.* Lond. 1827

2799 NAPOLEON, Museum, The History of France Illustrated from Louis XIV. to the end of the Reign and Death of the Emperor, by J. Sainsbury, *with facsimiles of autographs, &c.*, thick impl. 4to. *half morocco.* 1844

Privately printed; this is by far the most interesting and extensive collection of the relics of Napoleon, comprising Marbles, Bronzes, Gems, Decorations, Medallions, Drawings, Pictures, State Papers, Coins, Medals, &c.

Presentation copy from the author to J. H. Hackett, Esq., with autograph letter.

2800 ——— III. Briffault (*F. T.*) The Prisoner of Ham, Authentic Detail of the Captivity and Escape of Prince Napoleon Louis, 12mo. *cloth.* Lond. 1846

2801 ORLEANS (*Duke of*), Memoir of the Regency of, during the Minority of Lewis XVth. 8vo. *calf.* Lond. 1732

2802 PARIS, Bretez Plan de Paris gravé, par C. Lucas, 20 *fine large plates*, folio, *calf.* 1739

2803 ——— Curiosities de Paris, Versailles, etc., 2 vols. 12mo. Paris, 1778

2804 PETRE (Chevalier), Histoire des Guerres de la Vendée, royal 8vo. Paris, 1851

2805 PICTURES of the French, a Series of Literary and Graphic Delineations of French Character, by Jules Janin, Balzac, Cormenin, and other celebrated French authors, royal 8vo. *illustrated by upwards of* 230 *humorous and extremely clever wood engravings, cloth.* Lond. 1840

2806 RITCHIE (*Leitch*), Wanderings by the Seine, *twenty engravings from drawings by J. W. M. Turner*, 8vo. Lond.

2807 SANDERSON (*J.*) Sketches of Paris, in familiar letters to his friends, 12mo. Phil. 1838

2808 TROLLOPE (*Mrs.*) Paris and the Parisians, 2 vols. 1835, 8vo. *cloth.* N. Y. 1836

2809 TUSSAUD (*Mme.*) Memoirs of the French Revolution, 2 vols. 12mo. *cloth.* Phil. 1839

2810 WILSON (*W. R.*) Records of a Route through France and Italy, with Sketches of Catholicism, *cloth*, 8vo. Lond. 1835

FREE MASONRY.

2811 CARLISLE (*Rich.*) Manual of Masonry, 2 vols. 16mo. *cloth.* Lond. 1836

2812 COLE (*Samuel*), The Free Mason's Library, or General Ahiman Rezon, 8vo. *sheep.* Balt. 1826

2813 EARLY History of Free Masonry, illustrated by an English Poem of the Fourteenth Century. With Notes and Glossary by Halliwell, post 8vo. 1844

"There is nothing in this 'Early History' that the initiated will regret to read, and we trust that it will be read, not merely looked at, by the most discerning Masons."—*Freemason's Quarterly Review.*

2814 FELLOWS (*John*), An Exposition of the Ancient Mysteries and Free Masonry, 8vo. *half cloth.* N. Y. 1835

2815 FREE MASONRY, a Poem in three Cantos, showing it to be a deadly foe to equal liberty, and circumstances relative to the Abduction of Capt. Morgan, 12mo. *boards.* Leicester, 1830

2816 CARBONARI; Memoirs of the Secret Societies of the South of Italy, *curious Lithographs*, 8vo. *boards.* Lond. 1821

2817 KNAPP (*Sam. L.*) The Genius of Masonry, in three Lectures, 12mo. *half cloth.* Prov. 1828

PARKER on Free Masonry, *vide* Lot 1853.

GERMANY AND HOLLAND.

2818 BATAVIA Sacra, *numerous brilliant portraits,* folio, *calf.* 1714

2819 BEHRENS (*H.*) The Natural History of Hartz-Forest in His Majesty K. George's German Dominions, 8vo. *calf.* Lond. 1730

2820 BRACHELIUS (*Adolp.*) Historia nostri Temporiis, dat is Geschiedens onfes Tigdts., 1618–1654, thick 18mo. *half morocco.* Rotterdam, 1656

2821 CARR (*Sir J.*) Tour Through Holland, 8vo. *sheep.* Phil. 1807

2822 CHARLES V. Emperor of Germany; Edicts in German. folio, *old calf.* Worms, 1521

2823 CHAUCHARDS, Germany, 4to. *half calf.* Lond. 1800

2824 HISTORICAL and Literary Memoirs and Anecdotes, selected from the Correspondence of Baron de Grimm and Diderot and Duke of Saxe Gothe, between 1770 and 1790, translated, 2 vols. 8vo. *half calf.* Lond. 1814

2825 KUGHLER, (*F.*) Pictorial History of Germany during the Reign of Frederick the Great, including a complete History of the Silesian Campaigns and the Seven Years' War, royal 8vo. *with over* 500 *wood cuts, cloth.* Lond. 1845

2826 HANECONII (*Martini*), Fresca, seu de Viris rebusque Frisiæ illustribus, the prints cut out and mounted, with a portrait of Haneconius by P. A. Harling, *about* 54 *portraits, including Charles V., Philip II., Albert and Isabella, very curious,* 4to. Franck. 1620

2827 HOWITT (*W.*) Life in Germany, or scenes, impressions, and every-day life of the Germans, *illustrated with numerous engravings,* 8vo. *half calf, extra.* Lond. 1849

2828 ——— (*Wm.*) Rural and Domestic Life in Germany, 2 vols. 8vo. Phil. 1843

2829 LE Bas Allemagne, 2 vols. 8vo. *half calf.* Paris, 1838

2830 NETHERLAND Historian (The), True and exact relation of the Wars between the French King and the States General of the United Provinces, 12mo., 60 *curious plates by Romain de Hooghe,* &c., *calf, rare.* Amsterdam, 1675

2831 MAGNUS (*Olaus*), Beschreibung allerley Gelegenheyte, Sitten, Gebrauchen und Gewonheyten der Mitnachtigén Volker in Sweden, Elst unnd Westgothen, Norway, &c., *curious wood cuts,* 8vo. *stamped binding, hogs skin.* Strazburgh, 1657

2832 RHINE (*The*), its Scenery and Historical and Legendary Associations, 4to. *cloth.* Lond. 1845

2833 ROSCOE (*Thos.*) Belgium, or Picturesque Tour, 16 *fine steel plates, by Allan,* royal 8vo. *silk, gilt.* 1841

2834 STRADÆ (*Famianus*) de Bello Belgico decades duæ, 13 *fine plates,* 18vo. *calf.* Romæ, 1654

2835 STOPENDAEL (*Daniel*), Les delices du Water Graess ou diemer, mer pres de la ville d'Amsterdam, Dutch and French, 60 *plates, beautifully engraved, with descriptions by Broueriers, calf,* folio. Amsterdam, 1775

GREECE AND THE LEVANT.

2836 ANDERSON (*R.*) Observations upon the Peloponnesus and Greek Islands, 12mo. *boards.* Bost. 1830

2837 BYRON (*Lord*), Journey to Greece, 12mo. *calf, gilt, extra.* Paris, 1825

2838 CRŒSUS, King of Lydia, History of, 12mo. *sheep.* Edin. 1755

2839 DODWELL (*Ed.*) Views in Greece, engraved from the collection of drawings made in that country by Dodwell & Pomardi, 30 *fine coloured plates,* description in French and English, folio, *green morocco.* Lond. 1821

2840 Gillies' History of Greece, 8vo. *cloth.* Phil. 1841

2841 Lettres Atheniennes per M. Christophe, 2 vols. 12mo. *calf.* Paris, 1805

2842 Olin (*Stephen*), Greece and the Golden Horn, *plates, cloth,* post 8vo. N. Y. 1854

2843 Rostagna (*G. B.*) Viaggi del Marchese Gloron Francesca Villa in Dalmatia e Levante con la distinta relatione de successi in Candia, 4to. *plates.* Torino, 1668

Ces relations curieuses ont eut beaucoup de succès, on les a données deux fois en Français.

2844 Voiage de Levant Fait par le Commandement du Roy en l'année 1621, par le Sr. D(u) C(astel), 4to. *vellum.* .Par s, 1629

2845 Wordsworth's Greece, 8vo. *imperfect.* 1840

GREEK AND LATIN CLASSICS AND TRANSLATIONS.

2846 Anacreon Convivialia Semiambra Gr. et Lat. edente Spalletti, *plates, boards,* royal folio. Romæ, 1781

"This very splendid edition is printed from an ancient MS. of the tenth century. The type, comprehending the first sixteen pages, is a facsimile of the Vatican MS."—*Dibdin.*

2847 Anacreon, illustrated by Sir R. Ker. Porter, *with translations,* 22 *beautifully spirited engravings of Amatory Subjects, fine copy in green velvet,* 4to. Lond. 1805

2848 Appian, Auncient Historie and exquisite Chronicle of the Romanes Warres, both Civile and Foren, written by that noble orator Appian, of Alexandria, and translated by W. B., **Black Letter**, *calf, fine copy,* 4to. Lond. 1578

Heber's copy, with his note.

2849 Arrian's Voyage of Alexander, translated by Falconer, 4to. Oxford, 1805

2850 Cæsaris, Commentarii, *wood-cuts,* 18mo. Lugd. 1546

2851 Cæsar's Commentaries, first four Books, translated by J. Mair, *calf,* 12mo. Edin. 1777

2852 ——— Translated by Martin Bladen, *plates, calf,* 8vo. Lond. 1705

2853 Cicero, Those fiue questions which Marke Tullye Cicero disputed in his Manor of Tusculanum; written afterwards by him, in as many bookes, to his friend and familiar, Brutus, in the Latin tounge and nowe oute of the same translated and Englished by Iohn Dolman, studente and felowe of the inner temple, imprinted at Lôdō by Thomas Marshe, *rare, fine copy,* **Black Letter**, 8vo. Lond. 1561

2854 CLASSICAL Manual, being a Mythological, Historical, and Geographical Commentary on Pope's Homer and Dryden's Æneid, *cloth*, 8vo. Lond. 1833

2855 CURTIUS, History of the Wars of Alexander, translated by J. Digby, 2 vols. *calf*, 12mo. Lond. 1726

2855* DIBDIN (*T. F.*) Introduction to the Classics, *cloth*, 8vo. Lond. 1827

2856 DIOGENES Laertius, de vitis dogmatis et apophthegmatis, clavorum Philosophorum; G'k et Lat., ed. Meimobii et Gale, *with 24 fine portraits*, 2 vols. *calf*, *scarce*, 4to. Amst. 1694

For an account of the peculiarities of this excellent and beautiful ed. see Bibliog. Dict., vol. 3, p. 126.
"By far the most critical and perfect edition."—*Dibdin.*

2857 DIONYSIUS Halicarnassensis, Roman Antiquities, translated with notes and dissertations by Spelman, 4 vols. *half calf*, 4to. Lond. 1758

"A faithful and elegant translation, accompanied with very learned and valuable notes and useful dissertations."—*Clarke.*

2858 EPECTETI Enchiridion, Latinis versibus. adumbratum, per Edvardum Ivie, *vellum*, 8vo. Oxford, 1715

2859 GREEK Anthology, chiefly by G. Burges, A. M.; with Metrical Versions, by various Authors, *cloth*, post 8vo. Lond. 1846

2860 HERODOTUS: New and Literal Version by Cary, *cloth*, post 8vo. Lond. 1850

2861 HESIOD, The Works of, translated from the Greek, by Mr. Cooke, *portrait*, *rare*, 12mo. *calf.* Lond. 1763

HOMER, *vide* Chapman, in Old English Poetry.

2862 HOMER; The Iliads and Odysses of Homer, translated out of Greek into English, by Thomas Hobbes, of Malmsbury, &c., printed for Will Crooke at the Green Dragon without Temple-Barre, *scarce*, 8vo. *calf.* Lond. 1677

2863 —— Iliad, literally translated into English Prose, post 8vo. *cloth.* Lond. 1850

2864 —— Odyssey, 5 vols. *sewed*, *uncut*, 12mo. Lond. 1758

2865 HOMERIC Ballads and Comedies of Lucian, translated by W. Maginn, annotated by R. S. Mackenzie, *cloth*, post 8vo. Redfield, 1856

2866 HOMER, Koliades (C) Ulysse-Homere, ou de veritable auteur de l'Iliade et de l'Odyssée, *boards*, impl. folio. Paris, 1829

2867 HOMER; Enquiry into the Life and Writings of, 8vo. *vignette plates, calf, gilt.* Lond. 1736

"A fine effort of genius and learning."—*Gibbon.*

2868 —— Satire on the translations of, *half calf,* 8vo. Lond. 1733

2869 —— Vindication of, by J. B. S. Morritt, &c., 4 vols. 4to. York, &c., 1798

2870 HORATIUS: Forma Minima, *mor. gt,* 32mo. Sedani, 1627

"This edition is the smallest yet published; it is printed in a very minute character, and is now extremely rare."—*Moss.*

This rare little edition used formerly to sell for upwards of £5. 5s.

2871 HORACE: Translated by P. Francis, 2 vols. 12mo. *cloth.* Valpy, Lond. 1831

HORACE *vide* Fanshawe, &c., Old English Poetry.

2872 CASCALES (*Sig. Francisco*), Tablas Poeticas Horatii Q. Flacci, &c., 8vo. *calf.* Madrid, 1779

2873 JUSTINUS: Historiarium ex Trogo Pompeio, lib. XLIV., cum notis Isaac Vossii, 18mo. Elzevir, Amst. 1656

2874 JUSTIN: The Historie of Justine, containing a narration of kingdomes, from the beginning of the Assyrian Monarchy, unto the reigne of the Emperour Augustus, translated by G. W. Lond, printed by W. Jaggard, 1606; Suetonius' Historie of the Twelve Cæsars, Emperours of Rome, translated by Philêmon Holland, London, printed for Matthew Lownes, 1606; 1 vol. *original binding, broken, fine copies,* folio.

2875 JUVENAL Satires, literally translated into English Prose, 12mo. Oxford, 1841

2876 LIPSII (*Just.*) Opera Omnia, folio, *calf,* 4 vols. in 3, *ex-officina Plantin.* Antv. 1634

2877 LIVY: Romane History, also the Breviaries of L. Florus, translated by Philemon Holland, *old calf,* folio. Lond. 1600

"A most accurate translation."—*Lowndes.*

2878 —— Romische Historie, *curious wood-cuts, old oak binding,* folio. Mentz, 1514

2879 LONGINUS on the Sublime, translated by W. Smith, 8vo. *calf.* Lond. 1752

2880 —— On the Sublime, a translation of, by a Graduate of Trinity College, Dublin, 12mo. *cloth.* N. Y. 1823

2881 LUCAN'S Pharsalia, containing the Civill Warres be tween Cæsar and Pompey, translated into English by Sir Arthur Gorges Knight, folio, *fine copy, calf, extra, rare.* Lond. 1614

"Sir Arthur Gorges is the character meant for Alcyon in Spenser's Colin Clouts come home again."—*See long MS. note in this copy.*

2882 LUCAIN, La Pharsale de, 12mo. *calf.* Paris, 1682

2883 LUCIAN. Works translated by Dryden, 4 vols. *old calf,* 8vo. Lond. 1711

Lucian was the Voltaire of Antiquity—nothing was sacred from his Satire.

2884 ——— Part of Lucian made English, from the originall, in the yeare 1638, by Jasper Mayne, to which are adjoyned those other Dialogues of Lucian, translated by Hicks, *old calf,* folio. Oxford, 1663

2885 LUCRETIUS de Natura Rerum, an Essay on the first book of, interpreted and made English Verse by J. Evelyn, frontispiece by Hollar, *calf,* 8vo. Lond. 1656

2886 ——— Literally translated into English Prose, with Notes, by the Rev. J. S. Watson, to which is adjoined the Metrical Version of John Mason Good, *cloth,* post 8vo. Lond. 1848

2887 LUCREZIA della Natura delle cose, Tradotta da Allessandro Marchetti, 2 vols. *half calf, plates, after Cochin,* 8vo. Amst. 1756

A beautiful copy of the best edition of this most elegant and esteemed book.

"Il semble que Lucrèce ait transmis son génie a M. Marchetti; ou retronse dans le Poème Italien les mêmes beautés, les mêmes grâces, la même énergie; qúon admire dans le Latin."—*Journal des Scavans.*

OVID, *see also* Gower & Jones in English Poetry.

2888 OVIDIUS de Arte Amandi et de remedia amoris, *fine clean copy, in boards,* P. Marechal, folio. MCCCCXCVII

2889 OVID'S Epistles, Translated by Sir Carr Scrope, Bart. Dryden, Pooley, Tate, Mrs. Behn, Rymer, Settle, Otway, Butler, and others, frontispiece, *original binding, good copy,* 8vo. Lond. 1809

2890 OVID, Metamorphoses, Latin and French, by Du Ryer, *fine plates,* folio. Bruxelles, 1677

2891 OVIDI, Metamorphoseon, *fine plates after Sandrart, by Englebrecht,* folio, *calf.* Noribergæ.

2892 OVID'S, Metamorphosis, translated by George Sandys, *plates, old calf,* folio. Lond. 1640

Sandys is pronounced by Dryden to be the best versifier of the last age, and Pope affirmed that English Poetry owed much of its present beauty to his translations.

2893 ——— Metamorphoses, Literally translated, *cloth,* post 8vo. Lond. 1847

2894 ——— Tristia, First Book Translated by F. Arden, *boards,* 8vo. N. Y. 1821

2895 ——— Another copy.

2896 OVID's Heroides, Amours, Art of Love, &c., translated, *frontispiece, cloth,* post 8vo. Lond. 1846

2897 ——— Fasti, Tristia, Epistles, &c., Literally translated, *plates, cloth,* post 8vo. Lond. 1846

2898 PERSII, Satyricon ed. Casauboni, 8vo. *vellum.* Paris, 1615

2899 PERSIUS, Satires of, in English Verse, by T. Brewster, *calf,* 12mo. 1751

"A correct, easy, and elegant version."—*Lowndes.*

2900 PLAUTI (*M. Accid.*) Linguæ Lat. facile Princeps; Comœdiæ viginti; vivis pene imaginibus, recens excultæ, una cum luculentissimis commentariis Bernardi Saraceni, Jo. Pet. Vallæ, etc., nec non observationibus, Pii Bononuenfii Ugoletii et Grafaldii Scholis, etc., *very fine copy, clean, and filled with splendid wood-cuts, very rare, calf,* folio. Venetiis, 1578

This edition has never been described by any Bibliographical writer; the copy in the Vatican library was for a long time supposed to be the only one in existence.

2901 PLINY, Historie of the World, translated by Philemon Holland, *title and* 10 *leaves in vol.* 1 *damaged,* 2 vols. in 1, folio. Lond., *Adam Islip,* 1601

"All the philosophy which could be collected within the precincts of the Roman Empire, in its largest circle, and from the labors of anterior time, Pliny embodied in his work."—*Turner.*

The only complete translation of this "Encyclopædia of the Ancient World."

2902 QUINTIUS Curtius, History of the Wars of Alexander the Great, translated by John Digby, *revised by W. Young,* 2 vols. *calf,* 12mo. Lond. 1747

2903 ROSS (*A.*) Mystagogus Poeticus, or the Muse's Interpreter, Explaining the Historicall Mysteries and Mysticall Histories of the Ancient Greek and Latin Poets, &c. &c., 8vo. *original binding, beautiful copy,* 12mo. Lond. 1653

2904 SALLUSTIUS cum Comentar, Ven. 1511; Guarini Paralella ex. Plutarch, Brix. 1498; Statii Opera, cum Coment., Ven. 1498, in 1 vol. folio. v. y.

2905 SENECA, Tragedias, decim, 4to. *calf.* *Plautin Auto.* 1576

2906 ——— The Works of Lvcivs Annaevs Seneca, newly enlarged and corrected by Thomas Lodge, *calf,* folio. Lond. 1614

2907 SOPHOCLES, Tragœdiæ VII. Gr. et Lat. cum omnibus Græcis Scholiis, et annotationibus H. Stephani, folio, *old calf, gilt leaves, very neat.* Paris, *H. Stephani*, 1568

This handsome volume belonged to Edward Gibbon, the historian, and has his book plate.

"An edition," says Harles, "at the present day both rare and held in great estimation." "To each page are affixed the Scholia of the old Roman edition of 1518, and those of Turnebus' edition, corrected by Stephens."—*Dibdin.*

2908 ——— Electra, by Theobald, 8vo. Lond. 1714

2910 SUETONIUS, cum comment Beroaldi, folio, *old calf.* Paris, 1512

2911 TERENTII Comœdiæ, ad optimorum Exemplarium fidem recensitæ; Accesserunt Variæ Lectiones, 2 vols. 8vo. *large paper.* Lond. *Sandby*, 1751

"A beautiful and correct edition, adorned with engravings, representing the masks worn by the Actors in the different plays. At the end are several important various readings."—*Dr. A. Clarke.*

This is one of the Sandby classics. "The large paper copies, which are chiefly sought after, present to the eye one of the most splendid classical works this country has produced."—*Dibdin.*

2912 TERENTIUS, ad fidem Optimorum Editionem recensitus (edid. Brunck), *finely printed in large and beautiful type*, royal 4to. *half calf.* Basil, *J. Deeker*, 1797

This edition is very sumptuously executed with great typographical luxury.

2913 TYPHIODORUS, Destruction of Troy, translated by J. Merrick, 8vo. *calf.* Oxford, 1739

2914 VIRGIL, Opera, *splendidly printed, with plates by Hollar, Faithorne, Lombart, and others, morocco, extra gilt leaves, a superb volume*, folio. Paris, *typograph. regia*, 1641

2915 VIRGILII, Opera, *plates, vellum*, folio. 1725

2916 ——— Opera ex Cod. Mediceo Laurentiano descripta, ab Antonio Ambrogi, cum Versione Italica, *with numerous fine plates, from the celebrated Vatican Codex* 3 vols. royal folio, *morocco.* Romæ, 1763

"A very sumptuous edition."—*Dibdin.*

2917 VIRGIL, Bucolica et Georgica, 100 *beautiful plates, by Robert Edge Pine*, 8vo. *calf.* Lond. 1774

"This work was left unfinished by Old Pine, and was published by his son Robert; it is valuable chiefly for the elegance of the plates." —*Dibdin.*

2918 VIRGIL, Works of, translated by Lord Maitland, with preface by Dryden, 2 vols. 12mo. *half morocco.* Lond. n. d.

"Not mentioned by Lowndes."

2919 VIRGIL'S Æneidos: Thirteene Bookes of, the first twelve beeing the Worke of the Divine Poet Virgil Maro, and the thirteenth the Supplement of Maphæus Vegius, translated by Phaer and Twyne, **black letter**, 4to. *calf, extra, morocco back, very scarce.* *Bernard Alsop*, Lond. 1620

2920 VIRGIL, translated by Ogilby, *half morocco*, 12mo. Lond. 1649

2921 THEOBALD (*J.*) The Second Book of Virgil's Æneid, in 4 Cantos.

2922 MARTIN (*John*), Dissertations and Critical Remarks upon the Æneids of Virgil, 12mo. *half sheep.* Lond. 1770

2923 VIRGIL—Æneas, his Descent into Hell, as it is inimitably described by the Prince of Poets in the sixth of his Æneis, made English by John Boys, Esq., of Hode-Court, together with an ample and learned Comment upon the same, wherein all passages Criticall, Mythologicall, Philosophicall, and Historical, are fully and clearly explained; to which are added some certain Pieces relating to the Publick written by the Author, *rare*, 4to. *old calf.* Lond. 1661

Priced in the Bibliotheca Anglo-Poetica, £3 3*s.* 0*d.*

2924 FROMMEL (*C.*) 50 Bilder zu Virgils Æneide—China Historisch, Romantisch, Moralisch—2 vols. in 1, 4to. *half bound.* Carlsruhe, n. d.

2925 VIRGIL'S Works, translated into English Verse, by Pitt and Warton, with the Latin Text; Observations by Holdsworth and Spence; Warburton's Dissertation on the Sixth Book of the Æneid, &c., *plates*, 4 vols. 8vo. *old calf.* Lond. 1753

"An excellent translation of Virgil, illustrated with explanations of the difficult, and many curious and useful observations on the beautiful passages in them."—*Monthly Review.*

2926 XENOPHON'S Treatise of Hovsholde, imprinted at London in Fletestrete, by Thomas Berthelet, Printer to the Kynge's Most Noble Grace, *very rare, fine copy*, small 8vo. *calf*, **Black Letter.** Lond. 1537

*** On the back of the title is the following address "To the Reder." "This Boke of Householde, full of hyghe wisedom, written by the noble philosopher Xenophon, the Scholer of Socrates, the whiche for his swete eloquence, and incredyble facilitie, was surnamed Musa Attica, that is to say the songe of Athenes; is ryght counynly translated out of the Greke tonge into Englysshe, by Gentian Heruet at the desyre of Mayster Geffrey Pole, whiche boke for the wealthe of this realme, I deme very profitable to be red."

2927 XENOPHON, The Minor Works of, 8vo. *half cl.* Lond. 1813

2928 XENOPHON'S Expedition of Cyrus into Persia, translated from Xenophon by E. Spelman, *plates*, 8vo. Lond. 1811

See OLD ENGLISH POETRY.

HERALDRY.—*See also* PAGEANTS.

2929 FAVINE (*Andr.*), The Theater of Honour and Knighthood, or a Compendious Chronicle and Historie of the whole Christian World, *calf*, folio. Lond. 1623

"This work is the most valuable treatise we have in English upon the foreign Orders of Knighthood. There are other discussions upon Ceremonies, Combats, Precedence, &c., equally worthy the attention of the antiquary and historian."—*Lowndes.*

2930 NICOLAS (*Sir Harris*), History of the Orders of Knighthood of the British Empire, with an Account of the Medals, Crosses, and Clasps which have been conferred for Naval and Military Services, together with a History of the Order of the Guelphs of Hanover, 4 vols. impl. 4to. *splendidly printed and illustrated by numerous fine woodcuts of Badges, Crosses, Collars, Stars, Medals, Ribbands, Clasps, &c., and many large plates illuminated in gold and colours, portrait of Queen Victoria, cloth.* 1842

"Sir Harris Nicolas has produced the first comprehensive History of the British Orders of Knighthood; and it is one of the most elaborately prepared and splendidly printed works that ever issued from the press. The author appears to us to have neglected no sources of information, and to have exhausted them, as far as regards the general scope and purpose of the inquiry. The graphical illustrations are such as become a work of this character upon such a subject; at, of course, a lavish cost. The resources of the recently revived art of wood-engraving have been combined with the new art of printing in colours, so as to produce a rich effect, almost rivalling that of the monastic illuminations. Such a book is sure of a place in every great library. It contains matter calculated to interest extensive classes of readers, and we hope by our specimen to excite their curiosity."—*Quarterly Review.*

2931 WATERHOUSE (*E.*) A Discourse and Defence of Arms and Armory, showing the Nature and Rises of Arms an Honour in England from the Camp, the Court and the City, *fine frontispiece, clean copy in the original binding, rare,* 8vo. *calf.* Lond. 1660

2931* VERTOT (*Mons. D.*) The History of the Knights of Malta, *illustrated with the heads of the Grand Masters, and with maps and plans of Malta*, and a complete index to the whole, 2 vols. folio, *calf*, *very fine copy*. Lond. 1728

Reader, if you wish to realize what zeal, valor, fortitude, determination, and it may be fanaticism, can accomplish, read this renowned history of the still more renowned "Knights of Malta." It is illustrated with 70 fine portraits and 5 maps.

HISTORY IN GENERAL.—*See also* UNDER VARIOUS COUNTRIES.

2932 AUSTRIA and the Austrians, 2 vols. 8vo. Lond. 1837

2933 BRACHELII (*A.*) Historiarum nostri temporis, *many fine portraits*, *vellum*, 18mo. Amst. 1659

2934 BRYANT (*Jacob*), Observations and Enquiries relating to various parts of Ancient History, 4to. *calf*. Camb. 1767

2935 CHRONOLOGY, 12mo. *cloth*. N. Y. 1833

2936 DICTIONARY of Universal History, 18mo. *half calf*. Lond. 1823

2937 HISTORICAL Cabinet, 12mo. *sheep*. N. Haven, n. d.

2938 HONORIUS Augusta, dunensis, Christianus, ad Solitarii quandam de ymagine mundi, folio, *red morocco gilt, fine large margin, all the initials illuminated, some richly so*, 46 leaves, 30 lines each, **Black Letter**. Nuremberg, *Ant. Koburger*, MCCCCLXXII

2939 ILLUSTRATED Record of Important Events in the Annals of Europe during the Years 1812–13–14 and 15, *colored plates*, impe. folio, *russia extra*. Lond. 1815

2940 LLOYD (*L.*) The Marrow of Historie, or the Pilgrimage of Kings and Princes, &c., collected by one Lodowick Lloyd, one of the Gentlemen in Ordinary to Queen Elizabeth, and corrected and revived by R. C.—A. M. *rare*, **Black Letter**, 4to. Lond. 1653

2941 MEXIA (*Pedro*), Time's Storehouse, being the learned collections, judicious readings and memorable observations, not only divine, moral and philosophical, but also poetical, martial, historical and allegorical, by P. Sansovino, *many curious plates of Knighthood*, *&c.*, *engraved title*, *calf*, folio. Lond., *Wm. Laggard*, 1619

"This work contains much curious matter, the result of various and extensive reading, related in the quaint style of that age."—*Lowndes.*

2942 MIRROR of Time, 2 vols. 8vo. *boards*. 1834

2943 Miscellaneous Observations and Opinions on the Continent, *fine plates, large paper, boards.* Lond. 1835

2944 More (I.) A table from the beginning of the world to this day, wherein is declared in what yeere of the world everything was done, &c., sene and allowed by publike authoritie, printen by John Legate, printer to the Universitie of Cambridge, *scarce,* 8vo. Cambridge, 1593

2945 Munsteri (Seb.) Comographia Universalis, *many hundred curious woodcuts, including several large folding views of cities, towns, maps, &c., with those of the British Isles, very thick folio, half russia, wants title.* Basil. 1550

This curious ancient Cosmography extends to 1333 pages, and exhibits a very singular picture of the different nations of the world in the XVIth century; many of the woodcuts were engraved by R. Manuel, an artist of considerable merit, *vide Strutt's Dictionary of Engravers.*

2946 Price's Essays on the History of Arabia, 4to. *boards.* 1824

2947 Prideaux (*J.*) Introduction to Histories, 4to. *calf.* Oxford, 1655

2948 Rayment on Miraculous Events, 12mo. *half morocco.* Lond. 1801

2949 Shallus (*F.*) Chronological Tables, 12mo. *sheep, scarce.* Phil. 1817

2950 Taylor, (*W. C.*) The Revolutions, Insurrections, and Conspiracies of Europe, 2 vols. *cl.* Lond. 1843

2951 Tegg (*Thos.*) Dictionary of Chronology, 12mo. *cloth,* London, 1835

2952 Toone (*W.*) Chronological Historian, 2 vols. 8vo. *half calf.* Lond. 1826

2953 Valckenier (*P.*) Das Verwirrte Europa oder Policsche und Historische, 10 vols. in 3, folio, *numerous fine portraits and plates.* Amst. 1677

2954 Williams (*W.*) Primitive History from the Creation to Cadmus, 4to. *boards, uncut.* 1789

HISTORY OF THE STAGE.

2957 Actor (*The*), A Peep Behind the Curtain, being passages in the lives of Booth and some of his Contemporaries, 8vo. N. Y. 1846

2958 ——— Remonstrance, &c., 5 tracts, 1 vol. *half calf,* v. p.

2959 ——— Brainard's Remains, &c., 6 vols. *various,* 12mo.

2960 Addison (*J.*) Cato, a Tragedy, 4to. 1713, and six Tracts relating to the same, *scarce*, in 1 vol. 4to. v. y.

2961 Adventures of an Actor; comprising a Picture of the French Stage during fifty years, edited by Th. Hook, 2 vols. post 8vo. *half calf.* Lond. 1842

2962 ——— of an Actor in the character of a Merry Andrew, a Methodist Preacher, and a Fortune-teller, 12mo. Lond. n. d.

2963 ——— of a Dramatist on a Journey to the London Managers, 2 vols. 12mo. *half calf.* Lond. 1813

2964 Album of the Cambridge Garrick Club, *portraits and autographs*, 12mo. *half calf.* Camb. 1836

2965 Alacci (*Lione*), Drammaturgiâ (an alphabetical list of Plays), 4to. *half calf.* Venez. 1755

2966 Alwyn, or the Gentleman Comedian, 2 vols. in 1, 12mo. *half calf.* Lond. 1780

2967 American Actors, 21 *portraits of*, 4to. Circa, 1827

2968 Anecdotes Dramatiques, 3 vols. 12mo. *half calf.* Par. 1775

2969 Angelo's Pic-nic, or Table-talk, including numerous recollections of public characters who have figured in some part or another of the Stage for the last 50 years, 8vo. *cloth.* Lond. 1834

2970 ——— Another copy. Lond. 1834

2971 Annales Dramatiques, ou Dictionnaire Géneral des Theâtres, par une Société de gens lettres, 9 vols. 8vo. *half calf.* Paris, 1808

2972 Auger (*H.*) Physiologie du Theâtre, 3 vols. 8vo. *half calf.* Paris, 1839

2973 Authentic Memoirs of the Green Room, including Sketches Biographical, Critical, and Characteristic, 2 vols. in 1, 18mo. *half calf.* Lond. 1806

2974 Autograph Signatures of many celebrated Actors and other Persons connected with London Theatricals prior to 1833, cut from the Register of Drury Lane Theatre, wherein they were required to write their names.

This interesting volume is fully authenticated by Mr. J. H. Hackett, who presented it to Mr. Burton. These autographs are neatly mounted in 8vo. size.

2975 Autographs, Theatrical, pasted in an oblong 8vo. v. y

2976 Ballets, Weaver's Dramatic Entertainment on the Fable of Orpheus and Eurydice, 1718, and Loves of Venus and Adonis, as performed at the Theatre in Drury Lane, 1724, in 1 vol. 12mo. *half calf.* Lond. v. y.

2976* Baker, Biographica Dramatica, 2 vols. 8vo. *half calf.* 1782

2977 Bayley (*F. W. H.*) Wake of Extasy, a memory of Jenny Lind, *plates*, 4to. Lond. 1848

2978 Beard and Shebbeare, Letters which have passed between, *sd.* 8vo. Lond. 1767

2979 Beauchamps (*M. de*), Recherches sur les Theatre de France, 3 vols. 12mo. Paris, 1735

2980 Becket (*A.*) Dramatic and Prose Miscellanies, edited by Dr. Beattie, 2 vols. 8vo. *boards.* Lond. 1838

2281 Beckett (*G. A. à*) Quizziology of the British Drama, 12mo. *half calf.* Lond. 1846

2681* Betterton (*Thos.*) History of the English Stage. Lond. 1740

2982 Blasis (*C.*) Code of Terpsichore, the Art of Dancing, comprising its Theory and Practice, &c., translated by Barton, 8vo. *half calf.* Lond. 1830

2983 Bouterwek (*F.*) History of Spanish Literature, with Notes by Ross, *port.* 8vo. *cloth.* 1847

The best history of Spanish literature.

2984 Bowen (*Capt.*) Statement of facts in answer to Mrs. Gunning's Letters to His Grace the Duke of Argyll. Lond. 1791

2985 Brandon, Statement of facts relating to Covent Garden Theatre, *sd.* 8vo. Lond. 1823

2986 Brazie, Histoire des Petits Theatres de Paris, 2 vols. in 1, 18mo. *half calf.* Paris, 1838

2987 British Theatrical Gallery, a collection of whole length Portraits, with Biographical Notices by D. Terry, *prints colored*, 4to. Lond. 1825

2988 Brougham (*L.*) Bunsby Papers, 2d series, 12mo. *cloth.* N. Y. 1856

2989 Brown (*John*), The Stage, a Poem, 12mo. *half calf.* Lond. 1819

2990 Brunswick Theatre, Destruction of; Four Discourses on the Stage, &c. &c., 5 tracts, 12mo. v. p.

2991 Buckingham (*Duke of*) Rehearsal, 12mo. *half calf.* Lond. 1735

2992 Bunn (*Alf.*) Old England and New England, 12mo. *cloth.* Phil. 1853

2993 Burton's Theatre, Play Bills, *bound in* 10 *long vols.*

2994 ——— Play Bills for 1855, *bound.*

2995 Case of the Stage in Ireland, *sd.*, 8vo. Dub. n. d.

2996 Castil, Blaze, La Danse, et Les Ballets, 12mo. *half calf.* Paris, 1832

2997 Chiara (*P.*) Rosara, or the Adventures of an Actress, 3 vols. in 1, *half calf.* Lond. 1771

2997* Chapman (*J. K.*) The Court Theatre, a complete History of Theatrical Entertainments, Dramas, Masques, and Triumphs, at the English Court, from the time of King Henry VIII. to the present day, including the series of Plays performed before Her Majesty at Windsor Castle, Christmas, 1848, 1849, containing many curious particulars of our Early Dramatic Literature and art, *with highly finished and beautiful engravings on steel, by Finden, &c.*, small folio, *cloth gilt, gilt edges.* Lond. 1852

2998 Chetwood (*W. R.*) A General History of the Stage, from its Origin in Greece down to the Present Time, with the Memoirs of most of the principal performers that have appeared on the English and Irish Stage for these last fifty years, &c., *scarce*, 12mo. *half calf.* Lond. 1749

2999 Cibber (*Colly*), An Apology for the Life of, written by himself, interspersed with Characters and Anecdotes, &c., *portrait*, 8vo. *half calf.* Lond. 1822

One of the most interesting and readable autobiographies ever written, a model of that style of literature.

*** "The best book ever written on the subject of the theatre."—*Dunlap.*

3000 ——— The Tryal of, Remarks on, 1718; The Egotists, 3 *tracts*, 8vo. *calf.*

3001 ——— (*Theophilus*), Epistle to David Garrick, *sd.* 8vo. Lond. 1755

3002 Clive (*Mrs.*) Case of, Submitted to the Publick, *sd.* 12mo. Lond. 1844

3003 Colman (*Francis, and George Colman, the Elder*), Letters Addressed to, from Various Celebrated Men, with annotations and remarks, by George Colman, the younger, 4to. Lond. 1820

3004 Companion to the Theatre, 2 vols. *half calf*, 12mo. Lond. 1747

CONTROVERSY BETWEEN THE SUPPORTERS OF THE STAGE AND THOSE WHO ATTACKED IT ON THE GROUND OF IMMORALITY AND PROFANITY, &c.

3006 ANSWER to the Question, Is it Lawful to go to Plays? 1757; Sermon on the Stage, 1759; Observations on the Drama; Lawfulness of the Stage, 1787, 4 *tracts*, 8vo. Lond.

3007 BEDFORD (*A.*) Evil and Danger of Stage Plays, showing their Natural Tendency to Destroy Religion and Introduce a General Corruption of Manners, 8vo. *half calf.* Lond. 1705

3008 CAFFARO (*Father*), Defence of the Drama, *half calf*, 12mo. N. Y. 1826

3009 CALCRAFT (*John William*), A Defence of the Stage: or, an Inquiry into the Real Qualities of Theatrical Entertainments, 8vo. *half calf.* Dub. 1839

Presentation copy to J. W. Wallack, with author's autograph.

3010 CLARK (*Samuel*), The Fatal Vespers, a true and full Narrative of that Signal Judgment of God upon the Papists by the Fall of the House in Black Friers, London, upon the 5th of Nov., 1623, 4to. *paper.* Lond. 1657, *Reprinted*, Lond. 1817

3012 COLLIER (*J.*) A Short View of the Immorality and Profaneness of the English Stage, together with the sense of antiquity upon this argument, 8vo. *half calf.* Lond. 1698

3013 ——— The Stage Acquitted, a full answer to Mr. Collier; A Vindication of Charles I., 1699; A Defence of Dramatic Poetry, 1698; Amendment of Mr. Colliers' Citations, 1698, 3 vols. in 1, 8vo. *half calf.* v. d.

3014 CONSIDERATIONS on the Stage, 1809; An Impartial Appeal; Rebellion, or All in the Wrong, *portrait of Kemble, &c.*, 4 *tracts*, 8vo. Lond.

3015 COOPER (*Tho.*) The Arte of Giving, describing the trve nature and right vse of liberality, &c., *rare*, 12mo. *calf, neat.* Lond. 1615

*** Dicing, carding, cocke-fighting, beare-bayting, *stage-playes*, &c., are called "a practice of Satan to hinder bounty, by enticing men to exhaust their estates in vnlawfvll recreations."

3016 DRAKE (*Jas.*) Ancient and Modern Stages surveyed, in answer to Collier's view, 8vo. *half calf.* Lond. 1699

3016*DOUGLAS, a Tragedy; Tracts against Douglas; Tracts against the Stage; Twelve Tracts, 8vo. Lond. v. d.

3017 Filmer (*Dr.*) Defence of Plays, or the Stage Vindicated, against Collier, 12mo. *half calf*, Lond. 1707

3018 Law (*Wm.*) The Absolute Unlawfulness of the Stage Entertainment fully Demonstrated, 8vo. *half calf.* Lond. 1726

3019 ——— Another edition, 12mo. Lond. 1765

3020 Mansel (*R.*) Free Thoughts upon Methodists, Actors, and the Influence of the Stage (autograph of the author, Hill), 1814; Short struggle for Stage or no Stage, in answer to Best's Sermon, Sheffield, 2 vols. in 1, *half calf.* v. d.

3021 Northbrooke (*John*), Treatise, wherein Dicing, Dauncing, Vain Playes, or Enterludes, and other Idle Pastimes, &c., commonly used on the Sabbath Day, are reproved, 8vo. *half calf.* 1843

3022 Moser (*Justus*), Harlequin, or a Defence of Grotesque Performances, by Mr. Justus Moser, Councellor of the most high Court of Justice of Osnabruck, &c., translated by Warnecke, 12mo. Lond. 1766

3022* Ordinance of the Lords and Commons for the Utter Suppression of all Stage Playes and Interludes, five other ordinances, 3 *tracts*, small 4to. *full calf, very scarce.* Lond. 1647

3023 Prynne's (*Wm.*) Histrio-Matrix, the Player's Scourge, or Actor's Tragedie, showing that Stage Playes (the very Pompes of the Divell) ere Sinfull, Heathenish. Lewde, Ungodly Spectacles, &c., *thick* 4to. pp. 1050, *original old calf, very neat*, with Mr. William Prynne-his Defense of Stage Plays, 4 *leaves.* 1649

Prynne, for writing this extraordinary attack against "Plays, Interludes, and all the Pompes of the Divell," was tried in the Star Chamber, and sentenced "to have his book burnt by the common hangman, to be put from the Bar, to be forever incapable of his profession, to be turned out of the Society of Lincoln's Inn, to be degraded at Oxford, to stand in the pillory both at Westminster and in Cheapside, to lose both his ears, one at each place, to pay a fine of £5,000, and to suffer perpetual imprisonment." Unfortunate Wm. Prynne to receive such recompense for this his principal and daring work, and to swell and fortify which he had carefully read hundreds of old Latin Authors, and made more than One Hundred Thousand references to their pages.

3024 Rainoldes (*D.*) The Overthrow of Stage Playes, by the way of controversie betwixt D. Gaiger and D. Rainoldes, &c., wherein it is manifestly proved, that it is not onely unlawfull to bee an actor, but a beholder of these vanities, *rare*, 4to. Oxford, 1629

3025 RICHMOND, Calamity at, 1811, and 6 Tracts on the American Stage, 8vo. v. d.

3026 STAGE Condemned (*the*) 12mo. *half calf.* Lond. 1698

Written in support of Collies ; this copy has the Autograph of Sophia Hume, the Quaker Authoress. (?)

3027 STAGE (*The*) The High Road to Hell, &c., 1767 ; Theatrical Entertainments consistent with Society, Morality and Religion, in answer to the Stage, and 1768 2 vols. in 1, 8vo. L. v. d.

3028 STEELE (*Sir Richard*), The Theatre with the Anti-Theatre, &c., illustrated with historical anecdotes, by John Nichols, 2 vols. 8vo. Lond. 1791

3029 STYLES (*John*), Essay on the Character and Influence of the Stage on Morals and Happiness, 12mo. *half calf.* Lond. 1807

3030 SUTOR (*A.*) Essay on the Stage (*Contra*), 12mo. *half calf.* Aberdeen, 1820

3031 THEATRICAL Amusements: A Treatise on the Propriety of, in a Christian Community, 18mo. privately printed, Madras, 1826 ; Turnbull (Rev. R.) The Theatre in its Influence upon Literature, Morals, and Religion, Hartford, 1837 ; 2 vols. in 1, 18mo. *half calf.* v. d.

3032 Tracts against the Theatre, 12mo. v. y. 1765

3033 ——— against the Theatre, small 8vo. Lond. v. y.

3034 VANBRUGH ; A Short Vindication of the Relapse, and the Provoked Wife from Immorality and Prophaneness, (in reply to Collier) 8vo. *half calf.* Lond. 1687

3035 VINDICATION of the Stage, in answer to Collier, 4to. pp. 29, *half calf.* Lond. 1698

3036 WITHERSPOON (*J.*) Serious Enquiry into the Nature and Effects of the Stage, *half calf*, 12mo. N. Y. 1812

3037 COOKE'S Illustration to the British Theatre, 58 *fine plates*, 8vo. *half calf.* Lond. n. d.

3038 CRY (*The*), A New Dramatic Fable, 3 vols., vols. 1 and 3, 12mo. *calf.* Lond. 1754

3039 [CROKER] Familiar Epistles to Frederich J[one]s, Esq., on the Present State of the Irish Stage, 18mo. *half calf.* Dublin, 1804

3040 CUMBERLAND (*J.*) Theatrical Illustrations, 18mo. *half calf.* Lond. n. d.

3041 DANIEL (*G.*), Merrie England in the Olden Time, with humorous engravings, by J. Leech, 2 vols. post 8vo. 1842

3042 DARLEY'S Grecian Drama; a Treatise on the Dramatic Literature of the Greeks, 8vo. *calf.* Dublin, 1840

Contains a larger quantity of well-arranged matter than any single work hitherto published on the same subject.

3043 DAVIES' (*T.*) Dramatic Miscellanies, including Critical Observations on the Plays of Shakspeare, Anecdotes of Dramatic Poets, Actors, &c., 3 vols. post 8vo. *half calf, gilt.* 1785

3044 DEBURAU: Histoire du Théatre, a Quatre Sous, pour faire suite a l'Histoire du Theatre Français, par Jules Janin, 18mo. *half calf.* Bruxelles, 1836

3045 DIBDIN (*Charles*), Complete History of the English Stage, 5 vols. 8vo. *half calf.* Lond. 1800

3046 DIBDIN (*T.*) Last Lays of the Last of the Three Dibdins, 8vo. *half calf.* Lond. 1833

3047 DIBDIN (*C.*) Devil's Pocket-book, 8 Nos. *half calf.* 8vo. Lond. 1786

3048 DRAKE (*N.*) Shakspeare and his Times, royal 8vo. *half calf.* 1838

3049 DRAMA Recorded, or Barker's List of Plays, 12mo. *half calf.* Lond. 1814

3050 ——— Complete History of the, from the earliest period to the present time (by Dramaticus Censor), 8vo. Lond. 1793

3051 DRAMATIC Rights, or Private Theatricals and Pic-nic Suppers, Justified by fair Argument, by W. Cutspear, 8vo. *sewed.* Lond.

3052 DRAMATIC Scorpion, a Satire, 8vo. *half calf.* Lond. 1818

3053 DRURY Lane Play Bills for, 1827–8, in sheets.

3054 DUBLIN in an Uproar, or the Ladies Robb'd of their Pleasure, being a full and impartial account of the late remarkable tumult that happen'd at the Dublin Theatre, *sewed,* 8vo. Dublin, n. d.

3055 DUNLAP'S (*W.*) History of the American Theatre, 8vo. *half calf, interleaved.* Lond. 1833

The biographical sketches, criticisms, scenes, anecdotes, and facetiæ contained in this volume, will render it exceedingly popular; while, with the theatrical reader, the work will take a much higher grade, as affording a full and impartial history of that most checkered of all pursuits, the drama and its votaries.

3056 EDWARDS, Letter to Mr. Woodward on his Triumph over the Inspector, 8vo. *sewed.* Lond. n. d.

3057 EDWIN (*J.*) Eccentricities, collected from his MSS., and enriched with several hundred original anecdotes, 2 vols. 12mo. *half calf.* Lond. 1770

3058 EGAN (*Pierce*), Book of Sports and Mirror of Life; embracing the Turf, the Chase, the Ring, and the Stage; with Original Memoirs of Sporting Men, &c., *half calf.* Lond. 1831

3059 EGERTON'S Theatrical Remembrancer, 12mo. *half calf.* Lond. 1778

3060 ELLISTON (*R. W. and others*), Pamphlets on the London Theatre, various 4, 8vo. *half calf.* Lond. 1818

3061 ESSAY upon the Present State of the Theatre in France, England, and Italy, 12mo. Lond. 1760

3062 ESSAYS on Theatrical Performers, 12mo. *half calf.* Lond. 1807

3063 FENNELL (*James*), Statement of Facts relative to the late Disturbances at the Theatre Royal, Edinburgh, 8vo. *sewed.* Lond. 1788

3063*FLEURY, Memoire de la Comèdie Française, 1757 a 1820, 6 vols. 12mo. *half calf.* Bruxelles, 1835

3064 FLOWERS for Genius (*Miss Heron*), gathered on the Shores of the Pacific, 8vo. San Francisco, 1854

3065 FOOTE (*Horace*), Companion to the Theatre, and Manual of the British Drama, 18mo. *half calf.* Lond. 1829

3066 FOOTE (*S.*) Letter to, and Tracts on, 3 tracts, 8vo. v. d.

3067 FOREST Divorce Case, 8vo. N. Y. 1852

3068 FRENCH Stage, Tracts on the, 12mo. Paris, 1751

3069 GAISFORD (*John*), Theatrical Thoughts by, and Conundrums sent to him on the occasion of his Benefit, 8vo. *half calf.* Montreal, 1848

3070 GALLINI (*Giovanni-Andrea*), Treatise on the Art of Dancing, 8vo. Lond. 1762

GARRICK (*David*), Private Correspondence, *vide* Dramatic Biography, lot 1797.

3072 GARRICK, D—ry L—ne P—yh—se Broke open in a Letter to Mr. G——; 1748—Life and Death of D. Garrick, Esq., and Ed. Alleyn, v. 1779, 2 vols. in 1, 8vo. *half calf.* v. d.

3073 GARRICKIANA: Letter to David Garrick; Love in the Suds, 1772; Two Letters to Garrick, 1773; Garrick's Looking-Glass, a Poem; Pursuit after Happiness, a Poem; Ode to Dragon; Funeral Eulogium of Garrick; Monody on Garrick, &c.; 8 tracts, in 1 vol. 4to. *full calf.* Lond.

3074 GARRICKIANA: The Farmer's Return, 1762, *plate after Hogarth by Basire;* The Goddess of Health, a Poem, by Garrick, 1771; An Epistle to Garrick, by E. Lloyd, 1773; Pursuit after Happiness, 1777; Verses to the Memory of Garrick, 1779; Elegy on the Death of David Garrick, 1779; Dialogue between the Earl of C—d and Mr. Garrick, 7 rare and curious tracts, 4to. Lond.

3075 GAULTIER Garguille, Rencontre de Gautier Garguille avec Taburin en l'autre monde, et les entretiens qu'ils ont eus dans les Champs Elysées sur le nouveautés de ce temps, Par. 1634.—Apologie de Guillot Gorjio addressée à tous les beaux esprits, Par. 1634; 2 vols. in 1, 8vo. *half calf.* Paris, 1634

"All the works of this facetious person," says Brunet, "are rare."

3076 GENEST (*Rev. John*), Some Account of the English Stage, from the Restoration, 1660, to 1830, 10 vols. 8vo. Bath, 1830

This copy is inlaid with fine writing paper, and illustrated by a profusion of prints and portraits. The characters of all the Plays are published in this work, and all the original Actors are named, which makes it a very useful book of reference.

3077 GILLILAND (*Tho.*) The Dramatic Mirror and History of the Stage, Dramatic Writers, and Distinguished Performers, 2 vols. 12mo. *fine portraits, half calf.* Lond. 1808

3079 ——— Elbow Room, a Pamphlet containing remarks on the shameful increase of the private boxes of Covent Garden, 8vo. *sd.* Lond. 1804

3080 GODWIN (*Parke*), Vala, a Mythological Tale, 4to. *half calf.* N. Y. 1851

3081 GRATIANI (*G.*) Il Cromvele Tragedia, 5 *fine plates of scenes,* 4to. *half calf.* Bologna, 1671

3082 GREEN-Room, Secret History of, containing Authentic and Entertaining Memoirs of Actors and Actresses, 2 vols. 12mo. *half calf.* 1792

Best edition, containing anecdotes omitted subsequently.

3083 HAVE At You All, or the Drury Lane Journal, by Roxana Termagant, &c., 8vo. *half calf.* Lond. 1752

3084 HAWKINS (*Wm.*) Miscellanies, in Prose and Verse, with Strictures on the principal Performers of the two Theatres, 12mo. *half calf.* 1775

3085 HAMBURGISCHE Dramaturgie, 8vo. *half calf.* Hamburg, 1767

3086 HAWKINS (*T.*) Origin of the English Drama, illustrated in its various species, viz. Mystery, Morality, Tragedy, and Comedy, by Specimens from our earliest Writers, with Notes, 3 vols. 8vo. *calf.* Oxford, 1773

3087 HENSLOWE'S Diary, (Shakspearean Society,) 8vo. *half calf.* 1845

3088 HERVEY (*Ch.*) The Theatres of Paris, *illustrated with original portraits of eminent living Actresses by Lacauchie*, royal 8vo. *half morocco.* 1846

3089 ——— Another copy, *without plates*, 8vo. Paris, 1847

3090 HILL ( ) Actor, 12mo. *half calf.* Lond. 1750

3091 HIPPISLEY (*J. H.*) Chapters on Early English Literature, 8vo. *half morocco.* Lond. 1837

3092 HISTOIRE du Theatre François, 9 vols. 12mo. *half calf.* Paris, 1745

3093 HISTOIRE du Theatre de L'Opera Comique, 2 vols. 12mo. *half calf.* Paris, 1770

3094 HISTRIONIC Topography, or the Birthplaces, Residences, and Funeral Monuments of the most distinguished Actors, *plates by Storer, description by Brewer*, 8vo. *half calf.* Lond. 1818

HONE'S Works, *vide* Lot 2041.

3096 HITCHCOCK (*Robert*), Historical View of the Irish Stage, from the earliest period to the close of the season, 1788, 2 vols. 12mo. *half calf.* Dub. 1788

3097 HOLBROOK, The Dramatist, or Memoirs of the Stage, *sd.* 8vo. Birmingham, 1809

3098 HOUSSAYE (*Arsene*), Philosophers and Actresses, 2 vols. 12mo. *half calf.* Redfield, 1852

3099 IFFLAND (*A. W.*) Theorie der Schauspielkunst fur ausúbende, Kunstler und Kunstfreunde, 18mo. *half calf.* Berlin, 1815

3100 I CAPO d'Opera del Teatro antica e moderna, 12mo. *half calf.* Venez. 1789

3101 ITALIANS (*The*), A Defence of Kean; Reply to; Theatre Revolution; 4 tracts, 8vo. Lond.

3102 INIGO Jones, a New Life of, by P. Cunningham; Remarks on his Sketches for Masques and Dramas by Planché; Five Court Masques, edited from the original MSS. of Ben Jonson, J. Marston, &c. by J. P. Collier, *fac similes of drawings and portrait*, 8vo. *half calf.* 1848

3103 KEMP'S Nine Days' Wonder, performed in a Daunce from London to Norwich, with Notes by Dyce, 4to. *half calf.* Lond. 1840

3104 KALIDASAS Urvasi, a Drama, with notes by Ballensen, from the Sanscrit, 8vo. *half calf.* St. Petersburg, 1846

3105 LANDRIANA (*Paoli*), Osservazioni sui difetti predotti nei Theatré dalla, Milan, 4to. Milan, 1811

3106 LANGBAINE'S (*G.*) Account of the English Dramatic Poets, 8vo. *calf.* 1691

"Of all the early catalogues of the English Stage, Langbaine's is the only one to be relied on implicitly for its fidelity."—*Lowndes.*

3107 LEE (*Hy.*) Memoirs of a Manager, or Life's Stage with New Scenery, 2 vols. 12mo. *half morocco.* Taunton, 1836

3108 LESPES (*Leo*), Les Mysteries du Grand Opera, 8vo. *half calf.* Paris, 1843

3108* LETTERS which passed between Mr. West Digges, Comedian, and Mrs. Sarah Ward, 1752–59, 8vo. *half calf.* Edin. 1833

Only one hundred copies printed; contains much curious information relative to dramatic affairs at Edinburgh.

3109 LEWIS (*C. L.*) Comic Sketches, or the Comedian his own Master, 12mo. *half calf.* Lond. 1804

3110 LONDON Theatres, a Poem, and 4 others, 5 *tracts*, 8vo. Lond.

3111 LUCAS (*Hippolyte*), Historie Philosophique et Littéraire du Theatre Français, 12mo. *half calf.* Paris, 1843

3112 MACKLIN (*Charles, Comedian*), Apology for the Conduct of, *sd.* 12mo. Lond. 1773

3113 MAGASIN Pittoresque, *profusely illustrated with woodcuts*, 21 vols. *paper*, royal 8vo. Paris

3114 MANIERE de Juger des Ouvrages du Theatre, MS. of the XVIII. Century, small 4to. *half calf.*

3115 MARSHALL (*Thomas*), Lives of the most Celebrated Actors and Actresses, 12mo. *half calf.* Lond. 1847

3116 MATHEWS (*M. Chas.*) Lettre aux Auteurs Dramatiques de la France, 8vo. *half calf.* Lond. 1852

3117 MAXWELL (*Caroline*), The Actress, or Countess or no Countess, a novel, 4 vols. 12mo. Lond. 1823

3119 MOORE (*H. N.*) Fitzgerald and Hopkins, or Scenes and Adventures in Theatrical Life, 8vo. *half calf.* Phil. 1847

3120 NORTHALL (*W. K.*) Before and Behind the Curtain, 12mo. *half calf.* N. Y. 1851

3122 NOTES on Ben Jonson's Conversations with Wm. Drummond, of Hawthornden, 8vo. *half calf,* Shakspeare Society. Lond. 1842

3123 OPERAS, Enquiry into; The Opera Glass, &c., 3 *tracts*, 8vo. Lond.

3124 OPERA, The Spleen, in Four Cantos; The Orange Girl at Foote's; The Opera, a Poem; the Opera Rumpus, 4 *tracts*, 1768 to 1783, 4to. Lond.

3125 OULTON (*W. C.*) History of the Theatres of London, containing an Annual Register of all the new and revived Tragedies, Comedies, &c., 2 vols. *half calf*, 12mo. Lond. 1796

3126 ——— Beauties of Modern Dramatists, 2 vols. 12mo. Lond. 1800

3127 OULTON'S Hist. Stage, additions to, by Egerton, 12mo. Lond. 1803

3128 OXBERRY (*W.*) Actor's Budget of Wit and Merriment, consisting of Monologues, Prologues, Epilogues, Tales, Comic Songs, Jests, &c., *half calf*, 12mo. Lond.

3129 ——— Dramatic Chronology, containing the Names, Dates of Births, &c., of all the Actors and Actresses up to 1849, 12mo. *half calf.* 1849

3130 PALMER (*John*), Like Master Like Man, a novel, prefaced by George Colman, 2 vols. 12mo. *half calf.* Lond. 1811

3131 ——— Trial of John Palmer, Comedian. Lond. 1787

3132 PAMPHLETS on London Theatres, Royal, 8vo. 1809–10. Lond.

3133 ——— Letters to Mrs. Bellamy and Mrs. Siddons; Foote and Haynes Trial; Fanny Ellsler, &c., 5 *tracts*, 8vo. v. p.

3134 ——— A Poem to the Memory of Mrs. Cibber, 1766; The Theatres, by Sir M. Nipclose, 1772; The Eastern Theatre Erected, 1788; Verses to Mrs. Siddons, 1782, 4 *tracts*, 4to. Lond.

3135 ——— Twenty-Six Old and Curious Tracts on the Stage, in 5 vols. Lond. v. d.

3136 ——— The Theatres, a Poetical Dissertation, *plates;* The Cap, a Satiric Poem, by Peter Pindar; Theatrical Portraits; A Trip to Parnassus, 4 *tracts*, 1781 to 1788, 4to. Lond.

3137 ——— Poetical Tracts on the Stage, 8vo. Lond.

3138 ——— Historical, Critical, and Moral Dissertations on Masquerades, 4 *pamphlets.* 1751

3139 Pellicer (*D. C.*) Tratado Historico sobre el Origin y progresos de la Comedia y del Histrionismo en Espano, 18mo. *half calf.* Madrid, 1804

3140 Percy, Anecdotes of the Stage, 18mo. *half calf.* Lond. 1822

3141 Pettus & Arria, a Tragedy, to which is prefixed a letter to T. Sheridan on the present state of the English Stage, 8vo. pp. VIII. 76.

3142 Play Bills of the Theatre Royal, Newcastle, 8vo. *half calf.* Newcastle

3143 Playhouse Pocket Companion, a Theatrical Vade Mecum, 12mo. *half calf.* Lond. 1779

3144 Players (*The*), a Satyr, 1733; Catalogue of Theatrical Curiosities, 1748; Dramatic Rights, or Private Theatricals, 1802; *and two other tracts,* 8vo. *half calf.* v. d.

3145 Prologues and Epilogues Celebrated for their Poetical Merit, 12mo. Oxford (1789)

3146 Punch and Judy, with illustrations by George Cruikshank, 12mo. *half calf.* Lond. 1828

3147 Rebellion (*The*), or an Account of the Late Civil Wars in the Kingdom of Eloquence, 12mo. *sheep.* Lond. 1704

3148 Riccoboni (*Louis*), Histoire du Theatre Italien depuis la decadence de la Comedie Latine; avec un Catalogue des Tragedies et Comedies, &c., 8vo. *calf, very neat,* 17 *fine plates of costumes, &c.* Paris, 1728

3149 Rees (*J.*) Dramatic Authors of America, 12mo. Phil. 1845

3150 Rich's Register, or An Account of Plays acted at the New Theatre in Lincoln's Inn Fields, 1714; neat manuscript, *curious,* 4to. *half calf.*

3151 Ritchie (*Mrs.*) Mimic Life, or Before and Behind the Curtain, 12mo. *cloth.* Bost. 1856

3152 Robson (*Wm.*) The Old Play Goer, 12mo. *half calf,* Lond. 1846

3153 Ryan (*Richard*), Dramatic Table Talk, *plates,* 3 vols. 12mo. Lond. 1825

3154 Scarron (*M.*) Comic Romance, Translated by Oliver Goldsmith, 2 vols. Lond. 1775

3155 Secret History of the October Club, *half morocco,* by Mackenzie, 8vo. Lond. 1711

3156 Sismondi, Historical View of the Literature of the South of Europe, translated by Roscoe, 2 vols. 8vo. *half calf.* N. Y. 1827

3157 SKETCH of the History of the Theatres in the United States. This work is in *manuscript*, neatly written, and contains many curious reminiscences of the N. Y. Theatres, 2 vols. 4to. *half calf.*

3158 SMITH (*H. and J.*) Rejected Addresses, *half calf*, 12mo. Bost. 1841

3159 Sol. Smith's Theatrical Apprenticeship, *sewed* 12mo. Phil. n. d.

3160 SIX Tracts on the Stage. 8vo. v. d.

3161 STATEMENT of the Differences existing between the Proprietors and Performers of the Theatre Royal, Covent Garden, 8vo. *sewed.* Lond. 1800

3162 STEVENS (*G. A.*) Dramatic History, Master Edward (*Shuter*). Miss Ann (*Catley*), *half calf*, 12mo. Lond. 1785

3163 STEELE (*Sir R.*) Epistolary Correspondence, edited by John Nichols, 2 vols. 8vo. *half calf.* Lond. 1809

3164 TASTE of the Town, 8vo. Lond.

3165 THEATRE of the Greeks, 8vo. *half calf.* Camb. 1825

Contains a great body of information relative to the Rise, Progress, and Exhibition of the Drama, and an account of Dramatic Writers from Thespis to Menander.

3166 THEATRE (*The*), Nos. 1 to 11, 12mo. Lond. 1851

3167 THEATRICAL Bouquet, an Alphabetical Arrangement of Prologues and Epilogues, 12mo. Lond. 1778

3168 THEATRICAL Budget, a Peep into the Green-room, *colored prints*, 12mo. N. Y. 1828

3169 THEATRICAL Contribution of "Jacques" to the United States Gazette, 18mo. *half calf.* Phil. 1826

3170 THEATRICAL Dictionary, containing an account of all the Dramatic Pieces that have appeared from the commencement of Theatrical Exhibitions to the present time, *half calf*, 12mo. Lond. 1792

3171 THEATRICAL Journal, N. American Miscellanies, Becket's Dramatic Works, 3 odd vols.

3172 THEATRICAL Portraits, and other Poems, *half calf*, 12mo. Lond. 1822

3173 THEATRICAL Portraits, *small, whole lengths, neatly engraved, Garrick and others, mounted, in* 8vo. *Sayer, exc.* Lond. 1769

THEATRICAL Portraits, &c., *see* Prints.

3174 THEOPHRASTUS, Characters of, translated from the Greek, *and illustrated by physiognomical sketches*, royal 8vo. *half calf.* Lond. 1824

3175 THESPIAN Preceptor, 12mo. Bost. 1810

3176 THEW (*W.*) Poems on Various Subjects, chiefly theatrical, *half calf*, 8vo. Lond. 1825

3177 TOBY'S Character of Sir Rich'd Steele, &c., 4 tracts, 8vo. Lond.

3178 TOUCHARD LAFOSSE (*G.*) Chroniques, Secretes et Galantes de l'Opera, 1667–1845, 2 vols. *half calf*, 8vo. Paris, 1846

3179 TRACTS, Mrs. Galindo's Letter to Mrs. Siddons; Trial of Wright *v.* Barham, for Crim. Con., and Love Letters of Mrs. Piozzi to W. A. Conway, 3 vols. in 1, 8vo. *half calf.* v. d.

3180 TRACTS on the Stage, Three Sermons on; Three Tracts and Addresses on; Old Tracts on, by Mrs. Rowe and others, 4 vols. Lond. v. d.

3181 VAUXHALL Papers, edited by Bunn and Crowquill, 12mo. *half calf.* 1841

3182 VICTOR (*B.*) Original Letters, chiefly on Dramatic Subjects, 8vo. *half calf.* Lond. 1776

3183 ——— History of the Theatres in London and Dublin, from 1730, 3 vols. 12mo. *half calf.* Lond. 1741

3184 VILLANUEVA (*M. G.*) Origin, epocas y progresses del Teatro Español discurso Historica y un Compendio de la Historia General de los Teatros hasta la era presente, 8vo. Madrid, 1802

3185 WALKER (*J. C.*) Historical Memoir of Italian Tragedy, from the earliest period to the present time, with specimens and Analysis of the most celebrated Tragedies and Biographical Notices of the principal tragic writers of Italy, 4to. *half calf.* Lond. 1799

"Many notices of scarce Dramas may be gleaned from this work, as the author seems to have laboured with just and exemplary diligence in the illustration of his subject."—*Lowndes.*

Contains the Adamo of Andreini, from which Milton is said to have taken the idea of Paradise Lost.

3186 WATERS (*E.*) Statement of Matters relative to the King's Theatre, *sewed*, 8vo. Lond. 1818

3187 WHINCOP (*Thos.*) Scanderbeg, a Tragedy, with a List of Dramatic Authors and their Lives, 8vo. *calf.* Lond. 1747

The list of plays is by John Mottley, author of Joe Miller.

3189 WHYTE (*Samuel*), Collection of Poems, including the Theatre, a didactic essay, *plates*, *half calf*, *uncut*, 8vo. Dub. 1793

George Washington and several American ladies and gentlemen grace the subscription list to this interesting volume.

3190 Wilkes (*Mr.*) A General View of the Stage, 8vo. *half calf.* Lond. 1759

3191 Williams' (*David*) Letter to Garrick on his conduct as Actor and Manager at Drury Lane, with a preface and notes, 4to. *sewed.* Lond.

3192 Williams (*J.*) Pin-basket, or Children of Thespis, *half calf*, 12mo. Lond. 1797

3193 Wilson (*H. H.*) Theatre of the Hindus, Malati and Madhava, or the Stolen Marriage, translated from the Sanscrit by H. H. Wilson, Vikrama, Urvasi, Sig. Calidarsas, 8vo. Calcutta, 1826

3194 Woodward (*Henry, Comedian*), Letter to John Hill, *sewed*, 8vo. Lond. 1752

3195 ——— Another copy, 8vo. Lond. 1752

3196 Yates' Reminiscences, or Etchings of Life and Character, as performed at the Adelphi Theatre, *coloured plate*, *sewed*, 12mo. Lond.

COSTUME—ANCIENT, NATIONAL, CIVIL, AND THEATRICAL.

3200 African Costume, Description of the Manners and Customs of the Moors in Zahara, and of the Negro Nations, 45 *coloured plates*, 2 vols. 12mo. Lond.

3201 Baxter (*Thomas*), Illustration of Egyptian, Grecian, and Roman costume, in 40 outlines with descriptions, 8vo. *half calf.* Lond. 1810

3202 Bedolliere (*Emile de la*), Les industrie, les metiers, et professions en France, avec cent dessins par H. Monnier, 87 *plates, half calf*, 8vo. Paris, 1842

3203 Bonnard (*C.*) Costumes Historiques des XIII. XIV. et XV. Siecles, extraits des Monuments les plus authentiques de Peinture et de Sculpture, dessinés et gravés par P. Mercuri, 2 vols. royal 4to. *half calf, extra*, 200 *plates finely coloured.* Paris, 1829

Only a small number of copies were issued of this superb publication—they are already very scarce. The plates are very correctly drawn, and illuminated to resemble the original miniatures and paintings.

3204 Book of Costume, from the earliest period to the present time, by a Lady of Rank, illustrated with upwards of 200 *beautiful engravings on wood by Linton*, 8vo. *half calf.* 1847

The drawings are very artistical, and universally allowed to be the best yet produced in the department of Costume.

3205 BOUTELL (*C.*) Monumental Brasses of England, 149 *fine wood engravings*, with descriptions, *largest paper*, printed in folio, to range with Dugdale, &c., *half calf, extra*, pub. at £5 5*s.* 1849

"The amount of information conveyed in moderate compass, in the above attractive work, renders this collection of examples of Costume, of Decorative Designs, and of Heraldry, highly acceptable. They are marked by minute and faithful exactness, and their variety is striking."—*Archæol. Journal.*

3206 ——— Another copy, 8vo. Lond. 1849

3207 BRADFORD'S Sketches of the Country, Character, and Costumes of Portugal and Spain, made during the Campaign in 1808–9, folio, 56 *fine coloured plates, half calf.* Lond. 1810

3208 BROUGHTON (*T. D.*) Costume, Character, Manners, Domestic Habits, and Religious Ceremonies of the Mahrattas, 14 *coloured plates*, 4to. Lond. 1813

3209 BUSBY'S Costume of the Lower Orders of London, 4to. 24 *well engraved portraits*, with Biographical Anecdotes, *half calf.* Lond. 1819

3210 COLOURED Drawings from Characters in the French Ballet, 132 *plates, in the style of Watteaux*, from Garrick's collection, thick 4to.

3211 COLLECTION de Portraits des Artistes des Theatres de Paris, 71 *portraits*, fol. Paris.

3212 COLLECTION of the Dresses of different nations, ancient and modern, particularly old English dresses, after the designs of Holbein, Hollar, Vandyke, and others, with an account of the authorities from which the figures are taken, and some historical remarks on the subject, to which are added the habits of the principal characters on the English stage. Published by Thomas Jeffreys, Geographer to the Prince of Wales. 4to. *half calf.* Lond. 1757

Lowndes says the original price of this curious work was £20.

3213 COSTUMES of Austria, China, Switzerland, Russian Empire, Turkey, and Great Britain, upwards of 290 beautifully coloured plates, with descriptions, 6 vols. royal 8vo. 1813–14

A choice series of these valuable and interesting works, published at upwards of £30.

3214 ——— of the British Peasantry, Lithographs colored by hand, 21 *plates, half calf, extra*, folio. Lond.

3215 ——— et Annales des grands Théatres de Paris, *colored plates, half calf*, 2 vols. 4to. Paris, 1786

3216 Costumes du Moyen Age, d'Apres les Manuscrits, les peintures, et les Monuments, contemporains, 2 vols. 14 *colored plates*, royal 8vo. *half calf, extra.* Bruxelles, 1847

3217 ——— Civile et Militaires de la Monarchie François, depuis 1260 jusqu'a 1820, 380 colored plates of costume,arranged chronologically, 2 vols. imperial 4to. Paris, 1820

An interesting series of characteristic plates after Le Combe, lithographed by Delpech. Valuable as illustrations to the Autograph collector.

3218 ——— Français depuis Clovis, jusqu'a nos jours, par Cluguy, 160 *colored plates,* 2 vols. *half calf*, 8vo. Paris, 1834

3219 ——— de la Cour Français, *whole length portrait, colored*, 4to. Paris, 1854

3220 ——— of the Levant, Cent Estampes, qui répresentent les différentes Nations du Levant, avec deux nouvelles Estampes de Cérémonies Turques, 102 large and finely executed engravings of Costumes, by Scoten, &c., royal folio, *half calf.* Paris, 1714

One of the grandest of the old works of costume.

3221 ——— du Quadrille Historique des Modes Françaises, depuis Francois 1er jusqu'a nos jours, 17 *plates exquisitely colored*, folio, *half calf.* Paris, 1834

This splendid work was published at 5 guineas.

3222 ——— of the Netherlands, 18 *colored plates*, 18mo. Lond.

3224 ——— of the Russian Empire, colored plates, descriptions, in English and French, 70 *plates, half calf*, folio. Lond. 1814

3225 ——— Suisses: Nouvelle Collection de Costumes Suisses des XXII. Cantons; collection of the most original and interesting Swiss Costumes, drawn from nature; 60 exquisite and beautifully colored plates of Female Costume, 18mo. Zurich.

It requires long and careful inspection to decide whether these are not the most highly-finished drawings, so perfectly are they colored by hand.

3226 ——— of Tuscany, 40 *plates*, royal 4to. Paris, n. d.

3227 ——— de Theatre Français, a collection of 44 colored plates of Actors and Actresses in Character, 1 vol. *half calf*, large 4to. Paris, v. y.

3228 COSTUME, Sixteen Prints, Cries of Holland, *colored*, 4to. n. d.

3229 COTMAN'S Engravings of the Sepulchral Brasses in Norfolk and Suffolk, tending to illustrate the Ecclesiastical, Military, and Civil Costume of former ages, as well as to preserve Memorials of the most ancient Families in those Counties; with letter-press Descriptions, an Introductory Essay on Sepulchral Memorials, by several eminent Antiquaries, and a general Index, new and greatly enlarged edition, containing an Appendix to the Monumental Effigies in Norfolk, and numerous unpublished Brasses, in all 173 plates, two of which, being enamelled brasses, are splendidly illuminated, 2 vols. folio, *large paper*, *half calf*. Lond. 1839

"Cotman's work on Sepulchral Brasses is by far the most important publication on the subject."—*Dawson Turner*.

The style on which Mr. Cotman's Etchings are executed will be of itself a sufficient inducement to procure them a place in every good library. * * * His work on Sepulchral Brasses will be found particularly valuable to the Genealogist and the Antiquary."—*Upcott's English Topography*.

3230 COUTS (*Joseph*), Practical Guide for the Tailor's Cutting-room, 44 *plates*, royal 8vo. *half calf*, *extra*. Lond.

3231 CRYES of London, drawn by M. Lauron, containing 74 plates, several of noted characters: Jacob Hall, the Rope Dancer, Clarke, the Posture master, Mrs. Creswell, the old Bawd, John Kelsey, the Quaker; all noticed in Grainger, *rare*. Lond. 1711

Duke of Grafton's copy.

3232 CUMBERLAND (*G.*) Outlines from the Ancients, 81 *plates*, 8vo. Lond. 1829

2333 DAY and Davies' Illustrations of Mediæval Costume in England, collected from MSS. in the British Museum, 20 colored plates, with descriptions, 4to. *cloth*. Lond. 1850

3234 DETAILS of the Historical Bal Costume, given by the Queen at Buckingham Palace, *wood-cuts*, 4to. Lond. 1845

3235 FAIRHOLT (*F. W.*) Costume in England, a History of Dress from the Earliest Period to the XIXth Century, with Glossary of Terms, and upwards of 600 beautiful wood engravings, 8vo. *cloth*. Lond. 1846

This interesting volume comprises the Early Britons, the Romans in Britain, the Anglo-Saxons and Danes, the Normans, the Plantagenets, York and Lancaster, the Tudors, the Stuarts, William III. to 1800.

3236 EGYPTIAN Costume: Explanation of a series of prints relative to the Manners, Customs, &c., of the present inhabitants of Egypt, from drawings by Dalton, 22 *plates*, folio, *half calf.* n. d.

3237 FICORONII (*F.*) Dissertatio de Larvis Scenicis et Figuris Comicis Antiquorum Romanorum, 4to. 85 plates of Masks, etc. *half calf.* Rome, 1754

3238 FOSBROKE (*T. D.*) Synopsis of Ancient Arms and Armour, *plates*, 4to. Lond. 1824

3239 ——— Synopsis of Ancient Costume: Egyptian, Greek, Roman, British, Anglo-Saxon, Norman and English, 71 *figures*, *half calf*, *extra*, 4to. Lond. 1825

FLATTER'S Milton, *vide* Lot 2663.

3240 FRAGONARD (*Alex.*) Recueil de divers Sujets dans le style Grec. Paris, 1815

3241 FRENCH Costume, Theatrical, &c., colored plates, 4to.

3242 FRENCH Theatrical Costume, numerous colored plates, royal 8vo. Par. n. d.

3243 FROISSART Illuminated Illustrations of, a series of fac-similes from the drawings of the Illuminated Copies in the British Museum, the Bibliothèque Royale at Paris, &c., 74 plates, printed in gold and colours. 2 vols. in one super-royal 8vo. hf. bd. *uncut.* Lond. 1844

3244 GALERIE Théatrale ou Collection des Portraits en Pied des principaux Acteurs des trois premiers Theatres de la Capital, 3 vols. 4to. 144 colored plates. *half morocco.* Par. n. d.

3245 GALLERIE des Artistes, Dramatiques Composée, de 80 Portraits et Notices, 2 vols. 4to. *half calf.* Par. n. d.

3246 GUERARD (*J.*) Annales de la Danse, et du Theatre, 8 fine colored plates, folio, *half morocco.* Paris, n. d.

3247 HOPE (*Thos.*) Costume of the Ancients, illustrated in upwards of 320 beautifully engraved plates, containing representations of Egyptian, Greek, and Roman Habits and Dresses, 2 vols. royal 8vo., new edition, with nearly 20 additional plates, bds. 1841

"The substance of many expensive works, containing all that may be necessary to give to artists and even to dramatic performers and others engaged in classical representations, an idea of ancient costumes, sufficiently ample to prevent their offending in their performances by gross and obvious blunders."

3248 HISTORIE des Modes Franscaises, ou revolutions du Costumes in France, *half calf*, 12mo. Amst. 1773

3249 ITALIAN Costume, a volume containing 24 original drawings, by M. D. Vito, beautifully colored, and a few prints, in all 35, folio. v. y.

3250 LAMBRANZI (*Greg.*) Deliciæ Theatrale Cinquenti Balle de diversi Nation, a series of 50 engraved plates of droll ballet figures, with music at the top of each plate, *half calf*, 4to. Norimb, 1716

3252 LANE (*R. J.*) Portraits of Charles Kemble in various Characters, folio, *half morocco.* 1840

3253 LAONICI, Histoire de la decadence de l'Empire Grec, et establissement de celuy des Turcs. trad. par V. Barbonnois, &c., plusieur descriptions des accoustremens tant des magistrats, et officiers de la Porte de l'Empereur des Turcs, *curious whole length portraits, in all* 100 *plates*, fol. Par. 1616

3254 LECOMTE, Costumes de Theatre de 1600 a 1820, 104 *colored plates*, 4to. Par.

3255 LECOMTE (*H.*) Costume de l'Europe, 90 *colored plates of the Peasantry of Russia, Sweden, France, &c.*, 4to. Par. 1819

3256 LENS (*André*), Le costume ou essai sur les habillements et les usages de plusieurs Peuples de l'Antiquité, prouvé par les Monuments, *numerous plates*, 4to. *half calf.* Liege, 1776

3257 LEWIS (*J. O.*) The Aboriginal Portfolio, *a series of portraits and memoirs of the N. A. Indians*, 9 parts, folio. Phil. 1833

3258 MARTIN (*Charles and Leopold*), Civil Costume of England, from the Conquest to the present period, a series of sixty-one plates (mostly portraits of royal and noble persons, drawn from Ancient Manuscripts, Tapestries, &c.), beautifully illuminated in gold and colors, royal 4to. *half calf.* Lond. 1842

This elegant work, executed by two sons of the celebrated painter, John Martin, Esq., is the only one which presents the authentic costumes of various ranks of society, from the Norman Conquest to the present day. It is especially valuable to artists.

3259 MASON (*G. H.*) Costume of China, 60 *colored plates*, fol. *half calf.* Lond. 1799

3260 MASQUE Saal, *upwards of* 200 *singular engravings in Opera, Comedy, and Masquerade*, fol. *half vellum.* Beyreuth, 1729

3261 MEYRICK'S (*Sir S. R.*) Painted Illustrations of Ancient Arms and Armour, a Critical Inquiry into Ancient Armour as it existed in Europe, but particularly in England, from the Norman Conquest to the Reign of Charles II., with a Glossary, &c., by Sir Samuel Rush Meyrick, LL.D., F.S.A., &c., new and greatly improved edition, corrected and enlarged throughout by the Author himself, with the assistance of Literary and Antiquarian Friends (Albert Way, &c.), 3 vols. impl. 4to., *illustrated by more than* 100 *plates, splendidly illuminated, mostly in gold and silver, exhibiting some of the finest specimens existing in England, also a new plate of the Tournament of Locks and Keys, neatly half bound, morocco.* 1844

Sir Walter Scott justly describes this collection as "the incomparable Armoury."

"This most superb Archæological work is animated with numerous novelties, curious and historical disquisitions, and brilliant and recondite learning. Learning going to Court in the full, rich costume of the Order of the Garter. Plates as fine as the monuments of Westminster Abbey. Really and truly the work is admirably executed, and deserves every eulogy."—*Edinburgh Review.*

3262 ——— Engraved Illustrations of Ancient Arms and Armour, a series of 154 very highly finished Etchings of the Collection at Goodrich Court, Herefordshire, engraved by Joseph Skelton, and accompanied by Historical and Critical Disquisitions by the possessor, Sir Samuel Rush Meyrick, LL.D., &c., in 2 vols. impl. 4to. *portrait, half bound, morocco, uncut, top edges gilt.* Oxford, 1830

"We should imagine that the possessors of Dr. Meyrick's former great work, would eagerly add Mr. Skelton's as a suitable illustration. In the first they have the History of Arms and Armour; in the second work beautiful engrávings of all the details.

"This work cannot fail to be highly acceptable and useful to the Antiquary, Historian, and Artist. The plates are executed in outline, with a truth and delicacy that cannot be too highly praised."—*Gent's Mag.*

3263 ——— Costume of the Original Inhabitants of the British Islands, and the Gothic Nations, 24 *beautifully colored plates*, fol. *half calf.* Lond. 1821

3264 MILITARY Costume of Turkey, 30 *colored plates*, folio. Lond. n. d.

3265 ——— Costume of Bengal; Line of March of a Bengal Regiment of Infantry, *panoramic sheet.*

3266 MONNIER (*H.*) Galerie Theatrale, 24 *colored plates*, oblong 4to. Par.

3267 MILLER (*Capt.*) The Mock Gladiatory Manly Art of Self-defence, designed and engraved by Scotin and Gravelot, 31 *fine figures of Miller and his pupils, very scarce*, fol. Lond. 1759

3268 MOORE, Lalla Roûkh, Divertissement mêlé du chants et de Danses executé au chateau de Berlin, Jan. 24, 1822, 23 *colored plates*, 4to. Berlin, 1822

3269 MORELLI (*Cosimo*), Pianta, e spaciato del nuovo Teatro d'Imola, &c., 20 *plates*, la fol. Roma, 1780

3270 MODERN Costume. Scrap-Book; Plates of, Lond. v. d.

3271 NICOLAI (*N.*) Costume of Turkey, *many wood-cuts, after Titian*, 4to. Antorff, 1577

3272 PANTHEON Charivarique, collection des Portraits-charges d'artistes, journalistes, auteurs dramatiques, musiciens, acteurs, &c., 90 *most amusing plates*, fol. *half calf.* Par. 1838

3273 PINELLI (*Bart.*) Nuova Racolta di Costumi Pittoreschi, 50 *plates, half calf*, oblong 4to. Rome, 1816

3274 ——— Twelve Etchings of Picturesque Costumes of Rome; Adventures of Mazzaroni, an Italian Bandit, in all 27 plates, folio. Roma

3275 PLANCHE (*J. R.*) History of British Costume, 12mo. *half calf.* Lond. 1834

3276 PYNE (*W. H.*) Costume of Great Britain, 60 *colored plates*, folio. Lond. 1808

3277 RACINE (*Jean*), Theatre de Orné de cinquante sept, estampas, after Prudhon, Gérard, Girodet, Chaudet, Serangeli, &c., *plates finely engraved, calf, extra*, folio. Paris, 1813

3278 REHBERG (*Frederick*), Lady Hamilton's Attitudes, taken from nature, 26 *outline plates of figures and drapery from ancient statues, &c.*, in 1 vol. 4to. *cloth.*

3279 REPTON on Female Head Dress, 1835; Observations on the Fashion of Hats, &c., 1831; Douce on Female Head Dress, 1796, *plates*, in 1 vol. *half calf*, 4to. Lond. v. y.

3280 SATCHWELL (*R.*) Scripture Costume, *plates, colored*, 4to. *half calf.* Lond. 1819

3281 SERE (*Ferd.*) Histoire du Costume, et de l'Ameublement en Europe, 120 parts, 4to. Paris, 1856

This splendid work, now in course of publication, is full of most beautiful engravings, highly colored and illuminated (after the antique), of Costumes, Furniture, Antiquities, Vertu, etc. etc.

3282 SCULPTURE, Specimen of the Works of the best Ancient and Modern Sculptors, 16 *plates.* Lond. n. d.

3283 SHAW'S Dresses and Decorations of the Middle Ages, from the VII. to the XVII. Centuries, with an Historical Introduction and Descriptive Text to every Illustration, 2 vols. impl. 8vo. *consisting of* 85 *copperplates,* 7 *elaborate woodcuts, a profusion of beautiful Initial Letters, and examples of curious and singular ornament, enriching nearly every page of this highly decorated work, the plates colored, half calf, extra.* 1843

"The illuminations consist of colored plates, copied with fidelity from pictures, colored glass, jewelled ornaments, pieces of ancient armor, weapons, domestic ornaments, costumes, reliquaries, mitres, sceptres, crowns, &c., ard form a perfect museum of the curiosities of the curious vestiges of 500 years. The letter-press, by the eminent antiquary, Mr. Thomas Wright, explains the history, the use, and the application of all these things, and whether as a book of reference for artists, of instruction for antiquaries, or of illustration for those who read history, is important and almost indispensable for a right understanding of the subject on which it treats."—*Times,* Jan. 29, 1844.

3284 SMITH (*C. H.*) Ancient Costume of Great Britain and Ireland, from the VII. to the XVI. Century, selected from rare specimens and accompanied with suitable descriptions, *illustrated by upwards of* 60 *brilliantly colored and illuminated portraits,* folio, *half crimson morocco, gilt.* 1848

This work abounds with full length figures dressed in sumptuous robes, heightened with gold and various brilliant colors, showing the various costumes of those periods.

The illustrations are all taken from acknowledged authorities, but are arranged with artistic and pictorial taste, divested of that hard stiff manner which renders so many works on costume so unattractive to all but the professional student.

3285 ——— (*J. T.*) Cries of London, portrait and 30 fine etchings of the most remarkable itinerant traders, of Ancient and Modern Times, *from rare engravings and from the life,* with Descriptions by J. B. Nichols, royal 4to. *cloth.* Lond. 1839

3286 SOLVYN'S (*of Calcutta*) Costumes of Indostan, 60 *colored plates,* folio.

3287 SPANISH Costume, Colecion de Trajes de España, 70 *colored plates,* 4to. Lond.

3288 STONE (*Mrs.*) Chronicles of Fashion, from the Time of Elizabeth, illustrative of Manners, Amusements, Banquets, Costume, &c., *numerous engravings,* 2 vols. 8vo. Lond. 1846

3289 STRUTT'S (*Joseph*) Dresses and Habits of the People of England, from the Establishment of the Saxons in Britain to the present time, with an Historical and Critical Inquiry into every branch of Costume; new and greatly improved edition, with Critical and Explanatory Notes by J. R. Planche, Esq., F. S. A., 2 vols. royal 4to. 153 *plates, half bound olive morocco, gilt top, uncut.* 1842

3290 —— Regal Costume; the Regal and Ecclesiastical Antiquities of England, containing the most Authentic Representations of all the English Monarchs from Edward the Confessor to Henry the Eighth, together with many of the Great Personages that were eminent under their several Reigns, taken from Coeval authorities preserved in the Public Libraries and Cathedrals of Great Britain, new and greatly improved edition, with Critical and Explanatory Notes, by J. R. Planché, royal 4to. *illustrated by* 72 *engravings, carefully copied from ancient Manuscripts, Monuments, &c., all splendidly illuminated, half bound olive morocco, top gilt, uncut.* 1842

3291 —— Sports and Pastimes of the People of England, edited with Index, &c., by W. Hone, 140 *curious cuts from ancient illuminations, large paper, the cuts colored,* impl. 8vo. 1845

3293 TERENTII Comœdiæ recens. Cocquelinus, 2 vols. *plates, half calf,* la. folio. Romæ, 1767

Not only valued as an excellent edition, but for its splendid plates of costume.

3294 FOURTEEN Colored Drawings of Theatrical Costume, 4to.

3295 VECÉLLIO (*Cœsare*), Habito Antichi et Monderni di tutti il Mondo, *about* 420 *wood-cuts drawn by Titian, old vellum,* 8vo. Venet. 1598

3296 YOSY'S Switzerland and its Costume, containing an Account of all the Nineteen Cantons, a Description of Geneva, Neufchatel, the Boundaries, Road over the Simplon, with much useful information for Travellers, interspersed with Historical Anecdotes, Local Customs, Traditions, Superstitions, &c., *and illustrated by* 50 *beautifully colored plates of Swiss Costume,* 2 vols. 8vo. *half calf.* Lond. 1815

HISTRIONIC ART, GESTURE, AND ACTION—ELOCUTION, ORATORY, RHETORIC, &c.

3297 ACTING, An Essay on the Science of, by a Veteran Stager, 12mo. *half calf.* Lond. 1828

3298 AUSTIN (*G.*) Chironomia, Treatise on Rhetorical Delivery, and Investigation of the Elements of Gesture, 4to. *plates, the most elaborate work on the subject, half calf.* Lond. 1806

3299 BELL (*Sir Chas.*) Essays on the Anatomy of Expression, *fine plates, large paper*, 4to. Lond. 1806

3299* BURGER'S Leonardo und Blandine, ein Melodram, 2 vols. small 4to. *with* 160 *remarkably clever etchings of Theatrical Scenes and Attitudes,* and descriptive letter-press by Von Groz, *half morocco.* Augsburgh, 1783

This is undoubtedly the most elaborate work ever attempted on theatrical representation, elocution, &c., as the plates represent every *attitude, gesture of the dialogue*, &c., which occurs through the whole play. *Scarce and curious.*

3300 BROWNSMITH (*J.*) Dramatic Timepiece, or Perpetual Monitor, being a calculation of the length of time every Act takes in the Performing, 18mo. *half calf.* Lond. 1767

3301 DE JORIO (*And.*) La Mimica degli Antichi Investigata nel Gestire Napoletano, royal 8vo. *half calf.* Napoli, 1832

3302 DHANNETAIRE (*M.*) Observations sur l'Art du Comedien, 8vo. *half calf.* Paris, 1775

From J. P. Kemble's library, with his arms on side.

3303 DWYER (*J. H.*) Essay on Elocution, 12mo. *half calf.* Albany, 1853

3304 ——— Another copy. 1844

3305 ENGEL (*M.*) Idées sur le Gest et l'Action Theatrale; Suivies d'une Lettre, du même Auteur, sur la Peinture Musicale. Le tout traduit de l'Allemand. Avec trente-quatre Planches, 2 vols. 8vo. *half calf.* Paris, 1788

3306 ESSAY on the Science of Acting, by a Veteran Stager, 12mo. *half calf.* Lond. 1828

3307 HEDELIN (*Abbott of Aubignac*), Whole Art of the Stage; Rules of Dramatic Art, &c., large 4to. *half calf.* Lond. 1684

"A work displaying considerable learning."—*Lowndes.*

3308 HOLMES (*John*), The Art of Rhetoric made Easy, 8vo *calf.* Lond. 1739

3309 How (*J. W. S.*) Practical Elocutionist, 12mo. Phil. 1857

3310 Mayhew (*Ed.*) Stage Effect, or the Principles which Command Dramatic Success in the Theatre, 18mo. *half calf.* Lond. 1840

3311 Murdoch (*J. E.*) and W. Russell, Orthophony, or Vocal Culture in Elocution, 12mo. *cloth.* Bost. 1845

3312 Remond, Le Comédien Ouvrage divise en deux partes, Sainte Albine (M. Remond), 8vo. *half calf.* Paris, 1825

3313 Rede (*L. T.*) Road to the Stage, or Instruction for Obtaining Theatrical Engagements, 18mo. *half calf.* Lond. 1835

3314 Siddons (*Henry*), Practical Illustrations of Rhetorical Gesture and Action adapted to the Drama, &c. by Henry Siddons, 70 *fine plates expressive of the Passions, and representing Theatrical Costume, cuts, &c., half calf.* Lond. 1822

3315 Vates, or the Philosophy of Madness, being an Account of the Life, Actions, Passions, and Principles of a Tragic Actor, *part* 1, *all published*, 7 *plates*, by T. Landseer, 4to. Lond. 1840

3316 Walker (*J.*) Rhetorical Grammar, 12mo. 1787

INDIA.

3317 Burton (*R. F.*) Goa and the Blue Mountains, 8vo. *cloth.* Lond. 1851

3318 Coleman (*Ch.*) Mythology of the Hindus, 4to. *cloth.* Lond. 1832

3319 Coutumes des Indiens Orientaux, Conformité de, par Mr. de la C****, 16mo. *calf.* Brux. 1704

3320 Earl (*G. W.*) Eastern Seas, or Voyages and Adventures in the Indian Archipelago in 1832, 1833, and 1834, 8vo. *cloth.* 1837

3321 Forrest (*Lieut. Col.*) Month's Ramble through part of the High Pyrenees, 8vo. *plates by J. D. Harding*, all pub. Lond. n. d.

3322 Hamilton (*F.*) Account of the Kingdom of Nepal, and of the Territories annexed to this Dominion by the House of Gorkha, *map and plates of the Himalaya Mountains*, &c., 4to. *half calf.* Edinb. 1819

3323 Hindostan, the Shores of the Red Sea and the Himalaya Mountains, *illustrated in a series of views*, with description by E. Roberts, 2 vols. 4to. *cloth, gilt.* Lond. n. d.

3324 INDIA and Canton, Elliot's Views in, with Historical and Descriptive illustrations, royal 8vo. Lond. 1838

3325 MILL'S History of British India, 6 vols. 8vo. *half calf.* 1826

"Mill's 'History of British India' is one of those rare works destined to immortality."—*Athenæam.*

3326 RAFFLES (*Sir Stamford*), History of Java, its Antiquities, Literature, Commerce, &c. 2 vols. 8vo. and 4to. *atlas of engravings by Daniell, cloth.* Lond. 1844

3327 ROBERTS (*Ed.*) Embassy to the Eastern Court, 8vo. *cloth.* N. Y. 1837

3328 THUGS, or Secret Murderers of India; illustrations of the History and Practices of the Thugs; and Notices of some of the Proceedings of the Government of India for the Suppression of the Crime of Thuggee, from the papers of Captain Sleeman, 2 vols. 12mo. *cloth.* Phil. 1839

3329 TAVERNIER (*J. B.*) Les Six Voyages de, 4to. *old calf, stained.* Paris, 1677

"Tavernier will always continue among the most valuable travellers in the East."—*Pinkerton.*

3330 URQUHART (*D.*) Spirit of the East, 2 vols. 12mo. Phil. 1839

3331 WATTS (*Talbot*), Japan and the Japanese, 8vo. N. Y. 1852

3332 WILSON (*H. H.*) History of British India, vol. 1, 8vo. *cloth.* Lond. 1845

IRELAND.

3333 AINSWORTH (*Wm.*) An Account of the Caves of Ballybunion, County Kerry, *plates*, 8vo. Dub. 1834

3334 ANCIENT Irish Histories of Spencer, Campian, Hanmer, and Marleborough, 2 vols. impl. 8vo. *half morocco, uncut, from Goff's Library.* n. d.

3335 BARRINGTON (*Sir Jonah*), Personal Sketches of his own Times, 12mo. *cloth.* N. Y. 1853

3336 NORBERRY (*Bob*), or Sketches from the Note-Book of an Irish Reporter, *curious plates*, 8vo. *cloth.* Dub. 1846

3337 CARLETON (*Wm.*) The Black Prophet, a Tale of Irish Famine, 12mo. *col. boards.* Lond. 1847

3338 CARLETON (*W. H.*) Neal Malone, and other Tales of Ireland, in 2 vols. 12mo. *half cloth.* Phil. 1839

3339 CARR (*J.*) Stranger in Ireland, 8vo. Phil. 1806

3340 CLONEY (*Thos.*) Personal Narrative of those Transactions in the County Wexford, in which the Author was Engaged during the awful Period of 1798, 8vo. *boards.* Dub. 1832

3341 CROMWELL (*Thos.*) The Druids, a Tragedy, with Notes on the Antiquities and Early History of Ireland, 8vo. *boards.* Lond. 1832

3342 DAVIS (*Sir John*), Discoverie of the true Causes why Ireland never was subdued nor brought under the obedience of the Crown of England until the beginning of his Majesties raigne, 18mo. *calf.* Lond. 1747

3343 HALL (*Mr. and Mrs. S. C.*) Ireland, its Scenery, Character, Legends, Tales, &c., with upwards of 500 beautiful engravings on steel and wood, by Creswick, Harvey, &c., 3 large vols. royal 8vo. *cloth.* n. d.

This very beautiful work forms a complete cyclopædia of Ireland, its topography and picturesque scenery, antiquities, political state, and amusing traits of the manner, customs, and superstitions of its peasantry.

3344 HALL (*Mrs. S. C.*) Lights and Shadows of Irish Life, 2 vols. 12mo. *half cloth.* Phil. 1838

3345 IRISH Hudibras, or The Fingallian Prince; taken from the Sixth Book of Virgil's Æneids, and adapted to the present times, *fine clean copy, scarce,* 8vo. *calf.* Lond. 1689

3346 KING (*Dr. William, Record-Keeper in Ireland*), Remains, containing miscellaneous pieces in Verse and Prose, *with the portrait by M. v. Gucht, scarce,* 8vo. *calf.* Lond. 1732

3347 O'FLANAGAN, The Blackwater in Munster, 4to. *cloth.* Lond. 1844

3348 O'REGAN (*Wm.*) Memoirs of the Life of J. P. Curran, 8vo. *boards.* Lond. 1817

3349 PICNICS, or Legends, Tales, and Stories of Ireland, in 2 vols. 12mo. *half cloth.* Phil. 1837

3350 SAMPSON (*William*), Memoirs of, with a Sketch of the History of Ireland, 8vo. *sheep.* Leesburg, Va. 1817

3351 VALLANCEY (*Ch.*) Vindication of the Ancient History of Ireland, 8vo. Dublin, 1786

3352 WALKER'S Historical Memoirs of the Irish Bards, and on the dress, armour, and weapons of the Ancient Irish, &c., *uncut, with all the plates,* 4to. *half morocco.* 1786

3353 WILLIAMS (*E.*) Political History of Ireland, 8vo. N. Y. 1843

ITALY, ROME, &c.—*See also* ANTIQUITIES.

3354 ADVENTURES of a French Serjeant during his Campaigns in Italy, Spain, &c., 12mo. *boards.* Phil. 1826

3355 BARBAULT, les Plus Monuments de Rome ancienne ou recueil des plus beaux morceaux de l'antiquité, Romaine, 128 *plates*, folio, *vellum.* Rome, 1761

3356 BARDI, Views in Venice, oblong 4to. *half morocco.* Firenze.

3357 BATTISTA NANI, History of the Affairs of Europe in this present age, but more particularly of the Republick of Venice, Englished by Sir R. Honeywood, folio, *half calf.* Lond. 1673

3358 BOISSARDI (*T. T.* et Aliorum), Romanæ Urbis Topographia et Antiquitates, 6 vols. in 3, *vellum, illustrated with elegant figures by Theod. de Bry*, folio. Francof. 1597–1602

This elegant work contains over 500 fine engravings of Tombs, Statues, and Topographical Antiquities.

3359 BROCKEDON'S Italy, Classical, Historical, and Picturesque, with Descriptions, 60 *highly finished engravings from drawings by Stanfield, Roberts, Prout, &c.*, impl. 4to. *morocco gilt.* 1847

3360 CORIO (*Bernardi*), L'Historia de Milano, 4to. *vellum.* Venezia, 1554

3361 CORLEONE et Veronese, Delle Magnificenze de Roma, Antica e Moderne, 10 vols. in 4, oblong, *half calf.* Rome, 1747

3362 ELLET (*Mrs. E. F.*) Scenes in the Life of Joanna of Sicily, 12mo. *cloth.* Boston, 1840

3363 FLORENCE—Views of all the celebrated buildings in Florence, *ninety-two plates, proofs, half morocco*, oblong 4to. n. d.

3364 GUICCIARDINI, History of the Wars of Italy, translated into English by G. Fenton, folio, *calf.* Lond. 1599

"This historian represents man in his darkest colors. Their drama is terrific. The actors are monsters of perfidy, of inhumanity, and inventors of crimes which seem to want a name. They were all princes of darkness, and that age seemed to afford a triumph to Manichism. The worst passions were called in by all parties."—*D'Israeli.*

3365 GALANTI (*Ma.*) Napoli e Contorni, *plates*, 8vo. *half calf.* Napoli, 1821

3366 HISTORY of the Triumvirates of Rome, translated by Thos. Otway, 8vo. *calf.* Lond. 1686

3367 Italy, France, and Switzerland, *illustrated*, 4to. *morocco*, Lond. n. d.

3368 Latium, A Description of, or La Campagna de Roma, 4to. *cl.* Lond. 1805

3369 Macerone (*Fr.*) Interesting Facts relating to the Fall and Death of Joachim Murat, King of Naples, 8vo. *boards.* Lond. 1817

3370 Napier's (*Capt.*) Florentine History, from the earliest Records, 6 vols. post 8vo. *cloth.* Moxon, 1846

A valuable historical work, and the best history of Florence in the English language.

3371 Schlosser, History of Rome, translated from the German, 8vo. *cloth.* Phil. 1837

3372 Select and Choyce Observations, containing all the *Romane* Emperors, by H. Leigh, portraits inserted, 12mo. *calf.* Lond. 1657

3373 Tyrol, Allom's Views in the, 8vo. *calf, gilt.* Lond. n. d.

3374 Töpffer Nouveau voyages en *Z*igzaj *numerous fine woodcuts*, royal 8vo. *half morocco.* 1854

2375 Vedute de Venezia, A Series of Large and Splendid Engravings, Views in Venice, representing Public Festivals, Solemnities, Pageants, Ceremonies, &c., on a large scale, with an infinity of figures, &c., bound in one volume, oblong folio, *half calf, rare,* v. y.

3376 Viaggiana; or Detached Remarks on the Buildings Pictures, Statues, Inscriptions, &c., of Ancient and Modern Rome, 12mo. *boards.* Lond n. d.

JEST BOOKS.

3377 American Joe Miller, with humorous illustrations, *half calf*, 24mo. Phil. 1839

3378 Aristophanes, being a classic collection of true Attic Wit; containing Jests, Gibes, Bon-Mots, &c., *port. of Foote, scarce*, 12mo. Lond. 1768

3379 Attic Salt-Cellar, or Funny Magazine, No. 1. 18mo. Phil. 1842

3380 Ben Johnson's Jests, or the Wit's Pocket Companion, 12mo. *half morocco, rare.* 1789

3381 Ben Johnson's Last Legacy to the Sons of Wit, Mirth, and Revelry, Complete Jests, Riddles, Epigrams, &c. *half calf, scarce,* 8vo. Lond. 1756

3382 Button-Maker's Jests, wants title, *half calf*, *scarce*, 12mo. Lond.

George III. was called the Button-Maker.

3383 Daniel Gunston's Jests, &c., 12mo. Lond. 1780

3384 Doctor Merry-Man, or Nothing but Mirth, being a posie of pleasant poems and witty Jests, *half calf*, *scarce*, 12mo. Bow Churchyard, n. d.

3385 Gallery of Literary Morceaux, containing innumerable Anecdotes and Jests, 18mo. 1835

3386 Gems of American Wit and Anecdotes, or the American Joe Miller, 32mo. *cloth.* Lond. 1839

3387 Gras et Maigre, ou nouveau Merdia-Pissa-Foirilleyala, veritable code et art des crieurs pisseux et foireux, 18mo. *sewed.* n. d.

3388 Henry the Great, Collection of some brave actions and memorable sayings of, written in French by the Bishop of Rodez, 12mo. Lond. 1688

3389 Irish Miscellany, or Teagueland Jests, being a compleat collection of the most profound puns, learned bulls, elaborate quibbles, &c., by natives of Teagueland, *third edition, with the portrait of Joe Miller as Teague in the Committee*, *very rare*, 12mo. *calf.* Lond. 1749

3390 Jocorum atque seriorum cum-novorum, tum selectorum atque memorabilium recens, *Othone et Melandris*, 3 vols. in 2, 18mo. *vellum.* Francof. 1626

3391 Joe Miller's Jests, or a collection of the most brilliant Jests, and the most pleasant short stories in the English language, with considerable additions, original Edit. by J. Motley, 12mo. *half calf.* Lond.

3392 ——— Complete Jest Book, 12mo. *cloth.* *Bohn*, Lond. 1835

3393 Meier's Merry Philosopher; or Thoughts on Jesting, 12mo. *calf.* Lond. 1764

Dr. Shaw, the celebrated traveller, warmly recommended the perusal of this book to persons of literature and taste, and such was his fear of losing it, that he sent over to Germany for duplicates of the original.

3394 Merry Fellow's Companion, or American Jest Book, containing a choice selection of Anecdotes, Bon-Mots, Jests, Repartees, Stories, &c., 12mo. *very rare.* Harrisburg, 1797

3395 Irish Diamonds, or Irish Wit and Blunders, by John Smith, *plates*, 12mo. 1847

3396 THEATRICAL Jester, or Green Room Witticisms, &c., *uncut, rare*, 12mo. Lond. *circa*, 1770

3397 TOM PAINE'S Jests, being an entirely new and select collection of Patriotic Bon-Mots, Repartees, &c., *never before printed*, 8vo. Phil. 1794

JURISPRUDENCE.

3398 BALDI de Ubaldus di Peruzzio, a learned Lawyer of the 14th Century, born in Perugia, died 1400, aged 76; a work on Jurisprudence, *gothic letter*, apud Johãi: de Colon et apud Nicholaum Jenson, large fol. Rome, MCCCCLXXXI.

3399 BLOUNT'S Law Dictionary, folio, *calf*. Lond. 1670

3400 BROWN (*D. P.*) The Forum, vol. 2, 8vo. *cloth*. Phil. 1856

3402 GROTII (*H.*) de Jure Belli ac Pacis, 8vo. *old calf*. Amst. 1670

"The first example of a philosophical statement of National Law."—*Tenneman*.

3403 INSTRUCTOR Clericalis; Directing Clerks in the King's Bench, &c., 8vo. *calf*. Lond. 1697

3404 KINNIE (*Asa*), The most important parts of Blackstone's Commentaries in Question and Answer, 8vo. *sheep*. N. Y. 1838

3406 ——— Questions and Answers in Law, alphabetically arranged, with references to the most approved authorities, 11 vols. 8vo. *sheep*. 1852

3406* ——— Law Glossary, 12mo. *cloth*. N. Y. 1853

3407 LAW and Lawyers, or Sketches and Illustrations of Legal History and Biography, 2 vols. post 8vo. *cloth*. Lond. 1840

3408 LIBER Intrationum Omnibus Legum Angliæ, folio, **Black Letter**. Lond., *Henry Smyth*, 1546

This most curious and rare book is one of the earliest Law Books of Great Britain.

3409 MAGNA Charta, cum Statutis tum Antiquis, tum recentibus maxim opere animo tenendis, eam noniter excusa et summa diligentia emendata et correcta, 18mo. *calf*, **black letter**. Lond. 1602

Although the title of this book is in Latin, many of the statutes are in French and English.

3410 MONTESQUIEU, Commentarie sur l'Esprit de Lois, par Tracy, 8vo. *calf*. Paris, n. d.

3411 O'Brien (*Ed.*) The Lawyer—his Character and Rule of Holy Life, after the manner of Herbert's Country Parson, 12mo. *cloth.* Lond. *Pickering,* 1843

3412 Peel's (*Sir Robert*) Acts, Alphabetically Arranged, 12mo. *boards.* Lond. 1830

3413 Precedents: A Booke of Presidents, exactly written in Manner of a Register, Newlie Corrected, with Addicions of Divers Necessarie Presidentes, etc. 18mo. *old calf,* black letter. Lond. 1583

3414 Story (*Joseph*), A Familiar Exposition of the Constitution of the United States, 12mo. *cloth.* Bost. 1840

3415 Taylor (*Alfred S.*) Elements of Med. Jurisprudence, 8vo. *cloth.* Lond. 1843

3416 Young Lawyers' Recreations, 12mo. *old calf.* Lond. 1694

LITERATURE.—*See also* Bibliography.

3417 Art of Criticism, or the Right Method of Making a Right Judgment upon Subjects of Wit and Learning, 8vo. *calf.* Lond. 1705

3417* Athenæum, a Journal of Literature, 44 Nos. 4to. v. d.

3418 Beloe (*W.*) The Sexagenarian, or Recollections of a Literary Life, 2 vols. 8vo. *half calf.* Lond. 1817

"This work contains many amusing anecdotes of the author's literary contemporaries; and the freedom of his strictures is remarkable." —*Allibone's Dict. of Authors.*

3419 Berington (*Rev. Joseph*), The Literary History of the Middle Ages, with *portrait,* 12mo. *cloth.* Lond. 1846

A work of great merit, comprising a pleasant succession of notices on the chief writers of the continent from the fall of the Roman Empire.

3420 Biographical Dictionary of the Living Authors of Great Britain and Ireland, comprising literary memoirs and anecdotes of their lives, and a chronological register of their publications, etc., including notices of some foreign writers, etc., 8vo. Lond. 1816

"As accurate a list of the works of the authors living in 1816, as could possibly be compiled."—*Lowndes.*

3421 Bowles (*Jas.*) Letters to Dr. Percy on Don Quixote, 4to. *half calf.* Lond. 1777

3422 Browne (*R. W.*) History of Classical Literature, 8vo. *cloth.* Phil. 1852

3423 BACON (*Francis*), The Two Bookes of, on the Proficience and Advancement of Learning, Divine and Humane, 1st edition, small 4to. *sheep*, *scarce*. Lond. 1605

3424 BUCHAN (*Earl of*), Essays on the Lives and Writings of Fletcher, of Saltoun, and Thomson, 8vo. *boards*. Lond. 1792

3425 BURNET (*George*), Specimens of English Prose Writers from the Earliest Times to the Close of the 17th Century, with sketches, biographical and literary, including an account of books as well as their authors, with occasional criticisms, &c., 3 vols. *half calf*, *scarce*. Lond. 1807

"We regard these volumes as worthy of no small commendation."
Monthly Review.

3426 CARDELL on Language, and Croke on Rhyming Latin, 2 vols. 1828

3427 CRAIK (*G. L.*) Sketches of the History of Literature and Learning in England, 2 vols. 12mo. Lond. 1844

3427* CRITICK, Modest, or Remarks upon the most Eminent Historians, by one of the Society of Port Royal, 16mo. *calf*. Lond. 1689

3428 CLARK (*Willis Gaylord*), The Literary Remains of the late, including the Ollapodiana Papers, *sheep*, 8vo. N. Y. 1855

3429 CURTIS (*G. T.*) Treatise on the Law of Copyright, 8vo. *sheep*. 1847

3430 D'ISRAELI (*I.*) Curiosities of Literature, royal 8vo. *cloth*. 1844

3431 ——— (*I.*) Curiosities of Literature, 2d series, 2 vols. 8vo. *cloth*. Lond. 1824

3432 ——— The Literary Character Illustrated, 2 vols. *half calf*. Lond. 1822

3433 DUNLAP (*John*), History of Roman Literature, from its earliest period to the Augustan age, 2 vols. in 1, 8vo. Phil. 1827

3434 DUYCKINCK (*E. A. & G. L.*) Cyclopædia of American Literature, embracing Personal and Critical Notices of Authors, and selections from their writings, from the earliest period to the present day, 225 *portraits*, 425 *autographs, and* 75 *views of colleges*, 2 vols. royal 8vo. *folded*. N. Y. 1855

3435 ECCENTRICITIES of Life and Literature, 3 vols. Bost.

3435* Edwards (*E.*) Memoirs of Libraries, including a Handbook of Library Economy, 2 vols. royal 8vo. Lond. 1859

This important work has been in preparation during upwards of thirteen years. Neither France nor Germany can boast of a work treating the subject with a similar comprehensiveness; and in England the work has certainly had no predecessor. The volumes contain the following illustrations: eight copper-plates of the manuscripts of Herculaneum; thirty-four wood-cuts of interiors and exteriors of celebrated libraries; eight plates of fac-similes of the types employed by early printers; seven chromo-lithographic plates of book-binding, St. Augustine's Monastery, Canterbury, and several plans of ancient libraries.

3436 Fifty Years' Recollections of an Old Bookseller, 8vo. *cloth.* Lond. 1837

3437 Gautruche (*P.*) L'Histoire Pöetique, 18mo. *calf.* Amst. 1712

3438 Gilfillan (*George*), Third Gallery of Portraits, *cloth*, post 8vo. N. Y. 1855

3439 Gilman (*S.*) Contributions to Literature, *cloth,* post 8vo. Boston, 1856

3440 Grant (*James*), Walks and Wanderings in the World of Literature, 2 vols. 12mo. *boards.* Phil. 1840

3441 Griswold (*R. W.*) Prose Writers of America, with a Survey of the Intellectual History, Condition, and Prospects of the Country, 8vo. *cloth.* Phil. 1851

This interesting work comprises upwards of 70 biographical notices of American writers, with selections from their writings.

3442 Hall (*Th.*) Vindiciæ Literarum, 18mo. *old calf.* Lond. 1655

The author was a Puritan Divine, highly commended by Calamy.

3443 Harleian Miscellany, Collection of Scarce, Curious, and Entertaining Pamphlets and Tracts, selected from the Library of Lord Oxford, with Historical, Political, and Critical Annotations, by Oldys, 12 vols. 8vo. (*the only octavo edition*), *half morocco, gilt.* Lond. 1808

"I hardly know of any one collection, or set of volumes, likely to be productive of more varied entertainment."—*Dibdin.*

3444 Haywarde (*R.*) Prismatics, *fine wood engravings,* 12mo. N. Y. 1854

3445 Hales (*Richard*), Remarks on the Arabian Nights, 8vo. *sheep.* Lond. 1797

3446 Homer, Enquiry into the Life and Writings of, 8vo. *calf.* Lond. 1735

3447 IRELAND (*W. H.*) Scribbleomania, or the Printer's Devil's Polichronicon, a Sublime Poem, by Anser Pen-Drag-On, Esq., "Cacoethes scribendi," 8vo. *boards.* Lond. 1815

The witty writer in his apology for a preface says: "Sampson slew his thousands with the jaw bone of an ass; then wherefore should not I perform similar exploits with the quill of a goose?"

3448 KAMES (*Lord*), Elements of Criticism Abridged, by John Frost, 12mo. *sheep.* Phil. 1833

3449 LANDOR (*Walter Savage*), Imaginary Conversations of Literary Men and Statesmen, 3 vols. *cloth,* 8vo. Lond. 1826

3449* ——— 2d Series, 2 vols. *cloth,* 8vo. Lond. 1829

3450 MADDEN (*R. R.*) The Infirmities of Genius, 2 vols. 12mo. *boards.* Phil. 1833

3451 MENZEL'S History of German Literature, translated with Notes by T. Gordon, 3 vols. 12mo. *cloth.* Bost. 1840

"There is no higher name in the living literature of his country than Menzel; his History of German Literature is eloquent and popular at the same time."—*Blackwood's Mag.*

3452 MIRROR of Literature, Amusement, and Instruction, *with innumerable engravings,* from its Commencement in 1823 to December, 1839, *plates,* 17 vols. 8vo. *half calf.* Lond. v. y.

"The Mirror, with its choice engravings and inexhaustible varieties, is the most entertaining publication of the day."—*Atlas.*

"A storehouse of curious antiquarian knowledge. It has gone on improving from year to year.—*Penny Magazine.*

3453 MORGAN (*J.*) Phœnix Britannicus, 1 vol. 4to. *calf.* 1732

3454 MORRISON (*R.*) Horæ Sinicæ, translations from the popular Literature of the Chinese. Lond. 1812

3456 NEELE (*H.*) Literary Remains, consisting of Lectures on English Poetry, Tales, &c., 8vo. *sheep.* N. Y. 1829

3457 POOLE, Index to Periodical Literature, 2d and greatly enlarged edition, 8vo. *cloth.* N. Y. 1853

This most valuable book is now out of print. Its utility is inestimable.

3458 PRINCE (*J. H., Bookseller*) Life, Adventures, Pedestrian Excursions, and Singular Opinions of, *with portraits,* 12mo. *calf.* Lond. 1807

3459 OXBERRY (*William*), Comedian, The Flowers of Literature, a Collection in History, Biography, Poetry, and Romance, *fine portrait of Kean,* 4 vols. *half calf,* 12mo. Lond. 1822

3460 Letters from an English Traveller in Spain, in 1788, on the Origin and Progress of Poetry in that Kingdom, *portraits of the Poets,* 8vo. *boards.* Lond. 1781

3461 Maskell (*Rev. W.*) History of the Martin Marprelale Controversy, in the Reign of Queen Elizabeth, *portrait,* 8vo. *cloth.* Lond., *Pickering,* 1845

3462 Massey (*W.*) Origin and Progress of Letters, 8vo. *half calf.* Lond. 1768

3463 Mathias, Pursuits of Literature, a Satirical Poem, 4to. *half calf.* Lond. 1812

3464 ——— Another edition, *boards,* 8vo. Lond. 1801

3465 Memoirs of Literature, containing a large account of many valuable Books; also New Memoirs of Literature, Containing a large account of new Books (by Michael de la Roche), together, 14 vols. 8vo. *calf.* Lond. 1722–5

3467 Notes and Queries, 38 Nos. 4to. v. d.

3468 Philadelphia Book, or Specimens of Metropolitan Literature, 8vo. *full morocco, gilt edges.* Phil. 1836

3469 Reliquiæ Antiquæ, Scraps from ancient MSS., illustrating chiefly Early English Literature and the English Language, edited by Wright and Halliwell, *scarce, boards,* 8vo. Lond. 1839–1845

3470 Respublica Literaria, or the Republic of Letters, being a Vision, 12mo. *calf.* Lond. 1727

3471 Revue Literaire Française, several odd vols.

3472 Roberts (*W.*) History of Letter Writing, from the earliest period, 8vo. *cloth.* *Pickering,* 1843

"Mr. Roberts deserves credit for the diligence with which he has sought out original documents, many of which throw important light on this interesting portion of our history."—*Athenæum.*

3473 Soane (*G.*) New Curiosities of Literature and Book of the Months, *with several beautiful engravings after the great masters,* 2 vols. *cloth.* Lond. 1849

This is a work of popular information and amusement, containing a full and authentic record of the National Customs, Superstitions, Sports, &c., traced up to their earliest origins.

3474 Saunders, Salad for the Solitary, *woodcuts,* 8vo. N. Y. 1856

3475 ——— Salad for the Social, *woodcuts,* 8vo. N. Y. 1856

3476 Spence (*Joseph*), Anecdotes, Observations, and Characters of Books and Men, collected from the Conversation of Mr. Pope, with Notes by Singer, 8vo. Lond. 1820

"One of the most entertaining volumes of literary anecdote imaginable, which furnished Johnson with much of his biography of Pope and his contemporaries."—*Dibdin.*

3477 SMITH (*C. J.*) Historical and Literary Curiosities, consisting of Fac-similes of interesting Autographs, Scenes of remarkable Historical Events and interesting Localities, *engravings of Old Houses, Illuminated and Missal Ornaments, Antiques, &c.* 100 *plates, some illuminated*, thick 4to. *half morocco, Roxburgh style.* Lond. 1840

This is a very curious and interesting volume, including many objects not elsewhere represented. The plates are executed in a most artistic style.

3478 SAINT-PELAIE; Literary History of the Troubadours of the 12th and 13th centuries, 8vo. Lond. 1779

3479 STILLINGFLEET (Benjamin), Literary Life and Select Articles, plates, 3 vols. *calf*, 8vo. *half calf.* Lond. 1811

The Author was a distinguished Botanist.

3480 SYDNEY (Sir P.) Defence of Poetry, and Observation on Poetry and Eloquence, from the Discoveries of Ben Jonson, 8vo. *boards.* Lond. 1787

3481 TAYLOR (*W. of Norwich*), Historic Survey of German Poetry, interspersed with various translations, 3 vols. 8vo. *cloth.* Lond. 1830

3482 TIMPERLY, Encyclopedia of Literary and Typographical Anecdotes, *cloth*, royal 8vo. Lond. 1842

This comprehensive and truly valuable compilation—the labor of a practical printer—contains a vast fund of useful and curious matter, collected from every available source, and classed in such a manner, as to give an interesting account of the history of Printing, Anecdotes of Books, and Booksellers, notices of early Bibles, &c.

3483 TEGG (*Thos.*) Remarks on Talfourd's Speech on Copyright, pp. 23, 8vo. Lond. 1837

3484 TOWNLEY (*James*), Introduction to the Literary History of the Bible, 12mo. *boards.* Lond. 1828

3485 WRIGHT (*Thos.*) Essays on Subjects connected with the Literature, Popular Superstitions and History of England, in the Middle Ages, 2 vols. post 8vo. *cloth.* Lond. 1846

3486 WILLIS's Monthly Price-Current of Books, 84 Nos. 4to. v. d.

MAGAZINES, NEWSPAPERS, PERIODICALS, REVIEWS ANNUALS, &c.

3487 AINSWORTH (*W. H.*) Magazine, from 1842 to 1844, 6 vols. 8vo. *cloth.* Lond. v. y.

3488 AMERICAN Review, a Whig Journal of Politics and Literature, 1845, 2 vols. 8vo. N. Y. v. y.

3489 AMERICAN Whig Review, 12 Nos.

3490 ANNUAL Scrap Book, 12mo. *cloth.* Lond. 1838

3491 ATLANTIC Souvenir, 18mo. *calf.* Phil. 1826

3492 BEE (*The*), or Literary Weekly Intelligencer, 1791 to 1813, edited by J. Anderson, 18 parts, 8vo. *half calf.* Edinb. 1791, &c.

3493 BENTLEY'S Miscellany, 1838 to 1842, 10 vols. 8vo. Lond. v. y.

3494 ——— Idem, 45 Nos. odd, 8vo.

3495 BLACKWOOD'S Edinburgh Magazine, 15 volumes, 8vo. *sheep.* N. Y. 1833–1842

3496 ——— Edinburgh Magazine, 150 Nos. 8vo. N. Y. v. d.

3497 BRITISH Almanac and Companion, 1829–53, and Index to the same, 26 vols. 12mo. *cloth.* Lond. v. d.

3498 BURTON (*W. E.*) Gentleman's Magazine, or American Monthly Review, 7 vols. 8vo. *cloth.* Phil. 1837–40

3498* Ditto 3 vols. 2 *calf,* 1 *half calf.*

3499 ——— Gentleman's Magazine, 370 odd Nos. *sd.* 8vo. N. Y.

3500 CHRISTIAN Keepsake, 1838, '9 '40, 3 vols. *morocco, binding loose, plates.*

3501 DICKENS (*Charles*), Household Words, 27 Nos. 8vo. *sd.* Lond.

3502 EDINBURGH Review, from 1802 to 1840, 71 vols. 8vo. *cloth,* from 1841 to 1850 in 21 Nos. Lond. v. y.

3503 ——— Review, 40 Nos. odd. N. Y. v. d.

3504 ——— Review, Selections from, edited by Cross, 6 vols. 8vo. Lond. 1835

3505 ——— Review, Selections from, 5 Nos. odd, 8vo. Lond. 1835

3506 FOREIGN Quarterly Review, 1827 to 1846, 37 vols. 8vo. *half calf.* Lond. v. y.

3507 ——— Monthly Review, 20 Nos. Phil. n. d.

3508 FRIENDSHIP'S Offering, 18mo. *bds. plates.* Lond. 1826

3509 ——— Offering, 1827–36, 12mo. *bds.* 12 vols. *fine plates.* Lond. v. d.

3510 GENTLEMAN'S Magazine, 9 vols. 8vo. v. d.

3511 ——— SELECTION of Curious Articles from the Gentleman's Magazine (*Historical, Classical, Biographical, Critical,* &c.), edited by J. Walker, 4 vols. 8vo. *half vellum.* Lond. 1809

The plan of this work was suggested by the historian Gibbon, who says that "The Gentleman's Magazine contains a great number of literary, historical, and miscellaneous articles of real value, which might be revived to great advantage if properly chosen and classed."

3512 GENTLEMAN'S Magazine, edited by W. E. Burton, from July 1837 to July 1840, 6 vols. 8vo. *calf and half calf.* Phil. v. y.

3513 GILMAN (*C.*) Lady's Annual Register, 12mo. *cloth.* Bost. v. y.

3514 GODEY (*L. A.*) Lady's Book, vols. 2, 9, 10, 12, and 14, royal 8vo. *calf.* v. d.

3515 ——— Lady's Book, 100 odd Nos. Phil. v. d.

3516 GRAHAM'S Magazine, 6 parts, 8vo.

3517 HARPER'S New Monthly Magazine, from 1852 to 1855, from vol. 6 to vol. 11th, 6 vols. royal 8vo. N. Y. v. y.

3518 HARPER'S New Monthly Magazine, 70 odd Nos. from 1851–9, 8vo. N. Y. v. d.

3519 HEATH'S Book of Beauty for 1833–34–35, 3 vols. 8vo. *half morocco.* Lond.

3520 HUNT (*Leigh*), Journal, 150 parts, 8vo. N. Y. v. d.

3521 ——— The Indicator, 2 vols., and 5 others, 7 vols., cl. N. Y.

3522 ILLUSTRATED London News, a large parcel of, about 300 Nos.

3523 INTERNATIONAL Magazine, 25 Nos., 8vo. N. Y. v. d.

3524 JERROLD (*Douglas*), Illuminated Magazine, Vol. 1, May to October, *half calf*, 4to. Lond. 1843

3525 KIRKLAND (*Mrs.*) Union Magazine, Vols. 1, 2, and 3 in 1 vol. 1847

3526 KNICKERBOCKER Magazine, 5 vols. 8vo. v. d.

3527 KNICKERBOCKER Magazine, 37 Nos., various. v. d.

3528 LADIES' Companion, vol. 18, royal 8vo. *half calf.* 1843

3529 LADIES' Monthly Museum, or Polite Repository of Amusement and Instruction, 130 Nos., 8vo.

3530 LESLIE (*Miss*), The Gift, a Christmas and New Year's Present for 1839, 40, 45, and 48, 12mo. *roan.* Phil. v. d.

3531 LITERARY Museum, or a selection of scarce old Tracts, 8vo. *sheep.* Lond. 1792

3532 MCJILTON & Arthur's Baltimore Literary Monument, 8 Nos. Balt. v. d.

3533 MAGAZINES, various, 8vo. *half calf.* 1813

3534 MAGAZINES, various, 3 lots.

3535 MUSEUM of Nature and Art, 4 vols.

3536 NEW Monthly Magazine, 1831, 36, 39 and 40, 5 odd vols. *half calf.*

3537 NEW York Mirror, Lot of Nos. of.

3538 NEW Sporting Magazine, 12 vols. 8vo. *half calf, gilt.* 1831–37

3539 NEW York Review, 20 parts. N. Y. v. d.

3540 REPUBLIC of Letters, in 50 odd Nos. v. d.

3541 NORTH American Review, 1820 to 1832, and various Nos., in all 35 vols. 8vo. *half bound.* Boston, v. y.

3542 ——— British Review, various Nos. odd, 8vo. N. Y. v. d.

3543 ODD Fellow's Offering for 1850–51–52, *highly finished engravings,* 12mo. *half morocco, extra gilt.* N. Y.

3544 OLIO (*The*), or Museum of Entertainment, 2 vols. 8vo. *cloth.* Lond. n. d.

3545 ——— (*The*), vol. 10, 8vo. *half morocco.* 1833

3546 PARTERRE (*The*), 3 vols. 8vo. n. d.

3547 PENNY Magazine, for 1833, 4, 5, 7, 8, and 9, 6 vols. royal 8vo. *half calf.* v. d.

3548 PHILADELPHIA Saturday News, folio, *half calf.* 1836

3549 POLITICAL Magazine, 2 vols. 8vo. Lond. 1781–2

3550 PORTFOLIO and Companion to the Select Circulating Library from January to June, 1835, January to June, 1836, 2 vols. Select Library or Companion to the Portfolio, 1835 to 1837, 5 vols., in all 7 vols. *half morocco, uniform,* 4to. Phil.

3551 PUTNAM'S Monthly, 38 odd Nos. from 1853–57, *illustrated, sd.* 8vo.

3552 QUARTERLY Review, 1809 to 1834, 51 vols, 8vo. *half morocco, not uniform.* N. Y. v. d.

3553 ——— 50 parts odd, 8vo. N. Y. v. d.

3554 RETROSPECTIVE Review (consisting of Criticisms upon, Analyses of, and Extracts from Curious, Useful and Valuable Books), 16 vols. 8vo. complete, *half calf, scarce.* 1820–28

An excellent review of early, rare, and curious literature, by Sir Harris Nicholas, Southerne, Judge Talfourd, &c.

"To this work is mainly owing the increased interest shown in the study of Old English Literature, which forms so remarkable a characteristic of the intellectual taste of the present era. The sixteen volumes contain reviews and analyses, with copious extracts of several hundred rare and curious old books, including a very extensive series of the early English poets."

3555 ——— Review (New), consisting of Criticisms upon, Analyses of, and Extracts from curious, useful and valuable Old Books, 6 parts, 8vo. 1853–54

An admirable accompaniment and continuation of the old series, in 16 vols.; the articles are of the same length and character.

3556 ROYAL Magazine or Quarterly Bee, 8vo. *boards.* Lond. 1750

3557 SARTAIN'S Magazine, for 1849, 50, 51, 52, 4 vols. *plates*, royal 8vo. Phil. v. y.
3558 SHARPE'S London Magazine, a Parcel.
3559 TOKEN and Atlantic Souvenir, 8vo. Bost. 1838
3560 TOKEN and Souvenir, 3 vols. 12mo. v. d.
3561 TOWN and Country Magazine, vols. 14 and 16, 8vo. *half calf.* 1782-4
3562 UNITED States Democratic Review, 15 Nos. N. Y. v. d.
3563 WEEKLY Amusement (*The*), 8vo. *half calf.* 1764
3564 WESTMINSTER Review, various Nos. 8vo. N. Y. v. d.
3565 WHITLAW (*A.*) Republic of Letters, a Selection in Poetry and Prose, 4 vols. 12mo. *cloth, imperfect.* Glas. 1835
3566 WORLD (*The*), for 1753—1755, 2 vols. impl. 8vo. *uncut.*

MAN, MENTAL PHILOSOPHY, &c.

3567 ALLEN (*Col. Ethan*), Reason the only Oracle of Man, 12mo. *cloth, soiled.* N. Y. 1836
3568 ANALOGIES of Organized Beings, 8vo. *cloth.* Lond. 1831
3569 ANCIENT Fragments from the Chinese, Persian, &c. 12mo. *boards.* N. Y. 1835
3570 B. (*W.*) Philosopher's Banquet, newly furnished and decked forth, 18mo. *calf.* Lond. 1633
3571 BACHE (*Alex. Dallas*), Report on Education in Europe, 8vo. *cloth.* Phil. 1839
3572 BARLOW (*John*), Connection between Physiology and Intellectual Philosophy, 12mo. *cloth.* Lond. *Pickering*, 1842
3573 BARTLETT (*J.*) Aphorisms on Man, Manners, Principles, and Things, 18mo. *sheep.* Portsmouth, 1810
3574 BEATTIE (*Jas.*) Essay on Truth, 12mo. *cloth, gilt.* Lond.
3575 BLAKEY (*Robt.*) An Essay on Moral Good and Evil, 8vo. *boards.* Lond. 1831
3576 BLAKEY (*R.*) History of Moral Science, 2 vols. 8vo. *boards.* Edin. 1836
3577 BOISSARDI (*J. I.*) Theatrum Vitæ Humanæ, *illustrated with curious plates, and portrait of Boissard*, 4to. n. d.
3578 BRAITHWAIT (*Rd.*) Essays upon the Five Senses, 4to. *boards.* Lond. *reprint*, 1815
3578*BURTON (*Asa*), Essays on some of the first Principles of Metaphysicks, Ethicks, and Theology, *sheep*, 8vo. Portland, 1824

3579 BURTON (*Robert*), The Anatomy of Melancholy, last edition, with the original symbolical frontispiece, the quotations translated, author's life, &c., 8vo. *cloth.* Lond. 1830

3580 BURTON, Anatomy, &c., abridged, 8vo. *calf.* Lond. 1801

" 'Tis a book so full of variety of reading, that gentlemen who have lost their time and put to a push for invention may furnish themselves with matter for common or scholastical discourse and writing."—*Anthony à Wood.*

3581 CAMPBELL (*John*), Negro-Mania, being an Examination of the various Races of Men, 12mo. *cloth.* Phil. 1851

3582 CAPACITY and Extent of the Human Understanding, exemplified in the extraordinary case of Automathes, a young Nobleman who was accidentally left, in his infancy, upon a desolate Island, and continued nineteen years separate from all human society, 12mo. *sheep.* Lond. 1747

*** This book is mentioned by Gibbon, and noticed in Retro. Review.—*W. E. B.*

3583 CARDELL (*Wm. S.*) Essay on Language as connected with the Faculties of the Mind, and as applied to things in Nature and Art, sm. 8vo. N. Y. 1825

3585 CLIFFORD (*Martin*), An Apology for the Discourse of Humane Reason, 12mo. *calf.* Lond. 1670

3586 CLULOW (*William B.*) Aphorisms and Reflections, *cloth*, 8vo. Lond. 1843

3587 COMBE (*Geo.*) On Man, Foster on Decision of Character, and three other Works, 8vo. *cloth.* N. Y. 1835

3588 COMBE (*George*), Lectures on Moral Philosophy, *cloth*, 8vo. Boston, 1840

3589 COOPER (*Miss*) Rhyme and Reason of Country Life, 8vo. *cloth.* N. Y. 1854

3590 CORY (*J. P.*) Metaphysical Inquiry into the Method, Objects, and Result of Ancient and Modern Philosophy, 12mo. *cloth.* 1833

3591 DELEUZE (*J. P. F.*) Animal Magnetism, 12mo. Prov. 1837

3592 DODSLEY (*Robt.*) Economy of Human Life, illustrated by Harding, 12mo. *boards*, and Dean's Phil. of Life, 2 vols. Lond. 1806

3593 EDMONDS and Dexter on Spiritualism, 8vo. *cloth.* N. Y. 1853

3594 FORNEY (*Mr.*) History of Philosophy, 12mo. Glas. 1767

3595 GERARD (*Prof.*) Essay on Taste, and Dissertations on do. by Voltaire, D'Alembert, and Montesquieu, 8vo. *calf.* 1759

3596 HAI Ebn Yokdhan, The Improvement of Human Reason, exhibited in the Life of, how by meer light of nature to attain to the knowledge of God, translated from the Arabic, by S. Ockley, 8vo. *plates, calf, rare.* Lond. 1708

3597 HELVETIUS, Œuvres complettes, 5 vols. *calf*, 12mo. Lond. 1780

3598 HISTORY of Man, or the Wonders of Human Nature in relation to the Vices and Defects of the Sexes, 2 vols. in 1, 8vo. *half calf.* Edin. 1770

3599 HUTON (*Ph.*) Manual of the Physiology of Man, 12mo. *sheep.* Phil. 1828

3600 HUME (*David*), Treatise on Human Nature, 3 vols. 8vo. *calf.* Lond. 1739

3601 INSANE (*The*) World, 8vo. *boards.* Lond. 1818

3602 JONES (*Silas*), Practical Phrenology, 12mo. *cloth.* Bost. 1836

3603 LEMBERG (*Kritz*), Posthumous Works of, or the Wonders of Magnetism, 8vo. *boards.* Bost. 1843

3604 LOCKE (*John*), Philosophical Works of, with a Preliminary Essay and Notes, by J. A. St. John, 2 vols. *half calf, portrait.* Lond. 1854

3605 MACMAHON (*T. O'Brien*), An Essay on the Depravity of Human Nature against Hume and others, 16mo. Lond. 1774

3606 MAGNETISM in its Higher Relations to Humanity, 8vo. *cloth.* Lond. 1846

3607 MANDEVILLE (*Bernard*), World Unmasked, or the Philosopher the Greatest Cheat, to which is added the State of Souls Separated from their Bodies, translated from the French, 8vo. *calf.* Lond. 1736

3608 MORISON (*Alex.*) Outlines of Mental Diseases, *plates*, 8vo. *boards.* Lond. 1829

3609 MUSEUM (*The*), or Man as he is, *boards*, 12mo. Lond. 1814

3610 NEWNHAM (*W.*) Human Magnetism, 12mo. *cloth.* N. Y. 1845

3611 NORRIS (*John*), An Essay towards a Theory of the Ideal or Intelligible World, 2 vols. *calf*, 8vo. Lond. 1701

The chief of the English Platonic philosophers.

3612 PHILOSOPHY, Vite de Philosophis Moralissime, et delle loro elegantissime sententie (*Sine Loco*). (1551)

3613 PICKERINGS, History of the Races of Man, edited by Hall, *cloth*, post 8vo. Lond. 1851

3614 ROGERS (*T.*) The Anatomie of the Minde, a Philosophicall Discourse, newlie made and set forth by T. R. *very rare, from the library of Richard Farmer, with his autograph.* **Black Letter,** 8vo. *half calf.* Lond., *A. Maunsell,* 1576

*** Following the Preface is a poem of "Iosua Hutten to the Booke," after which is "Abraham Fowler's needeles Haedera," a curious poem, which concludes with the following lines :—

"The wyse that reade these fruitfull lines,
Where luckie blisse doth lurke,
Wyll wishe with mee, God guide his head,
That framde so fay're a worke."

3615 SARRAZIN (*Gen.*) The Philosopher, or Historical and Critical Notes, *fine portraits*, 2 vols. 8vo. *boards.* Lond. 1812

3616 SAVEREIN (*M.*) Histoire des Philosophes Modernes, 4 vols. in 2, small folio, *calf.* Paris, 1761

3617 SENAULT (*J. F.*) Use of the Passions, put into English, by Henry, Earl of Monmouth, *portrait by Marshal*, 8vo. Lond. 1671

3618 SPURZHEIM (*J. G.*) On Insanity, by Dr. Brigham, 8vo. *cloth.* Bost. 1835

3619 STONE (*W. D.*) Letter to Brigham on Animal Magnetism, 8vo. N. Y. 1837

3620 STRENGTH and Weakness of Human Reason, 12mo. *calf.* Lond. 1737

3621 STRODE (*Sir Geo.*) The Anatomy of Mortalitie, small 4to. *calf.* Lond. 1632

3622 TOWNSHEND (*Rev. C. Hare*), Facts in Mesmerism, 8vo. *cloth.* Lond. 1844

3623 TRACTS on Magnetism, 10 *pamphlets.*

3624 TRANSMIGRATION, an Essay of, in Defence of Pythagoras, *fine portrait*, 12mo. *old calf.* Lond. 1692

3625 WATTS (*Dr. Isaac*), Logic, or the Right Use of, 8vo. *old calf.* Lond. 1745

3626 ——— (*Rev. Joshua*), Remarkable Events in the History of Man, 8vo. *boards.* Lond. 1825

3627 WILKINS (*Bp.*) Mathematical and Philosophical Works, 2 vols. 8vo. *sheep.* Lond. 1802

3628 ——— Mercury, or the Secret and Swift Messenger, showing how a man may, with privacy and speed, communicate his thoughts to a Friend at any distance, *with portrait*, 12mo. *calf.* Lond. 1694

3629 ZIMMERMAN on Solitude, 12mo. *embossed, sheep.* N. Y. 1840

3630 ——— Another edition, 8vo. Lond. 1804

MUSIC.

3631 ANTHEMS, a collection of, by Composers of the Madrigalean Era, edited by Rimbault, 4to. Lond. n. d.

3632 BEETHOVEN, Life of, including his Correspondence and Remarks on his Musical Works, edited by J. Moscheles, 2 vols. 8vo. *cloth.* Lond. 1841

3633 BENNET (*J.*) Madrigals for Four Voices, edited by E. J. Hopkins, 4to. Lond. n. d.

3634 BLOW (*Dr. John*), Amphion Anglicus, containing compositions for one, two, three, and four Voices, with Accompaniments of Instrumental Music, &c., folio, *fine portrait, calf.* Lond. 1700

"So, whilst Apollo's race can sing,
Great Blow will be true Musick's King;
While silver Thames does ebb and flow,
Drink, drink a health to famous Blow."
Tom Durfey.

3635 BRITISH Musical Miscellany, or Delightful Grove, celebrated English and Scotch Songs, by the best Masters, small 4to. 6 vols. in 3, *half calf.* Lond.

3635* BURNEY (*Chas.*) General History of Music, from the Earliest Ages to the Present Period, 4 vols. 4to. *half calf, fine plates by Bartolozzi and others, from designs by Cipriani.* Lond. 1777

Sir William Jones says: "Dr. Burney gave dignity to the character of the modern musician, by joining it with that of the scholar and philosopher."

3636 BUSBY (*Thos.*) Concert Room and Orchestra Anecdotes of Music and Musicians, 3 vols. small 8vo. *with* 16 *plates, scarce, half calf.* 1825

3637 ——— (*Dr.*) General History of Music, from the Earliest Times, with the Lives of Eminent Composers and Musical Writers, Specimens, &c., 2 vols. 8vo. *half calf, gilt.* Lond. 1819

Condensed from the works of Sir John Hawkins and Charles Burney.

3638 BURNEY (*Dr.*) Account of the Musical Performances in Westminster Abbey and Pantheon, in Commemoration of Handel, *plates by Bartolozzi,* 4to. *half calf* 1785

3639 Byrd (*Wm.*) Book 1 of Cantiones Sacræ, edited by Wm. Horsley, 4to. Lond. n. d.

3640 ——— A Mass for Five Voices, edited by Rimbault, 4to. Lond. n. d.

3641 Callcott (*Dr.*) A Musical Grammar in four parts, 12mo. *half calf.* Lond. 1817

3642 Catel, Treatise on Harmony, 12mo. Bost. 1832

3643 Cherron et Fayolle, Dictionnaire Historique des Musiciens, 3 vols. 8vo. *half calf.* Paris, 1817

3644 Clio and Euterpe, or British Harmony, collection of celebrated Songs and Cantatas, *curiously engraven and embellished with designs to each Song*, 2 vols. royal 8vo. 400 *curious plates, showing the dresses, manners, &c. of the time, calf, rare.* Lond. 1762

3645 Collier (*Joel*), [i. e. John Bicknell], Musical Travels through England, 1774; Joel Collier, Redivivus, 1818, 2 vols. in 1, 12mo. *half calf.* v. d.

"The Musical Travels of Joel Collier, in which a slight attempt is made to ridicule Johnson, was ascribed to Soame Jenyns, but was written by Mr. Bicknell."—*Croker's Boswell's Johnson.*

"The object of this jeu d' esprit was to ridicule Dr. Burney. * * The family of Mr. Bicknell endeavoured to buy up all the copies."—*Dr. Fletcher.*

3646 Cornwall (*N. E.*) Music, as it was, and as it is, 12mo. *cloth.* N. Y. 1851

3647 Dictionary of Musicians, from the Earliest Ages, together with upwards of a Hundred Original Memoirs of Living Musicians; History of Music, &c. 2 vols. 8vo. *calf.* 1824

This work comprises the most important Biographical contents of the works of Gerber, Choron, Count Orloff, Dr. Burney, Sir John Hawkins, &c.

3648 Dowland (*J.*) First Book of Songs or Ayres, of Four Parts, edited by W. Chappell, 4to. Lond. n. d.

3649 Eastcott (*Rev. R.*) Sketches of the Origin, Progress, and Effects of Music, with an Account of the Ancient Bards and Minstrels, 8vo. *half calf.* Bath, 1793

3650 Ellet (*Mrs. E. F.*) Nouvellettes of the Musicians, *portraits*, 8vo. *cloth.* N. Y. 1851

3651 Este (*Thos.*) Whole Book of Psalms, with the Tunes, in Four Parts, edited by Rimbault, 4to. Lond. n. d.

3652 Forde (*Wm.*) An Essay on the Key in Music, 8vo. *boards.* Lond.

3653 GARDINER (*William*), The Music of Nature, or an attempt to prove that what is passionate and pleasing in the art of Singing, Speaking, and Performing upon musical instruments, is derived from the sounds of the animated world, with curious and interesting illustrations, 8vo. *cloth.* Bost. 1856

3654 GIBBONS (*O.*) First Set of Madrigals, edited by Sir Geo. Smart, 4to. Lond. n. d.

3655 ——— Fantasies, in Three Parts, by Rimbault, 4to. Lond. n. d.

3656 HANDEL (*G. F.*) Memoirs of the Life of, 12mo. *calf.* Lond. 1760

3657 HAWKINS (*Sir John*), General History of Music, 5 vols. 4to. *plates, half calf.* 1776

Hawkins's History having met with little success when first published—public attention being at the same time engrossed with Burney's work—only a small number of copies were sold, and the value, as a vast storehouse of curious and interesting information, of Hawkins's work having in recent times been proved, the commercial value has in consequence risen considerably, as complete copies are now very rare.

3658 HAYDN and Mozart, Lives of, translated from the French of Bombet, 8vo. *half calf.* Lond. 1818

3659 HAYLEY (*W.*) The Triumph of Music, a Poem, 1804, 2 vols. 4to.

3660 HILTON (*J.*) Ayres or Fa Las for three Voyces, edited by J. Warren, 4to. Lond. n. d.

3661 HOGARTH (*George*), Memoirs of the Musical Drama, 2 vols. 8vo. illustrated by capital portraits, including Madame Mara, Farinelli, Dr. Arne, Mrs. Billington, Catalani, &c. *cloth.* 1838

3662 ——— Musical History, Biography, and Criticism, 2 vols. 12mo. *half calf.* Lond. 1838

3663 HOOD (*Geo.*) History of Music in New England, 12mo. *cloth.* Bost. 1846

3664 ——— Another copy. Bost. 1846

3665 LUNN (*H. C.*) Musings of a Musician, 12mo. Lond. 1849

3666 MITFORD (*W.*) Inquiry into the Principles of Harmony in Language, 8vo. *cloth.* Lond. 1804

3667 MORLEY (*Thos.*) First Set of Ballets, edited by Rimbault, 4to. Lond. n. d.

3668 MOZART, Œuvres. in partitiones Quatuor. Tome II., 8vo. *boards.* Paris.

3669 MUSICAL Carcenet, 12mo. N. Y. 1832

3670 MUSICAL Companion for the Flute, sq. 12mo. Lond.

3671 MUSES' Delight, Songs, Duetts, &c. 8vo. *calf.* Liverpool, 1754

3672 MUSICAL Miscellany, a Collection of choice Songs, set to the Violin, &c., by the most Eminent Masters, 6 vols. 12mo., and curious collection of old English ballads, with the music, *calf*, *scarce.* Lond. 1729

An immense variety of the popular airs and melodies of the day, with curious anecdotes.

3673 ——— World, a Record of Musical Science, Literature, and Intelligence, 3 vols. 12mo. Lond. 1836

3674 MUSIC, &c. 4 vols.

3675 NIGHTINGALE (*The*), a Collection of Songs set to Music, selected by S. Larkin, 12mo. Portsmouth, 1804

3676 OPERAS, a Collection of old Italian and English Operas, comprising the Operas of Almahide, Clotilda, Hydaspes, Etearco, Rinaldo, Arsinoe, Camilla, Temple of Love, Rosamond (by Addison), &c., including those sung at the Introduction of the Italian Opera into England, by Scarlatti, Bononcini, &c., with all the songs of *Sig. Nicolini*, *Mrs. Tofts*, and other Artistes of the time, as mentioned in the *Tatler*, *Spectator*, &c., 2 vols. *with Frontispieces and Embellishments*, *in the original binding*, *lettered on the side*, *very scarce*, *if not unique*, folio. Lond. 1708–10

3677 PARKE (*H. P.*) Musical Memoirs, 2 vols. 12mo. *boards.* Lond. 1830

3678 PARTHENIA; or the first Musick ever printed for the Virginals, edited by Rimbault, 4to. Lond. n. d.

3679 PILKINGTON (*H. W.*) Musical Dictionary, 12mo. *boards.* Bost. 1813

3680 ——— Another copy, 12mo. 1813

3681 PURCELL (*H.*) Orpheus Britannicus; a Collection of the Choicest Songs, with Symphonies, a Thorough Bass, &c., for each, folio, *portrait*, *fine copy*, *old calf*, *gilt edges*, *scarce.* Lond. 1706

"An admirable Collection,—Purcell is as much the Pride of the English nation in Music as Shakspeare in the Drama, or Newton in Science."—*Dr. Burney*.

3682 ——— Bonduca, a Tragedy, edited by Rimbault, 4to. Lond. n. d.

3683 ——— Dido and Æneas, a Tragic Opera, edited by G. A. Macfarren, 4to. Lond. n. d.

3684 ——— Ode for St. Celia's Day, edited by Rimbault. Lond. n. d.

3685 QUARTERLY Musical Magazine and Review, 10 vols. royal 8vo. *half calf.* Lond. 1818, &c.

3686 RIMBAULT (*E. F.*) Bibliotheca Madrigalania, 8vo. Lond. 1847

3687 SOCIAL Companion, a Collection of Songs, *with plates,* 4to. *calf, no title.*

4688 THOUGHTS on the Use and Advantage of Music and other Amusements, 8vo. *half calf.* Lond. 1765

3689 WEELKES (*Th.*) First Set of Madrigals, edited by E. J. Hopkins, 4to. Lond. v. d.

3690 WILBYE (*J.*) First Set of Madrigals, edited by Jas. Turle, 4to. Lond. n. d.

3691 WILLIS (*N. P.*) Memoranda of the Life of Jenny Lind, 12mo. *cloth.* Phil. 1851

NOVELS, ROMANCES, TALES, ETC.

3692 ADVENTURES of Robin Day, 2 vols. *cloth,* 12mo. Phila. 1839

3693 AGATHONIA, a Romance, 12mo. *bds.* Lond. 1844

3694 AINSWORTH (*W. H.*) Jack Sheppard, a Romance in 2 vols. 12mo. *half cloth.* Phila. 1839

3695 ——— Saint James's, or the Court of Q. Anne, 3 vols. 12mo. *bds.* Lond. 1844

3696 ——— Windsor Castle, Illustrated by Cruikshank, 8vo. *cloth.* Lond. 1843

3696* ——— Another copy, *imperfect.* Lond. 1846

3697 ALEXANDER (*Gab.*) Wallace, the Hero of Scotland, and other Tales, 8vo. *half morocco.* N. Y.

3698 ALMACK'S, a Tale of English Society, 3 vols. in 1, 8vo. *half morocco.* N. Y. 1855

3699 AMATONDA, a Tale from the German of Anton Wall, 12mo. *sheep.* Lond. 1811

3700 AMERICAN Lounger, *bds.* 12mo. Phila. 1839

3701 ARNAUD (*M.*) Abbey of La Trappe, 12mo. Dublin, 1792

3702 ARTHUR CARRYL, a Novel, Cantos 1st and 2d, Odes, Epistles, to Milton, Pope, Juvenal, the Devil, &c., 8vo. N. Y. 1841

3703 ARNOLD (*T.*) Dramatic Stories, by, 3 vols. *bds.* 12mo. Lond. 1832

3704 ATTORNEY (*The*) or the Correspondence of John Quod, *illustrated,* 12mo. *cloth.* N. Y. 1853

3705 ARTHUR (*T. S.*) Ten Nights in a Bar Room, 12mo. *cloth.* N. Y. 1854

3706 BABBLER (*The*), a selection of Essays, 2 vols. 12mo. *calf.* Lond. 1767

3707 BALDWIN (*Joseph T.*) The Flush Times of Alabama and Mississippi, 12mo. *cloth.* N. Y. 1854

3708 BARLETTA (*Challenge of*), a Historical Romance, 12mo. *cloth.* N. Y. 1845

3709 BONDMAN (*The*), a Story of the Times of Wat Tyler, 12mo. *cloth.* Lond. 1833

3710 BARHAM (*Rev. Richard*) Cousin Nicholas, *illustrated*, 12mo. *cloth.* Buffalo, 1856

3711 BARNES (*Josiah*). The Old Inn, or the Travellers' Entertainment, 12mo. *cloth.* N. Y. 1855

3712 BAYLY (*T. H.*) Kate Leslie, 2 vols. 12mo. *bds.* Phila. 1838

3713 BECKFORD (*W.*) Vathek, 12mo. *boards.* Balt. 1834

3714 BELL-SMITH Abroad, 12mo. *cloth.* N. Y. 1856

3715 BEHEMOTH, a Legend of the Mound Builders, 12mo. *cloth.* N. Y. 1839

3716 BEHN (*Mrs. Aphra*), Histories and Novels, 8vo. *calf, scarce.* Lond. 1718

3717 BENNETT (*Emerson*), The Border Rover, 12mo. *cloth.* Phil. 1857

3718 BLACKBEARD, a Page from the Colonial History of Philadelphia, in 2 vols. 12mo. *cloth.* N. Y. 1835

3719 BLACKWATER Chronicle, a Narrative, &c., 12mo. *cloth.* N. Y. 1853

3720 BLESSINGTON (*Lady*), Works, Two Friends, the Repealers, Confessions of an Elderly Gentleman, &c., 2 vols. in 1, *cloth*, royal 8vo. Phil. 1838

3721 ——— Confessions of an Elderly Lady and Gentleman, in 2 vols. *boards*, 12mo. Phil. 1838

3722 ——— The Governess, 2 vols. 12mo. *boards.* Phil. 1838

3723 BRECKENRIDGE'S Modern Chivalry, or New Orlando Furioso, *illustrated*, 2 vols. 12mo. *boards.* Lond. 1844

3724 BRONTE (*Anne*), Tenant of Wildfell Hall, 2 vols. 12mo. N. Y. 1848

3725 ——— (*Charlotte*), Shirley, 12mo. *cloth.* N. Y. 1857

3726 BROWN (*C. B.*) Edgar Huntley, 12mo. *boards.* Bost. 1827

3727 BROWNE (*J. Ross*), Yusef, or the Journey of the Frangi, 12mo. *cloth, illustrated.* N. Y. 1853

3728 BULFINCH (*Thomas*), Age of Chivalry, Part 1; King Arthur and his Knights, Part 2; Mabinogeon, or Welsh Popular Tales, *plates*, 12mo. *cloth.* Bost. 1859

3729 BURTON, or the Sieges, a Romance, 2 vols. 12mo. *cloth.* N. Y. 1838

3730 BULWER LYTTON (*Sir E.*) Pelham, Disowned, Devereux, Paul Clifford, Eugene Aram, Pompeii, Rienzi, Pilgrims, Falkland, Leila, *with plates;* Ernest Maltravers, Alice, Lucretia, Zanoni, Last of the Barons, Harold, Night and Morning, Caxton's Calderon, My Novel, 6 vols. *half morocco, uniform,* 8vo. v. y.

3731 ——— Last Days of Pompeii, *cloth,* 8vo. N. Y. 1834

3732 ——— Ernest Maltravers, Alice, and Rienzi, 6 vols. 12mo. N. Y. 1837

3733 ——— Eva and Pilgrims, 12mo. Leipsic, 1842

3734 ——— (*Lady*), Behind the Scenes, 12mo. 3 vols. in 1, *cloth.* N. Y. 1854

3735 CABINET Album, a Collection of Original and Selected Literature, 12mo. *boards.* Lond. 1830

3736 CABINET Minister, 2 vols. *cloth,* 12mo. N. Y. 1839

3737 CAMPERDOWN, or News from our Neighborhood, 12mo. *cloth.* Phil. 1836

3738 CAMPBELL (*Alex.*) Sketches of Life and Character, *half roan,* 12mo. Edin. 1842

3739 CAPITALIST (*The*), and other Tales, 8vo. *half morocco.* N. Y. 1843

3740 CARLEN (*Emilie F.*) The Whimsical Woman, 12mo. *cloth.* N. Y. 1854

3741 CARLETON (*W. H.*) Father Butler and the Lough Deard Pilgrim, 2 vols. 12mo. *boards.* Phil. 1839

3742 CARLETON (*Wm*). Father Butler, 12mo. *cloth.* Dublin, 1839

3743 ——— The Black Prophet, Roby the Rover, &c., 3 vols. in 1, *half morocco.* N. Y.

3744 CERVANTES (*Miguel de*), Vida y Hechos del ingenias Hidalgo Don Quixote de la Mancha, 4 vols. 4to. *uncut.* Lond. 1738

3745 ——— History of that valorous and witty knight-errant Don Quixote of the Mancha, translated by T. Shelton, *old calf,* folio. Lond. 1652

3746 ——— Don Quixote, translated from the Spanish, and Account of the Author's Life, by Dr. Smollett, 2 vols. 4to. *splendid old edition, with 28 fine plates by Hayman ("The Stothard of the day"), calf.* Lond. 1755

3747 ——— Don Quixotte de la Mancha, by Chas. Jarvis, Esq., illustrated by Tony Johannot, 3 vols. 8vo. Lond. 1837

3748 CERVANTES (*Miguel de*), Don Quixotte, another edition, 4 vols. in 1, *half calf.* Lond. 1792

3749 ——— Les principales avantures de l'admirable Don Quixotte représentées en figures par Coypel, Picart and others, *with explanations*, 31 *plates*, 4to. La Haye, 1746

This is an elegant volume of illustrations.—*See also Prints.*

3750 CERVANTES' El Buscapie, 12mo. *cloth.* Lond. 1849

3751 CHANNER (*Capt.*) Arethusa, Jack Adams, and the Spitfire, 6 vols. 12mo. Phil. 1837

3752 CHANTICLEER, A Thanksgiving Story, 12mo. *cloth.* Bost. 1850

3753 CHANTICLEER, &c., 4 vols. *cloth*, 12mo.

3754 CHATEAUBRIAND (*Vicomte de*), Aben-Hamet, a Romance, 12mo. *boards.* Lond. 1826

3755 CHILDE Rocliff's Pilgrimage, and other Tales, 3 vols. 12mo. *cloth.* Lond. 1834

3756 CHOLLERTON, A Tale of our Own Times, by a Lady, 12mo. *cloth.* Lond. 1846

3757 CHORLEY (*W. F.*) Sketches of a Sea-port Town, *boards.* 12mo. Phil. 1836

3758 CLARK (*Louis Gaylord*), Knick Knacks from an Editor's Table, presentation copy, autograph of the author, *plates*, 12mo. N. Y. 1853

3759 CLEMENT FALCONER, or Memoirs of a Young Whig, 12mo. *half cloth.*

3760 CLARKE (*Mary Cowden*), Kit Bam's Adventures, 12mo. *cloth, plates.* Lond. 1849

3761 CLUB Book (*The*), being original Tales, 2 vols. 12mo. *soiled.* N. Y. 1831

3762 ——— Another Copy, 2 vols. in 1. N. Y. 1836

3763 COLLINS (*Wilkie*), The Dead Secret, 12mo. *cloth.* N. Y. 1857

3764 CONE Cut Corners, The Experiences of a Conservative Family in Fanatical Times, 12mo. *cloth.* N. Y. 1855

3765 COOPER (*J. F.*) Homeward Bound, Outward Bound, Pioneers, Prairie, and Deerslayer, 8 vols. 12mo. Phila. 1838–9

3766 ——— Last of the Mohicans, &c., 7 vols. 12mo. v. d.

3767 CRUIKSHANK'S (*George*) Omnibus, Illustrated with 100 Engravings on steel and wood, *cov. loose.* Lond. 1842

3768 CRYSTALINA, a Fairy Tale, by an American, 12mo. N. Y. 1816

3769 CURTIS (*G. W.*) Lotus Eating: a Summer Book, and Prue and I, 2 vols. 12mo. *cloth.* N. Y. 1852

3770 DAY'S History of Sandford and Merton, *plates*, 8vo. *cloth.* N. Y.

3771 DE FOE (*D.*) Life and Adventures of Robinson Crusoe, *Stothard's plates*, 2 vols. royal 8vo. large paper, *half morocco.* Lond. 1820

3772 DENISON (*Mrs. Mary A.*) What Not, 12mo. *cloth, illustrated.* Phila. 1855

3773 DESBORDES-BALMORE (*Madame*) Le Salon de Lady Betty, Mœurs Anglaises, 2 vols. 18mo. Brux. 1836

3774 DHU (*Helen*), Stanhope Burleigh, The Jesuits in our Homes, *cloth*, 8vo. N. Y. 1855

3775 DICKENS (*C.*) Hard Times, Haunted Man, Christmas Carol, David Copperfield, 4 vols. 8vo. N. Y. v. d.

3776 ——— Pickwick Papers, *extra set of plates, half morocco*, 8vo. N. Y. 1842

3777 ——— Oliver Twist, *plates, cloth*, 8vo. N. Y. 1842

3778 ——— Master Humphrey's Clock, illustrated by T. Sibson, 40 *plates.* Lond. 1840

3779 ——— David Copperfield, 2 vols., Bleak House, 2 vols. sewed, 4 vols. 8vo. N. Y. 1853

3780 ——— Dombey and Son, 15 Nos. 1817

3781 ——— Little Dorritt, 20 *plates, cloth,* 12mo. Phila. v. d.

3782 DISRAELI (*I.*) Romances by, 12mo. *half calf.* Lond. 1799

3783 DISRAELI (*B.*) Works of, in 1 vol. royal 8vo., *cloth,* Phila. 1837

3784 DIVERTING History of John Bull and Brother Jonathan, by Hector Bulbus, *cloth*, 12mo. N. Y. 1835

3785 DIXON (*Ed. H., M. D.*) Scenes in the Practice of a N. Y. Surgeon, *illustrated*, 12mo. *cloth.* N. Y. 1856

3786 DUMAS (*Alex.*) Monte Cristo, Edm. Dantes, Adventures of a Marquis, Paul Jones, Three Guardsmen, Three Mousquetaires, Bragelonne, Iron Mask, La Vallière, Memorandums of a Physician, Queen's Necklace, Six Years Later, or the Bastile, Countess de Charney, Iron Hand, Isabel of Bavaria, Two Dianas, Marguerite de Valois, Forty-five Guardsmen, Diana of Meridor, Thousand Phantoms, Silvandire, Genevieve, Secret Belt, Devil's Wedding Ring, Ascanio, D'Harmenthal, Regent's Daughter, Amaury, Fernande, Sketches in France, Corsican Brothers, Act of Corinth, Cecilia, Jailor's Daughter, George, Celebrated Crimes, collected in 15 vols. 8vo. *half morocco.* v. y.

3787 DOESTICKS, a "Deed without a Name," perpetrated by, 12mo. *cloth.* N. Y. 1856

3788 DUKE of Monmouth, in 2 vols. 12mo. *boards.* Phil. 1837

3789 DUMAS (*Alex.*), The Conscript, a Tale of the Empire, 12mo. *cloth.* N. Y. 1856.

3790 DUNLAP (*William*), Archers, or Mountaineers of Switzerland, 8vo. *sd.* N. Y. 1796

3791 EDGEWORTH (*Maria*), Castle Rackrent and Irish Bulls, 2 vols. in 1, *half sheep.* N. Y. 1834

3792 ELKSWATAWA; or the Prophet of the West, a Tale of the Frontier, 2 vols. 12mo. *cloth.* N. Y. 1836

3793 ELLEN GRANVILLE, by a Lady of Rank, 2 vols. 12mo. *half cloth.* Phil. 1838

3794 EVELYN (*Chetwood*), After Dinner Table-talk, 12mo. *cloth.* N. Y. 1850

3796 FAIR Puritan, Foresters, and Martin Faber, 3 vols. 24mo. *cloth.* v. d.

3797 FAMILY Quarrels, &c., 3 vols. 8vo.

3798 FELLOW Commoner, or Remarkable Escapes of a Predestinated Rogue, in 2 vols. 8vo. *half cloth.* Phil. 1838

3799 FIELDING, or Society, Atticus, or the Retired Statesman, and St. Lawrence, in 3 vols. 12mo. *boards.* Phil. 1837

3800 FENELON (*La Mothe*), Avantures de Telemaque fils d'Ulysse, *a magnificent edition, with plates by Picart, Gunst, Drevet, and others,* 4to. Amst. 1734

3802 FIRST of the Knickerbockers; a Tale of 1673, and Rose Clark, 2 vols. 12mo. *cloth.* N. Y. 1848–56

3803 GALT (*J.*) The Entail, or the Lands of Grippy, 2 vols. 12mo. *boards.* N. Y. 1823

3804 GAYTON (*Edmund*), Pleasant Notes upon the History of the renowned Don Quixote, original edition, folio, *half calf.* Lond. 1654

3805 GETTING Along, a Book of Illustrations, 2 vols. 12mo. N. Y. 1855

3806 GENTLEMAN Jack, &c., Novels, 8 vols. odd.

3807 GILMAN (*Caroline*), Recollections of a Southern Matron, 12mo. *sewed.* Charleston, 1852

3808 GEORGE a Green, Pindar of the Town of Wakefield, 12mo. London, *Pickering,* 1827

3809 GLASCOCK (*Capt. R. N.*) Land-Sharks and Sea-Gulls, in 2 vols. 12mo. *boards.* Phil. 1838

3810 GOETHE, Wilhelm Meister's Apprenticeship, 12mo. *cloth.* Bohn, 1855

3811 GOLDSMITH (*Oliver*), Vicar of Wakefield, 8vo. *cloth.* N. Y. 1850

3812 GRAZZINI (*A. F.*) Primà e seconda cena Novelle, 8vo. *half calf, uncut.* Milan, 1810

3813 GRIFFIN (*Gerald*), Works: Life, by his Brother; Tales of the Monster Festivals, 4 vols.; Tales of the Jury Room; Duke of Monmouth; Poems and Sonnets, 8 vols. 12mo. *cloth.* Lond. 1842

3814 GREENE (*Nathaniel*), Tales from the German, 2 vols. 12mo. *cloth.* Bost. 1837

3815 HANNAY (*Jas.*) Sketches in Ultra Marine, 12mo. *cloth.* Lond. 1854

3816 HARRY Coverdale's Courtship, &c., 2 vols. *paper.* N Y.

3817 HARRY Austin, or Adventures in the British Army, in 2 vols. 8vo. *boards.* Phil. 1838

3818 HAWTHORNE (*Nath.*) Twice told Tales, 2 vols. *cloth.* Bost. 1854

3819 HERALD (*The*), or Patriot Proclaimed, a collection of Essays, 2 vols. 12mo. *calf.* 1758

3820 HERBERT (*H. W.*) Roman Traitors and Warwick Woodlands, 3 vols. 1850

3821 HERBERT (*Henry*), Warwick Woodlands, or Things as they were there 20 Years ago, by F. Forrester, *illustrations*, post 8vo. Phil. 1850

3822 HINKLEY (*J.*) History of Rinaldo Rinaldini, 2 vols. 18mo. *cloth.* Phil. 1841

3823 HOLBERG (*Louis*), Niels Klun's Journey under the Ground, *curious plates*, 12mo. *cloth.* Bost. 1845

3824 HOFLAND (*Mrs.*) Czarina, Unloved One, Daniel Dennison, 8vo. *half morocco.* v. d.

3825 HOLE (*R.*) Arthur, or the Northern Enchantress, 8vo. *calf.* Lond. 1789

3826 HOOK (*Theodo.*) Sayings and Doings, Births, Deaths, and Marriages, Pascal Bruno, Gurney Married, and Cousin Geoffry, 8 vols. 12mo. v. d.

3827 HIGHWAYS and Byways, or Tales of the Roadside, by Grattan, complete in 3 vols. 12mo. *boards.* Boston, 1840

3828 HORACE Vernon and Hooton's Colin Clink, 2 vols. 12mo. 1839

3829 HOWARD Pinkney, and Howitt's Wood Leighton, 4 vols. 12mo. Phil. 1844

3830 HUET (*Monsieur*), A Treatise on Romances and their Originals, from the French, 18mo. *calf.* Lond. 1672

3831 HUNGERFORD (*James*), The Old Plantation, 12mo. *cloth.* N. Y. 1859

3832 INGLIS (*Henry D.*) The New Gil Blas, or Pedro of Penaflor in 2 vols. *half cloth*, 12mo. Phila. 1833

3833 ——— Rambles in the Footsteps of Don Quixote, plate by Cruikshank, *cloth*, 8vo. Lond. 1837

3834 IRVING (*W.*) Wolfert's Roost, *cloth*, 12mo. N. Y.

3835 JACK CONNOR, the Child of Twenty Fathers, 2 vols. 12mo. *calf.* Lond. 1753

3836 JAMES (*G. P. R.*) Philip Augustus; Richelieu; Mary of Burgundy; Collegians, Gentlemen of the Old School; Gypsy; Forest Days; False Heir; Arrabel Stuart; Rose D'Albret; Gowrie; Castle of Ehrenstein; Agincourt; Smuggler; Arrah Neil; Beauchamp; Heidelberg; Convict; Stepmother; Sir T. Broughton; Old Oak Chest; Thirty Years; Russell; Marc Graham; A Whim; Last of the Fairies; Woodman; Forgery; Henry Smeaton; Commissioner; The Fate; Aims and Obstacles; Pequinillo; Life of Vicissitudes; Agnes Sorel; Book of the Passions; Coeur de Lion; Henry Masterton; Ancient Regime; Charles Tyrrell, collected in 14 vols. *half morocco uniform*, 8vo. v. y.

3837 JAMES (*G. P. R. Esq.*) Gentleman of the Old School, in 2 vols., and Diary of an Ennuyée, 3 vols. v. d. 12mo. *cloth.* N. Y. 1839

3839 JANE LOMAX, or a Mother's Crime, 2 vols. 12mo. *half cloth.* Phila. 1838

3840 JERROLD (*Douglas*), Men of Character, 3 vols. 12mo. *boards, plates.* Lond. 1838

3841 JERROLD (*W. B.*) The Disgrace of the Family, illustrated, 12mo. *cloth.* Lond. 1848

3842 JOHNSON (*Charles*), Chrysal, or the Adventures of a Guinea, with curious and interesting anecdotes of the most noted persons in every rank of life, 2 vols. small 8vo. *sheep.* Balt. 1816

"A masterly but caustic satire, written by Charles Johnson."—*Lowndes.*

3843 KENNEDY (*George*), Horse Shoe Robinson, 2 vols. *cloth*, 12mo. Phila. 1856

3844 KINGSLEY (*Charles*), Sir Walter Raleigh and his Times, 12mo. *cloth.* Bost. 1859

3845 ——— Two Years Ago, 12mo. *cloth.* Bost. 1859

3846 KINGSLEY (*George*), Alton Larke, Taylor and Poet, an Autobiography, 12mo. *cloth.* N. Y. 1850

3847 KNOTT (*H. J.*) Novellettes of a Traveller, or Odds and Ends, taken from the Knapsack of Thomas Singularity, 2 vols. *cloth*, 12mo. N. Y. 1834

3848 LANDOR (*Walter Savage*), Pericles and Aspasia, 2 vols. *cloth*, post 8vo. Phil. 1839

3849 LANDON (*L. E.*) Works, containing Romance and Reality, Francesca Carrara, Traits and Trials of Early Life, Ethel Churchill, Book of Beauty, &c., 2 vols. in 1, *cloth*, royal 8vo. Phil. 1838

3850 LELAND (*Chas. G.*) Meister Karl's Sketch Book, 12mo. *cloth.* Phil. 1855

3851 LEMON (*Mark*), Betty Morrison's Pocket-Book, and other articles in prose and verse, *sewed*, 12mo. Lond. 1856

3852 LE SAGE, Adventures of Gil Blas of Santillane, translated by Smollett and *illustrated by Gigoux*, 2 vols. *cloth*, 8vo. Lond. 1836

3853 ——— Les Adventures de Monsieur Robert Chevalier dit de Beauchêne Capitaine de Filibustiers dans la Nouvelle, France, vol. 2, *half roan*, 12mo. Maestricht, 1780

3854 ——— Devil on Two Sticks, *with cuts*, 12mo. *calf.* Lond. 1778

3855 ——— Asmodeus, or the Devil on Two Sticks, *illustrated by Johannot*, *cloth*, royal 8vo. Lond. 1841

3856 LESLIE (*Miss*), Althea Vernon, and Pencil Sketches, 12mo. *cloth.* Phil. 1838

3857 LEVER (*Charles*), Jack Hinton, Neville, Tom Burke, Knight of Gwynne, Charles O'Malley, Arthur O'Leary, Horace Templeton, Kate O'Donohue, Maurice, St. Patrick's Day, Dodd Family, collected together and bound in 6 vols. *half morocco*, 8vo. N. Y. v. y.

3858 LIBRARY of Choice Reading, &c., 37 Nos. 12mo.

3859 LIGHT and Darkness, and 3 others, 12mo. *paper.* N. Y. 1855

3860 LITERARY Morceaux, 16mo. *cloth.* Lond. 1835

3861 LODORE, and 2 others, 3 vols. *half bound*, 12mo. N. Y. 1835

3862 LOFTY and the Lowly, &c. 6 vols. odd, 12mo.

3863 LONG Engagements, a Tale of the Affghan Rebellion, 12mo. *cloth.* Lond. 1846

3864 LONGFELLOW (*H. W.*) Hyperion, a Romance, in 2 vols. *boards*, 8vo. N. Y. 1839

3865 LOGAN, The Master's House, a Tale of Southern Life, 12mo. *cloth.* N. Y. 1854

3867 LOVER (*Samuel*), Barney O'Reardon, Handy Andy, Treasure Trove, Rory O'More, Tom Crosbie, 2 vols. *half morocco*, 8vo. N. Y.

3868 LUSIGNAN, or the Abbaye of La Trappe, 4 vols. 12mo. *half calf.* Lond. 1801

3869 MAGINN (*Wm.*) John Manesty, The Liverpool Merchant, 2 vols. *cloth.* Lond. 1844

3870 MAN of Two Lives (*The*), A Narrative written by himself, 2 vols. 12mo. *boards.* Lond. 1828

3871 MANNELLA, The Executioner's Daughter, a Story of Madrid, 3 vols. 12mo. Lond. 1837

3872 MANY Colored Life, or Tales of Woe and Touches of Mirth, 8vo. *cloth.* Lond. 1842

3873 MAIDEN and Married Life of Mary Powell, and Deborah's Diary, 2 vols. royal 8vo. Bost.

3874 MARET'S L'Ariane, 4to. *old calf.* Paris, 1643

3875 MARCOTTI (*L.*) The Blackgown Papers, 2 vols. 8vo. *cloth.* Lond. 1846

3876 MARRYATT (*Capt.*) Peter Simple, Jacob Faithful, Pirate, Three Cutters, Moonshie, Naval Officer, King's Own, Newton Forster, Pacha of many Tales, Japhet, Sea King, Poor Jack, Joseph Rushbrook, collected in three vols. 8vo. *half morocco.* Lond. v. y.

3877 ——— (*Capt.*) Complete Works, 2 vols. in 1, royal 8vo. N. Y.

3878 ——— (*Capt.*) Jacob Faithful, Naval Officer, and Phantom Ship, 4 vols. 12mo. Phil. 1839

3879 ——— Olla Podrida, 12mo. *cloth.* Lond. 1849

3880 ——— Pirate and Three Cutters, *wants plates,* 8vo. *cloth.* Lond. n. d.

3881 MAURICE (*Jacques*), K. N. Pepper, and other condiments, 12mo. *cloth.* N. Y. 1859

3882 MAXWELL (*W. H.*) Land and Sea, Bivouac, or Stories of the Peninsular War, 4 vols. *boards.* Phil. 1837

3883 ——— (*W. H.*) Novels and Stories, 3 vols. 8vo. *half morocco.* Phil.

3884 MAYHEW, Brothers, Plague of Life, Whom to Marry, &c., 8vo. *half morocco.* N. Y.

3885 MELVILLE (*Herman*), The Confidence Man, 12mo. *cloth.* N. Y. 1857

3886 ——— (*Herman*), The Piazza Tales, 12mo. *cloth.* N. Y. 1856

3887 MELVILLE (*Herman*), Redburn; His First Voyage, 12mo. *cloth.* N. Y. 1849

3888 MEPHISTOPHILES in England, or the Confessions of a Prime Minister, in 2 vols. 12mo. *boards.* Phil. 1835

3889 MILLER (*T.*) Fair Rosamond, or Days of K. Henry, 2d 12mo. *half cloth.* Phil. 1839

3890 MITCHELL (*J. K.*) Indecision, a Tale of the Far West, 12mo. *cloth.* Phil. 1839

3891 MITFORD (*M. R.*) Country Stories, 12mo. *boards.* Phil. 1838

3892 MOISSY (*M. de.*) Les Jeux, de la petite Thalie, 12mo. *half bound.* Berlin, 1773

3893 MORGAN (*Lady*, and Sir T. Charles), The Book without a name, 2 vols. 12mo. N. Y. 1841

3894 MONKLAND (*Mrs.*) Elvira the Nabob's Wife, 2 vols. 12mo. *boards.* Phil. 1839

3895 MY Aunt Pontypool, in 2 vols. 12mo. *boards.* Phil. 1836

3896 NEAL (*J.*) Down Easters, in 2 vols. 12mo. *cloth.* N. Y. 1853

3897 NEAL (*J. C.*) Charcoal Sketches, or Scenes in a Metropolis, *plates by D. C. Johnson*, 12mo. *cloth.* Phil. 1838

3898 ——— Another copy, imperfect. 1838

3899 NOVELS and Tales, 10 vols. 8vo.

3899* NEAL (*Lord*), A Romance, The Wizard's Grave, 12mo. *cloth,* N. Y. 1834

3900 NEWCASTLE (*Margaret, Duchess of*), The Description of a New World, called the Blazing World, written by the Thrice Noble, Illustrious, and Excellent Princesse, The Duchess of Newcastle ("dear old Madge Newcastle," Charles Lamb), folio, *old calf, gilt, very rare.* Lond. 1666

"The first part is Romancical, the second Philosophical, and the third is merely Fancy, or, as I call it, Fantastical."—*Preface.*

3901 NINETEENTH Century, &c., 26 vols. of pamphlets.

3902 NORTH (*W.*) Slave of the Lamp, and Nix's Mate, 3 vols. N. Y. 1855

3903 NOVELISTS' Magazine, 2 vols. 8vo. *cloth.* Phil. 1833

3904 NOVELS, a select collection of, 4 vols. 12mo. *half bnd.* Lond. 1720

3905 NOVELS, from the French, Cinq Mars, &c., 8vo. *half morocco.* N. Y.

3906 NOVELS, Translations, &c., 5 vols. *half morocco*, 8vo. N. Y.

3907 Novels, American, 2 vols. 8vo. *half morocco.*

3908 Novels, Various, 16 vols. 8vo. v. d.

3909 O'Hara Family, Bit o' Writin', and other Tales, 4 vols. 12mo. Phil. 1838

3910 Old Commander, Outlaw's Bride, Our Folks at Home, and Only Daughter, 6 vols. v. d.

3912 Out of the Depths, and others, 14 vols. 8vo.

3914 Palmerin of England, excellent and stately History of the famous and fortunate Prince Palmerin of England, translated by Anthony Munday, first and second parts in 2 vols. 4to. **Black Letter**, *vellum, fine copy, very rare,* printed by B. Alsop and T. Fawcet, in Grub strete. Lond. 1639

"Let Palmerin of England be preserved and kept as a singular piece, and let such another case be made for it as Alexander appropriated to preserve the works of Homer."—*Don Quixote.*

3915 Pardoe (*Miss*), River and the Desert, and City of the Sultan, 4 vols. 12mo. Phil. 1838

3916 Paris, or the Book of the Hundred and One, 2 vols. 12mo. *half cloth.* Bost. 1833

3917 Parterre (*The*), or Universal Story-Teller, *illustrated by engravings by S. Williams, cloth,* 4 vols. 8vo. Lond. 1840

3918 Percy (*Stephen*), Robin Hood and his Merry Foresters, *plates,* square 8vo. *cloth.* Lond. 1845

3919 Perils of Pearl Street (*The*), 12mo. *cloth;* and Penruddock, 3 vols. N. Y. 1834

3920 Pertet, Contes, 8vo. Lond. 1843

3921 Peter Pilgrim, or a Rambler's Recollections, in 2 vols. *cloth,* 12mo. Phil. 1838

3922 Petit (*Lizzie*), Household Mysteries, 12mo. *cloth.* N. Y. 1846

3923 Phantasmion, Prince of Palmland, 2 vols. 12mo. *half morocco.* N. Y. 1839

3924 Phœnix (*The*), or the History of Polyarchus and Argenis, from the Italian, 4 vols. *cloth,* 12mo. Lond. 1772

3925 Phœnisciana, or Sketches and Burlesques, 12mo. *cloth.*

3926 Pilkington (*Mrs.*) History of the Rockinghams, 12mo. *boards.* Lond. 1810

3927 Pickering's Nan Darrell, Prince and the Pedlar, Ruins of Prague, Pure Love, and Precaution, 8 vols. v. d.

3928 Pilgrim (*The*), or a Picture of Life in a Series of Letters, 2 vols. *calf,* 12mo. Lond.

3929 Poe (*Edgar A.*) Tales of the Grotesque, 2 vols. 12mo. N. Y.

3930 Potter (*Mary*) Pheleg Van Trundale, 12mo. *cloth.* N. Y. 1858

3931 Presbury (*B. F.*) The Master, or Love and Liberty, 12mo. *cloth.* Bost. 1859

3932 Prairie Scout, or Agatone the Renegade, a Romance of Border Life, *half cloth*, 8vo. N. Y.

3233 Psalmanazar (*George*), An Historical and Geographical Description of Formosa, with the Formosan Alphabet, 8vo. *calf.* Lond. 1704

3934 Quadroone, or St. Michael's Day, 2 vols. 12mo. *boards.* N. Y. 1841

3935 Quaker City and Others, Seven Pieces. v. d.

3936 Quod Correspondence, or the Attorney, 2 vols. 12mo. *half cloth.* Lond. 1842

3937 Rambles and Surprising Adventures of Captain Bolio, 32 *engravings*, 12mo. *cloth.* Lond. 1839

3938 Reade (*C.*) Love me Little, &c., and White Lies, 2 vols. 12mo. N. Y. 1859

3939 Reid (*Capt. Mayne*), The Scalp-Hunters and Rifle Rangers, 2 vols. 12mo. 1846

3940 Reynolds (*G. W. M.*) Works Collected: Pickwick Abroad, or a Tour in France, 1839; Life in Paris; Life in London; Ellen Munroe; Parricide; Faust; Court of London; Rosey Forster; Caroline of Brunswick; Venetia Trelawney; Mysteries of London; Joanna; Rosa Lambert; Kenneth; Royal Favorite; Rival Beauties; Glencoe; Pope Joan; Esther de Medina; Reformed Highwayman; Necromancer; Rye House Plot; Gypsey Thief; Angela Wildon; Timothy's Book Case; Seamstress; Mary Price; Eustace Quentin; First False Step; Robert Macaire; Lord Saxondale; Count Christoval; Soldier's Wife; Bronze Statue; Rose Somerville; Banker's Daughter; Old London; Loves of the Harem; Omar Pasha, 22 vols. *half morocco, uniform,* 8vo. v. y.

3941 Reveries of a Bachelor, by Ik. Marvel, 12mo. N. Y. 1850

3942 Reynard the Fox, Everdingen's History of Reynard the Fox, 24 *plates*, *cloth*, 4to. Lond. 1846

3943 Richard of York, or the White Rose of England, 3 vols. 12mo. *boards.* Lond. 1832

3944 Riley (*H. H.*) Puddleford and Its People, *illustrated*, 12mo. *cloth.* N. Y. 1854

3945 RITSON (*Joseph*), Fairy Tales, now first collected, 12mo. *cloth.* Lond. 1831

3946 ROBERT the Deuyll (Duke of Normandy), 12mo., *reprint by Pickering.* Lond. 1837

3947 ROCHIETTI (*Joseph*), Lorenzo and Oralaska, from Casal, 12mo. *half cloth.* Winchester, 1835

3948 ROMANCE of Octavian, Emperor of Rome, 12mo. *boards.* Oxford, 1809

3949 ROMANS Populaires Illustrés, par Bertoll, 2 vols. 4to. Paris, n. d.

3950 ROUE and Robber, 4 vols. *boards*, 8vo. Phil. 1836

3951 ROWCROFT (*Charles*), Tales of the Colonies, 12mo. *cloth.* Lond. 1847

3952 SACCHETTE (*Franco*), Novellé, 3 vols. *half russia, uncut.* Milan, 1804

3953 SAGE (*Le*), The Adventures of Gil Blas, translated by Smollett, *illustrated by Cruikshank,* 2 vols. 12mo. *cloth.* Lond. 1833

3954 SAINTINE (*M. D.*) Picciola, or Captivity Captive, *half cloth,* 12mo. Phil. 1838

3955 ST. PIERRE, Paul and Virginia, *embellished with illustrations and engravings in tint,* 8vo. *cloth, gilt.*

3956 ——— Paul and Virginia, Elizabeth, and Indian Cottage, 24mo. *cloth.* Lond.

3957 SAM Slick in Texas, Piney Woods Tavern, 12mo, *cloth.* Phil. 1858

3958 SAND (*Geo.*) Indiana, a novel, &c. 8vo. *half morocco.* N. Y.

3959 SCATTERGOOD Family, 7 vols.

3960 SCOTT (*Sir Walter*), Tales of, 12mo. *paper.* Paris, 1829

3961 SCUDERY (*Monsieur de*), Artamenes, or the Grand Cyrus, that Excellent Romance in Ten Parts, 10 vols. *old calf, ruled,* 12mo. Lond. 1691

3962 SEVARAMBIANS, The History of the, a People of the South Continent, 8vo. *calf.* Lond. 1738

"There is a want of moral and religious feeling in the book; but it is no ordinary work."—*Southey.*

3962* SEVEN Wise Men of Rome, Hystoria septem sapientii Rome; gothic letter; no pagination or signatures, *half calf,* 4to.; no place nor date: a note by Dr. Kloss states it to have been printed at Daventrie, 1475, by Richard Paffractium.

3963 SHANDY McGuire, &c., 2 vols. 12mo. N. Y. 1848

3964 SHELTON (*F. W.*) Up the River, *wood cuts,* 12mo. N. Y. 1850

3965 SHEPPARD Lee and Scourge of the Ocean, 4 vols. 12mo. *cloth.* Lond. 1836

3966 SIDNEY (*Sir Philip*), The Countesse of Pembroke's Arcadia, now the eighth time published, with some new additions, *first four leaves torn, old calf,* folio. Lond. 1633

"Among the contemporaries of Shakspeare, no one has so closely approached his peculiar excellencies or so nearly resembled him in some of his superlative endowments, as the author of the Arcadia." —*Retrospective Review.*

3967 SIMS (*W. G.*) Yemassee, Border Beagles, Richard Hurdis, Damsels of Darien, 6 vols. 12mo. 1839

3968 SISTER Anne, and others, 1 lot.

3969 SMEDLEY, Frank Farleigh, and other Tales, 5 vols. in 1, *half morocco.* N. Y.

3970 SMITH (*Albert*), The Pollbeton Legacy, 16mo. Lond. 1857

3971 ——— The Struggles and Adventures of Christopher Tadpole, *illustrated by Leech,* 8vo. *cloth.* Lond. 1851

3972 SMITH (*Horace*), Adam Brower, and other Tales, 8vo. *half morocco.* N. Y.

3973 SMOLLETT, The History and Adventures of an Atom, wants title p. of vol. 1, 2 vols. 12mo. *sheep.* Lond. 1769

3974 SOUTHEY (*Robt.*) The Doctor, 2 vols. in 1, 12mo. *cloth.* N. Y. 1836

3975 SOUTHWORTH (*Mrs.*) The Missing Bride, 12mo. *cloth.* Phil. 1855

3976 SOUVESTRE (*Emile*), Leaves from a Family Journal, 12mo. *cloth.* N. Y. 1855

3977 SPANISH Student, Stories, &c. 3 vols. various.

3978 SPENDLER'S Jew, Jesuit, Invalid, 8vo. *half roan,* N. Y. 1844

3979 STEPHENS (*Ann S.*) The Old Homestead, *cloth,* post 8vo. N. Y. 1855

3980 STONE (*W. L.*) Tales and Sketches, such as they are, 2 vols. 12mo. *cloth.* N. Y. 1834

3981 STORIES of a Bride, 2 vols. 12mo. *half roan.* N. Y. 1830

3982 STOWE (*H. Beecher*), The May-Flower, and Miscellaneous Writings, 12mo. *cloth.* Bost. 1855

3983 ——— Dred, 2 vols. 12mo. *cloth.* Bost. 1856

3984 STRANGER'S Grave (*The*), 12mo. *half sheep.* Bost. 1824

3985 SUE (*Eugene*), Mysteries of Paris, Wandering Jew, &c. 3 vols. *sewed.* N. Y. 1843

3986 SUE (*Eugene*), Martin the Valet; Mary Lawson; Wandering Jew; (Therese Dunoyer;) First Love; Mysteries of Paris; Gerolstein; Hotel Lambert; The Heaths; Fortune-Teller; Godolphin Arab; Sea Tales; De Survilles; Children of Love; Mysteries of the People; Hercules Hardy; Zulieka; Female Blue-Beard; Matilda; Temptation; Capital Sins; Pride; Envy; Anger; Voluptuousness, &c., collected in 9 vols. 8vo. *half morocco.* N. Y. v. y.

3988 SULLIVAN (*Robert*), Flittings of Fancy, 2 vols. 12mo. *half cloth, boards.* Lond. 1837

3989 TALES of College Life, and The New Tale of a Tub, 2 vols. *sq. paper.* Lond.

3990 TEMPLE of Gnidus, and Arsaces and Ismenia, 12mo. Lond. 1797

3991 THACKERAY (*W. M.*) Vanity Fair, Pendennis, Newcomes, Henry Esmond, Sketches in Ireland, Great Hoggarty Diamond, collected in 5 vols. 8vo. *half morocco.* N. Y. v. y.

3992 ——— History of Pendennis, in 5 parts, 8vo. N. Y.

3993 ——— The Confessions of Fitz-Boodle and Yellowplush Correspondence, 3 vols. 12mo. *cloth.* N. Y. 1852

3994 THORPE (*T. B.*) The Hive, or Bee-Hunter, a Repository of Sketches, *wood-cuts*, 12mo. *sewed.* N. Y. 1855

3995 TIECK (*Ludwig*), Tales from the "Phantasms," &c. 12mo. *cloth.* Lond. 1855

3996 TOM BROWN'S School Days at Rugby, by an Old Boy, 12mo. *cloth.* Bost. 1859

3997 TOM CRINGLE'S Log, 2 vols. 12mo. 2*d series, cloth.* Phil. 1833

3998 ——— Log, and others, 12 vols. 8vo.

3999 TOUGH Yarns by the Old Sailor, in 2 vols. 12mo. *boards.* Phil. 1835

4000 TROLLOPE (*A.*) Doctor Thorne, a Novel, 12mo. *cloth.* N. Y. 1858

4001 Two Flirts, or Adventures in a Country House, &c., and Tutti Frutti, 3 vols. Phil. 1838

4002 Two Years Before the Mast, 16mo. *cloth.* N. Y. 1841

4003 VANDELEUR, or Animal Magnetism, 2 vols. 12mo. *boards.* Phil. 1837

4004 VOLTAIRE (*M. de*) Romances, Novels, and Tales, 2 vols. 12mo. *half sheep.* Lond. 1806

4005 Warner (*Miss*), Hills of the Shatemuc, 12mo. *cloth.* N. Y. 1855

4006 Warren (*Samuel*), Ten Thousand a Year, 6 vols. 12mo. Phil. 1840

4007 ——— Diary of a Late Physician, 3 vols. 16mo. *cloth.* N. Y. 1854

4008 Wandering Jew, 9 parts, 8vo. N. Y. 1842

4009 Webber (*C. W.*) Tales of the Southern Border, 8vo. *cloth.* Phil. 1855

4010 Wentz (*Sara A.*) Smiles and Frowns, 12mo. *cloth.* N. Y. 1837

4011 Widow Bedott Papers, by Francis M. Whinker, 12mo. *cloth.* N. Y. 1856

4012 Wikoff (*Henry*), My Courtship and its Consequences, 12mo. *cloth.* N. Y. 1855

4013 Willis (*N. P.*) Al 'Abri, or the Tent Pitch'd, 12mo. *cloth.* N. Y. 1839

4014 ——— Fun-Jottings, 12mo. *cloth.* N. Y. 1853

4015 ——— People I have Met, 12mo. *cloth.* N. Y. 1850

4016 ——— Romance of Travel, 12mo. *cloth.* N. Y. 1840

4017 Wilson (*John*), The Trials of Margt. Lyndsay, 12mo. *cloth.* N. Y. 1845

4017*——— Recreation of Christopher North, 8vo. *cloth.* Bost. 1854

4018 Wise (*Lieut.*) Tales for the Marines, 12mo. *cloth.* Bost. 1855

4019 Woman of the World, 2 vols. *boards*, 12mo. Phil. 1838

4020 Yeast, a Problem, from Fraser's Magazine, 12mo. *cloth.* N. Y. 1851

4021 Young America, &c., 23 Nos.

4022 Zschokke (*Heinrich*), Alamontade and Dead Guest, 2 vols. 12mo. *cloth.* Phil. 1845

OCCULT SCIENCES.

4023 Aubrey's (*J.*) Miscellanies upon various Subjects, *new edition*, with Life, 8vo. *calf*, *scarce.* Lond. 1721

A most amusing collection of Fatalities, Omens, Dreams, Apparitions, Spirit Rappings, Prophecies, Magic, Visions, Converse with Angels and Spirits, Second Sight, Ecstacy, &c.

4024 Blagrave's Introduction to Astrology, 8vo. *calf.* Lond.

4025 Barrett's (*Francis*) Magus, or Celestial Intelligencer; a Complete System of Occult Philosophy, in Three Books; The Sciences of Natural Magic; Alchemy, or Hermetical Philosophy; The Nature, Creation, and Fall of Man; The Constellatory Practice, or Talismanic Magic; Magnetism and Cabalistical, or Ceremonial Magic, &c., *curious coloured engravings*, 4to. *calf, extremely rare.* 1801

4026 Calmet (*Augustine*), Phantom World, edited by Christmas, 2 vols. 8vo. *cloth.* Lond. 1850

Are profoundly interesting, inasmuch as the great and mysterious subjects of Astrology, Magic, Dreams, and Mesmeric Wonders are treated of in a way without a parallel.

4027 Fage (*John, Practitioner in Astrology*), The Sicke-men's Glasse, whereby one may give a true but infallible judgment of the life or death of a sicke bodye, &c., **Black Letter**, *rare, sewed*, 4to. Lond. 1606

4028 Gadbury (*Sir John*), The Works of that most excellent Philosopher and Astronomer, collected into one entire volume, 8vo. *sheep.* Lond. 1683

4029 Gaffarel (*J.*) Unheard of Curiosities concerning the Talismanical Sculpture of the Persians, the Horoscope of the Patriarchs, and the Reading of the Stars, sm. 8vo. *calf.* Lond. 1650

"A feast for an occult philosopher."—*Dr. A. Clarke.*

4029* Glanvil (*Joseph*), Saducisimus Triumphatus, or a full and plain Evidence concerning Witches and Apparitions, in eight curious Tracts, with additions, &c., by Henry More, D. D., 8vo. *calf.* Lond. 1700

A notice of this work, written to prove the existence of witches, will be found in the Retros. Rev., vol. 5, p. 87.

4030 Hill (*Tho.*) The Schoole of Skil, containing 2 Bookes: I. Of the Sphere; II. Of the Elements, &c., diagrams, small 4to. *sheep*, **Black Letter.** Lond. 1599

4031 History of Magic, containing the Autograph of Robert Southey, 1799—wants title—*half sheep*, 12mo. Lond. 1588

4032 Hutchinson (*Francis, D. D.*), An Historical Essay on Witchcraft, 8vo. *old calf.* Lond. 1718

"This work contains much interesting matter, and developes many celebrated impostures—a curious catalogue of the poor wretches burnt as witches."—*Lowndes.*

4033 Indigine (*Joannes*), Chiromanzey, Physionomey, Natural Astrology, Natural Influence of the Planets, &c., *curious wood-cuts of Palmistry, &c., by Lucas Cranach, in German, boards*, sm. folio. Franckfort, 1523

4034 LAMENT of Quinton McKell of Iron Gray, Soothsayer, 16mo. *privately printed.* N. Y. 1858

4035 LICHTENPERGER (*Johannes*), Prognostication, 4to. *half calf.* 1488

4036 MAGIC, Pretended Miracles, &c., 18mo. *cloth.* Lond.

4037 MATHEW (*Richd.*) The Unlearned Alchymist; His Antidote, or an explanation of the use, virtue, and benefit of my Pill, together with a precious Pearl in the midst of a Dung-hil, 16mo. *old calf*, torn. Lond. 1663

4038 MERLIN's Prophecies and Predictions, small 4to. *calf.* Lond. 1651

4039 MYSTERIES of Magic, 2 vols. in 1, 8vo. *boards.* Bost. 1833

4040 WEIDENFELD (*J. G.*) Four Books, concerning the secrets of the Adepts, or of the use of Lully's Spirit of Wine, &c., 4to. *calf.* Lond. 1685

4041 WITCHCRAFT, Three reprints of curious old Tracts relative to the execution of Witches, 8vo. *sewed.* Lond. v. y.

PAGEANTS, CORONATIONS, FUNERALS, FEASTS, PROCESSIONS, PROGRESSES, MASKS, MYSTERIES, SCENIC PANORAMAS, AQUATIC EXCURSIONS, FIREWORKS, BATTLES BY LAND AND WATER, TRIUMPHAL ARCHES, &C.

4052 ANCIENT Mysteries Described, Especially the English Miracle Plays, *plates*, 8vo. Lond. 1823

4053 BOCHII (*J.*) Historie narratio Profectionis et inaugurationis Alberti et Isabella, Oultremanni at the end, *beautiful plates*, folio. Plantin, Ant. 1602

4054 BUSENELLO (*Gio. Francesco*) Prospective of the Naval Triumph of the Venetians over the Turks, translated by T. Higgons, *calf*, 8vo. Lond. 1658

Each verse is divided by a crown and harp, a crown and fleur de lis, a crown and rose, it is dedicated to the celebrated Venetian Painter, Liberi, who is eulogized by Edmund Waller in some congratulatory verses at the beginning.

4055 CHINA, Suite de seize Estampes representant les Conquetes de l' Empereur de la chine, *oblong folio*, *curious plates.* Paris, 1785

4056 COLLECTIONS Relative to Claims at the Coronations of Several of the Kings of England, beginning with King Richard II., 8vo. *half calf.* Lond. 1838

4057 CORONATION, Faithful account of the Processions and Ceremonies observed in the Coronations of the Kings and Queens of England, &c., edited by Thomson, *additional plates* and MS. notes, 8vo. Lond. 1820

4057* CORONATION Service by T. Silver, Oxford, 1831, in 1 vol. *half calf*, 8vo. v. y.

4058 CORONATION, Walker (*Sir Edw.*) Circumstantial Account of the Preparations for the Coronation of King Charles the Second, *plates, half calf*, royal 8vo. Lond. 1820

4059 CORONATIONS, Form and Order of the Coronation of King Charles II. as it was done at Scoon, January 1, 1651, by Robert Douglas, 1660, Vinke's Reason of Faith, a Sermon, 1659, Rainbow's Funeral Sermon of the Countess of Pembroke, 1677, and many others, in 1 vol. 4to. Lond. v. y.

4060 CORONATION, Account of the Ceremonies observed at the, MS. title, 1727, Fireworks in St. James' Park for the Peace of 1748, in 1 vol. 4to. Lond. v. d.

4061 CORONATIONS, Ceremonies at the Coronation of Charles VI., Emperor of Germany, in German, several fine Portraits and large print of the Procession, folio. Frankf. 1712

4062 DANIEL (*Samuel*), Tethy's Festival, or the Queene's Wake, to solemnize the Creation of the High and Mighty Prince Henry, Prince of Wales, *half calf, very rare*, 4to. Lond. 1610

4063 DEKKER (*Tho.*) The Magnificent Entertainment given to King James, Annie his wife, and Henry F. the Prince, upon the day of his Majesties triumphant passage (from the Tower) through his honourable Citie and Chamber of London, 1603, with the Speeches and Songes delivered at the severall Pageants, 4to. Lond. 1604

A volume of the greatest rarity. Beloe heard of this as one of Dekker's works, but he had not seen any copy, (*Ance*, vol. 2, p. 158.) Rhode's copy sold for £16. The Bib. Ang. Poetica prices it at £8 8*s*.

4064 EGLINTOUN Tournament, a Righte Faithfull Chronique of the Ladies and Knights who gained worship at the Grand Tourney holden at his Castle by the Earl of Eglintoun, 12mo. *half morocco.* 1820

4065 FUNERAL Procession of Anne, Princess Royal of Great Britain, Dowager of Orange and Nassau, beautifully engraved by Fokke, description in French and Dutch, *large folio*, 8vo. Gravenhage, 1759

4066 HERAÆ (*C. G.*) Inscriptiones et Symbola, 8vo. *calf, numerous beautiful plates.* Noribergæ, 1721

4067 HONE (*W.*) Ancient Mysteries, 8vo. *half calf.* Lond. 1823

4068 JONSON (*Ben*), B. Jon: his part of King James, his Royall and Magnificent Entertainment through his Honorable Citie of London, Thurseday, the 15th of March, 1603; so much as was presented in the first and last of their Triumphall Arch's, 1604; A Particular Entertainment of the Queene and Prince, their Highnesse, at Althrope, Lord Spencer's, June 25th, 1603, as they came first into the Kingdome; in 1 vol., portrait of Ben Jonson by Vertue, also a very rare print of James I., on horseback, with view of London and London Bridge in the background, inserted, 4to. *half morocco, Duke of Roxburgh's fine copy, very scarce.* Lond. 1604

4069 LAUDER (*Sir T. Dick*), Memoirs of the Royal Progress of Queen Victoria in Scotland, 4to. *half calf.* Edinb. 1843

4070 LOUIS XV.: Sacre de Louis XV. Roy de France, &c., upwards of 50 very large and finely executed engravings of the ceremonies, processions, costumes, portraits, &c., original impressions, imp. folio, *calf.* Paris, 1722

The whole text of this interesting volume is engraved and printed on one side only, and each page surrounded by an engraved border.

4071 MARKLAND (*Abraham*), Poems on his Majestie's birth and restauration; his Highness, Prince Rupert's, and his Grace, the Duke of Albemarle's, Naval Victories; the late great Pestilence and Fire of London, *sewed,* 4to. Lond. 1667

4072 MARRIAGE du Prince Guillaume avec la Princesse Renée de Lorraine dans la ville de Munich l'an 1568: a series of engravings after Van Sickel, beautifully coloured in the style of the time, with a MS. title, *on vellum,* 15 *plates carefully mounted,* large folio, *half calf.* 1569

Highly interesting for the Costume, &c.

4073 MARRIAGE of Ferdinand and Maria; Descrizione delle Feste Celebrate in Parma l'annio 1769; per le Auguste Nozze di sua Altezza, Reale l'Infante Don Ferdinando colla reale Archiduchessa Maria Amalia, 40 *plates,* folio, *half calf.* Parma, n. d.

This splendid volume was printed at the Royal press for presents only.

4074 MARRIAGE of Napoleon; Description of the ceremonies and fêtes which took place on the Marriage of Napoleon and the Empress Marie Louise, folio, large and fine outline plates, by Percier and Fontaine, of the splendid ceremonies, festivities, &c., folio, *half calf.* Paris, 1810

4075 MURAT (M.) Rites of Funeral, Ancient and Modern, translated by P. Lorain, 12mo. *calf.* Lond. 1683

4076 NICHOLS (*J.*) The Progresses and Public Processions of Queen Elizabeth, 3 vols. 4to. *boards.* Lond. 1823

*** Nearly all the copies of the third volume were accidentally destroyed by fire.

4077 ——— Progresses, Processions, Festivities, and Pageants of King James I., his Queen, Family, and Court, *plates*, 4 vols. 4to. *half calf extra.* Lond. 1828

"The title-page of this work conveys a very imperfect idea of its contents, for instead of being a mere account of the progresses and festivities produced for the amusement of James I., it is in fact the domestic history of his reign. The research and tact which have been displayed in procuring and in dovetailing the discordant materials have seldom been equalled; and it would be difficult to name a compilation that will better repay perusal, though its chief value is as a book of reference for every person and circumstance connected with that reign."—*Retrospective Review.*

4078 ——— (*John Gough*), London Pageants; Part I—Account of Sixty Royal Processions and Entertainments in the City of London: No. II—a Bibliographical List of Lord Mayors' Pageants, *interleaved*, royal 8vo. Lond. 1831

4079 OGILBY (*J.*) Coronation of Charles II. The Entertainment of Charles II. in his Passage through the City of London to his Coronation. Containing an account of the whole Solemnity, the Triumphal Arches, Procession, Cavalcade, &c., by John Ogilby, folio, *fine plates by Hollar, including portraits of the distinguished men, Nobility, &c., calf, scarce.* Lond. 1662

"A splendid volume, published at the King's command."

4080 PEACHAM (*Henry*), Period of Mourning, disposed in sixe visions in memorie of the late Prince (Henry), with nuptiall Hymnes in Honour of the Marriage of Frederick Count Palatine and the Princess Elizabeth, 1613, *reprint*, 8vo. *half morocco.* Lond. 1789

4081 ACCOUNT of the Revels at Court in Queen Elizabeth's and King James's Reigns, Extracts from, with Introduction and Notes by P. Cunningham, 8vo. 1842

4082 ROBIN'S Panoramic Representation of the Queen's Coronation, Procession from the Palace to the Abbey, June 28th, 1838, *colored, in an octavo case.* Lond. 1838

4093 ROMANI (*Lauri*), Antiquis Urbis, splendor, 166 *plates of Triumphal Arches*, oblong 4to. Rom. 1612

4094 RUBENS, Pompa Introitus Ferdinandi Austriaci Hispaniarum Infantis, in Antverpiam, atlas folio, *consisting of* 43 *very large plates of Triumphal Arches, etc., engraved by Thulden, after paintings by Rubens.* Antv. 1635

4095 SANDFORD (*F.*) The History of the Coronation of King James II. and his Queen, folio, 30 *fine plates of the Ceremonial Procession* (*including many portraits of the nobles, &c.*), *Regalia, Rejoicings, &c., fine impressions, calf.* Lond. 1687

4096 SHARP (*Th.*) Coventry Mysteries. The Pageants or Dramatic Mysteries anciently performed at Coventry by the Trading Companies of that City; with a Dissertation illustrative of the Vehicle, Characters, and Dresses of the Actors, compiled, in a great degree, from sources hitherto unexplored; to which are added the Pageant of the Shearmen, the Taylors' Company, and other Municipal Entertainments of a Public Nature; an Essay on Minstrels and Waits, and a Glossary; *the whole embellished by copper-plates and wood-cuts* (*only* 250 *copies printed*), royal 4to. *half calf.* 1825

"The volume abounds with ingenious illustrations of many of those national and local customs, which are among the happiest associations of our younger years, the minstrels, waits, and puppets, which our infant feelings welcomed in their turn. The work is a most laborious and valuable addition towards a complete history of the early drama and the stage, and Mr. Sharp was eminently qualified to undertake and execute the arduous task, for which he is entitled to the gratitude of the literary world."—*Retrospective Review.*

4097 SYLVESTER (*Joshua*), An Elegie and Epistle consolatorie against immoderate sorrow for the immature decease of Sir William Sidney, Knight, &c., *half morocco,* 4to. *scarce.* Lond. 1613

4098 THOMSON (*Richard*), Faithful Account of the Processions and Ceremonies observed in the Coronations of the Kings and Queens of England, *plates,* impl. 8vo. *half calf.* Lond. 1820

4099 TOURNEUR (*Cyril*), Grief on the Death of Prince of Henrie, expressed in a broken Elegie, according to the Nature of such a Sorrow, 4to. Lond. 1613

4100 VANDER MEULIN, a large folio volume of 36 folding plates of Scenery, Battle Pieces, Pageants, &c., after this celebrated master, illustrative of scenes in the life of Louis XIV. of France, folio, *calf.*

POETRY—OLD ENGLISH, SCOTCH, AND FOREIGN.—
See also AMERICAN POETS, No. 235 TO 338.

> "Of battaile and of chivalry,
> Of ladies' love and druerie,
> Anon I wol you tell."—*Chaucer.*

4101 ADONIS (Imitation du Chant huitieme de l'Adone du Cavalier Marin), *beautiful frontispiece, title, and vignettes, sheep*, 8vo. Paris, 1775

4102 AKENSIDE (*Mark*), The Pleasures of Imagination, 18mo. *sheep.* N. Y. 1813

4103 ALEXANDER (*W., Earl of, Sterline*), Recreation with the Muses (Tragedies and Poems), *old binding*, folio. Lond. 1637

4104 AIKIN (*J.*) Essays on Song-writing, with a collection of such English songs as are most eminent for poetical merit, a new edition, with additions and corrections and a supplement, by R. H. Evans, *uncut,* 8vo. Lond. 1810

4105 ALLOT (*Robert*), England's Parnassus, or the choysest Flowers of our Moderne Poets, with their Poetical Comparisons, Descriptions of Beauties, Personages, Castles, Palaces, Mountaines, Groves, Seas, Springs, Rivers, &c., edited by Park, 4to. *half morocco.* Lond. 1814

The Roxburghe copy of the original edition of this volume sold for £21. It contains productions of Shakspeare, Spenser, Sidney, Drayton, Marlowe, Dekker, Davis, Marston, Chapman, Constable, Harrington, Lodge, Higgons, Gascoigne, Green, Peele, Middleton, Fraunce, Watson, Surrey, Wyat, Turberville, Churchyard, Daniel, Markham, Fairfax, Storer, Bastard, Weever, Kyd, Sackville, Fairfax, Warner, and many others.

4106 ANCIENT Metrical Tales, chiefly from original sources, edited by C. Hartshorne, M. A., post 8vo. *half morocco.* *Pickering*, 1829

Includes King Athelstane, K. Edward and the Shepherd, Florice and Blancheflour, Robin Hood, Cockwold's Dance, Doctour Double Ale, and several others.

4107 ANACREON, done into English out of the original Greek, attributed to Cowley, also to F. Willis; *see* MS. note, 8vo. *half morocco.* Oxford, 1683

4108 ANCIENT Gothic Church, and other Poems, 12mo. *bds.* Lond. 1842

4109 ANOMALICÆ, being Desultory Essays, 18mo. *half calf.* Whitby, 1798

4110 APOSTATE, Ecclesiastic, a Poem on the Rev. Mock-Patriot Parson H[or]ne. 1774

4111 ARDEN (*F.*) Ovid's Tristia, first book translated by, 8vo. *boards.* N. Y. 1821

4112 ARMSTRONG (*J.*) Miscellaneous Works, 2 vols. 12mo. *calf.* Lond. 1770

4113 ARIOSTO (*L.*) Orlando Furioso, 6 vols. 16mo. *sewed.* Venezia, 1811

4114 ——— Orlando Furioso, translated by Sir John Harington, *plates*, folio, *half calf.* Ludgate, 1591

4115 ——— Orlando Furioso, beautiful edition, printed by Baskerville, with fine plates by Bartolozzi, Grignon, &c. royal 8vo. *calf.* Birmingham, 1773

"I never see, or even think of the lovely edition of Baskerville, without the most unmixed satisfaction. Paper, Printing, Drawing, Plates, all delight the eye and gratify the heart of the thorough-bred bibliomanical virtuoso."—*Dibdin.*

"Ariosto has been, after Homer, the favorite poet of Europe. His grace and facility, his clear and rapid stream of language, his variety and beauty of invention, his very translations of subjects, so frequently censured by critics, but artfully devised to spare the tediousness that hangs on a protracted story, left him no rival in general popularity. Above sixty editions of the Orlando Furioso were published in the sixteenth century. There was not one, says Bernardo Tasso, of any age, or sex, or rank, who was satisfied with a single perusal." —*Hallam.*

4116 BAKER (*R.*) Cato Variegatus, or Catoe's Morall Distichs, translated and paraphrased, with variations of expressing in English verse, *rare*, 4to. Lond. 1636

Bibliotheca Anglo-Poetica, 1£ 18*s.*

4117 BARBER (*A. G.*), Fruit Garden, a Poem, 4to. *half calf.* Lond. 1754

4118 BARN-YARD Rhymes, showing what opinions the Turkey, the Cock, the Goose, and the Duck entertain on Allopathia, Homopathia, Electro-Galvanism, and the Animalculæ Doctrines, royal 8vo. *sewed.* N. Y. 1838

4119 BATTLE of Talavera, a Poem, *sewed*, 8vo. Lond. 1819

4120 BEAUMONT (*Sir John*), Bosworth Field, with a taste of the variety of other poems, set forth by his sonne, Sir Iohn Beaumont, *rare,* 8vo. *half morocco.* Lond. 1629

*** Following the dedication are commendatory verses by Ben Jonson, Michael Drayton, Francis Beaumont, and others. Dr. Kippis says, "It is plain that there was great harmony in his versification, and that it was much above the general cast of the age." Priced in the Bib. Ang. Poet. £2 5*s*., and sold in Lloyd's sale for £2 3*s*.

4121 ——— (*Joseph,* M. A., and ejected Fellow of St. Peter's Coll., Cambridge), Psyche, or Love's Mysterie, in XX Cantos, displaying the Intercourse betwixt Christ and the Soule, folio, *half calf.* Lond. 1648

Pope is reported to have said of this work, "there are in it a great many flowers well worth gathering; and a man who has the art of stealing wisely, will find his account in it."

"One of the most extraordinary Poems in this or any other language."—*Southey.*

4122 BELLMAN'S (*The*) Treasury, containing above one hundred verses, fitted for all humors and fancies, and suited to all times and seasons, 12mo. *very scarce, calf.* Lond. 1707

4123 BELL'S British Poets, Index to (being vols. 57 and 58), 18mo. *boards.* 1780

4124 BERANGER (*P. J. de*), Œuvres completes, illustrées, par Grandville, *plates, half morocco, uncut,* royal 8vo. Paris, 1811

4125 BERNARD (*Richard,* of Epworth, Lincolnshire), Terence in English, *half calf,* 4to. Lond. 1641

4126 BROOME (*Wm.*) Poems on Several Occasions, 8vo. *calf, ruled.* Lond. 1750

4127 BOILEAU, Le Lutrin, an Heroick Poem, Englished by N. O., *sewed,* 4to. Lond. 1682

4128 BOOK of Poetry, 18mo. *calf extra.* Phil. n. d.

4129 BOWDLER (*Miss*), Poems and Essays of the late, 18mo. *boards.* Lond. 1834

4130 BOYS (*John*), Æneas, his Errours, or his Voyage from Troy into Italy, an Essay upon the Third Booke of Virgil's Æneis, by John Boys, of Hode Court (Kent), 12mo. Lond. 1661

4131 BRETT (*Arthur*), Threnodia, on the Death of Prince Henry, Duke of Gloucester, *half morocco,* 4to. Lond. 1660

4132 BRINSLEY (*J.*) Translation of Virgil's Eclogues, with his Booke de Apibus, concerning the Government and Ordering of Bees, 4to. Lond. 1633

4133 BRAITHWAIT (*Richard*), Arcadean Princess, or the Triumph of Justice, *front. by Marshall, old binding*, 12mo. Lond. 1635

4134 BROME (*H.*) The Poems of Horace, consisting of Odes, Satyres, and Epistles, rendered into English verse by several persons, *old calf, fine copy in its pristine state, slightly wormed, portrait of Brome by Loggan, and of Horace by Dunstall, scarce*, 8vo. Lond. 1666

*** The translators to this volume were Brome, Cowley, Ben Jonson, Sir Thomas Hawkins, Sir Richard Fanshawe, &c. Lloyd's sale, £1 18*s.* Bib. Anglo-Poet. £4 4*s.*

4136 BRITISH Muse, or Tyranny Exposed, a Satire, occasioned by all the fulsom and lying Poems and Elegies that have been written on the Death of King James (2nd), with a smart Poem on the Generous articles of Limerick and Galway, 4to. *sewed.* Lond. (1691)

4137 BROOKS (*James G.*) Anniversary Poem before the Society of Phi Beta Kappa, New Haven, 8vo. *sewed.* 1826

4138 BROWNE (*William*), Britannia's Pastorals, *frontispiece by Hole*, sm. folio, *cloth.* Lond. 1613

With commendatory poems by Drayton, Selden, Davies of Hereford, Wither, Ben Jonson, &c. A copy of this scarce edition of this highly interesting poetical volume sold for £3 5*s.* at Bindley's sale, and for £3 3*s.* at Nassau's.

4138* ——— Britannia's Pastorals, edited, with Notes, &c., by Rev. H. Thompson, *reprint, half morocco.* 1845

"No book contains more original and accurate images, drawn from rural life and scenery. Remarkable for opulence, richness, and propriety of phrase."—*Retrospective Review.*

4139 BRUNONIAD, an Heroic Poem, 4to. *half calf.* 1789

4140 BRUNSWICK (*The*), a Poem, 8vo. *half calf.* Lond. 1829

4141 BUCK (*Geo.*) The Great Plantaganet, or a continued succession of that royall name from Henry the second to our sacred soveraigne King Charles, *rare*, 4to. Lond. 1635

Sold in Bindley's sale, £4; Bib. Anglo-Poetica, £4 10*s.*

4142 BULTEEL (*John*), A new collection of Poems and Songs, written by several persons; never printed before, *rare*, 8vo. Lond. 1674

4143 BULWER LYTTON'S (*Sir E.*) New Timon, a Poetical Romance, small sqr. 8vo. Phil. 1846

"One of the most remarkable poems of the present generation."—*Sun.*

4144 BURGES (*Sir T. B.*) Richard the 1st, a Poem, 2 vols. in 1, 8vo. *half calf.* Lond. 1801

4145 BURTON (*Johannes de Maplederham*), Sacerdos Parœcialis Rusticus, a Latin poem, 8vo. *sewed.* Oxon. 1757

4146 BUSH (*H.*) Vestriad, a Poem, 8vo. *half calf.* Lond. 1819

4147 BURNS' Works, Vol. I., &c., 14 vols.

4148 BUTLER'S Hudibras, edited by the Rev. T. Nash, D. D., *illustrated by 60 engraved portraits, and numerous fine wood-cuts,* 2 vols. 8vo. *half calf.* Lond. 1845

*** "The introduction of so many portraits of interesting personages, must give the best recommendations these volumes can obtain to the library of the man of taste."—*Art Union Journal.*

4149 BYRON (*Lord*), Works, by J. W. Lake, 8vo. *sheep.* Phil. 1858

4150 ——— Works, 8 vols. 18mo. *cloth.* Phil. 1839

4151 ——— Bride of Abydos, 8vo. *calf.* Lond. 1813

4152 ——— The Siege of Corinth, a Poem, 12mo. *sheep, torn.* N. Y. 1816

4153 BYRON—COLIN (*A.*) Historical Illustration of Lord Byron's Works, in a series of Etchings, 4 *plates,* royal 8vo. Lond. 1833

4154 CAMOENS (*Louis de*), The Lusiad, or Portugal's Historical Poem, newly put into English by Richard Fanshaw, Esq., *calf.* Lond. 1655

4155 ——— Lusiad, translated by Mickle, 4to. Oxford, 1776

The Portuguese regard Camoens as their Virgil, Horace, Ovid, and Martial. The subject of it is the conquest of the East Indies by the Portuguese; Vasco de Gama is the hero. He has the tender romance of Tasso, the picturesque of Ariosto, and connects these with the dignity of the heroic poet.

4156 CAREW (*Thomas*), Poetical Works, with Introduction, *finely printed,* 8vo. 12*s.* Edinb. 1824

Only 125 copies printed from the rare original edition of 1640.

4157 ——— Poetical Works of, 12mo. *half calf.* Lond. 1845

"Carew is pre-eminently beautiful, and deservedly ranks among the earliest of those who gave a cultivated grace to our Lyric Poetry." —*Campbell.*

"Sprightly, polished, and perspicuous, every part of his works displays the man of sense, gallantry, and breeding."—*Headly.*

4158 CARLISLE (*Earl of*) Tragedies and Poems, 8vo. *calf.* Lond. 1800

4159 CANE (*Miss*), now Mrs. Winscom, Poems on Various Subjects, 12mo. Bristol.

CARTWRIGHT (*Wm.*) Poems, *vide* Lots 928 and 929.

4161 CASIMERE, The Odes of Casimere, translated by G. H. [Hils]; *frontispiece by Marshall, very scarce*, 12mo. *half calf.* Lond. 1646

4162 LYRIQUES, Opuscules presentes a Lady Nelson, par M. Ceby, 12mo. *bds.* a Londres, 1801

4163 CHAPMAN (*Geo.*) Seaven Bookes of the Iliades of Homere, Prince of Poets, translated according to the Greeke in judgement of his best commentaries by George Chapman, Gent, printed by Iohn Windet, and are to be solde at the signe of the Crosse-keyes near Paules wharfe, *extremely rare*, 4to. *half russia.* Lond. 1598

*** This varies so considerably from the translation in folio that it may almost be considered a distinct work. Bright's copy sold for £6 6*s.* Pope says of Chapman's Homer: "There is a daring fiery spirit that animates his translation, which is something like what one might imagine Homer himself would have writ before he arrived to years of discretion."

"Brave language are Chapman's Iliades!"—*Bolton's Hypercritica.*

"Neither Warton, nor Ames, nor Herbert are acquainted with this edition."—*MS. Note.*

"Till I heard Chapman speak out loud and bold,
Then felt I like some watcher of the skies,
When a new planet swims into his ken."—*Keats.*

4164 ——— Funeral Song on the Death of Henry Prince of Wales, *sewed*, 4to. Kent, 1818

4165 CHAMBERLAYNE (*Wm.*) Pharonnida, an Heroick Poem, 3 vols. 8vo. *half morocco.* 1820

Southey, in a note to his "Joan of Arc," calls Chamberlayne a poet who has told an interesting story in uncouth rhymes, and mingles sublimity of thought and beauty of expression, with the quaintest conceits and most awkward inversions.

4166 CHATTERTON (*Thos.*) Poems supposed to have been written at Bristol, by Thomas Rowley and others, in the fifteenth century, 8vo. *half calf.* Cambridge, 1794

4167 TYRWHITT (*T.*) A Vindication of the Appendix to the Poems called Rowley's, in reply to answers of the Dean of Exeter, Jacob Bryant, Esq., and a third anonymous writer, with some further observations upon these poems, and an examination of the evidence which has been produced in support of their authenticity, *portrait*, *uncut*, 8vo. Lond. 1782

"The marvellous boy who perished in his pride."—*Wordsworth.*

4168 CHAUCER'S (*Geffray*) Workes, newlye printed, with dyvers Workes whych were never in print before, folio, **Black Letter**, *rough calf* (*wood-cut of the Knight's Tale and the Squire's Tale wanting; also the leaves after T. T.*), *fine tall copy.* Lond. *W. Bonham*, 1542

First complete edition of the entire works.

4169 CHAUCER (*G.*) The Workes of Geffrey Chaucer, newlie printed with diuers addicions, which were neuer in print before, with the siege and destruccion of the worthy citee of Thebes, compiled by John Lidgate Monke of Berie, as in the table more plainly doeth appere; *Wood-cuts of the Pilgrims, very rare*, **Black Letter**, folio. Lond. 1561

This scarce edition was edited and greatly enlarged by J. Stowe and James Shirley, who had painfully collected the works of Chaucer, Lydgate, and other writers.

4170 CHAUCER—The Works of our Ancient and Learned English Poet, Geffrey Chaucer, edited by Thomas Speght, *a very fine sound copy of this early and rare* **Black Letter** *edition, old calf, gilt, with portrait.* Lond. 1598

4171 CHAUCER'S Poetical Works, with an Essay on his Language and Versification, Notes and Glossary by Tyrwhitt, *portrait*, royal 8vo. *half calf.* Moxon, 1843

"In elocution and elegance, in harmony and perspicuity of versification, he surpasses his predecessors in an infinite proportion; his genius was universal, and adapted to themes of unbounded variety, and his merit was not less in painting familiar manners with humour and propriety, than in moving the passions, and in representing the beautiful or grand objects of nature, with grace or sublimity."—*Warton.*

4172 CLEAVLAND—Clievelandi Vindiciae, or Clieveland's genuine Poems, Orations, and Epistles, purged from the many false and spurious ones which had usurped his name, and from innumerable errours and corruptions in the true copies, &c., *portrait*, *scarce*, 8vo. Lond. 1677

Bib. Anglo-Poet., £1 11*s.* 6*d.*

*** Fuller says of Cleaveland that he was "a general artist, pure Latinist, exquisite orator, and excellent poet. All his poems are incomparable, so that to praise one, were to detract from the rest."

While the first edition and sheets of Paradise Lost were slowly struggling through the mists of bigotry and party prejudice into public reputation, the poems of Cleveland were poured forth in innumerable impressions. The reverse is now the singular contrast; and Cleveland has had the fate of those poets, described in Johnson's Life of Cowley, who, paying their court to temporary prejudices, have been at one time too much praised, and at another too much neglected.

4173 CHURCHILL'S (*C.*) Poems, 2 vols. 8vo. *half calf.* 1768

"Churchill has an exclusive right to the title of the British Juvenal."—*Headley.*

"Charles Churchill, the most striking personification of John Bull."—*Vide Gillfillan's Gallery of Portraits.*

4174 CLEVELAND (*John*), Character of a London Diurnal, with severall select Poems, *sewed*, 4to. Lond. 1647

4175 CLIFFORD (*A.*) Tixall Poetry, with Notes and Illustrations by Arthur Clifford, Esq., *fine, frontispiece*, 4to. *half morocco.* Edin. 1813

*** Containing poems by Sidney Godolphin, Sir Richard Fanshawe, Waller, Nat Lee, Dryden, &c.

COKAIN, *vide* Drama, Lot 965.

4176 COLERIDGE (*S. T.*) The Rime of the Ancient Mariner, 25 *poetic and dramatic scenes by D. Scott*, large folio, *cloth.* Edin. 1837

4177 CONSTANT Nymph (*The*), or the Rambling Shepherd, a Pastoral by a person of quality, 4to. *half calf.* Lond. 1678

COOPER'S Muses' Library, *vide* Shakspeariana.

4178 CORBET (*Bishop*), The Poems of, from the Edition of 1648, with Life, Biographical Notes, &c. by Octavius Gilchrist, post 8vo. *calf.* Lond. 1807

"The Poems of this great prelate, from their humorous merriment and pointed terseness, have more of a modern cast than any other works of the Elizabethan Age."

4179 COSTELLO (*L. S.*) Specimens of the early Poetry of France, from the time of the Troubadours or Trouveres to the Reign of Henry Quatre, *plates*, cr. 8vo. *cloth.* 1835

4180 COTTON (*Charles*) Burlesque upon Burlesque, or the Scoffer Scoft, being some of Lucian's Dialogues newly put into English fustian, for the consolation of those who had rather Laugh and be Merry than be Merry and Wise, *vellum*, 8vo. Lond. 1675

"This volume of Poems by the coadjutor of Isaac Walton, in the celebrated work upon angling, is of uncommon occurrence."

4181 COWLEY (*A.*) The Works of Mr. Abraham Cowley, consisting of those which were formerly printed and those which he designed for the press, now published out of the author's original copies, folio, *half morocco.* Lond. 1681

4182 Cowley (*A.*), Works, with Life by Clifford, portrait, 3 vols. 12mo. *half morocco.* Lond. 1721

A very complete edition of this Poet, with necessary Tables and divers Poems of eminent persons in praise of the author; and other considerable additions and improvements.

4183 ——— Select Works of, with Preface and Notes by the Editor (Bishop Hurd), 2 vols. small 8vo. *calf gt.* best Edition. Lond. 1772

"In all our comparisons of taste, I do not know whether I have ever heard your opinion of a poet very dear to me, though now out of fashion—Cowley."—*C. Lamb to Coleridge.*

4184 Coxe (*A. C.*), Saul, a Mystery, 12mo. *vel.* N. Y. 1845

4185 Crooked Sixpence, and 2 other Poems, 4to. 1743

4186 Creech (*T.*) Translations of Horace by T. Creech, *half morocco*, 8vo. Lond. 1684

4187 Cunningham (*A.*) Sir Marmaduke Maxwell, &c., 8vo. *boards.* Lond. 1822

4188 Dale (*Rev. Thomas*), The Poetical Works of, 12mo. *cloth.* Lond. 1836

4189 Dallas (*R. C.*) Poems, Lucretia and Moral Essays, with a Vocabulary of the Passions, 4to. *calf.* Lond. 1797

4190 Daniel (*Samuel*), First Foure Bookes of the Civile Warres betweene the Houses of Lancaster and Yorke, *two titles*, 4to. *half morocco, excessively rare.* Lond. 1595

"Sold at Sotheby's for £12."—*Lowndes.*

4191 ——— History of the Civil Wars between the Houses of York and Lancaster, published by John Daniel, his brother, 12mo. *half morocco.* Lond. 1767

4192 ——— The whole Workes of, in Poetrie, newly augmented, folio, *fine copy, in crimson morocco, extra gilt, most rare.* Lond. 1602

First complete edition sold at Bright's sale for £15.

"We find both in his poetry and prose such a legitimate and rational flow of language as approaches nearer the style of the 18th than the 16th century, of which, we may safely assert, that it will never become obsolete. He certainly was the Atticus of his day."

Headley.

"For sweetness and rhyming second to none."—*Drummond.*

4193 Davenant (*Sir William*), Gondibert, an Heroick Poem, 4to. *half morocco, gilt.* Lond. 1654

Priced £1 1*s.* in the Bibliotheca Anglo-Poetica.

Davenant was the godson of Shakspeare, and poet-laureat to Charles I. and II. He lived in habits of intimacy with Endimion Porter, Suckling, Carew, Habington, and other poets and wits of the time.

4194 DANTE, La Comedia Divina col Commenta di Ch. Landino, folio, *old vellum.* MCCCCXCVII.

This edition is not noticed by Burnet or Watts. Landino is one of the most prized of the old commentators.

"Landino, in his commentary on Dante, has preserved the remembrance of many historical facts, and related many circumstances indispensably necessary to the explanation of the divine comedia. His industry in the execution of a task so grateful to his countrymen, was rewarded by the donation of a villa or residence on the Hill of Casentino, in the vicinity of Florence, which he enjoyed under the sanction of a public decree."—*Roscoe's Lorenzo.*

This is also curious as being one of the first books in which copper-plates were introduced.

4195 ——— The Divina Commedia of Dante Alighieri, consisting of the Inferno, Purgatorio, and Paradiso, translated into English verse, with preliminary essays, notes, and illustrations, by the Rev. Henry Boyd, *portrait, uncut,* 3 vols. 8vo. *boards.* Lond. 1802

Bought at the Fonthill sale, £2.

"The secular aims, the greedy avarice, the nepotism, the shameful vices of the Popes whom Dante accuses—and he assailed none but wicked Popes—were all the more hateful to him, because they polluted the sanctity of the Church, while they inflamed the discords of his country. Such were the views which have caused Dante to be ranked as a partisan of the Ghibellines, although he repudiated—and it may be said with high reason—the charge of party—declaring that 'rectitude [see this passage in the treatise "*De Vulgari Eloquio*"], meaning inexorable justice—was his sole guide.'"

Athenæum.

4196 DAVIES (*Sir John*), Nosce Teipsum. This oracle expounded in two elegies: I. Of Humane Knowledge; II. Of the Soule of Man, and the Immortalitie thereof; *printed by Richard Field, for Iohn Standish, very rare,* 4to. Lond. 1602

⁎ See Bibliotheca Anglo-Poetica, where the 8vo. edition of 1619 was priced at £6 6*s.*

"A noble monument of learning, acuteness, command of language, and facility of versification."—*G. Ellis.*

4197 DAY (*John*), New Spring of Divine Poetrie, Acrostic Dedication to Mistress Ann Rudge, 4to. 1637

A very entertaining and scarce volume of Sacred Poems; containing The Worlde's Metamorphosis, Christ's Birth and Passion, and various other Meditations. Priced in the Bibliotheca Anglo-Poetica, £4 4*s.* See the Gentleman's Magazine for Jan. 1850.

4198 DELONEY (*Thomas*), Strange Histories, consisting of Ballads and other Poems, 1607, *half morocco, reprint,* 12mo. Lond. 1841

4199 DIBDIN (*C.*) Young Arthur, 8vo. *boards.* Lond. 1819

4200 DODD (*Dr., the unfortunate*), Poems by, "privately printed for the Author," post 8vo. *calf, gilt, scarce.* Lond. 1767

4201 DODSLEY'S Collection of Poems, by several hands, 6 vols. 12mo. *calf.* Lond. 1763

"The most popular poetical Miscellany ever published in England. Last edition was published in 1782." • *Vide* "Notes and Queries," vol. 2, p. 274.

4202 DRAYTON (*Michael*), England's Heroical Epistles, in the stile of Ovid's Epistles, 8vo. *half calf.* Lond. 1697

"Drayton is a sweet poet."—*Coleridge.*

4203 DRUMMOND (*W., of Hawthornden*), Select Poems of William Drummond; Life, by Sanford; Select Poems, by Giles and Phineas Fletcher, from Campbell; Select Poems, by William Habington; and Life, by Thomas Campbell, &c., in 1 vol. 12mo. *unbound.* n. d.

4204 ——— Poetical Works, now first published entire, edited by W. B. Turnbull, fcap. 8vo. *fine portrait, cloth.* 1856

"The sonnets of Drummond," says Mr. Hallam, "are polished and elegant, free from conceit and bad taste, and in pure, unblemished English."

4205 DRYDEN (*John*), Works of, 2 vols. folio, *calf.* 1701

4206 ——— The Medall, a Satyre against Sedition, 4to. *half morocco.* Lond. 1682

4207 ——— Absalom and Achitophel, a Poem, folio, *half morocco.* Lond. 1682

——— The Works of, now first collected, illustrated with Notes, Historical, Critical, and Explanatory, and a Life of the Author, by Walter Scott, Esq., 18 vols. 8vo., *vide* Lot 1063. Lond. 1808

"The style of Dryden was very superior to anything England had seen. . . . . He seems to have formed himself on Montaigne, Balzac, and Voiture; but so ready was his invention, so vigorous his judgment, and so complete his mastery over his native tongue, that in point of style, he must be reckoned above all three. He had the ease of Montaigne without his negligence and embarrassed structure of periods; he had the dignity of Balzac, with more varied cadences and without his hyperbolical tumour; the unexpected turns of Voiture, without his affectation and air of effort."—*Hallam.*

4207* ——— Tears of the British Muses on the Death of John Dryden, Esq., folio, *half morocco.* Lond. 1700

4208 Du Bartas (*G. Salust, Lord*), Bartas; his Devine Weekes and Workes, translated and dedicated to the King's most excellent Majesty, by Josuah Sylvester, *with portrait*, 4to. *half morocco.* 1611

"'This work,' says Dunster, 'contains the *prima stamina* of Milton's Paradise Lost.'

"Both the version of Sylvester, and his original poems, published with it, are remarkable for their inequality; for great beauties and glaring defects. His versification is sometimes exquisitely melodious, and was recognized as such by his contemporaries, who distinguished him by the appellation of *silver-tongued Sylvester.*"—*Drake.*

See Gentleman's Magazine, Aug. 1800, and Campbell's Specimens.

4209 Dunkin (*W.*) Works, 2 vols. 8vo. *calf.* Dublin, 1770

4210 Durfey (*Thomas*), Butler's Ghost, or Hudibras the Fourth, with Reflections on their Times, 8vo. *sheep.* Lond. 1682

Durfey, *see also* Lots 2260 to 2264, 3000 to 3005.

4211 Edwin and Angelina, *sewed*, 8vo. N. Y. 1797

4212 Ellis (*G.*) Specimens of early English Metrical Romances, to which is prefixed an historical introduction on the rise and progress of romantic composition in France and England, &c., *frontispiece*, 8vo. *first edition, calf, scarce.* Lond. 1790

4213 Ellis: Specimens of Early English Metrical Romances, with an historical introductioa, 3 vols. crown 8vo. *calf.* 1805

Contents: Merlin; Morte Arthur; Guy of Warwick; Sir Bevis of Hamptoun; Richard Cœur de Lion; Roland and Ferragus; Sir Otuel; Sir Ferumbras; Seven Wise Masters; Florice and Blauncheflour, Robert of Cysille; Sir Isumbras; Sir Triamour; Ipomydon; Layle Fraine; Sir Eglamour of Artois; Sir Eger, Sir Grahame, and Sir Gray Steel; Sir Degoré; Roswel and Lillian; Amys and Amylion.

4214 Falconer (*Wm.*) Shipwreck, by Wm. Falconer, *best edition, with fine marine plates, by Dodd*, royal 8vo. 1811

*** With the exception of Lord Byron, whose description of a shipwreck in Don Juan is only made more horrible by the mocking spirit of the narrator, we believe Falconer is almost the only poet who is any way successful in putting Sea life into verse, and making its perils and vicissitudes the subject of a poem.

4215 Fanshawe (*Sir R.*) Selected parts of Horace, Prince of Lyrics and of all the Latin Poets, the fullest fraught with excellent morality; concluding with a piece out of Ausonius, and another out of Virgil, now newly put into English, *rare*, 8vo. Lond. 1652

4216 FANSHAWE (*Sir R.*) Guarini's Il Pastor Fido, The Faithful Shepheard, with an addition of divers other Poems, etc., *rare, large copy, with both the titles, and portrait by Cross, in the original morocco binding, gilt edges,* 4to. Lond. 1648

4217 FARR (*Edw.*) Select Poetry, chiefly sacred, of the reign of King James the First, Selections from one hundred different authors, 12mo. *half morocco.* Cambridge, 1847

4218 ——— Another copy, *cloth.* Cambridge, 1848

4219 FELLOWS (*John*), The History of the Old and New Testament attempted in easy verse, 4 vols. 12mo. *plates, calf.* Lond. n. d.

4220 FERGUSON (*Robt.*) The Works of, with an Essay on his Genius and Writings, 12mo. *cloth.* Lond. 1851

4221 FLETCHER (*Thomas*), Poems on several occasions, and Translations wherein the First and Second Books of Virgil's Æneis are attempted, in English, *scarce,* 8vo. *calf.* Lond. 1692

4222 FLEMING (*Arthur*), Virgil: The Georgiks of Publius Virgilius Maro, otherwise called his Italian Husbandrie, gramaticallie translated into English meter, by A(rthur) F(leming), **Black Letter,** *very rare,* 4to. printed by T. O., for Thomas Woodcock. Lond. 1589

See the Bib. Ang. Poet., where a copy of this extremely rare book, wanting the last leaf, is priced £15 15s.

4223 FLUGEL (*Dr. J. G.*) Flowers of German Poetry, 12mo. *cloth.* Leip. 1835

4224 FONTAINE, Tales from, First Epistle of Horace, &c., 12mo. *half calf.* Lond. 1762

4225 FRY (*John*), Select Poems, and Poems to Mrs. Montagu, *various.*

4226 FULGOSI (*Baptista*), Anteros, *curious wood-cut,* small 4to. *sewed, Impressum Mediolani per L. M. Pachel,* MCCCCLXXXXVI.

Ce livre rare renferme deux dialogues contre l'amour ecrits en Italien, mèlé de passages late au verse du titre, est une figure en bois, &c.—*See Brunet.*

4227 FUGITIVE Pieces: Parnassian Shop, Valesco, Ferdinand Frank, Reliquiæ Juveniles, by Watts, 5 vols. 12mo. &c.

GASCOIGNE'S Works, *vide* Shakespeariana.

4228 GAY (*Mr. J.*) The Shepherd's Week, in Six Pastorals, and 4 other pieces, 12mo. *half calf, torn.* Lond. 1721

4229 GLANVILLE (*John*), Odes of Horace, imitated with relation to his Majesty (William III.) and the Times, 8vo. Lond. 1690

4230 GOMERSALL (*Robert*), Poems by, 12mo. *half morocco.* Lond. 1633

Priced £3 3*s.* in the Bib. Ang. Poet.

4231 GOSPEL Tragedy (*The*), an Epic Poem in Four Books, 12mo. *sheep.* Worcester, 1795

4232 GOULD (*R.*) Ludus Scacchia, a Satyr, with other Poems, *Printed by A. M., for Robert Clavel, at the sign of the Peacock in St. Paul's Church-yard, scarce,* 8vo. *half calf, stained.* Lond. 1675

*** The "other Poems" are "The Cyprian Virgin," "Strada's Nightingale," etc.

4233 ——— Poems, chiefly consisting of Satyrs and Satyrical Epistles. *Clean copy, in the original binding, scarce,* 8vo. *calf.* Lond. 1689

Includes "The Scourge for ill Wives," "Satyr on Women," and other curious Poems.

4233* GOWER, Ovid's Festivall or Romane Calendar, translated into English Verse equinumerically, by John Gower, *calf,* 12mo. Camb. 1640

A rare edition of this famous version, by the friend and contemporary of Chaucer.

4234 GRAY'S (*Thos.*) Poems, 8vo. *boards, with portrait.* 1784

4235 ——— Elegy on a Country Churchyard, 8vo. *cloth.* Phila. 1841

4236 ——— Murray (*John, Bookseller*), Letter to W. Mason concerning his Edition of Gray's Poems, *sewed,* 18mo. Lond. 1777

4237 GREEN (*Rob.*) Philomela, the Lady Fitz Water's Nightingale, 4to. *boards.* Lond. 1814

4238 ——— Four Letters and Certain Sonnets, especially touching Robert Greene and other parties by him abused, *London, imprinted by John Wolfe,* 1592, 4to. *half morocco, reprinted at the private press of Longman & Co.* Lond. 1814

4239 GREEN (*M.*) Spleen and other Poems, 12mo. *calf.* Lond. 1796

4240 GREVILLE (*Fulke, Lord Brooke*), Remains of, being Poems of Monarchy and Religion, 8vo. 1670

"Dryden formed his tragic style more upon Lord Brooke than upon any other writer."—*Southey.*

4241 GRIFFIN (*B.*) Fidessa, more Chaste than Kinde; a Collection of Sonnets, 8vo. *half morocco.* (*Reprint of* 1596,) 1815

Only One Hundred Copies of the reprint, with preface by the Rev. Dr. Bliss. Of the original work, it is believed that only two copies are in existence.

In Longman & Co.'s Catalogue, this reprint was marked £2 2*s.*

Remarkable as containing a Sonnet adopted by Shakspeare or imitated from him.

4242 HALL (*Bishop*), Satires and other Poems, edited by Peter Hall, 8vo. *cloth.* Lond. 1838

4243 HASLEWOOD (*Joseph*), Ancient Critical Essays upon English Poets and Poesy, by Puttenham, Gascoigne, Harvey, Spenser, K. James, Webb, Harrington, Meres, Campion, Daniel, and Bolton, edited by Haslewood, *woodcut portrait of Queen Elizabeth*, 2 vols. 4to. *calf, morocco backs.* Lond. 1811–15

Only 200 copies of these very curious Essays, some of which are of the greatest rarity, were printed, and nearly all the second volumes were destroyed at Bensley's fire. Published at £6 6*s.* in bds.

4244 HARTSHORNE'S Ancient Metrical Tales and Romances, from MS. sources, *William and the Werwolf*, *King Athelstan*, *Florice and Blanchefleur*, *&c.*, small 8vo., *half morocco.* Pickering, Lond. 1829

4245 HEADLEY'S Select Beauties of Ancient English Poetry, with remarks and a Biographical Sketch, by the Rev. Henry Kett, 2 vols. sm. 8vo. *half morocco.* 1810

"It shows research and discrimination, the preface abounds with curious learning and original thinking."—*Dr. Parr.*

"The work of a poetical and highly polished mind, which co-operated with Percy's Reliques in drawing attention to the then neglected Elizabethan poets."—*Bib. Manual.*

4246 HEYNES (*Thomas*), Triumphs of Royalty in the person of King Charles II., a Poem, *sewed*, 4to. Lond. 1683

4247 HERRICK (*R.*) Hesperides, or Work both Humane and Divine, *portraits*, 2 vols. *half calf*, 12mo. 1844

His flowers are not tied up into garlands, nor his fruit crushed into baskets, but spring living from the soil in all the dew and freshness of youth.

4248 HEYRICK (*Tho.*), Miscellany, Poems, &c., fine, clean copy, in the original binding, *scarce*, 4to. *calf.* Cambridge, 1691

*** Priced in Bib. Ang. Poet. £1 5*s.*

4249 HEYWOOD (*Thomas*), Troia Britannica, or Great Britaine's Troy, a Poem, divided into XVII. several Cantos, intermixed with many Pleasant Poetical Tales, folio, *half calf.* Lond. 1609

A most interesting collection of poems relating to Trojan and early British history.

4250 HOLYDAY (*Barten*), Survey of the World, *calf*, 12mo. Oxford, 1661

Bibliotheca Anglo-Poetica, £3 3*s*.

4251 ——— Juvenal and Persius, translated and illustrated as well with sculpture as with notes, *singular plates*, folio, *old calf.* Oxford, 1673

A writer of great learning and acuteness, whose translation and notes were so highly approved of by Dr. Johnson that he intended to republish it.

"Juvenal's genius from his unknown clime,
Came to the study, to impart his sense."

4252 ——— Persius, his Satires translated into English, 12mo. *half morocco.* Oxford, 1616

4253 HOMER, Iliads of, translated by George Chapman, introduction by W. Cooke Taylor, *wood-cuts after designs by Flaxman*, 2 vols. *cloth*, 8vo. Lond. 1843

HOMER, *vide* Chapman, Lot 4163.

4254 HOOD (*Thos.*) Poems, 12mo. *boards.* Phil. 1827

4255 HOPKINS (*Charles*), Epistolary Poems on several occasions, 8vo. *half morocco.* Lond. 1694

4256 HOPKINS (*John*), Amasia, or the Works of the Muses, a collection of Poems, 3 vols. in 1, portraits by Van Hove, *half morocco*, 8vo. Lond. 1700

4257 HORACE, Select parts of, translated into English Verse, by Richard Fanshawe, *original binding*, 8vo. *fine copy.* Lond. 1652

Nassau's copy sold for a guinea.

4258 HOWELL (*James*), Grecian Story, being an Historical Poem, in five books, to which is annexed the Grove frontispiece, containing portrait, 4to. *calf, extra.* Lond. 1684

4259 ——— Dodona's Grove, or the Vocall Forest, *with frontispiece*, folio, *half calf.* Lond. 1640

4260 HOWARD (*Sir Robt.*) Poems, viz.: A Panegyrick to the King, Songs and Sonnets, The Blind Lady, a Comedy, The fourth book of Virgil, Statius his Achilleis, with annotations, A Panegyrick to general Monck, *scarce*, 8vo. *half morocco.* Lond. 1660

Priced in the Bib. Anglo-Poetica, £1 10*s*.

4261 HUDDESFORD (*Geo.*) The Wiccamical Chaplet, a selection of Original Poetry, 12mo. Lond. 1804

4262 HUNT (*L.*) Amyntas, a Tale of the Woods, from the Italian, 12mo. Lond. 1820

4263 HYMN to the Nymph of Bristol Spring, 4to. 1751

4264 HYMN to the Dryads. 1796

4265 [JACOB'S] Poetical Register, or the Lives and Characters of all the English Poets, with an account of their Writings, portraits, 2 vols. 8vo. *calf.* Lond. 1723

4266 JONES (*John*), Ovid's Invective or Curse against Ibis, faithfully and familiarly translated into English Verse, both pleasant and profitable for each sort, sex, and age, 8vo. Oxford, 1658

*** Scarce. Priced in Bib. Ang. Poetica, £3 3*s.*

4267 KEMBLE (*John Philip*), Fugitive Pieces, 8vo. *morocco, gilt leaves, fine copy.* York, 1780

Excessively rare, being most rigorously and anxiously suppressed by the author, who boasted to a gentleman (to whom in vain he offered £10 10*s.* for his copy) that he had succeeded in destroying all the impressions but four copies.

4268 KENSINGTON Garden, a Poem, 4to. Lond. 1722

4269 KILLIGREW (*Anne*), Poems, *brilliant portrait by Beckett,* folio, *half calf.* 1686

*** "There are very few books in English poetry more rare than this." —*MS. Note.*

"Hear then a mortal muse thy praise rehearse
In no ignoble verse,
But such as thine own voice did practice here."
Dryden's Ode on the Death of Mrs. Anne Killigrew.

4270 LEAPOR (*Mrs.*) Poems, 8vo. *uncut.* Lond. 1748

Mrs. Leapor's genius must appear extraordinary to those who reflect that she was a poor uneducated girl, the daughter of a gardener in low laboring life. Her aunt was housekeeper to a gentleman of letters, and as Mrs. Leapor was fond of reading, the aunt supplied her with books from her master's library. She died at 25 years of age."—*MS. in the handwriting of Horace Walpole in the book.*

4271 LESLY (*G.*) Israel's Troubles and Triumphs, or, the History of their Dangers in and Deliverance out of Egypt. As it is recorded by Moses in Exodus, and turned into English Verse. Printed for the author, and sold by Nicholas Woolf, at his house in Star Court, Cheapside, *original binding, rare,* 8vo. *calf.* Lond. 1599

*** "Hearken to a Verser, who may chance Rhime thee to Good, and make a bait of Pleasure."

4272 LLOYD (*John*), Song of Songs, being a Paraphrase of the Canticles of Solomon, 8vo. *half morocco.* Lond. 1682

4273 LODGE (*Thos.*) Glaucus and Silla, with other Lyrical and Pastoral Poems, with a Preface by S. W. Singer, 8vo. *boards.* 1589, *reprint Chiswick*, 1819

This elegant volume includes all Lodge's verses from his various prose works. Only 250 copies printed.

4274 ——— A Fig for Momus, with an Autograph Note of Sir Alex. Boswell, 4to. *morocco, reprinted at the Auchinleck press.* 1818

Some of the poems in this volume are inscribed to Master E. Dig. (Digby); to reverend Colin (qu. Spenser?); to Master Samuel Daniel, Bolton, and Drayton.

4275 LYDGATE (*J. Monk of Bury*), Life and Death of Hector, his most famous Acts at the Siege of Troy, &c., last three leaves restored in fac-simile, folio. Lond., *T. Purfoot*, 1614

"This modern versification from the heroic couplet into six line stanza is generally attributed to T. Heywood; Fuller and other writers mistaking it for the original are amazed that the language is so much more intelligible than that of Chaucer."—*Dr. Farmer.*

4276 LYTERIA, a Dramatic Poem, 12mo. *cloth.* Lond. 1854

4277 MACAULAY; Lays of Ancient Rome, 4to. *calf, gilt edge.* Phil. 1853

"These Lays will add to Mr. Macaulay's great reputation. A stirring fancy, a fine imagination, run freshly and frankly through them, with the right homely, hearty wilfulness of the genuine ballad style. Life and passion are in every one of them."—*Examiner.*

4278 MACKAY (*Charles*), Songs for Music, Day and Night, by Allingham, 2 vols. 18mo. Lond.

4279 MARMION'S (*Shakerly*) Cupid and Psiche, or, an Epick Poem of Cupid and his Mistress, as it was lately presented to the Prince Elector, *reprinted at Chiswick*, 4to. 1820

The original edition of this curious and elegant poetical fable sold at Sotheby's, in 1817, for £6 16*s.* 6*d.*

4280 MASON (*William*), The English Garden, a Poem, 18mo. *cloth.* Lond. 1819

4281 MAITLAND, Virgil translated by, with a Prefatory Notice by Dryden, 2 vols., *vide* 2918.

Not mentioned by Lowndes.

4282 MAY (*Tho.*), Reigne of Henry II., written in seaven bookes, by his Majestie's commands, *very fine copy of this interesting historical poem*, 8vo. *bound in calf extra.* 1633

4283 ——— Victorious Reigne of Edward III., written in seaven bookes, by his Majestie's command, *fine impression of the scarce portrait, fine copy*, 8vo. *brown calf extra.* 1635

Inglis' copy of this interesting historical poem sold for £2 12*s.* 6*d.*, and Bindley's for £2 10*s.*

These two highly esteemed historical poems were written by the express command of Charles I.

4284 ——— Epitome of English History, wherein arbitrary government is displayed to the life, in the illegal transactions of the late times, under the tyrannick usurpation of Oliver Cromwell, &c., in prose, *very scarce, not mentioned by Lowndes, curious copper-plates*, 12mo. *calf.* Lond.

4285 ——— Lucan's Pharsalie; or the civill warres of Rome between Pompey the Great, and Ivlivs Cæsar. The whole ten Bookes Englished by Thomas May, Esquire, *fine engraved title, clean copy, in the original binding*, first edition, *rare*, 8vo. Lond. 1627

4286 ——— Continuation of the subject of Lucan's Historicall Poem on the death of Julius Cæsar, 2nd edition, *fine copy, vellum, original state*, 12mo. Lond. 1633

4287 ——— Lucan's Pharsalia, or the civill warres of Rome, betweene Pompey the Great and Ivlivs Cæsar, the whole tenne bookes Englished by Thomas May, Esq. A continuation of the subject of Lucan's historical poem, till the death of Julius Cæsar, *engraved title and portrait, pristine state*, 8vo. Lond. 1635

4289 ——— Mirror of Minds, or Barclay's Icon animorum, (prose,) 12mo. *calf.* Lond. 1633

4290 ——— Virgil's Georgicks, Englished by T. May, *calf extra, gilt*, sm. 12mo. Lond. 1628

Headley speaks very highly of May as a poet. He says, "His battle-pieces highly merit being brought forward to notice; they possess the requisites in a considerable degree for interesting the feelings of an Englishman; while in accuracy they vie with a gazette, they are managed with such dexterity, as to busy the mind with unceasing agitation, with scenes highly diversified and impassioned by striking character, minute incident, and alarming situation, &c.

4291 M'DONOUGH (*Capt. Felix*), Gratitude, a Poetical Essay, with other poems and translations, 12mo. *boards.* Lond. 1825

4292 MILTON (*John*), Paradise Lost, in 12 Books, plates by N. Burghers, after designs by Sir J. Medina, folio, *half morocco.* Lond. 1692

4293 ——— The Poetical Works of Mr. John Milton, containing Paradise Lost, Paradise Regained, Samson Agonistes, and his Poems on several occasions; together with explanatory notes on each book of the Paradise Lost, and a table never before printed, by Patrick Hume, portrait, and illustrated with singular plates by Medina, Lens, &c., folio, *half morocco.* Lond. 1695

"Hume's very elaborate commentary may be considered as the first attempt to illustrate an English Classic by copious and continued notes."—*Drake.*

4294 ——— Paradise Lost, a Poem, in 12 Books, *illustrated,* 2 vols. 4to. *calf.* Lond. 1749

4295 ——— Paradise Lost, with Notes, by John Marchant, 18mo. *old calf.* Lond. 1751

4296 ——— Paradise Lost, *plates,* 12mo. *half calf.* Lond. 1751

4297 ——— Paradise Lost, *plates,* 2 vols. 8vo. *large paper, calf.* Lond. 1802

4298 ——— Paradise Lost, translated into fifty-four designs, by J. J. Flatters, Sculptor, folio, *beautiful outline plates.* Lond. 1843

Published at 10 guineas.

4299 ——— Il Paradiso Perduba, 2 vols. 12mo. Parigi, 1758

4300 ——— The Fall of Man, or Milton's Paradise Lost, in prose, with critical and explanatory Notes, translated from the French, *plates, old binding, scarce, no title.* n. d.

The Notes in this "singular performance," as it has been called, are very copious.

"Above all the poets of this age, and in the whole range of English poetry, inferior only to Shakspeare. The first two books of his great epic are especially remarkable for their grandeur and sublimity; he invested his creations with the classic spoils of the mythology and superstitions of the ancient pagans, commingling with them the truths of the Christian religion."—*Chambers.*

"He possesses sublimity enough to command our fear, and gentleness enough to awaken our affection. He unites the fancy of Spenser to the majesty of Æschylus, and the delicate finish and grace of Canova to the bold and sweeping outlines of Michael Angelo. The humblest thought, subjected to the alchemy of Milton's genius, became transmuted into something precious and costly. He was an enchanter who changed all the earthen edifices of the imagination into pure gold."

4301 MILTON (*John*), Paradise Lost, with illustrations designed and engraved by J. Martin, impl. 8vo. *half morocco.* Lond. 1849

"More original, more self-dependent than Raffaelle or Michael Angelo, they perfected the style of others—Martin borrowed from none."
Sir E. L. Bulwer Lytton.

4303 ——— L'Allegro, and Il Penseroso, 30 fine etchings, as published by the Art-Union of London, folio, *bds.* Lond. 1848

4304 MINOT (*Lawrence*), Poems on interesting events in the reign of Edward the 2nd, written in 1352, published by Ritson, with a preface, dissertations, notes, and a glossary, 1st edition, *very rare*, 12mo. *half calf.* Lond. 1795

4305 MOLLINEUX (*Mary*), Fruits of Retirement, or Miscellaneous Poems, Moral and Divine, 18mo. *half morocco.* Lond. 1702

4306 MOORE (*Thos.*) Lalla Rookh, illustrated by Heath, royal 8vo. *cloth.* Lond. 1838

4307 MONTGOMERY (*J.*) Abolition of the Slave Trade, a Poem, with fine portraits of Wilberforce, Clarkson, and Granville Sharp, and 9 beautiful engravings after Sir R. Smirke, royal 4to. *half calf.* 1814

4308 MORFORD (*H.*) The Rest of Don Juan and Others, 9 parts, odd. v. d.

4309 MUSE'S Farewell to Popery and Slavery, or a collection of miscellany poems, satires, songs, &c., made by the most eminent wits of the nation, as the shams, intrigues, and plots of Priests and Jesuits gave occasion, 8vo. *fine copy, old calf.* Lond. 1690

4310 NAPOLEON Ballads, by Bon Gaultier; The Poetical Works of Louis Napoleon, *sewed*, 8vo. N. Y. 1852

4311 NEWTON (*Thos.*) Seneca, his Tenne Tragedies, translated into Englysh by Thomas Newton, **Black Letter**, *half calf*, imprinted by Thomas Marshe. Lond. 1581

Bindley's copy sold for £5 15*s.* 6*d.*

4312 NIBELUNGEN Lied, 8vo. Berlin, 1848

The Nibelungen Lied is the grandest poem produced in Europe during the Middle Ages, and justly considered the best Epic Poem of the German Literature. Original and German translations are placed on opposite pages, to facilitate the study of the Old German; all the more difficult words are found in the Glossary.

4313 NICHOLS (*John*), Collection of Poems, with Notes, Biographical and Historical, 12mo. *calf.* 1780

Mr. Nichols was assisted by Bp. Percy in making this elegant selection of English Poetry.

4314 NORMANDY (*Marquis of*), Essay on Poetry, Greenwich Hill, by Manning, &c., folio, *half morocco*. Lond. 1691–1700

4315 NUTBROWNE Maid, from the earliest edition of Arnold's Chronicle, edited by T. Wright, square 12mo., *half morocco*. Lond. 1836

4316 ——— Another copy, 12mo. Lond. *Pickering*, 1836

Very few copies of these curious pieces were printed from the original MSS., edited with copious Introductory Notes and Glossaries by T. Wright.

4317 OGILVIE (*J.*) Poems, 2 vols. 12mo. *sheep*. Lond. 1769

4318 OLDHAM (*John*), Poetical Works and Remains, 8vo. *half morocco*. Lond. 1695

The Poems of Oldham consists of Satire, Pindarics, occasional verses, and translations from Catullus, Ovid's Art of Love, &c. His spirited Satyrs gained for him the appellation of "the English Juvenal."

4319 OGILBY (*J.*) Homer, his Iliads translated, adorned with sculpture and illustrated with annotations, by John Ogilby; Homer, his Odysses translated, adorned with sculpture and illustrated with annotations, by John Ogilby, Esq., &c., portraits and numerous fine plates by Hollar and Lombart, 2 vols. folio, *old calf*. Lond. 1660–69

Sold at the Fonthill sale, with the Virgil, for £8.

Pope frequently spoke, in the later part of his life, of the exquisite pleasure which the perusal of Ogilby's Homer and Sandys' Ovid gave him, when a boy at school.

4320 OSSIAN: Mackenzie (*Henry*), Report of the Committee of the Highland Society of Scotland, appointed to inquire into the nature and authenticity of the Poems of Ossian, *half morocco*, 8vo. Edin. 1805

4321 ——— Progress of Dulness, 12mo. Carlisle, 1797

4322 OVERBURY (*Sir Thomas*), A Wife now the Widow of, being a most exquisite and singular Poem of the choice of a Wife; whereunto is added many witty Characters and Conceited Newes, small 4to. *calf, very scarce*. 1632

Priced in the Bibliotheca Anglo-Poetica, £4 4*s*., and sold at Lloyd's sale for £2 2*s*.

4323 PEELE (*George*), A Farewell, entituled to our Famous and Fortunate Generalls of our English Forces; Syr John Norris and Syr Francis Drake, Knights, and all theyr brave and resolute followers, whereunto is annexed a Tale of Troy, copied and spelling modernized, *in the handwriting of* A. Dyce, 4to. *half morocco*, from the edition printed in 1859

4324 PALINGENIUS (*M.*) Zodiake of Life, wherein are contained twelve severall labours, pointing out most lively the whole compasse of the World, &c., translated out of Latine into English, by Barnabie Googe, the title-page a fac-simile, by Harris, **Black Letter,** 4to. *calf, extra, fine copy, very rare.* *Robert Robinson,* Lond. 1588

Valued at £6 6*s.*, Bib. Anglo-Poetica.

"Googe's Zodiac of Palingenius was a favorite performance, and is constantly classed with the poetical translations of the period, by contemporary critics. The work itself was written by G. A. Manzolius, and contains sarcasms against the Pope, the Cardinals, and the Church of Rome."—*Ellis.*

Warton speaks very highly of the original work, both as regards its design and execution. The same elegant critic also observes that "Googe seems chiefly to have excelled in rendering the descriptive and flowery passages of this moral Zodiac;" and also, "it must be confessed that there is a perspicuity and freedom in Googe's versification."

4325 PROCTOR (*Thomas*), Gorgeous Gallery of Gallant Inventions, reprint, 4to. *half calf.* Lond. 1814

4326 PEARCH'S Collection of Poems, being a continuation to Dodsley's Collection, 4 vols. 12mo. *half bound, queer copy.* 1775

4327 PEGGE (*Mr.*) Observations on Dr. Percy's Account of Saxon Minstrels and others, curious antiquarian pieces, 4to. 1766

4328 PERCY'S Reliques of Ancient English Poetry, consisting of Old Heroic Ballads, Songs, and other pieces of our Earlier Poets, together with some few of later date, 3 vols. *half calf,* 12mo. 1844

"But above all, I then first became acquainted with Bishop Percy's 'Reliques of Ancient Poetry.' The first time, too, I could scrape a few shillings together, I bought unto myself a copy of these beloved volumes ; nor do I believe I ever read a book half so frequently, or with half the enthusiasm."—*Sir W. Scott.*

4329 PERU, a Poem, by Helen M. Williams, 4to. Lond. 1784

4330 PHAER and Twyne: The xiii. Bookes of Aeneidos, the first twelue beeinge the woorke of the diuine Poet Virgil Maro, and the thirteenth the Supplement of Maphaeus Vegius, translated into English Verse by Thomas Phaer, Esquire and Thomas Twyne, Doctor in Physicke, *original binding, large copy, beautiful state,* **Black Letter,** 4to. *calf, very rare,* by William How. Lond. 1584

*** First edition, with the supplement of Maphaeus Vegius.

4331 PHAER (*Thos.*) Another edition, 4to. *half morocco.* Lond. 1596

4332 PICKERING (*Amelia*), Sorrows of Werter, a Poem, 4to. Lond. 1788

4333 PIERS Ploughman: The Vision and Creed of Piers Ploughman, edited with Notes and Glossary, by Wright, 2 vols. 12mo. *cloth.* Lond. 1856

Robert Longlande, author of the poem called the Vision of Pierce Plowman, a secular priest, and a fellow of Oriel College, at Oxford. He flourished about the year 1350. This Poem is a satire on the vices of almost every profession; but particularly on the corruptions of the clergy and the absurdities of superstition. These are ridiculed with much humor and spirit, couched under a strong vein of allegorical invention.

4334 PLAUTUS' Comedies: Amphitryon, Epidicus, and Rudens, made English with critical remarks upon each Play, 12mo. Lond. 1716

4335 POEMS by Eminent Ladies, 12mo. *calf.* 1755

"We allow'd you Beauty, and we did submit
To all the Tyrannies of it.
Ah, cruel Sex! Will you depose us too in Wit?"—*Cowley.*

4336 POEMS and Translations, *half morocco*, 8vo. Lond. 1683

4337 POEMS: Monody on Mrs. Margaret Woffington, who died 1760; Verses to Mrs. Siddons, 1782; Three Poems, by Percival Stockdale, 1784; Epistle from Jas. Surface, 1780; The Struggles of Sheridan, 1790, 4to. Lond.

4338 POEMS and Miscellanies, 4to. *half calf.* v. d.

4339 POEMS—A curious collection bound in 1 volume, containing Cleaveland's Character of a London Diurnal, two editions, 1647; Answer to Waller's Painter, 1667; Denham's Cooper's Hill, 1642; Elegy on Sir John Sutlin (Suckling), 1642; Great Assizes of Apollo (by Geo. Wither), 1645; War Horns make room for Bucks with Green Bows, 1682; Mundas Muliebris, or the Ladies' Dressing Room, with the Fop-Dictionary, &c., *morocco*, 4to. Lond. v. y.

4340 POEMS, A collection of, by several hands, 2 vols. 8vo. *calf.* Dub. 1789

4341 POEMS—Epistle to a Friend, by McHenry; The Soliloquy, a Poem; Liberty, a Poem, by Thomson; The Pulpit Fool, a Satyr; The Trial for Murder, a Poem, 5 vols. 4to. Lond. v. d.

4342 POEMS, by Colgan, Hoffman, Quin, Bennett, Duck, Doolittle, Hunt, Duganne; On the 1st of May; To a Great Player, 10 vols. *various.*

4343 POEMS—Gotham, a Poem; Epistle to Hogarth, by C. Churchill; Independence; P. Pindar's Odes to Mr. Paine, author of the Rights of Man, 1 vol. 4to. *half calf.* Lond.

4344 POEMS—Gratulatio Acad. Cantab. de pace seren, Reg. Anne Auspiciis, 1713; Eusdon's Letter to Addison; Sewell's Epistle from Hampstead; The Conversation; Collins' Mistakes; Oats and the Dunghill, and the Woman of Taste, folio. v. d.

4345 POEMS—The Fate of Lewellyn, a Poem, 1777; Observations on English Poetry, 1782; Ode on the Royal Nuptials, 1761; Ode to Sir Peter Warren, 1747; Ode to the Incarnation, 1744, 5 pamphs. 4to. Lond.

4346 POEMS—Ode to the Genius of the Lakes, 1780; Poems, by Oram; Song of the King, by Lord Thurlow, 1824; Painting, a Poem in 4 Cantos, 1794; Congratulatory Odes, by R. Southey, 1814, 5 pamphs. 4to. Lond.

4347 POEMS—Psyche, a Dramatic Poem; Barnum's Parnassus; Present State of Wit; Quarter Day, 4 vols. *paper, various.*

4348 POEMS—Porcupine's Pelagius; The 'Piscopade, a Poem, 1748; Patriotism, a Mask-Heroic, in 5 Cantos, 1763; Probationary Ode, 1786; Poems, 1768, 4 pamphs. 4to. Lond.

4349 POEMS—Pye (*H. James*), Carmen Seculare for 1800; Smith (*C.*) Elegiac Sonnets; An Essay on Ancient and Modern Poetry; Battle of the Nile; Sonnets to Eminent Men, 5 vols. 4to.

4350 POEMS translated from the Asiatic language, 8vo. *calf.* Lond. 1777

4351 POEMS upon several occasions and to several Persons, by the author of the Censure of the Rota, a scarce poetical volume, 8vo. Lond. 1675

4352 POET'S Ramble after Riches, or a Night's Transactions upon the Road Burlesqued, &c., *scarce,* 4to. Lond. 1691

4353 POEMS of the Earls of Roscommon, Dorset, Halifax, and Sir Samuel Garth, 18mo. *calf.* Lond. 1750

4354 POEMS for Cold Weather, 4to. Lond. 1785

4355 POEMS, consisting of Indian Odes, 1775, 4to.

4356 Poetry of the World (*The*), 12mo. *calf*, 2 vols. in 1. Lond. 1795

4357 Poetry—Difference between Modern and Ancient, 4to. n. d.

4358 Poole (*J.*)—The English Parnassus, or a Help to English Poesie, containing a collection of all the rythming monosyllables, the choicest epithets and phrases, with some general forms upon all occasions, subjects, and themes, alphabetically digested, &c., *rare, plate*, 8vo. *half calf.* Lond. 1678

Valued in the Bibliotheca Anglo-Poetica at £1 5*s*.

4359 Pope's (*Alex.*) Works, edited by W. Roscoe, *best library edition*, 8 vols. *cloth*, 8vo. Lond. 1847

"Pope is the greatest moral poet of all times, of all climes, of all feelings, and of all stages of existence. The delight of my boyhood, the study of my manhood, perhaps, if allowed me to attain it, he may be the consolation of my age. *His poetry is the Book of Life.*"—*Lord Byron.*

4360 Pope (*Mr.*) The Rape of the Lock, 2d ed. *curious plates, paper.* Lond. 1714

The enlarged edition with the addition of the machinery.

4361 ——— (*Alex.*) The Dunciad, being vol. 6 of his works, 18mo. *calf.* Lond. 1754

4362 ——— Miscellaneous Poems, 2 vols. 12mo. *calf.* Lond. 1726

4363 ——— The Shade of, by Matthias, 2 tracts, 8vo. 1799

4364 Praed (*W. M.*) Poetical Works, 12mo. *Redfield*, 1854

4365 Priestley, The Sadducees, a Poem, 4to. 1778

4366 Puttenham (*Geo.*) The Arte of English Poesie, Contriued into three Bookes, the first of Poets and Poesie, the second of Proportion, the third of Ornament, *portrait of Queen Elizabeth, from the library of Thos. Jolley, Esq., original edition, very rare*, 4to. *half morocco.* Lond. 1589

***** Wood hints that "some have thought the book was written by Sir Philip Sidney, and Wharton has inferred from many passages that it was written much earlier than 1589. Oldys in 1736 spoke of this Treatise as then very scarce, and added "*I never saw but one of them, and this was in the curious library of James West.*" The Roxburghe copy sold for £16 5*s.* 6*d.*, and Col. Stanley's for £21.**

Mr. Gilchrist has drawn an able and comprehensive character of this work. He observes, "this is on many accounts one of the most curious and entertaining, and intrinsically, one of the most valuable books of the age of Elizabeth. The copious intermixture of contemporary anecdote, tradition, manners, opinions, and the numerous specimens of coeval poetry, nowhere else preserved, contribute to form a volume of infinite amusement, curiosity, and value."

4367 QUARLES (*Francis*), Divine Poems, *original binding*, 8vo. Lond. 1638

4368 ——— Divine Poems, History of Jonah, Esther, Job, &c., *half calf*, 8vo. Lond. 1717

4369 ——— Feast for Wormes, *half calf*, 12mo. Lond. 1664

"Quarles is an author not of such little merit as generally has been supposed; he is often eloquent, and sometimes extremely pathetic."—*Todd.*

4370 RIMBAULT (*Edward F.*) Cock Lorell's Bote, &c.

4371 RAYMOND (*Geo.*) Chronicles of England, a Metrical History, *fine portrait of Queen Elizabeth*, 8vo. *cloth.* 1842

4372 RICHARD de Hampole, Stimulus Conscientiæ, or the Prick of Conscience, an unprinted English Poem of the 14th Century, edited by Yates, &c. Lond. 1829

4372* RICHARDS (*Geo.*), Modern France and Matilda, 2 vols. 4to. Lond. 1795

4373 RITSON (*Joseph*), Robin Hood, a collection of all the ancient Poems, Songs, and Ballads, now extant relative to that celebrated English Outlaw, 2 vols. *half morocco*, 12mo. *Pickering*, Lond. 1832

4374 ——— Pieces of ancient popular Poetry, *half morocco*, *Pickering*, Lond. 1833

4375 RIVAL Beauties, 4to. 1774

4376 ROBIN Hood's Garland, being a complete history of all the notable exploits performed by him and his merry men, 28 *plates*, 12mo. *half calf.* York

4377 ROBERTS (*Dr.*) Poems by, on the Existence of God, &c. 12mo. *calf.* Lond. 1785

4378 ROBINSON (*Mrs. Mary*), The Poetical Works of, *with fine portrait by Reynolds* (the "Perdita" of George 4th), 3 vols. 8vo. *half calf.* Lond. 1806

Many very beautiful Sonnets, Poems, and Translations, from Petrarch, &c., occur in this interesting and popular collection.

4379 ROMAN de la Rose, par Guillaume de Lorris et Johan de Meun.

Cy est le Rommant de la Rose,
Ou tout l'art d'amour est enclose.

Gothic Letter, commencing sheet B., *woodcuts*, *old calf*, folio. Paris, 1531

"This famous poem is esteemed by the French the most valuable piece of their old poetry, and Chaucer's translation caused it to be equally valued in England."—*Warton.*

4380 Rolliad, or Probationary Odes for the Laureateship, 8vo. *sheep.* Lond. 1795

4381 Roscoe (*Wm. G.*) Poems by, 12mo. Lond., *W. Pickering*, 1834

4382 Roscommon (*Earl of*), Poems, Art of Poetry, by the Duke of Buckingham, and Poems by Richard Duke, *half morocco*, 8vo. Lond. 1717

4383 ——— Essay on translated Verse, *sewed*, 4to. Lond. 1684

4384 Rowe (*Mrs.*) Poems on several occasions, written by Philomela, *first edition, clean copy in the original binding, rare*, 8vo. Lond. 1696

*** Philomela was the poetical name of Mrs. Elizabeth Singer, afterwards Mrs. Rowe. Several of the poems were omitted in the subsequent editions, as savoring too much of the heat of youth.—*See Dunton's Life and Errors.*

4385 Ryan (*Richard*), Poetry and Poets, 3 vols. *half calf.* 12mo. Lond. 1826

4386 S. (*S.*) Loyal and impartial Satyrist, containing eight Miscellaneous Poems, Ghost of an English Jesuit, Looking on Father Petre's Picture, Grand Decision to the Memory of Cranmer, True Christian Philosopher, Comical Cabal, &c. *half calf*, 4to. Lond. 1694

4387 Sackville (*Thomas, Earl of Dorset*), Poetical Works of, containing Gorboduc, and Induction and Legend of Henry, Duke of Buckingham, *half calf*, 12mo. Lond. 1820

4388 Sadducees, a Poem, 4to. Lond. 1778

4389 Sandys (*George*), Ovid's Metamorphosis, translated into English Verse by George Sandys, *engraved title by Cecill, original calf binding, fine copy with Autograph of Sir H. Peyton.* Lond. 1626

George Sandys, the 6th son of Bishop Sandys, succeeded his brother Edwyn as Treasurer of Virginia, where he finished this "composure," dedicating it to King Charles the First (who had just come to the throne as Sandys returned); he says it was "snatcht from the howers of night and repose, for the day was not mine, but dedicated to the service of your Great Father, and yourselfe." His learning and virtues were not only commended by Lord Falkland and other contemporaries but by Dryden, who called him "the best versifier of the age," and by Pope, who declared that "English Poetry owed much to the beauty of his translations."———

4390 Schiller (*Fred.*) Don Carlos, a Dramatic Poem by, 12mo. *cloth.* Balt. 1834

4391 School of Politicks; or the Humours of a Coffee-House, *sewed*, 4to. Lond. 1691

4392 Scott (*Mr.*) Heaven, a Vision, 1760; Plane Truth, a Satire, 1748; The Pluralist, a Poem, 1769; Pleasures of Melancholy, 1747; The Pasquinade, with Notes Variorum. 1753

SCOTCH POETRY.

4393 Anderson (*Patrick, Physician to Charles I.*) Picture of a Scottish Baron Court, a Dramatic Poem, *half morocco*, 12mo. Edinb. 1821

4394 Barbour's Bruce, The Life and Acts of the most Victorious Conqueror, Robert Bruce, King of Scotland, by John Barbour, Archdeacon of Aberdeen, by Pinkerton, 3 vols., *calf.* Edinb. 1770

Copied exactly from the edition printed by Andro Hart in 1620. "Barbour adorned the English language by a strain of versification, expression, and poetical imagery far superior to his age."—*Warton.*

4395 Chalmer's (*George*) Poetic Remains of some of the Scottish Kings, now first collected, *portrait of James I., of Scotland, and fac-simile of his handwriting*, 8vo. *half calf.* Lond. 1824

4396 Drummond (*William of Hawthornden*) Poems of, with Life by Peter Cunningham, 8vo. *half calf.* Lond. 1833

"The great excellence of Drummond is unaffected feeling and unaffected language."—*Retrospective Review.*

4397 Dunbar (*W.*), Select Poems, 18mo. Perth, 1788

"The greatest poet that Scotland has produced."—*G. Ellis.*

4398 Falls of Clyde, or the Fairies, 8vo. *calf.* Edinb. 1806

4399 Hogg (*James*) Poetical Works, in 4 vols. 12mo., *boards, uncut.* Edinb. 1822

4400 ——— Songs by the Ettrick Shepherd, 12mo. N. Y. 1832

4401 Pinkerton (*J.*)—The Bruce; or, the History of Robert I. King of Scotland, written in Scottish verse by John Barbour. *The first genuine edition,* published from a manuscript dated 1489, with notes and glossary, *beautiful vignettes, fine copy,* 3 vols. 8vo. *half morocco.* Lond. 1790

4402 Pinkerton's Collection of Scottish Poems, 2 vols. 8vo. *boards.* Lond. 1786

4403 Scotch Poetry, a Collection of Original Poems by Robert M. Blacklock and other Scotch gentlemen, 12mo. *calf.* Edinb. 1760

4404 Scotia's Bards, Selections from Scottish Poetry, from the earliest to the present times, *with engravings*, 8vo. *cloth, gilt.* 1854

4405 Struthers (*John*), Poetical Works of, comprising the Peasant's Death, the Poor Man's Sabbath, the Plough, Dychmont, &c., &c., with an Autobiography, 2 vols. small 8vo.

"They are good works, and the works of a good man, who deserves well of his country, and whose name will not soon pass into oblivion." *Scottish Guardian.*

4406 Search after Claret, or a Visitation of the Vintners, a Poem, in two Cantos, *half calf*, 4to. Lond. 1691

*** Numerous London Taverns and Signs are named in these two Cantos, with the names of the landlords.

4407 Secundus (*J.*) Basia, or the Kisses, Latin and English Verse, 12mo. Lond. 1631

4408 Sedley (*Sir Charles*), Miscellaneous Works of, containing Satyrs, Epigrams, Court-characters, &c., to which is added the death of Marc Anthony, a Tragedy, edited by Capt. Ayloffe, 8vo. *calf.* Lond. 1702

4409 Sequel to Don Juan, 8vo. *cloth.* Lond. n. d.

4410 Sherburne (*Edward*), Poems and translations: Amorous, Lusory, Morall and Divine, *frontispiece, half morocco, extra, scarce.* Lond. 1651

Priced in the Bibliotheca Anglo-Poetica, £1 11s. 6d.

4411 ——— Seneca-Troades, or the Royal Captives, a Tragedy, translated by Edward Sherburne, *original binding,* 8vo. Lond. 1679

4412 Skelton (*John, Poet Laureat to Henry VIII.*) Poetical Works, (The Bowge of Court; Colin Clout: Why come ye not to Court, His Celebrated Satire on Wolsey; Philip Sparrow; Elinour Rummyng, &c.) with Notes, and an Account of the Author, by Rev. A. Dyce, 2 vols. 8vo. *half morocco, gilt top.* 1843

"The power, the strangeness, the volubility of his language, the audacity of his satire, and the perfect originality of his manner made Skelton one of the most extraordinary writers of any age or country."—*Southey.*

"Old Skelton's Philip Sparrow is an exquisite and original Poem." *Coleridge.*

4413 Smart (*C.*) Eternity of the Supreme Being, 4to. Camb. 1750

4414 Smith (*H. and J.*) Poetical Works, post 8vo. *cloth.* N. Y. 1857

4415 Slatyer (*Wm.*), Palæ-Albion: The History of Great Britaine from the first peopling of this Island to the present raigne of our happy and peaceful Monarke K. James, in English and Latin Verse, folio, *frontispiece containing several portraits, calf.* 1621

A book of great intrinsic worth and rare occurrence. Anthony a Wood says that the author was "in good esteem for his knowledge in English history and his excellent vein in Latin and English poetry."—*See Dr. Dibdin's Library Companion.* Sir M. Sykes' copy sold for £4 4*s*.

4416 Smyth (*Wm.*) English Lyrics, 18mo. Lond. 1801

4417 Solimani (*Julii*), Elogia, Ducum, Regum, inter regum, qui Bœmis, præfuerunt, beautiful miniature engravings of the Dukes and Kings of Bohemia to Ferdinand III., *vellum*, 4to. Pragæ, 1629

4418 Sotheby (*W.*) Oberon, a Poem, from the German of Wieland, 18mo. Lond. 1844

4419 Sotheby (*Wm.*) Farewell to Italy, and Occasional Poems. 1818

4420 Southey (*Robert, Poet Laureat*), Poetical Works, collected by himself, *sheep*, royal 8vo. N. Y. 1856

4421 Southwell (*Robert*), St. Peter's Complaint and other Poems, also Sketch of the Author's Life, by W. Jos. Walter, 12mo. *calf.* Lond. 1817

4422 ——— Mary Magdalen's Funeral Tears for the Death of the Saviour, *reprint of the original, thick paper, rare,* square 8vo. *boards.* Lond. 1823

4423 Spenser (*Edmond*), Faerie Queene, disposed into XII. Bookes, fashioning twelve Morall Vertues, folio, *curious wood-cut ornaments, calf.* Lond. *M. Lowndes,* 1609

This is the first edition of Spenser's Faerie Queene in folio: and also the first complete edition of the poem, as it contains six leaves at the end entitled "Two Cantos of Mutabilitie, which, both for Form and Matter, appeare to be parcell of some following Booke of the Faerie Queene, under the Legend of Constancie, never before imprinted."

This edition is so scarce that Lowndes was unable to quote the sale of any copy in the very numerous catalogues he referred to.

"Spenser's works are an inexhaustible mine of the richest materials, forming, in fact, the very bullion of our language; and it is to be lamented that they are so rarely explored for present use."
Headley.

4424 Spenser (*Edmund*), Workes of, edited by Todd, royal 8vo. *half calf.* Lond. 1845

The merits of Spenser are of so decided and exalted a nature, as to place him in spite of every deduction in the same class with Homer, Dante, Shakspeare, and Milton.—*Drake's Shakspeare and his Times.*

4425 SPENSER (*Edmund*), An Essay on the Life and Writings of, by John S. Hart, royal 8vo. *half morocco, gilt edges.* N. Y. 1847

4426 STATE Poems; Rowe on the sickness and recovery of Sir Robert Walpole; Ramble between Belinda, a Demi-Prude, and Cloe, a Court Coquette, &c., 8vo. *sewed.* Lond. 1716

4427 STEPHENSON (*J. Hall*) Crazy Tales, 4to. *half calf.* Lond. *privately printed*, 1762

4428 SUE (*Eugene*), The Preludes, a collection of Poems, *fine vig.* 12mo. *sewed.* N. Y. 1846

4429 SUCKLING (*John*), Fragmenta Aurea, a Collection of all the incomparable pieces written by, 8vo. *calf.* Lond. 1648

"For a perfect specimen of those men of 'wit and pleasure' who were 'about town' during the first Charles's time commend us to Sir John Suckling."

4430 SUKEY (a Poem on the Philosophy of the Mind, &c.), 8vo. *sewed.* Baltimore, 1821

4431 SYLVESTER (*J.*) The Parliament of vertues Royal, summoned in France, but assembled in England, for nomination, creation, and conformation of the most excellent Prince Panaretvs. A præsage of Pr. Dolphin; a portrait of Pr. Henry; a promise of Pr. Charles; also the Second Sitting of the Parliament of vertues, translated and dedicated to his Highness, by Iosvah Sylvester, &c., 2 vols. 12mo. *half morocco.* Lond. 1614

4432 TALE of the Basyn and the Frere and the Boy, **black letter**, two early Tales of Magic, from MSS. in the Library of the University of Cambridge, edited by T. Wright, sq. 12mo. *half calf.* Pickering, Lond. 1836

4433 ——— Another copy, sqr. 12mo. *half morocco.* Pickering, Lond. 1836

4434 TASSO'S Aminta, Englisht, with Ariadne's Complaint, in imitation of Auguillara, written by the Translator of Tasso's Aminta (John Reynolds), 4to. *with engravings on the title-page, sewed.* 1628

A very scarce poetical volume. At the end of the Aminta is a poem of "Venusses search for Cupid."

4435 ——— (*T.*) Godfrey of Bovlogne, or the Recouirie of Ierusalem; done into English heroicall verse by Edward Fairfax, gent., and now the second time imprinted and dedicated to his highnesse, together with the life of the said Godfrey, *portrait by W. Pass, rare*, fol. *half morocco.* Lond. 1624

White Knight's sale, £2 12*s.* 6*d.* Bib. Anglo-Poet, £2 2*s.*

4436 TASSO (*Torquato*), La Gerusalemme Liberata, *with very fine portraits*, 2 vols. Firenze, 1820

4437 ——— Godfrey of Bulloigne, or the recovery of Jerusalem, in English verse, by Edward Fairfax, with Essay by Leigh Hunt, and lives by C. Knight, 2 vols. 8vo. *half morocco.* N. Y. 1846

The masterly version of Fairfax, which for the last half century has been most undeservedly neglected, has not hitherto been superseded by any posterior attempts.—*Drake.*

4438 TATE (*Nahum*), Collection of Poems by several hands, 8vo. *half morocco.* Lond. 1685

4439 TAYLOR (*John, the Water Poet*), Workes, being sixty-three in number, collected into one volume by the author, with sundry new additions, corrected, revised, and newly imprinted, *frontispiece wanting, and corners of the bottom leaves mildewed*, fol. *very rare, calf, extra.* Lond. 1630

A copy of this volume produced fifteen guineas, at Col. Stanley's sale.—*Dibdin.*

An extremely curious collection, including, among other witty pieces, his Pennilesse Pilgrimage, or Journey (without money) from London to Edinborough—the Praise, Antiquity, and Commodity of Beggerie, Beggers, &c. Of all the oddities of his day, the greatest was Taylor the Water-Poet. He was a slang fellow, and a Skelton in his way. His pieces are replete with bizarre and barbarous wood-cuts.

4440 ——— Suddaine turne of Fortune's wheele, edited by Halliwell, 4to. *half morocco.* Brixton Hill, 1848

4441 THYNN (*Francis*), Debate between Pride and Lowliness, reprinted from the edition of Charlwood, edited by J. P. Collier, 8vo. *half calf.* Lond. 1841

4442 THYNNE (*Thomas, of Longleat, killed by Count Konigsmarck*), Directions to Fame, about an Elegy on the late; and an Eulogy on other most famous English worthies, *sewed*, 4to. Lond. 1682

4443 THOMSON'S Castle of Indolence, 12 *beautiful illustrations in outline by W. Rimer,* oblong folio, with the Poem, *cloth.* 1845

4444 TICKELL (*Mr.*) The Project, a Poem, 4to. 1778

4445 TILLBROOK (*Rev. S.*) Remarks on Southey's Vision of Judgment, 8vo. *paper.* Camb. 1822

TIXALL Poetry, *vide* Clifford, Lot 4175.

4446 TIPPER (*E.*) The Pilgrim's Viaticum; or, the Destitute, but not Forlorn; being a Divine Poem, digested from meditations upon the Holy Scriptures, *original blue morocco binding, gilt edges, very rare*, 8vo. Lond. 1698

4447 TODD (*Henry J.*) Illustrations of the Lives and Writings of Gower and Chaucer, *portrait*, 8vo. *half calf.* Lond. 1810

4448 TOWN Council (*The*), a Poem, 4to. 1774

4449 TRESHAM (*Henry*), Rome in the 18th Century, a Poem. 1799

4450 TRIBE of Levi, a Poem, *fine copy*, 4to. *half calf.* Lond. 1691

4451 TRIBE of Issachar, or the Ass Couchant, a Poem, satyrical, wood-cut of Passive Obedience and Non-resistance, *boards, uncut*, 4to. Lond. 1691

4452 TRISTAN: Recueil de ce qui reste des poemes relatifs a ses aventures, pub. par Michel, 2 vols. 12mo. *cloth.* Londres, *Pickering*, 1835

4453 TRIUMPH of Isis, an Elegy, 4to. n. d.

4454 TRIUMPH of Infidelity, a Poem (dedicated to Voltaire), 8vo. *half morocco.* *In the world*, 1788

4455 TUPPER (*Martin F.*) Hymn for All Nations, in 72 Languages, *curious*, 8vo. *paper.* Lond. 1851

4456 TURNER (*Sharon*), Inquiry respecting the early use of Rhime, 4to. (Soc'y of Antiq). 1802

4457 TUSSER (*Thomas*), Five Hundred Points of Good Husbandry, edited by William Mavor, 8vo. *half calf.* Lond. 1812

4458 VAIL (*John Cooper*), Poems, *sewed*, 8vo. N. Y. 1851

4459 VICARS (*J.*) The XII Æneids of Virgil, the most renowned laureat prince of Latine poets, translated into English deca-syllables; engraved title, are to be sold at the Angell in Popeshead alley, 12mo. *half morocco.* Lond. 1632

4460 VIDA'S Art of Poetry, translated into English Verse, 18mo. *calf.* Lond. 1742

4461 VOLTAIRE La Pucelle D'Orleans, *plates*, *calf*, 8vo. 1762

4462 W. (*J.*) English Iliads, or a Sea-Fight, received in a Poem, occasioned by the death of a person of honour, slain in the late war between the English and Dutch, 4to. *calf.* Lond. 1674

*** The author seems to have served under Lord Maidstone, the person alluded to in the title.

4463 WALLER (*Edmund*), Poems, the Works of, in verse and prose, published by Mr. Fenton, *Tonson's splendid quarto edition*, with portraits, vignettes, tail pieces, &c. by Virtue, *half morocco.* Lond. 1729

"Fenton's beautiful edition of this book has Virtue's best portrait of Waller, and other appropriate decorations from his brilliant graver." —*Dibdin's Library Companion.*

4464 WALLER'S (*Edmund*), Passion of Dido for Æneas, translated by Waller and Godolphin, 12mo. *half morocco.* Lond. 1658

4465 ——— Poems, &c., upon several occasions and to several persons, 12mo. *half calf.* Lond. 1682

"When he published these pieces he surprised the town as if a tenth muse had been newly born to cherish drooping poetry." *Clarendon.*

4465* WALKER (*Elias*), Enchiridion of Epictetus, translated frontispiece by Faithorn, *half morocco.* 8vo. Lond. 1695

4466 WALTERS, The Poet, a Metrical Romance of the Seventeenth Century, 8vo. *half morocco.* Phil. 1840

4467 WARNER'S Albion's England: a Historie of the same Kingdom from the Original, a Poem, with an Epitome in Prose, 4to. *half morocco, scarce.* Lond. 1612

The title and 6 leaves in the beginning, and last leaf, made good with MS.

This highly esteemed epitome of British History contains much good poetry and curious information. Priced in the Bibliotheca Anglo-Poetica £5 5*s.*; and sold at Townsley's sale for £6 6*s.*

"His tales, though often tedious, and not unfrequently indelicate, abound with all the unaffected, inardent, and artless ease of the best old ballads, without their cant and puerility."—*Headley.*

4468 WARTON (*Thomas*), History of English Poetry, including the Notes of Ritson, 4 vols. 8vo. *half calf.* Lond. 1840

"The most singular combination of extraordinary talents and attainments, uniting the deep and minute researches of the antiquary with the elegance of the classical scholar, and the skill of the practised writer; the style vigorous and manly, the observations acute and just, and the views of the subject extensive and accurate." —*Sir Egerton Brydges.*

4469 ——— Observations on the History of Poetry, 4to. 1782

4470 ——— Observations on the Fairy Queen of Spenser, 2 vols. 8vo. *half calf.* Lond. 1801

4471 WATTS (*Isaac*), The Psalms of David, imitated in the Language of the New Testament, 16mo. *calf.* Lond. 1765

4472 ——— Hymns and Spiritual Songs, in three Books, 18mo. *calf.* Lond. 1781

4473 WEBER (*H.*) Battle of Flodden Field, a Poem of the 16th Century, *plates,* 8vo. *calf.* Edin. 1808

——— Another copy, 8vo. *half morocco.* 1808

4474 WEAVER (*T.*) Plantagenets Tragicall Story, or the Death of King Edward the Fourth, with the unnatural voyage of Richard the Third, through the Red Sea of his Nephew's Innocent Blood to his Usurped Crowne, a Poem, 8vo. *with rare port. by Marshall, cf.* Lond. 1649

Lloyd's Copy of this scarce and elegant Poem sold for £3 15*s.*

4475 WEBSTER (*John*), A Monumental Columne erected to the living memory of the ever glorious Henry Prince of Wales, *cloth*, 4to. Lond. 1613

4476 WHITEHEAD (*Wm. Poet Laureat*), Plays and Poems by, 2 vols. 12mo. *sheep.* Lond. 1774

4477 WILD (*Dr.*) Rome Rhym'd to Death, 12mo. *half calf.* Lond. 1683

4478 WILSON (*John*), Lines to the Memory of Jas. Graham, 4to. 1811

4479 ——— City of the Plague, and other Poems, 8vo. *cloth.* Edin. 1817

4480 WINDSOR Stag, a Poem founded on Fact. 1777

4481 WITHERS' (*Geo.*) Abuses Strypt and Whipt, or Satyrical Essays, in Verse, 8vo. *half calf, MS. Title.* Lond. 1617

CONTENTS:—Epigrams—Abuses Strypt and Whipt—The Scourge, *with a curious wood-cut of a wild man or Satyr called "Vice's Executioner"*—Certaine Epigrams to the King, the Queene, the Prince, &c., to whom the Author gave any of his Books (including one to Henry Earle of Southampton and another to William Earle of Pembroke)—Prince Henries Obsequies or Mourneful Elegies upon his Death. It was for writing these spirited satires that Withers was committed to the Marshalsea, where he continued for several months.

4482 WITHER (*G.*) Prosopœia Britannica, or Britain's Genius, or Good Angel, personated, reasoning and advising touching the games now played and the adventures now at hazard in these Islands, presaging also some future things, a Poem, 8vo. *soiled copy, half morocco.* 1648

One of the scarcest of this author's numerous pieces, containing many striking passages and poetic personifications.
Towneley's copy sold for £3 13*s.* 6*d.*

4483 ——— Vaticinium Votivum, or Palaemon's Prophetick Prayer, lately presented privately to his now Majestie in a Latin poem, and here published in English, to which is annexed a paraphrase on Paulus Grebnerus's prophecie, with several elegies on Charles the First, the Lord Capel, the Lord Francis Villiers, *very rare*, 8vo. 1649

4484 WITHER (*G.*) Speculum Speculativum, or a Considering Glass, being an inspection into the present and late sad condition of these nations, with some cautional expressions made thereupon immediately after his Majesty's restoration, *in verse*, 8vo. *half russia, scarce.* Lond. 1660

This may be esteemed as one of the most curious of the author's numerous works, containing extracts, hymns, &c., selected from several of his former works.

4485 WRIGHT (*Abraham*), Parnassus Biceps, or several choice Pieces of Poetry, composed by the best wits that were in both the Universities before their dissolution, *half calf*, 12mo. Lond. 1656

In an Epitaph on some bottles of Sack and Claret laid in sand, page 63, he says:—

"A dozen Shakespears here inter'd do lye,
Two dozen Johnson's full of Poetry."

4486 YALDEN (*Tho.*) On the Conquest of Namur, *half morocco,* folio. Lond. 1699

4487 ZOUCHE (*Richard*), The Dove, or Passages of Cosmography, reprinted from the original edition of 1613, with a Memoir, and Notes collected and arranged by Richard Walker, 8vo. *half calf.* Oxford, 1839

POLITICS AND POLITICAL ECONOMY.

4488 BELLENDENUS, a Free Translation on the Preface to, containing animated strictures on the great political characters of the present time, 8vo. *calf.* Lond. 1788

4489 BENTHAMIANA, edited by J. H. Burton, 8vo. *cloth.* Phila. 1844

4490 BROUGHAM (*Lord*), Opinions of on Politics, Theology, Law, &c., 2 vols. 12mo., *cloth.* Phila. 1839

4491 CLAIMS of Labour, an Essay on the Duties of the Employers and Employees, 12mo. *cloth.* Lond. 1845

4492 COOKE (*G. W.*), The History of Political Parties in England, from the Rise of the Whig and Tory interests in the Reign of Charles Second, to the passing of the Reform Bill, with Biographical Sketches of the Ministers of State, &c., 3 vols. 8vo. Lond. 1836

4493 D'ANVERS (*Caleb*), a Dissertation upon Parties, 12mo. *half cloth.* Dub. 1735

4494 ——— Sedition and Defamation Displayed in a Letter to the Author of the Craftsman, 8vo. *calf.* Lond. 1731

4495 DEFOE (*D.*), True Born Englishman and 2 others. 1765, &c.

4496 FRENCH Louse, History of a, or the Spy of a new Species in France and England, giving a Key to the chief events of the year 1780, 8vo. *calf.* Lond. 1780

4497 GOVERNMENT, an Examination of the Patriarchal Scheme of, 8vo. *calf.* Lond. 1750

4498 GRANT (*J.*) The Bench and the Bar, 2 vols., *boards.* Phila. 1836

Comprising biographical, professional and anecdotal sketches of upwards of seventy of the most legal men of the day.

4499 HARRINGTON (*James*), The Commonwealth of Oceana, *first edition*, folio, *calf.* Lond. 1656

4500 ——— Oceana and Other Works, with an account of his Life by J. Toland, *portrait*, *old calf*, folio. Dub. 1737

"According to Hume, it is the only valuable model of a Commonwealth that has ever been offered to the public."—*Lowndes.*

4501 JUNIUS, Coventry's Critical Inquiry into the Author of, 8vo. *boards.* Lond. 1825

4503 LIGHT (*Col. Alex. W.*), a Plan for the Amelioration of the Poor, 8vo. *cloth.* Lond. 1831

4504 MALTHUS (*T. R.*), Political Economy, 8vo. *boards.* Lond. 1826

4505 MARKHAM (*Gerv.*), Way to get Wealth, containing six principal Vocations or callings, in which every good Husband or House-wife may employ themselves, 4to. *calf.* Lond. 1638

4506 MORE (*Sir Thomas*), Utopia, or the Happy Republic, a Philosophical Romance. The New Atlantis by Lord Bacon, 12mo. *cloth.* Lond. 1838

"We cannot appreciate too highly the spirit and originality of More's Utopia."—*Hallam.*

4507 POLITICAL Curiosities, including an account of the state of affairs in Europe, 12mo. *sheep.* Phil. 1796

4508 ——— Pamphlets for the years 1733, '4, '5, '9, the Contents written at the end of each vol. 8vo. *calf.* Lond.

4509 ——— Pamphlets, 8vo. *half calf.* Lond.

4510 RALEIGH (*Sir Walter*), The Mysteries of State Discabinated in Political and Polemical Aphorisms, published by John Milton, Esq., port. 18mo. *half calf.* Lond. 1658

4511 RICARDO (*D.*) Principles of Political Economy, 8vo. *boards.* Lond. 1817

4512 ——— Value; The Nature, Measures, and Causes of, in reference to Ricardo and others, 8vo. Lond. 1825

4513 ROBB'S Patriotic Wolves, 12mo. Edinb. 1797

4514 SCUDDERY (*Mons. de*), Curia Politiæ, or the Apologies of several Princes justifying to the World their most eminent actions, folio, *old calf.* Lond. 1673

4515 SEDGWICK (*T.*) Public and Private Economy, 12mo. *cloth.* N. Y. 1839

4516 TAYLOR (*James*), View of the money system of England from the Conquest, 8vo. *boards.* Lond. 1828

4517 TRACTS, a volume in which among others are the trial of Sir Chaloner Ogle, 1743; Letter to Thomas Carte, Historian, 1743; Memoirs of Card. Fleury, 1743.

4518 UTOPIA; Memoirs of a certain Island adjacent to the Kingdom of, by a celebrated author of that country, 12mo. *old calf.* Dublin, n. d.

4519 VOLNEY, Ruins of Empires, 16mo. *half cloth.* Bost. 1835

PORTRAITS—COLLECTIONS OF, *see also* ENGRAVINGS.

4520 BINET (*S.*) Vies des Principaux Fondateurs des Religions de l'Eglise, 40 *beautiful old portraits, engraved by C. and F. Galle*, small 4to. Anvers, 1634

4521 BIOGRAPHICAL MIRROR (*The*), by Harding, comprising a Series of Ancient and Modern English Portraits of Eminent and Distinguished Persons, with Memoirs, *upwards of* 150 *fine plates from scarce pictures and prints*, 3 vols. in 1, 4to. Lond. 1795

One of the best and most interesting portrait galleries, comprising for the most part portraits of distinguished persons of whom no other engravings are extant, and fac-similes of rare prints in the museums of eminent collectors. It forms an admirable companion to any History of England, the works of Pepys, Evelyn, &c.

4522 BOYDELL'S Heads of Illustrious Persons; Mary Queen of Scots, by Bartolozzi, &c., with biographical accounts of each, by John Watkins, large folio, *half morocco.* Lond. 1811

4523 BRITISH Gallery of Contemporary Portraits, series of 150 fine engravings of the most eminent persons now living or lately deceased, in Great Britain, with Memoirs, 2 vols. fol. *half morocco, fine impressions.* Lond. 1822

The portraits in this noble work, with few exceptions, do not occur in any other collection.

4524 Bromley (*H.*) Catalogue of Engraved British Portraits from Egbert, &c., 4to. *half calf.* Lond. 1793

4525 Byron Gallery, a Series of Ideal Portraits, Illustrative of Byron's Works, royal 8vo. *morocco.* Lond. n. d.

4526 Cæsars, Twenty-four heads, from Julius to Alex. Severum, 4to. *Venet. apud Donatum Bertellum*, folio. Venet. 1579

4527 Catalogue of a collection of Portraits, with prices, 8vo. *half calf.*

4528 Catalogue of Sir W. Musgrave's collection of Portraits, priced, 8vo. *half calf.* n. d.

4529 Catalogue of the Townely Granger collection of Portraits, 8vo. Lond. 1828

4530 Catalogue of S. Tyssen's collection of Portraits, 8vo. Lond. 1802

4531 Caulfield (*James*), Gallery of British Portraits, *large paper proofs, a few scarce prints inserted, Charles 1st by Smith, Death Warrant of Charles 1st, &c.*, large folio. Lond. 1814

4532 ——— Portraits, Memoirs, and Characters of Remarkable Persons, from the Reign of Edward III. to the Revolution, *upwards of* 100 *portraits of eccentric and notorious persons,* 3 vols. impl. 8vo. Lond. 1813

Calcographiana, *vide* Lot 2645.

4533 Cooper and Page, Fifty Wonderful Portraits engraved by, from authentic originals, 4to. *boards.* Lond. 1827

4534 Frenchmen, a collection of Portraits of, 4to. Paris, n. d.

4535 Gallery of English and Foreign Portraits, with Memoirs, published by the Society for the Diffusion of Useful Knowledge, 168 *fine portraits, brilliant impressions*, 7 vols. impl. 8vo. *cloth.* Lond. 1833–37

This interesting series is engraved in the highest style of art, in the same manner as Lodge's Portraits, to which it forms a very desirable companion. The Memoirs are well written; some have been attributed to the pen of Lord Brougham.

4536 ——— Another copy, 7 vols. *cloth.* 1833

4537 Harding's (*E.*) Portraits of George the Third and all the Royal Family, folio, *green morocco, silk linings, fine copy.* Lond. 1806

4538 Historic Gallery of Portraits and Paintings, 4 vols. 8vo. *cloth.* Lond. n. d.

Holbein's Portraits, *vide* Shaksperiana 4978.

4539 HOUBRAKEN and Vertue's Heads of Illustrious Persons of Great Britain, with their Lives by Birch, 100 *large and splendid portraits*, folio, *calf.* 1813

4540 ——— De Levens, Beschryvingen der Nederlandsche Konst Schilders en Konst Schilderessen, met een uytbreyding over de Schilder-konst der ouden, door J. C. Weyerman, 4 vols. 4to. *boards, uncut, brilliant plates.* 1729

4541 ITALIANS; Portraits of celebrated Italians, after drawings by Bettoni, beautifully engraved; amongst them are Bartolozzi, Raffaelle Morghen, Canova, and many others, about 40 in all, in one volume, 4to.

4542 KAY (*John*), Series of Original Portraits and Caricature Etchings (chiefly of Scotchmen), 2 vols. in 4 parts, royal 8vo. Edinb. 1842

4543 KIT-CAT Club, Portraits of the celebrated Persons composing the Kit-Cat Club, 48 *fine large mezzotinto portraits from the original paintings by Sir Godfrey Kneller*, 4to. Lond. 1821

"The Kit-Cat Club generally mentioned as a set of wits, were, in reality, the Patriots that saved Britain."—*Horace Walpole.*

4544 LODGE (*Ed.*) Portraits of Illustrious Personages of Great Britain, engraved from authentic pictures in the galleries of the Nobility, and the Public Collections of the Country, with Biographical and Historical Memoirs of their Lives and Actions, 10 vols. imperial 8vo. *fine impressions, cloth, gilt.* 1840

"Such a union of various talents, such a gallery of illustrious dead, was scarcely ever before presented to the public, in colours almost as vivid and sparkling as if the originals occupied the canvas whence their copies were taken."—*Dibdin.*

4545 NATIONAL Portrait Gallery of Illustrious and Eminent Personages, chiefly of the 19th century, 4to. *cloth, gilt.* Lond. v. d.

4546 PERRAULT (*Mr.*) Les Hommes Illustres de France, 89 beautiful Portraits of celebrities of the 17th and 18th centuries, *fine impressions*, folio, *calf.* Paris, 1696

There is no previous work to be put in competition with it; the principal engravers were Edelinck and Nanteuil, and they are worthy of the illustrious characters whose physiognomy will go down to posterity from the magic of their gravers.—*Dibdin.*

4547 PHYSIOGNOMICAL Portraits of Distinguished Characters, from undoubted originals, engraved in the line manner by the most eminent British Artists, with Biographies, royal 8vo. *half morocco.* 1824

With respect to the plates it is a very desirable copy.

4548 PORTRAITS of the British Poets, from Chaucer to Cowper and Beattie, 140 *highly finished engravings* by Finden, Warren, Pye, &c., India proofs, large paper, 2 vols. folio, *half morocco, gilt top.* 1824

This charming work, which is as interesting as it is beautiful, was published at no less a sum than £32. It is the only complete series in an elegant form, and is adapted to illustrate all editions of the poets, from octavo to folio size.

4549 PORTRAITS of the Princes of Holland; Principes Hollandiæ, Zelandiæ, &c., incisi et descripti auspiciis I. Scriverii; imp. folio, 38 *unusually large and remarkably fine portraits, after Titian, Rubens, and others,* engraved by Visscher, Zoutman, &c., *brilliant impressions.* Harlæm, 1650

One of the finest series of Historical Portraits ever executed, which quite puts to shame the miniature undertakings of the present day.

4550 PORTRAITS of Famous Men.

4551 SCOTT (*Sir W.*) Portrait Illustrations of the Waverley Novels, with Landscape Illustrations, royal 8vo. *half morocco.* *Tilt,* Lond. 1834

4552 THANE (*J.*) British Autography, a collection of authentic Portraits and fac-similes of the handwritings of Royal and Illustrious Personages, 3 vols. 4to. containing about 250 Portraits and as many Autographs, *fine copy, half morocco..* Lond. n. d.

4553 ——— 27 additional Portraits, folio. Lond. n. d.

Many of these portraits and autographs are from originals never before engraved, and not to be found in any other publication; the impressions in this volume are far superior to those usually seen.

4554 VENETIANA (*Augustino*), Illustrium Virorum extant in Urbe, 52 fine Portraits, folio, *calf.* Roma, 1569

4555 WOODBURN'S Gallery of Rare Portraits, comprising 200 fine Portraits of celebrated Englishmen, engraved by Cecil, Delaram, Faithorne, Vertue, White, &c., 2 vols. 4to. *morocco gilt, gilt leaves.* 1816

An admirable series of portraits illustrative of Clarendon and Burnet, printed either from the original plates or in exact fac-simile of the rare originals. Published at 15 guineas in boards—original subscriber's copy; complete sets are now of rare occurrence, as the book is generally cut up for illustration.

For Portraits of Actors, Literary Characters, Illustrious and Noted men, *see* PRINTS, &c. at the end.

SCOTLAND—*See* A FEW UNDER ENGLISH TOPOGRAPHY.

4556 ABERDEEN, Sum Notabill Thinges Excerpit from the Auld Recordes of the Hon. Citie of Aberdeen, 1565–1635, 8vo. *calf.* Edin. 1834

4557 Beattie (*Dr.*) Illustrated in a Series of Views, with descriptions, upwards of 100 highly finished engravings from drawings by Bartlett, good impressions, 2 vols. 4to. original edition, *half morocco, gilt leaves.* Virtue, 1836

4557* Boswell's Journal of Johnson's Tour to the Hebrides, 8vo. *calf.* Lond. 1813

4558 Hippolytus, Earl of Douglas, History of, 8vo., *wants title.*

4559 Mary Q. of Scots, Collections relative to the Funeral of, 8vo. *boards.* Edin. 1822

4560 Miscellanea Scotica, a collection of Tracts, relating to the History, Antiquities, Topography, and Literature of Scotland, 4 vols. 12mo. *boards, uncut.* Glasgow, 1818

4561 Murray's Scotch Scenery, part 1, 4to.

4562 Ritson (*Joseph*), Annals of the Caledonian Picts and Scots, and of Strathclyde, Cumberland, Galloway and Murray, 2 vols. post 8vo. *cloth, uncut.* Edinb. 1828

4563 ——— Memoirs of the Celts or Gauls, post 8vo. *cloth, uncut.* Lond. 1827

4564 Status Regni Scotiæ et Hiberniæ diversorum dictorum, 24mo. *Elzevir,* Lugd. 1627

4565 Scotland Delineated, a series of beautifully executed lithographic views of the magnificent scenery of the Highlands and Lowlands, including some views of the picturesque Street-architecture of the Cities and Towns, after the original drawings by Turner, Roberts, Stanfield, Creswick, Harding, &c., with Historical, Antiquarian and Descriptive Letter-press, by J. P. Lawson, mounted on drawing boards, and colored equal to the original drawings, in 6 parts, large folio. Edin. v. d.

This truly superb work forms a complete Gallery of the grand and picturesque scenery of Scotland, including nearly all the ancient castles, abbeys, mountains and rivers, which have been immortalized in the works of Sir Walter Scott.

4565* Scotland, Selection of Views in, 8vo. *half calf.* 1794

4566 Wallace (*Sir William*), The History of the Life and Adventures of, 8vo. *boards.* N. Y. 1820

SHAKSPEARIANA BURTONENSIS;

BEING A

CATALOGUE OF THE EXTENSIVE COLLECTION

OF

SHAKSPEARIANA

OF THE LATE

W. E. BURTON, Esq.,

OF NEW YORK.

FORMING PART OF

HIS VERY EXTENSIVE AND UNIQUE HISTRIONIC LIBRARY

ARRANGED UNDER THE FOLLOWING HEADS:

1. SEPARATE PLAYS; original editions and reprints; subsequent editions, alterations, adaptations, translations, Burlesques, &c.—arranged as in the collected editions of his works.
2. POEMS AND SONNETS, &c.
3. DOUBTFUL AND SPURIOUS PLAYS.
4. COLLECTED EDITIONS OF ALL HIS PLAYS; embracing all the first four folio editions and reprint of the first; and all the editions "*cum notis variorum*" from Rowe to Halliwell.
5. SHAKSPEARIANA—consisting of almost all the Biographers, Commentators, Imitators, Glossaries, Indices, Illustrations, Portraits, and Prints; with all old and modern authors who have from time to time alluded to, elucidated the text (or attempted to do so), by shedding their little lustre upon the brightest literary star that ever shone beneath the canopy of Heaven.
6. SHAKSPEARIAN RELICS; Statues, Busts, Models, casts of his Monument and Bust at Stratford, &c., including Clara Fisher's Museum, and the

CELEBRATED MULBERRY-TREE TEA CADDY,

one of the choicest souvenirs of the Tree in existence; and perfectly unique.

NEW YORK:
JOSEPH SABIN AND CO.
1860.

SHAKSPEARIANA.

ORIGINAL PLAYS AND SUBSEQUENT EDITIONS, ALTERATIONS, ADAPTATION OF PLAYS ON THE SAME SUBJECT; OPERAS, BURLESQUES AND TRANSLATIONS.

4567 Shakespeare (*Wm.*) Twenty of the Plays of Shakespeare, being the whole number printed in quarto, during his lifetime or before the restoration, collated when there were different copies, and published from the originals, by Geo. Steevens, Esq., 4 vols. *scarce, half morocco, gilt top*, quarto. Lond. 1766

Nassau's sale, £2 7*s*. White Knight's, £2 8*s*.

The Tempest—

4568 Tempest, altered from Shakespeare by Dryden and Davenant, three editions, 4to. *half morocco.* 1676, 1690, 1695

4569 Tempest, or the Enchanted Island, altered by J. P. Kemble, with additions from Dryden and Davenant, sewed, 8vo. Lond. 1806

4570 Tempest, an Opera, altered by Garrick, Songs from Shakespeare, Dryden, and others, 8vo. *half morocco.* Lond. 1756

4571 Virgin Queen, or a Continuation of the Tempest, altered from Shakespeare by Waldron, 8vo. *half morocco, gilt top, uncut.* Lond. 1707

Barnett (*M.*) The Tempest, as a Lyrical Drama, 8vo. *Vide* Lot 1415. 1856

4573 La Tempesta, an Opera, founded on the Tempest of Shakespeare, 4to. Phil: 1850

Merry Wives of Windsor—

4574 First Sketch of the Merry Wives of Windsor, the novels on which it is founded, with an Introduction and Notes, 8vo. *half morocco, gilt top.* Lond. 1842

COMEDY OF ERRORS—

4575 Comedy of Errours, altered from Shakespeare, by T. Hull, 8vo. *half morocco, gilt top.* Lond. 1793

4576 The Twins, or Which is Which, altered from Shakespeare's Comedy of Errors, by W. Wood, *half morocco, gilt top, uncut*, large paper. Edinburgh, 1780

LOVE'S LABOUR LOST—

4577 Love's Labour Lost, a wittie and pleasant Comedie, written by Wm. Shakespeare, 4to. *half calf.* Lond. 1631

4578 Love's Labour Lost, an old edition, wants title, &c., all after signature K 2, 4to. *half calf.*

MIDSUMMER NIGHT'S DREAM—

4579 Midsummer Night's Dream, altered from Shakespeare, by George Colman, two editions, 8vo. *half morocco.* Lond. 1763, 1777

4580 Midsummer Night's Dream, altered and new songs added by F. Reynolds, 8vo. *half morocco, gilt top.* Lond. 1816

4581 Midsummer Night's Dream, alterations, additions, and new Songs. Lond. 1816

4582 Midsummer Night's Dream, altered from Shakespeare by Garrick, with several new Songs, 8vo. *half morocco, gilt top, uncut.* Lond. 1763

4583 Another copy, 8vo. *boards.* Lond. 1763

4584 Fairies (*The*), An Opera, altered from Midsummer Night's Dream, with Songs from Shakespeare, Milton, Waller, Dryden, Lansdowne, Hammond, etc., 8vo. *unbound.* Lond, 1755

4585 Another copy, 8vo. Lond. 1755

4586 Midsummer Night's Dream, with illustrations, designed and modelled by W. Boynton Kirk, for a dessert service, manufactured by Kerr, Binns & Co., for the Dublin Exhibition of 1853, *thirteen plates*, 8vo. *cloth, gilt.* 1853

TAMING OF THE SHREW—

4587 Old Taming of a Shrew, upon which Shakspeare founded his Comedy, reprinted for the Shakspeare Society, from the edition of 1594, 8vo. *half mor. gilt top, uncut.* Lond. 1844

4588 A Cure for a Scold, a ballad Farce, in 2 acts, altered from Taming the Shrew, by T. Worsdale, 8vo. *half morocco, gilt top.* Lond. 1735

MERCHANT OF VENICE—

4589 Merchant of Venice, by William Shakspeare, with Notes and Illustrations of various Commentators, 12mo. *boards, uncut.* Dublin, 1805

4590 Jew of Venice, a Comedy, altered from Merchant of Venice by Lord Lansdown, 4to. *half morocco.* Lond. 1701

ALL'S WELL THAT ENDS WELL—

4591 All's Well that Ends Well, a Comedy, by William Shakspeare, 8vo. Lond. 1709

4592 All's Well that Ends Well, altered by J. P. Kemble, 8vo. Lond. 1793

MUCH ADO ABOUT NOTHING—

4593 Universal Passion, a Comedy, altered from Much Ado About Nothing, by James Miller, 8vo. *half morocco, gilt top.* Lond. 1737

AS YOU LIKE IT—

4594 Caldecott (*T.*) Hamlet and As You Like It, specimens for an edition of Shakspeare, *one hundred copies privately printed.* "Lady Jones, with Mr. Crowe and Mr. Caldecott's best respects," royal 8vo. *half morocco, uncut, top edges gilt.* Lond. 1819

4595 Love in a Forest, altered from As You Like It by Mr. Johnson, *sewed.* Lond. 1723

MEASURE FOR MEASURE—

4596 Measure for Measure, or Beauty the Best Advocate, altered from Shakspeare, with additions of several Entertainments of Music, by C. Gildon, 4to. *half morocco, gilt top.* Lond. 1700

CYMBELINE—

4597 Cymbeline, altered by W. Hawkins, 8vo. *half morocco, gilt top, uncut.* Lond. 1759

——— translated into German, *see* Kaufmann.

4598 Eccles (*Ambrose*), The Plays of Lear and Cymbeline, with Notes and Illustrations of various Commentators, to which are added, Remarks by the Editor, 2 vols. 1794; the Comedy of The Merchant of Venice, Dublin, 1805, together 3 vols. 8vo. *privately printed, fine paper, uncut, half green morocco, top edges gilt, scarce.* Lond. v. y.

WINTER'S TALE—

4599 Winter's Tale, a Play, altered from Shakspeare by Charles Marsh, 12mo. *half morocco, gilt top.* Lond. 1756

MACBETH—

4600 Macbeth, a Tragedy, by Shakspeare, *imperfect, wants all after page* 64. Lond. 1673

4601 Macbeth, a Tragedy, altered by Sir William Davenant, two editions in one vol., 4to. *half morocco, gilt top.* Lond. 1674

4602 Macbeth, a Tragedy, with Notes by Henry Rowe, two editions in one vol., 12mo. *half morocco. gilt top.* York, 1797

4603 Shakspeare's Macbeth, revised by J. P. Kemble, author's copy, 8vo. 1813

4604 Macbeth, with German Notes, by N. Delius, 8vo. *half morocco, gilt top.* Bremen, 1841

——— in German, *see* Kaufmann.

4605 Macbeth Travestie, a Burlesque, in 2 vols., by the author of Mammon and Gammon, two works in one vol. 12mo. *half morocco.* 1847, 1850

KING LEAR—

4606 King Lear, altered by N. Tate, four editions in one vol. 4to. *half morocco, gilt top.* 1681–89, 1699–1702

4607 King Lear, altered by George Colman, 8vo. Lond. 1768

4608 King Lear, altered by Colman, 8vo. *half morocco, gilt.* Lond. 1768

——— by Eccles, *see* under Cymbeline.

KING JOHN—

4609 Shakspeare (*W.*) The first and second part of the troublesome raigne of John, King of England, 4to. *very rare, half calf.* Lond. 1622

4610 Pieces of Antient English Poesie; The troublesome Raigne of King John, by Shakspeare; Marston's Metamorphosis of Pigmalion's Image and Satires, 12mo. Lond. 1764

4611 First and Second Part of the troublesome raigne of John, King of England, by Shakspeare, *imprinted at London, reprint,* 12mo. *half morocco, gilt top.* 1764

KING JOHN—*continued.*

4612 Papal Tyranny in the Reign of King John, a Tragedy, altered by Colley Cibber, 8vo. *half morocco, gilt top.* Lond. 1745

4613 King John, altered by R. Valpy, as it was acted at Reading School, London, 8vo. Lond. 1803

4614 Kynge John, A Play, in two parts, altered by John Bale, 4to. *half morocco, gilt top, reprint.* Lond. 1838

RICHARD THE SECOND—

4615 Life and Death of King Richard the Second, with New Additions of the Parliament Scene and the deposing of King Richard, by William Shakspeare, Jolly's copy, 4to. *half calf, rare.* . Lond. 1634

KING HENRY THE FOURTH—

4617 Historie of Henry the Fourth, with the humorous conceits of Sir John Falstaffe, newly corrected by Wm. Shakspere, 4to. *half calf, very scarce.* Lond. 1639

4618 King Henry the Fourth, with the Humours of Sir John Falstaffe, a Tragi-Comedy altered from Shakspere, by T. Betterton, 4to. *half morocco.* Lond. 1700

4619 Sequel of Henry the Fourth, with the Humours of Sir John Falstaffe and Justice Shallow, altered by Betterton, 8vo. *half morocco, gilt top.* Lond. n. d.

4620 Kenrick, Falstaff's Wedding. A Comedy, Sequel to the second part of King Henry the 4th, in imitation of Shakspere, 12mo. *half morocco, gilt.* Lond. 1766

4621 ——— Another edition, *half morocco.* Lond. 1773

4622 Henry IV., 8vo. *half morocco, gilt top, uncut.* Lond. 1845

KING HENRY THE FIFTH—

4623 Lord Orrery, History of Henry the 5th, and the Tragedy of Mustapha, Son of Soliman the Magnificent, pp. 44, folio, *half morocco.* Lond. 1690

KING HENRY THE SIXTH—

4624 The First Sketches of the second and third parts of Henry the Sixth, edited by J. O. Halliwell, 8vo. *half morocco.* Lond. 1843

KING HENRY THE SIXTH—*continued.*

4625 Richard, Duke of Yorke, or the Contests of Yorke and Lancaster, as altered from Shakespeare's three parts of Henry the 6th, by Soane, 12mo. *half morocco, gilt top.* Lond. 1817

KING RICHARD THE THIRD—

4626 King Richard the Third, revised by Colley Cibber, and adapted to the Stage by J. P. Kemble, his own copy, with MS. notes by himself. 8vo. Lond. 1811

4627 Richard the Third, from a Collection of Plays acted in Paris, *sewed,* 8vo. 1828

4628 True Tragedie of Richard the Third, from a unique copy, and the Latin Play of Richardus Tertius, from a manuscript edited by Baron Field, 8vo. *half morocco, gilt top.* Lond. 1844

4629 Richard the Third, Travestie, with annotations, 12mo. *half morocco, gilt top, uncut.* Lond. 1816

KING HENRY THE EIGHTH—

4630 Henry the 8th, altered from Shakespeare, by Grove, with several plates and portrait, 8vo. *half morocco, gilt top.* Lond. 1758

4631 King Henry the Eighth, revised by J. P. Kemble, Author's copy, 8vo. *half calf.* Lond. 1804

4632 Boker (*George H.*) Anne Boleyn, a Tragedy. Phil. 1850

PERICLES, PRINCE OF TYRE—

4633 Late and much admired Play, called Pericles, Prince of Tyre; with the true relation of the whole History, Adventures, and Fortunes of the saide Prince, written by Wm. Shakspere, 2d edition, 4to. *half morocco, very rare.* Lond. 1619

4634 Old Plays—Pericles, Prince of Tyre, printed 1714; The London Prodigal, Thomas, Lord Cromwell, The Puritan, and the Tragedy of Locrine, *plates,* 12mo. *half calf.*

4635 Kertland (*W.*) Foster-Child, or the Prince of Corinth, a Tragic Play, founded on (and adapted to the stage from) Shakspeare's Tragedy of Pericles, 4to. MS. 1820

TITUS ANDRONICUS—

4636 Titus Andronicus, or the Rape of Lavinia, altered from Shakspere by Edward Ravenscroft, 4to. *half morocco, gilt top.* Lond. 1687

TROILUS AND CRESSIDA—

4638 Troilus and Cressida; or, Truth Found Too Late; altered from Shakspere, by Dryden. Lond. 1679

4639 Troilus and Cressida; or, Truth Found Too Late; altered by John Dryden, 4to. *half morocco, gilt top.* Lond. 1679

4640 Troilus and Cressida, with an Introduction, and Notes Critical and Illustrative, by the Author of the Dramatic Censor, pamphlet. Lond. 1774

See Chaucer's Troilus and Cressida, translated by Kinaston. Lot 4817.

TIMON OF ATHENS—

4641 Timon of Athens, the Man-Hater, altered from Shakspere by Thos. Shadwell; two editions, first edition, 1678; second edition, 1703–4, 4to. *half morocco, gilt top.* Lond. 1678–1703

4642 Timon of Athens, altered from Shakspere by T. Love, *half morocco, gilt top,* 8vo. Lond. 1768

4643 Timon of Athens, a Tragedy, altered from Shakespeare by Cumberland, *half morocco, gilt top.* Lond. 1771

4644 Timon, a Play, edited by Alexander Dyce, 8vo. *half morocco, gilt top.* Lond. 1842

JULIUS CÆSAR—

4645 Julius Cæsar, a Tragedy, by Wm. Shakspere, *paper.* Lond. 1691

ANTONY AND CLEOPATRA—

4646 Antony and Cleopatra, a Tragedy, altered by Sir Charles Sedley, Bart., *half calf.* Lond. 1677

4647 ——— Another copy, *sewed.* Lond. 1677

4648 Antony and Cleopatra, Historical Play by Shakespeare, edited and fitted for the stage by abridging only, &c., by Edwd. Capell, 12mo. *russia, scarce.* Lond. 1758

4649 ——— Idem, *half morocco, gilt top,* 12mo. Lond. 1758

CORIOLANUS—

4650 Coriolanus, A Tragedy, altered by James Thomson, 12mo. *half morocco, gilt top.* Lond. 1749

4651 Coriolanus, or the Roman Matron, a Tragedy, altered from Shakspere by T. Sheridan, 12mo. *half morocco, gilt top.* Lond. 1789

4652 Coriolanus, or the Roman Matron, altered, *sewed,* no title.

ROMEO AND JULIET—

4653 Romeo and Juliet, a Tragedy, altered from Shakespeare by T. Cibber, to which is added a serio-comic apology for part of the life of Mr. T. Cibber, Comedian, written by himself, 8vo. *half morocco, gilt top.* Lond. 1748

4654 Romeo and Juliet, altered from Shakspere by Garrick, with notes and portrait, 8vo. *half morocco, gilt top.* Birmingham, 1770

4655 Romeo and Juliet, a Comedy, from the Spanish of Lopez de Vega, 8vo. *half morocco, gilt top.* Lond. 1770

4656 Julietta, translated from the Italian of Count Luigi da Porta, two versions in one vol.

HAMLET, PRINCE OF DENMARK—

4657 Tragical Historie of Hamlet, Prince of Denmark, by Wm. Shakespeare, 4to. 1603, reprint from the only known copy, it exhibits extraordinary variations from the received text, 8vo. *half morocco, top edge gilt.* Lond. 1825

4658 ——— Another copy, *half calf.* Lond. 1825

4659 Tragedy of Hamlet, Prince of Denmark, by Wm. Shakspere, small 4to. *crown morocco, rare.* Lond. 1637

4660 Tragedy of Hamlet, Prince of Denmark, by Wm. Shakspere, 8vo. Lond. 1703

4661 Hamlet, Caldecott, (*T.*) *see* As You Like It.

4661* Hamlet and As You Like it, a specimen of a new edition of Shakspeare, by Caldecott, *half morocco, top edge gilt*, royal 8vo. Lond. 1832

4662 Hamlet, a Dramatic Prelude, altered by James Rush, 12mo. *half morocco, gilt top.* Phil. 1834

4663 Ducis. Amleto, Tragedia, ad imitazione della Inglese di Shakespear, printed on blue paper, 8vo. Ven. 1774

4664 Valletta (Ignazio) Amleto, ricata in Italiano. 1839

4665 ——— Another copy.

4666 Cellenio (*Inarco*) Hamlet, Tragedia, con traducida é ilustrada con la vida de el autor, y notas criticas, 4to. *half morocco.* Madrid, 1738

4667 Poole—Hamlet Travestie, in Three Acts, with burlesque annotations, after the manner of Dr. Johnson and George Steevens, and the various Commentators, 12mo. *half calf.* 1817

HAMLET—*continued.*

4668 Hamlet Travestie, a Burlesque in 2 acts, with notes, 12mo. *half morocco, gilt top.* Oxford, 1849

OTHELLO, OR THE MOOR OF VENICE—

4669 Tragedy of Othello, the Moor of Venice, as it hath beene divers times acted at the Globe and at the Black Friers by his Majesty's Servants, written by Wm. Shakespeare, 4to. *half calf, cut close, rare.* Lond. 1622

4670 Othello, 4to. pp. 76. Lond. 1695

4671 Moor of Venice, with two Essays on Shakespeare, by Wolstenholme Parr. 8vo. *half morocco, g. t. u.* Lond. 1795

4672 Othello Travestie, with Burlesque Notes in the manner of the most celebrated commentators, and other curious appendices. 12mo. *half morocco, g. t. u.* Lond. 1813

4673 Another copy, *sewed.*

4674 Jennens (*Charles*), Shakspeare's Tragedies, King Lear, Othello, Julius Cæsar, Macbeth, and Hamlet, collated with the old and modern editions, 2 vols. *half morocco.* Lond. 1770-3

4675 Kauffmann (*Philip*), Lear und Macbeth, 12mo. *half morocco, g. t.* Berlin, 1830

4676 ——— Othello und Cymbeline, 12mo. *half morocco, g. t.* 1830

4677 Kemble's (*J. P.*) Editions, altered for representation, 7 vols. 8vo. *half morocco, l. c.* Lond. v. y.

4678 Valetta, Ignazio, Giulio Cesare, Coriolano, y Otello, ricata in Italiano, 12mo. *half morocco.* Firenzi, 1829

4679 Valpy (*K.*) Alterations of some of Shakspeare's Plays, 8vo. Reading, n. d.

DOUBTFUL AND SPURIOUS PLAYS.

4680 SIMMS (*W. G.*) A Supplement to the Plays of William Shakespeare; comprising the seven Dramas which have been ascribed to his pen, but are not included with his writings in modern editions, &c., edited, with notes and an introduction to each Play, by W. Gilmore Simms, Esq., *portrait and engravings, uncut, half morocco,* royal 8vo. N. Y. 1848

FAIRE EM—

4681 A pleasant Comedie of Faire Em, The Miller's Daughter of Manchester, with the Love of William the Conqueror, ascribed to Wm. Shakspeare, *scarce*, 4to. *half calf.* Lond. 1631

FIFTH OF NOVEMBER—

4682 Or the Gunpowder Plot, an Historical Play, supposed to be written by Wm. Shakspere, *paper.* Lond. 1830

MERRY DEVIL OF EDMONTON—

4683 Merry Devel of Edmonton, said by Kirkham to be by Shakspere, 4to. *very rare.* Lond. 1617

4684 Merrie Devill of Edmonton, reprint of an Elizabethan Drama, by an unknown author, 12mo. Lond. 1780

"I wish it could be ascertained that Drayton was the author, it would add a worthy appendage to his renown."—*C. Lamb.*

4685 Life and Death of the Merry Devill of Edmonton, with the Pleasant Pranks of Smug the Smith, Sir John, and Mine Host of the George, about the stealing of venison, 8vo. *boards.* Lond. 1819

MUCEDORUS—

4686 A most pleasant Comedie of Mucedorus, the King's Sonne of Valencia, and Amadine, the King's Daughter of Aragon, with the Merry Conceits of Mouse, amplified with new Additions, as it was acted before the King's Majestie at Whitehall, on Shrove Sunday Night, by his Highnesse's Servants, usually playing at the Globe, very delectable and full of conceited mirth, 4to. *half calf, very neat, and scarce.* Lond. 1668

Malone attributes this very rare and curious old Play or Droll to R. Green; but by others it is attributed to Shakspeare.

OLDCASTLE—

4687 First part of the True and Honorable History of the Life of Sir John Oldcastle, the Good Lord Cobham, written by Wm. Shakspere, *fine copy, very rare*, 4to. *morocco.* Lond. 1600

4688 Two Noble Kinsmen, written by Mr. John Fletcher and Mr. Wm. Shakspere, the first edition, 4to. *half calf.* 1634

4689 Whole Contention betweene the Two Famous Houses of Lancaster and York, divided into two parts, and newly corrected and enlarged, written by Wm. Shakspere, 4to. *very scarce.* Lond. *J. P.* 1619

4689* Double Falsehood, or The Distrest Lovers, written originally by Wm. Shakspere, revised by Theobald, first edition, published 1728, 8vo. *half morocco, gilt top, uncut.* Lond.

SHAKSPEARE.—POEMS, SONNETS, &c.

4690 SHAKSPEARE, all the Miscellaneous Poems of Wm. Shakspeare, which were published by himself in the year 1609, and now correctly printed from those editions, 2 vols. 12mo. *half morocco, gilt top.* Lond. 1710

4691 ——— Poems by Wm. Shakspeare, *with portrait,* 12mo. *morocco.* *Evans,* Lond. n. d.

4692 ——— Poems by William Shakspeare, with illustrative remarks, original and select, to which is prefixed a sketch of the Author's life, *plates, uncut,* 2 vols. 8vo. Lond. 1804

An elegant and copiously annotated edition by an unknown author.

4693 ——— Another copy, 2 vols. 8vo. *half calf.* Lond. 1804

4694 ——— Poetical Works, containing Venus and Adonis, Rape of Lucrece, Sonnets, Passionate Pilgrim, and A Lover's Complaint, *printed and embellished under the direction of C. Cooke, plates, calf,* 18mo. Lond. 1797

4695 ——— Sonnets, pp. 80, 18mo. *half morocco.* *Ball, Arnold & Co.,* Lond. 1840

4696 ——— Songs of Shakspeare, illustrated by the Etching Club, *large paper, beautiful designs, half calf.* Lond. 1843

4697 ——— Songs and Ballads of Shakespeare, illuminated by T. W. Gwilt Mapleson, Esq., 4to. *half morocco.* N. Y. n. d.

SHAKSPEARE—COLLECTED EDITIONS.

4698 SHAKESPEARE'S (*Mr. William*) COMEDIES, HISTORIES, AND TRAGEDIES, PUBLISHED ACCORDING TO THE TRUE ORIGINALL COPIES, FIRST EDITION, *exceedingly rare*, folio, printed by Isaac Jaggard and Ed. Blount. 1623

This copy has the original portrait by Droeshout, inlaid in a title, which is fac-similied by the inimitable Harris; the verses in front, also the last leaf, are by the same hand; otherwise it is as fine a copy as is generally seen—measures $12\frac{3}{4}$ inches high by $8\frac{1}{4}$ wide, *red morocco, extra, with gilt fillets inside, and gilt leaves*, bound by Bedford.

"Twenty-two out of the thirty-six Plays in this volume had never previously been published in any form whatever; of these it is the parent text; this circumstance alone imparts an extraordinary and inestimable value to this edition."

4698* SHAKESPEARE'S COMEDIES, HISTORIES, AND TRAGEDIES, THE CELEBRATED FAC-SIMILE REPRINT OF THE RARE FIRST EDITION, *with fine portrait after Droeshout's engraving*, folio, *calf extra*, printed by Ed. and J. Wright. Lond. 1807

4699 SHAKESPEARE (*Mr. William*) COMEDIES, HISTORIES, AND TRAGEDIES, PUBLISHED ACCORDING TO THE TRUE ORIGINALL COPIES, THE SECOND IMPRESSION, printed by Thomas Cotes for William Ashley, 8vo. Lond. 1632

This copy has the original title, with the portrait by Droeshout pieced at the bottom, and the inside; otherwise it is a tall and remarkable fine copy and such as is not commonly seen for sale, *elegantly bound in Russia, gilt leaves*, $13\frac{1}{4}$ *high by* $8\frac{7}{8}$ *wide.*

This rare edition, which at one time was thought to be more intrinsically valuable than its predecessor, is one of the best printed books of the period.

A leaf with ten metrical lines, signed "B. I." (Ben Jonson) "To the Reader," precedes the title page, in the centre of which is a portrait of Shakespeare *by Martin Droeshout*, the lines opposite referring to the same thus commencing:—

"The figure that thou here seest put,
It was for gentle Shakespeare cut."

This portrait has always been looked upon as the most satisfactory likeness of our *Immortal Bard.*

Stevens' copy sold for £18 18*s.*, and at Mr. Dunn Gardner's sale it brought £18 10*s.*

4700 SHAKESPEARE'S (*Mr. William*) COMEDIES, HISTORIES, AND TRAGEDIES, PUBLISHED ACCORDING TO THE TRUE ORIGINALL COPIES, THE THIRD IMPRESSION, original portrait and title, beautifully inlaid, the verses a reprint and part of the last leaf inlaid—*otherwise a very good copy*, printed for Philip Chetwind. Lond. 1663

It is $13\frac{1}{4}$ inches high by $8\frac{5}{8}$, beautifully bound in Russia, gilt leaves, and was formerly in the possession of J. W. Cole, the lessee of the Theatre Royal, Dublin.

This is considered of greater rarity than even the first edition, an account of the greater portion of the impression having been destroyed in the great fire of London. There is another *third* edition with the date 1664, but the one of 1663, as above, is the scarcest of all.

The publishers of the *fourth* edition in 1685, appear to have considered the destruction of the *third* edition so extensive as to entitle them to treat it as a non-entity; and accordingly say on their title-page, "*unto which is added Seven Plays never before printed in Folio*," though they had been previously printed in the third—a certain proof of its great rarity even in those days.

4701 SHAKESPEARE'S (*Mr. William*) COMEDIES, HISTORIES, AND TRAGEDIES PUBLISHED ACCORDING TO THE TRUE ORIGINAL COPIES, UNTO WHICH IS ADDED SEVEN PLAYS NEVER BEFORE PRINTED IN FOLIO, THE FOURTH EDITION, *portrait by Droeshout and verses beneath, a fine tall copy* $14\frac{3}{8}$ *by* $9\frac{1}{4}$, *Russia extra, gilt leaves,* printed for H. Heringman, E. Brewster, and R. Bently, &c. Lond. 1685

The same portrait was used for this edition as the third, after having been retouched; it has occupied the upper part of a leaf preceding the title having the initial lines beneath it. The work is printed in a large size, the prefatory matter occupying only four pages. Mr. Dunn Gardner's copy sold for £13.

This fourth edition, see above, contains the Seven Doubtful Plays, Pericles, London Prodigal, History of Lord Cromwell, Sir John Oldcastle, The Puritan Widow, A Yorkshire Tragedy, and Locrene.

4702 SHAKSPEARE'S Dramatic Works, revised, with Life by N. Rowe, portrait and numerous fine plates of characters by Vandergucht, Duchange, &c., large paper, 7 vols. *half morocco, gilt top, scarce.* Lond. 1709

The first 8vo. edition, and the first edition of Shakspeare, with plates.

4703 ——— Plays and Poems, by Alexander Pope, collated and corrected by him by the former editions, with Notes, printed in large type, fine portrait by Vertue, 7 vols. 4to. *half morocco, gilt top.* Lond. 1725

The seventh volume to this edition was added by Dr. Sewell. It contains Shakspeare's Poems, with Gildon's Essay on the Stage, and Remarks on Shakspeare. This volume is now *rare.*

This edition is much esteemed for its correctness and notes.

"The most striking instance of the growing popularity of the great Bard, was the enterprise of employing Pope to edit this first splendid edition of his works. 750 copies were printed at £6 6*s.*; but so little were the public prepared to sustain the undertaking, that the bulk of the edition was sunk among the booksellers to 16*s.* a copy."
Johnson's Lives.

4704 ——— Collated and corrected by the former editions by Alexander Pope, 8 vols. 12mo. *half morocco, gilt top.* Lond. 1728

The head of Shakspeare in this edition is said by Boaden to be that of King James.

4705 SHAKSPEARE The Works of, collated with the oldest copies, with Critical Notes, by Lewis Theobald, curious plates to each play, showing the theatrical costume of the day, *large paper copy*, with numerous MS. notes by the learned Styan Thirlby, 7 vols. *half morocco, gilt top, uncut.* Lond. 1733

4706 ——— Works, revised and corrected by Sir T. Hanmer, printed in large type, with plates by Gravelot after Hayman's designs, 6 vols. 4to. *half morocco, gilt top.* Oxford, 1744

4707 ——— Dramatic Works, with Glossary and various Readings, by Sir T. Hanmer, finely printed in large type with the series of engravings by Gravelot, from Hayman's celebrated designs, large paper, 6 vols. royal 4to. *half morocco, gilt top.* Oxf. Clar. Press, 1771

Particularly esteemed for its exceedingly large and beautiful type.

A copy of this edition was used by Mrs. Butler (Fanny Kemble) at her "Shakspeare Readings."

4708 ——— The Works of; the genuine text (collated with all the former editions, and then corrected and amended) is here settled; being restored from the *Blunders* of the first Editors, and the *Interpolations* of the two last, with a Comment and Notes, Critical and Explanatory, by Mr. Warburton, *portrait by Vertue*, 8 vols. 8vo. *half morocco, top gilt.* Lond. 1747

The present copy has MS. notes by the learned Styan Thirlby; it formerly belonged to Sir Edward Walpole, who lent the sixth volume to Dr. Samuel Johnson, which volume the Doctor did not return.

4710 ——— Dramatic Works, Dr. Johnson's Original Edition, with his Notes, and Illustrations of various Commentators, *portrait by Vertue*, 8 vols. 8vo. *half morocco, top edges gilt, uncut.* Lond. 1765

4711 ——— Mr. William Shakespeare, his Comedies, Histories, and Tragedies, set out by Himself in quarto, or by the Players his Fellows in folio, and now faithfully republished from those editions, with an Introduction, whereunto will be added Notes Critical and Explanatory, and a body of various Readings intire, by Capell; Prolusions, or Select Pieces of Ancient Poetry, etc., printed by Dryden Leach, fine copy, beautifully printed on fine paper, 10 vols. 8vo. *half morocco, gilt top.* Lond. 1768

*** Sold in Reed's Sale for £5 17*s.* 6*d.*, and in White Knight's for £11.

"Mr. Capell, I call the *patron* of Shakspeare; they who are acquainted with his Critical Writings will not scruple with me to pronounce him the Father of all legitimate commentary on Shakspeare."

Pursuits of Literature.

4712 SHAKSPEARE, with the Corrections and Illustrations of various Commentators, to which are added Notes by Samuel Johnson and George Stevens, with an Appendix, revised and augmented, 10 vols. and 2 vols. Prolegomena—12 vols. *half morocco, uncut, very rare in this state*, 8vo. Lond. 1778–80

This is the celebrated edition edited by Dr. Johnson, and is esteemed one of the best variorum editions of the last century.

4713 ——— Dramatic Works, Bell's excellent edition, large paper, with the various Prefaces, Dissertations, and Variorum Notes, numerous fine Portraits, and upwards of 100 beautiful Engravings of Scenes and Characters, proofs, 20 vols. post 8vo. *whole bound purple morocco, gilt leaves, contents lettered, fine copy.* 1786–8

4714 ——— Idem, Vol. 1, 18mo. 1788

4715 ——— Dramatic Works of, with Notes by Joseph Rann, A. M., 6 vols. *half morocco, gilt top*, 8vo. Oxford, 1786

4716 ——— Plays and Poems, with a historical account of the English Stage, by E. Malone, *portraits*, 10 vols. *fine paper, half morocco, stilted to match the large* 8vo. *set.* Lond. 1790

4717 ——— First American Edition, Johnson, vol. 1. Phil. 1795

4718 ——— Works, Bellamy's Edition, 8 vols. Portrait, Two Plates to each Volume, very rare, *half morocco, cut, top edges gilt*, 8vo. Lond. 1796

4719 ——— Works, Robinson's Edition, 7 vols., *large paper*, beautifully printed, very rare, not mentioned in Halliwell's Shaksperiana, *half morocco*, royal 8vo. Lond. 1797

4720 ——— Plays and Poems, from the text of Steevens, Robinson's Edition, no Notes, 8 vols. *calf*, 8vo. Lond. 1797

4721 ——— Basil Edition, with corrections and illustrations of various commentators, and the whole of the curious Prolegomena, Notes, &c., supposed to be edited by the celebrated Isaac Reed, 23 vols. *half morocco, gilt top*, 8vo. Basil, 1800

By a typographical error, the date of the first volume is MDCCCC.

4723 ——— Works, Miller's Edition, 2 vols. royal 8vo. *half morocco, uncut.* Lond. 1806

4722 SHAKSPEARE'S Dramatic Works, Bensley's fine Library Edition, handsomely printed on thick paper, 8 vols. 8vo. *half morocco, gilt top,* contents lettered. 1803

An excellent edition from the text of Steevens, with Life by Chalmers, and select Notes from the best Commentators.

4724 ——— Dramatic Works, with Notes of various Commentators, edited by Manley Wood, illustrated with numerous beautiful Engravings by Warren, Neagle, &c., *large paper*, 14 vols. 8vo. *half morocco, gilt top.* Kearsley, 1806

An elegant and scarce edition; the engravings are from designs by Stothard, Burney, Hamilton, Thurston, Loutherbourg, and other eminent painters.

4725 ——— Plays, printed from the Text of Johnson, Steevens, and Reed, Portrait and numerous beautiful vignette Plates to each Play, from designs by Smirke, Stothard, Westall, Thompson, Howard, Cook, &c., engraved by Fittler, Heath, Anker, Smith, and other eminent engravers, 6 vols. royal 8vo. *large paper, half bound dark green morocco, uncut, top edge gilt.* Lond. 1807

This edition is most beautifully printed by Ballantyne. The text, which is singularly correct, was edited by Sir Walter Scott. Copies on large paper are very scarce. Sabine's sold for £12 16*s*.

4726 ——— Dramatic Works, Ayscough's Edition, with the celebrated Index to the remarkable Passages and Words, fine Portrait by Sherwin, 3 vols. royal 8vo. *half morocco.* Lond. 1807

4727 ——— Dramatic Works, Portrait and Plates after Thurston, 12 vols. 12mo. *large paper, uncut, half morocco, and stilted to 8vo.* Lond. *Tegg*, 1812

4728 ——— Plays, with the Corrections and Illustrations of various Commentators, to which are added Notes by Samuel Johnson and George Steevens, revised and augmented by Isaac Reed, including the two vols. of Prolegomena, with a Glossarial Index, 21 vols. 8vo. *portraits and plates, russia, extra, gilt.* 1813

Perhaps this may be esteemed as the best and most useful of all the editions of Shakspeare. The proof sheets were most carefully corrected by Mr. Harris, librarian of the Royal Institution.

This excellent variorum edition includes the Doubtful Plays, Complete History of the Stage, a copious Glossarial Index, &c.

4729 ——— Dramatic Works, Wittingham's Edition, 24mo. 7 vols. *India paper, half morocco.* Chiswick, 1814

4730 SHAKSPEARE's Dramatic Works, edited by Isaac Reed, 10 vols. 8vo. *boards.* N. Y. 1817

4731 ——— Dramatic Works, Oxberry's Edition, the only one which is faithfully marked with stage business and stage directions, capital Portraits of the principal actors, in character, 4 vols. 12mo. *half morocco.* Lond. 1818–23

4732 SHAKSPEARE (*William*) WORKS, BOYDELL'S SPLENDID EDITION, 9 VOLS. FOLIO, CHOICE PROOFS OF ALL THE PLATES AND A SET OF THE ETCHINGS, MOST ELEGANTLY BOUND IN MOROCCO, GILT LEAVES. Lond. 1802

MISS BOYDELL'S OWN COPY.—These plates were all selected by the niece of the publisher, and it is presumed this is the choicest *copy* of the work extant, the result of one of the most patriotic and sumptuous undertakings that ever emanated from the liberality and spirit of any publisher before Alderman Boydell; combining at the same time employment and the greatest encouragement to every one concerned, from the elevated genius of the palette and maule-stick to the humble wielder of the folding stick.

4733 SHAKSPEARE (*W.*) BOYDELL'S LARGE SET OF ILLUSTRATIONS TO, CONSISTING OF ONE HUNDRED, AFTER THE PAINTINGS OF THE MOST CELEBRATED ARTISTS OF THE DAY; ENGRAVED BY SHARPE, HALL, BARTOLOZZI, SCHIAVONETTI, STOWE, OGBORNE, MIDDIMAN, AND OTHERS. THE WHOLE BEING THE MOST CHOICE PROOFS THAT EVER CAME FROM THE PLATES.

They are accompanied by the etchings of every print, with some variations. It is not usual to find more than eighty etchings in a set, but in this instance the set is complete within one or two, which is sufficiently or more than compensated, by the variations of KING LEAR by SHARPE and others, all in the first state as they were printed, loose in a portfolio with wrappers.

This splendid work is a noble monument to the genius of Shakspeare, formed by the united efforts of the most renowned British artists, aided and directed also by the munificence of Alderman Boydell. Among the paintings engraved in this superb series of illustrations are the works of Sir Joshua Reynolds, Romney, Opie, Smirke, Northcote, Stothard, Fuseli, Hamilton, Tresham, Westall, and other first rate British artists.

4734 BOYDELL's Shakspeare, a lot of odd sheets, letter-press.

4735 SHAKSPEARE (*W.*) Plays and Poems of, with Life of the Poet, and enlarged History of the Stage, with all the Prefaces and Essays of the various Commentators, Malone's edition, edited by James Boswell, 21 vols. including the 2 vols. of Prolegomena. Lond. 1821

——— Dramatic Works and Poems, with Life, Variorum Notes, and Preface by the Rev. W. Harness, 3 *fine portraits of Shakspeare*, 8 vols. 8vo. *half morocco, gilt top.* 1825

4736 SHAKSPEARE, Leipsic edition in English, *old calf.* 1824

4737 ——— Dramatic Works, Pickering's beautiful edition, 11 vols. post, 8vo. *half calf.* Lond. 1825

4738 ——— The Works of, Pickering's Diamond edition, the smallest ever published, *portrait from the print by Droeshout,* 9 vols. 48mo. *morocco, gilt, gilt edges.* Lond. 1825

*** This beautiful edition of Shakspeare was published under the patronage of Earl Spencer, and is one of the finest specimens of typography ever produced.

4739 ——— Plays, edited by Bowdler, with all the passages omitted which cannot be read aloud with propriety, 10 vols. 18mo. *half morocco, gilt top.* Lond. 1827

This admirable edition has met with deserved eulogy from all classes. The works of Shakspeare are now accessible to the domestic circle in a form which is free from the impurities of thought and expression sanctioned by the license of the times in which he lived.

4740 ——— Works of, with his Life, by Dr. Symmons, and notes and illustrations, by S. W. Singer, Esq., Whittingham's beautiful Chiswick edition, 60 *plates,* 10 vols. 12mo. *elegant copy, in half morocco, gilt top, uncut,* and contents lettered, *very scarce,* a large portion of the edition being lost by fire. Lond. 1826

4741 ——— The Dramatic Works of, *portrait,* 60 *exquisite woodcuts,* 8vo. *morocco, gilt top.* *Chiswick Press,* Whittingham, 1827

Very scarce. Like all the books that came from the celebrated "Chiswick Press," this is a beautiful specimen of typography and wood engraving.

4742 ——— Dramatic Works, with editorial and glossarial notes, a sketch of his Life, and an Essay on his writings, newly arranged by C. H. Wheeler, 8vo. *half morocco, uncut.* Lond. 1827

4743 ——— Dramatic Works, from the text of Johnson, Steevens, and Reid, *uncut, half morocco.* Lond., *Jones,* 1830

4744 ——— Slater (*E.*) Select Plays for Schools, selections from Shakspeare, 12mo. *half morocco, uncut.* Lond. 1836

4745 ——— Works, with the various Readings, Notes, History of the early English Stage, and Life, by J. Payne Collier, *fine portrait,* 8 vols. 8vo. *half morocco, gilt top.* Lond. 1844

The text in this edition is formed from an entirely new collation of the old editions ; it is the approved text of one who has dedicated much time and research to the subject.

4746 SHAKSPEARE, Bell's edition, *with plates and vignettes*, 7 vols. 48mo. *half morocco.*

4747 ——— Baudry's edition in English, 9 vols. 8vo. *half morocco, uncut.* Paris, 1843

4748 ——— Baudry's edition by Campbell, *many plates and cuts, half morocco, gilt top,* royal 8vo. Paris, 1848

4749 ——— Dramatic and Poetical Works, with Life by Barry Cornwall, and Notes by the best Commentators, *illustrated edition, with nearly* 1000 *engravings, from designs by Kenny Meadows,* 3 vols. impl. 8vo. *half morocco, gilt tops, fine uncut copy,* PRINTED ENTIRELY ON INDIA PAPER, ONLY TWELVE COPIES SO PRINTED. Lond. 1843

4750 ——— Plays and Poems, Valpy's Cabinet Pictorial edition, with Life, Glossarial Notes, &c., and 171 *plates engraved on steel after designs of the most distinguished British artists,* 15 vols. post 8vo. *half bd. morocco, contents lettered.* Lond. 1843

"This is at once the most delightful and elegant form in which Shakspeare has ever appeared."—*Morning Post.*

4751 ——— Dramatic Works and Poems complete, *with* 40 *portraits of the Heroines,* 8 vols. large paper, *half morocco top gilt.* Bost. 1850

4752 ——— Works, Hudson's edition, vols. 1 and 3, *cloth.* Boston and Cambridge, 1851

4753 ——— Knights cabinet edition of the Works of William Shakspere, Studies of Shakspere, Poems and notes, *uncut,* 12 vols. in 6, *morocco gilt,* 16mo. Lond. 1851

4754 ——— Halliwell's Folio. The Works of William Shakespeare, the Text formed by a new collation of the early editions, all the Novels and Tales on which the Plays are founded, copious Archæological annotations, and essay on the formation of the Text and a Life of the Poet, by J. O. Halliwell, F. R. S., numerous plates, fac-similes, wood-cuts, accurately taken from original sources, an original subscription copy, folio, *half bound.* 1854–6

The eighth and ninth volumes of the magnificent work are just ready. The purchaser of this copy will have the right of continuation to the whole work without further payment.

Only 150 copies are printed, and a number being assigned to every copy, the limit is most strictly maintained. All the engravings are also destroyed, so that the work must always be rising in price.

4755 SHAKSPEARE'S Plays, new Lansdowne edition, the Text from the early and best impressions, with Glossary, highly finished port. by Robinson, after that by Droeshout, thick 8vo. 1852

This elegant edition is printed in a novel and convenient style, the names of the characters being put at full length, in the centre of the text, in red ink.

4756 ——— Dramatic Works; the Text regulated by the old copies, and by the recently discovered Folio of 1632, containing early MS. emendations, edited by J. P. Collier, portrait of Shakspeare copied from the Folio Edition of 1623. Lond. 1853

4757 ——— The Dramatic Works of William Shakespeare, from the text of Johnson, Steevens, and Reed, with Glossorial Notes, Life, etc., a new edition, by William Hazlitt, Esq., The Supplementary Works of Shakespeare, comprising his Poems and Doubtful Plays, etc., 5 vols. 12mo. *cloth, gilt.* Lond. 1853

4758 ——— Dramatic Works, with Introductions and Notes by J. O. Halliwell, 80 plates, including Photographs of E. Forrest, Charles Kean, Phelps, Harley, Buckstone, and other eminent Actors, in character, 3 vols. impl. 8vo. in parts, *half calf.* 1858

4759 ——— The Plays of, with his Life, illustrated with many hundred wood-cuts from designs of Meadows, Harvey, and others, edited by Gulian C. Verplanck, with Notes, &c., 3 vols, royal 8vo. *half morocco.* N. Y. 1847

TRANSLATIONS.

4760 LA ROCHE (*Benj.*) Shakespeare, Œuvres completes, edition Illustrée, royal 8vo. Paris, n. d.

4761 ——— Another edition with preface, by Alexander Dumas, 2 vols. royal 8vo. *half morocco gilt.* Paris, 1844

4762 MICHEL (*L.*) Œuvres Completes de Shakespeare, 3 vols. royal 8vo. *half morocco.* Paris, 1837

4763 ——— Tragedia di, 14 vols. small 4to. *half morocco, gilt top, uncut.* Verona, 1817

4764 SHAKSPEARE, Dramatische Werke übersetzt von A. W. Schlegel and Ludw. Tieck, 12 vols. with fine steel engravings, *half morocco, gilt top.* Berlin, 1839

This translation into German by Schlegel and Tieck of the works of the great British Bard is a poetical production of the highest merit. In no other living language could Shakspeare's work be rendered similar to this translation.

4765 SHAKSPEARE, Another edition, 12 vols. *sewed.* Berlin, 1850

4766 ——— Schauspiele, neue gans ungear beitete ausgabe von J. Z. Eschenburg, 2 vols. thick 8vo. *thick paper, half morocco, gilt top.* Zurich, 1780

4767 ——— Ueber, W. Shakspeare Joh. Zoach, Eschenburg, *portrait*, 8vo. *half morocco.* Zurich, 1787

4768 ——— Eschenburg, Werke und Genius von Shakespeare, 8vo. *half morocco.* Zurich, 1787

4769 ——— Œuvres, traduites de l'Allemand, par Mde. Elise Voïart. Paris, 1826

4770 ——— Venus und Adonis, Tarquin und Lukrezia zwei gedichte Von Shakespeare, ans dem Englischen übersetzt H. C. Albrecht (with the English text), 8vo. *half calf.* Halle, 1783

SHAKESPEARIANA.

4772 ALEYN (*C.*) The Historie of that wise and fortunate Prince Henrie of that name, the seventh king of England, with that famed battaile fought between the sayd king Henry and Richard the Third, surnamed the Crookbacke, upon Redmoore Heath, neere Bosworth, in verse, *scarce*, 8vo. *calf.* Lond. 1683

Sold in Nassau's sale, £2 2*s*. Dodweswell, £2 12*s*. 6*d*.

4773 AMERICAN Whig Review, December, 1851, 8vo. N. Y. 1851

Containing an article on some Shaksperian and Spenserian MSS.

4774 ANNOTATIONS, Illustrative of the Plays of Shakespeare, by Johnson, Steevens, Malone, Theobald, Warburton, &c., 2 vols. in 1, *uncut, half morocco, top edges gilt*, 8vo. Lond. 1819

4775 ASCHAM (*R.*) The Schole-master, or plaine and perfite way of teaching children to understand, write, and speak the Latin Tong, **Black Letter**, 4to. Lond. *John Daye*, 1589

"A book that will be always useful, and everlastingly esteemed on account of the good sense, judicious observations, excellent characters of ancient authors, and many pleasant and profitable passages of English history, which are plentifully sprinkled therein."—*Dr. Campbell.*

AUBREY'S Miscellanies, *vide* Lot 4023.

AYSCOUGH (*S.*) Index to the remarkable passages and words made use of by Shakespeare, calculated to point out the different meanings to which the words were applied, also the Dramatic Works of Shakespeare, together, 3 vols. *calf, scarce,* 8vo. *vide* 4726.

4777 BABES in the Wood, Old English Ballad, *with coloured illustrations*, by the Marchioness of Waterford, 4to. *morocco.*

BAKER'S Biographia Dramatica, *vide* Lot 350.

4778 BANCROFT (*Thomas*), Two Books of Epigrammes, *half morocco*, 4to. *scarce.* Lond. 1639

Sold in Lloyd £10 10*s*. Priced in the Bib. Anglo-Poet. £20.

This rare volume contains 481 Epigrams and Epitaphs. The writer was a contributor to "Lachrymæ Musarum," 1650, in which his poem is thus inscribed: "To the never-dying memory of the noble Lord Hastings, &c., the meanest son of the Muses consecrates this Elegie." In the first Book occur two Epigrams on Shakespeare. "Shooke thy Speare" seems to allude to his crest, which was a Falcon supporting a Spear.

118. *To Shakespeare.*

Thy Muses, sugred dainties seeme to us
Like the fam'd Apples of old Tantalus ;
For we (admiring), see and heare thy straines,
But none I see or heare, those sweets attaines.

119. *To the Same.*

Thou hast so us'd thy Pen (or shooke thy speare),
That poets startle, nor thy wit come neare.

4779 BARRISTER'S (*A.*) Tour for Genealogy, containing curious fragments from a MS. collection, ascribed to Shakspeare, also Brewer's Histrionic Topography, 2 vols. in 1, *half morocco, gilt top, uncut,* Lond. 1811–18

4780 BARTON (*T. P.*) MS. List of Shakespeariana, in the possession of, 4to.

Mr. Barton's is the finest collection in the United States, and perhaps scarcely second to any other collection.

4781 BEAUTIES of Shakespeare, selected from his Works, to which are added the Principal Scenes in the same author, *rough leaves, half green morocco, top edges gilt,* 12mo. Lond. 1811

4782 BECKET (*A.*) Shakespeare's Himself Again, or the language of the poet asserted—being a full but dispassionate examen of the readings and interpretations of the several editors ; the whole comprised in a series of notes, sixteen hundred in number, with Autograph of the Author, &c., 2 vols. 8vo. *half morocco, gilt top.* Lond. 1815

4783 BEE (*The*), Or a Companion to the Shakspeare Gallery, 8vo. Lond. 1789

4785 BELL—Introduction to Shakespeare's Plays ; containing an essay on oratory (taken from Bell's edition). 12mo. *half morocco, gilt top.* Lond. 1773

Portraits of Shakespeare and Garrick.

4786 BIRCH (*W. T.*), An Inquiry into the Philosophy and Religion of Shakspeare, 12mo. *cloth.* Lond. 1848

4787 BLOUNT (*T. P.*) De Re Poetica: or Remarks upon Poetry, with characters and censures of the most considerable Poets, *clean copy, scarce,* 4to. *half morocco.* Lond. 1694

*** Containing characters of Chaucer, Shakespeare, Spenser, Sidney, Ben Jonson, Milton, Cowley, Waller, Donne, Suckling, &c.

4788 BOADEN (*J.*), A letter to George Steevens, containing a critical examination of the papers of Shakespeare: published by Mr. Samuel Ireland, to which are added extracts from Vortigern. (Interleaved and MS. notes by the author.) 8vo. *half calf.* Lond. 1796

4789 ——— An Enquiry into the authenticity of various pictures and prints, which, from the decease of the poet to our own times, have been offered to the public as portraits of Shakspeare, &c., 5 portraits, fine impressions, *proof, large paper, uncut,* 4to. *half calf.* Lond. 1824

4789* ——— Idem. *boards, uncut,* 8vo. Lond. 1824

4790 ——— On the Sonnets of Shakespeare, identifying the person to whom they are addressed, and elucidating several points in the poet's history, *uncut,* 8vo. *half morocco, gilt top.* Lond. 1837

4791 BOCATIUS, Tragedies of all such Princes as fell from theyr estates through the mutability of Fortune, translated by John Lydgate, Moncke of Bury., *in verse, morocco, gilt leaves, fine copy, curious plates,* folio. Lond. 1554

*** There are, perhaps, few books that have had so great an effect on the early literature of England as the present volume. Its popularity during the fifteenth and sixteenth centuries is shown by the numerous Manuscripts and editions, and to this popularity we owe the Mirror for Magistrates, written on the same plan, and intended as a continuation of it; the Legends and Barons Wars of Drayton, the Civil Wars of Daniel, the Legend of Wolsey, by Storer, and other Poems on the same model; but it is the Dramatic muse of the country that is chiefly indebted to it; since to it we trace the origin of the Historic Drama, which, rising in the Ferrex and Porrex of Sackville and Norton, acquired such strength in the hands of Marloe, and ultimately blazed forth with such splendor in the pages of Shakespeare, extremely rare.

*** Sold in the Roxburghe sale for 11*l.* 11*s.*, and in the Towneley for 10*l.* 5*s.*

4792 BOSWELL (*Jas.*) Biographical Memoir of Edmond Malone—not published, presentation copy, with author's signature, 8vo. *half morocco, gilt top, uncut.* Lond. 1814

4793 BOCCACIO (*J.*)—The Novels and Tales of the renowned John Boccacio, the first refiner of Italian prose; containing a hundred curious Novels, by seven honorable ladies, and three noble gentlemen, framed in ten days, woodcut title, fine copy, *old calf*, folio. Lond. 1620

The first English version of Boccacio, with curious wood-cuts; *rare.*

"Boccacio's soul was deeply imbued with the poetry of feeling and imagination, and this faculty is traced in his prose works far more than in his poetical compositions. In attentively perusing the De cameron, we not only admire the great versatility of the author's genius, combined as it is with an expert and decided hand in the management of details, but discover, besides a certain fixed design in plan and arrangement, a distinctly conceived and general ideality, framed and executed with judgment and intelligence."—*Schlegel.*

4794 BOURNE (*A. V.*) Poemata; Poems English and Latin (Ode Magistri Gulielmi, Shakespear, &c.) 12mo. 3*s.* 6*d.* Lond. 1734

What a sweet, unpretending, pretty-mannered, matter-ful creature!—Suckling from every flower, and making a flower of everything.—His diction all Latin, and his thoughts all English. Bless him!
Charles Lamb.

4795 BOWDLER (*Thomas*), A Letter to the Editor of the British Critic, occasioned by the censure pronounced in that Work on Johnson, Pope, Bowdler, Warburton, Theobald, Steevens, Reid, and Malone, &c., *uncut*, 8vo. *half morocco, top edge gilt.* Lond. 1823

4795* BOYDELL—Graphic Illustrations of the Works of Shakespeare, consisting of a series of prints, forming an elegant and useful companion to the various editions of his works, 100 large plates, fine impression, fine copy, 2 vols. folio, *boards, uncut.* Lond. 1793-1802

4795† ——— Another and smaller edition, 100 *plates*, 4to. *morocco.*

4796 ——— A Catalogue of the Pictures, &c., in the Shakespeare Gallery, Pall-Mall, fine copy, 8vo. *half morocco, uncut, top edge gilt.* Lond. 1790

4797 BRIEFE and True Relation of all what hath happened unto His Princeley Excellencie, Counte Maurice, of Nassau, Translated out of the Netherlandish Tongue according to the Coppie, printed by Hans Moermans. Hereunto is also annexed, the victorious taking of the strong cittie of Alba-regalis in the Nether Hungarie, by the Christians, with MS. notes and signature of Wm. Shakspere, 4to. *calf.* Lond. 1601

This is one of the pseudo Shakspearian library books, having a poem, notes and signature, pretending to be the handwriting of Shakspeare, by W. H. Ireland.

4798 Histrionic Topography, or the Birth-places, Residences, and Funeral Monuments of the most distinguished Actors, many interesting plates, 1 vol. large paper, not mentioned by Halliwell, 8vo. *half morocco uncut.* Lond. 1818

4799 Britton (*John*), Remarks on the Life and Writings of William Shakespeare, *only* 25 *copies, printed* 1814. Remarks, &c., revised and much enlarged, by J. Britton, *not printed for sale*, 1818. Remarks on the Monumental Bust of Shakespeare at Stratford on Avon, *wood-cuts*, PRINTED ON INDIA PAPER. "*Jos. Huslewood, Esq., from J. Britton, as a choice specimen of Typography,*" 1816. Another copy on common paper, 1816, *all presentation copies from J. Britton to Jos. Haslewood, with the original Autograph Letters, and the following Portraits inserted*—Copy of the *Droeshout Head, by Swaine*, ON INDIA PAPER: *Chandos Portrait, after Humphrey, by Scriven*, ON INDIA PAPER; *View of Shakespeare's House; Mezzotint Portrait by Turner; Bust by Scriven, after Boaden*, ON INDIA PAPER; *Copy of the Portrait by Marshall*, ON INDIA PAPER; *Mezzotinto by W. Ward, from the Bust*, in 1 Vol. *half green morocco, top edges gilt*, **Unique,** 8vo. Lond. *Whittingham*, v. d.

4800 ——— Remarks on the Life and Writings of Wm. Shakspeare, only 25 copies printed, a presentation copy from the Author, 12mo. *half morocco, uncut.* Lond. 1814

4801 Bruni, Epistole Heroiche Poesie del, Libri Due, La Madre Hebrea, Caterina D'Aragona, &c., *many fine plates*, 18mo. *vellum, fine copy.* Roma, 1627

One of the Epistles is to "Catarina D'Arragona del Arrige VIII. Re D'Inghiltaria," another "Cleopatra ad Octavio Cesare."

4802 Bunbury (*Miss*), The Star of the Court, or the Maid of Honor, and Queen of England, Anne Boleyn, 12mo. *half morocco.* Lond. 1844

4803 Burlesque Annotations on Shakspeare, with Bon Mots, Jeux d'Esprits, &c., of celebrated characters, Specimens of a Jest Book, by Marcus Spermaceti the Elder, 12mo. *half morocco, gilt top.* Lond. 1810

4804 Caldecott, *see* As You Like It and Hamlet, separate Plays.

4805 CAPELL'S (*E.*) Notes and Various Readings to Shakespeare, 3 vols. 4to. *portrait, half morocco, uncut,* printed for the Author. 1779–1800

"Mr. Capell, the editor, I call the Patron of Shakespeare. They who are acquainted with his critical writings on Shakespeare, and his accurate researches into this species of Antiquity, will not scruple with me to pronounce him the Father of all LEGITIMATE Commentary on Shakespeare."—*Matthias.*

4806 CAPELL (*E.*) Prolusions or select pieces of ancient poetry, compiled with great care from their several originals, and offered to the publick as specimens of the integrity that should be found in the editions of worthy authors, in three parts; containing: I. The Not-browne Mayde, Maister Sackvilles induction, and Overburys Wife. II. Edward the Third, a play thought to be writ by Shakespeare. III. Those excellent didactic Poems, entitled Nosce Teipsum, written by Sir John Davis, with a preface, *scarce, a very large copy, rough leaves, with the initials of Capell,* 8vo. Lond. 1760

Roxburghe sale, £1 12*s.* Bib. Anglo-Poet, £1 15*s.* White Knight's, £2 10*s.*

4807 CATALOGUES of the extensive Libraries, in print and MS. of Farmer and Steevens, with prices and names, portrait of Farmer, 8vo. *half morocco, gilt top.* Lond. 1798

4808 CATALOGUES of the Libraries of Mr. John Field and Jadis, 8vo. *half morocco.* Lond. 1827

CATALOGUES, *see* Halliwell.

4809 CATALOGUES of Dodd, Steevens, and Sabine's collection of Books, with portraits, 8vo. *half morocco.* Lond. 1797

4810 CATALOGUE of valuable [Shakespearian Books], 8vo. *half morocco, gilt top.* 1826–31

4811 CATALOGUE of a portion of the Library of an eminent collector, sold by Sotheby, 8vo. Lond. 1820

With many Shakespearian articles.

4812 CATALOGUE of part of John Tyrrel's "Shakespeariana," purchased by H. Rodd, and sold by him to W. E. Burton, 8vo. *interleaved, half morocco, gilt leaves,* only four copies printed on thick paper. Lond. 1850

4813 CHALMERS (*Geo.*) Another account of the incidents from which the title and a part of the story of Shakespeare's Tempest were derived, and the true era of it ascertained: evincing the original connection of the royal family with the poet's drama, only 40 copies printed, *rare,* 8vo. *half morocco, gilt top.* Lond. 1815

Sold at Rhodes' sale, for £3 13*s.* 6*d.*

4814 ——— An apology for the believers in the Shakespeare papers, which were exhibited in Norfolk-street. A Supplemental apology for the believers in the Shakespeare papers, being a reply to Mr. Malone's answer, which was early announced but never published; with a dedication to Geo. Steevens, and a postscript to T. J. Mathias, 2 vols. *uncut,* 8vo. *with MS. note and cuttings from Magazines inserted.* Lond. 1798

"It cannot be denied that, in both these volumes, there is a great mass of curious and useful intelligence, relating to Shakespeare; and, 'have them you must.'"—*Library Companion.*

4815 CHAUCER (*G.*) The workes of our ancient and learned English Poet Geffrey Chaucer, newly printed. In this impression you shall find these additions—1, His portraiture and progeny shewed; 2. His life collected; 3. Arguments to every booke gathered; 4. Old and obscure words explained; 5. Authors cited by him declared; 6. Difficulties opened; 7. Two bookes of his never before printed. Printed by Adam Islip, at the charges of Bonham Norton, full length port., &c., *rare,* Black Letter, folio, *half calf.* Lond. 1598

4816 ——— Godwin's Life of Geoffrey Chaucer, the early English Poet, including Memoirs of his near friend and kinsman, John of Gaunt, Duke of Lancaster, with sketches of the Manners and Opinions, Arts and Literature of England, in the fourteenth century, *portraits,* 2 vols. 4to. *uncut, boards.* Lond. 1803

Fonthill sale, £1 18*s.* Edward's, £1 12*s.*

4817 ——— Troilus and Cressida Amorum Troili et Cresseidæ, libri duo priores Anglico-Latini (published by Sir Francis Kinaston, the English text on the right, the Latin translation on the left), *rare,* Black Letter, 4to. Oxon. 1635

Gordonstown sale, £2 4*s.*

"The Troilus and Cressida of Chaucer, is the most beautiful Diary of Love ever written."—*Hartley Coleridge.*

4818 CHEDWORTH (*John Lord*), Remarks, Critical, Conjectural, and Explanatory, upon some of the obscure passages in Shakspeare's Plays, with remarks upon the explanations and amendments of the commentators in the editions of 1785, 1790, 1793, 8vo. *half morocco, gilt top, uncut.* Lond. 1805

Only one hundred copies, privately printed, all for presents.

4819 CLARKE (*Mrs. C.*) Complete Concordance to Shakspeare, a Verbal Index to all the Passages in his Dramatic Works, with plate of Shakspearian currency, Mrs. Clarke inserted, and a MS. list of Errata by Mr. Burton, 8vo. *half morocco, gilt top.* N. Y. 1846

4820 ——— Account of a Testimonial to, royal 8vo. privately printed, N. Y. n. d.

4821 ——— Another copy.

4822 ——— Shakspeare Proverbs, or the Wise Saws of our Wisest Poet, collected into a Modern Instance.

4823 ——— Lives of Shakspeare's Heroines, twelve numbers, *sewed.* N. Y. 1855

4824 CLEOPATRA: La Vita di Cleopatra reina d'Egitta, delle Conte Giulio Landi—con una oratione in lode dell' ignoranza, *fine clean copy, half morocco, gilt top.* Venezia, 1551

4825 COBLERIANA: or, the Cobbler's Melody, being a Collection of Miscellaneous Pieces, in Prose and Verse, Serious and Comic, *front.* (containing a Ballad on the Criticisms on the new edition of Shakspeare, &c.), 2 vols. 12mo. *calf, fine copy, very scarce.* Lond. 1768

"To Mr. G. Garrick—the gift of the Author, Dec. 1768."

4826 COLLECTANEA SHAKSPERIANA MSS., *a very valuable work*, 4 vols. folio. 1445-1796

This is perhaps the most extensive collection of memoranda ever got together towards furnishing material for a life of the Immortal Bard. The documents from which many of these extracts are taken, are dated from 1445 to a more recent period; they are all neatly mounted and on good paper, in four large volumes folio, and substantially bound in full calf. To a future biographer or editor of the Works of Shakspeare, these papers would no doubt be of great value and assistance.

4827 COLLET'S Relics of Literature, folding plates, characteristic signatures; a very curious and interesting volume, 8vo. *half morocco, gilt top.* Lond. 1823

CONTENTS.—The Praise of Kissing, by various authors; Roger Payne, the Eccentric Bookbinder; Singular Instance of a Man Selling his Body; Eccentric Advertisements; Ancient Value of Books; Book Destroyers; Singular Surnames, Epitaphs, Mottoes, Epigrams, Window Gleanings, &c. &c.

4828 Collier (*J. P.*) The History of English Dramatic Poetry to the time of Shakespeare, and Annals of the Stage to the Restoration, 3 vols. 8vo. *half morocco, uncut, top edges gilt.* Lond. 1831

4829 ——— Memoirs of the Principal Actors in Shakespeare's Plays, 8vo. *half morocco, gilt top.* Lond. 1846

4830 ——— New Particulars Regarding the Works of Shakespeare, in a letter to the Rev. A. Dyce, only fifty copies printed, 8vo. *half morocco, gilt top, uncut.* Lond. 1836

4831 ——— Notes and Emendations from the Early MS. Corrections in the Second Folio Edition, in the possession of J. P. Collier, fac-simile of the MS., 8vo. *cloth.* Lond. 1853

An indispensable accompaniment to the Works of Shakspeare.

4832 ——— The Poetical Decameron, or Ten Conversations on English Poets and Poetry, particularly of the Reigns of Elizabeth and James I., 2 vols. 8vo. *uncut.* Edinb. 1820

This copy once belonged to Charles Lamb.

4833 ——— Reasons for a new edition of Shakspeare's Works, containing notices of the defects of former impressions, and pointing out the lately acquired means of illustrating the Plays, Poems, and Biography of the Poet; also, Postscript to the Child's own Book (a Satire on the Reasons), 2 vols. in 1, 8vo. *half morocco, gilt top, uncut.* Lond. 1841

4834 ——— Shakespeare's Library: a Collection of the Romances, Novels, Poems, and Histories, used by Shakespeare as the foundation of his Dramas, now first collected, and accurately reprinted from the original editions, with introductory notices, 2 vols. 8vo. *half morocco, gilt top, uncut.* Lond. 1843

*** Containing Reprints of Greene's Pandasto, 1588; Lodge's Rosalynd, 1592; Hystorie of Hamblet, 1608; Appolinus, the Prince of Tyr, *from Gower's Confessio Amantis;* Rhomeo and Julietta, *from Paynter's Palyce of Pleasure*, 1567; Promos and Cassandra, 1582; Queene Cordilla, 1587; &c. &c.

4835 ——— Extracts from the Registers of the Stationers' Company, of Works entered for publication between 1557 and 1587, with Notes and Illustrations, 2 vols. 8vo. *half calf* (Shakspeare Soc.). 1848

A work of great value to all interested in bibliographical pursuits; many of the Old Ballads are printed entire, and are of the utmost rarity.

4836 Collins (*Rev. Mr.*) A Letter to George Hardinge, Esq., on the subject of a passage in Mr. Steevens' Preface to his Impression of Shakespeare, 4to. *scarce.* Lond. 1777

4838 ——— Another copy, 4to. Lond. 1777

4839 Cooper (*E.*) Muse's Library, being a choice collection of the best Ancient English Poetry, from the time of Edward the Confessor to the reign of King James the First, 8vo. *half morocco.* Lond. 1738

Include Poems by Langland, Gower, Chaucer, Lydgate, Barclay, Shakspeare, and a host of others, with Lives and Characters of the principal Old English Poets.

4840 Courtenay (*T. P.*) Commentaries on the Historical Plays of Shakespeare, 2 vols. 8vo. *half morocco, gilt top, uncut.* Lond. 1840

*** Originally published in Hook's New Monthly Magazine, from June 1838, to March 1839, under the title of "Shakspeare's Historical Plays considered Historically."

4841 Coventry Mysteries (*The*), edited by Halliwell, with fac-simile, 8vo. *half morocco.* 1841

A careful edition of the most interesting collection of the old Miracle Plays and Mysteries extant. It throws great light upon the origin and early history of the Drama.

Craft (*Zachary*), *vide* Kelsall, Lot 5009.

4842 Cranmer (*Archbishop*), Answer to a Craftie and Sophisticall Cavillation devised by Stephen Gardiner, against the true and godlye Doctrine of the Holy Sacrament, folio, *calf*, **Black Letter.** Lond. 1580

4843 Critical Reflections on the Old English Dramatic Writers, 8vo. *half morocco, gilt top.* Lond. 1761

4844 Croft (*John*), Annotations on the Plays of Shakespear (Johnson and Steevens' edition), 8vo. *half morocco, gilt top.* York, 1810

4845 Darcie (*Abm.*) Annales. The True and Royall History of the famous Empresse Elizabeth, and all the memorable things of her reign, small 4to. *engraved title, calf.* Lond. 1625

4846 Davis (*Thomas*), Dramatic Miscellanies, consisting of critical observations on several Plays of Shakspeare, with a review of his principal characters and those of various eminent writers, as represented by Garrick and others, with Anecdotes of Dramatic Poets, Actors, etc., 3 vols. 8vo. *boards, uncut.* Lond. 1784

4847 DAVIES (*John*), Microcosmos, The Discovery of the Little World, with the government thereof, 4to. pp. 300, *calf, gilt, fine copy, printed by Joseph Barnes.* Oxf. 1603

Two dedicatory Sonnets commence the volume; the first, "To my Most Deere and Dread Soveraigne James, by the Grace of God King of England, Scotland, France, and Ireland, be all heavenly and earthly happinesse." The second, "To the Sacred Queene of England's most excellent Maiestie," after which commendatory verses in Latin by J. Sandford, Robert Burrell, &c. At the end of Microcosmos is a poem of 22 pages, entitled "An Extasie," numerous dedicatory Sonnets to the Nobility, and others.

A writer in the European Magazine for Sept. 1793 (supposed to be Geo. Steevens), suggests that Davies was an associate of Shakspeare's, p. 215, note c, of his Microcosmos; where the initials "W. S. and R. B." occur, must doubtless have been intended for William Shakspeare and Richard Burbage, the latter of whom, in Oldys's MS. notes on Langbaine, is supposed to have been the painter of the Duke of Chandos' picture of our Bard. The same writer adds: "It is highly gratifying to observe that every new discovery tends to confirm the opinion, that Shakspeare was as estimable for the goodness of his private life as he was superior in genius to every one of his contemporaries."

Priced in the Bibliotheca Anglo-Poetica, £10 10*s*.

4848 DECKER (*T.*) Gull's Horn Book, new edition with notes, &c., by Dr. Nott, 4to. *fine copy in russia.* 1812

This work affords a greater insight into the fashionable follies and domestic life of Q. Elizabeth's day, than any other we have; it is the chief source from whence Sir W. Scott drew his descriptions of London life, &c., in the Fortunes of Nigel.

4849 DENNIS (*Mr.*) Essay on the Genius and Writings of Shakspeare, 8vo. *half morocco, gilt top.* Lond. 1712

4850 DESTRUCTION of the ancient and famous City of Troye, and Chronicle of the Wars between the Grecians and the Trojans, &c., written by Daretus, a Trojan, and Dictus, a Grecian; both present in the wars, &c., 4to. **Black Letter**, in 3 vols. *half calf, rare and curious.* Lond. 1607

"In the absence of Homer, the Trojan story was kept alive in the middle ages in the two Latin pieces attributed to Dares Phrygius and Dictus Cretensis, from whence this old Romance is taken. Shakespeare derived his Troilus and Cressida from an earlier edition of it."—*Warton.*

4851 DEVERELL (*Robert*), Hieroglyphics, and other Antiquities. In treating of which, many favorite Pieces of Butler, Shakspeare, and other great writers in Prose and Verse are put in a light now entirely new, by Notes, occasional Dissertations, *and upwards* of 200 *engravings in wood and copper*, 6 vols. 8vo. *half morocco, gilt top, extremely curious, rare.* Lond. 1816

4852 Dialogue between King Richard the 3d and his adopted Son, Richard the 4th, 8vo. *half morocco, gilt top.* Lond. 1744

4853 Dictionary of Quotations, in three parts, part the first, Shakspeare, 12mo. *uncut, half morocco, top edges gilt.* Lond. 1824

4854 Dodd (*Wm.*) The Beauties of Shakspeare, regularly selected from each Play, with a general index, digesting them under proper heads, illustrated with explanatory notes, and similar passages from ancient and modern authors, 2d edition, *scarce*, 2 vols. 12mo. *half morocco, gilt top.* Lond. 1757

4855 ——— Third edition, with the Author's last correction, 3 vols. 12mo. *half morocco, gilt top.* Lond. 1780

Best edition, with the *suppressed ironical dedication* to Lord Chesterfield; and additions both in the passages and notes.

4856 ——— Another edition, with Index, and illustrated, 18mo. Lond. 1824

4857 Dolby (*Thos.*) The Shakespearian Dictionary, forming a general index to all the popular expressions and most striking passages in the works of Shakespeare, from a few words to fifty or more lines; an appropriate synonyme being affixed to each extract, with a reference to the context. The whole designed to introduce the beauties of Shakespeare into the familiar intercourse of society, *portrait of Shakespeare*, 8vo. *half morocco.* Lond. 1832

4858 ——— Another edition, 12mo. *morocco extra.* Phil. 1851

4859 ——— Another copy, 12mo. *half morocco.* Phil. 1851

4860 Douce (*F.*) Illustrations of Shakespeare, and of ancient manners, with dissertations on the clowns and fools of Shakespeare, on the collection of popular Tales entitled Gesta Romanorum, and on the English Morris-dance, *engravings, uncut, scarce*, 2 vols. 8vo. *half morocco, gilt top.* Lond. 1807

"I look upon this work as a sort of Hortus Shakspearianus; the research and learning bestowed on it are immense."—*Dibdin.*

Combe's sale, £2 2*s.*; Nassau's sale, £2 12*s.* 6*d.*

4861 ——— Another edition, 8vo. *half morocco, gilt top.* Lond. 1839

"Replete with tasteful illustration and curious research."—*Dibdin.*

4862 DRAKE (*N.*) Shakspeare and his Times, including the Biography of the Poet, Criticisms on his genius and writings, a new chronology of his Plays, a disquisition on the object of his Sonnets, and a history of the manners, customs, and amusements, superstitions, poetry, and elegant literature of his age, *portrait, uncut*, 2 vols. 4to. *half morocco, gilt top*. Lond. 1817

"A masterly production, the publication of which will form an epoch in the Shakspearian history of this country. No work has hitherto appeared, and we may venture to pronounce that none can in future be produced, in which so much agreeable and well digested information, respecting Shakspeare and his times will be found."—*Gentleman's Mag.*

Strettell's sale, £5 15*s.* 6*d.*

4863 ——— Idem, inlaid in folio drawing paper.

4864 DRAKE (*Nathan*), Shakespeare's Character and Genius, by Coleridge, Campbell, Lessing, Lamb, Warton, Mackenzie, Dryden, Goethe, Sir Walter Scott, &c. &c., with Essay and Notes by Dr. Drake, UNCUT, *half morocco extra, top edges gilt*, 8vo. Lond. 1828

"A valuable accompaniment to every edition."

4865 ——— Noontide Leisure, or Sketches in Summer, including a Tale of the days of Shakspeare, 2 vols. 12mo. *half morocco, gilt top, uncut*. Lond. 1824

4867 DU BOIS (*Edward*), The Wreath, composed of selections from Sappho, Theocritus, Bion, and Moschus, to which are added some remarks on Shakspeare, *with frontispiece, half morocco, gilt top*, 8vo. Lond. 1799

4868 DUCK (*Arthur*), Life of Henry Chichele, Archbishop of Canterbury, who lived in the times of Henry V. and VI., Kings of England, translated from the Latin, 8vo. *portrait*. 1699

4869 DUFF (*Wm.*) Essay on Original Genius, on the Fine Arts and Poetry, 1767. Critical Observations on the Writings of the most celebrated Geniuses in Poetry, 1770, *half morocco, top edges gilt, cut, and stilted*, 8vo. Lond. v. y.

4870 DUNLOP (*J.*) History of Fiction, being a critical account of the most celebrated Prose Writers of fiction, from the earliest Greek romances to the Novels of the present day, 2 vols. Phil. 1842

4871 DUPORT (*Paul*), Essais Litteraires sur Shakspere, ou Analyse Raisonnée, scène par scène de toutes les pieces de cet auteur, 2 vols. *half morocco, top edges gilt, uncut*, 8vo. Paris, 1828

"A Block-head par excellence."—*C. Knight.*

4872 DYCE (*A.*) Remarks on Mr. J. P. Collier's and Mr. C. Knight's Editions of Shakespeare, 8vo. *uncut, half morocco, gilt top.* Lond. *Moxon*, 1844

4873 ——— Remarks on Mr. J. P. Collier's and Mr. C. Knight's Editions of Shakspeare, *uncut*, 8vo. *cloth.* Lond. 1844

"A plague o' both the Houses."—*Mercutio.*

4874 EDWARDS (*Thos.*) The Canons of Criticism and a Glossary, being a Supplement to Mr. Warburton's Edition of Shakespeare; The Trial of the Letter Y, *alias* Y. and Sonnets, LARGE PAPER, *seventh edition*, UNCUT, *half green morocco, top edges gilt*, 8vo. Lond. 1768

4875 EFFIGIES Poeticæ, or the Portraits of the British Poets, illustrated by Notes, Biographical, Critical, and Poetical, 2 vols. 4to. *half russia.* Lond. 1824

4876 EGERTON Papers (*The*), Collection of Public and Private Documents, illustrative of the Times of Elizabeth and James I., edited by J. Payne Collier, 4to. contains papers of great interest relating to Shakspeare and the early Drama, *cloth.* Lond. 1840

4877 ESSAYS by a Society of Gentlemen, at Exeter, on Literary fame and the Historical characters of Shakspeare, &c., *half morocco, gilt top*, 8vo. Exeter, 1796

4878 ESSAYS on Shakspere, Queen Elizabeth, &c., LARGE PAPER, 8vo. *half morocco, gilt top.* Lond. 1789

4879 ETYMOLOGIST (*The*), A Comedy in 3 Acts, 8vo. *half morocco.* Lond. 1785

Very satirical on Shakespeare's Commentators.

4880 EVANS (*John*), Progress of Human Life, Shakespeare's Seven Ages of Man, illustrated by a series of extracts in Prose and Poetry, WOOD-CUTS, *presentation copy*, UNCUT, *half morocco, top edges gilt*, 12mo. Chiswick, 1818

4881 ——— Idem, 12mo. *boards*, UNCUT. Lond. 1823

4882 EXHIBITION of the Shakspere Gallery at Pall Mall, London; list of prices attached, 8vo. Lond. 1805

4883 FAIRHOLT (*F. W.*) Home of Shakespear, *illustrated*, 33 *plates*, 8vo. *half morocco, gilt top.* Lond. 1847

4884 FARMER (*Richard*), Essay on the learning of Shakspeare, *first edition, Camb.* 1767; *second edition*, with large additions, *thick paper, Camb.* 1767; *third edition, presentation copy*, with autograph, "For Edward Malone from R. Farmer," Lond. 1789, in 1 vol. *half morocco, top edge gilt*, 8vo. Lond. v. d.

4885 FAMILIAR Verses, The Ghost of Willy Shakspeare to Sammy Ireland, *sewed*, 8vo. Lond. 1796

4886 FARREN (*G.*), Observations on the Laws of Mortality and Disease of, with an Appendix containing illustrations of the progress of mania, melancholia, crazyness, and demonomania, as displayed in Shakspeare's characters of Lear, Hamlet, Ophelia and Edgar, 1829. Essay on the Character of Shylock, 1833; Madness of Hamlet (Lond. *Mag.*), 1824; Madness of Ophelia (Lond. *Mag.*), 1824; Hamlet's Soliloquy, &c., with MS. notes, in 1 vol. 8vo. *half morocco, gilt top.* v. y.

4887 FELTON (*Sam.*), Imperfect Hints towards a new edition of Shakespeare, both parts, *uncut, half morocco, top edges gilt, rare*, 4to. Lond. 1787–8

4888 FIDDES (*Dr. R.*), The Life of Cardinal Wolsey, folio, fine portraits by Vertue, and *plates, splendid copy on large paper, calf gilt.* Lond. 1724

As a Collection of Facts this work is highly valuable.

4889 FISHER'S Warwickshire Antiquities.—A Series of Ancient Allegorical, Historical, and Legendary Paintings in Fresco, discovered on the walls of the Chapel of the Holy Cross, at Stratford-upon-Avon; ancient Seals, Stained Glass, &c.; 56 elaborate engravings, mostly coloured in imitation of the originals; also, a View of the Guild Chapel, and the adjoining house in which Shakspeare lived. Edited by John Gough Nichols, Esq.; royal folio, *half boards, morocco*, (pub. at 10*l.* 10*s.*) 1836

"These ancient fresco paintings are especially curious, as having been executed in England in an age of which, according to the opinion of Walpole, in his History of Painting, no specimens of the Art existed."—*Gentleman's Magazine.*

4890 FLOWERS of Shakespeare, Illustrations of those named by Shakespeare, *coloured*, 4to. *cl. gilt.* 1846

4890* FLORIO (*J.*) Queen Anna's New World of Words, or Dictionarie of the Italian and English Tongues, collected and newly much augmented by Iohn Florio, reader of the Italian vnto the soueraigne maiestie of Anna, &c.: whereunto are added certaine necessarie rules and short observations for the Italian Tongue, folio, *calf.* Lond. 1688

"For the variety of words was far more copious than any extant in the world at that time."—*Ant. à Wood.*

"Florio is Shakespeare's Holophernes, in Love's Labor Lost."

4891 FLETCHER (*G.*) Studies of Shakspeare, with Observations on the Criticism and Acting of his Plays, 8vo. *half morocco, gilt top.* 1847

Includes the Plays of King John, Macbeth, Cymbeline, As You Like It, Much ado about Nothing, and Romeo and Juliet.

4891* FORTESCUE (*Thomas*), The Foreste, or Collection of Historyes no lesse profitable than pleasant and necessary, doone out of French into English, *with table*, 4to. *morocco, fine copy.* Lond. 1576

The genius of these Tales may be discerned from their history. The book is said to have been written in Spanish, by Pedro de Mexia, thence translated into Italian, thence into French by Claude Cruget, a citizen of Paris, and lastly into English, by Thomas Fortescue.—Townley's copy sold for £4 17*s.* 6*d.*; Bindley's, £4, and Whiteknight's, £5 15*s.* 6*d.*

4892 GALERIE des Personages de Shakspere, reproduits dans les principales scénes de ses pieces, Paris; *beautiful illustrations, twenty-five plates,* par Pichot, royal 8vo. *morocco, gilt.* Lond. 1844

4893 GARRICK (*D.*), The Interview, or Falstaff's Ghost, a Poem inscribed to D. Garrick, Author's copy, 4to. *half morocco.* Lond. 1766

4894 GASCOIGNE (*George*) Whole Woorkes of, newlye compyled into one volume: that is to say, his Flowers, Hearbes, Weedes, The Fruits of Warre; the Comedie called Supposes; the Tragedie called Jocaster; the Steele Glasse; the Complaint of Philomene, &c., and the Pleasure at Kenilworth's Castle, **Black Letter** *very rare, interleaved,* in 4 vols. 4to. *imprynted by Abell Jeffes.* Lond. 1587

This rare and valuable work is quoted as having been sold as high as £27 6*s.* and is marked at £35, in the Bibliotheca Anglo Poetica.

Gascoigne's Works should always form part of a Shakspeare library.—In the Taming of a Shrew, Shakspeare has borrowed considerably from Gascoigne's comedy of the Supposes. "Shakspeare," says Mr. Chalmers, "obviously borrowed the names of two of his characters from the Supposes of Gascoigne, which was first acted in 1564, and published among his Workes in 1575 and 1587, adopting, moreover, from Gascoigne's comedy sentiments and language."—Such was the opinion also of Mr. Gifford, Warton, Dr. Farmer, &c. The Supposes was the first comedy written in English prose.

4895 GESTA Romanorum, **Gothic Letter**, *very rare, calf, antique,* 4to. Circa, MCCCCLXXIII

4896 GESTA Romanorum, translated from the famous Latin collection of Monkish Stories, with Notes, &c., by C. Swan, 2 vols. 12mo., *half morocco, scarce.* Lond. 1824

Shakespeare and several of our most celebrated Dramatists have been indebted to this work for the plots of their most admired plays.

4897 Ghost of Richard the 3d, a Poem printed 1614, and founded upon Shakspeare's Historical Play, reprinted from the only known copy in the Bodleian Library, with notes by J. P. Collier, 8vo. *half morocco, uncut.* Lond. 1844

4898 Gilchrist (*O.*), Examination of the Charges maintained by Malone Chalmers and others of Ben Jonson's enmity towards Shakespeare, 8vo. *half morocco, uncut.* Lond. 1808

4899 Gildon (*C.*) Letters and Essays by several Gentlemen and Ladies, with remarks on Rymer's Criticism on Shakespeare, 8vo. *half morocco.* Lond. 1696

4903 ——— The Complete Art of Poetry, in six parts, of the nature, use, excellence, rise, and progress of Poetry, &c.; at the end Shakesperiana, or the most beautiful topics, descriptions, and similes that occur throughout all Shakespeare's play, 2 vols. 12mo. *half morocco, gilt top.* Lond. 1718

4904 ——— Remarks on the Plays of Shakspeare, *large paper,* 4to. *half morocco.* Lond. 1725

4905 ——— Rise and Progress of the Stage, *large paper,* 4to. *half morocco.* Lond. 1725

4906 Gilliland (*Thos.*), Dramatic Mirror, containing the History of the Stage and of Country Theatres, including a critical account of all the Dramatic writers from 1660; and also of the most distinguished performers from the days of Shakspeare to 1807, *embellished with* 17 *elegant engravings, and portrait of author,* 8vo. 2 vols. *uncut, half morocco, top edge gilt.* Lond. 1808

4907 Gowrie Conspiracie, a Discourse of the unnaturall and vyle Conspiracie, attempted against the Kings Majesties Person, at Saint Johnstown, upon Twysday the fifth of August, 1600, 4to. *half mor.* Lond. 1603

One of the earliest accounts of this remarkable conspiracy, and written in a very clear and elegant dialect, sold at Gordonstoun sale, for £1 13*s*.

4908 Graves (*H. M.*), An Essay on the genius of Shakespeare, with critical remarks on the characters of Romeo, Hamlet, Juliet, and Ophelia: together with some observations on the writings of Sir Walter Scott, to which is annexed a letter to Lord ——, containing a critique on taste, judgment, and rhetorical expression, and remarks on the leading actors of the day, *uncut,* 8vo. *half morocco, gilt top.* Lond. 1826

4909 ——— Another Copy. 1826.

4910 GREENE (*Robert*), Greene's Arcadia, or Menaphon: Camilaes Alarum to slumber Euphues in his melancholy Cell at Silexedra, wherein are descyphered the variable effects of Fortune, the Wonders of Love, the Triumph of inconstant Fortune, 4to. *boards.* Lond. 1814

Interspersed with poems, and published by Thomas Nash, with a long and very curious preface *To the Gentlemen Students of both Universities*, with a lash at *some vaine-glorious tragedians*, and at Kydd's old Play of Hamlet: there are also interesting allusions to many of the poets and literary men of the time.

4911 ——— Pleasant and delightful History of Dorastus and Fawnia, pleasant for age to shun drowsie thoughts, profitable for youth to avoid wanton pastimes, and bringing to both a desired content, *half morocco, gilt top,* 4to. Lond. 1703

"The origin of the Winter's Tale."

4912 GREY (*Z.*) Critical, historical and explanatory notes on Shakespeare, with emendations of the text and metre, printed for the author, 2 vols. 8vo. portrait inserted, *half morocco, gilt top.* Lond. 1751, 1754, 1755

4913 ——— Remarks upon a late edition of Shakespeare's (Warburton's), with a defence of Sir T. Hanmer, 8vo. *half morocco.* Lond. 1751

GRIFFIN'S Fidessa, *vide* Lot 4241.

4914 GRIFFITH (*Elizabeth*), Morality of Shakespeare's Dramas Illustrated, *portrait, uncut, half morocco, top edges gilt,* 8vo. Lond. 1775

4915 GRINFIELD (*Thos.*) Remarks on the Moral Influence of Shakespeare's Plays, with illustrations from Hamlet, *engravings*, 8vo. *half morocco, gilt top.* Lond. 1850

4916 GROVE (*J.*) History of the Life and Times of Cardinal Wolsey, Prime Minister to Henry VIII., includes the whole of Cavendish's Life of Wolsey, fine portraits and plates, by Vertue, &c., *half morocco, gilt top*, 8vo. Lond. 1742

"One of the most interesting and valuable specimens of biography in the English language."—*Lowndes.*

4917 GUIZOT (*M.*) An Essay on the Life and Works of Shakespeare and his Times, with Notices of his Contemporaries, the Literature and the Drama of the Period, 8vo. *cloth.* Lond. 1852

An elegant and valuable contribution to Shakesperian Literature and the Drama.

4918 GUTHRIE (*Wm.*) An Essay upon Tragedy, with remarks upon the Abbè le Blanc, and observations on the English Stage, 8vo. *half morocco, gilt top.* Lond. [1750]

4219 ——— Another copy, 8vo. *half morocco, gilt top.* Lond. [1750]

4920 HALFORD (*Sir Henry*), Essays and Orations, with an account of opening the tomb of K. Charles I., 1833; Education and Conduct of a Physitian, 1834; On the Deaths of Eminent Persons, 1835; On the Deaths of Eminent Philosophers of Modern Times, 1836, &c., in 1 vol. *uncut, half morocco, top edges gilt,* 8vo. Lond. v. y.

4921 HALL (*Edward*), Chronicle; the Union of the two noble and illustre Famelies of Lancastre and Yorke, long in continual discussion, from the reigne of Henry IV., to that of Henry VIII., the undubitable flower and very heire of both the sayd linages, folio, **Black Letter**, wants 4 front leaves and Index, after "Edelfert," folio, *half calf.* 1570

It is to this Chronicle that Shakspeare is chiefly indebted in his Historical Plays, for not only the incidents, but frequently the very words of his characters. See Courtnay's Commentaries on Shakspeare's Historical Plays.

Col. Stanley's sold for £30 10*s.* and Heathcote's for £33 2*s.*

4922 HALLIWELL (*J. O.*) An Account of the only known Manuscript of Shakespeare's Plays, comprising some important variations and corrections in the Merry Wives of Windsor, obtained from a play-house copy of that play recently discovered, *sewed, uncut, half morocco, gilt top,* 8vo. Lond. 1843

4923 ——— Curiosities of Modern Shakespearian Criticism, 8vo. Lond. 1853

4924 ——— Illustrations of the Fairy Mythology of Shakespeare, 8vo. *half morocco, gilt top.* Lond. 1845

4925 ——— An Introduction to Shakspeare's Midsummer Night's Dream, UNCUT, 8vo. *half morocco, gilt top,* Lond. 1841

4926 ——— A New Life of Shakespeare, including many particulars respecting the Poet and his Family, never before published, illustrated with 76 Engravings on wood, of objects, most of which are new, from Drawings by Fairholt, 8vo. *half morocco, gilt top.* Lond. 1848

This work contains upwards of forty documents respecting Shakespeare and his family, *never before published*, besides numerous others indirectly illustrating the Poet's Biography. All the anecdotes and traditions concerning Shakespeare are here, for the first time collected, and much new light is thrown on his personal history, by papers exhibiting him as selling Malt and Stone, &c.

4927 HALLIWELL (*J. O.*) A New Boke about Shakespeare and Stratford-on-Avon, 4to. curious wood-cuts and facsimiles, ONLY 75 COPIES PRIVATELY PRINTED, *namely,* 50 *on ordinary paper, and* 25 *on thick paper, and this copy is No.* 5 *of those so printed, half morocco, gilt top.* 1850

This volume contains several curious, hitherto inedited, documents relating to Shakespeare and his Family, with facsimiles of the Poet's Marriage-bond with Anne Hathaway, &c. But what will render it of great interest to American readers, are Illustrations and Notes to Washington Irving's celebrated paper on Stratford-on-Avon. The illustrations include views of the Red Horse Inn, the "little parlour" in which Mr. Irving took up his above, the Jubilee Amphitheatre, the Room in which Shakespeare was born, and the Shop and Room at the birth-place; Charlecote, the Clerk's Dwelling, Exterior and Interior; Shakespeare's Matchlock, Hamlet's Sword, the Friar's Lantern, the Keeper's Lodge at Charlecote, and other scenes mentioned by Mr. Irving.

4928 ——— On the Character of Sir John Falstaff, as originally exhibited by Shakespeare in the two parts of King Henry IV.; presentation copy from the author to his brother, 12mo. *half morocco, gilt top, uncut,* only one hundred copies printed. Lond. 1841

4929 ——— Shakespeariana, a Catalogue of the early Editions of Shakespeare's Plays, and of the Commentaries, and other publications illustrative of his Works, *uncut,* 8vo. *half morocco, top gilt.* Lond. 1841

Indispensable to everybody who wishes to carry on any inquiries connected with Shakespeare, or who may have a fancy for Shakesperian Bibliography.—*Spectator.*

4930 ——— Another copy, with list of Works relating to Shakespeare, on sale by J. Russel Smith; Letters from Lord Jeffrey to Mr. Spalding, on Shakspeare, 1836; Catalogue of Shakspearian Books, &c., possessed by H. Jadis, Esq., *privately printed in* 1 *vol.* 8vo. v. y.

This copy has many MS. notes, numerous additions and corrections in the hand-writing of the late W. E. Burton.

4931 ——— Account of his Collection of Antiquities, Coins, MSS., Rare Books, Ancient Documents, and other Reliques, illustrative of the Life and Works of Shakespeare, *wood-cuts, large paper,* royal 4to. 1852

Only 80 copies privately printed.

4932 HALPIN (*Rev. T.*) Oberon's Vision in Midsummer Night's Dream, illustrated by a comparison with Lylie's Endymion, 8*vo. half morocco, uncut.* Lond. 1843

4933 HALSTED (*C. A.*) Life and Times of Richard the Third, as Duke of Gloucester and King of England, in which all the charges against him are carefully investigated and compared with the Statements of the Contemporary Authorities, *Portrait, and other illustrations,* 2 vols. 8vo. *half morocco.* Lond. 1844

"Many new lights are thrown on the career of Richard, many new facts elicited, and the injustice of four centuries vindicated by this intrepid and indefatigable champion of historical truth."—*Metropolitan Magazine.*

4934 HAMMOND (*H. J.*) Architectural Antiquities and Present State of Crosby Place, 4to. *cloth,* 15 *plates.* Lond. 1844

4935 HANMER (*Sir Thomas, Speaker of the House of Commons, and Editor of Shakspeare*), Correspondence, with a Memoir of his Life, edited by Sir H. Bunbury, 8vo. *calf.* Lond. 1838

Some interesting letters of Pope, Young, Garrick, and others; also other matter regarding Sir T. Hanmer's Edition of Shakespeare will be found in this volume.

4936 HARDING'S Shakspeare's Dramas Illustrated by an Assemblage of Portraits, Views, &c., with Biographical and Topographical Accounts, 2 vols. 4to. large paper, 150 fine plates by Harding, of all the Historical Characters and Localities of Shakspeare's Plays, *half calf extra.* Lond. 1811

"This rare and valuable Work is supplementary to the Editions of the Great Bard," and forms an appropriate companion to all.

4937 HARDINGE (*George*), Miscellaneous Works, in Prose and Verse, portrait, 3 vols. 8vo. *half morocco, top edges gilt.* Lond. 1818

4938 ——— Memoir and Essays on Shakspeare, from his Works, portrait, 3 vols. *half morocco, top edges gilt, uncut.* 1818

4939 ——— Another Essence of Malone, or the "Beauties" of Shakspeare's Editor, both parts, 8vo. *half morocco, gilt top.* 1801

4940 HARRIS (*J.*) Fac-similes of all the known Autographs of Shakspeare, from the originals in the Will, &c., also done upon a larger scale, showing at one view the manner in which the Poet invariably spelt his name, done by J. Harris, who is so well known for his accuracy in making fac-similes, on a sheet to suit a folio or 8vo.

4941 HARRISON (*Mr.*) The Infant Vision of Shakspeare, with an Apostrophe to the Immortal Bard, and other Poems, 1 vol. 4to. large paper, *half morocco, uncut.* Lond. 1794

4942 HART (*J. C.*) Romance of Yachting, 12mo. *half morocco, gilt top.* N. Y. 1848

4942*HARVEY (*Gabriel*), Four Letters and Certaine Sonnets, especially touching Robert Greene and other Poets by him abused, 4to. (reprint of 1592). Lond. 1814

"There is no tract in the English language which contains so many contemporary literary notices of the Elizabethan reign."—*Lowndes.*

HARVEY (*G.*) Pierce's Supererogation, *vide* Lot 5633.

4943 HAWKINS (*T.*) Origin of the English Drama, illustrated in its various species, viz. Mystery, Morality, Tragedy, and Comedy, by Specimens from our earliest Writers, with Notes, 3 vols. 8vo. *half morocco, gilt top, uncut.* Oxford, 1773

4944 HAYWARD (*Sir John*), Annals of the First Four Years of the Reign of Queen Elizabeth, edited by Bruce, 4to. *cloth.* Lond. 1840

4945 HAYLEY (*W., Cowper's Friend*), Memoirs of his own Life and Writings, edited by the Rev. J. Johnson, *fine portraits*, 2 vols. 4to. *half calf.* Lond. 1823

These interesting memoirs include extracts from his Private Correspondence, and unpublished Poetry, Memoirs of his Son, T. A. Hayley, the young sculptor, notices of Cowper and his Friends, &c.

4946 HAZLEWOOD (*Joseph*), A Collection of Scraps and Cuttings, illustrative of Shakspeare, collected by Mr. H., all neatly mounted, *unique*, 8vo. *calf, gilt.* n. d.

4947 HAZLITT (*W.*) Characters of Shakspeare's Plays, 8vo. *half mor. gilt top, uncut.* Lond. 1818

4949 HEATH (*C.*) Portraits of the Female Characters in Shakspeare's Plays, 45 very beautiful and highly finished line engravings by C. Heath, from drawings by the best Artists, royal 8vo. *half mor. gilt edges.* Lond. 1847

4950 ——— A Revisal of Shakspeare's Text, wherein the alterations introduced into it by the more modern Editors and Critics are particularly considered, 8vo. *half morocco, gilt top, with portrait.* Lond. 1765

4951 HENTZNER (*Paul*), Journey into England in 1598, translated by Horace Walpole, with Sir R. Naunton's Fragmenta Regalia, 8vo. portraits and plates, *half mor. gilt top.* Lond. 1797

"Honest Hentzner sets down the peculiarities of Englishmen in the Reign of Elizabeth with the same accuracy that Capt. Hall describes the Loo Choo Islanders."—*Retrospective Review.*

4952 HERBERT (*Edward Lord, of Cherbury*), The Life of, with his Correspondence, &c., 8vo. *half calf, gilt.* Lond. 1826

"The earliest and most curious specimen of autobiography known in our language."

4954 HEYWOOD, First and second parts of King Edward the 4th, reprinted from the unique black letter first edition of 1600, collated with one other in black letter, and with those of 1619 and 1626, with an Introduction and notes, by Barrow Field, *half morocco, gilt top.* Lond. 1842

4955 HIFFERNAN (*P.*) Dramatic Genius in five books, the first Book delineates the plan of a permanent Temple to be erected to the memory of Shakespeare, prose and verse, *very curious, half morocco, gilt top,* 8vo. Lond. 1772

4956 HIPPISLEY (*J. H.*) Chapters on Early English Literature, *uncut, half morocco, top edges gilt,* 8vo. Lond. 1837

HISTRIO-MASTIX, *vide* lot 1204.

4958 HOLBEIN'S Portraits of the Court of Henry the Eighth, a series of 80 exquisitely beautiful plates, engraved by Bartolozzi, Cooper, and others, and printed on tinted paper in imitation of the original and very highly finished drawings preserved in the Royal Collection at Windsor, with Historical and Biographical letter-press by Edmund Lodge, Esq., Norroy King of Arms, F.S.A. &c., published by John Chamberlaine, Esq., late Keeper of the Royal Collection of Drawings and Medals, impl. 4to. *elegantly hf. bd. turkey morocco, full gilt, edges gilt all round, with glazed paper, to the plates* (pub. at £15 15*s.*) Lond. 1828

This fine work was published under the patronage of K. George IV., with whom it was a special favorite.

4959 HOWARD (*F.*) The Spirit of the Plays of Shakespeare, exhibited in a series of outline plates, illustrative of the story of each Play, 483 *outline engravings on India paper,* 5 vols. in 8 parts, *uncut,* 4to. *half morocco, top gilt.* Lond. 1827–33

Published at £25 4*s.*

4960 ——— (*H.*) A Visionary Interview at the Shrine of Shakespeare, 4to. *half morocco.* Lond. 1756

4961 HOWARD'S Outlines to Much Ado, Merry Wives, Measure for Measure, and Richard II., 2 parts, 4to. Lond. 1828

4962 HOLINSHED (*Ralph*), Chronicles of England, Scotland, and Ireland, now newlie augmented and continued, with manifold matters of singular note and worthie memorie, to the year 1586, by John Hooker and others, 3 in 2 large thick vols. folio, **Black Letter**, *old calf.* 1586–7

This second and best edition of this very valuable work upon English history, was supervised, corrected and enlarged by Abraham Fleming, and his brother Samuel assisted in compiling the indexes (a very laborious work), and made other improvements.

"The Chronicle of Holinshed merits a high title. It is more full and complete than any of its predecessors, and less loaded with trifling matter. The 'Description of England' is the most interesting and valuable document, as a picture of the country, and of the costume and mode of living of its inhabitants, which the 16th century has produced."—*Dr. Drake.*

The great bard not only drew his materials from this Chronicle, but used much of his actual language in the composition of his historical dramas.

4963 HOWITT'S Homes and Haunts, or the Most Eminent British Poets, *with numerous beautiful woodcuts of famous localities, dwellings, etc.*, 2 vols. 8vo. *half morocco, gilt edges.* Lond. 1847

"The whole work is digested with ability and care. The numerous illustrations are chosen with infinite taste, and beautifully executed."—*Literary Gazette.*

4964 HUCKELL (*Rev. J.*) Avon, a Poem, in three parts, 12mo. pp. 59. Stratford on Avon, 1811

4965 HUNDRED MERRY TALES (*The*), or Shakspeare's Jest Book, *bds. uncut*, 12mo. 1831

4966 HUNT (*L.*) The Liberal, verse and prose from the south, 2 vols. in 1, 8vo. *half morocco.* Lond. 1822

*** This contains an essay on Shakespeare's Fools, Heaven and Earth a Mystery, &c.

4967 HUNTER (*J.*) Disquisition on the Scene, Origin, Date, &c., of Shakespeare's Tempest, privately printed, large paper, one of only two copies so printed; see the attestation of W. Pickering on the flyleaf, *morocco extra, sides richly tooled, gilt leaves*, by Hayday, small 8vo. 1839

4968 ——— New Illustrations of the Life, Studies, and Writings of Wm. Shakespeare, Supplementary to all the Editions, 2 vols. 8vo. *half morocco.* Lond. 1845

4970 HURDIS (*Jas.*) Cursory Remarks upon the Arrangement of the Plays of Shakespeare, occasioned by reading Mr. Malone's Essay on the Chronological order of those celebrated pieces, 8vo. *half morocco, uncut.* Lond. 1792

4971 ILLUSTRATIONS of Shakspeare and the British Drama, *many cuts*, 8vo. *half morocco*, *gilt*, *uncut*. Lond. 1831

4972 ILLUSTRATIONS of the Poets, from passages in the Life of Billy Vidkins, comic. Phil. 1849

4973 IRELAND (*S.*) Picturesque Views on the River Avon, royal 8vo. *with plates and woodcuts illustrating Shakespeare*, large paper copy, *half morocco*. 1795

IRELAND'S FORGERIES.

4974 IRELAND (*W. H.*) Shakspeare Papers, "Copies of Documents printed in my Four Guinea work, with other correspondence never published, in the handwriting of my father, Feb. 28, 1824, W. H. Ireland." MS. 4to. *half morocco*.

4976 ——— The Shakesperian Fabrications of Wm. Henry Ireland, 1796. "These are a part of the actual Papers written by Mr. Ireland, and given to me by the author, J. Caulfield." (The Printseller, author of Chalcographiana.) The original Forged Papers, Letters, &c., very neatly mounted, &c., with references to the page in the Confessions where each Document is described; among others are the famous Profession of Faith by Shakespeare, on hearing which read, Dr. Parr exclaimed, "Sir, we have very fine passages in our Church Service, and our Litany abounds with beauties, but here, Sir, is a man who has distanced us all!" (see it printed in Confessions, p. 58), Love Letter to Anna Hathaway, Promissory Note to J. Heminges, Facetious Letter to Cowley the Comedian, &c., with tracings from actual signatures to show the difference, &c., bound in 1 vol. folio, *half mor. unique*.

4977 ——— SHAKSPEARE'S KING LEAR.—Transcript of the Tragedy of King Lear, copied verbatim et literatim from the spurious MSS. given in by me to my father by my sister Anna Maria Ireland, now Mrs. Barnard, W. H. Ireland, 1824," also Autograph of Wm. Upcot, folio, *half mor*.

4978 ——— Chalmers (*George*), Apology for the Believers in the Shakespeare papers, 1797; Supplemental Apology, 1797; 2 vols. 8vo. *half morocco*, *uncut*, with MS. notes and cuttings from Magazines inserted. Lond. 1797–8

4980 IRELAND: Chalmeriana, a Collection of papers literary and political, 8vo. *half morocco, stilted* (reprinted from the Morning Chronicle). Lond. 1800

4981 ——— Authentic Account of the Shakespearian MSS. 8vo. *half morocco.* Lond. 1796

4982 ——— Sale Catalogue of the Library of, 8vo. *half morocco.* Lond. 1801

4984 ——— The Confessions of Wm. Henry Ireland, containing the particulars of his fabrication of the Shakespeare Manuscripts, together with Anecdotes and Opinions (hitherto unpublished) of many distinguished persons in the literary, political, and theatrical world [fac similes], *uncut,* 8vo. *half morocco, gilt top.* Lond. 1805

"The whole truth and nothing but the truth."

4986 ——— Miscellaneous Papers and Legal Instruments under the hand and seal of William Shakspeare, including the tragedy of King Lear, and a small fragment of Hamlet, from the original MSS. in the possession of Samuel Ireland, of Norfolk Street, *portrait and fac similes, uncut,* 8vo. *boards.* Lond. 1786

4987 ——— Another copy, 8vo. *half morocco, uncut.*

"The premature exposure of this literary forgery stopped the publication of this edition. The Copper Plates, Letter-press, &c., were defaced, broken up and sold for waste metal, and every remaining copy was torn up. From this statement it naturally results, that only 122 copies are extant, being those furnished to the Subscribers, added to which the usual numbers were remitted to the Universities, &c., and about half-a-dozen presented by Mr. Samuel Ireland to particular friends, making a total of 138 copies, which are all that remain to commemorate that most celebrated Imposition."—*Vide Wilson's Shakespeariana.*

4988 Philalethes [*Col. F. Webb.*], Shakespeare's MSS., in the possession of Mr. Ireland, examined respecting the Internal and External Evidences of their Authenticity, 8vo. *half morocco.* Lond. 1796

4989 MALONE (*E.*) Inquiry into the authenticity of certain Miscellaneous papers and Legal Instruments, &c., attributed to Shakspeare, 3 fac-similes of the handwriting of Shakspeare, Queen Elizabeth and the Earl of Southampton, large paper, 8vo. *half morocco, uncut, gilt top.* Lond. 1796

Author's presentation copy to Dr. Burney.

4990 PRECIOUS Relics, or the Tragedy of Vortigern, rehearsed, written in imitation of the Critic, 8vo. *half morocco, uncut.* Lond. 1736

4991 IRELAND (*S.*) Mr. Ireland's vindication of his conduct, respecting the publication of the supposed Shakespeare MSS., being a preface or introduction to a reply to the critical labors of Mr. Malone, 8vo. *half morocco, gilt top.* Lond. 1796

4992 ——— An investigation of Mr. Malone's claim to the character of scholar or critic; being an examination into his enquiry into the authenticity of the Shakespeare Manuscripts, paper, *uncut,* 8vo. *half morocco, gilt top.* Lond. 1797

4993 IRELAND (*W. H.*) Vortigern, an Historical Play, represented at Drury Lane, April 2, 1796, as a supposed newly discovered Drama of Shakespeare, a new edition, with an original Preface, 8vo. fac-simile, *half mor. gilt top.* Lond. 1832

The Preface is both interesting and curious, from the additional information it gives respecting the Shakespeare Forgeries, containing also the substance of his "Confessions."

4994 ——— Vortigern and Henry the II., 8vo. *half mor. stilted.* Lond. 1779

4994* ORIGINAL Letters of Sir John Falstaff, 18mo. *half mor.* Phil. 1813

4995 WOODWARD (*G. M. Caricaturist*), Familiar Verses from the Ghost of Willy Shakespeare to Sammy Ireland, to which is added Prince Robert, an Auncient Ballad, 8vo. *half mor.* Lond. 1796

4995* WYATT (*M.*) A Comparative View of the Opinions of Mr. James Boaden (editor of the Oracle), in February, March and April, 1795, and of James Boaden, Esq. (author of Fontainville Forest, and of a letter to George Steevens, Esq.), in February, 1796, relative to the Shakespeare MSS., by a friend to consistency, *uncut,* 8vo. *half mor. gilt top.* Lond. 1796

4996 ——— Another copy, *unbound.* Lond. 1796

4996* JACKSON (*Z.*) Shakspeare's Genius Justified, being restorations and illustrations of seven hundred passages in Shakspeare's Plays which have afforded abundant scope for critical animadversion, and hitherto held at defiance the penetration of all Shakspeare's commentators, with the original specimen pamphlet, 1818, *half mor. top edges gilt, uncut,* 8vo. Lond. 1819

*** Many of the emendations made in Collier's celebrated original folio are to be found in Zachary Jackson's suggestions.

4997 JAMESON (*Mrs.*) Characteristics of Woman, 2 vols. small 8vo. best edition; the only one embellished with the numerous and spirited etchings of the authoress, *mor. gilt top.* Lond. 1832

4998 JERNINGHAM (*Edward*), Poems, Shakspeare Gallery, &c., 2 vols. in 1, *half mor.* 12mo. Lond. 1796

4999 JONES (*Inigo*), Life of, by P. Cunningham, with Remarks on his Sketches for Dramas, by Planchè, and 5 Masques by Ben Jonson, etc., edited by Collier, fine portrait after Vandyke, and 15 fac-simile sketches, 8vo. 1848

This biography is more complete than any former one, and abounds in curious information respecting the customs of the period.

5000 JORDAN (*John*), Welcombe Hills, near Stratford on Avon, a Poem, historical and descriptive, 4to. Lond. 1777

JUBILEE—

5001 Colman (*George*), Man and Wife, or the Shakspeare Jubilee, 8vo. *half morocco, uncut.* Lond. 1770

5002 Garrick's Jubilee: Songs, Choruses, &c., *half morocco.* Lond. 1816

5003 Garrick Jubilee: Ode upon erecting a Statue to Shakspeare at Stratford-upon-Avon, 4to. *half morocco.* Lond. 1769

5004 Stratford Jubilee Comedy, Scrub's Trip, 8vo. *half morocco, gilt top.* Lond. 1769

5005 Jervis (*J.*) Court Detail of the Ceremonies attending the Shakspeare Club at Stratford-on-Avon, 1827, with an Account of Garrick's Jubilee, paper, 8vo. Stratford, 1827

5006 Jones (*George, the American Tragedian*), Jubilee Oration on Shakspeare, *Author's copy*, 12mo. *half morocco.* Lond. 1836

5007 ——— Idem, 12mo. *sewed.* Lond. 1836

5008 Account of the Second Commemoration of Shakspeare at Straford, 1830, 8vo. *half morocco, gilt top.* Leamington, n d.

5009 KELSALL (*C.*) The first sitting of the Committee on the proposed Monument to Shakspeare, carefully taken in short-hand by Zachary Craft, amanuensis to the Chairman, 8vo. *half morocco, gilt top.* Cheltenham, 1823

5010 KEMBLE (*J. P.*) Macbeth and King Richard the Third, an Essay in answer to Remarks on some of the Characters of Shakspeare, uncut, 8vo. *half mor., top edge gilt.* Lond. 1817

5011 ——— Authentic Account of the Retirement of, from the Stage; including the Addresses, Criticisms, Poems, &c., and an Account of the Dinner, with two beautiful portraits of Kemble, 8vo. *bds.* Lond. 1817

5012 KENILWORTH, The Princelye Pleasures of, 8vo. pp. 29. Lond. 1821

5013 ——— Festivities; comprising Laneham's Description of the Pageantry, and Gascoigne's Masques, represented before Queen Elizabeth, 1575, with engravings, 8vo. *half mor.* Warwick, 1825

5014 KENRICK'S Review of Dr. Johnson's New Edition of Shakespeare, in which the Ignorance or Inattention of that Editor is Exposed, and the Poet Defended from the Persecution of his Commentators, with the rare leaf at the end of the Review, 8vo. *half mor.* Lond. 1764

Chalmers says this is by a young man at Oxford, named Barclay.

5015 KNIGHT (*C.*) Studies of Shakspeare, forming a companion volume to the national edition of the Pictorial Shakspeare, fine frontispiece of portraits, 8vo. *half mor. uncut.* Lond. 1851

5016 ——— Essay on Henry VI. and Richard III., with postscript, royal 8vo. *half mor.* 1840

5017 LAMENTABLE and True Tragedie of M. Arden of Feversham, 8vo. Lond. 1776

5018 LAMB (*Charles*), Specimens of English Dramatic Poets, who lived about the time of Shakspeare, 2 vols. 8vo. *half calf.* N. Y. 1845

5019 ——— Tales from Shakspeare, designed principally for the use of Young Persons, by Miss and Charles Lamb, 20 large and beautiful wood-cut engravings by Harvey, fcap. 8vo. *half mor. gilt top.* Lond. 1831

"One of the most useful and agreeable companions to the understanding of Shakspeare which have been produced."

5020 LANGBAINE (*Gerard*), An Account of the English Dramatick Poets, or some Observations and Remarks on the Lives and Writings of all those that have published either Comedies, Tragedies, Tragi-Comedies, Pastorals, Masques, Interludes, Farces, or Operas, in the English Tongue, 8vo. *half mor. gilt top.* Oxford, 1691

LE NEVE, *vide* Neve, Lot 5069.

5021 LANDOR (*W. S.*) Citation and Examination of William Shakspeare, Euseby Treen, Joseph Carnaby, and Silas Gough, Clerk, before the worshipful Sir Thomas Lucy, Knight, touching deer stealing on the 19th day of September, in the year of grace 1582, now first published from original papers, to which is added a conference of Master Edmund Spenser, a gentleman of note, with the Earl of Essex, touching the state of Ireland, A. D. 1595, uncut, 12mo. *half mor. gilt top.* Lond. 1834

5022 LENNOX (*Mrs.*) Shakspeare Illustrated, or the Novels and Histories on which the Plays of Shakspeare are founded, collected and translated from the original authors, with Critical Remarks by the Author of the Female Quixote, 3 vols. 12mo. *half mor. gilt top, uncut, very rare in this state.* Lond. 1753–54

5023 LIDGATE (*J.*) The Life and Death of Hector—one, and the first of the most puissant, valiant, and renowned monarches of the world, called the nyne worthies; shewing his invincible force, together with the marvailous and most famous acts by him achieved and done in the great, long, and terrible siege, which the princes of Greece held about the towne of Troy, for the space of tenne years, and finally his unfortunate death after hee had fought a hundred mayne battailes in open field against the Grecians; the which heerein are all at large described, *engraved title,* folio, *calf.* Lond. 1614

Sold at Roscoe's sale, for £3 3s.

This is a modernization of the ancient heroic couplet into six-line stanzas, amounting to 30,000 lines, printed in double columns, generally attributed to Thomas Heywood.

Warton, in his History of English Poetry, speaks with great praise of this famous old Poem.

5024 LINES on Shakspeare, one leaf. n. d.

5025 LIFE of Macbeth, containing a Key to his Character, 12mo. *half mor.* Lond. n. d.

5026 LIFE and Death of Anne Bullen, Queen Consort of England, portrait, 8vo. *half morocco, gilt top.* Lond. 1820

5027 LONDON, Oblong Panoramic View of, by G. Visscherr, mounted in a portfolio, includes view of the Globe Theatre, &c.

5028 LOVEDAY (*Robert*), Hymen's Præludia, or Love's Masterpiece, being that much admired romance entitled Cleopatra, written originally in French, now rendered into English, folio, *half morocco.* Lond. 1674

5029 Lowndes, Shakspere and his Commentators, Extracted from the Bibliographer's Manual, presentation copy from Lowndes to the Duke of Buckingham, with autograph, portrait of Shakspeare, etc., 8vo. *half morocco.* 1821

Only Twenty-five copies so printed.

5030 Luders (*Alex.*) Essay on the Character of Henry the Fifth, when Prince of Wales, *front rough leaves, half morocco, top edge gilt,* 12mo. Lond. 1813

5031 Lylie (*John*), Euphues, the Anatomy of Wit, very pleasant for all gentlemen to read, and most necessary to remember; Euphues and his England, &c., containing his Voyages and Adventures, with sundry pretty discourses of honest Love, &c., by John Lylie, small 4to., **Black Letter,** *fine copy, calf extra, gilt edges, rare.* Lond. 1823

"Ah! that I had with me my 'Anatomy of Wit!' that all to be unparalleled volume! that quintessence of human wit! that treasury of quaint invention! etc."—*Sir Piercie Shafton—in "The Monastery."*

5032 ——— Euphues and Lucilla, or the Friend and Inconstant Mistress, to which is added Ephœbus, &c., *half calf,* 12mo. Lond. 1716

The only Rare Poet of that time, the wittie, comicall, facetious, quicke, and unparalleled John Lyly.

5033 Macdonell (*P.*) Essay on Hamlet, with copious original notes, 8vo. *half morocco.* Lond. 1843

5034 Madden (*F.*) Observations on an Autograph of Shakspere, and the orthography of his name, communicated to the Society of Antiquaries, by Sir Frederick Madden, in a letter to John Gage, Esq., *half morocco,* 8vo. Lond. 1838

5035 Mad Pranks and Merry Jests of Robin Goodfellow, reprinted from the edition of 1628, with an introduction by J. P. Collier, 8vo. *half morocco, uncut.* Lond. 1841

5036 Maginn (*W.*) The Shakspere Papers of the late William Maginn, annotated by Dr. Shelton Mackenzie, 12mo. *cloth.* N. Y. 1856

5037 Malone (*Edm.*) Inquiry into the Authenticity of certain Miscellaneous Papers and Legal Instruments published in 1795, and attributed to Shakspeare, Queen Elizabeth, and Henry, Earl of Southampton, illustrated with fac-similes of their handwriting, *largest paper, on which only* 25 *copies were printed for presents,* 8vo. *fine clean copy, bds, uncut, rare.* Lond. 1796

This was Malone's own copy with his Autograph, also that of the Elder Booth. It has extra proof plates.

5039 MALONE (*Edm.*) Supplement to Johnson and Steevens, Edition of Shakspeare 1778, with the Appendix and Second Appendix (which is rare), containing the genuine Poems and Seven Plays that have been ascribed to him, enriched with autograph letters and manuscript notes, by Steevens, Malone, Haslewood, and other commentators of the day, UNIQUE, 2 vols. in 3, *half mor. uncut.* 1780

5040 ——— A Letter to the Rev. Richard Farmer, D. D., &c., relative to the edition of Shakspeare published in MDCCXC and some late criticisms on that work, *large paper*, 8vo. *half mor.*, *gilt top.* Lond. 1792

5041 ——— Life of William Shakspeare, with an Essay on the Phraseology and Metre of the Poet and his Contemporaries, by James Boswell, LARGE PAPER, ONLY 21 COPIES, NOT PRINTED FOR SALE, *portraits on India Paper from Boaden's Enquiry added*, 8vo. *half mor.*, *uncut.* 1821

*** "This forms part of the 1st and the whole of the 2nd volume of Malone's edition of Shakspeare, published in 1821, in 21 vols. 8vo.; of this portion 21 extra copies were taken off at the express wish of the Editor, Jas. Boswell."

5042 ——— Historical Account of the Rise and Progress of the English Stage, of the Economy and Wages of the Antient Theatres in England, *half morocco, stilted*, *gilt top.* Basil, 1800

5043 MASON (*J. M.*) Comments on the Plays of Beaumont and Fletcher, with an Appendix, containing some further observations on Shakespeare, extended to the late editions of Malone and Steevens, *large paper, uncut*, 8vo. *half morocco, top gilt.* Lond. 1798

5044 ——— Comments on the several editions of Shakespeare's Plays, extended to those of Malone and Steevens, *uncut*, 8vo. *half morocco, top gilt.* Dublin, 1807

Last and best edition, only 250 copies printed.

5045 MATHIAS' Pursuit of Literature, a Satirical Poem, 8vo. *half morocco, uncut.* Lond. 1798

5046 MEETING of Gallants at an Ordinarie, or the Walkes in Powles, from a Black Letter Copy, edited by Halliwell, *half morocco*, 12mo. Lond. 1841

MIDDLETON (*Thos.*) Tragi-Comedie, called the Witch, *vide* Lot 1350.

5047 MILLS (*J. C.*) The Shakespearian Oracle, 12mo. *cloth.* N. Y. 1855

5048 MILTON and Shakspeare. Essay on Milton by Lauder; and Whalley on Shakspeare, with several other Tracts, 8vo. *sheep.* Lond. 1750

5049 MILTON (*John*), History of England, from the first Traditional beginning to the Norman Conquest, published from a copy corrected by the Author himself, folio, *half mor.* Amsterdam, 1694

5050 MIRROR for Magistrates—The Falls of Unfortunate Princes, and Chronicle Historie (in verse), of Men of Note, &c., since the first entrance of Brutus into this Island, &c., new Edition, by Joseph Haslewood, 150 *copies only printed,* 3 vols. 4to. *boards, uncut.* Lond. 1815

"The popularity of this famous poetical miscellany, the work of the chief wits of the time, and its influence on our national poetry, in the reigns of Elizabeth and James I., was very considerable. The Inductión, by Lord Buckhurst, is conceived with the vigor of a creative imagination, and was the model of Spenser."—*Warton.*

5051 MISCELLANEOUS Observations on the Tragedy of Hamlet, *scarce, sewed,* 8vo. Lond.

5052 MODERN Characters for 1778, by Wm. Shakespeare; Shakespeare's History of the Times, or the Original Portraits of that Author adapted to Modern Characters, in one volume, 12mo, *uncut, half morocco, top edges gilt.* Lond. 1778

5053 MONTAGU (*Mrs.*) An Essay on the Writings and Genius of Shakspeare, compared with the Greek and French Dramatic Poets, with some Remarks upon the Misrepresentations of Mons. de Voltaire, first Edition, *uncut,* 8vo. *half mor. top gilt.* Lond. 1769

5054 ——— Sixth and best edition, corrected, to which are added Three Dialogues of the Dead, *large paper,* royal 8vo. *half morocco.* Lond. 1810

5055 MONTAGUE (*F.*) Ages of Female Beauty, *fine steel plates,* 4to. *cloth.* Lond. n. d.

A pictorial adaptation of the "Seven Ages of Man."

5056 MONTAIGNE, The Essays, or Morall, Politicke, and Militarie Discovrses of Lord Michael de Montaigne, Knight of the Noble Order of St. Michael, and one of the Gentlemen in Ordinary of the French King's chamber, &c., *fine engraved title,* folio, *calf, gilt.* Lond. 1632

Translated by "The still resolute Iohn Florio," who is the original of Holofernes, in Love's Labour Lost.

Shakspeare is supposed to have been familiar with an earlier edition of this translation.

5057 MONTREAL Shakspearian Club, Constitution and By-Laws of, 12mo. 1847

5058 ——— Annual Reports of, for 1845 and 1847, 2 vols. 12mo. v. d

5059 MORGANN (*M.*) An Essay on the Dramatic Character of Sir John Falstaff, *large paper, half mor. top gilt, uncut*, 8vo. Lond. 1777

5060 ——— An Essay on the Dramatic Character of Sir John Falstaff, *thick paper, half mor. top gilt, uncut*, 8vo. Lond. 1815

"A more honorable monument to the memory of Shakespeare than any which has been reared to him by the united labors of his commentators."—*Dr. Symmons.*

5061 MORRIS's Essay towards fixing the True Standards of Wit, Humour, Raillery, Satire, and Ridicule, to which is added an Analysis of the Characters of an Humourist, Sir John Falstaff, Sir Roger de Coverly, and Don Quixote, 8vo. *half mor. gilt top.* Lond. 1744

5062 MOSES (*H.*) Illustrations of Ancient Costume, 4to. *half mor.* n. d.

5063 MOSSOP'S Part of King John, MS., *very curious*, 4to. *half mor.* 1754

5064 MOULIN (*I.*) Omtrekken eener Algemeene Litteratuur over William Shakespeare en deszelfs werken, 8vo., only 103 copies, *privately printed.* 1845

A very copious list of all the English and Foreign Writers on Shakespeare, pointing out the particular Essays in larger works and periodical literature.

5065 NARES (*R.*) Glossary of Words, Phrases, Names, Allusions, Proverbs, &c., in the Works of English Authors, particularly Shakspeare and his Contemporaries, 4to. *bds.* 1822

One of the most interesting and curious books of the kind ever published, and by far the best and most useful work wo possess for explaining and illustrating the obsolete language, and the customs and manners of the sixteenth and seventeenth centuries, and it is quite indispensable for the reading of the literature of the Elizabethan period.

5066 NAUNTON (*Sir Robert*), Fragmenta Regalia, Memoirs of the Court of Queen Elizabeth, new edition, by Dodd, *fine portraits, half mor.* Lond. 1824

5069 NEVE (*Philip Le*), Cursory Remarks on some of the Ancient English Poets, particularly Milton, 8vo., *scarce, half mor. gilt top.* 1789

Not published. Two hundred copies only printed for presents to the author's friends.

5070 New Readings of Old Authors, a Series of Humourous Illustrations of Shakespeare, by Seymour, 26 parts, 12mo. Lond. 1848

A master-stroke of rich humour, and the moral tendency unexceptionable.

5072 Nicholas (*Sir Harris*), Battle of Agincourt, and Expedition of Henry V. into France, *large paper* 8vo. *half mor.* Lond. 1833

5073 Oakley (*Ben.*) Selections from Shakespeare, *uncut*, 12mo. *half mor., gilt top.* Lond. 1828

5074 Ogilvie (*John D. D.*) Poems on Several Subjects; Day of Judgement; Odes to the Genius of Shakespeare, &c., *plates*, royal 8vo. *half mor. gilt top.* Lond. 1764

5075 Original Letters, &c., of Sir John Falstaff, selected from Genuine MSS. which have been in the possession of Dame Quickly and her Descendants near four hundred years, the second Edition, dedicated to Master Samuel Ireland, 12mo. *frontispiece, half mor.* Phila. 1813

This very curious little book was the joint production of James White and Charles Lamb.—*See Talfourd's Life and Letters of Lamb.*

5076 Outlines to the Tempest, *twelve plates*, 8vo. *half mor. gilt top.* Lond. 1825

5077 Patterson (*R.*), Letters on the Natural History of the Insects mentioned in Shakespeare's plays, with incidental notices of the Entomology of Ireland, woodcuts, 8vo. *half mor., top gilt.* Lond. 1838

5078 Pearce (*William*), Haunts of Shakespeare, a Poem, 4to. *half mor.* Lond. 1776

5079 Pendragon, or the Carpet Knight, his Kalendar, 12mo. *calf.* Lond. 1698

"A Poem in hudibrastic measure, intended as a satire on that active and mercenary writer in the cause of arbitrary power, Sir Roger L'Estrange."—*Lowndes.*

The following quotation appears on the title:

"Why let the Stricken Deer go weep,
The Hart ungall'd go play,
For some must watch while some must sleep;
So runs the world away."

5080 Percy (*Stephen*), Robin Hood and his Merry Foresters, *plates.* 1845

5081 Perrin (*M.*) Contes Moraux tirés des Tragedies de Shakespeare, 12mo. Lond. 1783

5082 PHILLIPS (*Edward, Nephew of John Milton*), Theatrum Poetarum Anglicanorum, containing the names and characters of all the English Poets from Henry III. to the close of Queen Elizabeth's reign, edited by Sir Egerton Brydges, *presentation copy*, *half mor.* Canterbury, 1800

5083 ——— Another Edition, one hundred copies only printed, edited by Sir E. Brydges, 8vo. *half mor.*, *uncut.* Geneva, 1826

"Contains criticisms far above the taste of the period, in which the hand of Milton may not obscurely be traced, as in the judgment on Shakespeare, Marlowe, &c."—*Warton.*

5084 ——— (*Edward, Nephew of John Milton*), The New World of Words, or a General English Dictionary, etc., frontispiece of portraits of Chaucer, Spenser, Sidney, Bacon, Selden, etc., folio, *calf, neat.* Lond. 1671

₊ Among the names of Learned Persons contributory to this Work, are, Ashmole, Evelyn, Dugdale, Boyle, Isaac Walton, Col. Venables, &c.

5085 PILGRIMAGE to Stratford-on-Avon, the Birthplace of Shakspeare, with portrait of Shakspeare, *plates*, 18mo. *half mor.* Lond. 1850

5086 PITMAN (*Rev. T. R.*) Shakspeare, for Schools, with notes from the best annotators, *half mor. t. g.* 8vo. Lond. 1834

5087 PLANCHÉ (*J. R.*) Costume of Shakspere, Historical Tragedy of King John, selected from the best authorities, 23 *coloured plates*, 12mo. *half mor. g. t. uncut.* Lond. 1823

5088 ——— Costume of Shakspere's Tragedy of Othello and Comedy of the Merchant of Venice, selected from the best authorities, 24 *plates*, 12mo. *half mor. g. t.* Lond. 1823

5089 ——— Costume of Shakspere's Tragedy of Hamlet, selected from the best authorities, 14 *col'd plates*, 12mo. *half mor. g. t.* Lond. 1825

5090 ——— Costume of Shakspere's Historical Play of King Henry the 4th, selected from the best authorities, 22 *col'd plates,* 12mo. *half mor. g. t. u.* Lond. 1824

5091 ——— Costume of Shakspere's Comedy of As You Like It, selected from the best authorities, 19 *col'd plates*, 12mo. *half mor. g. t.* Lond. 1825

5092 ——— Midsummer Night's Dream, Songs and Duets, 1840, and the Fairies, 1755, 2 vols. in 1, 8vo. *half calf.* v. d.

5093 PLUMPTRE (*J.*) Observations on Hamlet, and on the motives which most probably induced Shakespeare to fix upon the story of Amleth, from the Danish Chronicle of Saxo Grammaticus, for the plot of that Tragedy, being an attempt to prove that he designed it as an indirect censure on Mary Queen of Scots, 8vo. Cambridge, 1796

5094 ——— Another copy, 8vo. *half mor.* 1796

5095 POETICAL Farago, A miscellaneous assemblage of epigrams and other jeux d'esprits on Garrick's Picture, hung near the bust of Shakespeare, on Tibbald's (Theobald) pointing to Shakespear, on Shakespear and Voltaire, &c. 2 vols. in 1, *half mor. g. t.* 12mo. 1794

5096 POLIMANTEIA, or The Means lawful and unlawful to judge of the Fall of a Commonwealth, against the frivolous and foolish Conjectures of this Age, whereunto is added a Letter from England to her three Daughters, Cambridge, Oxford, Inns of Court, and to all the rest of her Inhabitants, persuading them to a constant Unitie of what Religion soever they are, for the Defence of our dread Soveraigne, and native Country, most requisite for this Time wherein wee now live, 4to. *half mor. g. t.* Camb., J. Legate, 1595

This work is of interest as containing the earliest allusion to Shakspeare *by name* in the printed literature of England.

5097 POLITEUPHIA, Wit's Commonwealth, 3d edition, 12mo. by John Bodenham, *printed by J. R. for N. Ling.* Lond. 1598

5098 ——— Another Edition, 12mo. *calf, gilt, f. c.* 1684

"A collection of sententious extracts from the Ancient Moral Philosophers."—*Lowndes.*

5099 PORTO (*Luigi da*), Romeo e Julietta, Storie de due Nobili Amanti çon la loro pietosa morti, avvenuta gia in Verona, &c., e scritta da Luigi da Porto, a neat manuscript of 40 pages, *half mor.* 4to.

5100 PRICE (*Thomas*), Wisdom and Genius of Shakspeare, with select and original notes, and Scriptural references, 12mo. *cloth.* Phil. 1839

5102 PYE (*H. J.*) Comments on the Commentators on Shakspeare, with preliminary observations on his genius and writings, and on the labors of those who have endeavored to elucidate them, with MS. notes by Judge Furman, *uncut*, 8vo. *half mor. g. t. stilted.* Lond. 1807

5103 PROSPECTUS of the Lansdowne Shakspere, 8vo. Lond. 1852

5104 QUELLEN des Shakespeare in Novellen, Marchen, und Sagen, 4 vols. 12mo. Berlin, 1831

5105 RALEIGH (*Sir Walter*), The Discoverie of the Empire of Guiana, with a relation of Manoa (which the Spaniards call El Dorado), and of the Provinces of Emeria, Arromaia, Amapaya, &c., performed in the year 1595, 4to. Lond. *R. Robinson*, 1596

Sold in Gordonstoun sale for £3; Jadis, £3.

From this rare tract Shakspeare derived his knowledge of the "still vexed Bermoothes."

5106 RECOLLECTIONS of the Scenic Effects of Covent Garden Theatre, dedicated to Mr. Macready; and outline illustrations of Werner, *paper*. Lond. 1839

5107 RETZSCH—Gallery to Shakspeare's Dramatic Works, in outlines, invented and engraved by Moritz Retzsch, 16 parts, oblong 4to. 1849

These beautiful plates illustrate Hamlet, Macbeth, Romeo and Juliet, King Lear, The Tempest, Othello, Merry Wives of Windsor, and King Henry IV.

5108 ——— Gallerie de Shakspeare, 70 plates, with explanations, translated from the German, oblong 8vo. Paris, 1828

5109 ——— Outlines to Shakspeare, seventh series; The Merry Wives of Windsor, 13 plates. Lond. 1844

5110 ——— Outlines, Explanatory Letter-press only, 6 parts, 4to. *cl.*

5111 RETVRNE from Pernassvs, or the Scourge of Simony, publickly acted by the Students in Saint Iohn's College in Cambridge, *rare, fine copy*, 4to. *half mor. interleaved.* 1606

*** Reprinted in "Hawkins's Origin of the English Drama," and is held in much esteem by the curious on account of its containing one of the earliest notices of Shakspeare:—

"Act I. Scene II.

"Who loues *Adonis* loue, or *Lucre's* rape
His sweeter verse contaynes hart robbing life,
Could but a grauer subiect him content,
Without loue's foolish lazy languishment."

"Act IV. Scene III.

"Few of the vniuersity pen plaies well, they smell too much of that writer *Ouid*, and that writer *Metamorphosis*, and talke too much of *Proserpina and Iuppiter*. Why heres our fellow *Shakespeare* puts them all downe, I and *Ben Ionson* too. O that *Ben Ionson* is a pestilent fellow, he brought vp *Horace* giuing the Poets a pill, but our fellow *Shakespeare* hath giuen him a purge that made him beray his credit."

5112 Rhodes (*W. B.*) Sale Catalogue of the Dramatic Library of, 10 days' sale, 8vo. *half mor.* Lond. 1825

5113 Ricardi Maydiston: Alliterative Poem on the Deposition of King Richard III., 4to. *half mor.* (Camden Society). Lond. 1838

5115 Rich (*Barnaby*), Eight Novels employed by English Dramatic Poets of the Reign of Queen Elizabeth, 8vo. *half mor. uncut* (Shakspeare Society). Lond. 1846

5116 Richardson (*W.*) Essays on Shakspeare's Dramatic Characters, of Richard the 3d, King Lear, and Timon of Athens, to which are added an Essay on the Faults of Shakespeare, and additional observations on the character of Hamlet, 2 vols. 18mo. *calf.* Lond. 1783

5117 ——— Essays on Shakspeare's Dramatic Character of Sir John Falstaff, and on his Imitation of Female Characters, to which are added some general observations on the Studies of Shakspeare, 16mo. *calf.* Lond. 1785

5118 ——— Another edition, 12mo. *calf.* Lond. 1789

5119 ——— Sixth Edition, large paper, *half mor. uncut.* Lond. 1812

5120 Riddle (*J. E.*) Illustrations of Aristotle, from the Dramatic Works of Shakspeare, post 8vo. *half mor.* Oxford, 1832

5121 Ritson (*J.*) Remarks, Critical and Illustrative, on the Text and Notes of the last edition of Shakspeare, 8vo. *half mor. gilt top, uncut.* Lond. 1783

5122 ——— Cursory Criticisms on the edition of Shakspeare published by Edmond Malone, 8vo. *half mor. gilt top.* Lond. 1792

5123 ——— The Quip Modest; Remarks on the Notes and Text of the last edition of Shakspeare, 8vo. *half mor. uncut.* Lond. 1788

5124 Rimbault (*E. F.*) "Who was 'Jack Wilson,' the Singer of Shakspeare's Stage?" An Attempt to Prove the Identity of this Person with John Wilson, Doctor of Music in the University of Oxford, A. D. 1644, 8vo. *half mor.* Lond. 1846

5125 Rodd (*Thos.*) Traditionary Anecdotes of Shakespeare, collected in Warwickshire in 1693, now first published from an old MS., 8vo. *half mor. gilt top.* 1838

5126 ——— MS. Essay on the Tempest, 8vo. *half mor.* n. d.

5127 ——— (*H.*) Remarks on the Chandos Portrait of Shakspeare, only 50 copies printed for private distribution, with a Letter, 8vo. Lond. 1849

5128 RODD (*H.*) Remarks on the Chandos Portrait of Shakspeare, not printed for sale, with a Letter by H. Rodd, 8vo. Lond. 1849

5129 ——— Sale Catalogue of Rare Prints and Books, illustrative of the works of Wm. Shakspeare, including the rare Portraits of the Bard, thick paper, 8vo. *half mor.* (only four copies so printed.) Lond. 1850

5130 RYMER (*Thos.*) Tragedies of the Last Age Considered, *half mor. gilt*, 12mo. Lond. 1678

5131 ——— Short View of Tragedy, its Original Excellency and Corruption, 8vo. *calf.* 1693

"Valuable for its historical matter; one of the earliest criticisms on Shakespeare."—*Retrospective Rev.*

The works of Rymer form one of the most laughable and amusing comments ever written upon Shakespeare. He has taken for his theme Othello, and after analyzing it through several pages, he winds up with the following summary: "There is in this play some burlesk, some humour, and ramble of comic wit—some show and some *mimickry* to divert the spectators; but the tragedy part is plainly none other than a bloody farce without salt or savour."

5132 SAVIOLO (*Vincentio*), His Practice, in two bookes, the first intreating of the use of Rapier and Dagger; the second of Honor and Honorable Quarrels, *woodcuts, calf gilt, fine copy,* 4to. *John Wolfe,* Lond. 1595

In the rule and order concerning the Challenger and Defender, it treats of "the manner and diversity of Lies," "Of Lies certaine," "Of conditional Lyes," "Of the Lye in generall," "Of the Lye in particular." It is the book referred to by Touchstone in Shakspeare's "As You Like It." See Reed and Steevens' Shakspeare, vol. 3, page 181. Sold at White Knight's sale for £5 15*s.* 6*d.*, Stretell's, £5 15*s.* 6*d.*, Stanley's £14 3*s.* 6*d.*

Saviolo's Practice throws considerable light on the affected manners of the gallants in the days of Elizabeth, and elucidates several passages in Shakspeare and Ben Jonson.

5133 SAYER's Dramatic Characters, or Different Portraits of the English Stage in the days of Garrick, 12mo. 38 *plates, calf, gilt, rare.* Lond. 1770

5134 SCHOOL for Satire, a volume of satirical poems, addressed to the various commentators on Shakspeare, Capell's Ghost, and others, 8vo. Lond. 1802

5135 SCHLEGEL (*A. W.*) A Course of Lectures on Dramatic Art and Literature, *uncut*, 2 vols. in 1, 8vo. *half mor.* Lond. 1840

5136 SECRET History of Mackbeth, King of Scotland, taken from a very ancient original MS., 12mo. *half mor. gilt.* Lond. 1708

5137 SECRET Passion, by the author of Shakspeare and his Friends, 3 vols. 8vo. *half mor. uncut.* Lond. 1844

5137* TALES from the Gesta Romanorum, 12mo. *half mor.* N. Y .1845

5138 SELOUS' Outline Illustrations to Shakspeare's Tempest, 12 *plates,* 4to. Lond. 1825

SEVEN AGES OF MAN.—*See* Lots 5147 to 5152.

5139 SEYMOUR (*E. H.*) Remarks, critical, conjectural, and explanatory, upon the Plays of Shakespeare; resulting from a collation of the early copies with that of Johnson and Steevens, edited by Isaac Reed, Esq.; together with some valuable extracts from the MSS. of the late Right Honorable John Lord Chedworth, &c. *uncut,* 2 vols. 8vo. *half mor.* Lond. 1805

5140 ——— (*H.*) Humourous Readings of Shakspeare, the four series complete, *upwards of* 200 *exceedingly humourous and clever drawings on stone, by this eminent caricaturist,* 2 vols. 12mo. *scarce, half mor.* 1841

Nothing so redolent of frolic, mirth, and fun, has ever before emanated from the brains of any one man; Alfred Seymour is the modern Hogarth.

5141 SHAKSPEARE Calendar, or Wit and Wisdom for every day in the year, edited by W. C. Richards, 12mo. N. Y. 1850

5142 ——— and his Times, Criticisms on his Genius and Writings, a new Chronology of his Plays, a Disquisition on the Objects of his Sonnets, and a History of the Manners, Customs, Amusements and Superstitions of his age, by Dr. N. Drake, port. and fac similes of autographs, 2 vols. 4to. *half mor. uncut.* 1817

This masterly production contains a mass of agreeable and well-digested information; and is particularly valuable for its full information on the contemporary writers and their works, the different editions, etc.

5143 ——— Gallery, Illustrating the Plays of Shakspeare, with seventy-nine beautiful plates, large paper, 4to. *half mor.* Lond. 1839

5144 ——— Historical Dramas, illustrated by Harding, authentic portraits of Royal and Noble Personages, Views of Towns, Castles, &c., by Schiavonetti and others, 2 vols. in 1, *binding broken,* 4to. Lond. 1811

5145 ——— Illustrated by a Series of Portraits and Views, with Biographical Anecdotes, to which are added Portraits of Actors and Editors, one hundred and fifty-eight plates, 2 vols. 8vo. *calf.* Lond. n. d.

5146 SHAKSPEARE Illustrated, or the Novels and Histories on which the Plays of Shakspeare are founded, collected and translated from original authors by Mrs. Lennox, 3 vols. 12mo. *half mor. uncut.* Lond. 1753

5147 ——— Illustrative Index to, in MS. 8vo.

5148 ——— Seven Ages of Man, illustrated by Gilbert, Claxton, &c., 4to. Lond. n. d.

5149 ——— Seven Ages of Man, illustrated with colored plates, folio, *half mor.* Lond. 1799

5150 ——— Seven Ages, illustrated by 12 beautiful wood engravings after designs by Sir David Wilkie, Mulready, Leslie, Calcott, Constable, Collins, Sir Edwin Landseer, &c., 4to. *cloth.* Lond., *Van Voorst* 1840

5151 ——— Maclise's beautiful designs to illustrate Shakspeare's Seven Ages, engraved by Goodall, 4to. Art Union, 1850

5152 ——— Seven Ages of Man, with illustrations by Kenny Meadows, 8vo. *unbound.*

5153 ——— Jest Books, with Preface and Glossary, by S. W. Singer, the 3 parts complete in 2 vols. 8vo. (only 250 copies printed), *half mor.* Chiswick, 1814–16

CONTENTS: Tales and Quicke Answeres very mery and pleasant to rede, *Berthelet*, 1530; Supplement to the Tales and Quicke Answeres, *Wykes*, 1567; A Hundred Mery Talys, *Rastell*, 1529.

The former book is most probably the one from which Benedick accuses Beatrice of stealing all her "good wit."

5153* ——— Jests, or the Jubilee Jester, being a curious collection of Jubilee and Jovial Songs, *frontispiece, half mor. rare*, 12mo. J. Robson, n. d.

Priced £1 11*s.* 6*d.* in a recent English Catalogue.

5154 ——— Laconics, a selection of Pithy Sentences, 12mo. *scarce.* Phil. 1853

5155 ——— Merry Tales, a new edition, 18mo. *half mor.* Lond. 1845

5156 ——— Newspaper, folio.

5157 ——— and his Friends, 3 vols. 12mo. *half mor. uncut.* Lond. 1838

5158 ——— Portfolio; a Series of 95 Graphic Illustrations, after designs by the most eminent British Artists, including Smirke, Stothard, Stephanoff, Cooper, Westall, Hilton, Leslie, Briggs, Corbould, Clint, *beautifully engraved by Heath, Greatbach, Robinson, Pye, Finden, Engleheart, Armstrong, Rolls, and others, India Proofs*, folio, *in a case, with leather back, stained.*

5159 SHAKSPEARE Repository, published by Fennel, 4to. 1853

5160 ——— Romances, collected and arranged by Shakspeare the 2d, 2 vols. in 1, 12mo. *half mor. g. t.* Lond. 1825

5161 SUNDRY Scrap Prints and Cuttings, many illustrative of Shakespeare and his Works.

5162 SHAKESPEARE Society Papers, *uncut*, 4 vols. 8vo. *half mor.* Lond. 1844–5

5163 ——— Will, copied from the original in the Prerogative Court, preserving the Interlineations and Facsimiles of the three Autographs of the Poet, with a few preliminary Observations, by J. O. Halliwell, 4to. *half mor. gilt top, uncut.* 1851

5164 SHERLOCK (*Martin*), Letters from an English Traveller, new edition with notes, *Charles Lamb's copy*, 8vo. *half mor.* Lond. 1780

5165 SHARPHAM (*Ed.*) Cupid's Whirligig, 4to. *green mor.* Lond. 1607

This play has been erroneously attributed to Shakespeare.

5166 SHORT (*C.*) Life and Humours of Falstaff, a Comedy formed out of the two parts of Shakespeare's Henry the 4th and Henry 5th, 12mo. *half mor., uncut.* Lond. 1829

5167 SIR Thomas More, a Play edited by A. Dyce, 1844; Marriage of Wit and Wisdom, an ancient interlude, edited by Halliwell, 1846, with illustrations to Shakspeare, in 1 vol. 8vo. *half calf.* Lond. v. y.

5168 SIX old Plays on which Shakespeare founded his Measure for Measure, Comedy of Errors, Taming the Shrew, King John, K. Henry IV. and K. Henry V., King Lear, *scarce*, 2 vols. in 1, *half mor., gilt top.* Lond., J. Nichols, 1779

5169 SKOTTOWE (*A.*)—The Life of Shakespeare; Enquiries into the Originality of his Dramatic Plots and Characters; and Essays on the Ancient Theatres and Theatrical Usages, 2 vols. in 1, *half mor.*, 8vo. Lond. 1824

5170 SONGS, Madrigals, and Sonnets; a gathering of some of the most pleasant flowers of Old English Poetry, including some of Shakespeare's, set in borders of coloured ornaments and vignettes, square 12mo., EVERY PAGE SURROUNDED WITH COLOURED BORDERS, *half mor.* Lond. 1849

5171 SKENE (*Geo.*) The Genius of Shakespeare, a Summer Dream, presentation copy by the author, 4to. *large paper, half mor.* Lond. 1793

5172 STAFFORD (*Wm.*) Compendium, or briefe examination of certayne ordinary complaints of divers of our Countrymen, in these our Dayes, by W. S. Gent, reprint from the edition of 1581, 8vo. *half morocco.* Lond. 1751

Prefixed to this edition is a ridiculous preface endeavoring to show that the tract was written by William Shakspeare, Gent., edited by J. Nichols.

5173 SPOOR (*Henrico*), Decorum et Heroum Virorum et Mulierum Illustrium Imagines Antiquæ, Illustratæ, 4to. *vellum.* Amsterdam, 1715

5174 STORER (*Thos.*), Life and Death of Cardinal Wolsey, reprinted from the editions of 1599, 4to. *half morocco.* Lond. 1815

5175 TAYLOR (*E.*) Cursory Remarks on Tragedy, on Shakspeare, and on certain French and Italian Poets, principally tragedians, 8vo. *half morocco, gilt top.* 1774

5176 ——— Another Copy. 1774

5177 ——— Picturesque Beauties of Shakspeare, *engraved on forty plates after Stothard and Smirke*, by Taylor, beautiful impressions, with the letter-press *uncut*, 1783-4. Shakespeare Gallery, containing a Select Series of Scenes and Characters (with criticisms and remarks), by Singleton, 1792, 50 *plates*, PROOFS, in 1 vol. *uncut, half morocco*, 4to. Lond. 1783-4

5178 THEOBALD.—Shakespeare restored; or, a specimen of the many errours, as well committed as unamended by Mr. Pope in his late edition of this poet, designed not only to correct the said edition, but to restore the true reading of Shakespeare in all the editions ever yet published, *scarce*, 4to. *half morocco, uncut.* Lond. 1726

5179 THURSTON (*T.*) Illustrations of Shakspeare, *thirty-eight engravings on wood, by Branston, from designs by T. Thurston*, 8vo. Lond. n. d.

5180 TODD (*H. J.*) Illustrations of the Lives and Writings of Gower and Chaucer, collected from authentic documents, *many plates*, 4to. *calf.* Lond. 1810

5181 TRACTS on Warburton, New Dunciad, Horatian Canons, with several of Warburton's own Notes, 4to. *half morocco.* Lond. 1750

5182 TRACTS, Hanmer's Letter on the Fools, Irving, Freron, &c., in 1 vol. *half morocco.* v. d.

5183 TREATISE on the Passions, with Critical Inquiry into the Theatrical Merit of Garrick, Quin and Barry; the first considered in the part of Lear, the two last opposed in Othello, 8vo. *half morocco.* n. d.

5184 TWEDDELL (*George*), Shakespeare, his Times and Contemporaries, 12mo. *half morocco.* Lond. 1852

5185 TWISS (*Francis*), Complete Verbal Index to the Plays of Shakspeare, adapted to all editions, 2 vols. 8vo. *half morocco, gilt top.* Lond. 1805

Exceedingly scarce, nearly the whole impression having been destroyed at Bensley's fire.

5186 TWYSDEN (*Sir R.*) An Account of Queen Anne Bullen, From a MS. in the handwriting of Sir Roger Twysden, Bart., 8vo. *half morocco.*

5186*ULRICI (*Hermann*), Shakspeare's Dramatic Art, and Relation to Calderon and Gœthe, translated from the German, 8vo. *half morocco.* Lond. 1846

5187 UPTON (*J.*) Critical Observations on Shakespeare, by John Upton, Prebendary of Rochester, first edition, with the reverie, or finely-imagined dream, which is omitted in the subsequent editions, 8vo. *half morocco, gilt top.* Lond. 1746

5188 ——— Idem, 2d edition, *large paper copy, half morocco, gilt top.* Lond. 1748

5189 VIEWS in Stratford-on-Avon, and its Vicinity, Illustrative of the Biography of Shakspere, accompanied with descriptive remarks, by Wm. Rider, folio, *half morocco.* Lond. 1828

5190 VOLTAIRE (*M. de*), Letters Concerning the English Nation, 8vo. Lond. 1733

"Letter 18th, p. 166, contains strictures on Hamlet, Julius Cesar, &c. No Frenchman can either understand or appreciate Shakspeare." *MS. note.*

5191 VOLTAIRE'S Letter to the French Academy, on the Merits of Shakspere, 12mo. *half morocco, gilt top.* Lond. 1777

5192 WALDRON (*F. G.*) Shakspearian Miscellany, containing Scarce and Valuable Tracts, Poetry, and Biographical Anecdotes, fine portraits of Actors, by Harding and Schiavonetti, &c., 4to. *half morocco, large paper.* Lond. 1802

Includes, Euphues' Golden Legacie, Life and Miracles of the Prophet Abraham, from an Arabic MS. &c.

5193 WALLACE (*Jas.*) Shakespearian Sketches, with MS. Notes, 12mo. *half morocco, gilt top.* Lond. 1795

5194 WALKINGTON (*Thomas*), Optick Glasse of Humors, or the Touchstone of Golden Temperature; or, the Philosopher's Stone to make a Golden Temper, 12mo. *neat.* Lond. 1664

Dr. Farmer, in his Essay on the Learning of Shakspeare, observes, "In the Merchant of Venice, the Jew, as an apology for his cruelty, rehearses many sympathies and antipathies for which no reason can be rendered. This incident is to be met with in the Optick Glasse of Humors."

5195 WALPOLE (*Horace*), Historic Doubts on the Life and Reign of King Richard III., *plates,* 4to. *half mor.* Lond. 1768

5196 WALPURGIS' Night and Walpurgis' Night-Dream, or Oberon and Titania's Golden Wedding Feast, 12mo. *half mor.* not published. n. d.

5197 WARD (*Rev. J., Vicar of Stratford-on-Avon*), Diary, from 1648 to 1678, edited from the original MS. by Dr. Severn, 8vo. *half mor. gilt top.* Lond. 1819

Ward was all but contemporary with Shakspeare; and part of the work throws much light upon disputed portions of his biography, and elucidates that relating to his death, of which hitherto we have been in ignorance.

5198 WARNER (*R.*) A Letter to David Garrick, Esq., concerning a Glossary to the Plays of Shakspeare, on a more extensive plan than has hitherto appeared; to which is annexed a specimen, author's copy, 8vo. *half mor. gilt top.* Lond. 1768

5199 ——— Another copy, 8vo. Lond. 1768

5200 WEAVER (*T. W.*) Plantagenet's Tragical Story, or the Death of Edward the 4th and Richard the 3d, a Poem, by T. W., with portrait by Marshall, 12mo. *half mor.* Lond. 1649

By some of the bibliographers the author is said to have been Whitchcot; not improbable, as Thomas Whitchcot was Governor of Windsor Castle about this period; and a portrait of him (painted in oil, with his own arms impaling those of his two wives in the corner), was sold a few years since, which corresponded exactly as to features, &c., with Marshall's engraving.

5200*a* WHALLEY (*P.*) An Enquiry into the Learning of Shakespeare, with remarks on several passages of his Plays, in a conversation between Eugenius and Neander, 8vo. *half mor. gilt top.* Lond. 1748

5200*b* WHATELEY (*Thos.*) Remarks on some of the Characters of Shakespeare, 8vo. *half mor.* Lond. 1785

5200*c* ——— Second Edition. Oxford, 1808

5200*d* WHATELEY (*Thos.*) Third edition, edited by Abp. Whately, 12mo. *half mor.* Lond. 1837

5200*e* WHELER (*R. B.*) Historical and Descriptive Account of the Birthplace of Shakspeare, with lithographic illustrations by C. F. Green, large paper, 4to. *half mor. uncut.* Stratford-on-Avon, 1824

5201 ——— History and Antiquities of Stratford-on-Avon, with Life of Shakspeare, embellished with 8 engravings, 12mo. *half mor. uncut.* Stratford, n. d.

5202 ——— Another copy, binding broken. n. d.

5203 WHITE (*Richard G.*) Shakspeare's Scholar, being Historical and Critical Studies of his Text, Characters, and Commentators, with an Examination of Collier's Folio of 1632, presentation copy, 8vo. *half mor.* N. Y. 1854

5205 WHITER (*W.*) A Specimen of a Commentary on Shakspeare, containing Notes on As You Like It; an attempt to explain and illustrate various passages on a new principle of criticism, &c., 8vo. *half mor. gilt top, uncut.* Lond. 1794

5206 WILSON (*J.*) Shakspeariana—Catalogue of all the Books, Pamphlets, &c., relating to Shakspeare, to which are subjoined an account of the early quarto editions of the great dramatist's plays and poems; the prices at which many copies have sold in public sales; together with a list of the leading and esteemed editions of Shakspeare's collected Works. Lond. 1827

5207 WILSON—An Analysis of the Illustrated Shakspeare of Thomas Wilson, Esq., portrait of Harris, as Card. Wolsey, proof before the letters, *rare, large paper*, 4to. *half mor. uncut.* Lond. 1820

*** Of the large paper copies, *only twenty-five were printed.* On the back of the title-page is "An attested copy, Wm. J. White, only twenty-five printed." The "Shakspeare" of which this is a description, was bound in twenty folio volumes, and contained fifteen hundred and twenty-five extra engravings, portraits, &c.

5208 WIVELL (*A.*) An Historical Account of the Monumental Bust of William Shakspeare, in the Chancel of the Church at Stratford-upon-Avon, Warwickshire, with critical remarks on the authors who have written on it, *plates*, 8vo. *uncut.* Lond. 1827

5209 ——— Inquiry into the History, Authenticity, and Characteristics of the Shakspeare Portraits, with the Supplement, 20 portraits of Shakspeare, 2 vols. in 1, 8vo. *bds.* Lond. 1827

5210 Woty (*W.*) The Stage, a Poetical Epistle, 4to. *half mor.* Lond. n. d.

5211 Wright (*Thomas*), The Passions of the Minde (from Haslewood's Library), 12mo. *calf.* *Printed by V. S. for W. B.*, Lond. 1601

"Sometimes I have seen Tarleton play the clowne, and use no other breeches than such sloppes, or slivings, as now many gentlemen wear; they are almost capable of a bushel of wheate, and if they bee of sacke cloth, they would serve to carry mawlt to the mill," &c. p. 298.

5213 Youth of Shakspeare, or Love and Genius, by the Author of Shakspeare and his Friends, 3 vols. 12mo. *half mor. gilt top, uncut.* Lond. 1839

SONGS, BALLADS, &c.—*See also Poetry, &c.*

—— Antique Ballads sung to crowds of old,
Now cheaply bought for thrice their weight in gold.

5214 Aiken (*J.*) Vocal Poetry, or a collection of English Songs, 12mo. *boards.* Lond. 1810

5216 Aikin's Essays on Song Writing, with collection of English Songs eminent for merit, 12mo. *boards.* Lond. n. d.

5217 Ainsworth (*W. H.*) Ballads, Romantic, Fantastical, and Humorous, illustrated by John Gilbert, *cloth*, 12mo. Lond. 1855

5218 ——— Another copy.

5219 Anthologie Françoise ou Chansons Choisies, depuis le XIII. Siècle jusqu' à présent, avec Les Chansons Joyeuses mises au Jour, with the music and engravings by Gravelot, 3 vols. small 8vo. *calf.* Paris, 1765

In the preface to the English Anthology by Ritson, it is said, the idea of that compilation originated from a sight of the elegant French Song Book, L'Anthologie Françoise.

5220 Beranger's Songs, with a sketch of his Life, 12mo. *cloth.* Lond. *Pickering,* 1837

5221 Bon Gaultier's Book of Ballads, 12mo. *cloth.* N. Y. 1852

5222 Book of British Ballads, edited by S. C. Hall, Esq., every page richly embellished with very highly-finished wood engravings, after designs by Creswick, Gilbert, Franklin, Corbould, &c., 2 vols. 8vo. *half mor.* Lond. 1844

5223 British Musical Miscellany, 6 vols. 8vo. *calf* Lond. n. d.

5224 BROME (*Alex.*) Songs and other Poems, *portrait*, 8vo. *calf.* Lond. 1668

5225 CHAMBERS (*Robert*), Popular Rhymes of Scotland, by, 12mo. *half mor.* Edin. 1826

5226 CHANSONS Populaires, Edition Illustrée, Patriotique, Satirique Romances, Rondes et Complaintes, 3 vols. imp. 8vo. *half mor.* Paris, 1848

5227 COOKE (*P. P.*) Froissart Ballads, 12mo. *boards.* Phil. 1847

5228 COSTELLO (*L. S.*) Specimens of the Early Poetry of France, from the time of the Troubadours and Trouveres to the reigne of Henri Quarte, *plates*, 8vo. *cloth.* Lond. *Pickering*, 1835

5229 DALRYMPLE (*A.*) Collection of English Songs, 8vo. *half mor.* Lond. 1796

5230 DIBDIN (*C.*) Mirth and Metre, 18mo. *sheep.* Lond. 1807

5231 DIBDIN (*Thos.*) Songs, Naval and National, with a Memoir and Addenda, illustrated by Cruikshank, 12mo. *cloth.* Lond. 1841

5232 DODD (*J. W.*) Ballads of Archery, Sonnets, &c. 12mo. *half calf.* Lond. 1818

5233 ——— Another copy, *half mor.* Lond. 1818

5234 DYER (*S.*) Songs and Ballads, 12mo. *cloth.* N. Y. 1857

5235 EVANS (*T.*) Old Ballads, Historical and Narrative, with some of modern date, now first collected and reprinted from rare copies and MSS., with notes and vignettes, *scarce*, 4 vols. 8vo. *half mor.* Lond. 1784

Sold in Sir M. M. Syke's sale for £2 7*s*.

5236 FRISKY Songster, a choice collection of Funny, Flash, and Love Songs, intended for Gentlemen's Parties only, 32mo. *cloth.* Lond.

5237 HARE's Book of British Songs, *plates*, folio. Lond, n. d.

5238 HUDSON (*Thos.*) Comic Songs, 8 parts, 12mo. Lond. 1824

5239 KING (*R. T.*) Selection from the early Ballad Poetry of England and Scotland, *half morocco*, 12mo. Lond. *Pickering*, 1842

5240 LINEN (*J.*) Songs of the Sea Shore, &c., 2 vols. N.Y.

5241 LONDON Singer's Magazine, 8vo. *boards.* Lond. n. d.

5242 LONDON Vocalist, an extensive and superior collection of Songs, *wood-cuts, half calf*, 12mo. Lond.

5243 McCARTY (*Wm.*) National Songs, Ballads and other Patriotic Poetry, chiefly relating to the War of 1812, 18mo. *boards*, pp. 144. Phil. 1846

5244 MINSTRELSY of the English Border, being a collection of Ballads and Border Legends, with illustrative notes by Sheldon, beautifully printed in the old style by Whittingham, square 8vo. *half morocco.* 1847

"Mr. Sheldon is a Border enthusiast; and he has done excellent and 'gentle' service to his favorite and most romantic districts. Some curious ancient ballads are for the first time collected. The book is quaintly but beautifully printed in proper ballad size; and the illustrative notes are full of information and interest."—*Examiner.*

5245 ——— Another copy, *cloth.* Lond. 1847

5246 MIRTH and Meter, 8 vols. *various.*

5247 MOTHERWELL (*Wm.*) Minstrelsy, Ancient and Modern, with an historical introduction and notes, *cloth*, 2 vols. 12mo. Boston, 1841

5248 NEWCASTLE Song Book, or Tyne Side Songster, Comic and Satirical Songs, in the Newcastle Dialect, 12mo. *plates, cloth.* Newcastle, 1842

5249 PARRY (*J. D.*) Legendary Cabinet, a collection of British National Ballads, Ancient and Modern, *half morocco*, 8vo. Lond. 1829

5250 POETRY of various Glees, Songs, &c., as performed by the Harmonists, 8vo. *calf.* Lond. 1798

5251 POLITICAL Ballads published in England during the Commonwealth, edited by T. Wright, *half morocco*, 12mo. Lond. 1841

5252 RIMBAULT (*G. F.*) A Little Book of Songs and Ballads, 8vo. *half morocco.* Lond. 1851

5253 RITSON (*J.*) Ancient Plays and Ballads, from the time of Henry III. to the Revolution, 2 vols. 8vo. *half mor.* Lond. 1829

"Ritson cannot be named without respect for his industry."—*Quarterly Review.*

5254 ——— Gammer Gurton's Garland, or the Nursery Parnassus, 12mo. *half calf.* Lond. 1810

5255 RODD (*Thomas*), Ancient Ballads, from the Civil Wars of Granada to the Twelve Peers of France, 12mo. *calf.* Lond. 1803

5256 ROXBURGHE Ballads, edited by John Payne Collier, post 4to. beautifully printed by Whittingham, and embellished with 50 *curious woodcuts, half bd. mor.* 1847

Nearly all the ballads contained in this very interesting collection are unique. They are printed from the extraordinary collection which belonged successively to the Duke of Roxburghe and Mr. Bright. At the sale of Mr. Bright's library, in 1845, they produced £535.

5257 SONGS and Carols, printed from a manuscript in the British Museum, edited by T. Wright, **Black Letter**, *half mor.* sqr. 12mo. Lond. *Pickering*, 1836

2258 ——— Another copy. Lond. 1836

5259 SONGS of Home and Happiness, 24mo. Lond. 1851

5260 SONGS for the Nursery, *woodcuts*, *cl.* sqr. 12mo. Glasg. 1847

5261 SONGS, Odes, and other Poems, on National Subjects, part 3, Military, *cl.* 12mo. Phil. 1842

5262 SONGS set to Music, a volume containing songs to the Opera of Arsinoe, Camilla, Thomyris, Temple of Love, Rosamond, Love's Triumph, in 1 vol. *old calf*, *very rare*, folio. Lond. *T. Walsh*, 1700

5263 SONG Books, various, a parcel of, 12mo.

5264 SONGS, a collection of, no title.

5265 STEVENS (*G. A.*) Lectures and Songs, 12mo. *half calf.* Lond. 1788

5266 TERPSICHORINA, or the Companion to the Opera, 18mo. 3 numbers. N. Y. 1828

5267 TURNAMENT of Totenham and the Feest, two early Ballads, printed from a manuscript preserved in the Public Library of the University of Cambridge, edited by T. Wright, **Black Letter**, *half mor.* sqr. 12mo. Lond. *Pickering*, 1836

5268 UNIVERSAL Songster, or Museum of Mirth, forming the most Complete, Extensive, and Valuable Collection of Ancient and Modern Songs in the English language, containing upwards of 5000 Songs, ancient and modern, *numerous comic illustrations by Cruikshank*, 3 vols. in 1, 8vo. *old calf.* Lond. 1825

5269 WAYS to Kill Care, a collection of original Songs, chiefly comic, by Young D'Urfey, *portrait*, *sheep*, *scarce*, 12mo. Lond. 1761

5270 WHIMS of the Day, an entertaining selection of the choicest Songs, 4 vols. 12mo. *calf, rare.* Lond. 1790

5271 WHISTLE Binkie, 24mo. *cl.* 1846

SPAIN AND PORTUGAL.

5272 DE ROCCA (*M.*) War of the French in Spain, 8vo. *boards.* 1823

5273 PRESCOTT (*W. H.*) Ferdinand and Isabella, 3 vols. 8vo. *cloth.* Bost. 1838

5274 ROBERTSON (*W.*) History of Charles V., 4 vols. 18mo. Montrose, 1818

5275 SARRAZIN (*Geo.*) History of the War in Spain and Portugal, 8vo. *calf.* Lond. 1815

5276 TURGUET (*L. de M.*) Generall Historie of Spaine, folio, *calf*, Southey's copy. 1612

5277 TWISS (*Richd.*) Travels through Portugal and Spain, *map and plates, including the Madonna and Child, by Bartolozzi, fine impressions,* 4to. Lond. 1775

5278 WATSON (*Rob.*) History of the Reign of Phillip II., 3 vols. 8vo., *calf.* 1779

SPORTS, GAMES, PASTIMES, &c.

5278*a* ARRIAN on Coursing, the Cynegeticus of the Younger Xenophon, translated with Classical and Practical Annotations, Appendix containing some account of the Caves Venatici of Classical Antiquity, 4to. *cloth.* Lond. 1831

5278*b* BERENGER (*St. Col. Baron de*), Helps and Hints how to Protect Life and Property, with instructions on Rifle and Pistol shooting, 8vo. *cl., plates.* Lond. 1835

5278*c* BLOME (*Richard*), Gentleman's Recreation in Arts and Sciences, Horsemanship, Hunting, Hawking, Fowling, &c., *plates, half calf,* dirty title and slightly damaged, folio. Lond. 1686

5278*d* ——— Gentleman's Recreations Abridged, 8vo. *old calf.* Lond. 1697

5278*e* BOOK of Sports, reprint of the Book of Sports allowable by Elizabeth, James I., and Charles (lawful to be played on Sunday before the Puritanic days of Cromwell) *long MS. note, sewed* 4to. Lond. 1817

5278*f* COMPLEAT Gamester; or how to Play at Billiards, Trucks, Bowls, and Chess, with the Arts and Mysteries of Riding, Racing, Archery, and Cock Fighting, 16mo. *sheep.* Lond. 1676

5279 CRACKS of the Day, edited by Wildrake, *portraits of 65 celebrated race horses,* from 1831 to 1840, *finely engraved, cl.,* royal 8vo. Lond. *circa* 1840

5280 ELLIOTT (*Wm.*) Carolina Sports, by Land and Water, 12mo. *cl.* Charleston, 1846

5281 FIELD Book (*The*), or Sports and Pastimes of the British Islanders, 8vo. *wants title.* Lond. 1833

5282 HOYLE'S Rules for Playing Fashionable Games, 18mo. *sheep.* N. Y. 1830

5283 Fouilloux (*Jacques du Jean de Franchieres et autres*) Venerie et Faucounerie, *many wood cuts, green mor., extra gilt top*, 4to. Paris, 1585

* This work is highly esteemed in France for its quaintness and simplicity of style, its author may be styled the Nimrod of France. This is the first edition with the Music or Calls of the Chase. Brunet quotes it at 80 fr.

5284 Johnson (*T. B.*) The Shooter's Companion, 12mo. *cloth.* Lond. 1834

5285 Krider's Sporting Anecdotes Illustrating the Habits of American Game, 8vo. *cloth.* Phil. 1853

5286 Lawrence (*John*), The Horse in all his Varieties and Uses, 12mo. *sheep.* Phil. 1830

5287 Lloyd (*L.*) Field Sports of the North of Europe, 2 vols. *half russia.* Lond. 1831

5288 Ludus Schacchiæ, Chesse-play, a game, both pleasant, wittie, and politicke; with certain briefe instructions thereunto belonging: translated out of the Italian into the English tongue; containing also therein, a pretty and pleasant poem of a whole game played at Chesse, written by G. B., 4to. *half morocco.* Lond. 1597

(Reprint Lond. 1810.) Large paper, only 25 printed.

5289 Maxwell (*W. H.*) Wild Sports of the West, with Legendary Tales, and Local Sketches, 2 vols. 12mo. *cloth.* N. Y. 1833

5290 Natural History, The Cabinet of American Rural Sports, with colored illustrations by Doughty, 2 vols. *half roan*, 4to. *very scarce.* Phil. 1830

5291 New Sporting Magazine from 1831 to 1837, 12 vols. 8vo. *half calf.* Lond. v. y.

5292 Piscatorial Reminiscences and Gleanings, by an old Angler and Bibliopolist, 12mo. *cloth.* Lond. 1835

5293 Radcliffe's Noble Science (Foxhunting) for the Use of the Rising Generation of Sportsmen, royal 8vo., beautiful woodcuts of Hunting, Hounds, &c., *cloth.* Lond. 1839

5294 Salter (*T. F.*) The Angler's Guide, with 88 fine cuts, 8vo. *cloth.* Lond. 1833

5296 Stud Book, containing Pedigrees of English Race Horses, 3 vols. in 1, *sheep.* 1834

5297 Venables (*Col. Robert*), The Experienced Angler, 20 *beautiful cuts on India paper*, 8vo. *half russia.* Lond. 1827

THEATRES—*See also* COSTUME.

5298 ARTAUD (*F.*) Description d'une Mosaique representant des Jeux du Cirque, folio. Lyon. 1806

5299 BRAYLEY (*E. W.*) Historical and Descriptive Accounts of the Theatres of London, *views of the theatres by Havell, colored*, 4to. Lond. 1826

5300 BURGESS (*Rev. R.*) Description of the Circus in the Via Appia near Rome, 12mo. *half calf.* Lond. 1828

5301 DESIGN for a New Theatre, Piazza, Tavern Houses, Buildings, and Streets, in Russell Street—Proposal of Richard Brinsley Sheridan and Thomas Linley, Esq., for rebuilding. MS. on a large roll, with the autographs of many of the Proprietors, including Sheridan, Holland, the Architect J. P. Kemble, George Grote, John Banister, Lancelot Shadwell, and other celebrated men connected with the Theatre.

5302 DUMONT (*Le Sieur*), Parallele de Plans des Plus Belles Salles de Spectacles d'Italie et de France, avec des details de Machines Theatrales, 64 plates, 12mo. *half calf.* 1774

5303 FONTANI (*Carlo*), L'Amfiteatro Flavio descritto e delineato, *with* 24 *fine engravings*, folio, *calf.* 1728

5304 ITALIAN Theatres, Descrizione del nuovo Siparo dell' Teatro alla Scala, Milan, 1821, *plate;* Morelli Teatro d'Imola, Imola, 1793; Projetto per il nuovo Teatro da Fabbricarsi in Venezia, 1790, in 1 vol. folio, *several plates.* v. y.

5305 KUSSEL (*Melchior*), Theatralische Vorstellingen, 36 beautiful etchings of Theatrical Scenery, equal to Callot, oblong folio.

5306 LOUIS (*M.*) Salle de Spectacle de Bordeaux, 22 *plates*, folio, *half calf.* Paris, 1782

5307 MAFFEI (*Marquis S.*) Compleat History of the Ancient Amphitheatres, particularly that of Verona, *adorned with sculptures*, 8vo. *half calf.* Lond. n. d.

5308 REMARKS on Theatres, and on the Propriety of Vaulting them with Brick and Stone, with Observation on the Construction of Domes and the Vaults of the Free and Accepted Masons, royal 8vo. *half calf.* Lond. 1809

5309 RICCABONI (*L.*) Historical and Critical Account of the Theatres in Europe, 8vo. Lond. 1741

5310 SANQUIRICO: A collection of Italian Aquatint Engravings of Drop Scenes, Tableaux, &c., oblong folio. 1823

5311 SAUNDERS (*G.*) A Treatise on Theatres, 4to. *half calf.* Lond. 1790

5312 ——— Another copy, 4to. *boards.* Lond. 1790

5313 STEPHENSON'S Patent Theatre Machinery, 10 *plates*, folio, *half calf.* n. d.

5314 THEATRUM Illustrata: Theatres of London at the time of Shakspeare, at some of which Shakspeare acted and was Manager, forming part of the celebrated publication, by Wilkinson, called Londina Illustrata, impl. 4to. Lond. 1825

5314*WYATT (*B.*) Observations on the Design for the Theatre Royal, Drury Lane, 18 *plates*, *half calf*, 4to. Lond. 1813

THEATRICAL AND DRAMATIC CRITICISM.—*See also* HISTORY OF THE STAGE.

5315 ALGAROTTI (*Count*), An Essay on the Operas, translated from the Italian. Glasgow, 1768

5316 ACTED and Unacted Drama, Hypercriticism Exposed, 1812; Beauties of Mrs. Siddons, 1786, &c. 5 Tracts, 8vo. Lond.

5317 BAKER (*Sir R.*) Theatrum Triumphans, or a Discourse of Plays, 18mo. *calf.* Lond. 1670

5318 BARRETT (*Rev. B.*) Pretensions to a Final Analysis of the Nature and Origin of Sublimity, Style, Beauty, Genius, and Taste, with an Appendix Explaining the Causes of the Pleasure which is derived from Tragedy, 8vo. *half calf.* Lond. 1812

5319 BETTY (*H. West, The young Roscius*), Three Tracts on, 8vo. v. d.

5320 BROWN (*John*), Letters upon the Poetry and Music of the Italian Opera, 18mo. *half calf.* Edin. 1789

5321 BYSTANDER (*The*), or Universal Weekly Expositor, by a Literary Association, 4to. *half calf.* Lond. 1790

5322 CIBBER, Egotist, or Colley upon Cibber, being his own picture retouched to so plain a likeness that no one now would have the face to own it but himself, 8vo. Lond. 1743

5323 COOKE (*W.*) Elements of Dramatic Criticism, with instructions for succeeding in the art of Acting, 12mo. *half calf.* Lond. 1775

5324 COMIC Natural History of the Human Race, 8vo. *half mor.* Phil. n. d.

This is a selection of the "Theatrical Genus," including Burton, Barnum, &c.

5324* ——— Various numbers of the same.

5325 COVENT Garden Journal, 2 vols. *plates, large paper, half calf.* Lond. 1810

5326 DAVIES (*T.*) Dramatic Miscellanies; consisting of critical observations on several plays of Shakespeare, with a review of his principal characters, and those of various eminent writers, as represented by Mr. Garrick and other celebrated comedians, &c. *uncut*, 3 vols. 8vo. *half calf.* Lond. 1784

5327 DIBDIN (*C.*) The Devil, a Review and Investigation of all Subjects whatever, vol. 1 (all pub.?) 8vo. *half calf.* Lond. 1786

"These papers are said to have been written by old Charles Dibdin; the early ones made a great noise, and were eagerly sought after by the town, but the remainder were quite neglected. A collection of them is now very scarce."—*J. Hotten.*

5328 DOWNES, Roscius Anglicanus, or an Historical Review of the Stage, with additions by Thos. Davies, 8vo. *half calf.* Lond. 1789

5329 Drama, The Article "Drama," from the Encyclopedia Britannica, written by Sir W. Scott, 4to. *half mor.* 1819

5330 DRAMA (*The*), or Theatrical Pocket Magazine, containing Biog., Essays, Criticisms, Poetry, Reviews, Anecdotes, Bon Mots, Chit Chat, &c., 7 vols. 18mo. *half calf.* Lond. 1821–25

5331 DRAMATIC Apellant, vol. 1, 8vo. *half calf*, also nine Plays. Lond. 1808

5332 DRAMATIC Censor, or Critical Companion, 2 vols. 18mo. *half calf.* Lond. 1770

5333 DRAMATIC Literature, Report of the Select Committee on, *half calf*, folio. Lond. 1832

5334 DRAMATIC Magazine with Plates, 2 vols. 8vo. Lond. 1829–30

5335 DRAMATIC Register for 1851 and 1852, in one vol., *half calf*, 12mo. Lond. n. y.

5336 DUTTON'S Dramatic Censor, 1 vol. 8vo. *bds.* Lond. 1800

5337 EVREMONT (*St.*) Mix't Essays upon Tragedies, Comedies, Italian Comedies, English Comedies, and Operas, 4to. *half calf.* Lond. 1687

5338 FRANKLYN (*Th.*) Dissertations on Ancient Tragedy, 1768

5339 GARDINER (*John*) on the Theatre, 8vo. Bost. 1792

5340 GILDON (*C.*) Comparison between the Two Stages, 8vo. Lond. 1702

5341 HAZLITT (*W.*), Lectures on Dramatic Literature, 8vo. Lond. 1821

5342 ——— Lectures on the English Poets, *half calf*, 8vo. Lond. 1818

5343 HOLCROFT (*Thos.*), The Theatrical Recorder, 2 vols. 8vo. *calf.* Lond. 1805

5344 HUNT (*Leigh*), Critical Essays on the Performers of the London Theatres, with Autograph of Baron Field, *calf*, 12mo. Lond. 1807

5345 JONSON (*B.*), Remarks on Three Plays of, by John Upton, 8vo. *half calf.* Lond. 1749

5346 LANGBAINE (*Gerard*), Momus Triumphans, or the Plagiaries of the English Stage exposed, *frontispiece of the Dukes Theatre, Lincoln's Inn Fields, very rare.* Lond. 1658

5346* LAW'S, Absolute Unlawfulness of the Stage Entertainments, *sewed*, 12mo. Lond. 1726

5347 LETTER of Compliment to the Ingenious Author of a Treatise on the Passions, so far as they regard the Stage, 12mo. *sewed.* Lond.

5348 LETTERS on the Drama, 8vo. *half calf.* Lond. 1796

5349 LETTERS on the Drama, 1796; Penn's (J.) Battle of Eddington, and Critical and Poetical Works, Poetical Miscellanies, Calsabigi's Letter to Alfieri on Tragedy, translated, 4 vols. in 1, 8vo. *half calf.* 1797, &c.

5350 MACKLIN—A Scotsman's Remarks on the Farce of Love a la Mode, 1760; Apology for the Conduct of Mr. Macklin, 1773, 2 tracts in 1 vol. 8vo. *half calf.* Lond. v. d.

5352 McDERMOT (*M.*) Philosophical Enquiries into the Source of the Pleasures derived from Tragic representations, 8vo. *half calf.* Lond. 1824

5353 MIRROR of Taste and Dramatic Censor, 4 vols. royal 8vo. *half calf.* Phil. 1810-11

5354 MONTHLY Mirror (*The*), Reflecting Men and Manners, with strictures on their epitome, THE STAGE, *numerous fine plates and portraits*, 30 vols. 8vo. *half calf.* Lond. 1795-1810

5355 ——— Another set, 28 vols. odd. v. d.

5456 MUNDUS Dramaticus (*The New Rosciad*), a Satire. Lond. 1852

5357 PHILLIPS (*E.*) Theatrum Poetarum Anglicanorum, containing the Names and Characters of all the English Poets from Henry III. to Q. Elizabeth, edited by Sir Egerton Brydges, 8vo. *half calf.* Canterbury, 1800

5358 PIZARRO, a Critique on the Tragedy of, *calf*, 8vo. pp. 40. 1795

5359 PLUMTRE (*J.*) Four Discourses on the Subjects Relating to the Amusements of the Stage, *half calf*, 8vo. Camb. 1809

5360 PROMPTER (*The*), A Weekly Miscellany, devoted to Public Amusement, edited by C. Mathews. The Prompter's Whistle includes a Memoir of W. E. Burton, 12mo. *half calf.* N. Y. 1850

5361 RAMBLE (*A*) Among the Musicians of Germany, giving some account of the Operas of Munich, Dresden, Berlin, &c., 8vo. *half calf.* Lond. 1828

5362 RAMBLER'S Magazine and New York Theatrical Register for 1809–10. N. Y. 1810

5363 REVUE Générale des Theatres de Londres et de Paris, 8vo. *half calf.* Lond. 1819

5364 RYMER (*T.*) Short View of Tragedy, with some reflections on Shakespeare, *half calf*, 8vo. Lond. 1693

5365 ROWE (*N.*) Remarks on the Tragedy of Lady Jane Grey, and five others, 6 Tracts, 8vo. Lond. v. d.

5366 SCHLEGEL, Lectures on Dramatic Art, translated by Black, 2 vols. 18mo. *half calf.* Lond. 1840

5367 STAGE (*The*), A Weekly Magazine of Generalities, pts. 1 to 14, in 1 vol. impl. 8vo. *half calf.* Lond. 1849

5368 STYLES (*John*), Essay, or the Character and Influence of the Stage on Morals and Happiness, *half calf*, 12mo. Lond. 1807

5369 TALLIS' Dramatic Magazine, 13 parts, royal 8vo. v. d.

5370 THEATRICAL Guardian, 4to *half cl.* Lond. 1791

5371 THEATRE (*The*), Or the Letters of Candidus on the Performance of the Edinburgh Stage in 1802, 18mo. *half calf.* Edinb. 1802

5372 THEATRICAL CENSOR (*The*), by an American, 12mo. *half calf.* Phil. 1805–6

5373 THEATRICAL Censor and Critical Miscellany, 8vo. *half calf.* Phil. 1806–7

5374 THEATRICAL Inquisitor, or Literary Mirror, 15 vols. 8vo. *half calf.* Lond. 1812–20

5375 THEATRICAL Journal and Musical Intelligencer, 9 vols. 8vo. *half calf.* 1839–48

5376 THEATRICAL Observer, 3 vols. 18mo. *half calf.* Dublin, 1821

5377 THEATRICAL Repertory, containing Criticisms on the Performances which were represented at Drury Lane and Covent Garden in 1801–2, 8vo. *half calf.* Lond. 1802

5378 THESPIAN Magazine and Literary Repository, *fine portraits by Condé,* 3 vols. 8vo. Lond. 1793

5379 THESPIAN Mirror, 13 numbers, with cutting from a Newspaper (The Post), stating the Editor was a boy 13 years of age, &c., *half calf,* 8vo. N. Y. 1806

5380 TIMOLEON, Remarks on the Tragedy of, wherein the Beauties and Errors are impartially considered, 8vo. pp. 28. [1697]

5381 VOLTAIRE (*M. de*), Critical History of Dramatic Poetry, 12mo. Lond. 1761

5382 WALDRON (*F. G.*) Candid and Impartial Strictures on the Performers belonging to Drury Lane and Covent Garden, 8vo. Lond. 1795

WALKER'S Italian Tragedy, *vide* Lot 3185.

5384 WEEKLY Amusement, from Dec. 1763—1765, *half calf,* 3 vols. 8vo. Lond. v. y.

5385 WHYTE (*S.*) Collection of Poems on Various Subjects, including the Theatre, a Didactic Essay, *plates,* 12mo. *half calf.* Dublin, 1792

THEOLOGY—BIBLES AND BIBLE PLATES.

5386 ALISON'S Sermons, 2 vols. 8vo., *boards.* Edin. 1815

5387 APOCRYPHAL New Testament, 12mo. *shp.* Bost. 1832

5388 ARMENIAN Prayers, a Book of, rubricated

5389 ART of Contentment, by the author of The Whole Duty of Man, 12mo. *calf.* Oxford, 1675

5390 ASGILL'S Argument on Eternal Life in Scripture, 12mo. *sheep.* Lond. 1700

5391 BATH-KOL, a Voice from the Wilderness, being an Humble Effort to Support the Sinking Truths of God against some of the principal Errors raging at this time, etc., 12mo. *sheep.* Bost. 1783

5392 BEDE (*The Venerable*), Ecclesiastical History of the English Nation from the coming of Julius Cesar till 731, 8vo. *calf.* Lond. 1723

5393 BELLARMIN (*Cardinal*), The Peace of Rome, 8vo. Lond. 1838

5394 BENTHAM (*Edvardi*), De Vita et Moribus Joh. Burtoni, 8vo. *sheep.* Oxon. 1771

5395 BIBLIA. Biblia Hebraica eorumdum Latina interpretatio Xantis Pagnini, recentur B. A. Montani, Novum Testamentum Græcum, in 1 vol. *thick oak and hogskin binding, stamped, curious brass corners and clasps*, fol. Antv. Plantin, 1584

5396 BIBLIA Latini, 8vo. **Black Letter**, in double columns, *wood cut initial heads, fine copy, hogskin.* Lugd. (1514)

5397 BIBLE in English, Genevan Version, wants title, *old calf*, 4to. **Black Letter.** n. d.

This is better known as the Breeches Bible.

5398 BIBLE, Holy Bible, containing the Old and New Testaments and the Apocrypha, embellished with engravings by eminent artists, from the designs of the most celebrated masters, ancient and modern, 6 vols. 4to. *red morocco*, 300 *splendid plates, fine copy.* Lond. 1815

5399 BIBLE, Devotional Family Bible, by A. Fletcher, *beautifully illustrated, imperial folio, in* 100 *Numbers complete.* Lond. n. y.

5400 BIBLE, The Holy Bible, in Irish and printed in Irish characters. Translated by Bp. Bedel, 12mo. Lond. 1830

5401 BIBLE PLATES, Sewel (A.) Historie des Olden en Newen Testaments, *beautiful plates*, folio, *calf.* 1722

5403 ——— Neue Künstliche Figuren Biblisher Historien, Gruntlich von Tobia Stimmer Gerissen, *one hundred and seventy-four woodcuts in woodcut borders*, by J. F. G. M., *fine impression, old calf, very rare*, 4to. Basel, 1576

5404 ——— Historiæ Sacræ Veteris et Novi Testamenta, Figures of the Bible in which almost every history of the Holy Scriptures is described, explanations in verse in five languages, Dutch, Latin, German, French, and English, engraved by Matthew Merian, Nicholas Visscher, etc., 2 vols. in 1, *calf, binding broken*, folio. Amst.

5405 ——— Sacred Histories of the Old and New Testament represented by very artificial figures, beautiful plates, with descriptions in English, Dutch, German, French, and Latin, folio. Amst. n. d.

5406 ——— Royaumont (*Sieur de*), History of the Old and New Testament, edited by Dr. Horneck, 260 Historical Sculptures, *old red morocco*, folio. Lond. 1705

5407 Bible Plates, Luykens, Prints to the Old and New Testament, 337 figures, 2 vols. *vellum*, 4to. Amst. 1712

Luykens' are undoubtedly the most picturesque and effective of all the Old Scripture prints.

5408 ——, Saurin Discours Historiques, Critiques, Theologiques, et Moraux sur les evenemens les plus memorables du Vieux et du Nouveau Testament, numerous beautiful prints by Hoet, Houbraken, and Picart, 6 vols. *large paper, rich old calf*, folio. Amst. 1720

5409 ——, Figures du Nouveau Testament, ou sont representées la Vie et les Actions les plus remarquables de Notre Seigneur Jesus Christ, depuis son incarnation jusqu'à sa glorieuse ascension, woodcuts, folio. Paris, 1724

5410 ——, Illustrations to the Bible by Basnage and Alewyns, numerous fine plates, folio. Amst. 1721

5411 ——, A large collection of Prints to illustrate the Old and New Testament, about 260 plates, large folio.

5412 ——, Fine Engravings to Illustrate the Bible after de Vos, by J. Wiercx, folio.

5412* ——, Franklin's Bible Cartoons illustrative of Scripture History, 16 plates, *cloth*, oblong 4to. N. Y.

5413 Bible Illustrations by Westall, Martin, &c., a series of exquisite woodcuts with descriptive letter press, 8vo. *morocco*. Lond, n. d.

5414 ——, La Trobe (*I. A.*) Scripture Illustrations, being a series of engravings on steel and wood, illustrative of the Geography and Topography of the Bible, 4to. *half morocco*. Lond. 1838

5415 ——, Illuminated Illustrations of the Bible, a series of fac-similes of ancient MSS. beautifully reproduced in gold and colors, royal 8vo., in 12 parts. Lond. 1846

5416 Biblia, Critica Biblica, or a Depository of Sacred Literature, 8vo. *calf*. Lond. 1824

5417 Brown's Concordance and other books, 4 vols. 12mo. v. d.

5418 Blakey (*R.*) Lives of the Primitive Fathers of the Christian Church, 8vo. *cloth*. Lond. 1842

5419 Boetius De Consolatione Philosophiæ, Rendorp copy, Black Letter, folio, *calf*, fine copy. Basilæ, 1570

5420 Bott (*Thos.*) Answer to Warburton's Divine Legation of Moses, 8vo. *calf*. Lond. 1743

5421 Brothers (*Richard*), The World's Dawn, or the Cabinet of Fate Unlocked, containing all the Ancient and Modern Prophesies, dedicated to William Wilberforce, Esq., portraits, vol 1, 8vo. *bds.* Lond. 1795

5422 Bruni (*Conradi*), De Hœreticis in genere, folio, *rough calf.* Mogunt, 1849

5423 Bryant (*Jacob*), Observations, &c., 4 vols. 4to. Eton, 1795

5424 Burder (*Wm.*) Religious Ceremonies, or the Forms of Worship, 8vo. *cl.* Lond. 1841

5425 Burges (*Cornelius*), A Sermon Preached to Parliament at the Fast, Nov. 17, 1640, small 4to. *vellum.* Lond. 1641

5426 Burnet (*B.*) History of the Reformation, 2 vols. folio. Lond. 1715

5427 Burton (*Rev. Charles*), Discourses on the Times, 8vo. *cl.* Lond. 1832

5428 Caunter (*Robt.*) Posthumous Records of a London Clergyman, 12mo. *cl.* Lond. 1835

5429 Caxton—A Lityll Treatise, shorte and abridged, spekynge of the arte and crafte to knowe well to dye, by Jhon Gerson; printed by William Caxton, 1480; reprinted in fac-simile from the original edition in the British Museum, in small folio. Lond. n. d.

An exact fac-simile of the singular Black-Letter Types of the Father of English Printing, so admirably executed as to have deceived several old Book Collectors.—To increase the attraction of this volume, it has been done up in a Vellum Cover, on which is a fac-simile of the "In Sponsalibus," or Marriage Service of the old Salisbury Missal, including the quaint old English forms (with the words *Boner* and *Buxsom*) printed in red and black letter; also, the large wood-cut of the Crucifixion, from the Canon of the Masse, so rare, from the general destruction at the Reformation; copied from the Mascall's almost unique copy of the first edition by Wynken De Worde.

5430 Chauveau (*F.*) Fifty-six Plates to illustrate the Bible Lucan, &c., 8vo. Par.

5431 Christian Keepsake for 1849, 8vo. *half mor.* Phil. 1849

5432 Chubbe (*Rev. John*), Miscellaneous Tracts of, Rector of Whatfield, 2 vols. 18mo. *calf.* Ipswich.

5433 Clement XI—Present State of the Court of Rome, or Lives of the Present Pope and College of Cardinals, 8vo. *calf.* Lond. 1706

5434 Clerk (*B.*) De Curiali sive Antico, etc., 12mo. *calf.* Comt. 1713

5435 CLISSOLD (*Rev. Aug.*) Practical Nature of the Doctrines of Emanuel Swedenborg, 12mo. *cloth.* Bost. 1839

5436 COBBETT (*Wm.*) Thirteen Sermons by, 16mo. *cloth.* N. Y. 1834

5437 COIT (*T. W.*) Puritanism, or a Churchman's Defence against its Aspersions, 8vo. *cl.* N. Y. 1845

5438 COGITANS (*John*), The Spiritual Mustard-Pot, and an Essay on the Origin of Religion, 12mo. *bds.* Troy, 1824

5439 COLLIER (*Jeremy*), The Emperor Marcus Antonius His Conversation with Himself, 8vo. *half calf.* Lond. 1708

5440 COUSTOS (*John*), The Mysteries of Popery Unveiled, by Anthony Gavin, 12mo. *sheep.* Enfield, 1821

5441 CROSS (*Marcus C.*) Museum of Religious Knowledge, 12mo. *cloth.* Phil. 1839

5442 CUSTOS (*Henrici*), Expositio super Oratione Dominica, et super Salutatione Angelica et super formulam Fidei Apostolica, written at Campen, 1415, large 4to. *calf, neat.* n. d.

5443 DEMOUSTIER (*C. A.*) Lettres a Emile sur la Mythologie, 6 vols. *old french calf,* 18mo. Paris, 1816

5444 DUNCAN (*Jon.*) The Religions of Profane Antiquity, 12mo. *cloth.* Lond.

5445 ECCE HOMO ! or a Critical Enquiry into the History of Jesus Christ, being a rational Analysis of the Gospel, 8vo. *boards.* Lond. 1813

5446 EUSEBII: Evsibii Cætariensis Episcopi Chronicon id est Temporvm Breviarvm incipit Fœliciter: Qvem Hieronymvs, etc., **Black Letter,** very rare, fine, large, clean copy, printed in red and black, from the Library of Robert Chambers, with his book-plate, 4to. *half calf.* Venetiis, MCCCCLXXXIII

5447 EVANS (*John*), Sketches of all Denominations of Religion, 12mo. *sheep.* Burlington, 1812

5448 EVENING Hours with my Children, or Conversations on the Gospel Story, 4to. *cloth.* N. Y. 1855

5450 FELLTHAM (*Owen*), Resolves, Divine, Morall and Politicall, 4to. *calf, engraved title.* Lond. 1647

5451 FINATI (*Giovanni*), Narrative of the Life and Adventures of, edited by Barker, 2 vols. 12mo. *half calf.* 1830

The author assumed the name of Mahomet, and made campaigns against the Wahabens for the recovery of Mecca.

5452 Forty Questions concerning the Soul, proposed by Dr. Walter, and answered by Jacob Behmen, 4to. *half calf.* n. d.

5453 Fox (*John*), Book of Martyrs, edited by John Cummings, 3 vols. royal 8vo. *cloth.* Lond. 1845

"The Book of Martyrs was, and yet is, one of the most extraordinary and popular Church histories in the world."—*Dibdin.*

5454 Gentleman's Religion, in 3 parts, Natural, Doctrinal, and Practical, 16mo. *vellum.* Dublin, 1730

5455 Guevara, The Diall of Princes, compiled by the Reuerende Father in God, Don Anthony, of Guevara Byshop of Guadix, Preacher and Chronicler to Charles the Fyst, Emperour of Rome, Englysshed oute of the Frenche, by Thomas North, seconde Sonne of the Lorde Northe, Ryght necessary and pleasant to all Gentylmen, and others whiche are louers of Vertue, **Black Letter**, *very rare, fine copy, in the original wooden boards, covered with calf stamped binding*, folio. *John Waylande*, Lond. 1557

*** With the Singular Dedication "To the Mooste hyghe and vertuouse Princesse Mary, &c."

5456 Hales (*Mr. John*), Golden Remains of the Ever-memorable, with his Letters from the Synod of Dort, 8vo. *calf.* Lond. 1688

5457 Harcourt (*L. Vernon*), The Doctrine of the Deluge, 2 vols. 8vo. *cloth.* Lond. 1838

5458 Harrington (*Sir James*), Horæ Consecratæ, or Spiritual Pastime, with the rare Portrait by Faithorne, small folio, *calf.* Lond. 1682

5459 Harris (*T. S.*) Arcana of Christianity, vol. 1, part 1, 8vo. *cloth.* N. Y. 1858

5460 Howitt (*Wm.*) Popular History of Priestcraft, 12mo. *boards.* Lond. 1834

5461 Hrosuite (*seu Hrosvithæ*), Illustris Virginis et moniarlis Germanæ Saxonica orte (Opera) nuper a Conrado Celte inventa, folio. Norimb. 1501

This rare volume is described by Brunet who says it sold for £4 16*s*. at Hibbert's sale.

5462 Innes (*John*), On the Miracles, 24mo. Lond. 1815

5463 Inquisition of Spain, the History of to the Reign of Ferd. VII., *half mor.* Phil. 1847

5464 Inquisition (*Spanish*), Records of Trans. from Original MSS. *nt. half mor.* 8vo. Bost. 1828

5465 Inquisition—Mysteries of the Inquisition in Spain, with Historical Notes by Fereal, *half mor.* 8vo. Phil. 1845

5466 Jenkyn (*Wm.*) A Sleeping Sickness a Distemper of the Times, small 4to. *calf.* Lond. 1847

5467 Jesuits, Instructive and Curious Epistles from, 12mo. *cloth.* Dublin, 1839

5468 Josephus, Translated by Whiston, royal 8vo. *cloth, plates.* Lond. n. d.

5468*a* Jesuit's Morals, Practices of, demonstrated by many remarkable histories of their actions, translated from the French by John Evelyn, folio, *calf.* Lond. 1670

5468*b* Keble (*Rev. T.*) Christian Year, 16mo. *cloth.* Phil. 1840

5469 Keith (*Rev. Alex.*) Evidence of Prophecy, 12mo. *cloth.* N. Y. 1832

5470 Kenrick (*Francis P.*) A Treatise on Baptism, 12mo. *cloth.* Balt. 1852

5471 Knapp (*L.*) Secret Discipline mentioned in Ancient Ecclesiastical History explained by Theodore Temple, 12mo. N. Y. 1833

5472 Koran (*The*), Translated from the original Arabic, with Explanatory Notes and a Preliminary Discourse by George Sale, 8vo. *calf.* Lond. 1844

"The Koran contains the most sublime poetical passages, far surpassing European poetry."—*Byron.*

5473 Leland (*Rev. Dr.*) View of Deistical Writers of England, in last and present century, 8vo. *cloth.* Lond. 1837

5474 L'Estrange (*Roger*), Interest Mistaken, or the Holy Cheat—against the Presbyterians—12mo. *half calf.* Lond. 1661

5475 Lewis (*John*), Ignis Cælestris, or an Interchange of Divine Love betweene God and the Saints, 1620; Perkins (W.) Foundation of Christian Religion, &c., 1651; Rules and Directions regarding the Lord's Supper, 1655, and other curious Tracts, in 1 vol. 18mo. Lond. v. y.

5476 Life of Jesus Christ, including his Apocryphal History, from the Spurious Gospels, unpublished MSS., 8vo. *bds.* Lond. 1818

5477 McIlvaine's Evidences of Christianity, 12mo. Phil. 1857

5478 Mahomet, Prideaux's, True Nature of Imposture Exhibited, in the Life of Mahomet, 8vo. *old calf.* Lond. 1716

5479 Mahometism fully Explained, translated by Mr. Morgan, 8vo. Lond. 1723

5480 Michelet, Spiritual Direction and Auricular Confession, 12mo. *cloth.* Phil. 1845

5481 Missionary Herald, 15 Nos., 8vo. N. Y. v. d.

5482 Moberly (*Geo.*) Sayings of the Great Forty Days, 12mo. *cloth.* Phil. 1850

5483 Munter (*Dr.*) Conversion and Death of Count Struensee. Lond. 1826

5484 Nash (*Thos.*) Christ's Tears over Jerusalem, whereunto is annexed a Comparative Admonition to London, 4to. *boards.* Lond. 1815

5485 New Testament in Dutch, Psalms set to music, 24mo. n. d.

5486 Nonius Marcellus, Peripateticus Tiburiensis, Doctrinade proprietate sermonorum, etc. Extremely rare. From the Harleian Library. The Capitals rubricated, and a Bishop's Arms painted in the margin. Very fine, large, clean copy. *Morocco extra, broad borders of gold, gilt edges,* folio. Venetius, *N. Jansen,* MCCCCLXXVI

*** Sir Mark Sykes' copy sold for £6 15*s*.

5487 O. (*J.*) A Present for Teeming Women, 18mo. *old calf,* wants title.

5488 Paley (*Wm.*) Natural Theology, 8vo. *bds.* Lond. 1809

5489 Palingenesia, or the World to Come, 8vo. 1824

5490 Pamphlets Relating to the Church of England, small 4to. (autograph of G. Furman.) Lond. v. d.

5491 Partridge (*M.*) Nunneries as they are, 12mo. *cloth.* N. Y. 1839

5492 Pyrerius, Men before Adam, or a Discourse upon the twelfth, thirteenth, and fourteenth verses of the fifth chapter of the Epistle of the Apostle Paul to the Romans, by which are proved that the first men were created before Adam, rare, fine copy, *calf, neat,* 8vo. London, printed in the year 1656

5493 Peters (*Hugh*), A Dying Father's Last Legacy to an Only Child, written during his imprisonment in the Tower, 18mo. *calf, with portrait, very scarce.* Lond. 1660

5494 PEREGRINI Sermones notables et Compendiosa de Templa et de Sanctu, 1495. Michaelis de Vngaria, Sermones Predicabiles, **Black Letter**, *clasps, wooden-boards.* Argent. MCCCCXC.

5495 PLATINA & SIR PAUL RYCAUT, Lives of the Popes of Rome, to the year 1682, 8vo. *calf.* Lond. 1704

5496 POOLE (*Matthew*), A Dialogue between a Popish Priest and an English Protestant, 18mo. *half calf.* Lond. 1670

5497 POPERY, Tales about, being a History of Papacy in all ages, *illustrated,* 8vo. *cloth.* Lond. 1842

5498 EMERLINE (*G. D.*) Frauds of Papal Ecclesiastics, 8vo. *boards.* N. Y. 1835

5499 PROPHETICAL Warnings of the Eternal Spirit, 16mo. *half calf.* Lond. 1708

5500 RALEIGH (*W.*) Sir Walter Rawleigh's Ghost, or his Apparition to an Intimate Friend, willing him to translate into English this learned book of L. Lessius, &c. Written against the atheists and polititians of these days, *portrait,* 12mo. *calf.* Lond. 1651

5500* RENNEL (*Major*), On the Voyage and Place of Shipwreck of St. Paul, 4to. 1824

5500† REYNOLDS (*John*), The Triumphs of God's Revenge against the Crying and Execrable Sin of Murther and Adultery, *many curious plates,* 4to. Lond. 1679

5501 RUPP (*J. D.*) An Original History of all Denominations in the United States, 8vo. *sheep.* Phila. 1844

5502 SAINTS, Vies des S. S. Peres des Deserts et des Saints Solitaires, *illustrated,* 12mo. *calf.* Amst. 1714

5503 SCRIPTURE History, *illustrated by beautiful engravings,* 25 Nos., sqr. 12mo. Lond.

5504 SERMONS, A Collection of Twenty-Three Sermons, mostly preached by the Clergymen to the Parliament from 1647 to 1648, many of whom were ejected upon the restoration of Charles 2d, *all fine copies,* in 1 vol. 4to. Lond. v. y.

5505 SHEPARD (*Thomas, of New England*), The Parable of the Ten Virgins, reprinted and carefully corrected in the year 1695, small folio, *half sheep.* 1695

5506 SOUTHWELL (*R.*) The Triumphs over Death: or, a Consolatorie Epistle for Afflicted Minds in the Affects of Dying Friends, 4to. *boards.* Lond. (reprint of 1595), 1814

5507 STOUGHTON (*Rev. John*), Fifteen Sermons upon Selected Occasions, small 4to. *old calf.* Lond. 1640

5508 STRAIT Gate, Sorrowing yet Rejoicing, &c., 7 vols.

5509 SWEDENBORG (*Emanuel*), Treatise on Heaven and Hell, 8vo. *boards.* Chester, 1800

5510 TAYLOR (*Isaac*), Fanaticism, 12mo. *boards.* 1824

5510* "THINGS New and Old," for the Glory of God, 8vo. *cloth.* 1845

5511 TODD (*Rev. H. J.*) A Vindication of the most Rev. Thomas Cranmer, 12mo. *cloth.* Lond. 1826

5512 TOOKE (*A.*) Pantheon, 12mo. Lond. 1810

5513 TROPHEA Ecclesiæ Anglicanæ, seu Sanctorum Martyrium antiquorum et recensior passiones ære expresse a Joanne Baptista de Cavalerii, 36 *plates, vellum,* folio, Rome, in collegio Anglico, 1584

This volume, which is very rare, belonged to Count Grassis, and has his autograph, also Gio. Cingari. The plates contain the Martyrdoms of Englishmen from the earliest period of Christianity to the deaths of Sir J. More, Bp. Fisher, Campion Sherman, and Briant.

5514 TURNLEY (*Joseph*), The Spirit of the Vatican, 8vo. *cloth.* Lond. 1845

5515 TYMME (*Thomas*), A Silver Watchbell, the Sound whereof is able to warn the most profane, worldly and careless Sinner to become a true Christian, &c., 12mo. *vellum.* Lond. 1614

5516 VALE (*G.*) Fanaticism, its Source and Influence in the case of Matthias, 12mo. N. Y. 1835

5517 WISE Virgin (*The*), A Wonderful Narration of the hand of God, in afflicting Martha Hatfield, 12mo. *old calf.* Lond. 1653

5518 UDALL (*N.*) Noli me Tangere is a Thinge to be Thovght on; or, Vox carnis sacræ clamantis ad Altari ad Aquilam sacrilegam, Noli me Tangere ne te perdam, with the curious frontispiece by Marshall, *clean copy, rare,* 4to. Lond. 1642

5519 VOLTAIRE, Letters to, by certain Jews, 2 vols. in 1, *sheep,* 8vo. Cincinnati, 1845

5520 VOLTAIRE (*M. de*), Philosophical Dictionary, in English, 6 vols. 12mo. *sheep.* Lond. 1826

5521 WATSON (*Rich'd*), Apology for the Bible, *sheep,* 16mo. Cam. 1828

5522 ——— Equanimity in Death, 4to. 1813

5523 WHOLE Duty of Man, Works of the author of, 12mo. Lond. 1682

"For my part," said Major Bellenden, "I have not read a book these twenty years except my Bible, the Whole Duty of Man, and Turner's Pallas Armanta."—*Old Morality.*

5524 WOOLASTON (*Wm.*) Religion of Nature Delineated, 4to. *calf.* Lond. 1724

VOYAGES AND TRAVELS IN GENERAL.

5525 BROWN (*Thos.*) Wanderer in Norway, 12mo. *boards.* Lond. 1816

5525*BRY (*Theodore and J. Israel de*), Twenty Plates to the Voyages to Candy, *half green morocco.* folio. Frankf. 1605

5526 ——— Twenty Plates to the Voyage in Ternate, Patani, &c., *half green mor.* folio. ib. 1606

5527 ——— Voyages to Guinea, Twenty Plates to, *half green mor.* folio. ib. 1603

5528 GOLOWNIN (*Capt.*) Memoirs of a Captivity in Japan, 3 vols. 8vo. *cloth.* Lond. 1824

5529 HARRIS (*John*), A Collection of Voyages and Travels, 2 vols. folio, *calf.* Lond. 1705

5530 HOLTHAUS' Wanderings of a Journeyman Tailor, 8vo. N. Y. n. d.

5531 LITHGOW (*W.*) The Rare Adventures and painful peregrination of long nineteen years Travayles from Scotland to the most famous Kingdoms in Europe, Asia, and Africa, 4to. no title, but has the curious frontispiece. Lond. 1632

5532 ——— Another edition. Lond. 1722

The chief interest of this book consists in the Personal narrative of the author.—*See Retr. Rev.* Vol. XI.

5532* QUIN'S Steam Voyage down the Danube, 12mo. 1836

5533 VAUGHAN (*W. O. G.*) Voyages, Travels, and Adventures of, 2 vols. 12mo. *boards.* Lond. 1760

5534 VOYAGES and Travels, a collection consisting of authentic writers in our Tongue, which have not before been collected in English, and combined with others of note in other Nations and Languages; the whole digested according to the parts of the World to which they particularly relate, illustrated with a great variety of cuts, prospects, ruins, maps, and charts, compiled from the Library of the late Earl of Oxford, 2 vols. folio. *calf*, Gibbons copy, best edition. Lond. 1745

5535 WESTON (*S.*) Englishman Abroad, 8vo. *half calf.* Lond. 1824

TRIALS, CRIMES, POLICE, PRISONS, &c.

5536 ADSHEAD (*Jos.*) Prisons and Prisoners, with illustrations, 8vo. *cloth.* Lond. 1845

5537 ALBOISE et Moquet, Les Prisons de l'Europe, *magnifique edition*, 8 vols. 8vo. *half mor., fine plates.* Paris, 1845

5538 ALHOY (*Maurice*), Les Bagnes, Histoire, Types, &c., profusely illustrated, 8vo. *cloth.* Paris, 1845

5539 ALLIRY et Lurime, Prisons de Paris, 8vo. *cl.* Paris, 1846

5540 AMERICAN Criminal Tracts, 2 vols. *neat half mor.*, 8vo.

5541 ANDRYANE (*Alexander*), Memoirs of a Prisoner of State in the Fortress of Spielberg; translated by F. Prandi, 12mo. *cloth.* Lond. 1838

5542 BARRINGTON (*George*), Account of a Voyage to New South Wales, History of N. S. Wales, including Botany Bay, the Customs and Manners of the Natives, &c., 8vo. *calf.* Lond.

By the famous Pickpocket, who was made superintendent of the Convicts, with his Life, Trial, Speeches, &c., *scarce and curious.*

5543 BECCARIA on Crimes and Punishments (attributed to Voltaire), 8vo. *sheep.* Lond. 1775

5544 BEE (*The*) Revived; or the Prisoner's Magazine, containing the Greatest Curiosities in Prose and Verse, 12mo. *half boards.* Lond. 1750

5545 BLANDY (*Mary*) Account of the Parricide of, and other Trials, 4to. Oxford, 1751, &c.

5546 CAUNTER (*H.*) Confessions and Crimes of Prisoners, 12mo. Phil. 1836

5547 CAUSES CELEBRES Ecclesiastiques, 18mo., wants title.

5548 CAUSES CELEBRES Nouvelles, 2 vols. 8vo. *half morocco.* Paris, 1845

5549 CAUSES CELEBRES English, or Reports of Remarkable Trials, *square* 12mo. *cloth.* Lond. 1844

5550 CAUSES CELEBRES, Celebrated and remarkable Cases of Criminal Jurisprudence, 6 vols. 8vo. *half cf.* Lond. 1825

5550* COLQUHOUN'S Treatise on the Police and Crimes of the Metropolis, 8vo. *bds.* Lond. 1829

5551 CRIMES des Empereurs D'Allemagne, avec cinq Gravures, 8vo. *calf.* A Paris, 1793

5552 CRIMES des Rois de France, 8vo. Paris, 1839

5553 CRIMINAL Calendar of the U. S., by Henry St. Clair, 8vo. Bost. 1835

5554 CRIMINAL Recorder, or an Awful Beacon to the Rising Generation of both Sexes, 12mo. *sheep.* Phila. 1810

5555 CUCKOLD's Chronicle (*The*), a Collection of Curious Trials in the 18th Century, *half morocco, neat, wants title.* Lond.

5555* DEATH Punishment, Articles on, vol. 2, 12mo. Lond. 1837

5556 DEVILS of London, the Cheats and Delusions of Romish Priests and Exorcists, 8vo. *calf.* Lond. 1703

5557 DODD (*Dr.*) Full and Particular Account of the Life and Trial of Doctor Dodd, 12mo. Lond. 1777

5558 DUDLEY (*Thos.*), The Tocsin, or a Review of London Police Establishments, 8vo. *half calf.* Lond. 1828

5559 DUMHOUDER (*Van Bragge*) Joost de Practyke in Criminele Saecken, 12mo. *vellum, curious wood cuts.* Rott. 1628

5560 DYING Speeches and Behaviour of Several State Prisoners, 8vo. *calf.* Lond. 1720

5560* FORREST Divorce Case, Testimony in, 12mo. Phil. 1850

5561 FORREST Divorce Case, and other Pamphlets, 13 in all.

5562 GILCHRIST (*Jas. P.*) Origin and History of Ordeals, Trials by Battle, &c., *half bd.* 8vo. Lond. 1821

5563 GORDON (*Lady Duff*), Criminal Trials, translated from the German, 12mo. *cl.* N. Y. 1846

5564 HILL (*Susannah*), The Art of Strangling, illustrated with several Anecdotes, with Memoirs of S. Hill, and a Summary of her Trial at the Old Bailey, 8vo. *half calf.* Lond. 1791

5565 JARDINE (*D.*) Criminal Trials during the Reign of Queen Elizabeth and James I., 2 vols. 12mo. *cl.* Lond. 1847

5566 JOURNAL D'Un Deporte non Juge ou Deportation, 2 vols. *half bd.* Paris, 1834

5567 LIVES and Exploits of English Highwaymen, 12mo. *cl.* Lond. 1839

5568 KIRBY's Wonderful and Eccentric Museum, a Magazine of Remarkable Characters, and Curiosities of Nature and Art, *with portraits of eccentric and notorious persons,* 3 vols. 8vo. *cl.* Lond. 1820

An extraordinary collection of curious biographies, narratives of credulity, and superstition, &c.

5569 LEAHY (*David*), On the State of Crime in Ireland, 8vo. *cl.* Lond. 1839

5570 MITCHELL (*James, a Conventicle Preacher*), Trial of, 4to. Lond. 1684

5570* MYNSHUL (*Geffray*), Essayes and Characters of the Prison and Prisoners, 12mo. *bds.* Edinb. 1821

5571 NEW Newgate Calendar, 12mo. *bds.* Lond. n. d.

5572 OLD Bailey Experience, or Criminal Jurisprudence, 8vo. *sheep.* Lond. 1833

5573 PELHAM (*Camden*), Chronicles of Crime, or the Newgate Calendar, 2 vols. *cl. gilt, plates.* Lond. 1841

5574 PEUCHET (*J.*) Memoires des Archives de la Police de Paris, 6 vols. *half calf,* 8vo. Paris, 1838

5575 ROBIN HOOD, the Noble Birth and Gallant Achievements of this remarkable Outlaw, 12mo. Lond., *Pickering,* 1827

5576 SAMPSON (*M. B.*) Rationale of Crime, and its Appropriate Treatment, 12mo. *cl.* N. Y. 1846

5577 SELFRIDGE (*Thos. O.*) Trial for Killing Chas. Austin, 8vo. *bds.* Bost. 1805

5578 SELECT Trials at the Old Bailey, 4 vols. *old calf.* Lond. 1764

5579 SKETCHES of Popular Tumults, 12mo. *cl.* Lond. 1837

5580 STEWART (*Virgil A.*) History and Adventures of, by H. R. Howard, 12mo. *cl.* N. Y. 1846

5582 TRIAL of Bullions, Cobbett, Ward, and others, 7 pamphlets.

5583 TRIALS for Murder, &c., 9 pamphlets. v. d.

5584 TRIAL of Algernon Sydney, Boroske, &c., 2 vols. 4to. Lond. v. d.

5585 WHITEHEAD (*C.*) Lives and Exploits of English Highwaymen, Pirates, and Robbers, 12mo. *cl.* Lond. 1839

TURKEY.

5587 KNOLLES, The General Historie of the Turks, from the original of their Empire fol. *cuts, old calf.* Islip, 1610

Called by Dr. Johnson the first of modern historians.

5588 LEWIS' Views of Constantinople, folio, *half morocco.*

5589 RYCAUT (*P.*) History of the Turkish Empire, folio, *calf.* 1680

WALES—*See also* ENGLAND.

5590 BENNETT (*G. J.*) Pedestrian's Guide through North Wales, 8vo. *cloth.* Lond. 1838

5592 PARRY (*J. H.*) Cambrian Plutarch, 8vo. *cloth.* Lond. 1834

WOMAN, MARRIAGE, &c.

5594 ALEXANDER (*Wm.*) History of Women, from the earliest antiquity to the present time, 2 vols. 8vo. *calf* Dublin, 1779

An account of almost every interesting particular concerning the sex among all nations.

5595 ART of Engaging the Affections of Wives to their Husbands, 8vo. pp. 79. Berwick, 1793

5596 BERAND, Les Filles Publiques de Paris, 2 vols. 16mo. Brux. 1839

5597 DIALOGUES Concerning the Ladies, to which is added An Essay on the Ancient Amazons, 12mo. *sheep.* Lond. 1785

5598 EDEN (*Adam*), A Vindication among the Ladies on foot, to abolish Modesty and restore the Native Simplicity of going naked, by Adam Eden. 12mo. *sewed.* Lond. 1755

5599 ELLIS (*Mrs.*) The Women of England, 2 vols. in 1, 12mo. *cloth.* Phila. 1839

5600 ESSAY in defence of the Female Sex, with the Characters of a Pedant, Squire, Beau, &c., 12mo. *calf.* Lond. 1697

5601 FLAG (*Wilson*), Analysis of Female Beauty, 12mo. *boards,* Bost. 1834

5602 FRY (*Caroline*), A Word to Women, 12mo. *cloth.* Phila. 1840

5603 GUYON (*M. l'Abbe*), Histoire des Amazones Anciennes et Modernes enrichie de Medailles, 2 vols. 12mo. *calf.* Paris, 1760

5604 HALE (*Mrs. S. J.*) Distinguished Women of every Age, with 230 *portraits*, 8vo. N. Y. 1853

HAYWOOD'S Exemplary Lives of Nine Women, *vide* Lot. 1195.

5605 JAMESON (*Mrs.*) Characteristics of Woman, Moral, Poetical, and Historical, *with engravings*, 8vo. *morocco, gilt.* N. Y. 1850

5606 KAVANAGH (*Julia*), Woman in France during the 18th Century, 12mo. *cloth.* Phila. 1850

5607 LE MOYNE, Galerie des Femmes Fortes, *with numerous full length portraits,* 2 vols. 12mo. in 1, *calf, gilt.* Paris, 1665

A rare edition, not generally noticed by Bibliographers; the portraits include Mary, Queen of Scots, Eleanor of Castile, Princess of Wales, Joan of Arc.

5608 ——— Heroic Women, translated, folio, *old calf.* n. d.

5609 L'ESTRANGE, Woman's Witchcraft, or the Curse of Coquetry, 12mo. *cloth.* Phil. 1854

5610 MCINTOSH (*M. J.*) Woman in America, 12mo. *cloth.* N. Y. 1850

5611 MADDEN (*Theod.*) Thelyphthora, or a Treatise on Female Ruin, in its causes, effects, &c., considered on the basis of the Divine Law, 2 vols. 8vo. *calf.* Lond. 1780

The controversy which this singular work occasioned lasted long, and was carried on with great keenness—in it the author maintains the lawfulness of polygamy as authorized by the Mosaic law, and therefore obligatory to Christians.

5612 ——— Hill (Rich.) The Blessings of Polygamy Displayed, in reply to THELYPHTHORA, 8vo. *bds.* Lond. 1781

5613 MATTHEWS (*Rich'd*), Act for Marriages in England, 12mo. *bds.* Lond. 1837

5614 MITCHEL (*John*), The Female; or, The Travels of Hephzibah, under the similitude of a Dream, *many plates*, 8vo. *sheep.* Lond. n. d.

5615 MORGAN (*Lady*), Woman and her Master, 2 vols. *cloth.* Phil. 1840

5616 POLLEN (*Thomas*), The Fatal Consequences of Adultery to Monarchies as well as Private Families, 12mo. *bds.* Lond. 1772

5617 POLYGAMY, Concubinage, Adultery, Divorce, &c., select and curious cases of, 12mo. Lond. 1736

5618 PROSTITUTION in Paris, 18mo. *cloth.* N. Y. 1845

5619 SAINTINE (*X. B.*) Woman's Whims, or the Female Barometer, translated by Fayette Robinson, *cloth.* 8vo. N. Y. 1850

5620 SEGUR (*J. A. de*), Les Femmes, leur condition et leur influence dans l'ordre social, 4 vols. 24mo. *sewed.* Bruxelles, 1827

SWEETNAM (*John*), Arraignment of Lewd, Idle, Forward, and Unconstant Women, *vide* Lot 1662.

5621 TAIT (*William*), An Inquiry into the cause, extent, and consequences of Prostitution in Edinburgh, 8vo. *cloth.* Edinb. 1840

5622 TRACTS from 1714 to 1720, 2 vols., containing several scarce ones relative to the Chevalier St. George (the Elder Pretender); the Dying Speeches of Col. Henry Oxburgh, James Shepheard, &c.; Dissertation upon Old Women, &c., 8vo. v. y.

5623 WALKER (*Alex.*) Woman Physiologically considered as to mind, morals, marriage, 12mo. *bds.* Lond. 1840

5624 ——— The Anthropological Works of, 3 vols. 12mo. *cloth.* N. Y. 1843

MISCELLANIES.

5626 ADAGIA Nonnulla Latino Anglica, 12mo. *sewed.* Edinb. 1723

5627 ADMIRANDA rerum admirabilium encomia, sive diserta et amœna Pallas disserens seria sub ludicra specia, &c., 12mo. *curious plates.* *N. Batavorun,* 1676

5628 ÆNEAS SILVIUS (*Pope Pius II.*) Ænee Silvii Piccolonomini qui et Pius Secundus fuit Epistole in Cardinalatu edite Lege fœliciter **Gothic Letter,** 4to., no page, date, place, or signature.

Mentioned by Brunet, who calls it a folio, and says it sold for 67 francs at La Valliere's. This is a fine copy, from the Duke of Sussex's sale.

5629 ANALYST (*The*), A Collection of Miscellaneous Papers, 12mo. *cl.* Boston, 1840

5630 ANDERSON (*J. S. M.*) Addresses on Miscellaneous Subjects, post 8vo. *cl.* Lond. 1849

5631 ARCHAICA and Heliconia, containing reprints of rare old English pieces of Prose and Poetry, edited by Park, Sir Egerton Brydges, and Haslewood, complete, in *half mor. and bds., uncut.* 1814–15

This was published at one hundred dollars without the binding. But a limited number were printed, and it is daily becoming more scarce. The original works are so rare, that it is a question if they could ever be collected; and if they could be got, the cost of them would almost purchase a tolerable library. The following is a list of the contents: ARCHAICA—Greene's Philomela; Greene's Arcadia; Southwell's Triumph over Death; Breton's Characters, and his Good and Bad; Nash's Christ's Tears over Jerusalem; Harvey's Four Letters and Sonnets touching R. Greene; Harvey's Pierce's Supererogation; Harvey's New Letter of Notable Contents; Braithwaite's Essay on the Five Senses. HELICONIA—Breton's Small Handfull of Fragrant Flowers; Proctor's Gorgeous Gallery of Gallant Inventions; Breton's Flourish upon Fancy; Handefull of Pleasant Delites, edited by C. Robinson; Whetstone's Life and Death of Francis Earle of Bedford; Phœnix Nest; Barnes's Spirituall Sonnets; Spirituall Sonnets by H. C.; Churchard's Funeral of Sir F. Knowles; Storer's Life and Death of Cardinal Wolsey; Allott's England's Parnassus; Churchyard's Good-will; Sad and Heavy Verses for the Losse of Archbp. Whitgift, by Churchyard.

In this set the Archaica is in 9 parts, boards, and the Heliconia 9 parts in 7 vols. half morocco; it will be sold as in 16 vols.

5632 ANDREWS (*J. P.*) Anecdotes, Ancient and Modern, 8vo. *calf.* Lond. 1789

5633 ANDREW'S Cesar, &c., 5 vols.

5634 BAUDII (*D.*) Epistolæ et Orationes, 12mo. *calf.* Amst. *Elzevir*, 1662

5635 BEARDS—Guhlingii (*G. F.*) Dissertatio de Barba Deorum ejusdem, de causis Barbæ Deorum, in 1 vol. 4to. *half calf.* Vitemb. 1725

Polonius.—"This speech is somewhat too long."
Hamlet.—"It shall to the barber's with your beard."

5636 BELL (*Major James*), Letters from Wetzlar, written in 1817, 12mo. *half roan.* Lond. 1821

5636*a* BEASLEY (*Rev. F. W.*) The Duellist, a Poem, 12mo. Phil. 1841

5636*b* BOOK of Curtesye, edited by J. O. Halliwell, 8vo. *half mor.* Lond. 1841

5637 BOWEN (*B. B.*) Blind Man's Offering, 12mo. *cl.* N. Y. 1853

5638 BRETON (*Nicholas*), Characters, and the Good and the Bad, 4to. pp. 37. Lond. *reprint*, 1815

5639 BRITISH Authors, and Children's Books, &c., 6 vols.

5640 BRITISH Essayists, edited by Alexander Chalmers, complete in 45 vols. 12mo. *calf.* Lond. 1808

5641 BULLIONS' Latin Reader, &c., 10 vols.

5642 BURGESS (*George*), The Last Enemy, 12mo. *cl.* Phil. 1850

A curious book on the various modes of death.

5642*BURKE (*Edmund*), Works, 7 vols. 8vo. *half calf.* Bost. 1826

"Burke was a writer of the first class, and excelled in almost every kind of prose composition."—*Edinburgh Review.*

5643 BURTON (*Edmund*), Ancient Characters, deduced from Classical Remains, 8vo. *calf.* Lond. 1763

5644 BUTLER (*Samuel*), The Genuine Remains of, with notes by Robert Thyer, portraits and plates, 2 vols. 8vo. *half calf, scarce.* Lond. 1822

5645 CARLYLE (*Thomas*), Critical and Miscellaneous Essays, 2 vols. *cloth*, 8vo. Boston, 1838

5646 ——— Past and Present and 2 others, 3 vols. 12mo. v. d.

5647 ——— Sartor Resartus, *cloth*, 12mo. Boston, 1837

5648 CAMPANUS (*J. A.*) Opera Omnia continentur tractatus V., Orationes XV., Epistolarum IX., libri, Vita Pii, Historia Brachii, Epigrammatum libri VIII., a Michaele Ferno, Meladioni, collecta et edita; qui et auctoris vitam scripsit: cum signaturis. Characteribus Venetiis, Eucharius Silber alias Franck, Romæ, folio, *rare, fine, large, clean copy, in the original oaken binding covered with stamped calf*, from the Library of the Duke of Sussex, with his Book-plate, folio. Venet. MCCCCXCV

*** See the Bibliotheca Spenceriana.

5648* CASTIGLIONE (*Il conte Baldesare*), Le sue opera volgare e Latine, recorrette ed. illustrate da G. A. G. Volpi, *portrait*, 4to. *half russia.* Padova, 1766

5649 CATO Moralissimus, Elegantissimo Commento, Rob de Euromode, *rare*, **Black Letter**, 8vo. Circa, MCCCCLXXXVI

5650 COKE (*Roger*), Detection of the Court and State of England, during the reigns of James I., Charles I. and II., and James II., also the Interregnum, 3 vols. 8vo. *calf.* Lond. 1719

"A sort of secret history, engaging to an Englishman, naturally inquisitive, curious, and greedy of scandal."

5651 CLEMENTS (*G.*) Customs Guide, 12mo. Lond. n. d.

5652 COBBETT (*Wm.*) Advice to Young Men, 18mo. *cloth.* N. Y. 1831

5653 COLERIDGE (*S. T.*) Works, 8vo. *sheep.* Phil. 1843

5654 COLTON Lacon, Vol. I., and other books, 12 vols.

5655 COLMAN (*Geo.*) Works, Prose on several occasions accompanied with some pieces in verse, 3 vols. 12mo. *calf.* Lond. 1787

5656 CONVERSATIONS on Nature and Art, 12mo. *cloth.* Phil. 1839

5657 COWLEY (*Abraham*), Prose Works of, 8vo. *half calf.* Lond. 1826

5658 DE FOE (*Dl.*) Works of, with his Life, by Chalmers, Prefaces, Notes, &c., by Sir Walter Scott and others, complete in 20 vols. 12mo. *cloth.* Oxford, 1840

This is the most complete edition of De Foe ever published; it is now quite scarce.

5659 DE QUINCEY (*Th.*) The English Opium Eater, 16mo. *boards.* Phil. 1843

5660 DESTOUCHES (*J.*) Œuvres choisies, 3 vols. 24mo. *half mor.* Paris, 1826

5661 **Dinckmut—Buch der Geschopffe, &c.,** Printed with large grotesque type, numerous large engravings, the full size of the page, illustrative of the "Mouth of Hell," "The Serpent tempting Eve," "The Confession," &c., *extremely rare, fine large copy,* folio, *calf,* antique style, *red edges;* Gedrucket und feliglichen vollen det dises buch von Conrado Dinckmut zu ulm an nechsten samstag nach sant Michels tag anno domini MCCCCLXXXIII. iar. io. Ulm. 1483

5662 EDWARDS (*B. B.*) Year Book, or Manual of Reference, 12mo. Phil. 1838

5663 ENGLISHMEN, The Candor and Good-nature of, exemplified, with Essays on the principal virtues prefixed, *half sheep,* 8vo. Lond. 1777

5664 ENGLISH and American Tracts, 24 *pieces.* v. y.

5665 ESSAYS from Montaigne, 12mo. *sheep.* Lond. 1800

5666 FERDOSAE, Episodes, the Shah Nameh, &c., royal 8vo. Lond. 1815

5667 FIELDING'S (*Henry*) Works, 8 vols. 8vo. *calf, gilt.* Lond. 1771

"Of all the works of imagination to which English genius has given origin, the writings of Henry Fielding are perhaps most decidedly and exclusively her own."—*Sir Walter Scott.*

"The prose Homer of human nature."—*Lord Byron.*

5668 FORDE (*Thos.*) Fœnestra in Pectora, or Familiar Letters, 8vo. *half bound.* Lond. 1660

5669 GOOD Child's Library, 9 vols. sq. 12mo. *col'd plates.* Lond.

5670 HEDGE'S Logic, and other Books, 9 vols.

5671 HEMAN'S Reader, &c., 7 vols.

5672 HOLY Trinity Guild, &c., 2 vols. 8vo.

5673 HOPKINS (*John*), Notions of Political Economy, 12mo. *half calf.* Bost. 1833

5674 IRVING (*Washington*), Works, 2 vols. *cloth,* royal 8vo. Phil. 1840

5674* JUNIUS' Letters, 12mo. *half calf.* N. Y. 1821

5675 KRISS Kringle's Book and Howitt's Picture Book, 2 vols.

5676 LADIES' Companion, &c., 4 vols.

5677 LAMARTINE, Œuvres Completes de, royal 8vo. Tournai, 1850

5678 LAMB'S (*Charles*) Works complete, containing his Letters, Essays of Elia, Poems, Plays, &c., with Life of the Author, royal 8vo. *cloth.* Moxon, 1846

5680 LE Blazon des Heretiques, 8vo. *half mor.,* only 50 copies reprinted. Paris, 1833

5681 Lounger's Common-place Book, or Miscellaneous Collections in History, Criticisms, &c., 2 vols. 12mo. *cloth.* Lond. 1838

5683 Lower (*M. A.*), English Surnames, Essays on Family Nomenclature, Historical, Etymological, and Humorous, with Illustrative Anecdotes, 2 vols. post 8vo. *cuts, cloth.* Lond. 1850

5684 Merrywater (*George*), Kings the Devil's Viceroys and Representatives on Earth, 8vo. *half calf.* Lond. 1838

5684* Miscellaneous Pamphlets, about 25 in a parcel. v. d.

5685 Murphy (*Arthur*), Works of, complete, 7 vols. 8vo. *calf, gilt.* Lond. 1786

5686 Moore (*Chas.*) A Full Inquiry into the Subject of Suicide, to which are added two Treatises on Duelling and Gaming, 2 vols. 4to. *sheep.* Lond. 1790

"An excellent work."—*Lowndes.*

5686* Music Books, &c., 3 vols. v. d.

5687 National Jubilee and others, 8 vols.

5688 Neville (*Henry*), Shuffling, Cutting, and Dealing in a Game at Pickquet acted from 1653—58, first edition, 4to. *half morocco.* Lond. 1659

So rare that it was reprinted in the Harleian Miscellany.

5689 Nimrod, A Discourse upon Certain Passages of History and Fable, 8vo. *boards.* Lond. 1826

5690 Noctes Vaticanæ, 4to. *vellum, uncut.* Mediolani, 1748

5690* Pamphlets, Select: I. Sketches of Moscow and St. Petersburg, *with nine colored engravings,* by Paul Sverrin. II. Jeffery's Review of the Conduct of the Prince of Wales. III. The Riots in Birmingham, 1791. IV. The Case of Jane Marie and Cruelty of James Ross, 1808. V. Alex. Whistelo, a Black Man, being a remarkable case of bastardy, 8vo. *half bound.* v. d.

5691 Peccorone (*Il*) di Sig. Giovanni Fiorentino, 2 vols. *half russia, uncut.* Milan, 1804

5692 Perotti (*Nicholai*), Cornucopiæ, *rare, fine, large, clean copy, in the original oaken boards, stamped calf binding.* Nicolai Peroti Eruditissimi uiri Cornvcopiæ seu comentariorum linguæ Latinæ. Impressorum Venetiis per Magistrum Paganinium de paganinis brixiensum, folio. Venet. MCCCCLXXXIX

5693 Perrin's Fables, &c., 7 vols.

5694 Philopoena, or Friendship's Offering, 4to. *cloth, gilt.* N. Y. 1854

5695 PHONOGRAPHY and other Pamphlets, 17 vols.

5696 PICUS MIRANDULÆ (*Joan, Francis*), De appetitu, De elementis, &c., *elegant wood-cut titles by Holbein, with his name, sewed*, 4to. Basil, 1568

5697 POE (*E. A.*) Miscellaneous Works, vol. 4, 12mo. *cloth.* N. Y. 1858

5698 POLWHELE (*Rev. R.*) Reminiscences in Prose and Verse, 3 vols. in 1, 12mo. Lond. 1836

5699 PUCKLE (*Jas.*) The Club, or a Gray Cap for a Green Head, 18mo. *cloth, gilt.* Chiswick, 1834

5700 RALEIGH (*Sir Walter*), Remains of, 18mo. *sheep.* Lond. 1702

5701 QUARLES (*Francis*), Argalus and Parthenia, 8vo. *half morocco.* Lond. 1684

5702 RECORDE (*Robert*), Castle of Knowledge, containing the Explication of the Sphere, both Celestial and Material, &c., with sundry pleasant proofs, and certain new denominations not written before in any vulgar works, *fine copy*, folio, *calf, panelled.* Lond., *Reginald Wolfe*, 1556

Fine and perfect specimen of old English typography.

5702* SABRINAE Corolla in hortulis Regiae Scholae Salopiensis contexuerunt tres viri floribus legendis. Editio Altera, 8vo. Lond. 1846

5703 ST. EVREMOND (*M. de*), The Works of, made English, with his Life, by Des Maizeux, and Memoirs of the Duchess of Mazarin, 3 vols. 8vo. *boards.* Lond. 1722

"The fame of St. Evremond, as a brilliant star, during a long life, in the polished aristocracy of France and England, gave for a time a considerable lustre to his writings, the greater part of which are such effusions as the daily intercourse of good company called forth."—HALLAM.

5704 SANDS (*R. C.*) Writings of, in Prose and Verse, 2 vols. in 1, 8vo. *half calf.* N. Y. 1835

5705 SEQUESTER (*Vibius*), de Fluminibus, Fontibus Lacubus, &c., ex recensione, F. Hesselii, 8vo. *bright old calf gilt.* Rotterd. 1711.

5706 SCHILLER, Werke, vols. xi. and xii. 12mo. Stuttgart, 1858

5707 SMITH (*Richard Penn*), Miscellaneous Works collected by his son, Horace W. Smith, 8vo. *cloth.* Phila. 1856

5708 SONDERLAND (*J. B.*) Bilder und Randzeichnungen zu Deutschen Dichtungen, *forty large and very elaborate and ornamental engravings, with Ballads, &c.*, royal folio. Dusseldorf, n. d.

5709 SPECTATOR, Complete, *with eight portraits*, royal 8vo. *cloth.* Lond. 1850

5710 SCUDAMORE (*Lord*), Homer A-la-mode, a mock poem upon the first and second poems of Homer's Iliads. Oxd. 1665

5711 SUIT of Armour, for youth, *plates*, 12mo. *fine calf.* Lond. 1824

5712 SUMMER Book, 12mo. N. Y. 1851

5713 SUPPLICACYON for Beggars, reprinted from the original edition of 1534, 12mo. *half mor.* Lond. *Pickering*, 1845

5716 TOFTE (*Robert*), Honours Academie, or the famous pastorall of the Faire Shepheardesse Julietta, with divers comicall and tragicall histories in prose and verse, *half mor.* fol. Lond. 1610

5717 TYLER (*Robt.*) Works, comprising the Last Man; Elements of the Beautiful; and Death; 12mo. *cloth.* Phila. 1839

5718 VOLTAIRE, The Works of M. De Voltaire, translated from the French, with notes historical and critical, by Smollet, Francklin, and others, 24 vols. 12mo. *calf.* Lond. 1762–65

5719 WALPOLE (*Horace, Earl of Olrord*), Works of, edited by Robert Berry, Esq., containing his correspondence, Royal and Noble Authors, Anecdotes of Painters, Tragedy of the Mysterious Mother, Castle of Otranto, Historic Doubts on Richard III., Description of Strawberry Hill, &c., with *numerous plates, portraits, views, &c.*, 5 vols. 4to. *half bound.* Lond. 1798

Considerable portions of Walpole's writings are not published in octavo, and can only be procured in this edition.

5720 WATERLOO, Guide to the Model of the Battle of, Maps and Plans, with other Pamphlets on Panoramas, 8vo. *half bound.*

5721 WHIGS and Democrats, a pamphlet, with others.

MANUSCRIPTS, LETTERS, AUTOGRAPHS, &C.

SOME OTHER CURIOUS MSS. WILL BE FOUND UNDER VARIOUS DEPARTMENTS.

5722 STAR CHAMBER, Treatise of the Court of Starrechamber in a legible hand, 530 pages, folio; at the end is a sheet entitled a Dissertation on the Old Court of Star Chamber, *unbound.*

5723 MISSAL, Part of an Old Missal, curious illuminated capitals of the XIV. century, 12mo. *much worn.*

5724 COMMON Place Book, Opening Address for the Coburgh Theatre, several comic songs, &c., *cloth*, 8vo.

5725 VENICE. Stolfi Chronica de Veneti, Manuscript from the Library of the Duke of Sussex, folio, *half vel.*

5726 POEMS and Songs, chiefly amorous and gallant, in an old hand; the writer appears to be Richard Archard, from his name being written twice in the volume, 1650 and 1657, also several receipts and accounts of money paid to various persons at different times, *old calf, clasps,* 18mo.

5727 KEMBLE (*J. P.*) Project, or a New Way to fill an Empty Purse, a Ballad Farce, not printed, *calf*, 4to.

5728 STAGE. Manuscript Tracts on the Stage, curious and old, 3 vols. 4to.

5729 DUBLIN Theatre, Diary of the Theatre in Dublin, 1733, neatly written, 4to. *half calf.*

5730 SIAMESE Manuscript, a Siamese Book of the Laws of Marriage, a good specimen of Siamese writing in an oblong volume, in folds, written with a soft white substance on black paper.

A MS. note appended, describes it accurately. "Siamese MSS. are very seldom met with, and this is a good specimen." "The mighty King Ra-mah-te-bo-de-se-pram-chak-ra-pat-te-ra-chat-te - ra - cha - bo - pit, deigned to express his royal mind and set his seal to these laws, in the year 1904 of the Siamese era."

CURIOUS AND IMPORTANT LETTERS AND INSTRUCTIONS, &c., TO AND FROM THE SECRET COMMITTEE OF CONGRESS, IN THE WAR OF 1776.

5731 THOMPSON (*Chas.*) Extract from the Minutes of Congress, by order of Congress, for appointing a Commissioner or Agent to the Courts of Vienna and Tuscany, signed by John Hancock and Secretary Thompson.

5732 FRANKLIN (*Benjamin, Silas Deane, and Arthur Lee*), Autographs to a Document dated Paris, 1777, relative to taking the French ship Fortune by an American Privateer.

5733 DEANE (*Silas*), Letter in the handwriting of Silas Deane announcing the arrival of Dr. Franklin at Paris, with eulogium, &c.

5734 ——— Letter to the Committee recommending the bearer, a French gentleman, named L. Dusauley, as a gentleman likely to be of good service to the cause of the Americans, in Silas Deane's hand. 1776

5735 JAY (*John*), Letter from Madrid, 1780, of three leaves, addressed to Silas Deane, partly in figures, which are deciphered by another hand, containing much important matter.

5736 DEANE (*Silas*), Letter and initials, to Messrs. Morris and Lee, &c., regarding a letter from Dr. Franklin announcing two prizes, &c.

5737 ——— Long letter respecting the Amphitrite, also reflecting on the conduct of Monsieur E. Du Coudray, directed to Messrs. Morris and others.

6738 TALLMADGE (*B.*) Letter to Mr. Deane from Bedford, Oct. 15, 1782, respecting the army and the enemy, "England expects a peace, but her pride and haughty spirit can hardly brook the idea of asking it at the hands of the Bourbon House."

5739 HANCOCK (*John, and Charles Thomson, Sec'y*), autographs to a printed circular relating to the fitting out vessels, &c.

5741 IZZARD (*Rd.*) to Henry Laurens, Esq., long letter of four leaves on large folio paper, full of interesting matter: "Mr. Lee assures me he has discovered that his despatches to Congress have been opened by one of his colleagues. I think you will rejoice with me that these gentlemen are soon to act in different departments," &c.

5742 DEANE (*Silas*), Letter to Dr. Franklin, Dickenson, &c., Nov. 9, 1776, "a warr appears evidently at hand, and will, probably, be general; all Europe have their eyes on America," &c., not signed.

5743 ——— Letter on the arrival of General Lee to Mons. Girard: "The British Ministry are resolved on something, I know not what, for in addition to the spies they already have in Paris, they have giv'n one Col. Mercer, a Virginian, a pension of four hundred pounds per annum on condition of his receiving it in France, which is in effect to be rewarded and exiled at the same instant," &c., initials only.

5744 ——— A letter, not signed, sent by Mons. Brongian, "a gentleman of family; his zeal for engaging in the American cause induces him to embark for our country, and to quit for the present his prospects of preferment here (Paris), which are very good."

5745 D'HARCOURT (M.) Letter from Havre, August 17, 1777, to Mr. Deane.

5746 HANCOCK (*John and Charles Thomson,*) Attestation to a Resolution of the Commissioners of the Courts of France and Spain to consult together and prepare a Treaty of Commerce and Alliance, &c.

5747 DEANE (*Silas*), Letter dated Dec. 3, 1776, relating to Capt. Burnell, lately seized by the English, Cherbourg to his Excellency (President Hancock).

"I sent forward your bills, a large part of which were protested, and that intelligence arrived of the loss of Canada," &c. "The late affair at Long Island, of which we had intelligence in October, and the burning of New York, the report of Tarleton's having crossed the lakes, &c., has absolutely ruined our credit," &c.

5748 ——— Advice of Sending One Thousand Pounds Sterling to Barnabas Deane, Esq.

5749 ——— Letter, Nov. 29, 1776, Recommending Col. Conway to (John Hancock).

5750 IZZARD (*Ralph*), Long and Important Letter on folio paper—to Congress, April 11, 1778.

5751 DEANE (*Silas*), A Long and very Important Letter, Oct. 1, 1776.

"The Ministry had become extremely uneasy at your absolute silence, and the bold assertions of the British ambassador that you were accommodating matters, aided by the black and villainous artifices of two of our countrymen here, had brought them to apprehend not only a settlement between the two countries, but the most serious consequences to the West Indies should we unite with Great Britain," &c.

5752 DEANE (*Silas*), Long Letter to Lord George Sackville Germaine, one of the Principal Secretaries of State to the King of Great Britain, Paris, 1777, relative to the seizure of the Snow, Dickenson, and other Vessels, demanding a restitution of those Vessels, &c.

5753 DUPLICATE of a Letter written by Silas Deane, Nov. 6, 1776, with information and questions on a variety of subjects.

5754 DEANE (*Silas*), Dec. 3, 1776, Letter on the Loss of Canada, &c., and Postscript, in all six leaves.

5755 DEANE (*Silas*), Letter to Franklin, March 8, 1776.

"Employ must be found for the forces of Great Britain out of the United States of North America. The Caribs of Saint Vincent, if set a going, may be supplied through Martinico with stores. The Mountain Negroes of Jamaica, if set a going, might employ a great number of their forces; this is not employing slaves, which, however, the example of our enemies authorize," &c., not signed.—To Messrs. Franklin, Harrison, &c., Oct. 8, 1776.

5756 ——— Letter, Dec. 6, 1776, suggesting the employment of "the Duc de Broglio to take the lead of your armies, and strike panic into their enemies," &c.

5757 DE VERGENNES, Letter to Mr. Deane, (March 26, 1778), on his Departure, "Hoping he will inspire the same sentiments in his own country as he has in France, assuring him of his true interest in his welfare and of that of his country," &c.

5758 CHALONER (*John*), Letter on Business to Barnabas Deane, April 27, 1782.

5759 HANCOCK (*John and Charles Thomson*), Signatures to Minutes of Congress, relating to Capt. Sullivan, and Lord Howe's meeting the Gentlemen of Congress, but not as Members of Congress, &c., Sept. 1, 1776.

5760 HANCOCK (*John*), Additional Instructions to Benjamin Franklin and Silas Deane and Commissioners from the United States of America to the King of France, Oct. 16th, 1776.

5761 DU COUDRAY (M.), Havre, 14 xbre., Letter on the Departure of Silas Deane, full of the highest esteem for himself and Dr. Franklin, also the esteem of the Duc de Rochefoucault, his friend, &c. *See* 5737.

5762 DEANE (*Silas*), Recommendation of Mons. Ladarine to Richard Peters and one other.

5763 BRITTON (JOHN), Two Notes to T. Hill, his Remarks on the Life and Writings of Shakspeare.

5764 NEWARK (THE STATE OF,) A Document on Parchment, Containing the Autographs of about 60 Attornies, who have sworn their allegiance to the State from 1790 to 1792.

5765 AUTOGRAPHS of Robert Carey, Earl of Monmouth, and W. Alexander, Earl of Sterling, part of a bill, 1618.

5766 WM. CECIL, the Great Lord Burghley, Signature, dated 1598, (the year of his death,) and Ro. Cecyll, Lord Salisbury, his son, Signature to Official Documents.

5767 ROBERT CECIL, Earl of Salisbury, Henry Howard, Earl of Northampton, Gilbert Talbot, Earl of Shrewsbury, autographs of.

5768 DOCUMENT on Parchment, for the Pay of the Board of Gentlemen Pensioners of Queen Elizabeth, signed by Lord Hunsdon.

5769 SIR Erasmus and Lady Dryden, Two Accounts to Lady-day 1709, and Michaelmas 1712.

5770 EPITAPH for Mrs. Creed (who founded a School at Ashton), by Mr. Jones.

5771 HENRY THE EIGHTH, King of England. Warrant to Sir Andrew Windsore, "Keeper of our Grete Wardrobe," to deliver "seven broode yardes of clothe, for a gowne, to our well beloved Chaplain, Jeffrey *Wren*," *on vellum, with the King's full Signature, very rare.*

5772 THOMAS HOWARD, Earl of Suffolke, Sir Fulke Greville (Lord Brooke), to part of a document, 1617.

5773 THOMAS SACKVILLE, Lord Buckhurst, (author of the Induction to the Mirror for Magistrates and Gorboduc —"the best English Poet between Chaucer and Spenser") Lord High Treasurer, Document and Signature, dated 1603, *when he was* 75, (he died æt. 80, 1608,) *fine and rare.*

5774 SALE of a Share of Covt. Garden Theatre, note of Buckstone.

5775 SOUTHAMPTON (Henry Wriothesley, Earl of, Patron of Shakspeare)—Signature to a Receipt for Six Hundred Pounds, Received of Philip Burlamachi, for the Levying, Conducting, and Transporting the Regiment under his Command to the States of the United Provinces.

5776 SIR Christopher Wren, Signature to Receipt for £500.

5776* SONGS—A MS. Collection of, containing many original, by Mr. Burton and others, copied by him, including some not adapted for the press.

ENGRAVINGS.

PRINTS, THEATRICAL PORTRAITS, PORTRAITS OF LITERARY CHARACTERS AND CELEBRATED MEN, RARE ETCHINGS, PRINTS FOR BIBLICAL ILLUSTRATION, SHAKSPEARIAN SCRAPS, COSTUMES, ETC.

5777 Portraits to Walpole's Painters and Engravers.

5778 Australian Views, by Captain Wallis, engraved by Preston, a convict, on the copper used to bottom vessels—12 large plates, *sewed*, folio, Lond. 1820, damaged by nails in the packing.

5779 Plates to Dibdin's Bibliographical Tour, proofs, rare—17 plates.

5780 Animal Kingdom, by W. Hawkins, arranged according to Cuvier, colored, folio.

5781 Budget of Fun, a newspaper for 1831.

5782 Shakspeare, illustrations to, from Boydell—6 plates.

5783 Comic Natural History of Man, colored plates.

5784 Michael Angelo, Giulio Romano, David, Raphael, Poussin, and Tintoret, engraved by Perelle—6 plates.

5785 Views in Venice—20 plates.

5786 Art Union Prints, in outline—8 plates.

5787 Views in Florence, colored—10 plates.

5788 Plates to illustrate Richardson's History of Pamela, after Highmore, a very fine set and rare—12 plates.

5789 Dante, Tasso, Poliziano, Alfieri, and one other, engraved by Raphael Morghen, &c., all fine and rare—5 plates.

This set was purchased at the sale of Dr. Jarvis's collection.

5790 Small German plates, neatly mounted on brown paper, to illustrate Shakspeare and Life of Frederick the Great—34 plates.

5791 Sacred Subjects, by old masters—10 plates.

5792 Set of Pastoral Subjects, by Claudine Stella, *sewed*, oblong folio—15 plates.

5793 Portfolio of cuttings, scraps, play bills, notes, &c., one by Fanny Kemble.

5794 A very large number of Theatrical Portraits, Scraps, MSS., &c., loose in a Portfolio.

5795 Don Quixote, six plates after Coypel, very fine, and one other—7 plates.

5796 Don Quixote, illustrations to, after Coypel, by Vander Gucht—24 plates.

5797 Ferogio; Une Année de Voyage, &c.—17 plates.

5798 Decorations for Theatres, &c., German and Italian—19 plates.

5799 Planché (J. R.), Continental Gleanings, folio.

5800 Wilkie Gallery, 6 numbers, folio, containing 18 plates.

5801 Tower of London, after the fire in 1841, by Cater and Oliver.

5801* Aldegraver, set of 12 plates of a Westphalia Wedding in 1538—1 wanting.

5802 Views of London and Old London Bridge, copied from Visscher, &c.—8 plates.

5803 Drawings by W. Y. Ottley for the Tempest, &c.—5.

5804 Brady and D'Avignon's Gallery of Illustrious Americans, 12 numbers (No. 11 wanting), fine portraits, with memoirs. N. Y. 1849, &c.

5805 Royal Gems from the Galleries of Europe, with notes, by S. C. Hall—7 parts.

5806 Conservatoire de Danse Moderne, colored plates.

5807 Album of Villa Architecture, No. 1.

5808 Portraits of Oxford Founders—24 plates.

5809 Ecclesiastical and other English Views, by Hearne and Byrne, &c.—33 plates.

5810 John Kemble, by Sharpe, proof; Charles Kemble, by Lane; and Garrick, by Laurie, all scarce, in a portfolio—3 plates.

5811 Views of Egypt, and 3 of Obelisk, bound by Bleau, folio—27 plates.

5813 Book-plates and Illustrations to Popular Authors—a parcel.

5814 Turner and Girtin, River Scenery, in a folio—17 plates.

5815 Don Quixote, plates to, after Alken, engraved by Teitten.

5816 Views of Theatres, &c., some drawings—a parcel.

5817 Foreign Theatres—a large parcel.

5818 Life of Morland, by Blagden, large folio. Lond. 1806

5819 Pictures of Life and Character, by John Leech, from Mr. Punch's collection, a series of comic pieces, oblong folio.
5820 Another copy, imperfect.
5821 Carter's Views in the Island of Barbadoes.
5822 View of London before the Great Fire—2 sheets.
5823 Porson's Devil's Walk, by Landseer, curious and spirited etchings—10 plates.
5824 French Caricatures—a parcel.
5825 Spanish Costume, colored—10 plates.
5826 Views of Herculanæum and Pompeii, by Roux—4 plates.
5827 Pond's Eccentric Characters, a series of etchings—24 plates.
5828 Portraits of Siddons and Kemble, &c., after Lawrence—7 plates.
5829 Foreign Portraits, Salmasius and others—a parcel.
5830 Illustrations to Shakspeare, inlaid, royal 8vo. in a green morocco cover.
5831 Another lot.
5832 Theatrical Characters, Kean, &c.—a parcel.
5833 Literary Characters—a parcel.
5834 Book plates and sundries.
5835 Book plates, &c., do.
5836 Etchings by Prevost—8 plates.
5837 Theatrical and scrap prints—a parcel.
5838 Book plates—a parcel.
5839 Theatrical plates and portraits—a large parcel.
5840 Plates to Inchbald's Theatre, 8vo.
5841 Copies of rare prints from Ottley's work—30 etchings.
5842 Corner's Portraits of Painters, on India paper—a parcel.
5843 Dusseldorf Kunster Album, Poesie.
5844 Views and scraps—a parcel.
5845 Etchings, Ponte Salario, by Rosene, &c., 7.
5846 Morning and Evening, after Tavernor.
5847 King John Signing the Magna Charta, &c.—6 plates.
5848 Portraits of Celebrated Characters—8 plates.
5849 Campbell the Poet, Morton the Dramatist, Lawrence, Artist, Bannister, Comedian, all fine—4 plates.
5850 The Old Pretender and his Sister, Butler the Poet, &c., 14.
5851 Shakspearian Prints—3 plates.
5852 Do. and scraps.
5853 Portrait of Col. Charles May.

5854 Views in Italy—12 plates.
5855 The Denoument, &c.—2 plates.
5856 Original Drawings by Kobell, Watelet and Spillman, 4.
5857 Drawing of a Gleaner, G. T. Van Den Bergh, fine, 1.
5858 Nymphs Bathing; at the Toilet, &c.—7 plates.
5859 Labours of Hercules, after L. Giordani, &c.—12 fine etching.
5860 Miscellaneous Prints for scrapbook, &c.—20 plates.
5861 Concert of Birds, by Earlom, very fine, mezzotint engraving.
5862 Conversations and other subjects—8 plates.
5863 France Illustrated—6 plates.
5864 Napoleon, Portraits and Prints, relating to—10 plates.
5865 Napoleon's Coronation, colored—5 plates.
5866 ——— Historical Events, a set of 12 colored plates.
5867 ——— Historical Prints, 20 plates of his career.
5868 Philip 4th of Spain, Emperor Maximilian, &c., fine prints by Visscher, folio—20 plates.
5869 Declaration of Independence, after Trumbull and Key, 2.
5870 Costume of about 300 characters, on six sheets, 6.
5871 John Gilpin, after Stothard.
5872 The Four Seasons, after Van Goyen, by Wierotter, and a set by Perelle—8 plates.
5873 Another set, very fine, by J. Van-der-Velde, 4.
5874 Les Coulisses de L'Opera, or Opera slips and Cirque Olympiques, colored—2 plates.
5875 Garrick, Palmer, Burton, and Webster as President, Abel Drugger, Subtle, and Fane, after Zoffany, fine, 1.
5876 Outlines to Shakspeare—12 plates.
5877 Sir Walter Raleigh and his Wife.
5878 Wouvermans, Les Capucins, very fine—2 plates.
5879 Breughel D'Enfer, grotesques Diableries—2 plates.
5880 Lear, after West, by Sharpe and two others—3 plates.
5881 Sportman's Bothie, &c.—2 plates.
5882 The Queen's Pets, and others—12 plates.
5883 Sporting Prints, finely engraved—19 plates.
5884 Seven etchings of Landscapes, by Koken, 7.
5885 Another set, 7.
5886 Singular Events, &c.—7 plates.
5887 Views in Italy—28 plates.
5888 Old Man and Woman, and Landscapes—4 plates.
5889 Industry and Idleness, &c.—a parcel.

5890 Banks of the Loire, by Perez, &c., various.
5891 Shakspeare's Statue, five; Portrait of Wallack, twelve in all—17 plates.
5892 Neapolitan Costume, a series of fine drawings, 15.
5893 Etchings by Salvator Rosa and Poussin, 2.
5894 Etchings by Berghem and Ridinger—7 plates.
5895 Etchings by Sebastian Bourdon, &c.—7 plates.
5896 Theatrical Subjects—6 plates.
5897 Will of John Duff; Original MS., Satyrical, 1.
5898 Toper, after Gerhard Dow, and others—10 plates.
5899 Miscellaneous, 8.
5900 Poussin, &c., various—4 plates.
5901 Ostade, Rubens, and Claude, rare etchings—3 plates.
5902 Battle of Zutphen, after Cooper, 1.
5903 Woodcuts to Martin Luther's Bible, and numerous other wood cuts,initial letters, &c., mounted on oblong, blue paper, several hundred.
5904 Bible Prints, by Killian, neatly mounted—a large parcel.
5905 Etchings by Hutin—11 plates.
5906 Landscapes, by the Old Masters, Landscapes by Perelle, &c.—14 plates.
5907 Painters' Etchings, all fine, and scarce—33 plates.
5908 Lady Hamilton's attitudes—12 plates.
5909 Pinelli's plates to Berneris, "Il meo Patacea"—52 plates.
5910 Venus and Cupid, by Bartolozzi and others, some fine and rare—11 plates.
5911 Berghem, &c., some scarce—13 plates.
5912 Raffaelle, Francia, Carlo Dolci, L. Caracci, &c., fine engravings after celebrated pictures by—6.
5913 Eight prints colored and mounted, from Tomkin's Gallery.
5914 Maddox, the actor, balancing the straw (see Davies's Life of Garrick), scarce, Maddox, Liston, &c.—parcel
5915 Foreign and English Views—do.
5916 Theatrical—do.
5917 Various Old Masters—6.
5918 Miscellaneous—parcel.
5919 Heads to Birch's Lives of Illustrious Persons, engraved by Houbraken and Vertue—about 100.
5920 Foreign Portraits—a large parcel.
5921 English Portraits—do.
5922 Views Foreign and English—do.
5923 Foreign Portraits—do.
5924 English and Foreign Topography—do.
5925 Portraits of Literary and other characters—do.

5926 English Portraits—a large parcel.
5927 Do. Theatrical, &c.—do.
5928 Do. do.
5929 Do. do.
5930 Portraits of Literary characters from the Monthly Mirror—about 100.
5931 Theatrical Portraits—a parcel.
5932 Foreign Portraits—do.
5933 English do.
5934 Do. do.
5935 Do. do.
5936 Nanteuiel, Portrait of Louis XIV., very large sheet, one of this artist's largest and choicest works, fine and very rare.
5937 Nanteuiel, Archbishop of Narbonne, fine—1.
5938 Two Bassi Relievi, of a frieze, by Langor.
5939 Nuptials—2.
5940 Columbus, after Wilkie, fine—1.
5941 Macbeth, after Zuccarelli, by W. Woollett, very fine—1
5942 Holy Family, after Raffaelle, Schugler, very fine—1.
5943 Gates of Calais, Hogarth, scarce—1.
5944 La Vierge aux Anges, after Titian, by Sadler, fine—1.
5945 Garrick as Richard III.
5946 Garrick as Macbeth, fine.
5947 La Belle Ferronniere, colored—1.
5948 Laertes and Ophelia, after West—1.
5949 Death of Cardinal Wolsey—1.
5950 Macklin and Mrs. Pope as Shylock and Portia—1.
5951 Lear, etched by Barry—1.
5952 Garrick and Miss Bellamy as Romeo and Juliet, after Wilson, by Ravenet, fine—1.
5953 Timon of Athens, and 1 other—2.
5954 Cæsar and Cleopatra—1.
5955 Falstaff and Recruits—1.
5956 Bunbury's Illustrations to Shakspeare, a set inlaid to the size of Boydell's large series—20.
5957 Garrick as Richard III.—2.
5958 Garrick as Richard III., in the tent scene, by Hogarth, fine early impression, and very rare in this State—1.
5959 Boydell. Shakspeare sacrificed by Alderman Boydell, a large caricature, by Gillray, colored, very rare—1.
5960 Mrs. Pritchard as Hermione, after Robert Edge Pine, by Aliamet, whole length, fine and scarce—1.
5961 Shakspeare Nursery, after Fuzeli—1.
5962 Merry Wives of Windsor, Mrs. Ford and Mrs. Page, after Cause, colored—1.

5963 Illustrations to Shakspeare—6.
5964 Do. do.—6.
5965 Do. do.—4.
5966 Death of Cæsar, a beautiful engraving after Carracci, by Fontana, fine—1.
5967 Caius Marius, proof—1.
5968 Francis I. and Reine Marguerite, 1.
5969 Babington's Conspiracy, 1.
5970 Napoleon, 3.
5971 Etchings, &c., 5.
5972 Drawing, 1.
5973 View of Boston, 1.
5974 View of New York, 1.
5975 The Ferry Boat, by Thompson, 1.
5976 Bolton Abbey in the Olden Time, after Landseer, proof, 1.
5977 Engravings for Scrap-books, a parcel.
5978 Various Scrap Prints, do.
5979 Foreign Portraits, do.
5980 Portraits, various, do.
5981 Bible Prints, do.
5982 Foreign Prints, do.
5983 Shakspeare Prints, do.
5984 Scenic and other Prints, *colored.*
5985 Bewick's (the wood engraver), last Work, framed with Play-house bill, 2.
5986 Engravings framed and glazed after Rembrandt, small, 1 glass broken, 3 plates.
5987 Large Portfolio, green morocco.
5988 Do. flaps.
5989 Do. do.
5990 Do. do.
5991 Do. superior, with Bramah Lock.
5992 Six Prints to illustrate Shakspeare, *on strainers.*
5993 Scraps in a portfolio.
5994 Do. do.
5995 Do. in a wrapper.
5996 Do.
5997 Historiographic Chart of the Mississippi River.
5998 Roll of Prints, some torn.
5999 April the First, a parcel.
6000 Ledger made for Nashville Mutual Fire Ins. Co., large folio.
6001 Ledger made for Gentleman's Magazine, with alphabet, large fol.
6002 Pamphlet Cases, assorted, in all 6.

CURIOSITIES.

SCULPTURE IN MARBLE, MODELS, MEDALS, CASTS, ANTIQUITIES, SHAKSPEARIAN RELICS, LIBRARY FURNITURE, ETC.

6003 A full length Plaster Statue of Thomson's Musidora.

6004 A full length Plaster Statue of The Venus de Medicis. In good condition.

6005 A beautiful Plaster Group, representing Samson and the Philistines.

6006 A beautiful Plaster Group, representing the "Rape of Lecrece." It rests on a handsomely carved stand, and the whole is about five feet in height.

6007 A large figure of Cupid, in marble. In good condition.

6008 A large Plaster Flower Stand, beautifully carved. Festoons of flowers and grapes, with cupids in pairs squeezing and sucking the grapes, and garlands of flowers surrounding the base.

6009 Pair of large Plaster Pitchers, beautifully wreathed with flowers.

6010 A small Plaster Flower Stand, carved with festoons of grapes and flowers and groups of cupids.

6012 A beautifully carved Bacchanalian Group of three figures, in case with glass cover, perfect.

6013 A Bust of the celebrated Comedian John Reeve, very rare.

6014 Plaster Cast of the face of Oliver Cromwell, taken after death.

6015 Five Idols of the Californian Indians.

6016 Large pair of silver Mexican Spurs.

6017 Plaster Cast of Venus and Cupid Sleeping, in half open shell.

6018 An ancient Mexican Vase dug up by the Americans while making trenches the morning after Gen. Scott entered Chapultepec.

6019 Indian War Club, used by the inhabitants of the North West Coast, cut entirely by shells.

6020 Indian Paddle, used and made the same as No. 6019.

6021 Large Stone Nubian Face, representing Comedy, the key-stone to the Pompeii Theatre.

6022 Plaster Statuette of Hercules.

6023 Pair of Statuettes of Females with Flowers, representing Ceres and Pomona.

6024 Small Figure of a Female, in marble, reclining on couch.

6025 Two pieces of ancient marble cutting.

6026 A large and fine fossil specimen of an Ammonite, the "Cornua Ammonis," very curious.

6027 Handsome case of Medallions, comprising 48 portraits of celebrated persons.

6028 Metal Watch of a British Officer, dug up at Bunker's Hill.—A curious old fashioned metal watch and chain, dug up in the vicinity of Bunker's Hill. The works are entire. The pinchbeck coating of the case eaten off. The centre of the dial-plate, with the hands have been renovated. The hour and minute circle is of the original piece. Maker's name, Clarke, of London.

6029 Washington's Repeater.—Silver repeating watch, in embossed or open filigree case, with striking bell and machinery complete, double cases, engraved, maker, S. Dechamme, London. This watch was worn by Washington during his encampment at Valley Forge. It passed into the hands of Mrs. Allston, Burr's well known daughter, and from that family into the hands of the late owner.

6030 Talma's Repeater, presented by Napoleon.—Large sized, heavy gold repeater, in perfect order. A coronation souvenir from the great Napoleon to his friend Talma, the well known tragedian. The outside case of thick gold, is engraved with the Imperial crown and an Italian cypher of "N. 1." The back of the inside case is of thick gold, with a circle of open work, having as a centre the ten franc casting of the Imperial coinage, the head of Bonaparte, with "Le 2 Mai, 1809, Souvenir pour Talma, de Napoleon Bonaparte." The maker's names Vauchu, Freres, and the register 10,801. It is capped and jewelled. The hands are duplex, porcelain face, on which is inscribed "Faite, par l'ordre de Napoleon I., Empereur des Français, 1809." A letter of authentication accompanies this highly interesting relic.

MEDALS, BADGES, COINS, &c.

6031 Royal Badge of Distinction, worn by the Acting Governor of New York, under British Rule, being the head (en medaillon) of George III., and the British Arms, in reverse. This handsome ornament is cast in solid silver, and is three inches in diameter. It was unavoidably left behind by the last British Governor in his hurry on Evacuation Day. In red morocco case.

6032 A capital copy of the "Great Clay Medal," with its magnificent Head and beautiful Reverse; in bronze. Purple morocco case.

6033 Large, extra sized, bronze medal, in honor of Alex. Von Humboldt. Head in very high relief, and beautiful reverse, Berolini, 1828.

6034 Handsome silver medal, struck in commemoration of John Phillip Kemble. In high relief. In red morocco case.

6035 Pair of Medals, struck in honor of the celebrated return of the Bourbons to the Government of France, 1825; solid silver.

6036 Pair of Silver Medals struck in honor of the marriage of Napoleon with Marie Louise, 1813.

6037 Curious Roman Silver Medal, large size.

6038 Medal struck in commemoration of the entrance of the British Army into Madrid, Aug. 12, 1812; bronze.

6039 Bronze Medal struck in commemoration of the arrival of Lieutenant-General Sir R. Abercrombie with the British Army in Egypt, March 8, 1801.

6040 Medal (bronze) struck to commemorate Lieutenant-General Lord Hill at Almaraz, May, 19, 1812.

6041 Medal, in bronze, struck in honor of Madame Lavalette for her admirable conduct in aiding the escape of her husband on the morning of his intended execution.

6042 Bronze Medal struck in honor of the successes of the East India Company against Napoleon in Egypt, 1804.

6043 Medal (bronze) struck to commemorate the battle of the Cowpens, Jan. 17, 1781.

6044 Bronze Medal struck in memory of John Locke, 1704.

6045 Medal (bronze) struck to commemorate the position of the British Army on the Tagus, 1810–11.

6046 Bronze Medal struck in memory of Sir Francis Bacon.

6047 Medal (bronze) struck to commemorate the production of Milton's "Paradise Lost."

6048 Medal struck in commemoration of Benjamin Franklin (bronze).

6049 Medal struck in commemoration of Major General Lord Hutchinson at the delivery of Egypt, Sept. 2, 1801; bronze.

6050 Bronze Medal struck to commemorate Henry William, Marquis of Anglesey, at the charge of the British at Waterloo, June 18, 1815.

6051 Bronze Medal struck in commemoration of Arthur, Duke of Wellington, and the capitulation of Pampeluna, Oct. 31, 1813.

6052 Bronze Medal struck in memory of Sir Isaac Newton.

6053 Bronze Medal struck in commemoration of the declaration of the Congress of Vienna, Feb. 26, 1815.

6054 Large Bronze Medal struck in honor of the celebrated actor, George Frederic Cooke, 1805.

6055 Medal (dark bronze) in honor of the celebrated sculptor, Antonio Canova—high relief—1827.

6056 Medal (bronze) struck to commemorate Lieut.-General Sir T. Picton, at Badajos, April 6, 1812.

6057 Bronze Medal struck in commemoration of the death of Sir John Moore, at Corunna, Jan. 16, 1809.

6058 Bronze Medal in commemoration of Marshal-General Lord Beresford, at the battle of Albuera, May 16, 1811.

6059 Medal struck to commemorate Lieutenant-General Lord Lyndoch at St. Sebastian, Aug. 31, 1813.

6060 Medal (bronze) struck in commemoration of the celebrated General John Churchill, Duke of Marlborough.

6061 Bronze Medal struck in commemoration of Tristram Coffin, "the first of the race that settled in America" in 1642.

6062 Large Bronze Medal, in high relief, with two portraits of the Bourbon Princes, bearing the inscription, "L. P. Alb. D'Orleans Comte de Paris Prince Rl. L. C. P. R. D'Orleans Duc de Nemours."

6063 Handsome unknown Medal.

CLARA FISHER'S SHAKSPEARIAN CABINET.

MODELS.

6064 I. The House in which Shakspeare was Born. In Henley Street, at Stratford-upon-Avon, in Warwickshire, on the 23d of April, in the sixth year of the reign of Elizabeth, 1564, was born William Shakspeare. The model represents the building in the state it appeared at the time of his birth, with pointed roofs to the garret windows, a style of building much prevailing in the time of Elizabeth.

6065 II. Birth-place of Shakspeare, in the state it was seen at the time Garrick gave the celebrated jubilee, in September, 1769, in honor of Shakspeare; the garret windows had been taken away, and the exterior much altered.

6066 III. The Same House, as it appeared in 1827, at the last jubilee, held in honor of Shakspeare.

Half of the building has been new fronted with brick work, and two small bow windows added to the ground floor.

6067 IV. The Grammar-school at Stratford-upon-Avon, in which Shakspeare received his education. A desk (rudely formed), is still preserved in the school-room, and shown as "Shakspeare's writing desk."

6068 V. Anne Hathaway's Cottage, at Shottery, about a mile from Stratford-upon-Avon, resided Anne Hathaway, afterwards the wife of Shakspeare. The cottage is still standing, as represented by the model.

6069 VI. The Remains of a Church. At Luddington, near Stratford-upon-Avon, formerly stood a church, where Shakspeare and Anne Hathaway were married; now a blacksmith's shop.

6070 VII. DAISY-HILL FARM HOUSE. This building was formerly the game-keepers' lodge, at Charlecot Park, in which Shakspeare was confined the night he was detected attempting to steal a deer, from the domains of Sir Thomas Lucy, a magistrate, before whom he was conveyed the next morning by the gamekeepers.

6071 VIII. CHARLECOT HALL, the seat of Sir Thomas Lucy, built in the early part of the reign of Queen Elizabeth, situate about six miles from Stratford-upon-Avon.

The severe conduct of Sir Thomas Lucy, on this occasion, is said to have driven Shakspeare from his native Stratford to London, in or about the year 1585 or 1586, a circumstance which laid the foundation of his after fame and fortune.

6072 IX. THE GLOBE THEATRE, where most of Shakspeare's plays were originally performed, and in which theatre he was himself an actor.

The building was situated on the Surrey side of the river Thames, near the commencement of the present Southwark iron bridge; and when plays were acting a flag was displayed from the top of the building. This is engraved in Aggas's map of London about 1570.

6073 X. THE FALCON INN, BANKSIDE, a house celebrated for having been the resort of Shakspeare, Ben Jonson, and most of the authors and wits of those days; it stood near the Globe Theatre.

6074 XI. THE FORTUNE THEATRE, in which several of Shakspeare's plays were performed. This building was purchased by Alleyn, the actor, and by him made into a theatre, about the year 1599. The exterior, as represented in the model, is still standing in Golden-lane, not far from the well-known brewery in that neighborhood.

6075 XII. THE CROWN INN AT OXFORD, an inn frequented by Shakspeare in his journeys between London and Stratford-upon-Avon, then kept by Mr. Davenant, the father of Sir William Davenant, godson of Shakspeare.

6076 XIII. THE FALCON INN AT BIDFORD. This inn (situate about six miles from Stratford-upon-Avon), is now the poorhouse at Bidford. It is reported that Shakspeare and a party of jolly fellows from Stratford, got so overcharged with the strong ale of the landlord, that he and his companions (unable to return home) laid themselves down, and slept all night in a field, by the roadside, under a large crab-tree.

6077 XIV. SHAKSPEARE'S CRAB-TREE. About a mile from the inn, where the merry meeting, above alluded to, took place, in the way to Stratford-upon-Avon, stood (till very recently) a large venerable crab-tree, under whose shade the party slept till the next morning; the circumstance getting known in the neighborhood, the tree has been called "Shakspeare's crab-tree" ever since.

6078 XV. THE FALCON INN AT STRATFORD-UPON-AVON, kept by a person named Julius Shawe, a subscribing witness to Shakspeare's will.

6079 XVI. NEW PLACE, The residence of Shakspeare, at Stratford-upon-Avon, which he purchased in the year 1597.

He repaired and remodelled it, agreeable to his own taste, at considerable expense. In the garden, behind the house, grew the celebrated mulberry tree, said to have been planted by Shakspeare's own hand. To this mansion he retired from the fatigues and bustle of public life, about the year 1613, and there ended his mortal career in peace and tranquillity, on the 23d of April, 1616, his birth-day, at the age of fifty-two.

"We ne'er shall look upon his like again."

6080 XVII. THE CHURCH AT STRATFORD-UPON-AVON—Under the north side of the chancel, this great ornament of dramatic literature lies buried; a flat stone covers his remains, on which (very rudely cut) are the following lines, said to have been written by himself:

"Good friend, for Jesus' sake forbear,
To dig the dust enclosed here!
Blessed be the man that spares these stones,
And curst be he that moves my bones."

6081 XVIII. The Life of Shakspeare, as written by N. Rowe, Esq.—his Portrait engraved by Sharpe—his Works arranged in chronological order, as entered at Stationer's Hall—Names of the Actors in his Plays—Copy of his Will—and Fac Simile of his Handwriting—Engraving of his Monument at Stratford-upon-Avon—and Copies of Epitaphs belonging to his Family, *in a glass case.*

6082 XIX. A Bust of Shakspeare, taken from the monument in the church at Stratford-upon-Avon.

6083 XX. The Armorial Bearings of Shakspeare, with a Copy of the Patent from the Herald's College, proving his right, by the warlike achievements of his forefathers, to such honourable distinction.

SHAKSPEARIAN RELICS, &c., COLLECTED BY MR. BURTON.

6084 A GOBLET carved from the celebrated Mulberry Tree.

6085 ANOTHER, very fine and rare.

*** Garrick's Goblet, formed of the same wood, and of the same size, sold for £100 sterling. Christie (the most learned and most gentlemanly man who ever graced the rostrum of the Knights of the Hammer), observed, when selling that Cup, that it ought to be bought for the Dramatic Fund, and handed round after their annual dinner filled with "good old wine," then afterwards sent round for subscriptions, when no doubt, he said, it would overflow with their charitable donations.

Major Sirr's Cup sold for £17, and Brandon's (*box-office keeper of Drury Lane*) for £10.

6085* Singular old Delft Mug, dated 1604. This was dug up in the garden of Shakspeare, and it is supposed was his. It is 11 inches high.

6086 Shakspeare Medal, struck in commemoration of the celebrated Boydell edition of the Poet's Works, 1803, *silver, very rare.*

6087 The Great English Shakspeare Jubilee Medal, in very high relief, struck in silver.

6088 Great English National Shakspearian Medal.

6089 A beautiful Model of the Monument of Shakspeare, made from the Mulberry Tree, enclosed in a handsomely carved wood case, with glass doors.

6090 Statuette of Shakspeare in Parian Marble, of modern workmanship.

6091 Another Statuette, different position.

6092 Statuette of Shakspeare of old Chelsea China, *very scarce.*

6093 Figure of Falstaff leaning on his cane, *in Parian marble.*

6094 BUSTS OF ANCIENT AND MODERN POETS, WARRIORS, POLITICAL AND LITERARY CHARACTERS, *life size*, will be sold in pairs, to suit private buyers.

6095 Piece of Oak from Shakspeare's House at Stratford, during the repairs of 1857, brought by C. V. A.

6096 Shakspeare's Mulberry Tree, a piece from the same block as the one presented by the Rev'd Thos. Rackett (one of David Garrick's executors) to the British Museum.

6097 Piece of Tile from Shakspeare's House, brought by C. V. A., 1857.

6098 Statue of Shakspeare, full length, executed by Thom, in the same style as his celebrated groups of Tam O'Shanter and Old Mortality.

6099 Colossal Statue of Shakspeare, carved in Wood, saved from the conflagration of the Park Theatre.

6100 Bullock's Cast of the Bust of Shakspeare, taken from his Monument at Stratford-on-Avon, on carved stand.

6101 Cast of the face only, from the same, mounted on black marble.

This very accurate cast was done by stealth at the "witching time of night," by two young men, who, it is supposed, applied a silver key to the guardian of the sanctuary. It had a great sale.

6102 A reduced Copy of the Monument of Shakspeare in the Church of Stratford-upon-Avon, painted as the Monument now is; this is a good memento of the Poet, and very desirable as an ornament to the Library of a collector of Shakspeariana.

6103 SHAKSPEARE'S MULBERRY TREE. As a specimen of the far-famed Mulberry Tree, the following lot may challenge every known relic, not excepting the celebrated Casket, formerly Garrick's. The following is a copy of a cutting from the Catalogue of a former possessor of whom it was purchased by Mr. Burton :—

SHAKSPEARIAN RELIC.—H. Rodd has for sale a magnificent memento of the famed "Mulberry Tree" It is undoubtedly the finest specimen extant as a work of art, and it is in the purest state of preservation, being a most ornamental as well as most useful piece of furniture, viz. a TEA CADDY. The design might be attributed to Hogarth, as the "line of beauty" is strongly developed throughout, and the appropriateness of the devices and carving are such as in no way to derogate from the great subject it is intended to commemorate. The front has the head of Shakspeare in an oval of branches and fruit of the Tree, in very high relief, whilst boughs of the same are gracefully waving on each side—the trunk forming the ends, whilst the branches are running and entwining themselves over the top and sides—on the lid is the Coat of Arms of Shakspeare in an elegant shield—the centre of the three inner cases has the whole length figure of Shakspeare, from the statue by Schemaker, with the speech of "the Cloud-Capped Towers" beautifully enamelled; the side cases have carved on each a Mulberry Tree; the handle is of silver. Altogether it is considered an unique specimen of the celebrated Mulberry Tree planted by the hand of Shakspeare. Price FIFTY GUINEAS.

FURNITURE TO SMALL LIBRARY.

6104 A Mahogany Book Case, about 5 feet wide by 7 feet high, with glazed doors above, and folding doors below, capable of holding a considerable number of volumes.

6105 Another Case corresponding.

6106 Another.

6107 Another.

6108 Round Library Table, with Rack.

6109 Carpet.

6109* Six Chairs, covered with horsehair.

6110 Pier Table.

6111 Small Table.

6112 Double Mahogany Book Case.

IN LARGE LIBRARY.

6112* A MAGNIFICENT SIDEBOARD OF SOLID CARVED OAK, IN THE ELIZABETHAN STYLE. This splendid piece of furniture is composed of ancient oak carvings of Female Figures, deeply cut cornice, carved doors, &c., with back board and shelves at the top.

Cost the late Mr. Burton $400.

6112† MARBLE TOP TABLE, ON CARVED OAK STAND—The Venetian style of the de Medicis period, in perfect condition—a very beautiful and rare piece of furniture.

6113 Gothic Book Cases. The fittings of the Library in a room of about 30 feet square; about 120 feet run, composed of Book Cases, with glazed folding doors in the early Gothic style, the bottom compartments with shelves and fall down doors, about 12 feet high. These will be sold as one Lot, or divided to suit buyers.

6113* Large Gothic Book Case, painted oak, glazed doors.

6114 Gothic Dwarf Book Case, glazed doors, capable of containing large books of prints.

6115 Large Kneehole Library Table, about 5 feet square, with drawers, &c.

6116 Large Carpet, of Gothic pattern, fitted to the room, about 90 square yards, more or less.

6117 Large Library Arm Chair, carved with eagles' heads, &c.

This was Mr. Burton's favorite chair.

6118 Two Small French Pattern Chairs, with curious seats
6119 One large handsome easy Lounge.
6120 A similar lot.
6121 Three Library Steps.
6122 Large Billiard Table.
6123 Fire Proof Safe.
6124 Do.
6125 Do.
6126 Lot of Wood Cuts.
6127 Steel and Copper Plates.
6128 Gas Fixtures, consisting of Four Bronzed Gas Chandeliers.

VALUABLE OIL PAINTINGS.

(NOT SOLD WITH MR. BURTON'S GALLERY.)

6129 ZUCCARELLI—A Landscape.
6130 ——— The Companion.
6131 T. WILSON, JR.—Portrait of Shakspeare.
6132 VAN VELZE—Landscape, &c., very fine in effect.
6133 GIOTTO—St. Elizabeth.
6134 UNKNOWN—A Political Caricature.
6135 ROBBE OF BRUSSELS—Goats, Sheep, &c., in a Landscape, on panel.
6136 MIGNARD—Louis XV.
6137 ——— The Queen of Louis XV.
6138 P. VECCHIO—St. John in the Wilderness.
6139 GAINSBOROUGH—Cottage, Bridge, &c. A fine specimen purchased by Mr. B.'s Grandfather.
6140 DAVID—Whole length portrait of the Emperor Napoleon. Capital copy of the original picture by.
6141 VANDYSK—Margarette, Duchess d'Orleans. A fine portrait from Mr. Clark's.
6142 JOLIVET—Grand Landscape of Forest Scenery. The work by a French Nobleman, an amateur artist, was exhibited in the Louvre, 1845; it was purchased at the sale of the Marquis d'Allegre, in Paris, 1849.
6143 MIGNARD—Portrait of a Lady in Rich Dress, with Cupid and a Dove. One of the celebrated beauties of the Court of Louis XIV.
6144 GIULIO ROMANO—The Synod of the Gods.
6145 ——— Bacchus and Ariadne.
6146 CHAMBAUX—Rock of Lorelei.
6147 UNKNOWN—A Sacrifice, on panel.
6148 CLESSING—View of Cyprus.
6149 WILKINS—A Storm.
6150 GLESSING—Old Cottage and Bridge.
6151 SULLY—Portrait of Shakspeare, formerly in the Proscenium of the Chestnut Street Theatre.

MURILLO.

6152 THE HOLY FAMILY—Believed to be original by this Master. Arthur, the well known art agent for Lord Cowley, offered $5,000 for it to take to Europe; and Clark, who for many years held one of the most valuable collections of old pictures in the United States, valued it as Murillo, and catalogued it as by that Master. It is grand, in both design and color, and is decidedly of the Spanish school. This is certainly no copy, for no other like treatment of the subject is known.

E. LANDSEER AND COUNT D'ORSAY.

6153 QUEEN VICTORIA ON HORSEBACK (*Life Size*)—The Figure and Landscape by D'Orsay--the Horse by E. Landseer. It was brought to the United States for exhibition, and valued by the Count D'Orsay at $7,500. Mr. Burton had in his possession, at the time of his death, an autograph letter from D'Orsay acknowledging its genuineness, which has been mislaid by his family since his decease; if found, it will be handed to the purchaser. There however can be no doubt of its originality, as the picture is well known.

6154 PAUL VERONESE—Paolo Cagliari, called Paolo Veronese, was born at Verona, in 1532, and died in 1588.

FINE GALLERY PAINTING OF A MAN BETWEEN VIRTUE AND VICE—This is supposed to be a portrait of the artist. A replica of the celebrated picture, formerly in the collection of the Duke of Orleans, the Italian part of which was bought by Mr. Bryan, who was authorized by the Duke of Bridgewater, the Earl of Carlisle, and the Marquis of Stafford, to purchase it for £43,000 sterling. That picture was valued at 350 guineas, and was purchased by T. Hope, Esq. An engraving, with an account of the picture, will be found in the Galerie du Palais Royal dit Duc d'Orleans, 3 vols.

Price from a Price list
made by Samuel Agnew,
No. 1126 Arch Street,
Philadelphia, Pa

PROSPECTUS

OF AN

AMERICAN

Bibliographer's Manual.

Respectfully announces to Librarians and Book-buyers in general, that he has in preparation and will proceed to publish, if the proposition meets with the co-operation and support such a project requires,

A

BIBLIOGRAPHICAL DICTIONARY

OF ALL BOOKS RELATING TO AMERICA,

From its discovery to the present time, with their current or approximate value.

The work will be arranged after the plan of Brunet and Lowndes, *i. e.* an alphabetical arrangement of Authors and the first word of anonymous publications; the articles *a, an,* or *the* excepted—to be followed by an analytical or finding index, which will make the work at once general and special, *e. g.* Supposing the following work: (25 Abbott (*John,*) Natural History of the rarer Lepidopterous Insects of Georgia, edited by J. E. Smith, M. D., illustrated by numerous plates of butterflies in their various states, and of the plants on which they feed; 2 vols. folio, London, 1796, 7), to be No. 25, in the general order; it will appear in the index under various heading thus:—

Botany—Abbott & Smith, ... No. 25
Entomology—Abbott & Smith, ... " 25
Georgia, Insects of—Abbott & Smith, ... " 25
Insects, *vide* Entomology.
Natural History—Abbott & Smith, ... " 25
Plants, *vide* Botany.
Smith (J. E.), Natural History, Ga., ... " 25

Thus every book will be so analyzed as to its contents, that the searcher for any work on a given subject, or by a given author, cannot fail to find it.

The materials used as sources of information are the various works of Faribault, Rich, Terneaux Compans, Asher, Aspinwall, Jewett, White Kennett, Boucher de la Richardiere, Pinelo, Ludewig, Thomas, Munsell, Poole, Roorbach, Warden, Muller, &c.; also, catalogues of various public and private collections, while the Dictionaries of Brunet, Lowndes, Ebert, Cailleau, and others will be searched for all they have on the subject; indeed, no pains will be spared to make the work as complete and thorough as possible.

The extent of the work cannot at present be estimated, but it is proposed to issue it to subscribers in octavo volumes of the size and style of the Oxford edition of Ebert's Bibl. Dict. at $5 per volume, of 500 pages, and pro rata; this price to be increased to non-subscribers 20 per cent.

☞ Gentlemen having the titles of any very uncommon book or books, are respectfully requested to furnish a transcript of the same, and suggestions and subscriptions will be alike thankfully received by

JOSEPH SABIN.

www.ingramcontent.com/pod-product-compliance
Lightning Source LLC
LaVergne TN
LVHW020930110826
845150LV00004B/814